영단기 토익
실전 1000제 RC

vol.1

머리말

취업, 졸업, 승진······
토익 시험을 보는 목적과 목표 점수는 달라도 토익 시험을 준비하는 분들이 반드시 접하게 되는 교재가 있다면, 아마도 <영단기 토익 실전 1000제> 시리즈 같은 실전 문제집일 것입니다. 실전 문제집을 통해 토익에 출제되는 문제 유형들을 익히고, 시간을 안배하는 연습을 하고, 부족한 부분을 파악하고, 자신의 점수를 가늠해 볼 수 있기 때문이죠.

이렇게 다양한 목적을 충족시켜야 하는 실전 문제집이기에, 영단기 연구소에서 여러분이 최신 출제 경향이 반영된 토익 문제로 실전에 대비할 수 있도록 <영단기 토익 실전 1000제 1 LC/RC> 개정판을 출간하게 되었습니다.

<영단기 토익 실전 1000제 1 LC/RC>에는 출제진급 연구원과 숙련된 원어민들이 신토익 시행 이후 정기 토익 전 회차의 출제 경향을 철저히 분석한 결과를 바탕으로 기출과 가장 흡사하게 만든 1,000문제가 수록되어 있습니다. 이 1,000문제를 고난도 문제의 비중을 달리하며 10회분의 모의고사로 구성하여 시험이 어렵게 출제되는 달에도, 쉬운 달에도 이 한 권으로 여러분이 실전에 완벽하게 대비할 수 있게 하였습니다. 또한, 여러분이 틀린 문제를 확인할 때 쉽게 이해할 수 있도록 명확하고 친절한 해석/해설을 담은 해설집을 함께 제공합니다.

기출을 기반으로 만든 최고의 문제로 구성된 <영단기 토익 실전 1000제 1 LC/RC>를 10일 동안 하루에 한 회씩, 실제 시험을 보듯 문제를 풀어보며 실전 감각을 키우고 틀린 문제는 해설을 확인하며 부족한 점을 보완한다면, 여러분은 시험장에서 자신 있게 문제를 풀어 나가는 자신을 발견하게 될 것입니다.

영단기 연구소가 여러분의 토익 조기 졸업을 기원합니다!

영단기 연구소 드림

목차 및 학습 플래너

문제집 페이지	TEST	공부한 날	TEST 시간	점수	해설집 페이지	복습
8	**TEST 01**	☐월 ☐일	시작 시각 ☐시 ☐분 종료 시각 ☐시 ☐분 75분 내에 완료했나요? ○ l ×	맞은 개수 _____ 환산 점수 _____	2	○ l ×
38	**TEST 02**	☐월 ☐일	시작 시각 ☐시 ☐분 종료 시각 ☐시 ☐분 75분 내에 완료했나요? ○ l ×	맞은 개수 _____ 환산 점수 _____	24	○ l ×
68	**TEST 03**	☐월 ☐일	시작 시각 ☐시 ☐분 종료 시각 ☐시 ☐분 75분 내에 완료했나요? ○ l ×	맞은 개수 _____ 환산 점수 _____	45	○ l ×
98	**TEST 04**	☐월 ☐일	시작 시각 ☐시 ☐분 종료 시각 ☐시 ☐분 75분 내에 완료했나요? ○ l ×	맞은 개수 _____ 환산 점수 _____	65	○ l ×
128	**TEST 05**	☐월 ☐일	시작 시각 ☐시 ☐분 종료 시각 ☐시 ☐분 75분 내에 완료했나요? ○ l ×	맞은 개수 _____ 환산 점수 _____	86	○ l ×
158	**TEST 06**	☐월 ☐일	시작 시각 ☐시 ☐분 종료 시각 ☐시 ☐분 75분 내에 완료했나요? ○ l ×	맞은 개수 _____ 환산 점수 _____	107	○ l ×
188	**TEST 07**	☐월 ☐일	시작 시각 ☐시 ☐분 종료 시각 ☐시 ☐분 75분 내에 완료했나요? ○ l ×	맞은 개수 _____ 환산 점수 _____	128	○ l ×
218	**TEST 08**	☐월 ☐일	시작 시각 ☐시 ☐분 종료 시각 ☐시 ☐분 75분 내에 완료했나요? ○ l ×	맞은 개수 _____ 환산 점수 _____	148	○ l ×
248	**TEST 09**	☐월 ☐일	시작 시각 ☐시 ☐분 종료 시각 ☐시 ☐분 75분 내에 완료했나요? ○ l ×	맞은 개수 _____ 환산 점수 _____	169	○ l ×
278	**TEST 10**	☐월 ☐일	시작 시각 ☐시 ☐분 종료 시각 ☐시 ☐분 75분 내에 완료했나요? ○ l ×	맞은 개수 _____ 환산 점수 _____	190	○ l ×

영단기 토익 실전 1000제 **개정판**

문제집과 해설집 합본
토익을 공부하는 수험생들의 의견을 적극 수용하여 별도로 판매하던 문제집과 해설집을 합본하였습니다.

최신 경향 100% 반영
신토익 시행 이후 정기 토익 전 회차의 출제 경향을 완벽 분석하여 반영했습니다.

대박달/쪽박달/평달 구분
고난도 문제의 비중에 따라 TEST별로 대박달/쪽박달/평달을 구분하여, 자신의 점수를 좀 더 실전에 가깝게 예측해 볼 수 있습니다. 각 TEST 시작 페이지에서 TEST의 난도를 확인할 수 있습니다.

영단기 토익 실전 1000제 1 RC **사용법**

STEP 1

RC 실전 TEST 풀기

최신 경향을 반영한 100% 새로운 문제!

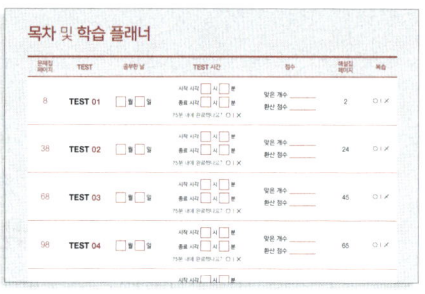

잠깐! TEST를 시작하기 전에 ❶

시작 시각과 종료 시각을 적으세요.
시계까지 옆에 챙겨두었다면 당신은 완벽한 토익커입니다.

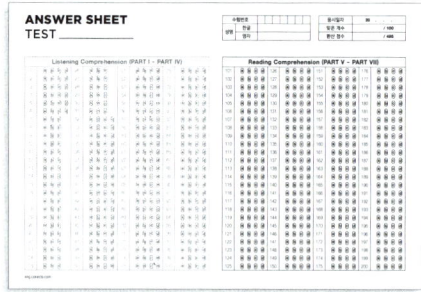

잠깐! TEST를 시작하기 전에 ❷

맨 뒤에 수록되어 있는 Answer Sheet 중 한 장을 잘라냅니다. 이제 마킹이 잘 되는 뭉뚝한 연필을 들고 시험을 시작해 볼까요?

+
시험장 환경에
최대한 가까워지는
구성으로
실전 감각 기르기

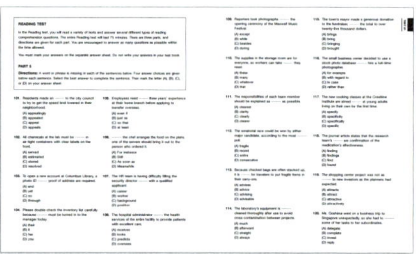

토익 RC 실전 TEST 10회분

<영단기 토익 실전 1000제 1 RC>는 최신 출제 경향을 완벽 분석하여 제대로 정밀하게 반영하였습니다. 정기 토익 시험에 응시하기 전 실전 TEST 10회분을 모두 풀고 꼼꼼히 복습하여 진정한 토익 고수가 되어 보세요.

STEP 2

채점하기

자신의 실력을 확인하자!

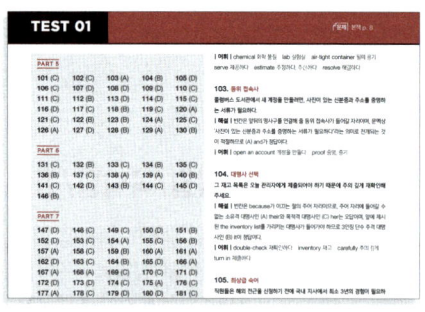

정답표

TEST를 마친 후 해설집의 정답표를 보고 채점하세요.

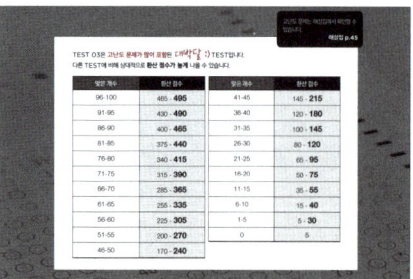

점수 환산표

맞은 개수를 확인한 뒤, 각 TEST 시작 페이지에 있는 점수 환산표에서 자신의 점수를 확인하세요.
* 주의: 예를 들어, 맞은 개수가 96-100이면 465점에서 495점 사이를 받을 수 있다는 의미이지 96개이면 465점을, 100개이면 495점을 받는다는 의미는 아닙니다. 본 교재에서 제공하는 점수 환산표는 절대적인 것은 아니며 대략 자신의 점수를 가늠해 볼 수 있는 지표입니다.

STEP 3
복습하기

상세한 해설을
확인하며,
실력을 키우자!

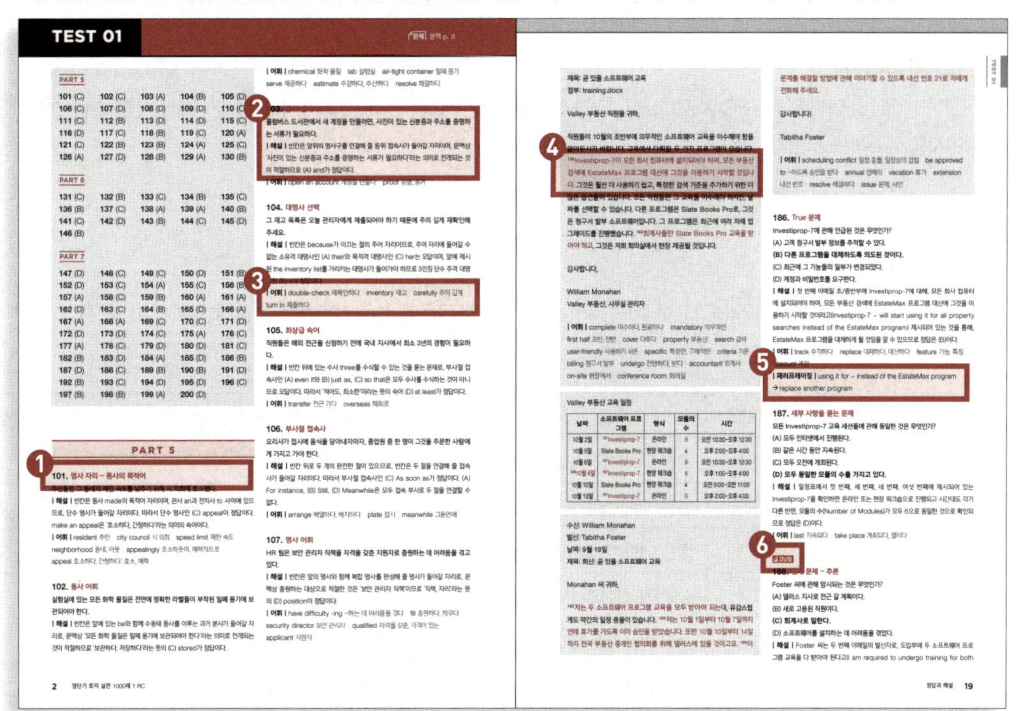

❶ 문제 유형	실전에 자주 출제되는 문제 유형, 또는 자신이 취약한 유형이 무엇인지 알 수 있도록 모든 문제에 문제 유형을 표기하였습니다.
❷ 해석 및 해설	정확하고 자연스러운 해석을 수록하여 지문과 문제 내용을 완벽하게 이해하고 넘어갈 수 있습니다. 또한, 정답 및 오답의 이유를 명확하게 파악하고 충분히 독학할 수 있도록 친절하고 자세한 해설을 제공하였습니다.
❸ 어휘	지문 및 문제에서 사용된 단어와 어구의 뜻을 수록하여 토익 중요 어휘까지 한번에 학습할 수 있습니다.
❹ 정답 단서	지문에서 정답을 선택하는 데 단서가 되는 부분을 해당 문제 번호와 함께 표시하였습니다. 단서를 통해 빠르게 정답을 찾는 연습을 할 수 있습니다.
❺ 패러프레이징	지문-질문 또는 지문-보기 간 패러프레이징이 된 부분을 따로 제시하여 정답을 찾는 데 결정적인 패러프레이징 표현을 하나하나 학습할 수 있습니다.
❻ 고난도 마크	토익 만점을 위해 반드시 맞추어야 하는 고난도 문제에 별도 표기하여 해당 문제를 더욱 철저히 학습할 수 있도록 하였습니다. 틀렸더라도 좌절 금지! 한 회 한 회 풀어 나가며 자신의 실력을 발전시켜보세요.

토익 시험의 모든 것

토익 소개

TOEIC 시험이란?
TEST OF ENGLISH FOR INTERNATIONAL COMMUNICATION의 약자로, 모국어가 영어가 아닌 사람이 일상적인 생활 또는 업무에서 의사소통이 가능한지를 평가하는 시험입니다.

시험 구성
❶ 전반적인 개요
듣기(LC) 4개 파트 100문제와 읽기(RC) 3개 파트 100문제로 총 7개 파트에 걸쳐 200문제가 출제됩니다. 200문제 모두 선택지 중에서 정답을 찾는 객관식 문제로 출제됩니다.

구성	PART 구성	출제 내용	문항 수	시간	점수
LC (Listening Comprehension)	PART 1	사진 묘사(사진 보고 문제 풀기)	6	45분 내외	495점
	PART 2	질문-대답(질문 듣고 답변 고르기)	25		
	PART 3	짧은 대화(두세 사람의 대화를 듣고 질문에 답하기)	39		
	PART 4	설명문(전화 메시지, 연설문, 안내 방송, 일기예보 등을 듣고 질문에 답하기)	30		
RC (Reading Comprehension)	PART 5	문장 빈칸 채우기(하나의 문장 안에 있는 빈칸에 알맞은 말(문법&어휘) 고르기)	30	75분	495점
	PART 6	지문 빈칸 채우기(짧은 지문 안에 있는 빈칸에 알맞은 말(문법&어휘&문장) 고르기)	16		
	PART 7	싱글 지문(1개의 지문을 읽고 질문에 답하기)	29		
		더블 지문(2개의 지문을 읽고 질문에 답하기)	10		
		트리플 지문(3개의 지문을 읽고 질문에 답하기)	15		
총계			200	약 120분	990점

❷ 출제 범위 및 주제
일상생활 및 업무에 대한 영어 의사소통 능력을 평가하기 때문에 특정 분야의 전문 지식 또는 이와 관련된 어휘는 출제하지 않습니다. 국제 업무 환경에 맞게 다양한 국가의 지명과 성명이 등장하며, 듣기 평가에서는 미국, 영국, 호주 발음이 고르게 섞여 출제됩니다. 다음 주제를 참고해 봅시다.

기업 일반	이사회, 편지, 공지, 전화, 팩스, 이메일, 사무실 장비 및 가구, 사무실 규정, 계약, 협상, 합병 및 인수, 판매, 보증, 사업 계획, 회의, 노사 관계
공식 연회	식사 및 연회, 장소 예약
엔터테인먼트	영화, 공연, 전시
재무	은행 업무, 투자, 세금, 회계, 청구
의료	건강 보험, 병원 방문 및 예약
부동산	건설 및 보수 내역, 부동산 구매 및 임대, 기타 설비
제조	제품 조립, 공장 경영, 품질 관리
인사	모집, 고용, 퇴임, 승진, 급여, 일자리 지원서, 구인 광고, 연금, 시상
구매	쇼핑, 주문, 배송, 송장
기술	전자 장비, 기술 지원, 컴퓨터, 연구실과 관련 장비
여행	교통 관련 일정, 교통 관련 각종 공지, 렌터카, 호텔 예약, 연착 및 취소

시험 가이드

1. 토익 접수 방법
- 토익 시험의 인터넷 접수 기간을 한국 TOEIC 위원회 사이트(www.toeic.co.kr)에서 확인합니다.
- 사이트에서 인터넷 접수를 선택하고 시험일, 고사장, 수험 정보 등의 정보를 입력합니다.
- 시험 접수 시 최근 6개월 이내 사진(JPG 형식)이 필요하오니 미리 준비합니다.

TIP 시험 전 약 12~13일부터는 특별 추가 접수에 해당하여 약 5천원 정도의 추가 비용이 발생합니다. 미리 시험을 접수하는 것이 좋습니다.

2. 시험 당일 꼭! 챙겨야 할 준비물
- **규정 신분증**
  성인의 경우, 주민등록증, 운전면허증, 기간 만료 전 여권, 공무원증 등이 인정됩니다. 중고등학생에 한하여 학생증(국내 학생증만 허용)도 신분증으로 인정됩니다.
- **연필 (볼펜, 사인펜은 No!)**
  연필 끝을 뭉뚝하게 만들어 준비하면 답안 마킹을 더 쉽게 할 수 있습니다.
- **지우개**
- **아날로그 손목시계 (전자식 시계는 No!)**

3. 입실 전 유의사항
- 시험 시간이 오전일 경우 오전 9:20까지, 시험 시간이 오후일 경우 오후 2:20까지 입실합니다.

TIP 오전 시험은 오전 9:50 이후, 오후 시험은 오후 2:50 이후로는 절대 입실할 수 없으니 꼭 시간을 지켜 미리 입실합니다.
시험 시간 직전에는 독해 문제를 풀기보다는 듣기 연습을 충분히 하여 귀를 훈련시키는 게 더 효과적입니다.

4. 시험 진행 안내

오전 시험	오후 시험	시험 진행
9:30~9:45 (15분)	2:30~2:45 (15분)	답안지 작성 오리엔테이션
9:45~9:50 (5분)	2:45~2:50 (5분)	쉬는 시간
9:50~10:05 (15분)	2:50~3:05 (15분)	신분증 확인
10:05~10:10 (5분)	3:05~3:10 (5분)	문제지 배부, 파본 확인
10:10~10:55 (45분)	3:10~3:55 (45분)	듣기 평가 (LC)
10:55~12:10 (75분)	3:55~5:10 (75분)	독해 평가 (RC)

5. 성적 확인 및 성적표 발급 방법
- 시험일로부터 10일 후 낮 12시에 한국 TOEIC 위원회 사이트(www.toeic.co.kr)에서 성적 확인이 가능합니다.
  (토요일 시행 시험 등 일부 회차 시험은 11일 후에 발표될 수 있습니다.)
- 성적 수령은 온라인 출력이나 우편 수령을 택할 수 있습니다.
- 온라인 출력 시, 성적 유효 기간 내 홈페이지를 통해 출력 가능합니다.
- 우편 수령 시, 성적 발표 후 접수 시 기입한 주소로 성적표가 우편 발송됩니다. (약 7~10일 소요)
- 온라인 출력과 우편 수령은 1회 발급만 무료이며, 이후에는 유료로 발급됩니다.

TEST 01

PART 5 · PART 6 · PART 7

준비하기

손목시계　　뭉뚝한 연필과 지우개　　Answer Sheet

토익 RC는 75분 동안 진행됩니다.
반드시 75분 이내에 문제 풀이와 답안지 마킹을 완료하세요.

고난도 문제는 해설집에서 확인할 수 있습니다.
해설집 p.2

TEST 01은 **고난도 문제가 평균적으로 포함**된 *평달* TEST입니다.
환산 점수가 중간값으로 나올 수 있습니다.

맞은 개수	환산 점수	맞은 개수	환산 점수
96-100	465 - 495	41-45	145 - 215
91-95	430 - 490	36-40	120 - 180
86-90	400 - 465	31-35	100 - 145
81-85	375 - 440	26-30	80 - 120
76-80	340 - 415	21-25	65 - 95
71-75	315 - 390	16-20	50 - 75
66-70	285 - 365	11-15	35 - 55
61-65	255 - 335	6-10	15 - 40
56-60	225 - 305	1-5	5 - 30
51-55	200 - 270	0	5
46-50	170 - 240		

READING TEST

In the Reading test, you will read a variety of texts and answer several different types of reading comprehension questions. The entire Reading test will last 75 minutes. There are three parts, and directions are given for each part. You are encouraged to answer as many questions as possible within the time allowed.

You must mark your answers on the separate answer sheet. Do not write your answers in your test book.

PART 5

Directions: A word or phrase is missing in each of the sentences below. Four answer choices are given below each sentence. Select the best answer to complete the sentence. Then mark the letter (A), (B), (C), or (D) on your answer sheet.

101. Residents made an ------- to the city council to try to get the speed limit lowered in their neighborhood.
    (A) appealingly
    (B) appealed
    (C) appeal
    (D) appeals

102. All chemicals at the lab must be ------- in air-tight containers with clear labels on the front.
    (A) served
    (B) estimated
    (C) stored
    (D) resolved

103. To open a new account at Columbus Library, a photo ID ------- proof of address are required.
    (A) and
    (B) yet
    (C) so
    (D) through

104. Please double-check the inventory list carefully because ------- must be turned in to the manager today.
    (A) their
    (B) it
    (C) her
    (D) you

105. Employees need ------- three years' experience at their home branch before applying to transfer overseas.
    (A) even if
    (B) just as
    (C) so that
    (D) at least

106. ------- the chef arranges the food on the plate, one of the servers should bring it out to the person who ordered it.
    (A) For instance
    (B) Still
    (C) As soon as
    (D) Meanwhile

107. The HR team is having difficulty filling the security director ------- with a qualified applicant.
    (A) career
    (B) worker
    (C) background
    (D) position

108. The hospital administrator ------- the health services of the entire facility to provide patients with excellent care.
    (A) receives
    (B) looks
    (C) predicts
    (D) oversees

109. Reporters took photographs ------- the opening ceremony of the Maxwell Music Festival.
(A) except
(B) while
(C) besides
(D) during

110. The supplies in the storage room are for everyone, so workers can take ------- they need.
(A) these
(B) many
(C) whatever
(D) that

111. The responsibilities of each team member should be explained as ------- as possible.
(A) clearest
(B) clarity
(C) clearly
(D) clearer

112. The senatorial race could be won by either major candidate, according to the most ------- poll.
(A) fragile
(B) recent
(C) entire
(D) consecutive

113. Because checked bags are often stacked up, it is ------- for travelers to put fragile items in their carry-ons.
(A) advises
(B) advice
(C) advising
(D) advisable

114. The laboratory's equipment is ------- cleaned thoroughly after use to avoid cross-contamination between projects.
(A) much
(B) afterward
(C) straight
(D) always

115. The town's mayor made a generous donation to the fundraiser, ------- the total to over twenty-five thousand dollars.
(A) brings
(B) bring
(C) bringing
(D) brought

116. The small business owner decided to use a stock photo database ------- hire a full-time photographer.
(A) for example
(B) with regard to
(C) in case
(D) rather than

117. The new cooking classes at the Crestline Institute are aimed ------- at young adults living on their own for the first time.
(A) specify
(B) specificity
(C) specifically
(D) specific

118. The journal article states that the research team's ------- are confirmation of the medication's effectiveness.
(A) finding
(B) findings
(C) find
(D) found

119. The shopping center project was not as ------- to new investors as the planners had expected.
(A) attracts
(B) attract
(C) attractive
(D) attractively

120. Ms. Ooshima went on a business trip to Singapore unexpectedly, so she had to ------- some of her tasks to her subordinates.
(A) delegate
(B) complete
(C) invest
(D) reply

GO ON TO THE NEXT PAGE

121. The security guard refused Mr. Dillon ------- because he could not provide a valid employee badge.
(A) admits
(B) admittedly
(C) admittance
(D) admitting

122. ------- Top Gardening changed the checkout procedure on its Web site, its online sales have gone up dramatically.
(A) Why
(B) Since
(C) Whether
(D) Still

123. ------- the bank transfer be made after 5 P.M., you can expect it to be processed the following working day.
(A) As much as
(B) Should
(C) Everything
(D) Whenever

124. With the recent complaints of safety violations, Colbert Airlines will probably have ------- passengers than usual.
(A) fewer
(B) longer
(C) each
(D) neither

125. The files will be deleted -------, so please confirm that you do not need them before selecting this action.
(A) favorably
(B) substantially
(C) permanently
(D) forcefully

126. Marquee Couriers increased the hourly wage for delivery drivers ------- fill the positions more quickly.
(A) in order to
(B) similarly
(C) moreover
(D) in any case

127. The airline representative apologized for the cancellation but explained that it was due to factors ------- the company's control.
(A) between
(B) against
(C) throughout
(D) beyond

128. By the end of the year, the state's health department ------- over five thousand restaurants to check for food safety violations.
(A) has inspected
(B) will have inspected
(C) will be inspected
(D) has been inspected

129. During his keynote speech, Dr. Grayson ------- the role of nonprofit organizations in reducing poverty worldwide.
(A) emphasized
(B) assumed
(C) hesitated
(D) conserved

130. The Grand Villa neighborhood is known for having the city's largest ------- of high-end boutiques.
(A) mobilization
(B) concentration
(C) recipient
(D) commodity

PART 6

Directions: Read the texts that follow. A word, phrase, or sentence is missing in parts of each text. Four answer choices for each question are given below the text. Select the best answer to complete the text. Then mark the letter (A), (B), (C), or (D) on your answer sheet.

Questions 131-134 refer to the following letter.

November 16

Dear Ms. Charron,

It was a pleasure meeting you in person this morning to learn more about your desire to outsource Eastway Shipping's bookkeeping. -------. I understand that you no longer wish to handle these types of tasks. I am
                                 131.
confident that our dependable certified accountants can take on the -------. I hope that your questions and
                                                                         132.
concerns ------- during our meeting. If not, please feel free to contact me at 555-7966 with further inquiries.
          133.
In addition, I have enclosed a brochure of our services for you to -------.
                                                                    134.

Warmest regards,

William Satterfield

---

131. (A) I will delete the error from the October invoice right away.
(B) Please call my office if the items do not arrive on time.
(C) Your accounting needs can easily be handled by our experienced team.
(D) The business transports goods to distribution centers all over the world.

132. (A) incident
(B) role
(C) outcome
(D) progress

133. (A) addresses
(B) addressing
(C) were addressed
(D) had addressed

134. (A) translate
(B) review
(C) recommend
(D) oversee

Questions 135-138 refer to the following press release.

Mercury Fashions Fall Line

Mercury Fashions offers luxurious apparel that fits your lifestyle. On September 1, we ------- our new line of fall fashions at a runway show at Sapphire Plaza. We closely follow the latest fashion trends, so we plan to have clothes dominated by the hottest colors to help you show your style. These cutting-edge designs are flattering to a wide range of body types. -------, we have new accessories like scarves, handbags, and hats that you can mix and match. -------. Visit www.mercuryfashions.com for a sneak peek. These beautiful items will be in ------- high-end department stores on the same day as the runway show.

135. (A) have revealed
(B) have been revealing
(C) are going to reveal
(D) revealed

136. (A) Even
(B) Also
(C) Rather
(D) Merely

137. (A) Our design team is always standing by you to meet your custom requests.
(B) The tags should be removed before wearing them.
(C) Create dozens of your own looks as you want.
(D) Our headquarters will relocate in the city of New York.

138. (A) most
(B) which
(C) their
(D) soon

Questions 139-142 refer to the following letter.

October 9

Ralph Benton
874 Everette Way
Coral Springs, FL 33065

Dear Mr. Benton,

Thanks to the collaborative ------- of you and your team, Otis Rentals has become the number one car rental agency in Florida. Our market share has grown from 15% to 41% in just three years under your leadership. -------.
139.

140.

On behalf of Otis Rentals, I would like to invite you to transfer to our Texas branch, where you would take on the role of regional manager. This region ------- the most competitive one in the country, but I believe that you are up to the challenge. The preferred start date is November 15. -------, we can be somewhat flexible if more time to make arrangements is needed.
141.
142.

Sincerely,

Lucille Walsh, Chief Operations Officer
Otis Rentals

---

139. (A) efforts
(B) reports
(C) panels
(D) visits

140. (A) I will take a trip to Florida for the first time.
(B) Such an accomplishment is rarely seen in our field.
(C) Please confirm which job candidate you prefer.
(D) It had four doors and a spacious trunk in the back.

141. (A) considers
(B) was considered
(C) is considered
(D) considering

142. (A) Consequently
(B) Besides
(C) For example
(D) However

Questions 143-146 refer to the following article.

(October 12)—Rapid Insurance, one of the nation's largest providers of homeowners insurance, has announced a change at the executive level. Lillian Howes has been selected by the Rapid Insurance board as the company's new CEO. She ------- James Loftin, who held the position for thirteen years.
143.

"Mr. Loftin will leave the company to work in the charity sector, and we wish him all the best in his -------
144.
endeavors," said Rapid Insurance spokesperson Anna Gilley. Investors are pleased with the change, as Ms. Howes is no stranger to Rapid Insurance's operations. "Ms. Howes ------- worked as the managing director
145.
of the company before becoming the chief operating officer three years ago," commented Ms. Gilley.

"-------"
146.

143. (A) has been succeeded
(B) succeeds
(C) would have succeeded
(D) was succeeding

144. (A) constant
(B) accurate
(C) future
(D) distant

145. (A) authentically
(B) suddenly
(C) regrettably
(D) previously

146. (A) We plan to look into the matter carefully.
(B) We believe the transition will be a smooth one.
(C) The new insurance package has become popular.
(D) The board will make the final decision soon.

PART 7

Directions: In this part you will read a selection of texts, such as magazine and newspaper articles, e-mails, and instant messages. Each text or set of texts is followed by several questions. Select the best answer for each question and mark the letter (A), (B), (C), or (D) on your answer sheet.

Questions 147-148 refer to the following information.

Excitement and thrills are just around the corner!

Director Nick Murray revealed in a recent interview that the sequel to the popular *The Warrant* is coming out on July 29. The movie, called *The Warrant 2: Deadly Search*, stars Eric Jackson and will be playing in theaters nationwide.

Baxter Theater is holding a special promotion for the movie. Book your ticket at www.baxter99.com by July 20, and you'll be sent a voucher to download one of the eighteen songs from *The Warrant 2*'s soundtrack.

147. According to the information, what will happen on July 29?
(A) A celebrity will be interviewed.
(B) A price will decrease.
(C) A theater will have a grand opening.
(D) A film will debut.

148. How can a free music voucher be obtained?
(A) By purchasing tickets for a group
(B) By completing a survey
(C) By making an online reservation
(D) By arriving at a site early

Questions 149-150 refer to the following e-mail.

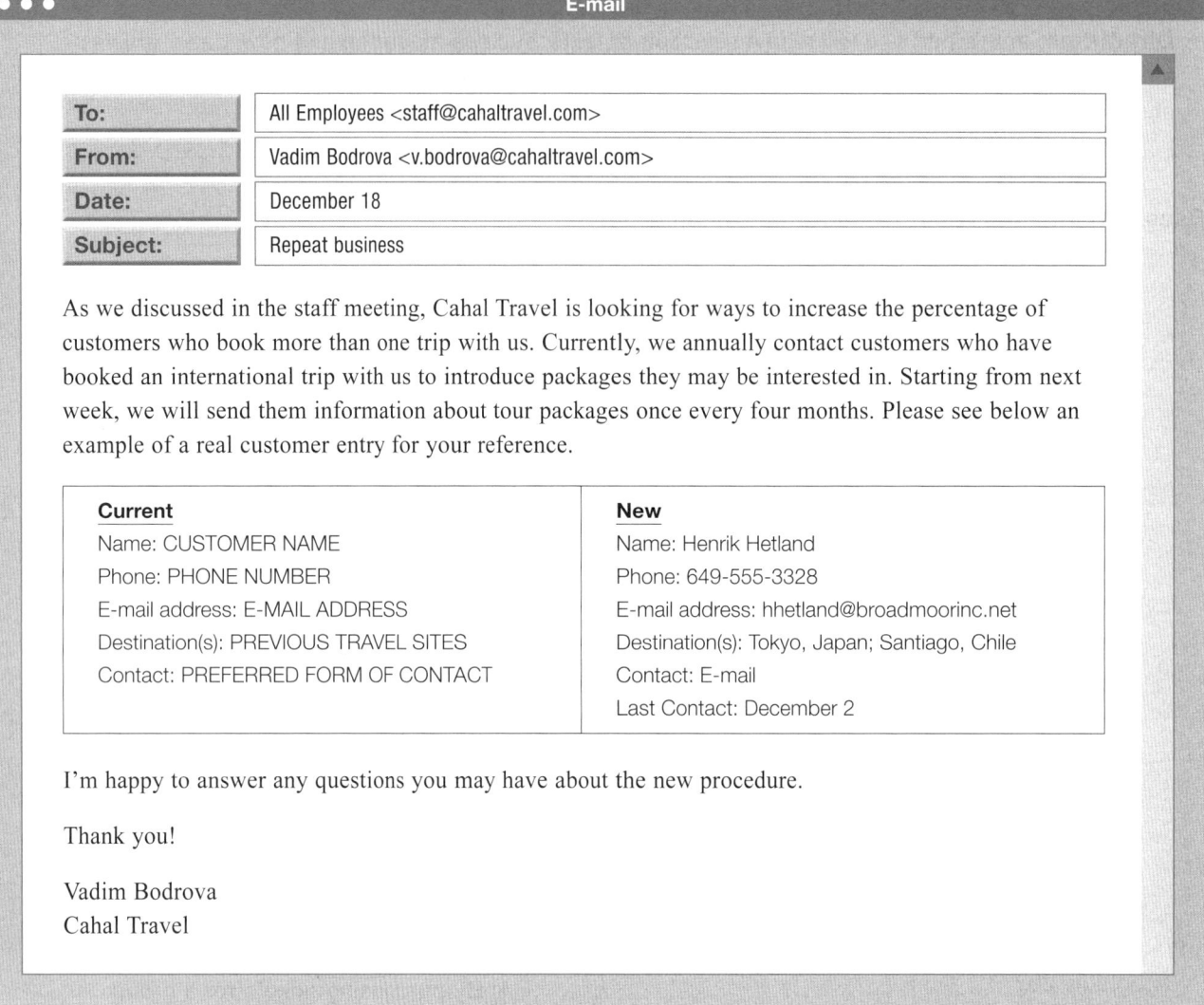

149. What will the business change?
    (A) The processing fee for booking a trip
    (B) The size of the groups for tour packages
    (C) The frequency of contacting past customers
    (D) The requirements for new vacation planners

150. Who most likely is Mr. Hetland?
    (A) A job candidate
    (B) A travel agent
    (C) An airline employee
    (D) An overseas traveler

Questions 151-152 refer to the following online chat discussion.

Stewart Bowser [9:24 A.M.]
Do you have a minute? I'm trying to reserve a time slot for Joseph Harris to have a checkup with Dr. Pritchard, but there is a problem. It looks like he has been entered into the system twice. I'm not sure which file to use.

Delilah Gibbs [9:25 A.M.]
That sometimes happens if someone inputs new patient information without saving the changes properly. However, there could also be two people with the same name.

Stewart Bowser [9:26 A.M.]
Good point. How can I tell if that's the case?

Delilah Gibbs [9:27 A.M.]
Look at the birth date to confirm the patient's identity. Then you'll know whether or not you have the right one.

Stewart Bowser [9:28 A.M.]
Of course! Thank you!

---

151. What is Mr. Bowser trying to do?
(A) Change an address
(B) Make an appointment
(C) Bill a patient
(D) Contact a doctor

152. At 9:28 A.M., what does Mr. Bowser most likely mean when he writes, "Of course"?
(A) He knows a patient personally.
(B) A computer is working fine.
(C) He is willing to help Ms. Gibbs.
(D) A solution is obvious.

Questions 153-155 refer to the following e-mail.

To: Hans Edgren <h.edgren@lincoya.com>
From: Amherst Bank <accounts@amherstbank.com>
Date: December 9
Subject: Amherst Bank Credit Card

Dear Mr. Edgren,

I am writing to inform you that the limit on your Amherst Bank credit card has been raised from $1,800 to $2,500. —[1]—. We are taking this action because you have had no late payments on your account for the past year. Your account's interest rate will also be lowered by two percent. —[2]—.

If you are satisfied with these conditions, your service contract will be automatically updated, and no further action is needed. However, should you wish to return to the previous credit limit and interest rate, please inform the bank by calling 1-800-555-7799. —[3]—. Thank you for being an Amherst Bank customer. —[4]—.

Sincerely,

Benjamin Elliot
Account Services, Amherst Bank

---

153. Why did Mr. Elliot send the e-mail to Mr. Edgren?

(A) To check some unusual activity on a credit card
(B) To remind him that a credit limit has been reached
(C) To notify him of account changes on his credit card
(D) To ask him to pay the monthly bill on his account

154. What is Mr. Edgren asked to do?

(A) Contact the company if he wants to reset some terms
(B) Update his billing address on the account
(C) Verify that he approved some recent purchases
(D) Provide a reason for making a late payment

155. In which of the positions marked [1], [2], [3], and [4] does the following sentence best belong?

"Confirmation of your request will then be sent by e-mail."

(A) [1]
(B) [2]
(C) [3]
(D) [4]

Questions 156-157 refer to the following memo.

To: All Magnolia Advisors Staff
From: Kwang-min Hwang
Date: October 24
Subject: Financial data

Magnolia Advisors is responsible for an increasing amount of sensitive financial data from our clients. Because of this, the executive committee has decided to make changes to improve the protection of confidential files and prevent unauthorized access. On November 6, card readers will be installed on the doors of all file storage rooms, and employees will be issued key cards. In addition to denying entry to those without cards, the card readers will keep a record of who is entering the room and when. If a card reader malfunctions, please see Maintenance Director Jim Abbott in his office. Should you have questions or concerns about the change, feel free to call me at extension 23.

156. What is the purpose of the memo?
(A) To describe computer software that stores digital files
(B) To notify employees of increased security measures
(C) To congratulate the staff on meeting a financial goal
(D) To introduce a new policy regarding client interactions

157. What does Mr. Hwang recommend doing if a device is not working?
(A) Visiting a maintenance employee
(B) Reporting a problem by e-mail
(C) Calling him at his office
(D) Ordering some replacement equipment

Questions 158-160 refer to the following e-mail.

To: Ellie Jarvis <elliejarvis@boylestoninc.com>
From: GTP Cleaning <info@gtpcleaning.com>
Date: January 19
Subject: Order #49025

Dear Ms. Jarvis,

On behalf of GTP Cleaning, I would like to apologize for an issue with your order (#49025) that has put its delivery behind schedule.

The following products are in stock and will be dispatched today, arriving at your mailing address within 2–3 days:

Brightex Wood Polish, 9.7-oz. canister
McGraw All-Purpose Cleaner, 32-oz. bottle
Trumbull Scouring Pads, pack of 6
Avery Window Cleaner, 26-oz. bottle, new non-toxic formula

The following item is currently out of stock:

Freida Pod, pack of 3 2.5-oz. air-freshener units, Cherry Blossom fragrance

We will not receive replacements for the out-of-stock item at our warehouse for 4 to 6 weeks. If you take no action, this item will be shipped as soon as it becomes available again. There will be no additional charge for the separate shipment. Please note that there are variations of the same air-freshener, such as Calming Lavender and French Vanilla. Please click here to check out the complete list on our Web site, as you may find something you prefer. If so, you can adjust the order in your account anytime before the final item is shipped.

Thank you for your patronage!

Leon Espinoza
GTP Cleaning

---

158. Why was the e-mail sent?

 (A) To offer a refund
 (B) To approve a request
 (C) To explain a delay
 (D) To promote a product

159. What is mentioned about the Freida Pod?

 (A) It has been discontinued.
 (B) It is available in multiple scents.
 (C) It has non-toxic ingredients.
 (D) It is the most popular product.

160. What does Mr. Espinoza ask Ms. Jarvis to do?

 (A) View some alternative options online
 (B) Check the quantity of her order
 (C) Resend the payment for the current order
 (D) Provide feedback after testing a product

Questions 161-163 refer to the following article.

Cantrece Shopping Center Wins National Award

March 22—Cantrece Shopping Center has been honored with the prestigious Conifer Prize in a ceremony held last night at the San Mateo Hotel. The award is presented annually to a company or organization whose building follows eco-friendly practices, uses sustainable building materials, and reduces energy consumption. The shopping center is an exemplary model for all of these categories. Solar panels on the building's rooftop supply over 80% of the building's needs. In addition, skylights reduce the need for daytime lighting, and a rainwater collection system provides water for flushing toilets and cleaning. The building's designer, Yolanda Knapp, was present to accept the award at the ceremony, and she said she and her colleagues will continue to strive to create functional structures that use resources responsibly.

The judging panel that selects the winner of the Conifer Prize is continually looking for companies that meet their criteria. If you would like to recommend a company to be considered for this prize, please visit www.coniferprize.com.

161. For what did the Cantrece Shopping Center receive an award?
(A) Its environmentally friendly design
(B) Its contributions to charity
(C) Its unique products for sale
(D) Its record number of customers

162. Where does Ms. Knapp most likely work?
(A) At a magazine publisher
(B) At a shopping center
(C) At a real estate agency
(D) At an architectural firm

163. According to the article, what can be done on the Web site?
(A) Downloading a list of selection criteria
(B) Viewing photographs from previous winners
(C) Nominating companies for future awards
(D) Reading the interview with Ms. Knapp

Questions 164-167 refer to the following e-mail.

To: Sylvia Reid <s.reid@harringoninc.com>
From: Chris Alexander <chris_alexander@modoccorp.com>
Date: February 19
Subject: Modoc Corp.

Dear Ms. Reid,

It was a pleasure meeting you at the recent Cosmetics Retailers Trade Expo in San Francisco. As promised, I'm sending you the current catalog for Modoc Corp. —[1]—.

I understand that you are looking for ways to boost sales in your shop, and I believe that our products can help you reach this goal. —[2]—. We have a variety of face creams, cleansers, and other skincare products. One of our best sellers is Meridian, a lightweight moisturizer that is intended for daily use. Customers love it because it is fragrance-free, so they don't have to worry about how it might combine with their perfume or other beauty products. —[3]—.

Should you have any questions, I would be happy to answer them anytime. —[4]—. You can reach me at this e-mail address or at 248-555-0973.

Warmest regards,

Chris Alexander

---

164. What is the purpose of the e-mail?

(A) To thank Ms. Reid for a demonstration
(B) To follow through on a request
(C) To register for a trade expo
(D) To set up a business meeting

165. What is implied about Ms. Reid?

(A) She tried some free samples.
(B) She lives in San Francisco.
(C) She developed a new perfume.
(D) She works in the field of cosmetics.

166. What benefit of Meridian is mentioned?

(A) It does not have any odor.
(B) It is environmentally friendly.
(C) It lasts for a long time.
(D) It comes in various sizes.

167. In which of the positions marked [1], [2], [3], and [4] does the following sentence best belong?

"I'm sure you'll find that it has numerous items you'll be interested in."

(A) [1]
(B) [2]
(C) [3]
(D) [4]

Questions 168-171 refer to the following online chat discussion.

Kelly Ward [1:30 P.M.]	Good afternoon. I've invited Esther Tsao to this chat, as she has volunteered to assist with the planning.	
Esther Tsao [1:31 P.M.]	I'm happy to be a part of this event. My roofing business, which has now been closed, always sold a lot of materials from our booth at the conference over the years.	
Kelly Ward [1:32 P.M.]	I'm glad to hear that. Now you'll be able to participate from the other side of things.	
Herbert Inez [1:34 P.M.]	We're glad to have your help. Adding a second day for the first time creates some unique challenges. For example, the only site I found that is available for the weekend of October 8th is Orchard Hall. It's not as conveniently located as Toliver Plaza, where we've held the event before, but it's much more affordable.	
Kelly Ward [1:35 P.M.]	That's perfect. Could you contact Orchard Hall today so that we can put down a deposit and lock in the dates?	
Herbert Inez [1:36 P.M.]	Sure. And I'll try to negotiate a discount for conference attendees staying on site.	
Esther Tsao [1:38 P.M.]	Has the guest speaker for the evening session been selected yet?	
Kelly Ward [1:39 P.M.]	We have invited Marcel Dillon to do it.	
Esther Tsao [1:40 P.M.]	He would be fantastic! I saw photos of the latest building he designed in New York, and it is a masterpiece.	
Herbert Inez [1:42 P.M.]	I agree. I'm sure a lot of people will be interested in hearing what he has to say.	
Kelly Ward [1:43 P.M.]	Exactly! I expect to get confirmation from him sometime this week.	

168. What is indicated about Ms. Tsao?
(A) She has participated in the conference as a vendor.
(B) She is responsible for decorating the booths.
(C) She will give a presentation at the conference.
(D) She plans to put her business up for sale.

169. What is suggested about this year's conference?
(A) Its venue is conveniently located.
(B) Its admission rates will be raised.
(C) It will be longer than previous ones.
(D) It will be held in New York.

170. At 1:35 P.M., what does Ms. Ward mean when she writes, "That's perfect"?
(A) She is glad that Mr. Inez has finalized a contract.
(B) She likes the event dates that Mr. Inez selected.
(C) She is satisfied with the venue they will use.
(D) She thinks the guest speaker will do a great job.

171. Who most likely is Marcel Dillon?
(A) A journalist
(B) A fashion designer
(C) An event planner
(D) An architect

Questions 172-175 refer to the following Web page.

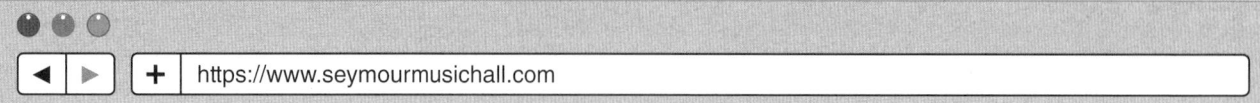

Seymour Music Hall
Go Beyond the Music!
Spring is the perfect time to visit Seymour Music Hall and enjoy music-related programs and activities. Every Wednesday at noon, we offer a free concert to the public to showcase the talents of students taking lessons in our music tutoring program.

Hours of Operation:
Monday–Thursday 10 A.M.–6 P.M. / Friday 11 A.M.–8 P.M. / Saturday–Sunday 11 A.M.–7 P.M. / Closed on all major holidays.

Current Exhibits:
Music Through the Ages (permanent collection): Rio Room
Modern Jazz: Amber Room
Instruments Across the Globe: Dunbar Room

Lectures:
March 16, 6:30 P.M.
Ranjeet Sardar, the conductor of the Surat Symphony Orchestra, discusses how to choose the instrument that is right for you based on your interest and physical attributes. This information can be especially helpful for children who are joining an orchestra or band for the first time.

April 20, 6:30 P.M.
Jihee Kim, who has been creating designs for album covers and concert posters for over a decade, explains how she translates the emotions of the music into pictures.

May 18, 7:30 P.M.
Archie Bouley, curator of the "Modern Jazz" exhibit on display in the Amber Room, discusses her research methods. Her goal for the exhibit was to show how jazz trends develop and change.

172. What is indicated on the Web page about Seymour Music Hall?

(A) Its exhibits change every month.
(B) It is offering free music lessons.
(C) Its on-site lectures require tickets.
(D) It is open to the public daily.

173. What is NOT a topic that is covered in Seymour Music Hall's current exhibits?

(A) Trends in a particular genre
(B) International musical instruments
(C) The history of music
(D) Modern recording techniques

174. Who most likely is Ms. Kim?

(A) A film producer
(B) A music critic
(C) A graphic designer
(D) A professional musician

175. What will lecture attendees learn about in April?

(A) Capturing feelings in visual form
(B) Improving music-playing techniques
(C) Researching famous musicians
(D) Selecting a musical instrument

Questions 176-180 refer to the following e-mail and letter.

To: Raul Wolfe <r.wolfe@wolfetiles.com>
From: Kelly Wagner <kellywagner@anokabank.com>
Date: March 19
Subject: Business Loan through Anoka Bank

Dear Mr. Wolfe,

My name is Kelly Wagner. I am following up on the appointment you had on March 4 regarding a loan for your dress-making business. I understand that you originally met with Constance Gauthier, but she has transferred to another branch, so I am taking over for her. As I'm sure Ms. Gauthier explained, the loan amount is dependent on your business's financial situation. Your business needs at least $125,000 in annual earnings for each of the past two years to be issued a $25,000 loan. If your annual earnings for each of the past two years have been $200,000 or more, then you would be eligible to receive $40,000.

The next step in processing your application is for you to send documents for verification. I will need a copy of your business plan, documents showing the salary payments to employees, your sixteen-digit business license number, and an overview of your business account for the past two years.

If the loan is approved, you will be notified by mail, and the loan amount will be deposited into your bank account three days after the approval date. As soon as the funds are deposited, you can access them for any business purpose.

Warmest regards,

Kelly Wagner

Raul Wolfe
524 Boswell Court
San Diego, CA 92101

April 7

Dear Mr. Wolfe,

We are pleased to inform you that Anoka Bank approved your business loan request this morning. Enclosed you will find a copy of the loan agreement, which you should retain for your records. A lump sum of $40,000 will be deposited in your bank account, and the payments will begin from May 15. A payment of $864.79 will be automatically taken from your account on the 15th of every month for a period of 60 months (five years). If you prefer, you may make larger payment in order to pay the loan off early.

Should you have any questions, please feel free to contact your designated loan officer, Kelly Wagner, at 555-7947, extension 24.

Thank you for being an Anoka Bank customer!

The Anoka Bank Loans Team

176. What is implied about Ms. Wagner?
    (A) She recently transferred to a new branch.
    (B) She is Ms. Gauthier's supervisor.
    (C) She has not met Mr. Wolfe in person.
    (D) She would like to reschedule a meeting.

177. What is NOT requested by Ms. Wagner for Mr. Wolfe's application?
    (A) The original business license
    (B) A business plan
    (C) Payment records
    (D) An account summary

178. When will Mr. Wolfe be able to access the loan funds for the first time?
    (A) On April 7
    (B) On April 8
    (C) On April 10
    (D) On April 15

179. What is suggested about Mr. Wolfe's business?
    (A) It operates in more than one city.
    (B) It opened two years ago.
    (C) It will undergo a building project.
    (D) It earned at least $200,000 last year.

180. According to the letter, what part of the loan agreement is flexible?
    (A) The lump sum amount
    (B) The monthly due date
    (C) The interest rate
    (D) The duration of payments

Questions 181-185 refer to the following Web page and e-mail.

José Acevedo knew that he wanted to be a writer from a very young age. As a young boy growing up in Toronto, where he still lives today, he wrote short stories for his family and friends. He received a university degree in journalism before working at the *Toronto Daily Herald*. During that time, he was awarded the McKinley Prize, which is given for top reporting in a newspaper format. Mr. Acevedo then started publishing his own books, and he has four titles to date.

Plastic Universe, published 2012
A look into the modern world's addiction to plastic and its effects on wildlife and the environment. The book helped to further the discussion across the country on plastic use and its downsides.

Wind Revolution, published 2015
The book traces the history of wind turbines and their growing popularity as a sustainable energy source. It also outlines how individuals can get involved with using turbines on their own property.

Catching Up, published 2016
Acevedo interviews Toronto City Council members to investigate their efforts to adopt laws to the changing needs of the public, especially regarding technology and the environment.

Texas Treasures, published 2017
An undercover investigation into the oil industry in the U.S. state of Texas. Acevedo examines essential topics such as worker health, environmental protection, and corporate greed.

E-mail

To:	José Acevedo <contact@joseacevedo.com>
From:	Namiyo Sawada <n.sawada@zlproductions.com>
Date:	August 30
Subject:	Documentary

Dear Mr. Acevedo,

I am currently working on a documentary, and I believe that the details from your latest book would be a great addition to my film. Your insights would be highly valuable to our viewers. I first became familiar with your work when my book club read your debut novel, and I have followed your career since then. I wanted to introduce myself first, but I will call you tomorrow to arrange a time to meet, if you are interested. I can come your way so you don't have to travel.

Warmest regards,

Namiyo Sawada
ZL Productions

181. Who are the intended recipients of the McKinley Prize?

(A) Novelists
(B) Film directors
(C) Newspaper journalists
(D) Environmental activists

182. What is implied about Mr. Acevedo?

(A) He installed wind turbines on his property.
(B) He spoke with his local politicians.
(C) He has opened a new office in Texas.
(D) He will teach a university course.

183. Which book does Ms. Sawada want to feature in a documentary?

(A) *Plastic Universe*
(B) *Wind Revolution*
(C) *Catching Up*
(D) *Texas Treasures*

184. What does Ms. Sawada hope to do on August 31?

(A) Set up an appointment
(B) Attend a meeting
(C) Release a video
(D) Announce a book club

185. In the e-mail, the word "way" in paragraph 1, line 5, is closest in meaning to

(A) method
(B) style
(C) feature
(D) direction

Questions 186-190 refer to the following e-mails and schedule.

---

e-mail

To: All Valley Realty Employees
From: William Monahan
Date: September 18
Subject: Upcoming software training
Attachment: training.docx

Dear Valley Realty Employees,

Please be aware that employees will be required to complete mandatory software training in the first half of October. There are two programs that will be covered by the training. Investiprop-7 must be installed on all company computers, and we will start using it for all property searches instead of the EstateMax program. It is much more user-friendly, and there are more options for adding specific search criteria. All employees must complete the training, but they can select the date. The other program is Slate Books Pro, which is billing software. The program has recently undergone several upgrades. Only accountants need to take the Slate Books Pro training, and it will be provided on-site in our conference room.

Thanks,

William Monahan
Office Manager, Valley Realty

Valley Realty Training Schedule

Date	Software Program	Format	Number of Modules	Time
October 2	Investiprop-7	Online	6	10:30 A.M.–12:30 P.M.
October 5	Slate Books Pro	On-site workshop	4	2:00 P.M.–4:00 P.M.
October 6	Investiprop-7	Online	6	10:30 A.M.–12:30 P.M.
October 8	Investiprop-7	On-site workshop	6	1:00 P.M.–4:00 P.M.
October 10	Slate Books Pro	On-site workshop	4	9:00 A.M.–11:00 A.M.
October 13	Investiprop-7	Online	6	2:00 P.M.–4:00 P.M.

To: William Monahan
From: Tabitha Foster
Date: September 19
Subject: RE: Upcoming software training

Dear Mr. Monahan,

I am required to undergo training for both software programs, but I'm afraid I have some scheduling conflicts. I have already been approved to take my annual vacation from October 1 to October 7. I'll also be in Dallas from October 10 to 14 for the National Realtors Convention. Please call me at extension 21 so we can talk about how to resolve this issue.

Thanks!

Tabitha Foster

186. What is mentioned about Investiprop-7?
    (A) It can track customer billing information.
    (B) It is intended to replace another program.
    (C) It has recently changed some of its features.
    (D) It requires an account and password.

187. What is the same about all Investiprop-7 training sessions?
    (A) They are all held on the Internet.
    (B) They last for the same amount of time.
    (C) They all take place in the morning.
    (D) They have the same number of modules.

188. What is implied about Ms. Foster?
    (A) She plans to transfer to the Dallas branch.
    (B) She is a newly hired employee.
    (C) She works as an accountant.
    (D) She had difficulty installing the software.

189. When will Ms. Foster most likely undergo training?
    (A) On October 6
    (B) On October 8
    (C) On October 10
    (D) On October 13

190. Why is Mr. Monahan asked to call Ms. Foster?
    (A) To provide an updated schedule
    (B) To discuss solutions to a problem
    (C) To confirm attendance at a convention
    (D) To approve a vacation request

Questions 191-195 refer to the following Web page, order form, and e-mail.

Hampstead

For the past twenty years, Hampstead has been supplying landscaping materials and equipment in the Culver City area. We're open annually from early spring to mid-fall, and we can help you create the outdoor space of your dreams whether you are shopping for your business or your family home.

We work hard to provide affordable goods, with a wide range of options to suit all tastes and budgets. We try to source our goods from businesses in and around Culver City whenever possible, as this supports the local economy and reduces pollution caused by transportation. In addition to our product line, we also offer

- Free local delivery on all orders exceeding $35
- Garden design services (whether ornamental or for crops)
- Fast and easy ordering by phone or online
- Referrals for landscaping professionals in your area

We accept returns for any reason within 30 days of the delivery date. Bagged items such as soil and wood chips must be unopened. If you receive damaged goods or the wrong item, we will reimburse you for the return shipping costs. Otherwise, you must cover those costs yourself.

Hampstead

Name: Ray Casper **Order Date:** May 24 **Delivery Date:** May 26
Delivery Address: 442 Emerson Road, Culver City, CA 90230

Description	Product ID	Price Per Unit	Qty.	
Solar LED path lights (pack of 4)	NR5472	$29.99	10	$299.90
Raised garden bed, wooden frame (48' x 96' x 5.5')	HL195	$99.99	3	$299.97
Shredded wood mulch (50-lb bag)	HL3810	$8.99	5	$44.95
Grey stones (20-lb bag)	PS024	$23.49	5	$117.45
Metal garden edging (black, 75-ft roll)	AE638	$319.49	1	$319.49
For questions or comments about your order, please e-mail info@hampstead4u.com.			Subtotal	$1,081.76
			Tax	$64.90
			Delivery	$0.00
			Total	**$1,146.66**

E-mail

To:	Ray Casper <r.casper@lomaxltd.com>
From:	Mara Brewer <m.brewer@lomaxltd.com>
Date:	June 2
Subject:	Landscaping

Hi Ray,

Thanks for ordering the materials that the maintenance team needs for the landscaping work in front of our building. I've used goods from a variety of stores, and these items from Hampstead are by far the best I've seen. I'm sure they will last for a long time. We are making steady progress on the changes, but we're running low on rocks, so I've ordered more of those. Also, one of the garden beds had a crack in it when it arrived, so we should exchange it. It would be best for you to contact Hampstead about that, since you placed the original order.

Thanks!

Mara

191. What is true about Hampstead?
(A) It has branches in several cities.
(B) It provides a rental service.
(C) It is operated by a family.
(D) It is a seasonal business.

192. Which aspect of Hampstead is mentioned on the Web page?
(A) Cultivating its own plants
(B) Supporting local businesses
(C) Hiring experienced crew members
(D) Training landscaping professionals

193. What does Ms. Brewer like about Hampstead?
(A) It delivers items quickly.
(B) It offers a long warranty.
(C) It has high-quality goods.
(D) It carries a wide selection.

194. Which product has Ms. Brewer ordered?
(A) NR5472
(B) HL195
(C) HL3810
(D) PS024

195. How will Hampstead most likely respond to Mr. Casper's request?
(A) By providing express delivery
(B) By making a free repair
(C) By issuing a full refund for a product
(D) By reimbursing shipping costs

Questions 196-200 refer to the following advertisement, form, and e-mail.

Bryson Camping Spring Sale

Stock up on essential goods at our Spring Sale. One week only—April 2–8.

All Kolbert sleeping bags $29.99 each	10% off all Hathaway flashlights	60% off select outdoor stoves	$15 off all Forestlife backpacks	30% off all Benson 2- and 3-person tents

Coupons cannot be used with certain sale prices.
Check our Web site for details.

Bryson Camping
Customer Inquiry/Comment Form

Customer Name: Rachel Barry
Company Name (if applicable): Adventure Tours
E-mail Address: rachelb@adventuretoursltd.net
Loyalty Card Number (if applicable): 7625003
File Upload: receipt.jpg

Inquiry/Comment: I recently purchased a large order of supplies for our customers' overnight camping trips. This included 5 Renway sleeping bags, 20 Hathaway flashlights, 8 Benson tents (the 3-person size), and 3 Forestlife backpacks. I saw on your Web site that most of these items are now being offered at discounted prices because of your Spring Sale. I have uploaded a copy of my receipt for review. I hope you will apply your 30-day price match to my order so that I can take advantage of the discount.

To	Rachel Barry <rachelb@adventuretoursltd.net>
From	Bryson Camping <inquiries@brysoncamping.com>
Date	April 4
Subject	Bryson Camping Customer Inquiry/Comment

Dear Ms. Barry,

Thank you for contacting Bryson Camping. You are correct that we refund the difference if the price drops within 30 days of the purchase date. However, some of the sale prices are not as low as what you have already received. For example, you got half off the Benson tents because the product was first offered at an introductory rate, as it was new to the market. You also received a bulk discount on items that were ordered in groups of ten or more. Therefore, you will only receive a partial refund for the Forestlife products. It will be sent along with a new receipt for those items within five business days.

We would love to know what you think about our inquiry process via the attached survey. If you send it back, you will be entered into a prize drawing for a $50 store voucher.

Justin Dugan
Customer Service Agent, Bryson Camping

196. What is implied about Ms. Barry?
(A) She was recently hired as a tour guide.
(B) She was misinformed about a store policy.
(C) She made a purchase before April 2.
(D) She visited the store 30 days ago.

197. Why does Ms. Barry want the business to review a receipt?
(A) To issue a refund for damaged items
(B) To process a request for a price change
(C) To confirm that some items were not shipped
(D) To check whether an employee made an error

198. According to Mr. Dugan, why was Ms. Barry given a discount on the Benson items?
(A) She signed up for a loyalty club program.
(B) She took advantage of a product launch.
(C) She purchased a large number of goods.
(D) She presented a discount coupon.

199. For which items will Ms. Barry receive a new receipt?
(A) Backpacks
(B) Flashlights
(C) Sleeping bags
(D) Tents

200. What has Mr. Dugan sent with the e-mail?
(A) Some survey results
(B) A store voucher
(C) Some discount codes
(D) A feedback form

Stop! This is the end of the test. If you finish before time is called, you may go back to Part 5, 6, and 7 and check your work.

TEST 02

PART 5 · PART 6 · PART 7

준비하기

손목시계

뭉뚝한 연필과 지우개

Answer Sheet

토익 RC는 75분 동안 진행됩니다.
반드시 75분 이내에 문제 풀이와 답안지 마킹을 완료하세요.

TEST 02는 **고난도 문제가 적게 포함**된 쪽박달 :(TEST입니다.
다른 TEST에 비해 상대적으로 **환산 점수가 낮게** 나올 수 있습니다.

고난도 문제는 해설집에서 확인할 수 있습니다.
해설집 p.24

맞은 개수	환산 점수		맞은 개수	환산 점수
96-100	**465** - 495		41-45	**145** - 215
91-95	**430** - 490		36-40	**120** - 180
86-90	**400** - 465		31-35	**100** - 145
81-85	**375** - 440		26-30	**80** - 120
76-80	**340** - 415		21-25	**65** - 95
71-75	**315** - 390		16-20	**50** - 75
66-70	**285** - 365		11-15	**35** - 55
61-65	**255** - 335		6-10	**15** - 40
56-60	**225** - 305		1-5	**5** - 30
51-55	**200** - 270		0	5
46-50	**170** - 240			

READING TEST

In the Reading test, you will read a variety of texts and answer several different types of reading comprehension questions. The entire Reading test will last 75 minutes. There are three parts, and directions are given for each part. You are encouraged to answer as many questions as possible within the time allowed.

You must mark your answers on the separate answer sheet. Do not write your answers in your test book.

PART 5

Directions: A word or phrase is missing in each of the sentences below. Four answer choices are given below each sentence. Select the best answer to complete the sentence. Then mark the letter (A), (B), (C), or (D) on your answer sheet.

101. The national media ------- ignored the report on bridge safety and recommendations.
    (A) large
    (B) largest
    (C) largely
    (D) larger

102. The new security system can provide ------- by phone when a window or door has been opened.
    (A) alertly
    (B) alerts
    (C) alert
    (D) alerted

103. Employees will be reimbursed ------- for the expenses they incurred during the business trip.
    (A) soon
    (B) very
    (C) many
    (D) about

104. Ms. Herrera and Mr. Lee set up most of the centerpieces for the banquet ------- because the rest of the team got stuck in traffic.
    (A) theirs
    (B) their
    (C) their own
    (D) themselves

105. Applications for the engineer position will be accepted only ------- March 31, so don't forget to submit yours.
    (A) until
    (B) without
    (C) against
    (D) throughout

106. The mechanic ------- that the tires on the vehicle were heavily worn and in need of replacement.
    (A) noting
    (B) note
    (C) noted
    (D) to note

107. The stunning white sands of Sheridan Beach ------- thousands of tourists every year.
    (A) exhibit
    (B) attract
    (C) improve
    (D) feature

108. Before using any ingredients in his dishes, Chef Montague checks that they are ------- from preservatives.
    (A) to free
    (B) freely
    (C) free
    (D) freedom

109. The budget prepared by Mr. Elliot does not account ------- changes in currency rates, so it was considered inaccurate.
(A) for
(B) through
(C) of
(D) upon

110. The state government recently formed a ------- to explore strategies for preventing air pollution.
(A) relationship
(B) committee
(C) barrier
(D) politician

111. As we have had some problems with our distributor, the phone model is ------- for the next few weeks.
(A) occupied
(B) rearranged
(C) unavailable
(D) correct

112. Ms. Harvey, whose sculptures are on display at the gallery, has worked as a professional artist ------- more than forty years.
(A) for
(B) to
(C) at
(D) of

113. Mr. Mueller was surprised that the suggestion most favored by the management team was in fact -------.
(A) his
(B) himself
(C) him
(D) he

114. Reporters pointed out that ------- of the remarks made by the company's CEO were incorrect.
(A) what
(B) other
(C) several
(D) even

115. Many online retailers may consider ------- their security measures so that sensitive customer data cannot be stolen.
(A) to modify
(B) modifies
(C) modifying
(D) modified

116. The Carlyle Research Library houses the most ------- collection of manuscripts produced by novelist Ann Ortega.
(A) extends
(B) extensive
(C) extended
(D) extension

117. ------- the city planner has finalized the plans for the roadwork, a more accurate estimate can be provided.
(A) Upon
(B) After
(C) Not only
(D) Whether

118. The campaign manager believed that Joan Moore's writing style fit the needs of the speechwriter role -------.
(A) routinely
(B) constantly
(C) perfectly
(D) urgently

119. The company was nominated for several awards in its field, and this has led to increased investor -------.
(A) enthuse
(B) enthusiastic
(C) enthusiasm
(D) enthusiastically

120. The database is password protected so that it can only be accessed by employees who are ------- to use it.
(A) complied
(B) preferred
(C) researched
(D) authorized

GO ON TO THE NEXT PAGE

121. The magazine costs $1.95 per issue via a subscription, ------- the newsstand price is nearly three times that amount.
    (A) whether
    (B) all
    (C) approximately
    (D) whereas

122. Six companies entered bids for the construction of the city's recreation center, and ------- met the required criteria for the project.
    (A) both
    (B) all
    (C) anyone
    (D) everything

123. Ms. Lee confirmed that a fifteen-foot cargo truck would be ------- for moving her belongings and furniture.
    (A) occasional
    (B) flexible
    (C) sufficient
    (D) eligible

124. Most offices in the area only recycle paper, glass, and plastic, but Logan Inc. has collection containers for cardboard -------.
    (A) such as
    (B) long enough
    (C) even so
    (D) as well

125. Visitors to the Santa Rosa Resort ------- tip the housekeeping staff $5 per night's stay.
    (A) mutually
    (B) customarily
    (C) sharply
    (D) perfectly

126. The Horace Institute's ------- of lectures for first-time managers has been extremely popular.
    (A) behavior
    (B) movement
    (C) series
    (D) route

127. The scales developed by Condor Laboratories weigh both liquids and solids ------- unprecedented precision.
    (A) around
    (B) unlike
    (C) toward
    (D) with

128. The new machinery installed at Bonfoy Manufacturing is capable of ------- hundreds of yards of fabric per day.
    (A) produce
    (B) producer
    (C) producing
    (D) produces

129. Fire department personnel will check the building thoroughly to ------- the structure is sound before allowing people back into it.
    (A) calculate
    (B) ensure
    (C) accept
    (D) retain

130. This new navigation system can recalculate the best route ------- by factoring in real-time traffic.
    (A) automates
    (B) automatically
    (C) automation
    (D) automating

PART 6

Directions: Read the texts that follow. A word, phrase, or sentence is missing in parts of each text. Four answer choices for each question are given below the text. Select the best answer to complete the text. Then mark the letter (A), (B), (C), or (D) on your answer sheet.

Questions 131-134 refer to the following letter.

Daniel Vance
1749 Oxford Court
Tulsa, OK 74106

January 7

Dear Mr. Vance,

I'm writing regarding your recent order of a Montclair stereo system, which was supposed to be delivered on December 20 but did not arrive until January 2. We are very sorry that this item -------. We agree that you are
                                                                                                                131.
entitled to compensation due to the -------. Firstly, we will refund all shipping charges for this merchandise.
                                     132.
We will also credit your account in the amount of $50 to help make up for any issues that resulted ------- our
                                                                                                     133.
error. -------. The credit will be posted on your account by January 15.
       134.

Sincerely,

The Finwood Electronics Customer Service Team

---

131. (A) had to delay
(B) will be delayed
(C) is delaying
(D) was delayed

132. (A) absence
(B) disadvantage
(C) inconvenience
(D) shortage

133. (A) from
(B) onto
(C) among
(D) until

134. (A) Our warehouse team will check for the item.
(B) The sale will run for as long as supplies last.
(C) We hope you will be satisfied with this proposal.
(D) Both payments are printed on last month's statement.

Questions 135-138 refer to the following article.

Jobs Report Released
January 3

Figures gathered by the city's Department of Labor indicate that the employment rate is up in Lawton. -------, the city is at an all-time low for unemployment. This is partially thanks to the opening of the Marquette manufacturing facility six months ago. The factory, which employs nearly 150 people, uses laser cutters to fashion custom-made components out of ------- such as wood, metal, and plastic. -------. Therefore, new jobs become available regularly. City officials ------- the upturn in the manufacturing sector will lead to growth in other local businesses as well.

135. (A) Otherwise
 (B) In fact
 (C) Nonetheless
 (D) On the contrary

136. (A) productions
 (B) advantages
 (C) expenses
 (D) materials

137. (A) Reports on job conditions are prepared once per quarter.
 (B) The factory provided data about its staffing procedures.
 (C) Each product comes with a money-back guarantee.
 (D) The demand for the company's goods has been rising.

138. (A) believing
 (B) believe
 (C) are believed
 (D) believes

Questions 139-142 refer to the following e-mail.

To: All staff
From: Loni Jordan
Date: November 2
Subject: Staff awards

Hello Everyone,

The year has gone by quickly, and it is almost time again for our ------- ceremony to present awards to employees. This is the perfect opportunity ------- the hard work and dedication of our staff members. Of course, we can also enjoy socializing together over a delicious meal. Our usual place is Newton Hall, but it is already fully booked for December. I'm looking for another facility that has a ------- of one hundred people, as the entire staff will be in attendance and some employees may choose to bring their spouses. Most likely, we will use the ballroom at the Violet Hotel. -------. The catering company we're using can accommodate vegetarians, vegans, and more. You will be given more information as the event date approaches.

Sincerely,

Loni Jordan
Events Committee, Sanders Inc.

139. (A) closing
(B) debut
(C) annual
(D) recruitment

140. (A) will recognize
(B) to recognize
(C) recognizing
(D) having recognized

141. (A) space
(B) capacity
(C) result
(D) sample

142. (A) The final seating chart can be downloaded.
(B) This delay will not happen again.
(C) Thank you for volunteering to assist with the planning.
(D) Please let me know if you have dietary restrictions.

Questions 143-146 refer to the following memo.

To: All Sunset Hair Salon Employees
From: Geneva Curtis, General Manager
Date: Wednesday, May 31
Subject: Hair-washing area

The plumber we hired to install two new sinks in our hair-washing area has taken several sick days and will now complete the work on June 4 instead of June 1. Given this unexpected ------- 143., we will not be able to easily handle the high volume of customers that have already made reservations. To keep up with the demand, please complete the hair-washing for your customers as quickly as possible, especially if you are using the high-pressure tap ------- 144. to the storage closet. I ------- 145. any problems this might cause with your customers, but we will only have to put up with it for a few days. ------- 146..

143. (A) structure
(B) situation
(C) treatment
(D) hesitation

144. (A) furnished
(B) adjacent
(C) essential
(D) comparable

145. (A) to regret
(B) regrets
(C) was regretting
(D) regret

146. (A) Let me know what style you prefer.
(B) Please tell them to come back soon.
(C) The change will be well worth it in the end.
(D) Each session should only take a few minutes.

PART 7

Directions: In this part you will read a selection of texts, such as magazine and newspaper articles, e-mails, and instant messages. Each text or set of texts is followed by several questions. Select the best answer for each question and mark the letter (A), (B), (C), or (D) on your answer sheet.

Questions 147-148 refer to the following business card.

Elaine's Alterations

529 Cambridge Avenue ◆ 555-3223
Elaine Smith, Owner

Custom alterations for suits, dresses, and more.
Quick Hemming Service: Trousers shortened while you wait!

Mon. – Fri.: 9 A.M. – 6 P.M. / Sat.: 10 A.M. – 4 P.M.

---

147. What service can be performed within a short time?

(A) Repairing torn suit jackets
(B) Replacing missing buttons on clothing
(C) Adjusting the length of trousers
(D) Taking measurements for custom dresses

148. What is suggested about Elaine's Alterations?

(A) It offers a money-back guarantee.
(B) It only has one employee.
(C) It sells a variety of fabric.
(D) It is closed on Sundays.

GO ON TO THE NEXT PAGE

Questions 149-150 refer to the following e-mail.

To: Larry Morgan <morgan.l@crescentinc.com>
From: Celeste Ross <ross.c@crescentinc.com>
Date: December 2
Subject: Monthly Meeting

Dear Mr. Morgan,

I am writing to inform you that the monthly managers meeting scheduled for December 3 has been pushed back by half an hour, so it will begin at 3:30. This is due to a scheduling conflict with the conference room. We still expect the meeting to last approximately one hour. If there is anything you think should be covered at the meeting, please e-mail me by the end of the day. That way, I can formally add it to the agenda.

See you tomorrow!

Celeste

149. What has changed about a meeting?

(A) The date
(B) The location
(C) The start time
(D) The duration

150. Why should Mr. Morgan write to Ms. Ross?

(A) To suggest a topic for discussion
(B) To confirm his attendance at a meeting
(C) To provide a copy of the agenda
(D) To warn her about a scheduling problem

Questions 151-152 refer to the following text-message chain.

Ivan Mathiasen [9:20 A.M.]
I sent you an e-mail with the business proposal for Seneca Hospitality. I'm wondering if you've had a chance to check it out.

Amina Behane [9:23 A.M.]
I have a major customer visiting my office soon, but I can take a quick look now.

Ivan Mathiasen [9:24 A.M.]
Thanks. I just want to make sure that I've covered everything.

Amina Behane [9:25 A.M.]
There are a few adjustments to be made, but that's normal. I've had to coach your other team members on the same issues. Let's meet after lunch to discuss it.

Ivan Mathiasen [9:26 A.M.]
Okay, I'm free anytime.

Amina Behane [9:27 A.M.]
That's her now. I'll call you when I'm done.

151. What is implied about Ms. Behane?
(A) She requested some updated figures.
(B) She had some trouble receiving an e-mail.
(C) She is Mr. Mathiasen's supervisor.
(D) She used to work for Seneca Hospitality.

152. At 9:27 A.M., what does Ms. Behane mean when she writes, "That's her now"?
(A) An important client has arrived.
(B) A career coach is highly recommended.
(C) A colleague can answer questions.
(D) A coworker will cover Ms. Behane's duties.

Questions 153-154 refer to the following instructions.

Don't ever miss another episode of your favorite television show again with the Vision-HD smartphone app. The Vision-HD smartphone app allows you to remotely program your smart TV to record a program, and it can be used up to seven days in advance.

1. Visit www.myappstore.com/visionhd and download the app. This app is free to all users, but there are some optional in-app purchases available.
2. Input your customer number from your cable service provider. You can find the number on the top of your billing statement.
3. That's all! Begin using the app and enjoy television on your own schedule!

153. What has the Vision-HD smartphone application been designed to do?
(A) Set a device to record television shows
(B) Show reviews for popular TV programs
(C) Stream videos from the Internet
(D) Improve the image quality of videos

154. What do customers need to provide when signing up for the service?
(A) An ID card
(B) A customer number
(C) An e-mail address
(D) A down payment

Questions 155-157 refer to the following review.

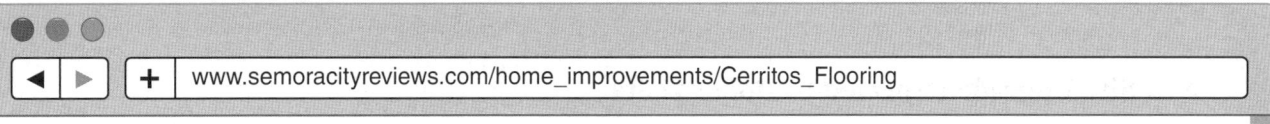

Business: Cerritos Flooring
Rating: 5/5

Reviewer: Ruben Ives

I would highly recommend Cerritos Flooring to anyone who is considering having hardwood floors installed. When choosing a company, I just went for the cheapest one, so I wasn't sure whether the quality of the work would be good enough. However, I was pleasantly surprised. I only had to wait a few days to get an appointment, and the crew arrived in the morning on time and with all of the tools they needed. They performed the work efficiently. What I really thought was amazing was that they vacuumed and cleaned up everything before they left. No one would even be able to guess that they had been there! I've had the new floor for two weeks, and it looks fantastic. I'm sure it will look as good as new for many years to come.

The one thing I would suggest is to make sure your corridor is empty prior to your appointment. I forgot to do this, which made bringing in the supplies somewhat difficult for the workers, as they were being very careful not to break anything along the way.

155. Why did Mr. Ives select Cerritos Flooring?

(A) It had the lowest prices.
(B) It was recommended by a friend.
(C) It had a good reputation.
(D) It was nearest to his home.

156. What impressed Mr. Ives most about the service?

(A) It was available on the same day as ordering.
(B) The work comes with a warranty.
(C) It was completed ahead of schedule.
(D) The crew did not leave behind a mess.

157. What does Mr. Ives suggest doing?

(A) Booking a morning appointment
(B) Checking the floor after two weeks
(C) Removing items from a hallway
(D) Reporting broken items to the company

Questions 158-160 refer to the following article.

Web Site Upgrade Expected to Boost Visits

(February 22)—The Maywood city government has launched an upgraded version of its Web site to appeal to more residents. This is the first major change to the site in more than fifteen years.

As before, visitors to the site can search for activities by date, as well as access a database of community-related documents. The most noticeable new feature is an online gallery where registered users can upload images of community activities. —[1]—.

Some residents expressed concern about the cost of upgrading the Web site, as the city spent over $20,000 for the project. "With a population as small as ours, it's difficult to justify investing in something that was already working perfectly," said Joshua Quentin, a business owner in Maywood. —[2]—.

City officials hope that the new Web site will create a renewed interest in Maywood's local activities. —[3]—. For example, the annual Summer Singing Contest and the Riverside Litter Collection Day are opportunities this month for residents to get together. The Web site also has the technology to broadcast live video streams, a system that will debut during next week's debate among candidates for state senator. —[4]—. It will also be used to broadcast the regional festivals throughout this year.

158. What has been added to the city's Web site?

(A) A collection of photographs
(B) An interactive calendar
(C) A search engine
(D) A video-recording feature

159. What is NOT indicated as an upcoming event in Maywood?

(A) A music competition
(B) A sports race
(C) A political debate
(D) A cleanup project

160. In which of the positions marked [1], [2], [3], and [4] does the following sentence best belong?

"Nonetheless, most people thought the site was outdated and that the change was necessary."

(A) [1]
(B) [2]
(C) [3]
(D) [4]

Questions 161-163 refer to the following e-mail.

To: Madison Seneca <mseneca@professionaltraining.net>
From: Davi Gomez <gomez_davi@blaine-inc.com>
Date: January 29
Subject: Professional Training: February Event

Dear Ms. Seneca,

As you know, Professional Training will hold its next training event on Friday, February 12. We had scheduled you for two one-hour talks. Unfortunately, one of them has been removed from the schedule due to low enrollment figures. Therefore, you will only be giving the following talk: "Using the Power of the Web to Advertise Your Business." According to the contract, you are entitled to 50% of the speaking fee for the talk that is not going forward, due to the late notice. You are welcome to attend one of the other talks or workshops on that day at no charge, and I highly encourage you to do so. Please e-mail me back by February 6 to let me know your top choice so that I may issue you a pass.

Sincerely,

Davi Gomez

161. Why did Mr. Gomez send the e-mail?
(A) To check enrollment figures
(B) To approve a presentation suggestion
(C) To report a cancellation
(D) To register for a training event

162. What does Ms. Seneca most likely specialize in?
(A) Contract negotiation
(B) Energy production
(C) Business loans
(D) Online marketing

163. What is Ms. Seneca encouraged to do by February 6?
(A) Upload a presentation file
(B) Plan a travel schedule
(C) Select an activity to attend
(D) Provide a list of participants

GO ON TO THE NEXT PAGE

Questions 164-167 refer to the following article.

PENNSWOOD, January 19—An independent firm has reviewed the state's economic figures and estimated that the number of visitors to the state has dropped by 7.3 percent compared to last year, with revenues from this sector reaching approximately $3.2 billion. —[1]—.

A variety of businesses, such as hotels and restaurants, are directly affected by these figures, as they heavily depend on spending from tourists to keep them in business. —[2]—. "If my rooms are vacant," says hotel owner Mathew Ledford, "I can't keep my staff working full-time."

Tourism Director Kathleen Renfrow said that the recently released figures should be put in context. "Last year was the 100th celebration of the erection of the Human Freedom Monument," she said. "That event brought in many more tourists than usual, so it's not a fair comparison. To get a better picture of how we are performing, it would better to compare the figures to those of two years ago. —[3]—. Our office is continually looking for ways to generate interest in our state, and we have a variety of activities—such as boating festivals and sports tournaments—to raise our profile."

In order to make these types of events a success, adequate funding is needed. Fortunately, it seems likely that the tourism industry will be a top priority in budgetary considerations. All three people running for governor this fall—Melvin Ramey, Ann Alvarez, and Luke Zimmer—have publicly shown support for investing in the state's tourism industry as a way of generating tax income and enriching communities across the state. —[4]—.

164. What is the article mainly about?
    (A) A proposed tax on tourism businesses
    (B) A reduction in tourism
    (C) An ad campaign for tourists
    (D) A new tourist attraction

165. According to Ms. Renfrow, what special event was held last year?
    (A) An anniversary of a monument
    (B) A music awards show
    (C) An outdoor boating festival
    (D) A sports tournament

166. Who most likely is Ms. Alvarez?
    (A) A political candidate
    (B) A hotel owner
    (C) A financial advisor
    (D) A tourism director

167. In which of the positions marked [1], [2], [3], and [4] does the following sentence best belong?

    "When doing so, you see that they are almost equal."

    (A) [1]
    (B) [2]
    (C) [3]
    (D) [4]

Questions 168-171 refer to the following online chat discussion.

Heather Teodros [4:25 P.M.]
Thanks for covering the first day of the arts festival at Wyatt Park for me, everyone. How did things go?

Arnaldo Guevara [4:26 P.M.]
We got a lot of photos of the booths and activities, and we had interviews with the event coordinator as well as a number of artists and visitors. We've already got a summary of what we're going to print in the paper.

Heather Teodros [4:27 P.M.]
I'd like a copy of that once it's ready.

Arnaldo Guevara [4:29 P.M.]
Of course. Everyone we spoke with really enjoyed the event. As an added bonus, it brought in a lot of people from out of town. That's always good for the local economy.

Ganesh Bhagat [4:31 P.M.]
Exactly. I know that city representatives were trying to grab more attention for our community.

Sharon Moyer [4:32 P.M.]
I hope the rest of the event goes smoothly.

Ganesh Bhagat [4:33 P.M.]
Well, it's supposed to be rainy for the next few days, so that may negatively affect the turnout.

Heather Teodros [4:34 P.M.]
Fortunately, they're using all of the picnic shelters at the event site, so most of the booths are protected.

Arnaldo Guevara [4:35 P.M.]
The daily weather report said that there will be scattered showers, so that's not too bad.

168. Who most likely is Ms. Teodros?
    (A) An event planner
    (B) A professional artist
    (C) A journalist
    (D) A city official

169. At 4:27 P.M., what does Ms. Teodros most likely mean when she writes, "I'd like a copy of that once it's ready"?
    (A) She would like to read an outline of some information.
    (B) She is interested in seeing a complete list of participants.
    (C) She wants to create a feedback survey for the event.
    (D) She will send some cards to VIP visitors.

170. What positive comment was made about the event?
    (A) It provided discounts to art club members.
    (B) It attracted non-resident visitors.
    (C) Its admission fee was reasonable.
    (D) Its parking situation was well organized.

171. What is implied about Wyatt Park?
    (A) It is the town's largest park.
    (B) It received some negative reviews.
    (C) It releases a daily report.
    (D) It has some covered structures.

Questions 172-175 refer to the following job posting.

Now Hiring: Senior Administrative Assistant

Salco Community College is seeking a full-time senior administrative assistant. Preference will be given to candidates who can start immediately.

The senior administrative assistant is responsible for a variety of tasks to help keep the office running smoothly, and this position would be ideal for a person who likes changing activities frequently and who can work under pressure. Duties include responding to information requests from the community; booking flights, hotels, and vehicle rentals for staff members' business trips; contributing content to a monthly newsletter; and monitoring the office's expenditures. An annual salary of approximately $28,000 (negotiable) is offered along with four weeks of paid vacation and medical insurance.

To apply, send a résumé and cover letter to hr@salcocc.edu on or before April 7. Our hiring committee will review the applications on April 8, and successful applicants will be contacted the following day to set up an interview. Interviews will most likely be held on April 11. Those who come to our office for an interview will also be asked to take a computer-based skills examination. Questions about the hiring process may be directed to the e-mail address listed above. We also accept inquiries by phone at 555-7931 during regular business hours.

172. What is implied about Salco Community College?

(A) Its number of full-time students has risen.
(B) It provides services at more than one campus.
(C) Its budget has recently been increased.
(D) It needs to fill a position quickly.

173. What is NOT mentioned as a duty of the position?

(A) Increasing a newsletter's circulation
(B) Providing information to the public
(C) Keeping track of spending
(D) Coordinating travel arrangements

174. When will successful candidates initially be contacted?

(A) April 7
(B) April 8
(C) April 9
(D) April 11

175. According to the job posting, what will some applicants be required to do?

(A) Take a test on site
(B) Submit letters of recommendation
(C) Present a portfolio of work
(D) Complete an online application

Questions 176-180 refer to the following online article and forum comment.

the Asheville Herald, May 25, "Fresh Flow Dance Group Prepares for Summer Season"

With fast-paced rhythms and perfectly synchronized dance moves, Fresh Flow, a contemporary dance troupe based in Asheville, has amazed audiences across the country. Those who attend Fresh Flow's performances will be treated to a spectacular show. They may even find themselves invited onto the stage or urged to dance along in the aisles. The group has recently announced its summer schedule, which will include shows four times a week at the Kiernan Theater throughout June and July.

Fresh Flow was formed by Dario Varela, who graduated ten years ago from the Saldivar School of Arts with a bachelor's degree in Performing Arts. He started the group several years after graduation as a way to promote dance activities in Asheville.

Tickets for Fresh Flow performances can be purchased online through the Fresh Flow Web site or at the Kiernan Theater box office. Sunday performances are geared specifically toward children and families. In addition to adding more child-friendly tunes, the group also makes adjustments to the facility. For example, screens broadcasting the show live are set up in the lobby, as some children may find the music and movement overwhelming and need to take a break.

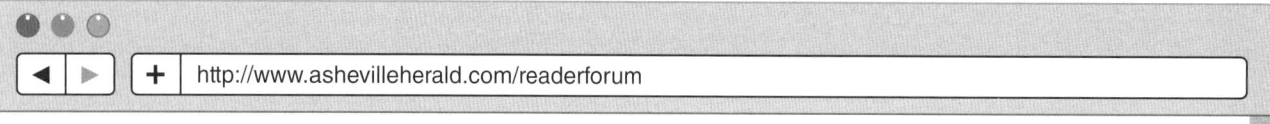

I appreciated your recent article about Fresh Flow. This group is so talented, and its members find ways to make the art of dance more interesting to the general public. I remember watching a Fresh Flow show for the first time a few years ago. The precision of the dancers was amazing, and I loved the beautiful costumes designed by the group's founder himself. Since that performance, I have attended many other Fresh Flow shows, sometimes using the choreography as inspiration for the moves that I teach to my own students. My only criticism of the group is that the announcements of its bookings always seem to come at the last minute. I think most people prefer to plan ahead rather than just buy tickets on a whim.

– Melissa Nash

176. What is implied about Fresh Flow?
   (A) It will give four weekend performances.
   (B) It is funded by the city.
   (C) It encourages audience participation.
   (D) It was founded ten years ago.

177. What is suggested about Sunday performances?
   (A) Seating is available on a first-come, first-served basis only.
   (B) The tickets are offered at a lower price than usual.
   (C) There is a special segment performed by children.
   (D) Their dances and contents are suitable for children to watch.

178. What is implied about Mr. Varela?
   (A) He has costume design skills.
   (B) He used to work at the Saldivar School of Arts.
   (C) He provides private dance lessons.
   (D) He is a personal friend of Ms. Nash.

179. What is most likely true about Ms. Nash?
   (A) She grew up in Asheville.
   (B) She works as a dance instructor.
   (C) She had an interview with *the Asheville Herald*.
   (D) She has visited the Kiernan Theater.

180. What change would Ms. Nash most likely be in favor of?
   (A) Promoting shows further in advance
   (B) Giving autographs to audience members
   (C) Adding more performances on weekends
   (D) Allowing ticket bookings by phone

Questions 181-185 refer to the following e-mail and text message.

To: Colin Vogel <vogelcolin@blevinsinc.com>
From: Flores Air <bookings@flores-air.com>
Date: April 28
Subject: Flores Air Flight

Dear Mr. Vogel,

Thank you for booking a flight with Flores Air. Please find your itinerary below.

Passenger: Colin Vogel
Booking Confirmation: GS595867
Departure: Atlanta, May 6, 7:32 P.M.
Class: Business

Flight: F950
Seat: 15C
Arrival: London, May 7, 8:47 A.M.

Boarding begins one hour before departure. As a Platinum Member, a status granted to passengers who traveled at least 100,000 miles with us last year, you are entitled to earn 2,500 bonus frequent flyer miles on this flight. These will be automatically added to your account on the flight day.

Baggage Information:

	1 Carry-on	1st Checked Bag	2nd Checked Bag	3rd Checked Bag
Economy Class	Free	$25.00	$35.00	$50.00
Business Class	Free	Free	$25.00	$35.00
First Class	Free	Free	Free	$25.00

Passengers with flight delays between one and two hours will be given complimentary drinks (bottled water, soda, coffee, and tea) at the gate. For delays of two hours or more, passengers will be issued a voucher for a free lunch/dinner, which can be used at participating restaurants in the airport.

To: Colin Vogel, 793-555-0899
From: Flores Air, private number
Date: May 6, 3:51 p.m.

The departure of Flores Air's flight F950 with service to London has been postponed due to severe weather. It will now depart three hours later than originally scheduled, at 10:32 P.M. This is our only flight to London departing today, so it is not possible to take a different flight. We're sorry for any inconvenience this may cause.

181. What is indicated about Mr. Vogel?
 (A) He charged the cost of a flight to his company's account.
 (B) He flew over one hundred thousand miles last year.
 (C) His office is currently based in Atlanta.
 (D) His flight was partially paid for with rewards points.

182. How much will Mr. Vogel pay for a second checked bag?
 (A) Free
 (B) $25.00
 (C) $35.00
 (D) $50.00

183. What is the purpose of the text message?
 (A) To outline a cancellation policy
 (B) To announce a flight delay
 (C) To explain a gate change
 (D) To confirm a seat request

184. What is Mr. Vogel eligible to receive?
 (A) A shuttle ticket
 (B) A partial refund
 (C) A seat upgrade
 (D) A meal voucher

185. In the text message, the word "take" in paragraph 1, line 5, is closest in meaning to
 (A) travel on
 (B) remove
 (C) catch on
 (D) collect

Questions 186-190 refer to the following advertisement and e-mails.

Assistant Needed

Wallenberg Real Estate has an opening for a real estate assistant to join the team at the Newport branch. A real-estate license is not required, as this position does not involve advising clients or negotiating terms. The job consists of setting up for open houses, posting new listings on our Web site, and gathering data about homes and land rights from governmental databases and public records. This position is part-time only, and the successful candidate will be able to set his or her own hours. Please send résumés to Alice Prescott at a.prescott@wallenbergre.com.

	E-mail
To:	Alice Prescott <a.prescott@wallenbergre.com>
From:	Candace Steiner <steinerc@hillhaven.net>
Date:	April 20
Subject:	Real Estate Assistant

Dear Ms. Prescott,

I am interested in the real estate assistant position that was recently posted in the Classified Ads section of the *Newport Herald*. Although I have never worked for a real estate firm, I spent three years as a receptionist at the office of Linden Insurance, so I am used to administrative duties. I was particularly attracted to the job at Wallenberg because I am taking classes at the Montford Institute part-time, so the working conditions are perfect for me.

I am a hard worker, and I am able to learn new tasks quickly. Attached you will find my current résumé along with an extra file detailing the software programs in which I am proficient. Because of these skills, I believe I would require very little training to get started. I hope we can meet in person to discuss the position further, as I am considering real estate for my future long-term career.

Sincerely,

Candace Steiner

To: Randall Santiago <r.santiago@wallenbergre.com>, Stella McCord <s.mccord@wallenbergre.com>, Joseph Duncan <j.duncan@wallenbergre.com>
From: Alice Prescott <a.prescott@wallenbergre.com>
Date: April 24
Subject: Open position for real estate assistant

Good morning,

Thank you all for taking the time to sit in on the interviews this week. Since we didn't get the chance to make a final decision about the job candidates, I thought we could do it by e-mail. I believe that Ms. Steiner would be the best person for this position, so I think we should make her a job offer. I thought she was friendly and easygoing in the interview. Most importantly, the information she organized in her supplemental file is exactly what we need to avoid having to do a lot of training. Please let me know what you think!

Thanks!

Alice Prescott

---

186. What is indicated in the advertisement as a responsibility of the position?

(A) Setting up contracts
(B) Answering phones
(C) Researching properties
(D) Designing a Web site

187. What is true about Ms. Steiner?

(A) She is familiar with selling homeowners' insurance.
(B) She is currently employed by a real estate agency.
(C) She has enrolled in a licensing program.
(D) She has experience in an office setting.

188. According to Ms. Steiner, what attracted her to the position?

(A) The job duties
(B) The flexible working hours
(C) The convenient location
(D) The generous vacation time

189. Why did Ms. Prescott send the e-mail?

(A) To ask about the availability of some interviewers
(B) To introduce a newly hired staff member
(C) To inform coworkers of an interview change
(D) To recommend a candidate for a position

190. What characteristic of Ms. Steiner is Ms. Prescott most interested in?

(A) Her experience in the real estate field
(B) Her knowledge of software programs
(C) Her ability to work on short notice
(D) Her strong people skills

Questions 191-195 refer to the following article, invitation, and e-mail.

STAUNTON (April 10)—Bringing together his passion for fitness and his natural people skills, Fabio Souza is launching a 24-hour gym in the Valley Lane neighborhood of Staunton. Mr. Souza has a wealth of experience as a certified personal trainer, as he was employed by TCB Fitness in Hillcrest for ten years. He took note of the positive aspects of that business and incorporated them into his own gym.

The new gym, which is called Loxley, will feature state-of-the-art workout equipment, engaging group classes, and monthly health seminars. The building, which is located on Kyle Avenue, is beautifully designed, with clean lines and an expert use of color. In fact, Mr. Souza started his career as an interior designer at Canton Inc. However, after his father was diagnosed with a heart condition, Mr. Souza started to understand the importance of exercise.

"I wanted to create a fun and supportive environment for people in order to help them to get in shape," said Mr. Souza in a recent interview.

Loxley is set to open on May 1. Its services will be available to those with memberships only, at a cost of $600 annually.

Celebrate our grand opening!

LOXLEY
~ a full-service gym open around the clock ~

Friday, May 1
Special Activities*: 9 A.M.–7 P.M.

* Enjoy tours of our facility, free yoga classes, and free fitness consultations.
  Sign up for a one-year membership for $500.

To: Fabio Souza <f.souza@loxleygym.com>
From: Bonnie Tolbert <bonnietolbert@bairdcorporation.net>
Date: April 18
Subject: Loxley

Dear Fabio,

Thank you for the invitation for the grand opening of your gym. It's wonderful to see that you've followed your dream. Way to go! I remember that you always wanted to have your own business, even back when we were coworkers at TCB Fitness.

I wish I could be there in person on the opening day. Unfortunately, I'll be out of town on business. However, I plan to visit you and check out Loxley as soon as I can after that. I wish you all the best on your new venture!

Take care,

Bonnie

---

191. Why was the article written?
(A) To promote the opening of a new fitness facility
(B) To announce classes for personal training certification
(C) To highlight a variety of working opportunities in Staunton
(D) To explain a new trend in the exercise community

192. What motivated Mr. Souza to change his career path?
(A) The inheritance of his father's company
(B) An on-the-job injury
(C) The illness of a relative
(D) A downturn in the job market

193. What is indicated about the May 1 event?
(A) It features discounted membership rates.
(B) It will have refreshments available to visitors.
(C) It includes free massages for participants.
(D) It will run tours of the site once per hour.

194. What is the purpose of Ms. Tolbert's e-mail?
(A) To thank Mr. Souza for a job offer
(B) To accept an invitation
(C) To sign up for a membership
(D) To congratulate Mr. Souza

195. What is true about Ms. Tolbert?
(A) She is an investor in Loxley.
(B) She recently moved to Staunton.
(C) She is an experienced interior designer.
(D) She used to work in Hillcrest.

Questions 196-200 refer to the following article, e-mail, and outline.

Small Changes Can Make a Big Difference

LONGVIEW (January 15)—Local entrepreneur Gwen Langston has volunteered to put on a free workshop on making and using eco-friendly household cleaners. The workshop is open to everyone, and it will be held at 7:30 P.M. on January 21 in room 103 of the Longview Community Center.

Langston has dedicated her life to helping the environment. She operates a small shop downtown called Reclaim Depot, which exclusively sells goods made from recycled or salvaged materials. Her shop is also a collection point for certain unwanted items.

"Many people dump paint, automotive fluids, expired medicines, and more down the drain. These harmful chemicals often end up in our water supply. I hope everyone living in the Longview area will be motivated to use our collection point for their chemical waste to make sure these substances do not end up in the wrong place," said Langston.

No registration is required for the workshop. However, attendees should note that seating is available on a first-come, first-served basis.

To: <stafflist@longviewquarterly.com>
From: <editor@longviewquarterly.com>
Date: January 17
Subject: Opportunity

Dear Staff,

Gwen Langston will host a workshop on January 21. I stopped by her shop this morning to find out if she would be interested in participating in a brief interview for our publication. Fortunately, she's willing to do this, so I need one of you to cover this story. I'm sure our readers will be interested in her advice.

Christopher Mitchem
Chief Editor, *Longview Quarterly*

Longview Quarterly
Spring Issue

Title	Article Description	Writer
Ditch the Toxins	Tips for cleaning your home without the use of harsh chemicals and toxins	Enrico Padovano
Heart Healthy	A collection of low-fat and low-sodium recipes that still pack a flavorful punch	Danielle Laprade
Collecting for Cash	Harness rainwater easily for home use to save money and help the environment	Jeff Wofford
Longview Pride	A look at what local politicians are doing to get tourists interested in our little city	Victoria Fomina

196. What is the article mainly about?

(A) A volunteer opportunity
(B) A business's grand opening
(C) An educational event
(D) An environmental regulation

197. According to the article, what activity does Ms. Langston wish that residents would do?

(A) Dispose of chemicals responsibly
(B) Review the products from her business
(C) Use energy-efficient household appliances
(D) Pick up litter in public areas

198. What is suggested about Mr. Mitchem?

(A) He is collecting some goods for recycling.
(B) He conducted a job interview this morning.
(C) He will accompany a coworker to a workshop.
(D) He has visited Reclaim Depot.

199. What article would be best for people wanting to make use of a natural water source?

(A) Ditch the Toxins
(B) Heart Healthy
(C) Collecting for Cash
(D) Longview Pride

200. Who most likely interviewed Ms. Langston?

(A) Mr. Padovano
(B) Ms. Laprade
(C) Mr. Wofford
(D) Ms. Fomina

Stop! This is the end of the test. If you finish before time is called, you may go back to Part 5, 6, and 7 and check your work.

TEST 03

PART 5 · PART 6 · PART 7

준비하기

손목시계

뭉뚝한 연필과 지우개

Answer Sheet

토익 RC는 75분 동안 진행됩니다.
반드시 75분 이내에 문제 풀이와 답안지 마킹을 완료하세요.

TEST 03은 **고난도 문제가 많이 포함**된 대박달 :) TEST입니다.
다른 TEST에 비해 상대적으로 **환산 점수가 높게** 나올 수 있습니다.

고난도 문제는 해설집에서 확인할 수 있습니다.
해설집 p.45

맞은 개수	환산 점수	맞은 개수	환산 점수
96-100	465 - **495**	41-45	145 - **215**
91-95	430 - **490**	36-40	120 - **180**
86-90	400 - **465**	31-35	100 - **145**
81-85	375 - **440**	26-30	80 - **120**
76-80	340 - **415**	21-25	65 - **95**
71-75	315 - **390**	16-20	50 - **75**
66-70	285 - **365**	11-15	35 - **55**
61-65	255 - **335**	6-10	15 - **40**
56-60	225 - **305**	1-5	5 - **30**
51-55	200 - **270**	0	5
46-50	170 - **240**		

READING TEST

In the Reading test, you will read a variety of texts and answer several different types of reading comprehension questions. The entire Reading test will last 75 minutes. There are three parts, and directions are given for each part. You are encouraged to answer as many questions as possible within the time allowed.

You must mark your answers on the separate answer sheet. Do not write your answers in your test book.

PART 5

Directions: A word or phrase is missing in each of the sentences below. Four answer choices are given below each sentence. Select the best answer to complete the sentence. Then mark the letter (A), (B), (C), or (D) on your answer sheet.

101. The sales team had a ------- time adjusting to the new software than the finance team did.
    (A) hardest
    (B) hardly
    (C) hard
    (D) harder

102. Mr. Marlowe admitted ------- mistake to the team as soon as it was discovered.
    (A) he
    (B) him
    (C) his
    (D) himself

103. To send another wire transfer to the same person, ------- input the amount and then click the "Confirm" button.
    (A) simply
    (B) closely
    (C) nearly
    (D) quite

104. The quality of Logan Manufacturing's goods has been consistent ------- the last two decades.
    (A) by
    (B) up
    (C) for
    (D) to

105. The vehicle's preliminary testing process includes accelerating the engine ------- it starts to overheat.
    (A) seldom
    (B) until
    (C) besides
    (D) whereas

106. The two business partners work perfectly together due to their complementary talents and mutual -------.
    (A) admiring
    (B) admiration
    (C) admirably
    (D) admires

107. Kendra Fabiano, the author of the book about ancient Egypt, ------- published a book on the Roman Empire.
    (A) however
    (B) always
    (C) previously
    (D) accordingly

108. Linden Studios was granted ------- rights to produce a film based on the popular novel *Holding On* by author Rita Palmer.
    (A) excluding
    (B) exclusive
    (C) exclude
    (D) excludes

109. These silk curtains, fabulous by -------, look even better with a lace netting behind them.
(A) theirs
(B) them
(C) themselves
(D) they

110. The ------- of the uniforms for new employees is paid for by the departmental budget.
(A) cost
(B) benefit
(C) contribution
(D) value

111. The company hopes to improve its image by having a ------- writer on staff who can draft press releases.
(A) reluctant
(B) talented
(C) compatible
(D) various

112. Midnight Blue is the best-selling laundry detergent ------- families with young children.
(A) unlike
(B) among
(C) along
(D) into

113. Salespeople who have read Professor Vance's book report that they are more ------- in their negotiation skills now.
(A) confidences
(B) confident
(C) confidence
(D) confidently

114. The Madison Culinary Institute ------- affordable courses on food preparation techniques for beginners up to professionals.
(A) passes
(B) takes
(C) completes
(D) offers

115. The server brought out Mr. Baker's dessert before he had ------- finished the main dish.
(A) then
(B) else
(C) even
(D) very

116. ------- the poor weather, very few people turned up for the gallery's auction supporting local painters and sculptors.
(A) As long as
(B) Due to
(C) Given that
(D) Even if

117. This diagram will help you understand the pros and cons about public and private insurance -------.
(A) cautions
(B) options
(C) motivations
(D) removals

118. Ms. Allan took a scenic train ride across the country, during which she ------- many unique landscape features.
(A) photograph
(B) will be photographing
(C) photographed
(D) to photograph

119. The warehouse team will be short-staffed all week, ------- be sure to allow additional time for requests to be processed.
(A) whereas
(B) so
(C) while
(D) only

120. The front desk employees at Marlin Hotel strive to respond to guests' requests in a timely manner, ------- they need.
(A) anybody
(B) everyone
(C) whatever
(D) however

121. For details about your latest transactions or ------- funds from your account, use the ATM near the bank's entrance.
(A) withdrew
(B) withdraws
(C) to withdraw
(D) withdrawal

122. Hiring an event planner can be an effective way to take care of ------- between the venue and the suppliers.
(A) appreciation
(B) indication
(C) coordination
(D) formation

123. The popularity of his weekly podcast gave a ------- boost to financial expert Ken Ramsey's book sales.
(A) valid
(B) successive
(C) considerable
(D) frank

124. The amount of traffic to a Web site will ------- improve if the owner invests in ads on social media.
(A) substantiating
(B) substantially
(C) more substantial
(D) substantial

125. The opening of a public library in the small community of Yorktown was made ------- by financial support from residents.
(A) generous
(B) famous
(C) possible
(D) evident

126. The homeowner wants to hire a plumber ------- company can provide a ten-year guarantee on the new pipes.
(A) where
(B) who
(C) that
(D) whose

127. The flowers are kept in a greenhouse because they are ------- to fluctuations in temperature.
(A) threatened
(B) vulnerable
(C) feeble
(D) limited

128. A government grant was given to the Arlene Theater to improve the ------- of its facility for people in wheelchairs.
(A) accessible
(B) accessibility
(C) accessed
(D) accessibly

129. Unless the traveler has paid for additional features, the cruise's welcome packet ------- two meal cards and two room keys.
(A) contained
(B) will contain
(C) has contained
(D) containing

130. The musical was praised by critics for its creative ------- of Renaissance poetry into its song lyrics.
(A) intermission
(B) accessory
(C) method
(D) incorporation

PART 6

Directions: Read the texts that follow. A word, phrase, or sentence is missing in parts of each text. Four answer choices for each question are given below the text. Select the best answer to complete the text. Then mark the letter (A), (B), (C), or (D) on your answer sheet.

Questions 131-134 refer to the following information.

Setting Up Direct Debit

Paying your utility bills by automatic direct debit guarantees that you will never be late. Additionally, many utility companies offer a discount for direct debit customers, which is a great way to ------- your monthly costs. After signing into your account, click the Direct Debit button. Select the company you wish to pay from the drop-down menu. -------. Next, ------- input your customer ID code. You may choose which date of each month you would like the payment to be made. This can be changed at any time by adjusting the ------- on your account.
131.
132.
133.
134.

131. (A) predict
 (B) monitor
 (C) lower
 (D) display

132. (A) To get the best interest rate, talk to one of our bank tellers.
 (B) A meter reading must be provided in the case of disputes.
 (C) If your desired option isn't there, you may enter it manually.
 (D) Click on the tab to read our latest customer reviews.

133. (A) most careful
 (B) carefully
 (C) careful
 (D) carefulness

134. (A) savings
 (B) settlement
 (C) settings
 (D) specialty

Questions 135-138 refer to the following e-mail.

To: All Gilbert Inc. Employees
From: Courtney Austin
Date: Monday, June 30
Subject: Urgent Repairs

Some technicians from Putnam Construction will visit our office to ------- urgent repairs on the ceiling tiles in the copy room. -------. Should you need items copied, please use the print shop across the street or take care of it tomorrow. Several cracked tiles will be removed, and an issue with exposed wiring will be resolved. ------- their time on site, the work crew may be using noisy tools. Those of you near the site of the work may wish to move to a different workstation temporarily. We ------- that this is an inconvenience. Thank you for your patience.

135. (A) cancel
 (B) divulge
 (C) acquire
 (D) perform

136. (A) You will be notified about which company was selected.
 (B) This area will be off limits for the rest of the day.
 (C) The amount of paper used should be reduced.
 (D) Please let me know if you would like an invitation.

137. (A) When
 (B) Lastly
 (C) During
 (D) Soon

138. (A) will understand
 (B) are understanding
 (C) understand
 (D) had understood

Questions 139-142 refer to the following notice.

Employees at Bellshire Department Store should be aware of promotional activities aimed at raising the brand awareness for Cobblestone Inc.'s ------- .
                                                                    139.

A demonstration area will be set up on the second floor, where shoppers can attend information sessions. ------- will be conducted by a Cobblestone Inc. representative, who will show the benefits of items such as
140.
cast-iron frying pans. The sessions will be held a few times a day and last ------- half an hour.
                                                                        141.

You may get asked questions about Cobblestone Inc.'s soup pots and other merchandise, so please review the product descriptions. ------- . Cobblestone Inc. will supply us with additional merchandise to avoid
                              142.
shortages.

139. (A) cookware
     (B) furniture
     (C) electronics
     (D) apparel

140. (A) Either
     (B) Anything
     (C) Each
     (D) Enough

141. (A) roughed
     (B) rough
     (C) roughly
     (D) roughness

142. (A) Some customers have returned goods that were damaged.
     (B) Employees should practice their presentations in advance.
     (C) Sales of the items being demonstrated are expected to increase.
     (D) We would like you to write clear explanations for all of them.

Questions 143-146 refer to the following Web page.

Visitor Information

Skyway Botanical Garden maintains the health of its plants and flowers by ------- the moisture within the
                                                                            143.
glass greenhouses. Many species that we house cannot survive in dry conditions. -------, sprinklers are in
                                                                                 144.
operation intermittently. For the safety of visitors, we temporarily close sections that are being watered. The
sections may remain closed for some time after the sprinklers turn off so that visitors do not walk on -------,
                                                                                                        145.
possibly slippery, paths. -------. While this rule may seem strict, it prevents damage, making the garden
                          146.
more beautiful.

---

143. (A) defending
(B) eliminating
(C) monitoring
(D) acquiring

144. (A) At the same time
(B) For this reason
(C) After all
(D) In contrast

145. (A) damply
(B) dampness
(C) dampen
(D) damp

146. (A) In addition, visitors are not permitted to touch the plants.
(B) Our experienced guides can identify each flower.
(C) Photos may be taken at any time with or without a flash.
(D) Therefore, the hours of operation will be extended in the summer.

PART 7

Directions: In this part you will read a selection of texts, such as magazine and newspaper articles, e-mails, and instant messages. Each text or set of texts is followed by several questions. Select the best answer for each question and mark the letter (A), (B), (C), or (D) on your answer sheet.

Questions 147-148 refer to the following receipt.

Tabor's

February 28, 11:41 A.M.	Mechanic: John Prieto
Order: 04976	Model: 4-door Crestin

Oil Change – Incl. 1 liter of synthetic oil	$29.99
Tire Puncture Repair	$12.99
Brake Test	$5.99
Tire Pressure Check	$3.99
Subtotal	$52.96
Tax	$4.38
TOTAL	**$57.34**

We'd love to hear about your experience at Tabor's! Visit our Web site and submit the order number above to complete our survey. After you are finished, you can download a voucher for a free brake test with the purchase of any other service.

---

147. What kind of business most likely is Tabor's?

(A) A vehicle repair shop
(B) A car dealership
(C) A car rental agency
(D) A driving institute

148. How much can survey respondents save with the voucher?

(A) $3.99
(B) $4.38
(C) $5.99
(D) $12.99

Questions 149-150 refer to the following e-mail.

To: Marion Knox
From: Fernando Lugo
Date: March 19
Subject: Takeaway Cups

Dear Marion,

I'm glad that you will be able to take on our project. As I said on the phone, our coffee house has developed new recipes for some cold drinks, and we would like to serve them in special cups. Please keep the following suggestions in mind:

Text: Summer Fun at Bueno Café!
Images: Bueno Café logo as well as 2–3 images associated with summer
Size: 2 x 3 inches for the printed area

Our logo is usually printed in navy blue, but for this project, we're open to other ideas. We'd like to see what you come up with. Please send your first drafts to me by March 31, as I need to have some prototypes mocked up by April 3 to be shown to a consumer feedback panel. Thanks a lot!

Fernando

149. What does Ms. Knox most likely specialize in?
(A) Market analysis
(B) Graphic design
(C) Creating recipes
(D) Managing finances

150. What is true about the new cups?
(A) They will be smaller than those for other drinks.
(B) They will be shown to consumers on March 31.
(C) Their material should be recyclable.
(D) Their color scheme hasn't been decided yet.

Questions 151-152 refer to the following advertisement.

Move Monthly Magazine

Looking for a hobby that is enjoyable as well as good for your health? *Move Monthly Magazine* can help you navigate the wonderful world of running! We understand that most of our readers have never set foot on a treadmill, let alone entered a long-distance race. That's not a problem! Our articles will help you get motivated and find the right running workout for you. Unlike many other sports magazines, which are filled with as much as fifty percent advertising, we give you an ad-free experience. Each issue offers workout routines specially designed by professional athletes and coaches. Just find your level, follow the steps, and watch your running times improve. Visit www.movemonthlymag.com to subscribe.

151. Who most likely is the intended audience of the magazine?

(A) Sportswear designers
(B) Professional athletes
(C) Beginning runners
(D) Shoe salespeople

152. According to the advertisement, what can be found in the magazine?

(A) Recommended routes
(B) Sports advertisements
(C) Training schedules
(D) Product reviews

Questions 153-154 refer to the following text-message chain.

Nella Lettiere [7:52 A.M.]
I've just arrived at the airport in Toronto, but the car rental agency lost my reservation. There are no vehicles available, and a cab to Vance Plaza would be very expensive. What can I do?

Kwangseok Jang [7:55 A.M.]
I've got it. Instead of going straight to the conference, take the free shuttle from exit 5 to the Eldridge Hotel.

Nella Lettiere [7:56 A.M.]
Thanks! I didn't know that was an option.

Kwangseok Jang [7:57 A.M.]
What time is the first presentation?

Nella Lettiere [7:58 A.M.]
Not until ten o'clock. That'll give me time to drop off my bags and then head over on foot.

153. At 7:55 A.M., what does Mr. Jang most likely mean when he writes, "I've got it"?
(A) He will take care of passing along a message.
(B) He thought of a way to resolve a problem.
(C) He has the document that Ms. Lettiere needs.
(D) He can send a confirmation number to Ms. Lettiere.

154. What is implied about the Eldridge Hotel?
(A) It charges a fee for a transportation service.
(B) It did not process Mr. Lettiere's reservation correctly.
(C) It is hosting an industry conference.
(D) It is within walking distance to Vance Plaza.

Questions 155-157 refer to the following memo.

To: All customer service representatives
From: Kenneth Greer, Distribution Manager
Date: January 15
Re: Urgent

Over the weekend, the IT team installed new billing software on all computers. —[1]—. The software is designed to make it easier to track customers' monthly usage of electricity and gas. When the software was installed, the default date—January 1—was used instead of the correct installation date. —[2]—. This caused the bills for January to be automatically sent out to customers again. —[3]—.

We believe the issue has been resolved, but we won't know for certain until the next series of bills is sent out. —[4]—. Receiving a second bill is likely to upset and confuse customers, so we are expecting a lot of people to contact us in the next few days. Please make sure you answer any calls forwarded to you.

155. What is the memo mainly about?
 (A) Why some billing errors have occurred
 (B) Why a service has become more expensive
 (C) How to install some new software
 (D) How to check the level of energy usage

156. What does Mr. Greer want employees to do?
 (A) Report problems to the IT department
 (B) Handle customer complaints
 (C) Back up information on their computers
 (D) Attend an informational meeting

157. In which of the positions marked [1], [2], [3], and [4] does the following sentence best belong?

"Unfortunately, that won't be for a few more weeks."

 (A) [1]
 (B) [2]
 (C) [3]
 (D) [4]

Questions 158-160 refer to the following form.

Sunshine Curtains

Overview of Services

Customer: Jason Elsner
Curtain Type: Pencil pleat
Fabric: Pink Garden Flowers (#298)
Description: Replacement of curtain panel (fee waived; see below)
Order taken by: Denise Cowen
Order assigned to: Rose Navarro

Size (L x W): 152 cm x 165 cm
Seams: Section 1 (top 10 cm), Section 2 (left-hand side 5 cm), Section 3 (right-hand side 5 cm), Section 4 (bottom 10 cm)

Section 1: Pencil pleat with hook loops every 5 cm
Section 2: Pale pink fringe (color P21)
Section 3: Extra strip of lining for reinforcement
Section 4: No special instructions

Comments: This panel replaces one in a set that had a tear in the fabric.

158. Who most likely is Ms. Cowen?
  (A) A fabric designer
  (B) A sales clerk
  (C) An interior decorator
  (D) A seamstress

159. Where does the customer want additional fabric?
  (A) At the top
  (B) At the bottom
  (C) On the right-hand side
  (D) On the left-hand side

160. Why will a service be provided to Mr. Elsner for free?
  (A) An employee noted the wrong measurement.
  (B) A coupon was used at the time of purchase.
  (C) The item sustained some damage.
  (D) The wrong fabric was used for a project.

Questions 161-163 refer to the following customer review.

Ezell Apparel Review
Posted by Sherry Kaplar, 3 days ago

I am a regular shopper at Ezell Apparel, and I always have a great experience every time I shop there. Recently, I purchased some linen trousers that fit me perfectly except for being too long. I was able to use the shop's on-site service to rectify this problem. I made the purchase on a Sunday, and an employee took my measurements. Someone from the store called me on Monday afternoon to let me know the trousers were ready. I asked for them to be delivered to my home for a small fee, rather than having to make the trip back to the store, and they arrived the very next day. The service from start to finish was impeccable.

I usually purchase casual clothing, but a lot of people don't realize that Ezell Apparel has an extensive business wear section. One of my friends recently started a job and needed to update her wardrobe. She was able to find everything she needed under one roof.

161. What is suggested about Ezell Apparel?
(A) It offers a generous return policy.
(B) It offers an alteration service.
(C) It has more than one branch.
(D) It has promotions regularly.

162. When was Ms. Kaplar's item delivered?
(A) On Sunday
(B) On Monday
(C) On Tuesday
(D) On Wednesday

163. The word "update" in paragraph 2, line 2, is closest in meaning to
(A) modernize
(B) notify
(C) renovate
(D) assess

GO ON TO THE NEXT PAGE

Questions 164-167 refer to the following article in a company newsletter.

Personnel Corner

by Neil Reece

This month, we'd like to congratulate Dennis Kennedy on signing up his 50th new client of the year. Mr. Kennedy is the first advertising executive to reach this impressive milestone, so we are very proud of him. We expect many more great things from Mr. Kennedy in the future.

It's no surprise that clients are drawn to Mr. Kennedy's inventive ad campaigns. He also assisted his team in adopting practices to protect sensitive client information. Through his hard work, he has helped the company to develop a reputation for excellence and reliability. Because of this, current clients have recommended our business to their friends and acquaintances, helping us to build our customer base steadily.

164. Why was the article written?

(A) To introduce a valued client
(B) To congratulate an award winner
(C) To announce a job promotion
(D) To recognize an employee's achievement

165. What does Mr. Reece indicate about Mr. Kennedy?

(A) He wants to start his own business.
(B) He is certified in his field.
(C) He will change to a new team.
(D) He has creative ideas.

166. The word "sensitive" in paragraph 2, line 2, is closest in meaning to

(A) fragile
(B) confidential
(C) thoughtful
(D) subtle

167. What is suggested about the business?

(A) It is a leader in the industry.
(B) It holds client appreciation events.
(C) It has grown by word of mouth.
(D) It plans to open a new branch.

Questions 168-171 refer to the following online chat discussion.

Patrick Kincaid [9:31 A.M.]
Good morning. This is Patrick from Meridian Enterprises. You made a claim for damages to your roof.

Alicia Tidwell [9:33 A.M.]
Yes, that's correct. The high winds from the recent storm blew off some of the shingles and loosened others.

Patrick Kincaid [9:34 A.M.]
Would this afternoon be a good time to assess the damage and see what is covered under the policy we sold you?

Alicia Tidwell [9:35 A.M.]
Sure. What time should I expect you?

Patrick Kincaid [9:36 A.M.]
I need to assess a claim in Rosebank at 1 P.M., but getting back to Hadley could take anywhere between one to two-and-a-half hours, depending on traffic.

Alicia Tidwell [9:37 A.M.]
It doesn't matter much on my end. I'm working from home, so I don't have to make any special arrangements.

Patrick Kincaid [9:38 A.M.]
I'm glad to hear that. Normally, the work would be carried out only by me, but I'll have a new employee with me. She will assess the damage as well so that I can check her accuracy.

Alicia Tidwell [9:39 A.M.]
That's no problem.

168. Where most likely does Mr. Kincaid work?
  (A) At an interior design studio
  (B) At a repair shop
  (C) At a construction company
  (D) At an insurance agency

169. What is implied about Mr. Kincaid?
  (A) He is waiting for some paperwork.
  (B) He thinks the assessment could take over two hours.
  (C) He cannot guarantee an arrival time.
  (D) He will contact Ms. Tidwell again at one o'clock.

170. At 9:37 A.M., what does Ms. Tidwell mean when she writes, "It doesn't matter much on my end"?
  (A) She can postpone a meeting to another day.
  (B) She does not mind meeting at a different location.
  (C) She is planning to be home all afternoon.
  (D) She has prepared enough funds for the work.

171. What does Mr. Kincaid say is unusual about the visit?
  (A) The appointment will last longer.
  (B) Some special tools will be required.
  (C) It will incur an additional charge.
  (D) More than one employee will be present.

Questions 172-175 refer to the following e-mail.

E-mail

To:	Finn Carmichael <f_carmichael@victoriainbox.com>
From:	Myrna Kerr <myrna@becketthistory.org>
Date:	July 10
Subject:	Beckett County Museum of History

Dear Mr. Carmichael,

On behalf of the Beckett County Museum of History, I would like to thank you for your financial contributions throughout the years to help the museum improve its services. Without the generosity of the public, we could not serve the thousands of people who visit the museum annually. —[1]—.

Through last year's fundraiser, we were able to purchase temperature-controlled display cases to protect our oldest and most fragile documents. —[2]—. The previous year, we launched a Web site with information about the museum, including an interactive video tour.

Looking forward, we plan to undergo structural changes at our facility. We will add ramps at both entrances and widen some of the doorways to accommodate visitors who use wheelchairs. This is a very ambitious project. —[3]—. We have applied for some government grants, and the city will chip in funds from the municipal budget. However, we still have a shortfall. We rely on locals like you to help us make up the difference. Anything you can share would be greatly appreciated. —[4]—.

Sincerely,

Myrna Kerr
Director, Beckett County Museum of History

172. Why is Mr. Carmichael receiving this e-mail?

(A) Because he has experience working at a museum
(B) Because he is a member of the city council
(C) Because he is an expert in history
(D) Because he donated funds to the museum

173. What is suggested about Mr. Carmichael?

(A) He signed up for a museum membership.
(B) He donated some documents to the museum.
(C) He is currently residing in Beckett County.
(D) He is willing to give a talk at the museum.

174. What project will begin at the museum soon?

(A) Launching an informational Web site
(B) Installing temperature-controlled displays
(C) Adding more items to the collection
(D) Improving accessibility to the building

175. In which of the positions marked [1], [2], [3], and [4] does the following sentence best belong?

"It entails a three-week closure of the facility, not to mention the considerable costs."

(A) [1]
(B) [2]
(C) [3]
(D) [4]

Questions 176-180 refer to the following article and letter.

Community Update
By Adrienne Morton

WOODHILL (March 13)—Lynn Theater is finally ready to begin an ambitious project to restore the building to its original condition, Managing Director Fred Lloyd confirmed. The exterior of the building will be pressure washed to remove decades of pollution buildup. However, the majority of the changes will be happening inside. Interior designer Zeming Jiang has viewed old photographs of the theater in an effort to recreate its previous magnificence. All of the theater's seats, totaling just over one thousand, will be replaced in order to maximize the comfort of the audience and comply with fire safety regulations. The walls of the main auditorium will be repainted, with some parts having gold leaf applied, and all damaged woodwork will be repaired. The theater's lobby area is also set to undergo a spectacular transformation. The current gift shop will be reduced to its former size. About fifteen years ago, a portion of the lobby was sectioned off to extend the gift shop, but this change will be reversed.

The work has been made possible by the generous donations of Woodhill's businesses as well as private citizens. Finance Director Glen Bowers, who was in charge of the fundraising campaign, expected the goal to be reached within one year. However, due to a downturn in the local economy and competition from other charity projects, it took two-and-a-half years of ongoing efforts. The theater will be closed for the work, but the Woodhill Community Theater Troupe will still perform plays temporarily at Mercer High School.

To the Editor of the *Woodhill Herald*:

Your recent article on Lynn Theater seemed to lack one of the details that readers would be most interested in—how long the site will be unavailable. The Woodhill Community Theater Troupe is just one of the many groups that make use of the facility. For example, Indira Vaknis and I started a city band, which often gives concerts at the theater, and we had not been informed of any changes in advance of the article.

While I'm pleased that the theater will be revamped, the proposed changes to the lobby are a mistake, in my opinion. This will significantly hinder the theater's ability to generate additional revenue. I hope readers will contact the interior designer of the project directly to suggest alternative plans.

Sincerely,

Francesco Lund

176. What is the purpose of the article?
(A) To promote a community theater show
(B) To explain ways to donate to a fundraiser
(C) To recruit members for an acting troupe
(D) To announce a restoration project

177. What is indicated about the fundraising campaign?
(A) It was overseen by the theater's director.
(B) It ran longer than expected.
(C) It gathered funds for other charities.
(D) It was only supported by businesses.

178. What information did Mr. Lund think should have been included in the article?
(A) The total of funds needed
(B) The process for buying theater tickets
(C) The duration of the closure
(D) The changes to be made at a site

179. What does Mr. Lund indicate in his letter?
(A) He is concerned that the seats will be uncomfortable.
(B) He thinks the gift shop should not be made smaller.
(C) He does not like the use of gold leaf in the lobby.
(D) He wants the old photographs of the theater to be kept.

180. Whom does Mr. Lund encourage readers to contact?
(A) Mr. Lloyd
(B) Ms. Jiang
(C) Mr. Bowers
(D) Ms. Vaknis

Questions 181-185 refer to the following Web page and form.

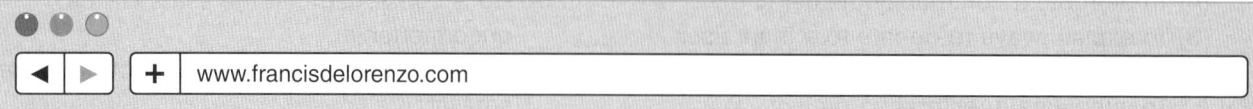

Francis Delorenzo is a leading provider of career coaching services. Mr. Delorenzo has a wealth of experience in the business world, working as a junior accountant and later a lead financial consultant at Magnolia Inc. While there, he developed an interest in counseling and returned to Anaheim University to receive a master's degree in the field. He worked as an administrative assistant to Dr. Diana Whitlam part-time during his studies to gain insights into the field. Upon receiving his master's degree, he began his own counseling business to help others reach their full potential and find a rewarding career path.

If you're thinking about transitioning to a new field, or if you want to find the best way to move to the top of your current field, Mr. Delorenzo can help. Clients from across the country have benefitted from using Mr. Delorenzo's services, in which he creates a program designed solely for each client's specific needs and goals. To read what past clients said about the service, click here to follow the link.

If you are interested in booking Mr. Delorenzo's services, please call 647-555-8703. Mr. Delorenzo is also available for interviews and public appearances. E-mail info@francisdelorenzo.com to request a booking form. After completing and submitting the form, you will be contacted by Media Director Sheila Tanner (for television and radio appearances) or Press Officer Satoya Kouno (for lectures and print media interviews).

Francis Delorenzo Booking Form

Name: Violet Richardson
E-mail Address: vrichardson@molinopublishing.com
Company/Organization: Boyar Inc.
Phone: 497-555-8217
Type of Event: Interview for *Take Control* magazine, a publication that provides tips on organizing your personal and professional life
Proposed Dates: The interview can be done by phone anytime in August.
Comments: When I was switching careers, a coworker introduced me to Mr. Delorenzo's services. I have attended several lectures since then and found them to be invaluable. I know our readers could learn a great deal from Mr. Delorenzo.

181. What is NOT mentioned as a job held by Mr. Delorenzo?

(A) Assistant
(B) Financial advisor
(C) University professor
(D) Accountant

182. What does the Web page indicate about Mr. Delorenzo's services?

(A) They are tailored to each individual client.
(B) They are available after an initial consultation.
(C) They are in high demand by financial professionals.
(D) They are recommended for part-time workers.

183. What can visitors do by clicking on the link?

(A) Read some career advice
(B) Request a booking form
(C) View customer testimonials
(D) Sign up for a counseling session

184. What is true about Ms. Richardson?

(A) She wants to visit Mr. Delorenzo in August.
(B) She will be contacted by Mr. Kouno.
(C) She used to work with Mr. Delorenzo.
(D) She is the founder of Boyar Inc.

185. How did Ms. Richardson first hear about Mr. Delorenzo?

(A) By reading a magazine article
(B) By attending a lecture
(C) By watching a television program
(D) By getting a colleague's recommendation

Questions 186-190 refer to the following online message board, e-mail, and Web page.

http://www.eventplanningworld.com

Home >> Woodbridge >> Venues >> Member Questions

QUESTION

General / **Specific:**   **Charleston Plaza**

Member: Devin Hume [October 3]

Question: Is Charleston Plaza worth the high booking fee?

RESPONSE

Member: Harold Vela [October 4]

My insurance company recently used Charleston Plaza for our annual appreciation banquet for investors. The facility is modern and sophisticated, so it is ideal when you need to make a good impression on the guests.

On the event day, there was a brief power outage that delayed the start time of the presentations. Even though it was not Charleston Plaza's fault, the venue provided us with complimentary cookies and muffins by way of apology. A few days later, I received a card written by hand at my office. It was from Maria Martin, and she thanked me for my booking and apologized once again for the inconvenience. I was very impressed with this personal touch.

To: All executive staff
From: Maria Martin
Date: October 28
Subject: Hospitality Conference

Dear Executive Staff Members,

As the assistant manager of Charleston Plaza, I have learned a lot about dealing with the public. I am so thankful that you have selected me to attend the upcoming Regional Conference of Hotels. This will be a great way for me to network with people in a similar role and to learn more about improving the experience of our customers. I know that my immediate supervisor, Ayaan Tavada, found the event to be particularly informative last year. In fact, thanks to networking at this event, he was offered a position on the Woodbridge Tourism Board.

I will make the most of my time at the conference and use it to enhance my professional development.

Warmest regards,

Maria Martin

www.woodbridge.gov/tourism

Woodbridge Tourism Board Committee Heads Confirmed

Finance and Auditing Committee: Siddhi Vadekar, Randolph Inn
International Outreach Committee: Tai Lian, Dalroy Hotel
Hospitality Business Development Committee: Ayaan Tavada, Charleston Plaza
Events and Activities Committee: Riet Maat, Dalroy Hotel

The Woodbridge Tourism Board seeks to promote the tourism industry in Woodbridge by supporting local businesses, hosting activities, and advertising to out-of-town visitors. Meetings are held on the first Monday evening of every month and are open to the public. For meeting times and locations, please call 555-4997.

186. What does Mr. Vela mention about Charleston Plaza?
    (A) It is used by his company once per year.
    (B) It served his group some free food.
    (C) Its equipment was not set up properly.
    (D) Its Web site has a modern design.

187. What is indicated about Mr. Vela?
    (A) He works for one of the largest insurance companies in the region.
    (B) He was unable to give a presentation to his guests on the event day.
    (C) He attracted new investors with Charleston Plaza's help.
    (D) He received a hand-written message from the assistant manager.

188. What is the purpose of the e-mail?
    (A) To show appreciation for an opportunity
    (B) To encourage staff members to attend an event
    (C) To request funding for professional development
    (D) To recruit volunteers to work at a conference

189. Which committee is led by Ms. Martin's boss?
    (A) Finance and Auditing
    (B) International Outreach
    (C) Hospitality Business Development
    (D) Events and Activities

190. What is suggested on the Web page?
    (A) Committee heads are elected by the public.
    (B) Most board members are business owners.
    (C) Mr. Lian and Ms. Maat are coworkers.
    (D) The group meets every Monday evening.

Questions 191-195 refer to the following Web page, e-mail, and schedule.

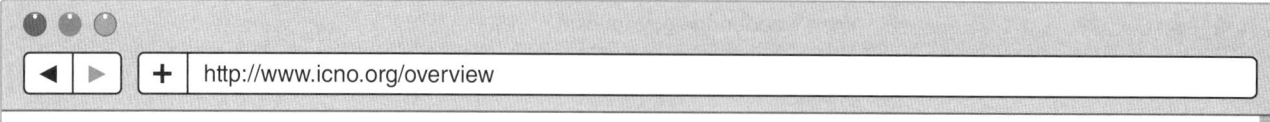

International Conference of Nonprofit Organizations (ICNO)
Saturday, June 18 ♦ Beacon Convention Center

ICNO is held annually to help nonprofit organizations maximize their effect and truly make a difference. After record attendance at last year's event in London, we are looking forward to further success at the conference in Berlin this year. There will be informative booths providing support services, a wide range of lectures, and an optional dinner during which you can meet and talk to others in the field.

We are also very pleased to include question-and-answer sessions for the first time. Whichever one you go for, you are sure to learn a great deal.

Q&A Sessions (Creston Room)
Volunteer Recruitment / 9:30 A.M.–10:30 A.M.
Social Media Marketing / 11:00 A.M.–12:00 noon
Corporate Donations / 1:30 P.M.–2:30 P.M.
Reducing Overhead Expenses / 3:00 P.M.–4:00 P.M.

To: Lucy Thurman
From: Conrad Riley
Date: June 9
Subject: ICNO

Dear Lucy,

The ICNO event planner has asked me to host a question-and-answer session at their upcoming event. I would like you to book a one-way ticket for me for June 18. I don't need a return ticket, as I'll be staying in Berlin a few extra days for a vacation and making my own arrangements. Even though I live near both Balanitis Station and Rehbach Station, I'd like to depart from Balanitis Station because it is a better facility. I should arrive between 9:30 and 10 in the morning so that I have plenty of time to get to the conference venue for my eleven o'clock session. Please keep in mind that the budget limit is €30.

Thank you!

Conrad

Ticket Search Results: 1 Adult, One-Way, Leipzig to Berlin, June 18

Departure Station	Departure Time	Arrival Time	Price	Operator
Balanitis	7:56 A.M.	9:36 A.M.	€34.00	Breite
Balanitis	8:01 A.M.	9:41 A.M.	€29.00	TRX
Rehbach	7:55 A.M.	9:48 A.M.	€27.00	Schwartz
Rehbach	8:12 A.M.	10:05 A.M.	€28.00	Davoser

191. What is NOT indicated about ICNO?
    (A) It is held once a year.
    (B) Its presenters can receive awards.
    (C) Its event venue changes.
    (D) It has networking opportunities.

192. In the Web page, the phrase "go for" in paragraph 2, line 1, is closest in meaning to
    (A) operate
    (B) depart
    (C) transport
    (D) choose

193. To whom did Mr. Riley most likely send the e-mail?
    (A) A personal assistant
    (B) A train company employee
    (C) An event planner
    (D) A conference venue owner

194. What topic will Mr. Riley cover at the conference?
    (A) Volunteer recruitment
    (B) Social media marketing
    (C) Corporate donations
    (D) Reducing overhead expenses

195. Which company will Mr. Riley most likely use on June 18?
    (A) Breite
    (B) TRX
    (C) Davoser
    (D) Schwartz

GO ON TO THE NEXT PAGE

Questions 196-200 refer to the following advertisement, letter, and voucher.

Don't miss the Keystone Appliances Mega Sale!

Keystone Appliances is pleased to launch the Gaviota brand of appliances. These goods are available exclusively at Keystone Appliances! We are excited to show you all the features of these products, so we are holding a special event at the Artesia Branch on Saturday, January 8. All day long, customers can enjoy complimentary refreshments and amazing discounts not only on Gaviota products but also on other goods throughout the store. Keystone Loyalty Club Members will receive an additional 5% off their purchase. Furthermore, those who watch our employees demonstrate the features of any Gaviota product will be given an entry form for our prize drawing.

Don't miss your chance to see these amazing new products from Gaviota!
    G60: A chrome microwave for style and functionality
    H103: An energy-efficient dryer with a moisture sensor for automatic shutoff
    K24: A smart refrigerator featuring a Fast-Freeze™ setting
    T990: A nearly silent dishwasher with a spacious interior

Get these new products and more at Keystone Appliances from January 8!

Carol Cortez
989 Mill Street
San Jose, CA 95136

Dear Ms. Cortez,

Congratulations! You are the winner of the grand prize in the January 8 drawing for Keystone Appliances customers. Enclosed you will find your prize, a five-hundred-dollar voucher. At Keystone Appliances, we do our best to create a positive experience for our customers. In light of this, we have just added more delivery drivers to our team, meaning you can receive your goods faster than ever before. We hope you enjoy spending the voucher, and we look forward to serving you soon!

Sincerely,

Sydney Hansen
Store Manager, Keystone Appliances [Artesia Branch]

Keystone Appliances Voucher

Issued: January 8
Amount: $500.00
Description: Prize Drawing

This voucher can be used in person at any Keystone Appliances retail location. If the full amount is not used, the holder will be issued a new voucher with the remaining balance. Please note that the voucher is not valid toward the purchase of Gaviota's K24. Expiration date: October 31.

196. What was the purpose of the January 8 event?
    (A) To recognize a national holiday
    (B) To celebrate an anniversary
    (C) To introduce a new brand
    (D) To prepare for a store relocation

197. What has Keystone Appliances recently done?
    (A) Expanded its delivery staff
    (B) Lowered its delivery charges
    (C) Purchased more delivery vehicles
    (D) Widened its delivery area

198. What is implied about Ms. Cortez?
    (A) She purchased an appliance on January 8.
    (B) She signed up for a loyalty program.
    (C) She watched a product demonstration.
    (D) She made a complaint about a purchase.

199. What new product cannot be purchased with the voucher?
    (A) A microwave
    (B) A dryer
    (C) A refrigerator
    (D) A dishwasher

200. What is true about the voucher?
    (A) It can be returned to the manufacturer for cash.
    (B) It is valid until the end of the year.
    (C) It cannot be used online.
    (D) Its value must be spent in a single purchase.

Stop! This is the end of the test. If you finish before time is called, you may go back to Part 5, 6, and 7 and check your work.

TEST 04

PART 5 · PART 6 · PART 7

준비하기

 손목시계  뭉뚝한 연필과 지우개   Answer Sheet

토익 RC는 75분 동안 진행됩니다.
반드시 75분 이내에 문제 풀이와 답안지 마킹을 완료하세요.

고난도 문제는 해설집에서 확인할 수 있습니다.
해설집 p.65

TEST 04는 **고난도 문제가 평균적으로 포함**된 *평달* TEST입니다.
환산 점수가 중간값으로 나올 수 있습니다.

맞은 개수	환산 점수	맞은 개수	환산 점수
96-100	465 - 495	41-45	145 - 215
91-95	430 - 490	36-40	120 - 180
86-90	400 - 465	31-35	100 - 145
81-85	375 - 440	26-30	80 - 120
76-80	340 - 415	21-25	65 - 95
71-75	315 - 390	16-20	50 - 75
66-70	285 - 365	11-15	35 - 55
61-65	255 - 335	6-10	15 - 40
56-60	225 - 305	1-5	5 - 30
51-55	200 - 270	0	5
46-50	170 - 240		

READING TEST

In the Reading test, you will read a variety of texts and answer several different types of reading comprehension questions. The entire Reading test will last 75 minutes. There are three parts, and directions are given for each part. You are encouraged to answer as many questions as possible within the time allowed.

You must mark your answers on the separate answer sheet. Do not write your answers in your test book.

PART 5

Directions: A word or phrase is missing in each of the sentences below. Four answer choices are given below each sentence. Select the best answer to complete the sentence. Then mark the letter (A), (B), (C), or (D) on your answer sheet.

101. Hobbs Manufacturing ------- all of its employees to take annual equipment operation courses.
    (A) recovers
    (B) appears
    (C) requires
    (D) claims

102. ------- bonus check will be issued on the same day as the salary payment for December.
    (A) He
    (B) His
    (C) Him
    (D) Himself

103. ------- a board member, Ms. Lessing is eligible to vote on a number of issues that affect the corporation.
    (A) On
    (B) At
    (C) To
    (D) As

104. Plympton Freight's trucks carry heavy ------- across the country.
    (A) loader
    (B) load
    (C) loaded
    (D) loads

105. Several board members were not ------- convinced that further funding for the project is necessary.
    (A) occasionally
    (B) preferably
    (C) equally
    (D) completely

106. Ms. Romero ------- Mr. Miller's training duties while he is away from the office on medical leave.
    (A) handled
    (B) is handled
    (C) will handle
    (D) to handle

107. The employees at Sweet Story Bakery always seem to have a more ------- attitude on Friday.
    (A) cheerfully
    (B) cheerful
    (C) cheer
    (D) cheers

108. The writing styles of the two authors are ------- similar, so people often confuse them.
    (A) broaden
    (B) broad
    (C) broadly
    (D) broadness

109. The blog claims that it gives consumers tips and tricks for always finding the best deal -------.
(A) available
(B) straight
(C) ready
(D) durable

110. The policies listed in the company's handbook apply to all employees, unless ------- specified.
(A) once
(B) about
(C) otherwise
(D) few

111. A fine may be imposed on those ------- do not clean up after their dog in the park.
(A) when
(B) who
(C) why
(D) where

112. Most customers were not ------- with the quality of the product, but a few people did return it.
(A) disappointing
(B) disappointed
(C) disappoint
(D) disappointment

113. In the manager's -------, the assistant manager will create the weekly schedule and handle all customer complaints.
(A) instance
(B) ability
(C) possession
(D) absence

114. The keypad lock on the laboratory's main door may need to be replaced if the problem -------.
(A) persist
(B) persisting
(C) persists
(D) had persisted

115. Once the merger was finalized, employees at Vertox Tech spread the good news -------.
(A) usually
(B) rigidly
(C) swiftly
(D) logically

116. Next week, the safety inspector will examine the factory for the third time ------- the discovery of the mechanical problem.
(A) around
(B) since
(C) until
(D) below

117. The ------- nature of the charity's fundraising department makes it a pleasant place to work for all volunteers.
(A) cooperation
(B) cooperative
(C) cooperated
(D) cooperatively

118. Board members think it would be risky to make changes to the management team right before heading ------- an initial public offering.
(A) with
(B) between
(C) into
(D) about

119. ------- the next three days, the abandoned lot on Carson Street will be transformed into a beautiful garden.
(A) Sustaining
(B) Toward
(C) Over
(D) Given

120. Thanks to the help of his coach, Vincent Salinas is ready to participate in marathons -------.
(A) competes
(B) compete
(C) competitively
(D) competitive

121. By including rich -------, the author creates a unique world that the reader can easily imagine.
(A) detailing
(B) detailed
(C) detailers
(D) details

122. During his participation in the summer internship program, Mr. Pineda ------- at identifying potential gaps in the market.
(A) prepared
(B) excelled
(C) instructed
(D) guaranteed

123. Belmont Enterprises is considering providing language ------- and a cultural studies program for employees working overseas.
(A) instructor
(B) instruction
(C) instructed
(D) instruct

124. ------- the amount of money received during the fundraising dinner, the museum staff may reach out to corporate donors.
(A) As much as
(B) Whether
(C) Because
(D) Depending on

125. Liveta Apparel has ------- to recycle or donate all of its unsold clothing at the end of each season.
(A) despite
(B) promptly
(C) promised
(D) prior

126. After putting off making a decision about whom to hire, the manager ------- selected the candidate from the best university.
(A) steadily
(B) eventually
(C) thoroughly
(D) formerly

127. Voters have mixed opinions about the proposed ------- of the chapel, as the cost is over $10 million.
(A) to restore
(B) restorable
(C) restoration
(D) restore

128. Last-minute purchase items such as snacks and batteries are ------- placed near the checkout aisle to increase their sales.
(A) strategize
(B) strategic
(C) strategy
(D) strategically

129. Mr. Roth's suitcase ------- to have been taken by another passenger by mistake because a very similar bag was left behind.
(A) vacates
(B) relieves
(C) appears
(D) arranges

130. Due to the popularity of Kim Welsh's book, Avalon Pictures is delighted with the ------- of acquiring the movie rights.
(A) preference
(B) distress
(C) prospect
(D) summary

PART 6

Directions: Read the texts that follow. A word, phrase, or sentence is missing in parts of each text. Four answer choices for each question are given below the text. Select the best answer to complete the text. Then mark the letter (A), (B), (C), or (D) on your answer sheet.

Questions 131-134 refer to the following memo.

From: Theo Jaworski
To: All Staff Members
Date: September 22
Re: Main entrance

In an attempt to reduce -------, the configuration of the security checks at the main entrance will be
                         131.
changed. The new system will be ------- on Monday, October 4. From the morning of that date, employees
                                  132.
will use the express line when entering the building, and they will simply have to show their employee ID

badge. -------.
       133.

------- complaints regarding the entry process should be directed to the security office. Your comments will
134.
be taken into consideration for future changes.

131. (A) wait
 (B) waited
 (C) waiting
 (D) waiter

132. (A) announced
 (B) instituted
 (C) overturned
 (D) persuaded

133. (A) In-house materials must be kept there at all times.
 (B) The photos submitted by some employees were not recent enough.
 (C) Visitors will use the standard line and may be asked questions.
 (D) The delay was caused by an error in our security software.

134. (A) Former
 (B) These
 (C) Further
 (D) Any

Questions 135-138 refer to the following article.

TORONTO (April 10)—Company employees ------- product testers for the new music-streaming service
                                        135.
Melody Mix by Canadian company Arrington Inc. have provided mixed reactions to the service. Preliminary
users state that the service's Recommendation function does not work as planned. For example, a user
who regularly listens to hard rock may receive suggestions for classical music songs. Industry experts
have ------- that the company will delay the release of the service to rectify this issue. Arrington Inc. has a
     136.
reputation for creating an ------- experience for its customers, as demonstrated by the 15 million users of its
                          137.
current music service. -------.
                       138.

135. (A) even if
     (B) however
     (C) as well as
     (D) whereas

136. (A) analyzed
     (B) demanded
     (C) speculated
     (D) argued

137. (A) enjoying
     (B) enjoyable
     (C) enjoy
     (D) enjoyably

138. (A) Visit the Web site to sign up for this loyalty program.
     (B) Arrington Inc. may relocate its headquarters soon.
     (C) Company salespeople were pleased to win the award.
     (D) Melody Mix is projected to have triple that figure.

Questions 139-142 refer to the following e-mail.

To: Photography Team
From: Ermanno Mancini
Date: August 10
Subject: Upcoming photo shoot

Dear Photography Team,

The next photo shoot for the Navagio beachwear line will take place on Thursday, August 13. The models will be prepped and ready by nine o'clock. -------139., all photographers should arrive by seven o'clock to help scout locations and set up the equipment. The photos will be taken with just men, just women, or a -------140..

I expect the photo shoot to take about four hours. -------141.. This will allow us additional time if needed. I must -------142. the importance of keeping all food items away from the photo shoot area, as they can attract seagulls.

139. (A) Likewise
(B) If possible
(C) For example
(D) On the other hand

140. (A) combination
(B) combine
(C) combining
(D) combined

141. (A) The new equipment helps us to be more efficient.
(B) However, you should plan to be at the site all day.
(C) We will check the weather report to decide the date.
(D) Fortunately, the client loved the look of the photos.

142. (A) avoid
(B) discover
(C) appreciate
(D) stress

Questions 143-146 refer to the following article.

December 10—At an event yesterday evening in New York, designer Claudia Larmon ------- a new line of jewelry. The collection, known as Eternal Sparkle, has fashionable and modern necklaces, rings, and earrings that are suitable for a variety of occasions, both casual and formal. The jewelry only uses gemstones ------- fair-trade sources. -------. Ms. Larmon encourages everyone to be responsible consumers, saying, "Make your purchase through ------- jewelry experts to ensure that the stones are authentic and produced with fair labor practices."

143. (A) visited
(B) shopped
(C) launched
(D) hired

144. (A) since
(B) up
(C) into
(D) from

145. (A) Other companies are paying close attention to the new regulations.
(B) This was accomplished through months of research on Ms. Larmon's part.
(C) Customers often choose gemstones based on color rather than price.
(D) There has been a trend toward more simplified jewelry in the fashion industry.

146. (A) certifies
(B) certify
(C) certified
(D) certificate

PART 7

Directions: In this part you will read a selection of texts, such as magazine and newspaper articles, e-mails, and instant messages. Each text or set of texts is followed by several questions. Select the best answer for each question and mark the letter (A), (B), (C), or (D) on your answer sheet.

Questions 147-148 refer to the following notice.

Notice to Spadaro Customers:

Spadaro has been proud to be the area's only seller of antique dining tables, bookcases, and other furnishings for over twenty-five years. For our customers' convenience, we offer a delivery service to anywhere in the southwest region. As all of our items are over one hundred years old, we need highly skilled delivery drivers who are used to handling delicate items. This can only be accomplished by paying a premium wage. Therefore, we have recently increased the delivery charges by fifteen percent. For those using this service, we hope that you understand that we are working to ensure the safe transport of your items.

147. What does Spadaro sell?

(A) Food
(B) Electronics
(C) Furniture
(D) Books

148. What is the announced in the notice?

(A) A change in delivery fees
(B) A wider delivery area
(C) A delayed delivery schedule
(D) A new delivery method

Questions 149-150 refer to the following text message chain.

Helen Montoya [10:06 A.M.]
Hi, Cameron. I just found out that my train back from Strasburg has been canceled.

Cameron Reagan [10:08 A.M.]
Does that mean you're not coming back to the office?

Helen Montoya [10:09 A.M.]
I'll be there, but I have to take the bus instead. That means I'll be about forty-five minutes late for the group interview for the open position. And it's too late to reschedule.

Cameron Reagan [10:10 A.M.]
Don't worry. I'll have the candidates take the computer-based personality test first. That'll take at least half an hour. Then we'll just need to have a short break before beginning the interviews.

Helen Montoya [10:11 A.M.]
That'll do. Thanks a lot! I'll text you when I get closer.

149. What problem does Ms. Montoya have?
 (A) She has to change her travel plans.
 (B) She must cancel an interview session.
 (C) She does not know how to get to a site.
 (D) She has misplaced some meeting notes.

150. At 10:11 A.M., what does Ms. Montoya mean when she writes, "That'll do"?
 (A) The computer program is good enough.
 (B) A candidate should be selected quickly.
 (C) There are sufficient supplies for an activity.
 (D) Mr. Reagan's suggestion will work.

Questions 151-153 refer to the following job advertisement.

Finesse Language Center
finesselanguage.com ♦ 349-555-3165

From April 1, Finesse Language Center will stay open two hours later to add more classes to keep up with the growing demand for our classes. As a result, we are seeking a part-time receptionist to assist in covering the additional opening times. Shifts will range from 4 to 6 hours every Monday through Saturday, except national holidays.

The ideal candidate must be fluent in both English and Spanish to best serve our students. In addition, we require the receptionist to have a familiarity with using computers and be able to keep documents and schedules well organized. If you would like to apply for the position, please prepare a résumé and letter of recommendation from a past or current employer and upload them on our Web site.

151. Why is the language center seeking a receptionist?
   (A) A new branch of the business will open.
   (B) An experienced employee will retire soon.
   (C) The site's business hours will be extended.
   (D) The number of incoming calls has increased.

152. What is NOT a requirement of the position?
   (A) Basic computer knowledge
   (B) Willingness to work holidays
   (C) Organizational skills
   (D) Ability to speak two languages

153. How can people show interest in the job?
   (A) By making a phone call
   (B) By e-mailing a résumé
   (C) By applying online
   (D) By visiting the center

Questions 154-155 refer to the following e-mail.

---

e-mail

To: Christie Layton <layton.c@bridge-post.com>
From: Video View Direct <support@videoviewdirect.com>
Date: August 31
Subject: RE: Account #49762

Dear Ms. Layton,

Regarding your inquiry, our system automatically locks customers out of their video streaming accounts after a password is entered incorrectly three times. We believe this is what happened in your case. To reset your account, follow the steps below.

1. Click here to follow the link to the correct page on our Web site.
2. Enter your account number (#49762) and the temporary password 9B770QW. Click on "Reset" to choose a new password, and enter it twice.
3. You will then see an optional questionnaire about which movies and genres you like. We urge you to provide this information, as it will help our system to give you better movie recommendations.
4. We will send confirmation by e-mail that you have successfully reset the account.

Thank you for your patronage!

The Video View Direct Customer Service Team

---

154. What is suggested about Ms. Layton in the e-mail?

(A) She is a new customer of Video View Direct.
(B) She wants to upgrade a monthly service.
(C) She had difficulty accessing her account.
(D) She is currently working as a film director.

155. What is Ms. Layton encouraged to do?

(A) Indicate her preferences online
(B) E-mail the customer service team again
(C) Change her account password regularly
(D) Recommend the business to others

Questions 156-158 refer to the following e-mail.

To	Sandra Huynh <shuynh@cmai.com>
From	Trifon Glazkov <tglazkov@kenzieco.com>
Date	May 24
Subject	Arrangements

Dear Ms. Huynh,

As you know, I will be away from the office nearly all of June while I travel to South Korea to tour major firms as well as take some vacation time. —[1]—. I will send you a list of our computer programs currently in development and the contact information for the individual programmers working on each one. This is for your reference only, as Ruben Fletcher will be handling all of my regular duties while I am away.

Mr. Fletcher has been the second-in-command for our team for two years, and he has good working relationships with all of the employees. —[2]—. He will get together twice a week with each team leader to monitor progress. We sat down for several hours yesterday and made a detailed plan to prepare for a number of contingencies. —[3]—. However, as it stands, I am completely confident that everything will run smoothly. I will be checking my e-mail somewhat infrequently while away, but Mr. Fletcher can be reached at rfletcher@kenzieco.com. —[4]—.

Sincerely,

Trifon Glazkov

---

156. What kind of business does Mr. Glazkov most likely work for?

(A) A software company
(B) A financial institution
(C) A tour operator
(D) A magazine publisher

157. According to Mr. Glazkov, what will Mr. Fletcher do?

(A) Hold regular meetings
(B) Create a detailed plan
(C) E-mail a list
(D) Run a new branch

158. In which of the positions marked [1], [2], [3], and [4] does the following sentence best belong?

"Without it, I would be concerned about such a long absence."

(A) [1]
(B) [2]
(C) [3]
(D) [4]

Questions 159-160 refer to the following brochure.

Enterprise Inc.

Proudly serving Wilmington and the surrounding area.

Overview of services:
– Shredding and disposal of company documents
– Pick-up service for your convenience
– Recycling as much of your waste as possible

Prices are based on volume, so please call us at 555-0387 for an estimate. We have been disposing of confidential documents for years and can ensure that your data is secure at all times.

Customer Testimonials:
"When my dental practice switched over to digital records, it was so convenient to have Enterprise Inc. pick up our old documents for us. And the staff was friendly and helpful."
— Lauren Tedesco, *5th Street Dental*

"Before relocating my business, I wanted to get rid of unneeded paper files. I called Enterprise Inc., and they were able to send a truck the very same day. I'll definitely use them in the future!"
— Charles Merrill, *Merrill Accounting*

159. What is indicated about Enterprise Inc.?
(A) It provides advice on Internet security.
(B) It has experience handling private information.
(C) It recycles all kinds of waste.
(D) It has been in business for over a decade.

160. What benefit of the service does Mr. Merrill mention?
(A) The convenient location
(B) The low prices
(C) The fast response
(D) The friendly staff

Questions 161-163 refer to the following article.

Business Corner
by Diana Keith

BLACKWELL (May 23)—The local economy in Blackwell is booming, and experts have a high degree of confidence that this trend will continue. Businesses have seen steady increases every quarter for the past three years, thanks in part to ad campaigns run by the municipal government to attract skilled workers to Blackwell. The technology sector has particularly benefitted from this practice, and the impressive growth in various industries is getting attention. "I started looking at Blackwell for my investments because of the positive trend in growth, and I also know the businesses here have good community support," said Paul Crawford of Burnley Co.

According to Gabrielle Velez, a former economics professor and current city council member, "The flow of more money into Blackwell results in business expansion, more jobs, and more spending—a cycle that can keep going upwards."

---

161. The word "degree" in paragraph 1, line 1, is closest in meaning to

(A) temperature
(B) amount
(C) order
(D) scale

162. What does the article mention about Blackwell's local government?

(A) It has been working to promote the town.
(B) It purchases shares in local businesses.
(C) It has recently upgraded its technology.
(D) It plans to offer more tax breaks for companies.

163. Who most likely is Mr. Crawford?

(A) A city council member
(B) A business investor
(C) A university professor
(D) A new Blackwell resident

GO ON TO THE NEXT PAGE

Questions 164-167 refer to the following article.

Companies that have been in business for decades must find a way to strike a balance between their long history and their future vision. —[1]—. One such company, Winthrop Communications, is taking a chance on younger consumers. The company was founded in the early seventies with a business model based on providing landline telephone services, but it now has a new focus on cell phone technology. As a result, Winthrop is planning to adjust the image and color of its logo for a more modern appearance. "It's time to abandon the dull gray and outdated graphics and create something more upbeat and recognizable," said Winthrop spokesperson Melanie Myers.

"Rebranding always comes with risks," said industry analyst Malcolm Collins. "However, with Winthrop's shift from landlines to a mobile network, the timing is favorable. This kind of changeover offers the best window of opportunity, and companies considering similar action should keep that in mind. —[2]—."

Consumers are sure to get a lot of exposure to the new logo on account of Winthrop's ambitious marketing campaign. Karen Ramirez has been put in charge of the campaign. Ramirez has focused her-twenty-year career on tech-related marketing, and she has built a reputation for creating quirky ads that consumers talk about and share on social media. —[3]—.

While it may take time for consumers to start associating Winthrop with modernity and progress, Winthrop CEO Jamie Beck believes it is worth the effort and expense. —[4]—. "We're not the same company we were at the founding, and we need to start reflecting this in our brand image," Beck commented. The performance of Winthrop's soon-to-be-released smartphone is sure to provide an indication of whether or not the company is ready to compete in the new world of communications.

164. What is the article mainly about?

(A) A change in a company's logo
(B) A challenge facing the smartphone market
(C) A newly introduced product
(D) A trend in consumer purchasing

165. What does Mr. Collins recommend doing?

(A) Constructing more cell phone towers
(B) Making advertisements more colorful
(C) Researching target markets carefully
(D) Taking advantage of a transition period

166. What is mentioned about Ms. Ramirez?

(A) She has won awards for her commercials.
(B) She helped to design a new smartphone.
(C) She specializes in promoting technology brands.
(D) She suggested shortening the company's name.

167. In which of the positions marked [1], [2], [3], and [4] does the following sentence best belong?

"The company hopes to get a boost from word-of-mouth referrals."

(A) [1]
(B) [2]
(C) [3]
(D) [4]

Questions 168-171 refer to the following online chat discussion.

	Alem Semere (10:10 A.M.)	I'd like to hear your thoughts on improvements we can make to the process of receiving fire safety certification. The committee meeting is on Thursday.
	Itsuka Mitani (10:11 A.M.)	How about having businesses fill out their information online? That would save time on completing reports.
	Philip Kowal (10:12 A.M.)	We would have to completely overhaul our online system, as it's currently set up for inspectors only.
	Alem Semere (10:13 A.M.)	That's true. It would require a major portion of the budget. But our department has to find some way to clear the backlog by the end of the quarter.
	Philip Kowal (10:14 A.M.)	Well, we can't afford to hire more inspectors.
	Itsuka Mitani (10:15 A.M.)	We could send inspectors alone instead of in pairs, and they could take photos if they needed a second opinion.
	Philip Kowal (10:16 A.M.)	Right! I'm sure the employees wouldn't mind visiting properties alone.
	Alem Semere (10:17 A.M.)	Wonderful! I'll explain the details when I speak at the meeting.

168. What is the discussion about?

(A) Recruiting more businesses
(B) Training new inspectors
(C) Adjusting a certification procedure
(D) Implementing an online billing system

169. What is implied about the writers?

(A) They oversee a group of trainees.
(B) They hold meetings once per quarter.
(C) They teach fire safety classes.
(D) They are behind schedule on their work.

170. At 10:16 A.M., what does Mr. Kowal most likely mean when he writes, "Right"?

(A) He agrees that Ms. Mitani's strategy will be helpful.
(B) He believes Ms. Mitani is capable of handling a project.
(C) He needs more information about a schedule.
(D) He would like the latest photos sent to Ms. Mitani.

171. What does Mr. Semere plan to do on Thursday?

(A) Review some fire safety regulations
(B) Upload a new online form
(C) Present a plan to committee members
(D) Hire more inspectors for a task

GO ON TO THE NEXT PAGE

Questions 172-175 refer to the following notice.

"Movement and Light"
December 9, 7 P.M.–10 P.M.

Sparkle Studio is once again hosting its year-end dance show at Anaheim Auditorium. The routines that will be performed on stage were developed by choreographer Maria Osborne. The keen observer will notice the South American influence that is common to all of the dances, as Ms. Osborne studied cultural traditions in Venezuela and Chile for three years before moving back to her U.S. hometown of Atlanta. Following the show, there will be a question-and-answer session with Ms. Osborne and some of the dancers.

Admission to the event is free, but we do accept financial contributions to help support our programs. Staff members will be positioned at the door to collect these. We are a non-profit organization dedicated to spreading the joy of dance, so any support you can give would be greatly appreciated. You can visit our Web site at www.sparklestudio.org to find out more about our studio and to view clips from last year's show. Visitors are encouraged to park in Anaheim Auditorium's main lot, which will not impose the usual $5.00 parking charge on that evening after 5 P.M.

172. Why was the notice written?

(A) To solicit feedback from volunteers
(B) To advertise a dance class
(C) To announce a studio relocation
(D) To promote an annual performance

173. What is indicated about Ms. Osborne?

(A) She will give a dance lesson on December 9.
(B) She used to live overseas.
(C) She is the founder of Sparkle Studio.
(D) She has performed at Anaheim Auditorium before.

174. What is mentioned about the Sparkle Studio's Web site?

(A) It provides driving directions.
(B) It was upgraded recently.
(C) It features video clips.
(D) If has sign-up forms.

175. What is NOT true about the event?

(A) It will be broadcast online.
(B) Donations will be collected on-site.
(C) Audience members can ask questions.
(D) The parking fee will be waived.

Questions 176-180 refer to the following announcement and e-mail.

Lorelei Electronics is recalling approximately 250,000 wall-plug chargers that accompanied three of its digital cameras—L57, EZ-Shoot, and P990. The cameras were sold in retail stores in the U.S., Canada, and Mexico between February and July of this year. The chargers were made of fragile plastic that can split when dropped even from a very low height, exposing the internal wiring.

Lorelei executives decided to order the voluntary recall immediately after a salesperson at a Lorelei retail shop discovered the issue. No injuries have been reported in relation to the device.

Customers who own one of these chargers are advised to stop using it immediately. The faulty devices will be replaced at no charge with a new one made with more durable materials. Customers in the U.S. and Mexico should take the item to any store that carries Lorelei products, including department stores. If a replacement is not immediately in stock, it will be shipped to the address provided by the customer. Customers living in Canada should return the item by mail. For further information, visit www.loreleielectronics.com.

To: Ralph Lindquist <lindquistr@ashworthco.net>
From: Lorelei Electronics Customer Service <service@loreleielectronics.com>
Date: October 15
Subject: RE: Inquiry
Attachment: label.docx

Dear Mr. Lindquist,

Thank you for your inquiry regarding the recall of our camera chargers. Based on the information you gave me, you should return the device by mail. Attached you will find an address label that can be printed out and attached to the padded envelope so that you do not have to pay postage. Please note that we currently have a lot of people dealing with the recall, so if you send in the item within the next two weeks, you will receive the replacement in seven days. However, if you wait until November or later, it could take up to four weeks to process your request due to the reduction in staff.

Sincerely,

Megan Jeffries
Customer Service Agent, Lorelei Electronics

176. Why is the product being recalled?
    (A) The wrong wires were used.
    (B) The item can crack easily.
    (C) The device overheats when plugged in.
    (D) The plastic may emit chemicals.

177. How did Lorelei Electronics find out about the problem?
    (A) By being informed by an employee
    (B) By receiving a complaint from an injured customer
    (C) By carrying out a routine inspection
    (D) By getting a warning from the product's designer

178. In the announcement, the word "carries" in paragraph 3, line 4, is closest in meaning to
    (A) endorses
    (B) sells
    (C) transports
    (D) achieves

179. What is suggested about Mr. Lindquist?
    (A) He wants to return a camera.
    (B) He bought more than one device.
    (C) He made his purchase online.
    (D) He lives in Canada.

180. How long will it take to get a replacement if the return is made in October?
    (A) One week
    (B) Two weeks
    (C) Three weeks
    (D) Four weeks

GO ON TO THE NEXT PAGE

Questions 181-185 refer to the following job advertisement and e-mail.

Open Positions at Commonwealth Solar Corporation

Commonwealth Solar Corporation (CSC) is known across the sustainable energy sector for its dependable service for supplying and installing residential solar panels. Originally headquartered in Newcastle, we moved our base of operations to Sydney two years ago to accommodate our rapid growth. We also have a branch in Perth, and all of our goods are supplied by Bladin Manufacturing in Melbourne. We are accepting applications for positions in Perth until January 20, after which time we will devise a rough schedule of interviews.

Distribution Manager: Oversees the storage and distribution of goods, ensuring that items are supplied by the target date. Strong problem-solving skills are essential along with basic computer proficiency.

Business Development Manager: Grows the customer base by identifying sales leads. Files accurate reports by due dates. University degree in a business field required. Must have excellent communication skills and computer skills.

Installation Technician: Completes installation projects at customers' homes within a strict time limit, following all safety standards. Valid driver's license required.

Interested applicants should fill out the Web-based application at www.commonwealthsol.com.au. Those who meet the qualifications will be invited to a group interview, at which they should turn in two letters of reference from a current or former supervisor. Candidates who attend the second round of interviews will be asked to take a computer-based personality test following the interview.

E-mail

To:	Milla Jacobs <m.jacobs@commonwealthsol.com.au>
From:	Ira Braun <braunira@quickinbox.com.au>
Date:	February 8
Subject:	Interview

Dear Ms. Jacobs,

Thank you for inviting me to the second round of interviews for the business development manager position. I look forward to discussing my skills and career history in greater detail. As you know, I am currently living in Bunbury, but I am willing to relocate for the right job opportunity. Also, if it would be helpful for me to meet some of the staff at your headquarters, I will be visiting a friend in that same neighborhood next week and would be happy to stop by. Please let me know if this would be useful to your decision-making process.

All the best,

Ira Braun

181. What is indicated about CSC?

(A) It has job openings at several branches.
(B) It operates a manufacturing facility.
(C) It was founded two years ago.
(D) It has a reputation for reliability.

182. In the job advertisement, the word "rough" in paragraph 1, line 6, is closest in meaning to

(A) unpleasant
(B) approximate
(C) uneven
(D) challenging

183. What is mentioned as a skill needed for all of the positions?

(A) Strong communication skills
(B) The ability to meet deadlines
(C) A degree from a university
(D) Experience working with computers

184. What most likely is NOT something that Mr. Braun has done?

(A) Submitted professional references
(B) Completed an online form
(C) Taken a personality test
(D) Attended a group interview

185. Where does Mr. Braun plan to visit a friend?

(A) Sydney
(B) Newcastle
(C) Bunbury
(D) Perth

Questions 186-190 refer to the following memo, e-mail, and information.

To: All Sutter Branch Employees
From: Isabelle Pearce, Sutter Branch Manager, Silva Corporation
Date: February 26
Re: Branch closing

The board of directors has voted to shut down the Lindbergh branch on March 9. Employees at that branch will be reassigned to our branch, including Director of Operations Scott Harley. Their first day of work will be Tuesday, March 13. We will hold a welcome reception on that day so that you have a chance to get to know them.

Although it is always disappointing to suffer a branch closure, this is the best way to keep the company in operation by reducing overhead expenses. Furthermore, the office building in Lindbergh will be sold, which will provide us with additional capital. Because of this, our branch will be able to carry out a special one-time project. We are accepting suggestions for improvements from employees. If you have an idea you would like to share, please e-mail HR Manager Jade Ingram at j_ingram@silva-corp.com. Submissions must be received by March 20 so that a report can be prepared by March 22.

To: Mariette Plante <m_plante@silva-corp.com>
From: Jade Ingram <j_ingram@silva-corp.com>
Date: March 23
Subject: Summary report

Dear Ms. Plante,

As you know, I've been asked to summarize the suggestions from employees regarding possible improvements that can be made here at the Sutter branch, outlined in the attached report. This was made possible by the help of the former Lindbergh Director of Operations. Ms. Pearce reviewed the results yesterday. She determined that the most popular option, a parking lot expansion, would not be feasible due to the space limitations of our property. However, there were also plenty of votes for an on-site cafeteria, so she wants to go forward with that option. In Ms. Pearce's view, it is a practical project that would have numerous benefits, including raising company morale and reducing the number of employees who return late from their lunch break. I will keep you updated on further developments as they arise.

Sincerely,

Jade Ingram

Employee Survey Results / Compiled by Jade Ingram / Submitted March 22
Topic: Suggestions for branch improvements
Total number of respondents: 218

Topics that were suggested at least thirty times are listed below. A complete list is included on the second page of this report.

Expand the parking area	87
Add an on-site cafeteria	62
Upgrade computers and other office equipment	38
Host a company retreat for employees	31

186. According to the memo, what will happen on March 13?

    (A) Employees will meet new coworkers.
    (B) A branch will shut down.
    (C) A new service will be available.
    (D) Survey results will be announced.

187. According to the memo, what will cause the Silva Corporation to have surplus funds?

    (A) The popularity of a product
    (B) A government grant
    (C) The sale of a building
    (D) A tax refund

188. What is suggested about Ms. Ingram's assignment?

    (A) She plans to delegate it to a member of the Lindbergh team.
    (B) She missed the original deadline for the work.
    (C) She requires information from Ms. Plante to complete it.
    (D) She received assistance from Mr. Harley.

189. In the e-mail, the word "view" in paragraph 1, line 6, is closest in meaning to

    (A) scene
    (B) examination
    (C) vision
    (D) opinion

190. How many people suggested the project that Ms. Pearce approved?

    (A) 87
    (B) 62
    (C) 38
    (D) 31

Questions 191-195 refer to the following proposal forms and memo.

Gem Interiors: Project Proposal Form
Date: March 4

Customer: Lawrence Consulting, 597 Duncan Avenue, Cincinnati, OH 45229

Description of Work:
Installation of carpeting in a commercial building. Materials include foam underlay and nylon carpet (product: Azar 3535). Gem Interiors keeps our prices low by having customers do the preparation work, such as removing and disposing of old tiles or carpets, themselves.

Payment Information:
The total charge for this project will be $28,350. We will honor this quote for 30 days, after which time the price may change. A 10% deposit is due on the first day of installation, and the remainder is due one week after the work is completed.

Technician: _Brian Harmon_   Customer Signature: _____
Approved by: _Edwin Prichard_   Date: _____

Carpetland Proposal
Date: March 4

Customer: Lawrence Consulting
Point of contact: Chad Theisen, 555-4633
Location of work to be performed: 597 Duncan Avenue, Cincinnati, OH 45229

Carpetland proposes to install carpet [5,500 square feet] at the above property for a total of $32,500. This amount includes material, labor, and the removal/disposal of the current flooring.

A $4,000 deposit must be made at the time of reserving a work date. The remaining balance should be paid on the day the work starts. This quote is valid for 2 weeks from the date on this form.

To: All Lawrence Consulting Employees
From: Chad Theisen, Branch Manager
Date: March 7
Subject: New carpeting

The third-floor offices will have their carpeting replaced starting from March 10. The project will take about three days. We hope the change will make the working environment more pleasant thanks to the noise reduction, as more sound waves are absorbed. In preparation, before leaving work on March 8, all third-floor employees should clear their personal items and put them in a box with their name on it. A temporary office space will be set up on the fifth floor. Please note that our own maintenance team will be working on the floor on March 9 to pull up the existing tiles.

Thank you for your cooperation!

---

191. Who most likely is Mr. Prichard?
(A) A supervisor at Gem Interiors
(B) A carpet designer
(C) A construction crew foreman
(D) A safety inspector

192. When must customers make the first payment to Carpetland?
(A) Two weeks after a bill is sent
(B) Within one week of the project's completion
(C) On the day the work begins
(D) When a booking is made

193. What is true about both carpet companies?
(A) Their offers are valid for a limited time.
(B) Their crew members have a lot of experience.
(C) They provide a discount for giving a referral.
(D) They require the customer's signature.

194. What are employees working on the third floor asked to do?
(A) Designate whether they want to work from home
(B) Move their office furniture to another room
(C) Place their belongings in labeled containers
(D) Make recommendations regarding carpet colors

195. What is implied about Lawrence Consulting?
(A) Its maintenance team will take March 10 off.
(B) It will have its carpets installed by Gem Interiors.
(C) It will be closed for three days in March.
(D) It has used Carpetland in the past.

Questions 196-200 refer to the following text message, article, and review.

From: Bumati Kapil, 894-555-2009 (10:25 A.M.)
To: Jerome Quinn, 468-555-1373

Hi, Jerome. I'm here at the former Ritter Chapel with Clarence Wells, the representative from TJ Glass. It seems the repairs of the stained-glass windows are going to be more complicated than we thought. Mr. Wells says that their company is not experienced enough to deal with this kind of project and that we'll have to find someone that specializes in stained-glass restoration. Can you come here now to discuss this further and meet with the electrician, who will be here soon?

Timor Café to Find Home in Unexpected Setting

COVINGTON (June 9)— Timor Café has designated the building that was once Ritter Chapel as its home, and renovations are underway to prepare the site for the café's grand opening scheduled for July 12. The café's owner, Jerome Quinn, purchased the building earlier this year, and the structure is being restored as historically accurate as possible. After services at the chapel were terminated about a decade ago, the building was sold to the city. City officials had planned to use it as a public library, but budget cuts halted the renovation work, leaving the city's acquisition sitting idle for many years. Jerome Quinn purchased the site with the plan to add a coffee shop to his portfolio of establishments in Covington.

The café will sell premium hand-crafted coffee drinks along with fresh pastries. Mr. Quinn believes that customers will enjoy the unique atmosphere, which includes impressive stonework and gorgeous stained-glass windows. To learn more, visit www.timorcafe.net.

www.aroundcovington.com/visitorreviews

| HOME | EVENTS | THINGS TO SEE | **REVIEWS** |

Restaurants and Dining >> Coffee Shops >> Timor Café

Reviewed by Sabrina Lin

I went to Timor Café's grand opening on August 3, and I was very impressed with my overall experience there. The baristas were very knowledgeable about coffee beans, and they explained the subtle flavor differences of each type that the café had. My coffee was superb, and it was accompanied by a delicious blueberry muffin. I was a bit disappointed that the café did not offer wireless Internet, but the distinct chapel décor still made the visit well worth it.

196. What is the purpose of the text message?
 (A) To request an increase in the budget
 (B) To explain why a business cannot do a task
 (C) To get a reference for a glass company
 (D) To ask Mr. Quinn to select building materials

197. Where did Ms. Kapil want Mr. Quinn to meet her when she sent the text?
 (A) At a building materials supply store
 (B) At a glass maker's office
 (C) At a real estate firm
 (D) At a proposed site for a coffee shop

198. What does the article imply about Mr. Quinn?
 (A) He owns several businesses in the area.
 (B) He has a background in historical research.
 (C) He is working as a city official.
 (D) He designed the interior of the café himself.

199. What is mentioned in the article about Ritter Chapel?
 (A) It has been converted to a library.
 (B) It was previously owned by the city.
 (C) It is located near city hall.
 (D) It was considered to be unsafe.

200. What does Ms. Lin imply about the café in her review?
 (A) Its Internet was too slow.
 (B) Its staff members were busy.
 (C) Its opening was delayed.
 (D) Its seats were comfortable.

Stop! This is the end of the test. If you finish before time is called, you may go back to Part 5, 6, and 7 and check your work.

TEST 05

PART 5 · PART 6 · PART 7

준비하기

손목시계

뭉뚝한 연필과 지우개

Answer Sheet

토익 RC는 75분 동안 진행됩니다.
반드시 75분 이내에 문제 풀이와 답안지 마킹을 완료하세요.

> 고난도 문제는 해설집에서 확인할 수 있습니다.
> **해설집 p.86**

TEST 05는 **고난도 문제가 적게 포함된** 쪽박달 :(TEST입니다.
다른 TEST에 비해 상대적으로 **환산 점수가 낮게** 나올 수 있습니다.

맞은 개수	환산 점수	맞은 개수	환산 점수
96-100	**465** - 495	41-45	**145** - 215
91-95	**430** - 490	36-40	**120** - 180
86-90	**400** - 465	31-35	**100** - 145
81-85	**375** - 440	26-30	**80** - 120
76-80	**340** - 415	21-25	**65** - 95
71-75	**315** - 390	16-20	**50** - 75
66-70	**285** - 365	11-15	**35** - 55
61-65	**255** - 335	6-10	**15** - 40
56-60	**225** - 305	1-5	**5** - 30
51-55	**200** - 270	0	5
46-50	**170** - 240		

READING TEST

In the Reading test, you will read a variety of texts and answer several different types of reading comprehension questions. The entire Reading test will last 75 minutes. There are three parts, and directions are given for each part. You are encouraged to answer as many questions as possible within the time allowed.

You must mark your answers on the separate answer sheet. Do not write your answers in your test book.

PART 5

Directions: A word or phrase is missing in each of the sentences below. Four answer choices are given below each sentence. Select the best answer to complete the sentence. Then mark the letter (A), (B), (C), or (D) on your answer sheet.

101. Moray Lab equipment has proven ------- when handling hazardous materials.

(A) effect
(B) effected
(C) effective
(D) effectively

102. Mr. Becker only ------- the finest organic ingredients for his cooking.

(A) speaks
(B) uses
(C) stays
(D) becomes

103. The deadline for the ad was postponed ------- next week because of the new client requests.

(A) in
(B) by
(C) out
(D) until

104. Mr. Porter's diagrams makes it easier for ------- students to learn the basic concepts of chemistry.

(A) he
(B) his
(C) him
(D) himself

105. Before ------- branches overseas, Tinker Inc. has decided to upgrade its domestic facilities in Chicago and Detroit.

(A) launch
(B) launched
(C) launching
(D) launches

106. ------- the performance continues to sell out, it will run for an extra week.

(A) Or
(B) How
(C) Else
(D) If

107. *The Tungsten Review* is the second ------- established journal among professional chemists.

(A) high
(B) most highly
(C) height
(D) more highly

108. The new power tool from Heavy Hack Manufacturing ------- industrial safety standards in the test.

(A) related
(B) exceeded
(C) managed
(D) responded

109. The embassy is open five days a week, ------- visitors cannot obtain services without an appointment.
(A) once
(B) what
(C) but
(D) for

110. According to the memo, the management extended the ------- to employees' family members.
(A) invited
(B) invitations
(C) invitational
(D) inviting

111. The availability of items on sale is ------- to vary among locations.
(A) upcoming
(B) obvious
(C) likely
(D) clear

112. The new multi-vitamin from Austin Pharmaceuticals is meant for ------- suffering from chronic fatigue at work.
(A) both
(B) them
(C) those
(D) whose

113. At Bennington Corp., Ms. Heisman has been doing well as a group member as well as working ------- as a Web designer.
(A) independency
(B) independence
(C) independent
(D) independently

114. The new location on the main downtown strip of Main Street is expected to earn a ------- profit for the company.
(A) repetitive
(B) massive
(C) sturdy
(D) reliant

115. The recent ------- of Duluth Motors has significantly increased Border Auto's production capacity.
(A) acquiring
(B) acquires
(C) acquired
(D) acquisition

116. The new mobile app enables motorists to ------- vacant parking spaces near Central Stadium.
(A) locating
(B) location
(C) locate
(D) located

117. A confirmation e-mail will be sent to your registered address ------- we have received your order.
(A) since
(B) during
(C) once
(D) above

118. ------- of the all company's interns include restocking their office's printers with paper and toner.
(A) Obligations
(B) Allowances
(C) Procedures
(D) Donations

119. The city council members of Schenectady are ------- several proposals for a new city beautification project.
(A) review
(B) reviews
(C) reviewing
(D) reviewed

120. ------- the rise of obese children, many public schools have discontinued offering soft drinks.
(A) Ahead of
(B) Due to
(C) Prior to
(D) Along with

GO ON TO THE NEXT PAGE

121. The construction of a new public art gallery was a major ------- in increasing tourism.
    (A) report
    (B) duty
    (C) choice
    (D) factor

122. Any applications submitted after the deadline are not ------- for financial aids for prospective students.
    (A) consider
    (B) considered
    (C) considering
    (D) considers

123. Please direct any inquires ------- our new language program to Ms. Simpson, academic advisor.
    (A) following
    (B) between
    (C) concerning
    (D) across

124. The finance analyst concluded that the business venture was a success ------- a well-planned budget.
    (A) totally
    (B) thanks to
    (C) even though
    (D) as long as

125. Ms. Saunders will take over the responsibility of keeping the account information -------.
    (A) confide
    (B) confidential
    (C) confidentially
    (D) confiding

126. Last semester, Darcey University ------- six-month intensive foreign language courses for students who were interested in studying abroad.
    (A) instituted
    (B) demonstrated
    (C) applied
    (D) identified

127. ------ in the office, Mr. Bae is now serving as a fulltime programmer who works remotely from his home.
    (A) Fewer
    (B) Together
    (C) Rarely
    (D) Close

128. Although she was hired at Jordan Corporation just six months ago, Ms. Bishop ------- got the promotion to store manager.
    (A) whomever
    (B) nevertheless
    (C) while
    (D) additionally

129. So far, the commercial property on Marshal Street is the only one ------- to accommodate our needs.
    (A) tentative
    (B) excessive
    (C) adequate
    (D) provisional

130. Bryce Co. has announced its plans to decrease its waste production ------- until it meets the new government standard.
    (A) supportively
    (B) voluntarily
    (C) incrementally
    (D) alternatively

PART 6

Directions: Read the texts that follow. A word, phrase, or sentence is missing in parts of each text. Four answer choices for each question are given below the text. Select the best answer to complete the text. Then mark the letter (A), (B), (C), or (D) on your answer sheet.

Questions 131-134 refer to the following article.

Ashmore Steps Up at KC Airlines

METRO VALLEY, November 10—A spokesperson for KC Airlines confirmed that CEO Oliver Norris has ------- from his position due to health reasons. Board Chairman David Ashmore will take over the role temporarily while a replacement is being sought. -------. He was CEO of the airline Freize for six years before becoming a member of the KC Airlines team. -------, he also served as president of an import-export business for several years on the 90s. The board is considering both internal and external applicants for the position. Experts predict that Melissa Hargrove, a senior official ------- the company's largest ever acquisition, is most likely to be offered the job.

131. (A) declined
 (B) resigned
 (C) emerged
 (D) refrained

132. (A) The competitive market has contributed to the issue.
 (B) KC Airlines is one of the largest domestic air carriers.
 (C) Mr. Ashmore has previous experience running a company.
 (D) Board members voted unanimously to change the logo.

133. (A) Consequently
 (B) Rather
 (C) Otherwise
 (D) Furthermore

134. (A) who negotiated
 (B) that negotiates
 (C) whose negotiation
 (D) is negotiating that

Questions 135-138 refer to the following e-mail.

To: Amy Davis
From: Paul Kane
Date: January 18
Subject: Follow-Up on Carson Gallery Visit

Dear Ms. Davis,

Thanks for your advice regarding the Carson Gallery. Based on your comments, we ------- a stack of baskets near the gift shop entrance. As you pointed out, it was ------- difficult for shoppers to take all of their items to the counter. Now people can carry more items with them. In addition, we think your suggestion to reroute the line for the special exhibits is a great idea. From next month, it will run alongside the bulletin board. -------.

Next month, we plan to concentrate ------- attracting more visitors to the site.

Warmest regards,

Paul Kane

135. (A) added
(B) will add
(C) are adding
(D) add

136. (A) only
(B) somewhat
(C) soon
(D) rarely

137. (A) It was the only change we could implement at this time.
(B) The gift shop was too small for the items we wanted to include.
(C) This would encourage patrons to read our posters for upcoming events.
(D) We hope local artists will consider working with our gallery.

138. (A) for
(B) on
(C) with
(D) to

Questions 139-142 refer to the following information.

Enclosed you will find your purchase from Stockton Cookware. We strive to provide top-quality kitchen tools to help chefs of all abilities be -------. We offer a money-back guarantee on all of our products,
                                                                    139.
allowing customers to return items that do not meet their standards. Please note that requests for refunds or exchanges ------- within 60 days of the original purchase. -------. Your refund will be issued to your credit
                        140.   141.
card or made in cash, depending on how the original purchase was made. We appreciate your patronage. Thank you for ------- with us!
                 142.

139. (A) inspires
     (B) inspiration
     (C) inspire
     (D) inspired

140. (A) will receive
     (B) are receiving
     (C) have been received
     (D) must be received

141. (A) The receipt provides you with the total price.
     (B) This can be done by mail or at a retail store.
     (C) We are rated number one in the country.
     (D) Sorry that your requested item was discontinued.

142. (A) cooking
     (B) buying
     (C) meeting
     (D) using

Questions 143-146 refer to the following article.

In contrast to its usual dependence on word-of-mouth advertising, Fresh-Berry is taking an ------- approach to marketing its new dairy-free desserts. -------. Public Relations Director Christopher Diehl announced that the company would add at least three more product lines to its selection, starting with desserts. This is the first change in Fresh-Berry's products since its founding seven years ago. -------, company officials are intent on making it a success by investing heavily in advertising. The desserts are expected to hit the shelves early next year. The Fresh-Berry team is still working on the dessert recipes, which are expected to include the most popular -------.

143. (A) outstanding
(B) entire
(C) immediate
(D) aggressive

144. (A) The plan has worked well for the past few years.
(B) More and more businesses are entering the crowded market.
(C) The business is already known for its breakfast smoothies.
(D) The ingredients are certified as coming from organic farms.

145. (A) Even so
(B) Likewise
(C) For example
(D) Therefore

146. (A) flavors
(B) prices
(C) advertisements
(D) portions

PART 7

Directions: In this part you will read a selection of texts, such as magazine and newspaper articles, e-mails, and instant messages. Each text or set of texts is followed by several questions. Select the best answer for each question and mark the letter (A), (B), (C), or (D) on your answer sheet.

Questions 147-148 refer to the following Web page.

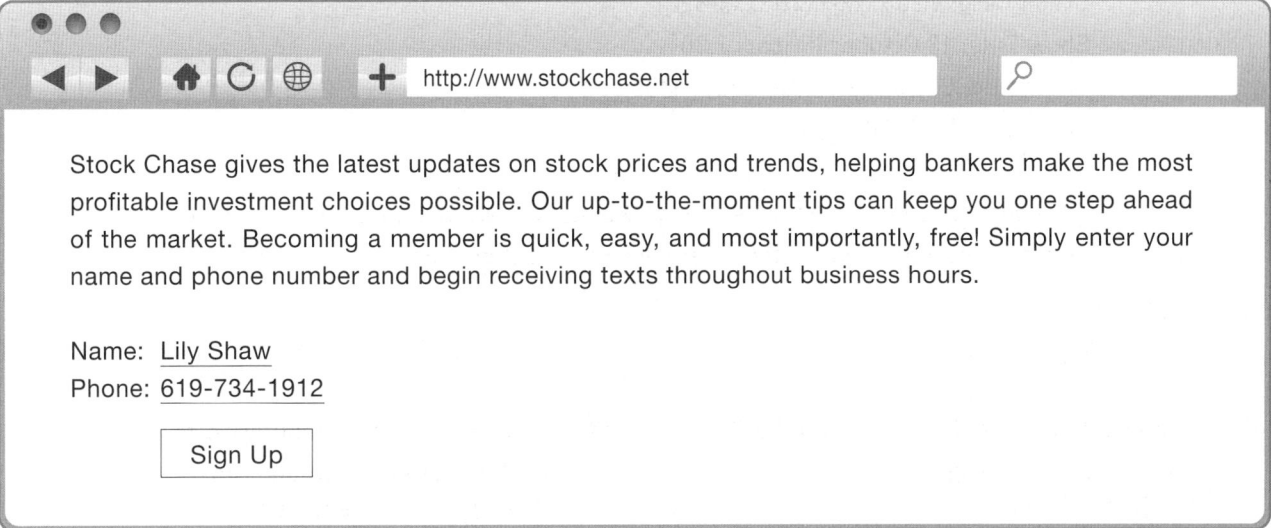

147. Who is the Web page most likely intended for?

(A) Truck drivers
(B) Store owners
(C) Investment bankers
(D) Security guards

148. What can be inferred about Ms. Shaw?

(A) She will receive updates from Stock Chase.
(B) Her name will be posted on a Web site.
(C) Her investments are highly profitable.
(D) She is an employee of Stock Chase.

GO ON TO THE NEXT PAGE

Questions 149-150 refer to the following receipt.

Receipt #4385-0118

Refer to this number for customer service issues

Customer: Jonathan Hurst
Credit Card: Visa xxxx-xxxx-xxxx-6201
Show Date: 13 October (Friday) 7:30
Show Title: Life of Byron (Comedy / Musical)
Seating: D-19, D-20

It is best to come to the theater early. Guests who arrive late will have to wait until the intermission to enter. There are no exceptions to this rule.

149. What event is scheduled for 13 October?
(A) A museum opening
(B) A book signing
(C) A theatrical performance
(D) A race competition

150. What is Mr. Hurst encouraged to do?
(A) Complete a feedback form
(B) Arrive to the venue early
(C) Visit a souvenir shop
(D) Wait for the intermission

Questions 151-152 refer to the following text message chain.

Evelyn Berger <3:38 P.M.>
Sorry I missed your call. I was giving a presentation in a meeting. What's up?

Randy Avalos <3:41 P.M.>
I just wanted to let you know that I've fixed the problem with our online shopping page.

Evelyn Berger <3:42 P.M.>
Great. So all of the links are active now?

Randy Avalos <3:42 P.M.>
Yes. When you click on the link, it takes you to the product description. I've also made the font size for the prices larger so they're easier to read.

Evelyn Berger <3:44 P.M.>
That's perfect. Thanks. I was worried that there might be some negative comments from customers about the broken links.

Randy Avalos <3:47 P.M.>
I haven't received any.

Evelyn Berger <3:48 P.M.>
All right. That's a relief. Thanks for taking care of that so quickly.

151. What does Mr. Avalos say he has done?
(A) Placed an order online
(B) Raised the product prices
(C) Made changes to a Web site
(D) Written some product descriptions

152. At 3:47 P.M., what does Mr. Avalos imply when he writes, "I haven't received any"?
(A) He is waiting for approval.
(B) A shipment will arrive late.
(C) He is dissatisfied with a service.
(D) A problem was not noticed.

Questions 153-154 refer to the following memo.

To: Palmore Department Store Employees
From: Jeffrey Dye
Date: September 6
Re: Break Rules

Although all employees are entitled to break times during their shifts, there are some rules that are expected to be followed. There have been some complaints recently, so I want to make sure that everything is clear.

If you stay on store property during your break time, be aware that customers might think that you are there to assist them. To avoid any misunderstandings, please use one of the employee break rooms while on break. We appreciate your cooperation and understanding. If there are any questions regarding this, please direct them to your immediate supervisor.

153. What is the main purpose of the memo?
 (A) To announce a temporary store closure
 (B) To request some feedback
 (C) To introduce a new dress code
 (D) To clarify a policy

154. What are employees are reminded to do?
 (A) Take a break in designated areas
 (B) Work remotely from their homes
 (C) Keep their uniforms tidy and clean
 (D) Collect detailed customer opinions

Questions 155-157 refer to the following advertisement.

Southern Pacific Explorer – Find Heaven on Earth!

Step aboard any one of our fine ships and relax while exploring the waters of the Southern Pacific Ocean. All of our boats are fully equipped with all of the facilities you could possibly want while on vacation. Marvel at sights such as the Great Barrier Reef, dolphins, and whales during an adventure at sea. Whenever you get hungry you can enjoy a meal at any time of day or night with our 24-hour buffet. During the day, do some poolside sunbathing on our forward deck. If you prefer to swim indoors, our boats have an indoor exercise pool as well. Every night our ballroom features live music from 8 P.M. to midnight for you and your significant other to dance to. If you're bringing kids, then enjoy one of the fairy tale puppet shows that have been named "Most Fun Child Entertainment" by *Parenting on Vacation Magazine.* They take place hourly from 10 A.M. to 6 P.M. If you want privacy, you are always able to return to your sound-proofed bedroom with a window to the ocean outside. During the 4 hour stay at Creon Island, you can enjoy the marine leisure activities with nominal fees. Please get the price information and reserve a spot by asking your room assistant.

155. What is being advertised?

    (A) A tour group
    (B) A travel agency
    (C) A vacation resort
    (D) An ocean cruise

156. What is stated about Southern Pacific Explorer?

    (A) It employs lifeguards around the clock.
    (B) It has different facilities depending on each boat.
    (C) It provides award-winning entertainment.
    (D) It outscores its competitors on customer satisfaction.

157. What can be purchased for an extra fee?

    (A) Marine activities
    (B) Babysitting services
    (C) Live theater tickets
    (D) Digital film streaming

Questions 158-160 refer to the following e-mail.

To: Rachel Medrano <rachelm@center-post.com>
From: Amil Sankar <amilsankar@llk1.com>
Date: September 1
Subject: Response needed

Dear Ms. Medrano,

As discussed at the quarterly tenants meeting, the owner of Atlas Apartments is making security upgrades to the facility. Each unit will be equipped with a video intercom system, which will allow you to see who is standing at the entrance before buzzing the person in. — [1] —. The device will be installed inside your home by a technician on September 7 between 9 A.M. and noon. If you are not present during the work, it is not a problem. — [2] —. The building manager has a copy of all tenants' keys and can let the technician in. However, in this case, you will need to fill out the attached consent form for us to enter your apartment. Simply e-mail it back to me at this address.

The video intercom system is part of a larger plan to improve security at Atlas Apartments. — [3] —. We will install security cameras in all elevators and corridors, put motion-sensor lights in the parking lot, and hire another security guard so that there are always two on duty. — [4] —. That's because they are being paid for by the rent increases that went into effect last year.

If you have any questions about the changes, please feel free to contact me by e-mail or by calling the rental office at 555-8330.

Sincerely,

Amil Sankar
Tenant Liaison, Atlas Apartments

---

158. Why did Mr. Sankar send the e-mail to Ms. Medrano?

(A) To invite her to a tenants meeting
(B) To request information about her availability
(C) To inform her of an installation plan
(D) To request feedback about security measures

159. What should Ms. Medrano do if she will not be home on September 7?

(A) Reschedule a visit for another day
(B) Return a completed document to Mr. Sankar
(C) Leave her key with the building manager
(D) Ask a neighbor to do a task

160. In which of the positions marked [1], [2], [3], and [4] does the following sentence best belong?

"There is no direct charge to tenants for these upgrades."

(A) [1]
(B) [2]
(C) [3]
(D) [4]

Questions 161-163 refer to the following e-mail.

From: Pamela Robbins <custserv@atlantacabs.net>
To: Stephen Reynolds <s.reynolds@qmail.net>
Subject: Inquiry #20149 Response
Date: 17 May

Dear Mr. Reynolds,

One of our drivers has turned in a backpack that matches the description of the one you reported missing. You must have forgotten it in the cab when you got out.

For safety reasons, it is our company policy to not open any items that are left in our vehicles. We ask that you come to our main office to identify and claim your bag. Our regular office hours are from 8 A.M. to 6 P.M. Monday through Saturday. The office is NOT open on Sundays. When you come to claim your bag, we will ask you to sign a release form. This is a standard security procedure. We will also make a photocopy of your ID.

Please note that we only keep recovered items for two weeks, so you have until next month to retrieve your bag. Feel free to call us at 555-2867 if you have any further questions.

Pamela Robbins

Customer Service Representative, Atlanta Cabs

---

161. What did Mr. Reynolds most likely ask about?

(A) Ride availability
(B) Extra fees
(C) A lost personal item
(D) Office hours

162. According to the e-mail, what will Mr. Reynolds have to provide?

(A) His work schedule
(B) His personal belongings
(C) His identification
(D) His receipt

163. What is Mr. Reynolds asked to do?

(A) Gather more information
(B) Visit Ms. Robbins' office soon
(C) Provide a delivery address
(D) Contact a driver

Questions 164-167 refer to the following online chat discussion.

	Clara Mills [9:09 A.M.]	Hello, everyone. I've got an issue that we need to discuss. I just came from the production floor, and our order for Seneca Fashions needs to be put on hold.
	Thao Phan [9:10 A.M.]	What happened? We're supposed to send the samples for those dresses by Friday because the company is having a photo shoot with some models.
	Clara Mills [9:11 A.M.]	I was looking over the fabric that arrived, and I noticed that it was the wrong color. It's slightly darker than the other pieces in the line. I've contacted the fabric manufacturer and they can send the right fabric by Tuesday.
	Hedra Penhale [9:11 A.M.]	That means we'll be late in fulfilling Seneca Fashions' order. The owner, Ms. Lin, is going to be so upset.
	Kenny Carini [9:12 A.M.]	But it's never happened before.
	Thao Phan [9:13 A.M.]	Right. I don't think it will affect our reputation that much. We have a long track record of being reliable.
	Clara Mills [9:13 A.M.]	And we'll only be a few days late if we can find people who are willing to put in extra hours.
	Thao Phan [9:14 A.M.]	I can take care of that.
	Clara Mills [9:15 A.M.]	Thanks. Let me know what's decided and I'll post the updated schedule in the break room.
	Hedra Penhale [9:16 A.M.]	And thank you, Clara, for spotting the problem with the colors. That could have been a very costly mistake!

SEND

164. Where most likely do the writers work?
    (A) At a modeling agency
    (B) At a clothing factory
    (C) At a fashion magazine
    (D) At a textile manufacturer

165. At 9:12 A.M., what does Mr. Carini most likely mean when he writes, "it's never happened before"?
    (A) He is surprised that the problem occurred.
    (B) He refuses to take responsibility for an error.
    (C) He thinks a customer will be understanding.
    (D) He doesn't know how to resolve the issue.

166. What does Mr. Phan say he will do?
    (A) Post an updated schedule
    (B) Inspect some goods carefully
    (C) Recruit employees to work overtime
    (D) Hold a meeting with Ms. Lin

167. What is suggested about Ms. Mills?
    (A) She prefers the goods to be darker.
    (B) She will select some new colors.
    (C) She saved the company a lot of money.
    (D) She helped Ms. Penhale finish a project.

Questions 168-171 refer to the following article.

TOPEKA (December 19) – A charity concert is being planned for New Year's Eve right here in Topeka. The upcoming concert, Magic of Music, will raise funds for local afterschool programs that teach children things like music and self-expression through art. It will feature several famous bands along with some local bands. Tickets can be purchased in advance on the event's Web site, www.magicofmusic.com, and cost $30 for adults and $20 for children.

Kate Dickerson, the organizer of the concert, has extensive experience with organizing events to sponsor charities. Not long ago, she planned the amateur soccer tournament Kicking for Cures to raise money for cancer research. In an interview about the event's success, Ms. Dickerson indicated that in order to plan a successful fundraiser you have to make whoever buys a ticket feel good about themselves. "It's important to compliment people for supporting the cause," she said.

When asked why she chose Topeka for Magic of Music, Ms. Dickerson said that it was a central location for the bands who volunteered to play. "I'm so grateful to the artists coming to perform. I wanted to minimize the amount of time they have to spend travelling to get here," she told reporters at a press conference promoting the event. Like most events planned by Ms. Dickerson, Magic of Music has already drawn a lot of public attention.

168. What is the main focus of the article?
 (A) An environmental organization
 (B) A fundraising event
 (C) A sports competition
 (D) An afterschool program

169. According to the article, what did Ms. Dickerson recently do?
 (A) She started an afterschool program.
 (B) She performed on stage.
 (C) She joined a soccer team.
 (D) She organized a sports event.

170. What does Ms. Dickerson say is the most important part of organizing events?
 (A) Recognizing the participants
 (B) Making tickets affordable
 (C) Donating all proceeds
 (D) Inviting celebrity guests

171. Why did Ms. Dickerson choose Topeka for the concert location?
 (A) She has many personal connections in the city.
 (B) She was asked for help by public school teachers.
 (C) She wants to make travel convenient for performers.
 (D) She could not afford a more famous venue.

Questions 172-175 refer to the following article.

Local Organization Announces Scholarship Opportunities

October 8—The Texas Agricultural Association (TAA) has announced plans to offer five scholarships of $5,000 each. The mission of this organization is to provide assistance to those working in the farm industry. — [1] —. This is done through networking with members, trying to pass protective legislation, and monitoring markets closely.

— [2] —. Applications for the scholarships will be accepted from October 15 to November 1. Applicants must live in the state of Texas and must have completed an undergraduate program and be working toward a graduate degree. — [3] —. All successful candidates will be chosen based on merit. The scholarships can be used for both on-campus university students and distance education students.

Applications can be completed online at http://www.texasagrassoc.org/scholarship. — [4] —. They should be accompanied by a short piece of writing explaining the applicant's educational and career goals. A committee of eight TAA members will meet to select the winners of the scholarships. Questions regarding the scholarships should be directed to Robin Hatcher at r.hatcher@texasagrassoc.org.

172. According to the article, what is the main goal of TAA?

(A) To grow environmentally friendly food
(B) To support farm workers
(C) To teach people about agriculture
(D) To develop farming technologies

173. What is NOT indicated about the scholarships?

(A) They are intended for graduate-level students.
(B) They are only given to students in a certain location.
(C) They will be awarded on November 1.
(D) They can be used for traditional or online education.

174. According to the article, what should be included with the application?

(A) An application fee
(B) A university transcript
(C) A personal essay
(D) A reference letter

175. In which of the positions marked [1], [2], [3], and [4] does the following sentence best belong?

"They do not need to be a TAA member in order to apply."

(A) [1]
(B) [2]
(C) [3]
(D) [4]

Questions 176-180 refer to the following e-mail and receipt.

To: VIP Customer Mailing List
From: Annie's Outfitters
Date: 4 October
Subject: Last Chance! Closing Sale!

After being in business for five decades, Annie's Outfitters will be closing its doors for good. We want to thank all of the loyal customers we have had throughout that time. As one last thank you and farewell, we will be holding a closing sale, and everything must go!

The closing sale will be officially announced next week, but since you are our VIP customers, you can enjoy the final clearance sale prices of 50% off before anyone else. We hope to see you for one final shopping spree at our store. Please keep in mind our last day of business is October 25. Until then, all purchases with a subtotal of $100 or more qualify for free gift wrapping. If you have a $15 discount coupon from completing a survey form after a previous purchase, this is a final chance to use it!

Annie Cosenza
Owner, Annie's Outfitters

Date: 12 October   **Time: 16:42**

Item Description	Regular Price ($)	Your Price ($)
Pearl Earrings	30.00	15.00
Fall Jacket (Leather, Size M)	80.00	40.00
Ruby Bracelet	20.00	10.00
High Heels (Silver, Size 6)	50.00	25.00
Subtotal:		90.00
Tax:		9.00
Gift Wrapping:	2.00 (x4)	8.00
Other:		-15.00
Total:		$92.00

Tender: Credit (xxxx-xxxx-xxxx-4913)   Name on Card: Samantha Henson
Thank you for shopping at Annie's Outfitters!
Product reviews can be found at www.anniesoutfitters.com!
* No returns or exchanges for items purchased at clearance sale price*

176. Why was the e-mail sent?
    (A) To introduce a new monthly membership
    (B) To express thanks to survey participants
    (C) To announce a store closure
    (D) To promote a seasonal sale

177. What is most likely true about Ms. Henson?
    (A) She paid with a store credit card.
    (B) She filled out a customer survey.
    (C) She used to work at Annie's Outfitters.
    (D) She checked product reviews online.

178. What is indicated about the items on the receipt?
    (A) They were sent to different addresses.
    (B) They cannot be refunded.
    (C) They have positive customer reviews.
    (D) They were ordered online.

179. How could Ms. Henson have an extra charge waived?
    (A) By waiting for a sale to start
    (B) By joining a membership
    (C) By using a coupon
    (D) By purchasing more items

180. What is NOT mentioned about Annie's Outfitters?
    (A) It offers an express shipping option.
    (B) It displays reviews of products online.
    (C) It will no longer accept returned merchandise.
    (D) It allows coupons to combine with sale prices.

GO ON TO THE NEXT PAGE

Questions 181-185 refer to the following notice and e-mail.

Empire Country Club Membership

Membership	Standard	Prince	Emperor
Fee (monthly)	$500	$950	$1,600
Golf Course Access	O	O	O
Basic Spa Access (Hot tub, Steam room)	O	O	O
Personal Parking Space*	X	O	O
Full Body Massage	X	O	O
Fishing Pier Access	X	X	O

Any walk-in visits are not accepted. Please make a reservation in advance.

*Parking spaces are for regular-sized vehicles ONLY. Large vehicles such as limousines must be parked separately from the regular parking lot.

Members are allowed to bring up to 3 guests when coming to the club. For any more than that, there is a $100 fee per visit per extra person.

From: Sadie Long <slong@empirecc.net>
To: Lindsay Alexander <l.alexander@cmail.net>
Subject: RE: Guests Visit
Date: 3 September
Attachment: Membership Details

Dear Ms. Alexander,

In response to your request to host friends, of course you may. Your membership allows you to bring up to 3 people with you without any extra fee. More than that, however, would incur an extra fee. Each of the people that you bring will have the same accesses as you, meaning that you are all allowed to enjoy all but our fishing facilities.

As for your transportation, the regular parking lot is not large enough to accommodate your transportation. You have to ask your driver to drop you off at the clubhouse and park in the West lot, which is normally used by employees.

I attached a copy of your membership details for your reference. If you still have any questions or comments, feel free to contact me by e-mail or phone.

Sincerely,

Sadie Long
Membership Coordinator, Empire Country Club

181. What is indicated about the Empire Country Club?

    (A) It provides a complimentary valet service.
    (B) It is conveniently located downtown.
    (C) It has recently been renovated.
    (D) It is available by appointment only.

182. What does standard membership include?

    (A) A reserved place to park
    (B) Massages upon request
    (C) Entry into a spa facility
    (D) The opportunity to fish

183. In the e-mail, the word "incur" in paragraph 1, line 2 is closest in meaning to

    (A) advance
    (B) proceed
    (C) generate
    (D) request

184. What can be inferred about Ms. Alexander?

    (A) She scheduled a group massage.
    (B) She pays a monthly fee of $950.
    (C) She will be charged an extra $100.
    (D) She did not read her member contract.

185. What is suggested about Ms. Alexander's group?

    (A) They plan to travel to the clubhouse by a large vehicle.
    (B) They are going to visit Empire Country Club on a weekend.
    (C) They will have to pay a separate entry fee.
    (D) They want to sign up for a membership.

GO ON TO THE NEXT PAGE

Questions 186-190 refer to the following advertisement, instructions, and review.

Special offer for all Web Access Academy members! 40% off selected courses!*

- 304: PhotoMaster Level 3 / *Using photo manipulation software* – Stevie Dawson takes you through the more advanced techniques for manipulating images for online use.
- 115: Essentials Level 1 / *Computer language basics* – Gary Marlow conducts our best-selling program for those who are new to computer programming.
- 346: Find Yourself Level 3 / *Search Engine Optimization (SEO)* – Harry Miles, our top-rated instructor, gives you a detailed look at getting your Web site listed highly on all major search engines.
- 108: Commercial Skills / *Create your own Web site templates* – Janet Sedley shows you how to create templates to save you time over multiple Web sites.

Please note that courses may require a software download.

Enroll and pay here.

*Applies to August courses only. You must have completed at least one class from Web Access Academy.

Congratulations! You are now signed up. Please follow the instructions below:

1) Go to www.webwizard.org/downloads and input "WEBAA33" in the box.*
2) When the download finishes, click Install and wait for the program to install. It will open automatically when finished.**
3) Download the following document here and make sure you have read it by the time your first video session begins.

If you have any difficulties, please check our course forums for help. Many questions have already been answered, but you can also post your own questions.

*Please note that this program is only free for download before July 31.
**Older computers may have difficulty running some programs. Read equipment requirements here.

www.webaccessacademy.com/reviews

Name: David Murray
Date: September 3

Comment: I took the Find Yourself course and based on my experience with it I would highly recommend this course. Because of the small lesson modules, it's perfect for someone who is working. I did have difficulty getting the Web Wizard program to run properly. After getting no response to my question on the forums, I e-mailed the instructor directly and was very pleased with how quickly I got a response. The information provided helped me to solve the problem completely. I'd also like to note that, while I got Web Wizard for free as part of the course, I'm not sure if I would pay the $120 they usually charge. Otherwise, I am fully satisfied. Thanks!

186. Which course would be best for computer programing beginners?
 (A) 304
 (B) 115
 (C) 346
 (D) 108

187. What is NOT mentioned as a step in the instructions?
 (A) Installing a computer program
 (B) Paying by credit card
 (C) Entering a code
 (D) Reading a document

188. What problem does Mr. Murray mention?
 (A) A computer program was not working correctly.
 (B) The forums were difficult to understand.
 (C) The course schedule was poorly organized.
 (D) The tutor support was slower than expected.

189. What can be inferred about Mr. Murray?
 (A) His registration was completed after August 1.
 (B) He is a highly experienced programmer.
 (C) He downloaded a program before July 31.
 (D) His computer needs to be upgraded.

190. Who did Mr. Murray contact?
 (A) Stevie Dawson
 (B) Gary Marlow
 (C) Harry Miles
 (D) Janet Sedley

Questions 191-195 refer to the following e-mail, article, and text message.

To: Sherman Library Board Members <board@sherman-library.org>
From: Katherine Milford <milfordk@sherman-library.org>
Date: July 2
Subject: Upcoming Meeting

Dear Board Members,

I am writing to remind you that our next library board meeting will be Thursday, July 16, at 7 P.M. I appreciate everyone's flexibility in moving the meeting back by a week to accommodate my travel schedule. The main topic on the agenda will be deciding what to do with our surplus funds. As you all know, a member of the community made a generous financial donation to the library. At last month's meeting, we selected two potential projects on which the money could be spent—adding self-service checkout stations to some of our branches or implementing an online reservation system. These will be listed on the voting ballots as Self-Service and Reservation System, respectively. In order to move forward with one of these projects, and abandon the other one, a majority of the board members must vote in favor of it. If this fails to happen, we will discuss both projects again at the August meeting, which is currently scheduled for August 15. However, I hope we can reach an agreement this month.

I look forward to seeing you all on July 16!

Sincerely,

Katherine Milford
Chair, Sherman Library Board of Directors

Sherman Library to Offer New Service

July 20—Sherman Library and its staff have faced a number of challenges, including budget cuts, staffing issues, and even a natural disaster. Employees were concerned about the constant pressures put on the library and many stated that they couldn't take it anymore. However, now the library is getting some much-needed relief with a recent donation for special projects. Board members voted last week to implement an online reservation system for patrons. This will allow anyone with a locally issued library card to reserve books online and be notified via text message when they are ready.

Patrons may sign up for a trial of the system, and those who participate will be expected to complete a detailed survey about their experience in order to improve the system. The trial period will run for the entire month of September, and the system will most likely be rolled out to all members in mid-November.

To: Josephine Kuhn 433-555-6780
From: Sherman Library 433-555-1025
Received: Wednesday, September 6, 10:52 A.M.

Reservation Notification: 2 of 3 requested books available
Borrower Name: Josephine Kuhn
Library Card Number: 89578542134758
The following items are now available for pickup at Sherman Library:
Fiction: 209578   *Down Cedar Street*   Posner, Sarah
Fiction: 249503   *The Investigator*   Wetzel, Richard

Your items will be held until Tuesday, September 12. If not collected, they will be returned to the shelves for general checkout. Your other item is expected to be ready in 3 days.

191. Why does Ms. Milford thank the e-mail recipients?
    (A) They completed a requested project early.
    (B) They provided useful suggestions.
    (C) They agreed to change a meeting date.
    (D) They donated money to the library.

192. In the article, the word "take" in paragraph 1, line 3, is closest in meaning to
    (A) endure
    (B) move
    (C) require
    (D) use

193. What is suggested about the Self-Service project?
    (A) It will be discussed at the August meeting.
    (B) Less than half of the board members voted for it.
    (C) It was more expensive than initially planned.
    (D) The majority of library patrons were against it.

194. What is implied about Ms. Kuhn?
    (A) She is a member of the board of directors.
    (B) She will be asked to give feedback.
    (C) She currently has three books checked out.
    (D) She recently applied for a library card.

195. How long will Ms. Kuhn's items be held?
    (A) 2 days
    (B) 3 days
    (C) 1 week
    (D) 2 weeks

Questions 196-200 refer to the following notice, e-mail, and ticket.

JD TRANSPORTATION PASSENGER NOTICE

JD Transportation is pleased to announce the following changes to our services, effective February 1:

- New Routes Added:

    Lincoln City ↔ Deleon / Regular service every weekday morning

    Lincoln City ↔ Clementon / Express service five times a day, Mon.–Thurs.

    Lincoln City ↔ Hargis Valley / Express service Mon. mornings and Thurs. evenings

- Bus Upgrades: All Express buses will feature free Wi-Fi. Complimentary refreshments will be served on routes to and from Deleon. Some buses will be equipped with televisions.

- Fare Changes: At the same time as these changes occur, we will raise our fares by approximately 5%. This is our first fare change in five years, and we are committed to keeping fares down. There is still no charge to refund an unused ticket.

E-mail

To:	Yemane Girma <ygirma@ecvmail.com>
From:	Eunyoung Jang <jangeunyoung@broaddusinc.net>
Date:	February 10
Subject:	Your visit to Broaddus Inc.

Dear Mr. Girma,

Everyone here at Broaddus Inc. is looking forward to your visit on February 28. We believe that our staff will find your workshop to be informative and rewarding. Please let me know if there are any special materials you need me to prepare.

I have made the necessary travel arrangements for you. You will arrive at the regional airport in Lincoln City. Rather than having someone pick you up there, we ask that you take the bus. It will be much faster because there are designated bus lanes which avoid the heavy traffic. The bus terminal is connected to the airport, so you just need to show the attached confirmation at the counter to pick up your ticket. Your flight arrives one hour before the bus leaves, so there should be more than enough time to catch the bus. The journey is about two hours, and I will meet you when you arrive at the final stop. You don't have to follow any luggage restrictions for the bus, so whatever you brought on the plane will be fine.

I will send details about your hotel booking later this week.

Sincerely,

Eunyoung Jang

Ticket Reservation Confirmation

Passenger Name: Yemane Girma   **Travel Date:** Tuesday, February 28
Journey: Lincoln City to Clementon, Express Bus #282
Departure Time: 2 P.M.
Seat: 12A
Payment Status: Paid

Tickets that have not been picked by ten minutes before the departure time may be given to standby passengers. Visit our Web site for more information.

196. What is NOT indicated about JD Transportation?
    (A) Some of its routes are only available in the morning.
    (B) Its ticket prices will increase in February.
    (C) Some of its buses will have TV screens.
    (D) It will offer more buses on weekends.

197. What is the purpose of Mr. Girma's visit to Broaddus Inc.?
    (A) To accept an award
    (B) To attend a job interview
    (C) To train staff members
    (D) To inspect a facility

198. In the e-mail, the word "follow" in paragraph 2, line 7, is closest in meaning to
    (A) understand
    (B) go after
    (C) copy
    (D) adhere to

199. When does Ms. Jang expect to meet Mr. Girma on February 28?
    (A) At 1 P.M.
    (B) At 2 P.M.
    (C) At 3 P.M.
    (D) At 4 P.M.

200. What is implied about Mr. Girma?
    (A) He requested a seat by the window.
    (B) He will have Internet access during his journey.
    (C) He will pay for the ticket when he picks it up.
    (D) He is eligible to receive free snacks during his trip.

Stop! This is the end of the test. If you finish before time is called, you may go back to Part 5, 6, and 7 and check your work.

TEST 06

PART 5 · PART 6 · PART 7

준비하기

손목시계

뭉뚝한 연필과 지우개

Answer Sheet

토익 RC는 75분 동안 진행됩니다.
반드시 75분 이내에 문제 풀이와 답안지 마킹을 완료하세요.

TEST 06은 **고난도 문제가 많이 포함된** 대박달 :) TEST입니다.
다른 TEST에 비해 상대적으로 **환산 점수가 높게** 나올 수 있습니다.

맞은 개수	환산 점수	맞은 개수	환산 점수
96-100	465 - **495**	41-45	145 - **215**
91-95	430 - **490**	36-40	120 - **180**
86-90	400 - **465**	31-35	100 - **145**
81-85	375 - **440**	26-30	80 - **120**
76-80	340 - **415**	21-25	65 - **95**
71-75	315 - **390**	16-20	50 - **75**
66-70	285 - **365**	11-15	35 - **55**
61-65	255 - **335**	6-10	15 - **40**
56-60	225 - **305**	1-5	5 - **30**
51-55	200 - **270**	0	5
46-50	170 - **240**		

고난도 문제는 해설집에서 확인할 수 있습니다.
해설집 p.107

READING TEST

In the Reading test, you will read a variety of texts and answer several different types of reading comprehension questions. The entire Reading test will last 75 minutes. There are three parts, and directions are given for each part. You are encouraged to answer as many questions as possible within the time allowed.

You must mark your answers on the separate answer sheet. Do not write your answers in your test book.

PART 5

Directions: A word or phrase is missing in each of the sentences below. Four answer choices are given below each sentence. Select the best answer to complete the sentence. Then mark the letter (A), (B), (C), or (D) on your answer sheet.

101. Please call the housekeeping office, rather than the front desk, if ------- want more towels or other supplies.
 (A) yours
 (B) your
 (C) you
 (D) yourself

102. The spokesperson ------- with brief answers at the press conference yesterday.
 (A) is responding
 (B) responds
 (C) responded
 (D) to respond

103. Even regular visitors could ------- recognize the hotel's lobby after it had been renovated.
 (A) scarce
 (B) scarcer
 (C) scarcest
 (D) scarcely

104. Lecture attendees may stay late after the talk to ------- research methods with the guest speaker.
 (A) focus
 (B) dictate
 (C) discuss
 (D) fund

105. Building permit requests without a full address will no longer be -------.
 (A) intended
 (B) earned
 (C) perceived
 (D) accepted

106. The board members did not understand the ------- of some of the terms in the contract.
 (A) meanly
 (B) meaning
 (C) meant
 (D) mean

107. The evening gowns have a ------- similar design even though they were created by two different fashion houses.
 (A) remark
 (B) remarking
 (C) remarks
 (D) remarkably

108. Using an ------- during international summits is a good way to avoid communication issues between parties.
 (A) interpretation
 (B) interpret
 (C) interpreter
 (D) interpreted

109. The battery in the new Mahlon smartphone lasts longer ------- most others on the market.
(A) of
(B) than
(C) to
(D) across

110. To keep up with customer demand, the café needs a ------- supply of freshly baked bread throughout the day.
(A) popular
(B) simple
(C) steady
(D) rigorous

111. Although the weather is supposed to be cold, the event planners ------- expect a big crowd.
(A) last
(B) still
(C) next
(D) more

112. Following Ms. Anderson's resignation, a new CEO was ------- appointed by the board.
(A) promptly
(B) prompt
(C) prompter
(D) promptest

113. So far, Fleming Design Co. ------- over fifty thousand dollars to local community projects.
(A) is contributing
(B) was contributed
(C) will contribute
(D) has contributed

114. The Cameron Theater held ------- for its upcoming play, which will be performed in June.
(A) auditions
(B) position
(C) examinations
(D) interest

115. Despite strong tourist activity in the area, a ------- number of restaurants have trouble staying in business.
(A) surprised
(B) surprisingly
(C) surprising
(D) surprise

116. Many of Cobre Bank's customers are taking out mortgages because interest rates are ------- lower than ever before.
(A) historically
(B) urgently
(C) actively
(D) repeatedly

117. The Platinum Pass gives concertgoers ------- access to the backstage lounge area before and after the show.
(A) excluding
(B) exclusively
(C) exclusion
(D) exclusive

118. Although employees ------- are prohibited from entering the contest, their family members are eligible.
(A) they
(B) themselves
(C) them
(D) their

119. As the vacuum cannot be easily reached in the attic, please store it in the downstairs closet -------.
(A) rather
(B) likewise
(C) instead
(D) particularly

120. Discussions regarding the new logo stalled because the team members could not agree on a ------- that would reflect the company's identity.
(A) degree
(B) belief
(C) route
(D) style

GO ON TO THE NEXT PAGE

121. We will announce the name of the person who is taking over the vice president's position ------- the contract is finalized.
(A) well
(B) rather
(C) once
(D) like

122. Guests of people staying at the Willow Inn should visit the front desk to ------- a short-term parking pass.
(A) obtain
(B) attach
(C) reach
(D) gather

123. City roads ------- with barricades will be open to the public right after the marathon race.
(A) to block
(B) that block
(C) blocked
(D) were blocked

124. A pump system will be installed in the basement to get rid of ------- water that may collect throughout the rainy season.
(A) excess
(B) valid
(C) adequate
(D) distilled

125. Neither of the ------- at the meeting wanted to be the first to suggest pricing terms for the licensing agreement.
(A) negotiability
(B) negotiable
(C) negotiators
(D) negotiation

126. ------- the newly installed packaging machinery, the plant will be able to increase output by as much as ten percent.
(A) To
(B) At
(C) With
(D) About

127. The sales team hopes ------- its previous record this month by adding more clients to the customer base.
(A) to be broken
(B) having broken
(C) breaking
(D) to break

128. Mechanics are advised to check the current price of replacement parts ------- providing an estimate for repairs.
(A) aside from
(B) according to
(C) prior to
(D) as of

129. The warehouse manager has not yet learned ------- some of the shipping crates were damaged in transit.
(A) what
(B) why
(C) whom
(D) whenever

130. The seams of all bike shorts made by GTR Apparel are double stitched to improve -------.
(A) preference
(B) familiarity
(C) attempt
(D) durability

PART 6

Directions: Read the texts that follow. A word, phrase, or sentence is missing in parts of each text. Four answer choices for each question are given below the text. Select the best answer to complete the text. Then mark the letter (A), (B), (C), or (D) on your answer sheet.

Questions 131-134 refer to the following information.

Community Art Contest Information

Those selected for the judging panel cannot have family members participating in the contest. This will ensure that judges will be ------- from bias. All submissions must meet the requirements for entry. -------.
131.   132.
Submissions will be accepted on Saturday, February 6, at the Dubois Center. ------- for the yellow signs
                                                                              133.
directing participants to the collection point. Artists are permitted to leave their canvases wrapped. When it comes time for judging, the paintings will be ------- unwrapped by our staff to avoid any damage.
                                                                         134.

131. (A) unlike
 (B) free
 (C) obvious
 (D) low

132. (A) Interest in art has been growing in the community.
 (B) Selecting a theme was difficult for event planners.
 (C) Detailed guidelines are provided on the Web site.
 (D) We are sorry that your artwork was rejected.

133. (A) Look
 (B) Pay
 (C) Call
 (D) Account

134. (A) slows
 (B) slowing
 (C) slowed
 (D) slowly

GO ON TO THE NEXT PAGE

Questions 135-138 refer to the following memo.

From: Roberta Galvan

To: All Celestine Insurance Employees

Date: July 13

Re: Renovations

We have hired a company to carry out some renovations on the third floor of our building due to the ------- condition of the carpeting and wallpaper there. The work is scheduled for July 28 to August 1. On the first day of the project, employees who work on the third floor ------- to workspaces in other parts of the building. ------- the work is being performed, the conference room will be off limits. Therefore, team leaders should try to postpone meetings if they can. -------.
135.
136.
137.
138.

135. (A) stable
 (B) easy
 (C) sufficient
 (D) poor

136. (A) were moving
 (B) move
 (C) had been moved
 (D) will be moved

137. (A) During
 (B) Occasionally
 (C) While
 (D) For the moment

138. (A) The equipment was noisier than we expected.
 (B) The crew members are known for their professionalism.
 (C) Otherwise, they will have to find a place off-site.
 (D) Each floor has a different decorative style.

Questions 139-142 refer to the following e-mail.

To: Jay Williamson
From: Kristie Aldridge
Date: November 4
Subject: Broadway Gym

Dear Mr. Williamson,

Thank you for signing up for a membership to Broadway Gym. To show our appreciation for your patronage, we are offering you one complimentary ------- with a nutritionist so you can plan a diet that matches your fitness goals. Once you start working out, we ------- your progress on a number of health indicators.

139.   140.

I know you were interested in signing up for the Pilates class, but, unfortunately, it is already at full capacity. -------, you have been placed on a waiting list. There are a number of other classes that might suit your interests. -------.

141.   142.

Warmest regards,

Kristie Aldridge
Membership Coordinator

139. (A) badge
(B) license
(C) session
(D) invoice

140. (A) have tracked
(B) were tracking
(C) will track
(D) tracked

141. (A) On the other hand
(B) For this reason
(C) In the same way
(D) All things considered

142. (A) Our locker rooms have been renovated recently.
(B) In case you are interested, I have attached a complete list.
(C) Nevertheless, the instructors have a great deal of experience.
(D) We would appreciate your feedback on the Pilates class.

Questions 143-146 refer to the following memo.

To: All Viridian Mattresses Employees
From: Damon Boswell, HR Director
Date: November 6
Re: Mavis Ferguson

As I announced in last week's staff meeting, Mavis Ferguson, the sales director for our region, ------- to our overseas branch in Lisbon at the beginning of January. Her goal is to make Viridian Mattresses the number-one mattress brand in Portugal. -------. She has the perfect combination of talent, determination, and experience.

Dwight Wolcott will ------- Ms. Ferguson in the role. He has been working as the assistant sales director for several years, so it will likely be a smooth transition.

A farewell party will be held for Ms. Ferguson on December 14 to thank her for her ------- service. Invitations for this event will be sent out next month. I hope to see you all there.

Damon

143. (A) was to transfer
    (B) would transfer
    (C) will be transferring
    (D) transferred

144. (A) You are welcome to apply for the job opening.
    (B) Several major clients are thinking about moving there.
    (C) A reception will be held in Conference Room A.
    (D) We are certain that she has the ability to achieve it.

145. (A) accomplish
    (B) succeed
    (C) restore
    (D) welcome

146. (A) distinguished
    (B) impressed
    (C) apparent
    (D) promising

PART 7

Directions: In this part you will read a selection of texts, such as magazine and newspaper articles, e-mails, and instant messages. Each text or set of texts is followed by several questions. Select the best answer for each question and mark the letter (A), (B), (C), or (D) on your answer sheet.

Questions 147-148 refer to the following product description.

Lawson Farms Lemon Curd

Our lemon curd is perfect as a spread for toast and other baked goods or mixed into yogurt. We use real butter and ripe lemons to give you a fresh boost of flavor. Before opening, the product should be kept in a cool, dry place. After opening, refrigerate the product at or below 5°C with the metal lid tightly sealed.

Allergen advice: If you are allergic to any of the ingredients listed on the label, do not consume this product.

Made in Spain
Volume: 350 ml
Packaging notes: The plastic pot can be recycled. We now offer the same volume but with a pot made from 30% less plastic.
Not intended for export.

147. What information is given in the product description?
   (A) How to store the product
   (B) Where to recycle the packaging
   (C) Which ingredients may affect allergies
   (D) How long the product lasts

148. What is suggested about Lawson Farms Lemon Curd?
   (A) It is distributed domestically and internationally.
   (B) It is now 30% larger than before.
   (C) Its lid is made of plastic.
   (D) Its packaging has recently changed.

Questions 149-150 refer to the following e-mail.

To: Joyce Farley <jfarley@dawsonmail.com>
From: Centennial Cosmetics <orders@centennialcosmetics.net>
Date: August 30
Subject: Order #9258

Dear Ms. Farley,

Thank you for purchasing goods from Centennial Cosmetics. Our research team is continually making improvements to our products to help our customers keep their skin looking young and healthy. That's why it's no surprise that professional models make our products part of their daily skincare routines and advocate using them. No matter what your skin type is, we recommend testing the product on a small area first to make sure that you are not sensitive to any of the ingredients.

We don't want you to miss any Centennial Cosmetics news! Please register for our monthly newsletter with product information, special deals, and style tips. You may do so by clicking "News" on our homepage.

Sincerely,

Zachary Mosquera
Customer Service Manager, Centennial Cosmetics

149. What is mentioned about the company's products?

(A) They are designed specifically for young consumers.
(B) They are made from natural ingredients.
(C) They are recommended by professionals.
(D) They come with a money-back guarantee.

150. What does Mr. Mosquera ask Ms. Farley to do?

(A) Write a product review
(B) Provide a receipt
(C) Join a mailing list
(D) Confirm a shipping address

Questions 151-152 refer to the following instructions.

How to Set Up Call Forwarding on the Colton Telephone System

Take advantage of this option when you will be away from your office phone. Calls can be routed to your cell phone or to the phone of a coworker.

1. First, lift the receiver. When you hear the dial tone, type in the call forwarding command code, which is *72. Then input the number of the phone you are calling from to set up this system.
2. Second, listen for a series of beeps, after which you should type in the ten-digit destination number (where you would like the calls to be forwarded). If the number is not accepted, you will hear one long tone.
3. Stay on the line until the call is answered at the destination number, either by a person or by voicemail.
4. Hang up the phone. You will be automatically called back within about thirty seconds and given a four-digit cancellation code by a recorded message. We recommend writing it here for your reference: __4258__
5. To cancel call forwarding at any time, dial *72 and then input the cancellation code.

151. What does the series of beeps indicate?
 (A) That the destination number has been accepted
 (B) That the user should input the destination number
 (C) That the number of origin is already in use
 (D) That the number of origin's calls will be forwarded

152. What is NOT required to do in order to set up a call forwarding service?
 (A) Enter a customer account number
 (B) Wait for a return call
 (C) Type in the command code
 (D) Input a destination phone number

Questions 153-154 refer to the following text message chain.

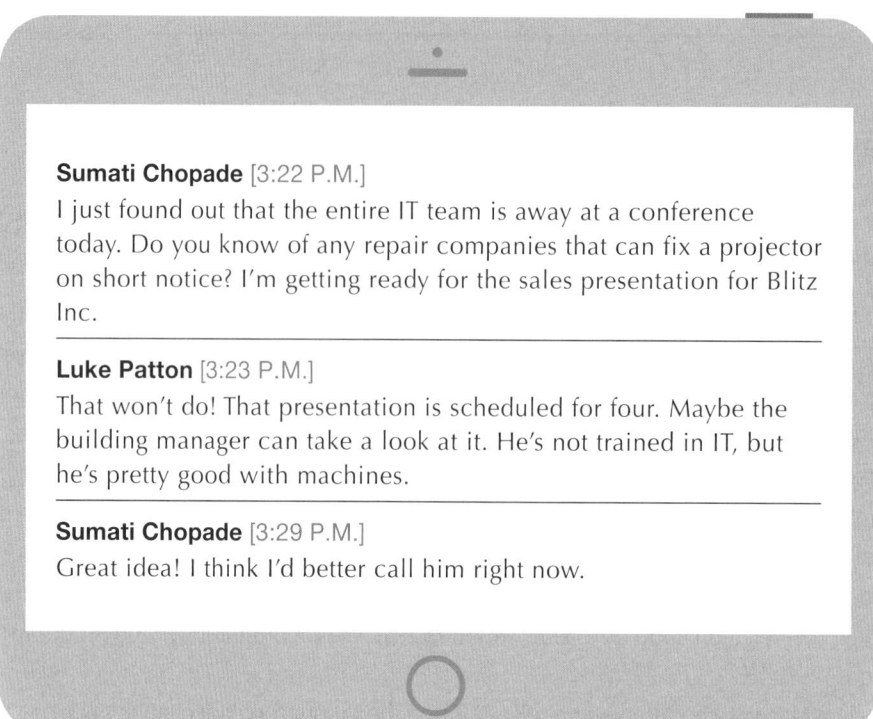

Sumati Chopade [3:22 P.M.]
I just found out that the entire IT team is away at a conference today. Do you know of any repair companies that can fix a projector on short notice? I'm getting ready for the sales presentation for Blitz Inc.

Luke Patton [3:23 P.M.]
That won't do! That presentation is scheduled for four. Maybe the building manager can take a look at it. He's not trained in IT, but he's pretty good with machines.

Sumati Chopade [3:29 P.M.]
Great idea! I think I'd better call him right now.

153. Why is Ms. Chopade contacting Mr. Patton?

(A) To invite him to a conference
(B) To ask for a professional referral
(C) To request some sales figures
(D) To apologize for a mistake

154. At 3:23 P.M., what does Mr. Patton most likely mean when he writes, "That won't do"?

(A) He forgot to order some replacement parts.
(B) He thinks there is not enough time to resolve a problem.
(C) He is worried that a presentation did not go well.
(D) He is concerned that a room is too small.

Questions 155-157 refer to the following invitation.

The Sacramento History Museum Cordially Invites You to

A Journey Through Time

Saturday, December 9

7:30 P.M., Main Lobby and Lecture Room

The Sacramento History Museum strives to preserve historical documents and artifacts that have shaped the area's culture and history. We are pleased to host this event as a way to show our appreciation to everyone who has donated funds for the museum's upkeep. The event will feature live music, refreshments, and a presentation in the lecture room by Monica Sheenan, who directs the day-to-day operations of the museum. Local artist Todd Leday has generously provided us with a painting that will be used in a prize drawing for all attendees. This invitation is valid for up to three people, and it must be presented at the entrance on the event day. It is not necessary to confirm your attendance in advance. However, as we cannot predict the number of guests that will use each invitation, we do recommend arriving early to guarantee a spot in the lecture room.

155. Who would most likely receive this invitation?

(A) Antique collectors
(B) History professors
(C) Financial supporters
(D) Art instructors

156. The word "directs" in line 5, is closest in meaning to

(A) manages
(B) shows
(C) focuses
(D) aims

157. What is suggested about the event?

(A) It will be used as a fundraiser for the museum's collection.
(B) Each guest is required to have his or her own invitation.
(C) It will include a painting demonstration as entertainment.
(D) It has a limited seating area.

GO ON TO THE NEXT PAGE

Questions 158-160 refer to the following notice.

NOTICE TO KETTLER HOTEL GUESTS

The swimming pool area located on the western side of the building will be closed from October 20 to 24. —[1]—. We are installing a heating system in the pool so that it may be used in all seasons, not just summer. Although this is a temporary inconvenience, we know that the final result will be a feature that our guests will enjoy immensely. —[2]—.

We apologize for any inconvenience this work may cause. If you had planned to use the swimming pool during your stay, whether for fitness or recreational purposes, please come to the hotel's front desk. —[3]—. There you will be issued a free pass to use the swimming pool at the Clarkdale Community Center (limit one per guest per day). We have worked out this compromise to minimize disruptions to our guests' plans. The facility is in our neighborhood, and you can get there on foot within about twenty minutes. —[4]—.

Should you have any concerns about the change, please speak to the hotel manager on duty. Thank you for your understanding.

---

158. Why is the Kettler Hotel making a change?

(A) To provide a view of an outdoor area
(B) To expand the size of a swimming pool
(C) To increase the number of guest rooms
(D) To make an amenity available year-round

159. According to the notice, what can guests receive from the front desk?

(A) A construction schedule
(B) An admission pass
(C) A food voucher
(D) A partial refund

160. In which of the positions marked [1], [2], [3], and [4] does the following sentence best belong?

"Alternatively, the hotel shuttle runs at the top of each hour."

(A) [1]
(B) [2]
(C) [3]
(D) [4]

Questions 161-163 refer to the following post.

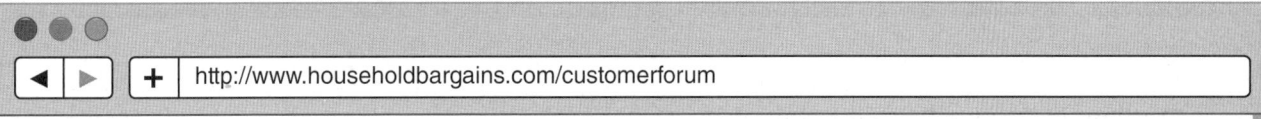

Broken Items
Posted by Angie Dodd 2 days ago

Last week, I used the Household Bargains Web site to order a set of ceramic dishes made by Elite Tableware. They were delivered this morning by the Cordova courier service. Unfortunately, I did not check the product right away. When I opened the box this afternoon, I discovered that two plates in the set were cracked. I called both Cordova and the manufacturer but could not get any information about getting a resolution. I'd love to hear your ideas on what to do next, as there is no customer service number for this Web site that I could find. From my Internet search, I found that the company will only accept returns under certain conditions. I'm wondering if the policy applies in my particular case.

161. What is NOT mentioned as an action taken by Ms. Dodd?

(A) Researching a policy online
(B) Returning items of an order
(C) Calling a courier service
(D) Contacting Elite Tableware

162. Why did Ms. Dodd write the post?

(A) To ask for product recommendations
(B) To update an earlier review of merchandise
(C) To offer advice about caring for ceramic dishes
(D) To get suggestions from other customers

163. The word "applies" in line 7, is closest in meaning to

(A) utilizes
(B) submits
(C) refers
(D) creates

Questions 164-167 refer to the following article.

Stadium in Derosa Remains Nameless
by Mark Graham

(March 25)—The construction of a baseball stadium in Derosa went smoothly all the way to completion, but the facility still lacks one key component—a name. The stadium was originally supposed to be named Yancey Stadium, after a naming rights agreement was reached with Yancey Automotive. —[1]—. City officials are, therefore, accepting new bids from commercial partners.

Interested parties should download the application materials from the city's Web site. Bids and the proposed name can be submitted anytime before April 19. —[2]—. A committee made up of city council members and Derosa residents will review the bids and select a short list of five. Those five companies must provide proof of financing in order to prevent having the same problem again. The naming rights will be granted to the highest bidder. —[3]—.

Finalizing the legal name of the stadium could take a few months. —[4]—. As the stadium is set to host the first tournament of the season, the Regional Baseball Opener, the facility will be officially known as Derosa Stadium in the meantime.

Companies do not have to be based in Derosa in order to be considered. For example, Marais Beverages has already submitted an application, with the proposed name of Marais Stadium. Inquiries about this or any other stadium matters can be referred to Oliver Shaw at oliver_shaw@derosacity.gov.

---

164. What is the purpose of the article?

(A) To explain a bidding process
(B) To recruit baseball players
(C) To introduce a new company
(D) To announce a construction decision

165. What does the article mention about the stadium?

(A) Its construction suffered from delays.
(B) It has been assigned a temporary name.
(C) It was partially funded by Yancey Automotive.
(D) It is unable to host a regional tournament.

166. What is suggested about Marais Beverages?

(A) It will sell beverages at the stadium.
(B) It is currently based in the city of Derosa.
(C) It obtained some forms from a Web site.
(D) It wanted to change some contract terms.

167. In which of the positions marked [1], [2], [3], and [4] does the following sentence best belong?

"Due to financing errors, funding for the endeavor fell through."

(A) [1]
(B) [2]
(C) [3]
(D) [4]

Questions 168-171 refer to the following text message chain.

Nazario Boni [12:23 P.M.]	The technician stopped by this morning, and he examined the broken pottery oven.
Taylor Johnson [12:25 P.M.]	Thanks for coming in early to let him into the studio. Was he able to get it working again?
Nazario Boni [12:26 P.M.]	Unfortunately, no. He said he is able to do it, but not today as promised. He needs to order a new component, and the delivery could take a few days.
Taylor Johnson [12:27 P.M.]	That's too bad.
Nazario Boni [12:28 P.M.]	Is it a problem for your pottery class? Will your students still be able to do their work?
Taylor Johnson [12:29 P.M.]	Don't worry. I can bake their projects in the smaller oven after class. They can come back the next day to pick them up.
Nazario Boni [12:31 P.M.]	The session is scheduled for just one day. Wouldn't it be a hassle for them to return to the studio?
Taylor Johnson [12:33 P.M.]	They're in the area.
Nazario Boni [12:34 P.M.]	Okay, that's good. I suppose we can deliver the final projects by mail to anyone who cannot come back in person.
Taylor Johnson [12:35 P.M.]	Exactly.
Nazario Boni [12:36 P.M.]	We'd better let the students know about this. I can put a note on our homepage.
Taylor Johnson [12:38 P.M.]	Thanks, that would be helpful.

168. What has caused a delay?

(A) A part needs to be ordered.
(B) A product has been discontinued.
(C) A shipment has been lost.
(D) A budget request was rejected.

169. Who most likely is Ms. Johnson?

(A) A music teacher
(B) An art instructor
(C) A repair technician
(D) A salesperson

170. At 12:33 P.M., what does Ms. Johnson most likely mean when she writes, "They're in the area"?

(A) She is expecting a shipment soon.
(B) She believes that delivery fees will be low.
(C) She thinks a change will not be inconvenient.
(D) She has enough time to visit some clients.

171. What does Mr. Boni offer to do?

(A) Provide a partial refund
(B) Work additional hours
(C) Purchase new equipment
(D) Post a message online

Questions 172-175 refer to the following e-mail.

E-mail

To:	Danielle Kaye <d_kaye@rothinsurance.com>
From:	Samuel Barbosa <samuel@alfrescodesigns.com>
Date:	February 7
Subject:	Flanigan Building

Dear Ms. Kaye,

Thank you once again for choosing Alfresco Designs for the rooftop garden project at the Flanigan Building. I know that you had originally requested violets as the main flower in the garden. However, these grow best in shade, but the area will mostly have full sun. Therefore, I would recommend using daylilies instead. I know that you wanted the project to be completely finished before your successor takes over, so I want to make sure we keep moving ahead with the details.

Also, I still need you to decide whether you want to have a grassy area installed in the northern half of the rooftop. While this has a very attractive appearance and can help to insulate the building, the planning will require the advice of a licensed structural engineer due to the additional weight. The sooner you can let me know your decision, the sooner I can contact someone.

I have attached a catalog of outdoor chairs and tables that you might want to add to this project. Please look over the options and choose the ones you like best prior to our next meeting. That way, we can see how we're doing on the budget. I look forward to meeting with you on February 13.

Sincerely,

Samuel Barbosa
Project Manager, Alfresco Designs

172. What is one reason that Mr. Barbosa sent the e-mail?

(A) To set up an appointment to view a building
(B) To propose some changes to a project
(C) To check the status of an order
(D) To recommend a local supplier

173. What is suggested about Ms. Kaye?

(A) She likes the appearance of daylilies.
(B) She lives in the Flanigan Building.
(C) She is able to increase a budget.
(D) She plans to leave her job soon.

174. Why does Mr. Barbosa inquire about the grassy area?

(A) To determine whether a professional needs to be consulted
(B) To finalize the number of days for the work
(C) To express the need to purchase insulation materials
(D) To suggest moving it to a different part of the roof

175. What should Ms. Kaye do by February 13?

(A) Request a catalog
(B) Send a signed contract
(C) Select some furniture
(D) Finalize a budget

GO ON TO THE NEXT PAGE

Questions 176-180 refer to the following memo and form.

To: All Employees
From: Marcel Bélair, HR Manager
Date: January 10
Re: Let's get creative!

The Carolina Enterprises HR team is always looking for ways to make the working environment more fun and enjoyable. In light of this, we plan to hold monthly craft sessions on the last Wednesday of every month. These will take place here in our building's conference room at 4 P.M. As the session will overlap with your regular working hours, your immediate supervisor must approve your participation by signing the participation form.

In each session, you will be taught how to make a new craft by Leona Haigh from the MK Art Institute. The first session will be held on Wednesday, January 30, and the crafts for the first four months are already planned. They are—in order—a yarn doll, a beaded picture frame, a mini painting, and a no-sew tote bag.

Full-time employees, whether salaried or paid by the hour, can participate for free. Others will be asked to pay a small fee to help cover the cost of materials. Please sign up in advance by completing the form that is available in the HR office.

Monthly Craft Session Sign-Up Form

Name: Jeremy Steele
Department: Marketing
Team Leader: Kylie Knight
Participation Date/s (check all that apply): Jan. 30 [✓]   Feb. 27 [✓]   Mar. 27 [✓]   Apr. 24 [ ]
Participation Fee: Paid [✓]   Not Applicable [ ]
Processed by: HR Employee Thomas Malloy

176. Why did Mr. Bélair send the memo?
 (A) To introduce an activity for staff members
 (B) To encourage following safety precautions
 (C) To solicit creative feedback from employees
 (D) To announce a mandatory training event

177. Where will a session be held?
 (A) At convention center
 (B) At an art gallery
 (C) At Carolina Enterprises
 (D) At the MK Art Institute

178. What will participants learn about on January 30?
 (A) A yarn doll
 (B) A picture frame
 (C) A mini painting
 (D) A tote bag

179. Why was Mr. Steele charged a fee?
 (A) He lost some company materials.
 (B) He signed up for more than one session.
 (C) He is a salaried employee.
 (D) He does not work full-time at the company.

180. Who should sign Mr. Steele's form?
 (A) Mr. Bélair
 (B) Ms. Haigh
 (C) Ms. Knight
 (D) Mr. Malloy

GO ON TO THE NEXT PAGE

Questions 181-185 refer to the following e-mail and advertisement.

---

e-mail

To: Earl Pierce <e.pierce@evanston.com>
From: Jaqueline Fleming <j.fleming@evanston.com>
Date: May 19
Subject: Team training

Dear Mr. Pierce,

I have researched some businesses training options following the team training idea that you proposed. Attached you will find the course that I believe would be best suited for your needs. The course is run by an expert in the field, and the institute is only a two-hour drive from our offices, so your team would not need to stay overnight. The course begins at 10 A.M., and it lasts until 5 P.M. You would receive $20 per person for lunch from our company, and gas can be purchased on the company card. I think the mini group session would be particularly helpful, as you and your team are the perfect size to fill one group.

I am giving my official approval to go forward with this training, so please register your team for a date that suits you. Should you have any difficulties in doing so, just let me know.

Sincerely,

Jaqueline Fleming

Business Workshop at the Alder Institute: Improving Communication

One-day workshops held on-site at the Alder Institute, 780 Holgate Street, Oakland, CA 94703. Available dates: June 4, June 7, June 12, June 18, June 21, June 26, July 8

Taught by Rosina Owen, former head of human resources at the multinational firm Lander Solutions, this workshop will help you to develop communication skills as well as identify the communication styles of others. The instructor uses a hands-on approach, urging participants to try the techniques for themselves through role-play activities and more. Mini group sessions with six people help to facilitate further discussion and solidify the ideas. Individuals or groups that are too small will be combined to form a group of six.

The workshop is from 10 A.M. to 4 P.M. on the dates listed above, and there is a participation fee of $80 per person. Register at www.alderinst.com.

181. Why was the e-mail sent?
(A) To request a budget increase
(B) To report a schedule change
(C) To accept a proposal
(D) To confirm a registration

182. In the e-mail, the word "run" in paragraph 1, line 2, is closest in meaning to
(A) conducted
(B) hurried
(C) competed
(D) flowed

183. What is implied about Mr. Pierce?
(A) He used to work at the Alder Institute.
(B) His position is in human resources.
(C) He oversees five other people.
(D) His office is based in Oakland.

184. What information about the workshop provided by Ms. Fleming was incorrect?
(A) The available dates
(B) The participation fee
(C) The topics covered
(D) The ending time

185. What is indicated about Ms. Owen?
(A) She has a university degree in communications.
(B) She encourages attendees to participate actively.
(C) She is the Alder Institute's newest employee.
(D) She was the founder of Lander Solutions.

Questions 186-190 refer to the following postcard, form, and e-mail.

Titan Fitness Center
~ October Boost ~

Recommend 2 or more friends to take our welcome tour on October 15, and you'll receive one of the thank-you gifts below:

Option A: A free Titan Fitness Center T-shirt (4 sizes available)
Option B: Coupon for 60% off at our on-site juice bar (no expiration date)
Option C: Free locker upgrade (pending availability)
Option D: Half-price entry to one of our group fitness classes

We are making this offer to show appreciation to our longest-attending customers, those who have been with us for at least five years.

Cynthia Avila
702 Kessla Way
Charleston, SC 29403

Titan Fitness Center
Customer Comment Form

We are dedicated to giving you the best workout experience possible. Please share your comments so we can better improve our service.

Today's Date: *November 5*
Name: *Cynthia Avila*

Branch (if applicable): *Downtown*
E-mail Address: *cynthia.avila@alhambra.com*

Comment Type: [ ] Suggestion [ ] Inquiry [ ] Compliment [X] Complaint
Have you contacted us before about this comment? If so, when and how? *Yes, by phone on November 2*

Details: *I met the conditions for your October Boost promotion last month. For the thank-you gift, I requested half-price entry to one of your classes, and your reception desk employee said it would be deducted automatically. So, I was surprised to see the full charge for the Zumba class I took when I received my monthly bill on November 1. Please look into this matter. Thanks!*

To: Cynthia Avila <cynthia.avila@alhambra.com>
From: Titan Fitness Center <support@titanfitcent.com>
Date: November 6
Subject: Your comment form

Dear Ms. Avila,

I'm very sorry that you were not reimbursed properly for participating in our October Boost promotion. Our records show that you did select the class option, but for some reason, you were sent a juice bar coupon instead. I have now issued a credit in the amount of $15.50 (half the class fee) to your account, so this will appear on your next bill. In addition, I'll mail you one of our Titan Fitness Center T-shirts by way of apology. And, of course, please feel free to use the coupon if you still have it.

Thank you for your understanding,

Ryan Lapira
Manager, Titan Fitness Center (downtown branch)

---

186. Why most likely was Ms. Avila sent the postcard?
    (A) She booked a session with a personal trainer.
    (B) She completed a customer questionnaire.
    (C) She helped a business design a T-shirt.
    (D) She is a long-term member of a gym.

187. What did Ms. Avila most likely do in October?
    (A) Underwent a health consultation
    (B) Recruited friends to take a tour
    (C) Renewed her membership
    (D) Changed to a different locker

188. When did Ms. Avila first notify the business of a problem?
    (A) October 15
    (B) November 1
    (C) November 2
    (D) November 5

189. What was Ms. Avila given by mistake?
    (A) Option A
    (B) Option B
    (C) Option C
    (D) Option D

190. What does Mr. Lapira say he will do?
    (A) Inform Ms. Avila of new promotions
    (B) E-mail a schedule of Zumba classes
    (C) Ask a coworker for more information
    (D) Send a free item of clothing

Questions 191-195 refer to the following advertisement, schedule, and e-mail.

Don't miss the music and fun at the Willmore Folk Festival!
Saturday, June 17 – Sunday, June 18

The 5th Annual Willmore Folk Festival is a community celebration of folk music. This popular event draws visitors from across the country, and there is no entrance fee. Past events have taken place at Terrace Park. However, thanks to the dramatic growth of this event, this year the festival has been moved to Ridgewood Park to accommodate more performers.

This year's schedule includes folk music star Martin Hancock as well as the McDowell Brothers Band. Event planners are also still looking for a few local groups, as morning performances are reserved for musicians from right here in Willmore. Both professional and amateur bands are welcome. Contact Zan Tian at 555-3316 for more information.

The event starts at 10 A.M. and runs until 8 P.M. on both days. Visitors should note that concession stand supplies will be severely limited, so bringing snacks or a packed lunch is suggested. For a complete list of the bands that will be playing, updated daily, visit www.willmorefolk.org.

Willmore Folk Festival
Schedule for Saturday, June 17 [Final]

START TIME	PERFORMER	LOCATION
10:00 A.M.	The Butterfly Crew	East Stage
11:00 A.M.	John Ramos	Freedom Stage
1:00 P.M.	Sandra and the Strummers	South Stage
2:30 P.M.	Maria Noyola	East Stage
4:30 P.M.	The McDowell Brothers Band	South Stage
6:30 P.M.	Kyle Crabtree	Freedom Stage

Benches are available only at the main stage. For other stages, audience members may stand or sit on their own blankets. All seating is available on a first come, first served basis.

To: Zan Tian <tian.z@verdurapost.com>
From: Maria Noyola <marianoyola@ezmail.com>
Date: June 3
Subject: Willmore Folk Festival

Dear Ms. Tian,

I wanted to thank you once again for inviting me to perform at the Willmore Folk Festival. On the stage, I will need three guitar stands, as I often switch instruments depending on what song I'm playing. Please also place two microphones on the stage, one for vocals and the other for my acoustic guitar. If possible, I would like to have a stool so that I have the option of sitting or standing while performing. I will bring my instruments to my assigned performance area 45 minutes before my show, so please meet me there. I'm not very familiar with Ridgewood Park, so could you also let me know how far of a walk it is from the main entrance?

Thank you!

Maria

191. What is NOT indicated about the Willmore Folk Festival?

(A) It includes international performers.
(B) It has been held four times before.
(C) It will have a new location this year.
(D) It does not charge for admission.

192. What are event attendees recommended to do?

(A) Sign up for text updates
(B) Take public transportation
(C) Reserve a seat in advance
(D) Bring their own food

193. What is implied about The Butterfly Crew?

(A) It will perform on the event's second day.
(B) Its members live in Willmore.
(C) It gave a performance last year.
(D) Its show will last for two hours.

194. What is the purpose of the e-mail?

(A) To request a scheduling change
(B) To invite a musician to an event
(C) To provide setup instructions
(D) To promote a music CD

195. Where does Ms. Noyola want to meet Ms. Tian on June 17?

(A) At the East Stage
(B) At the Freedom Stage
(C) At the South Stage
(D) At the main entrance

Questions 196-200 refer to the following advertisement, e-mail, and invoice.

Relax and refresh at Portillo Spa in beautiful Valparaíso, Chile!

Take a break from the hectic pace of modern life with Portillo Spa's Luxury Package. You'll arrive at the spa on Saturday morning and get pampered by our attentive staff until you leave on Sunday evening. The package includes a one-night stay in a room at our five-star hotel, three meals a day, and a variety of massages and beauty treatments. If you need to ride our shuttle to and from the airport, this package allows you to do so for free. There is also an optional Mountain Yoga Experience offered for an additional fee. You'll be transported up the mountainside for high-altitude yoga and fantastic views. You must provide a note from your physician to participate in this activity due to the slightly lower oxygen levels. Book your Luxury Package today by calling 1-800-555-9771. Please note that groups of 10 or more people must make reservations at least three weeks in advance.

To: Javiera Yanez <javierayanez@portillo-spa.com>
From: Matias Alvarado <matias@alvaradoltd.com>
Date: March 2
Subject: Invoice

Dear Ms. Yanez,

I am sending the February invoice for the Mountain Yoga Experience activity that you outsourced to our company. The participation numbers have been low for the past few months due to the cold weather, but that will soon pass. Participants have given us a lot of positive feedback. In fact, Ms. Ivonne Sousa said that it was the highlight of her weekend. Please note the extra charge that was incurred from the February 12 group, as the group size was larger than expected and we had to rent a bus at the last minute because we couldn't use our van. All other charges on the invoice were previously approved. To get even more people involved, you might want to consider changing the two-day package to three days so that people have more time for special activities.

Sincerely,

Matias

Alvarado Ltd.
Laguna Verde Headquarters Phone Number: 22864-8430

Customer: Portillo Spa
Date of Issue: March 2

Invoice Month: February
Payment Account: Porvenir Bank, 64870459

Monthly Charges		TOTAL:
Driver/Transportation	54,000 CLP	174,930 CLP
Heater Rental	23,000 CLP	
Yoga Instructor	30,000 CLP	Due:
Additional Expenses	40,000 CLP	March 31
VAT	27,930 CLP	

---

196. What is NOT mentioned as a part of the Luxury Package?
(A) All meals during the stay
(B) Beauty products to take home
(C) Overnight hotel accommodations
(D) Transportation from the airport

197. What is implied about Ms. Sousa?
(A) She reserved her room at least three weeks in advance.
(B) She attended a special event on February 12.
(C) She provided a physician's note to the spa.
(D) She recently visited Valparaíso for the first time.

198. In the e-mail, the word "pass" in paragraph 1, line 3, is closest in meaning to
(A) end
(B) succeed
(C) dispatch
(D) exceed

199. What does Mr. Alvarado recommend doing?
(A) Hiring an additional yoga instructor
(B) Adding more off-site activities
(C) Canceling events in cold weather
(D) Extending the duration of a package

200. Why was Portillo Spa charged 40,000 CLP?
(A) Mr. Alvarado gave extra transportation to Ms. Sousa.
(B) Mr. Alvarado had to rent a special vehicle.
(C) Mr. Alvarado hosted an extra group in February.
(D) Mr. Alvarado had to pay for a damaged heater.

Stop! This is the end of the test. If you finish before time is called, you may go back to Part 5, 6, and 7 and check your work.

TEST 07

PART 5 · PART 6 · PART 7

준비하기

손목시계

뭉뚝한 연필과 지우개

Answer Sheet

토익 RC는 75분 동안 진행됩니다.
반드시 75분 이내에 문제 풀이와 답안지 마킹을 완료하세요.

TEST 07은 **고난도 문제가 적게 포함**된 쪽박달 :(TEST입니다.
다른 TEST에 비해 상대적으로 **환산 점수가 낮게** 나올 수 있습니다.

맞은 개수	환산 점수	맞은 개수	환산 점수
96-100	**465** - 495	41-45	**145** - 215
91-95	**430** - 490	36-40	**120** - 180
86-90	**400** - 465	31-35	**100** - 145
81-85	**375** - 440	26-30	**80** - 120
76-80	**340** - 415	21-25	**65** - 95
71-75	**315** - 390	16-20	**50** - 75
66-70	**285** - 365	11-15	**35** - 55
61-65	**255** - 335	6-10	**15** - 40
56-60	**225** - 305	1-5	**5** - 30
51-55	**200** - 270	0	5
46-50	**170** - 240		

고난도 문제는 해설집에서 확인할 수 있습니다.
해설집 p.128

READING TEST

In the Reading test, you will read a variety of texts and answer several different types of reading comprehension questions. The entire Reading test will last 75 minutes. There are three parts, and directions are given for each part. You are encouraged to answer as many questions as possible within the time allowed.

You must mark your answers on the separate answer sheet. Do not write your answers in your test book.

PART 5

Directions: A word or phrase is missing in each of the sentences below. Four answer choices are given below each sentence. Select the best answer to complete the sentence. Then mark the letter (A), (B), (C), or (D) on your answer sheet.

101. All buyers from Richard's Auto Dealership can have their cars ------- inspected based on their maintenance schedules.

(A) regular
(B) regularity
(C) regulation
(D) regularly

102. This diet program assists and encourages ------- to lead a healthy lifestyle.

(A) your
(B) yours
(C) you
(D) yourselves

103. Access to River Road has been restricted ------- heavy rain and flood warnings.

(A) though
(B) wherever
(C) because of
(D) such as

104. After this baseball season ends, the ------- of Cooperstown Ball Park's seats will begin.

(A) replaces
(B) replaceable
(C) replacement
(D) replaced

105. Residents were ------- of the plan to spend city funds on upgrading Hayden Park.

(A) support
(B) supportively
(C) supportive
(D) supporting

106. All events at Bedford Festivals are subject to change without prior -------.

(A) notice
(B) belief
(C) need
(D) report

107. The opening ceremony is running later than expected, so the ------- morning sessions will be delayed for 20 minutes.

(A) schedule
(B) scheduled
(C) scheduling
(D) schedules

108. *Fields of Friends*, a gardening guidebook by Reader's House, will be ------- into multiple languages next year.

(A) translated
(B) organized
(C) trained
(D) involved

109. It is ------- to change your computer log-in password every three months for security purposes.
(A) impressed
(B) reluctant
(C) mandatory
(D) bountiful

110. The server had to relay the diners' request to the kitchen ------- when he heard one of them was allergic to seafood.
(A) swift
(B) swifter
(C) swiftly
(D) swiftest

111. According to the ------- of your warranty, all incurred expenses and fees will be covered.
(A) repairs
(B) comments
(C) terms
(D) cards

112. Allison Barr gained professional ------- in customizing shoes through the apprenticeship at Harman's Footwear.
(A) responsibility
(B) feedback
(C) expertise
(D) foundation

113. The board of Jenkins Manufacturing announced its plan to reduce emissions by 20% ------- three years.
(A) around
(B) between
(C) before
(D) within

114. Due to the financial crisis, ------- management has decided to sell the company to Geyser Corp.
(A) we
(B) our
(C) us
(D) ourselves

115. All employees of Bentley Chemical are eligible for full insurance benefits once they have ------- one full year at the company.
(A) completed
(B) expired
(C) predicted
(D) permitted

116. Our company conducts employee performance reviews -------, during which employees can speak openly with their supervisors.
(A) highly
(B) boldly
(C) clearly
(D) annually

117. The market for digital investments is ------- despite the fact that many people still prefer stocks and gold.
(A) emerge
(B) emerged
(C) emerging
(D) emerges

118. Booklets at Amherst Used Car contain a list of car brands and information that is ------- to payment options or car leases.
(A) comparable
(B) directed
(C) skilled
(D) relevant

119. The wrist watch developed for extreme sports enthusiasts is resistant against water, even ------- 100 meters deep.
(A) out
(B) under
(C) from
(D) among

120. Your parking permit should be ------- whenever you enter the reserved parking area.
(A) verify
(B) verified
(C) verification
(D) verifying

121. Please note that all vending machines throughout this building require ------- change.
(A) exact
(B) exacted
(C) exactly
(D) exactness

122. The sales manager will hold a department luncheon in ------- of meeting their quarterly sales quota early.
(A) deliverance
(B) celebration
(C) perspective
(D) competence

123. Be sure to submit expense reports by the 20th each month ------- you can be reimbursed without delay.
(A) due to
(B) as long as
(C) so that
(D) in addition

124. Danielle's Outlet trains its employees in case of emergencies they might ------- on the job.
(A) depend
(B) conclude
(C) evaluate
(D) encounter

125. Ms. Hawthorn was called to pick up her badge that -------.
(A) misplace
(B) misplaces
(C) was misplaced
(D) misplaced

126. The supply manager's responsibility is to make sure that all office goods are ------- used.
(A) productively
(B) production
(C) produce
(D) productive

127. Even though German Tech Company increased the prices of its laundry machines, customers ------- think of them as the most affordable ones.
(A) still
(B) quite
(C) much
(D) ago

128. ------- you haven't earned the required credits for graduation, you need to meet your academic supervisor.
(A) Meanwhile
(B) Shortly
(C) Regarding
(D) If

129. This coming Friday evening is ------- Ms. Min's retirement party is scheduled to be held.
(A) it's
(B) who
(C) on
(D) when

130. Please avoid contacting anyone on leave unless an issue needs ------- attention.
(A) immediate
(B) insufficient
(C) careless
(D) customary

PART 6

Directions: Read the texts that follow. A word, phrase, or sentence is missing in parts of each text. Four answer choices for each question are given below the text. Select the best answer to complete the text. Then mark the letter (A), (B), (C), or (D) on your answer sheet.

Questions 131-134 refer to the following notice.

NOTICE TO ALL EMPLOYEES

You are entering an active area of the production floor. For your -------, you must wear protective gear in this area at all times. This includes hard hats, gloves, and eyewear. ------- to comply with the regulations
131.   132.
could result in personal injury as well as a fine for the company. If you do not have the necessary gear, please ------- with your immediate supervisor. You should also check the condition of your gear to try to find
              133.
damage. -------. Thank you for your cooperation.
          134.

131. (A) safer
 (B) safety
 (C) safely
 (D) safe

132. (A) Closure
 (B) Precaution
 (C) Disruption
 (D) Failure

133. (A) speak
 (B) speaks
 (C) spoken
 (D) speaking

134. (A) As expected, it held up well in the preliminary tests.
 (B) Each employee received one upon starting work.
 (C) If you do, it should be replaced as soon as possible.
 (D) There is extra time available if you need it.

GO ON TO THE NEXT PAGE

Questions 135-138 refer to the following e-mail.

To: Ivy Acuna <acunai@woodlandinteriors.com>

From: Frank Dotson <dotsonf@woodlandinteriors.com>

Date: April 6

Subject: Our meeting

I would like ------- for missing our scheduled meeting this morning. I know that you are busy, and I'm sure
           135.
it was a great inconvenience to you. -------, my return flight from Vancouver was delayed, so I got back into
                                      136.
town much later than I had originally expected. We still need to go over the interior design for the property
on Carter Street. -------. I can drop by your office tomorrow afternoon around 3. I hope you find that -------.
                  137.   138.
If not, we can find another time that works.

Sincerely,

Frank Dotson

---

135. (A) being apologized
(B) apologizing
(C) apologized
(D) to apologize

136. (A) Namely
(B) Moreover
(C) Unfortunately
(D) Nonetheless

137. (A) The attachment he sent did not open.
(B) You should contact the Vancouver office.
(C) This will be much easier to do in person.
(D) Our project received the highest rating.

138. (A) accepted
(B) acceptable
(C) acceptably
(D) acceptance

Questions 139-142 refer to the following advertisement.

Volunteers Wanted:

Helpful Hearts is currently seeking volunteers for its programs to help the elderly. Tasks range ------- visiting people in their homes and assisting with household chores to providing rides to appointments. You're sure to find something that suits your schedule and interests. By volunteering with Helpful Hearts, you can truly make a ------- in another person's life. -------. Even just two hours a week is sufficient. If this sounds appealing to you, why not give it a try? You can visit our Web site at www.helpfulhearts1.org to learn more about us and ------- testimonials from our volunteers and participants.

139. (A) from
(B) toward
(C) through
(D) within

140. (A) comment
(B) difference
(C) choice
(D) prediction

141. (A) There are various group sizes working for us.
(B) We don't ask for a large time commitment.
(C) Training is provided to newcomers if requested.
(D) You do not need special skills to volunteer.

142. (A) are browsed
(B) browsed
(C) browsing
(D) browse

Questions 143-146 refer to the following e-mail.

To: Quinn Gleason <gleasonq@camdencslting.com>
From: Christina Cruz <cruzc@camdencslting.com>
Date: December 17
Subject: Workshop

I've ------- the information I gathered from the staff members who took your Organizational Skills Workshop last week. -------. For example, the majority of attendees said they would like to take one of your workshops in the future, and all of them said they found the information to be helpful. The main complaint was about the equipment you used to show the videos. People said they could ------- hear the audio track. Because of this problem, they couldn't understand ------- was being said. Let's keep this issue in mind for next time.

Sincerely,

Christina

---

143. (A) authorized
(B) emphasized
(C) strategized
(D) analyzed

144. (A) Sadly, attendance was lower than ever.
(B) I am happy to prepare the materials for you.
(C) Overall, the feedback was very positive.
(D) This will be the last session of the year.

145. (A) bare
(B) bared
(C) barely
(D) barer

146. (A) what
(B) that
(C) which
(D) such

PART 7

Directions: In this part you will read a selection of texts, such as magazine and newspaper articles, e-mails, and instant messages. Each text or set of texts is followed by several questions. Select the best answer for each question and mark the letter (A), (B), (C), or (D) on your answer sheet.

Questions 147-148 refer to the following text message.

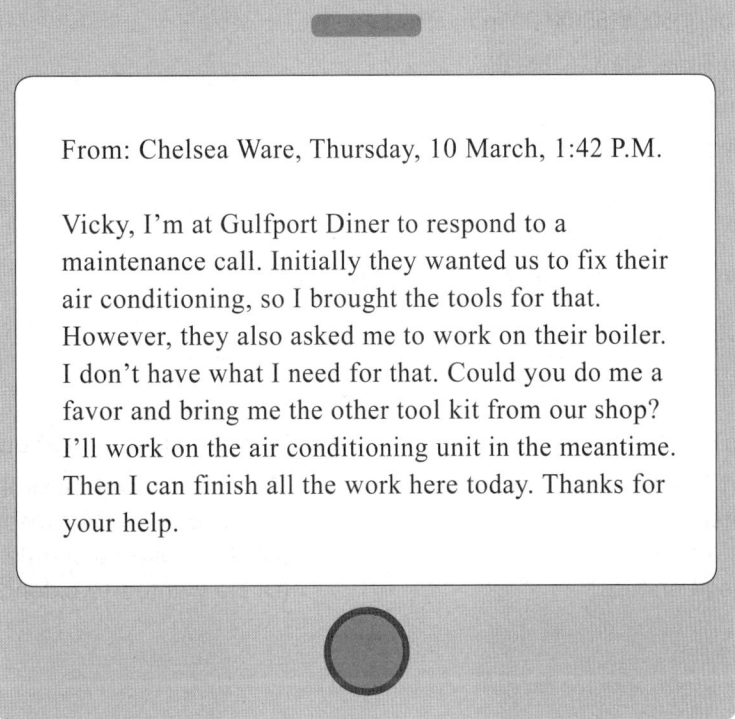

From: Chelsea Ware, Thursday, 10 March, 1:42 P.M.

Vicky, I'm at Gulfport Diner to respond to a maintenance call. Initially they wanted us to fix their air conditioning, so I brought the tools for that. However, they also asked me to work on their boiler. I don't have what I need for that. Could you do me a favor and bring me the other tool kit from our shop? I'll work on the air conditioning unit in the meantime. Then I can finish all the work here today. Thanks for your help.

147. What does Ms. Ware say is a problem?

(A) She is unfamiliar with a system.
(B) She cannot find a location.
(C) She has too much work.
(D) She received another request on a site.

148. What did Ms. Ware ask Vicky to do?

(A) Give some instructions
(B) Order a replacement part
(C) Bring some tools
(D) Attend a weekly meeting

Questions 149-150 refer to the following receipt.

Tokyo Airport

Private Resting Area

Customer Name: Yun Zhen Li

Room Type: Single Bed, Shower

First Hour: 1,500¥ (500¥/ 30 min. after)

Check-in Time: May 16, 0620

Check-out Time: May 16, 0850

Total Charge: 2,700¥*

*(Air VIP Member Discount Applied)

Thank you for staying with us! Visit us again next time!

---

149. What did Mr. Li do on May 16?

(A) Used an airport facility
(B) Stayed in a hotel
(C) Departed from Tokyo
(D) Cancelled a membership

150. What is suggested about Mr. Li?

(A) He got a first class flight upgrade.
(B) He is an Air VIP member.
(C) He booked a shuttle to downtown.
(D) He wanted to extend his stay.

Questions 151-152 refer to the following text message chain.

Jacob Perkins [1:03 P.M.]
Are you at the Waycross Convention Center yet? I know you were worried about missing the bus.

Sarama Bisrat [1:06 P.M.]
Fortunately, I was able to catch it. I should be at the center soon. We just passed the Crystal Mall.

Jacob Perkins [1:07 P.M.]
Great. Are you expecting any packages while you're away from the office?

Sarama Bisrat [1:08 P.M.]
Just one from Braxton Manufacturing. It doesn't contain anything time-sensitive.

Jacob Perkins [1:09 P.M.]
All right. Usually I open packages for people when they're gone. But I'll just leave it on your desk.

Sarama Bisrat [1:10 P.M.]
That seems best to me.

151. Where most likely is Ms. Bisrat when she sends the messages?
(A) In an office
(B) At a conference venue
(C) On a bus
(D) At a shopping mall

152. At 1:10 P.M., what does Ms. Bisrat mean when she writes, "That seems best to me"?
(A) She plans to come back to the office to complete an urgent task.
(B) She does not want Mr. Perkins to open a package.
(C) She thinks it is a good idea to contact Braxton Manufacturing.
(D) She wants a delivery to be stored in Mr. Perkins' office.

Questions 153-154 refer to the following information.

Timberland Marketing Expense Reimbursement Policy

- All reimbursement requests must be made via company form AC232.
- Acceptable reimbursements include meals for clients, business travel, office supplies, and others approved in advance.
- Original receipts must be included whenever possible.
- Reimbursements will be deposited on the first of the following month, provided that the request is submitted within the first two weeks of the current month.

Each team has its own budget. Please check with your team leader before making any purchases or charges that you expect to be reimbursed for.

---

153. What does every reimbursement request require?

(A) An official form
(B) A budget report
(C) A team leader's signature
(D) A travel itinerary

154. What is mentioned about Timberland Marketing?

(A) It reimburses expenses after two weeks.
(B) It pays its employees every other week.
(C) It assigns individual team budgets.
(D) It issues company credit cards to employees.

Questions 155-157 refer to the following invoice.

Jacobson's Warehouse
449 Victoria Court
Standish, ME 04084

Billing Information
Debra Collins
73 Hawthorne Lane
Standish, ME 04084
Expected Arrival: 7 April (after 1 p.m.)

Shipping Information
SAME

Code	Item	Price
*1612-0938	Dehumidifier	$69.00
8704-9225	Electric Fan	$21.00
7000-1643	Toaster (2-slot)	$16.00
2099-5815	Digital Clock	$8.00
0000-0000	Discount Coupon	-$15.00

*Due to its large size, this item will be shipped separately. Please allow an extra 1-2 days for delivery.

---

155. What kind of business is Jacobson's Warehouse?

(A) A restaurant
(B) A courier service
(C) An appliance store
(D) A furniture manufacturer

156. What is scheduled to happen on 7 April?

(A) An inventory will be checked.
(B) A discount coupon will expire.
(C) A partial order will be delivered.
(D) An appliance will be assembled.

157. What is indicated about the dehumidifier?

(A) It will arrive at a later date.
(B) It ships directly from the factory.
(C) It includes an extended warranty.
(D) It is not eligible for a free delivery.

Questions 158-160 refer to the following article.

International Business Gazette: Business Briefings, November 9
By Ansel Routhier

The long-expected union of Tanty Technologies and Invert Solutions has been confirmed following a meeting of the shareholders late last night. Newly appointed CEO Daniel Hardwick said that the arrangement would allow the newly-formed corporation, which will trade under the name "Tanty Solutions," to access the important Association of South East Asian Nations (ASEAN) region. — [1] —.

While many industry observers predicted the move as long ago as last year, negotiations had temporarily stalled due to copyright issues regarding Invert Solutions' banking software. — [2] —. With the court case being resolved in favor of Invert Solutions last month, the final barrier to the partnership was removed. — [3] —.

The same observers have predicted that revenues will rise immediately for the new corporation, with the sale of Tanty Technologies' robust financial prediction computer programs to Invert Solutions' Asian customer base. Additionally, many European and American customers of Tanty Technologies have expressed strong interest in the flexibility of Invert Solutions' products. — [4] —. The rest of the industry is watching carefully to see whether the transition will solidify a market giant or leave room for start-ups to gain ground.

158. Why was the article written?

(A) To announce a corporate buyout
(B) To report on a business merger
(C) To describe a shareholder policy
(D) To outline a recent software trend

159. What kind of company most likely is Invert Solutions?

(A) A corporate consulting firm
(B) A software developer
(C) A computer manufacturer
(D) An Internet security company

160. In which of the positions marked [1], [2], [3] and [4] does the following sentence best belong?

"These factors are examples of how the strengths of each company will be drivers of success."

(A) [1]
(B) [2]
(C) [3]
(D) [4]

Questions 161-164 refer to the following Web site.

National Census Bureau

The national census is conducted annually to get a general understanding of the various demographics in our country. The questions cover a broad spectrum including age, gender, race, income, family size, marital status, and other topics. It is important that people answer the questions honestly and to the best of their ability and knowledge. Although it is not mandatory, we appreciate those who respond to our questionnaire.

Census data is helpful to many kinds of social and scientific research and has been cited in many publications. If you are interested in using any of the statistics that our bureau has collected, you must first obtain permission. Please contact us at admin@ncb.gov and be sure to include your name, the intended use of our data, and the name of the publication you intend to use it in. Most requests are responded to within two business days. There is no charge for using census data once permission has been granted.

161. The word "general" in paragraph 1, line 1 is closest in meaning to

(A) organized
(B) basic
(C) leading
(D) simple

162. What is NOT indicated about the census participants?

(A) They should all have U.S. citizenship.
(B) They are asked to be honest.
(C) They are willing to take a survey.
(D) They belong to varied groups.

163. What is stated about the National Census Bureau?

(A) It is funded by the government.
(B) It employs a large research team.
(C) It charges a fee for using its data.
(D) It has supplied data to multiple publications.

164. How can one get permission to cite collected data?

(A) By conducting research
(B) By paying a small fee
(C) By sending a request by e-mail
(D) By filling out a form

Questions 165-167 refer to the following article.

SANTEE, CA (3 NOVEMBER)—Finley Foods, a major snack producer, has announced a special contest. First, people will be asked to submit their ideas for a new potato chip flavor. The company will select five flavors and begin selling them in small sample pack sizes. Then, after one month, it will hold an online poll to determine which flavors should stay as a permanent addition to the brand. The first place winner to submit the most popular new flavor will be offered a position as a senior flavor specialist at one of Finley Foods' production and packaging sites. All other top submissions will receive a cash bonus based on how well their flavor sold.

165. What is the main purpose of the article?

    (A) To advertise a job opening
    (B) To promote a snack-making brand
    (C) To publicize a competition
    (D) To announce a leadership change

166. Who will select the most popular flavor?

    (A) A CEO of Finley Foods
    (B) The people who cast votes
    (C) Representatives from Finley Foods
    (D) A group of chefs

167. What is stated about the first place winner?

    (A) The largest amount of cash will be awarded.
    (B) The local newspaper will feature the winner.
    (C) The winner will be invited to tour the factory.
    (D) An employment opportunity will be given.

Questions 168-171 refer to the following online chat discussion.

	Aruna Jadhav [9:03 A.M.]	Chris Edwards in the IT department has just confirmed that his team has successfully removed the virus that affected our computer network. We did lose some of our design files in the process, though, right?
	Gustave Tanguay [9:04 A.M.]	That's correct. Unfortunately, we were late getting the newly created logo to Valmeyer Manufacturing because we only had an earlier version of the file backed up.
	Camilla Calvacante [9:06 A.M.]	That's a shame.
	Riley Eldershaw [9:07 A.M.]	Yeah, it could negatively affect our reputation. We have to be stricter about making employees back up their work.
	Aruna Jadhav [9:08 A.M.]	I agree. All we can do now is provide a partial refund to the Valmeyer Manufacturing account by way of compensation. Has anyone done that yet?
	Camilla Calvacante [9:10 A.M.]	I plan to do that today, but I wanted to know what amount would be appropriate. Valmeyer Manufacturing is a regular client, so I was thinking around $250.
	Gustave Tanguay [9:11 A.M.]	That sounds reasonable. Aruna, do we have that?
	Aruna Jadhav [9:12 A.M.]	Yes. There's enough in our corporate bank account to cover that.

168. Where most likely do the writers work?

(A) At an accounting firm
(B) At a manufacturing facility
(C) At a computer retail store
(D) At a graphic design firm

169. What problem is mentioned in the discussion?

(A) A cost has increased.
(B) An employee was absent.
(C) A shipment was damaged.
(D) A deadline was missed.

170. What will Ms. Calvacante most likely do later today?

(A) Send a letter of apology to a customer
(B) Lead a meeting for the staff members
(C) Issue a refund to a client account
(D) Update an online price list

171. At 9:11 A.M., what does Mr. Tanguay mean when he writes, "do we have that"?

(A) He is trying to find a missing document.
(B) He is wondering if there are enough funds.
(C) He needs the contact information for a client.
(D) He wants to confirm an account number.

Questions 172-175 refer to the following advertisement.

Spring Sale at Rashid Gentlemen's Tailors

Mr. J. Rashid, current CEO and son of Rashid Gentlemen's Tailors' founder, is pleased to announce that Master Tailor Joseph McPherson will be visiting the business and working on site until April 4. Having spent over 30 years in the Paris fashion district, Mr. McPherson is known worldwide for providing the perfect stitching and fit. — [1] —. So, this is a rare opportunity to purchase these one-of-a-kind goods.

To celebrate the event, Rashid Gentlemen's Tailors will be including a set of three complimentary dress shirts with any order of two custom-made suits. — [2] —. These will be hand fitted to the customer's specifications, just like all the suits we have produced for over six decades, and they will be available in a wide range of colors and styles. — [3] —. From April 4 onwards, Rashid Gentlemen's Tailors will be offering a full shirt-making service for the first time in our history, and these items will be available made-to-order or from a selection off-the-rack. — [4] —.

Our overseas customers with measurements already on file will be able to take advantage of this opportunity as well. Simply log in and place an order through your online account at www.rashidgtailors.com using code MCP1022 in the appropriate section.

172. Who most likely is Mr. McPherson?

(A) A clothing distributor
(B) A company's CEO
(C) A tailoring intern
(D) A guest professional

173. What is NOT suggested about Rashid Gentlemen's Tailors?

(A) It is a family-owned business.
(B) Its promotion will include free items.
(C) It has been in business for over 60 years.
(D) It currently makes formal shirts.

174. What is recommended for foreign buyers?

(A) Booking appointments in advance
(B) Ordering through a Web site
(C) Sending their measurements via e-mail
(D) Placing their suit orders early

175. In which of the positions marked [1], [2], [3] and [4] does the following sentence best belong?

"He usually caters exclusively to celebrities and high-level politicians."

(A) [1]
(B) [2]
(C) [3]
(D) [4]

Questions 176-180 refer to the following memo and schedule.

ATTN: All Employees
SUBJECT: Week of January 9 – 13
DATE: Monday, January 2

The schedule for repainting our offices has been finalized. Attached is a schedule of the work that will take place. Please pull all furniture away from the walls to the center and cover them with given cloths on the evening of the day before your scheduled date so that the painters can work without obstructions. Although the paint should be dry after one day, it is best to plan on leaving your office for two days, except for the paintwork that will be done on Friday.

During the time your offices are being painted, please use Room 716, our main meeting room, as a temporary office. If you plan on using the meeting room next week, be sure to coordinate with whoever will be temporarily working there. Since it is the only room in our office with a microphone and speakers, holding a meeting there could be very distracting to anyone trying to use it as a temporary office space. Please contact management if you have any questions regarding this matter.

Office Painting Schedule (January 9 – 13)

Monday, January 9	Room 704 (Michelle Cox)
Tuesday, January 10	Room 714 (Teddy Boyle)
Wednesday, January 11	Room 705 (Jessica Ramsey)
Thursday, January 12	Room 715 (John Hack)
Friday, January 13	Room 706 (James Holder & Danielle Atchison)

176. What is the main purpose of the memo?

(A) To give directions to the new office location
(B) To announce a temporary workspace change
(C) To gather feedback on the work environment
(D) To specify what work needs to be done

177. What are the employees asked to do for the scheduled work?

(A) Package their personal belongings
(B) Bring their own brushes
(C) Cover their desks
(D) Oversee some workers

178. What is mentioned about Room 716?

(A) It is the largest room in the building.
(B) It will undergo renovations.
(C) It is equipped with a sound system.
(D) It can be reserved via the company's Web site.

179. When will Mr. Hack most likely move some furniture?

(A) On Monday, January 9
(B) On Tuesday, January 10
(C) On Wednesday, January 11
(D) On Thursday, January 12

180. What is implied about Ms. Atchison?

(A) She has accepted a position at another company.
(B) She shares an office with a coworker.
(C) She will be moving to a new office.
(D) She has recently been promoted to management.

GO ON TO THE NEXT PAGE

Questions 181-185 refer to the following brochure and e-mail.

Byron Marketing
www.byronmarketing.net

Brand recognition is the key to running a successful business. Let Byron Marketing help make your business known. Our services include:

Print – The traditional option, this includes posters, flyers, and newspaper ads. Consult with one of our representatives for recommendations on the amount of copies that would be appropriate for your business.

Radio – Since most people listen to the radio while in the car or office, this is the ideal choice if your target audience is working age. You can choose which stations to broadcast your company's commercial on.

Television – This is a great option for reaching young audiences such as children. The combination of exciting audio and visuals can grab and keep their attention.

Internet – Work with one of our graphic designers to decide the window dimensions that best suit your marketing needs. Then select the sites you want to advertise on.

We offer a free initial consultation during which you can select which services you would like us to provide. Follow-up consultations will be charged based on duration and number of services involved. All of our ad ideas will be presented for approval before final drafts are produced. E-mail us at custserv@byronmarketing.net or call us at 555-3189 to schedule a meeting.

---

e-mail

To: Byron Marketing Customer Service <custserv@byronmarketing.net>
From: Genevieve Wagner <gwagner@wagner.net>
Subject: Ad Campaign
Date: January 6

Hello, I'm the owner of Wagner Dolls. Just over a month ago I started my business, and I think that I need to run an ad campaign to promote it here. I think that kids in the area would really enjoy the handmade dolls that I sell. However, I need to find a way to get the word out about my products. Commercials produced by your company have made Lil' Truckers' Toy Shop famous, and I hope you can do the same for my business. I would like to meet with a representative of your company a week from today to discuss what you can offer. Thank you.

Sincerely,

Genevieve Wagner
Owner, Wagner Dolls

181. In the brochure, the word "running" in paragraph 1, line 1 is closest in meaning to

(A) hurrying
(B) moving
(C) operating
(D) broadcasting

182. What is NOT suggested about Byron Marketing?

(A) It offers online consultation.
(B) It shows its customers rough drafts.
(C) It develops custom service plans.
(D) It creates ads for multiple platforms.

183. What is indicated about Wagner Dolls?

(A) It has done business with Byron Marketing before.
(B) It specializes in imported goods.
(C) It opened for business last year.
(D) It creates custom designs on request.

184. Which option would Ms. Wagner be most interested in?

(A) Print
(B) Radio
(C) Television
(D) Internet

185. What can be inferred about Lil' Truckers' Toy Shop?

(A) It sells toys that are made by hand.
(B) It is the most successful toy store in the region.
(C) It conducts most of its business online.
(D) It has a contract with Byron Marketing.

GO ON TO THE NEXT PAGE

Questions 186-190 refer to the following advertisement, form, and e-mail.

Hometown Appliances · 451 Pine Street
One stop for all your household needs!

Hometown Appliances has the area's largest selection of appliances for the kitchen, laundry room, and more. In celebration of our second anniversary, we are offering two special deals for customers throughout the month of February. Enter code NYT1030 on your order form to claim free delivery. You can also get 50% off installation fees using code NRL2997. Customers who sign up for our newsletter will also receive a free sample of EverShine household cleaner. To register, visit www.hometownappliances.com.

Hometown Appliances Order Confirmation #860175

Name: Johnathan Holt
Order Date: February 3
Items:

1) MaxHome coffee machine	$499.00
2) EasyClean vacuum cleaner	$120.00
3) Durham bread-making machine	$140.00
4) Kessler handheld food mixer	$69.99

Billing Address: 317 Terra Cotta Street, Ulen, MN 56585
Shipping Address: Same as above

Subtotal:	$828.99
Promo code (if applicable):	NYT1030
Total (includes delivery, installation, and taxes):	$878.73
Payment	Credit Card ************6767
Installation type	None

Please note that all bank transfers must be marked with your reference number(s) in order for your order to be processed.

Replacement Guarantee If an item ordered through Hometown Appliances is defective, we will replace it free of charge. Please contact our customer service team for information about our refund policy.

To: Hometown Appliances <customerservice@hometownappliances.com>
From: Johnathan Holt <j.holt@readymail.com>
Date: February 10
Subject: Order #860175

To Whom It May Concern:

I would like to report an issue with the Durham product I ordered from you last week. The power cable is not properly attached to the base. I have not tried to plug it in, as it does not seem safe to do so. I am not sure if this falls under your Replacement Guarantee or if it is just subject to a refund. I would prefer the former, if possible, because I like the features of this particular device. This is a much better option for me than receiving a refund check in the mail. I have used Hometown Appliances in the past many times without any issues, so I'm sure this minor problem is no reflection on your usual level of quality.

Yours sincerely,

Johnathan Holt

186. What is true about Hometown Appliances?
    (A) It has upgraded its Web site.
    (B) It has been open for over one year.
    (C) It has launched some new products.
    (D) It has moved to a new location.

187. How did Mr. Holt pay for his merchandise?
    (A) By in-store credit
    (B) By bank transfer
    (C) By check
    (D) By credit card

188. What is implied about Mr. Holt's order?
    (A) It was delivered for free.
    (B) It had an incorrect price.
    (C) It had discounted installation.
    (D) It was not applicable to taxes.

189. According to Mr. Holt, which item has a problem?
    (A) The coffee machine
    (B) The vacuum cleaner
    (C) The bread-making machine
    (D) The handheld food mixer

190. What does Mr. Holt want Hometown Appliances to do?
    (A) Credit his online account
    (B) Change his mailing address
    (C) Send a replacement product
    (D) Upgrade an existing order

GO ON TO THE NEXT PAGE

Questions 191-195 refer to the following e-mail, form, and article.

---

e-mail

To: Goodwin Solutions Employees
From: Joanne Pruett
Date: September 12
Subject: Communication Workshops
Attachment: sign-up request.docx

Goodwin Solutions will host a month-long communication workshop in October for full- and part-time employees who have worked for the company for at least twelve months. Due to the limited number of spots available, please only sign up if you can promise that you will not miss any parts of the workshop. It will be conducted every Thursday in October from 6 P.M. to 8 P.M., so it will not interfere with any work obligations assigned by your supervisor. A variety of topics will be covered by experienced lecturers.

If you are interested, please submit a completed copy of the attached request form to Rafael Vaughn at r.vaughn@goodwinsol.com no later than September 19. Mr. Vaughn will evaluate the forms and choose the successful applicants on September 22.

Communication Workshop Sign-Up Request

Name: Tony Henning
Department: Public Relations
Work e-mail: t.henning@goodwinsol.com

Why are you interested in this workshop? The main difficulty of my job is navigating the communication gap with my international clients, as the approach I should take varies depending on the culture. I would love to learn more about this.

Do you have any scheduling conflicts with the sessions? No

Goodwin Solutions Company News
November Edition

Workshop Deemed Great Success

In response to employee requests, Goodwin Solutions hosted a month-long workshop on communication. Various communication topics were covered over the course of four weeks, with presentations by senior staff members at Goodwin Solutions. "I was honored to be a presenter for this project," said Kevin Terrell. "Not only did it give me the opportunity to share my expertise with others, but also I became better acquainted with some of the staff members."

Participants in the program had overwhelmingly positive responses in the post-workshop feedback survey, with one hundred percent of them saying they would recommend it to others. "I learned so much," said Tony Henning, who works in the PR department. "I was particularly pleased with Kristie Fultz's talk, which helped me with the biggest challenge of my job, so I feel much more confident. In addition, I was able to network with other staff members and develop closer relationships with them."

Plans for a new workshop are already underway, and the details will be announced in the next newsletter.

191. What is true about the workshop?
    (A) Participants must commit to attending all sessions.
    (B) Participants must get approval from their supervisor.
    (C) It is held at the company once per year.
    (D) It is intended for public relations employees only.

192. How will the participants in the program be determined?
    (A) By giving a presentation to a panel
    (B) By passing an online test
    (C) By attending a group interview
    (D) By being assessed by Mr. Vaughn

193. What is implied about Mr. Henning?
    (A) He is being considered for a promotion.
    (B) He is currently employed as a part-time worker.
    (C) He has worked for Goodwin Solutions for more than a year.
    (D) He has recently lost some of his clients.

194. What is suggested about Ms. Fultz?
    (A) She will create the schedule for the next workshop.
    (B) She covered some of Mr. Terrell's duties.
    (C) She gave a presentation on cultural differences.
    (D) She has a lot of experience in marketing methods.

195. What advantage of the workshop do Mr. Terrell and Mr. Henning both mention?
    (A) Building confidence
    (B) Getting to know coworkers
    (C) Improving sales figures
    (D) Sharing knowledge

GO ON TO THE NEXT PAGE

Questions 196-200 refer to the following article, letter, and voucher.

Tree-Planting Project to Commemorate Arbor Day
by Carol Rollins

April 18—Trevino City will hold its first-ever event to celebrate Arbor Day, a holiday that recognizes the impact of trees on public health and the environment. Trees will be planted at four parks throughout the city, and these have been paid for through a combination of municipal funds and private donations. Volunteers are needed for clearing and preparing the planting area as well as planting and watering the new trees. Individuals who participate as volunteers will receive a voucher for a free tree to plant on their own property. Community groups are also encouraged to take part in the project, in which case the group leader will be given a voucher for ten trees to be shared with the group members. Planting will take place according to the following schedule:

Monday, April 25: Maxwell Park, picnic area
Wednesday, April 27: Spring Park, near north parking lot
Friday, April 29: Avoca Park, along jogging path
Saturday, April 30: Cedar Park, near east playground

For more information, visit www.trevinocity.gov/events.

Anastasia Whitcomb
207 Timbercrest Road
Omaha, NE 68102

Dear Ms. Whitcomb,

Thank you for your participation on the first day of our Arbor Day tree-planting project. Because of volunteers like you, we were able to realize our dream of improving the environment here in Trevino City by unleashing the benefits of health-giving trees. From fresh oxygen and shade to natural homes for birds and insects, trees truly are a gift that keeps on giving. Enclosed you will find a voucher that can be used at Eastside Nursery.

We would like to show as many pictures as possible from the event, so if you have any to share, please visit www.trevinocity.gov/events to upload them. We plan to make this event an annual tradition, and we hope you will consider participating in next year's event.

Warmest regards,

Lonzo Tocci

Eastside Nursery Product Voucher

This voucher entitles the holder to __10 complimentary tree saplings__.

The voucher is valid from May 1 and can be used for any of the above item types in stock. Not for use with other offers. Offer valid only at the Union Street branch, as the Victoria Lane location does not carry trees.

Issued to __Anastasia Whitcomb__ by __Lonzo Tocci [Trevino City]__
Code: 3959

---

196. Where did Ms. Whitcomb volunteer for a project?
    (A) At Avoca Park
    (B) At Cedar Park
    (C) At Maxwell Park
    (D) At Spring Park

197. In the letter, the word "realize" in paragraph 1, line 2, is closest in meaning to
    (A) achieve
    (B) understand
    (C) notice
    (D) confirm

198. What does Mr. Tocci ask Ms. Whitcomb to do?
    (A) Reserve items at Eastside Nursery
    (B) E-mail her some pictures
    (C) Share her opinions
    (D) Post images on a Web site

199. What is true about the voucher?
    (A) It should be submitted online.
    (B) It cannot be combined with other offers.
    (C) Its expiration date is on May 1.
    (D) It can be used at two different branches.

200. What is suggested about Ms. Whitcomb?
    (A) She lost her first voucher.
    (B) She was a group leader.
    (C) She plans to participate next year.
    (D) She placed a special order.

Stop! This is the end of the test. If you finish before time is called, you may go back to Part 5, 6, and 7 and check your work.

TEST 08

PART 5 · PART 6 · PART 7

준비하기

손목시계

뭉뚝한 연필과 지우개

Answer Sheet

토익 RC는 75분 동안 진행됩니다.
반드시 75분 이내에 문제 풀이와 답안지 마킹을 완료하세요.

고난도 문제는 해설집에서 확인할 수 있습니다.
해설집 p.148

TEST 08은 **고난도 문제가 평균적으로 포함**된 평달 TEST입니다.
환산 점수가 중간값으로 나올 수 있습니다.

맞은 개수	환산 점수	맞은 개수	환산 점수
96-100	465 - 495	41-45	145 - 215
91-95	430 - 490	36-40	120 - 180
86-90	400 - 465	31-35	100 - 145
81-85	375 - 440	26-30	80 - 120
76-80	340 - 415	21-25	65 - 95
71-75	315 - 390	16-20	50 - 75
66-70	285 - 365	11-15	35 - 55
61-65	255 - 335	6-10	15 - 40
56-60	225 - 305	1-5	5 - 30
51-55	200 - 270	0	5
46-50	170 - 240		

READING TEST

In the Reading test, you will read a variety of texts and answer several different types of reading comprehension questions. The entire Reading test will last 75 minutes. There are three parts, and directions are given for each part. You are encouraged to answer as many questions as possible within the time allowed.

You must mark your answers on the separate answer sheet. Do not write your answers in your test book.

PART 5

Directions: A word or phrase is missing in each of the sentences below. Four answer choices are given below each sentence. Select the best answer to complete the sentence. Then mark the letter (A), (B), (C), or (D) on your answer sheet.

101. Please call ------- immediately at this 24-hour customer service hotline if your credit card is lost or stolen.
(A) we
(B) our
(C) us
(D) ourselves

102. Team members are ------- that the project manager extended the deadline from April 1 to April 10.
(A) thank
(B) thankful
(C) thankfully
(D) thanks

103. Ms. Henderson ------- that visitors wear an ID badge at all times during their visit.
(A) insists
(B) insisting
(C) to insist
(D) to be insisted

104. The parking lot located on Marron Street will be closed until ------- notice.
(A) effective
(B) constant
(C) periodic
(D) further

105. Job seekers who are ------- in the position should e-mail their résumé with cover letter and references to Ashley Waller.
(A) interesting
(B) interested
(C) interests
(D) interest

106. The software has been recently updated, ------- there are some changes to the menu items.
(A) lastly
(B) so
(C) because
(D) then

107. Information about the drug is ------- available to patients through the hospital's Web site.
(A) ready
(B) readily
(C) readier
(D) readiest

108. After receiving several orders with overly ripe fruits, Beechwood Catering's owner tried to find a new food -------.
(A) presenter
(B) container
(C) supplier
(D) diner

109. Spot-on Delivery will switch to hybrid vehicles to minimize ------- fuel expenses.
    (A) rising
    (B) closing
    (C) limited
    (D) yielding

110. The start time for the training will not be ------- until Ms. Rudd checks everyone's schedules.
    (A) concluded
    (B) persuaded
    (C) decided
    (D) entitled

111. Author Betty Glynn generated interest in her new novel ------- participating in several television interviews.
    (A) by
    (B) to
    (C) of
    (D) as

112. All funds should be allotted and spent ------ according to a well-planned budget.
    (A) wise
    (B) wisely
    (C) wisdom
    (D) wiser

113. After a few moments of -------, Ms. Wickham realized that the sign on the podium had a misprint.
    (A) observer
    (B) observative
    (C) observation
    (D) observe

114. Crosby Manufacturing was ------- bankruptcy last year, but the new CEO has turned the company around.
    (A) with
    (B) close to
    (C) along
    (D) nearby

115. Experts ------- regard Belleview Hotel as the best value for business travelers in Austin.
    (A) wider
    (B) widely
    (C) widen
    (D) widest

116. The main conference room is large ------- to seat the entire sales and finance teams at the same time.
    (A) even
    (B) enough
    (C) just
    (D) still

117. Ms. Russell did not attend the banquet because her doctor put her on a ------- diet.
    (A) restriction
    (B) restrict
    (C) restrictive
    (D) restrictively

118. Following the exhibit's grand opening, there will be a private ------- for the major donors.
    (A) malfunction
    (B) direction
    (C) occupation
    (D) reception

119. Sheila Slater gave a talk that was based on questions written by the audience members -------.
    (A) herself
    (B) themselves
    (C) ourselves
    (D) yourself

120. As the airline ticket prices far exceeded the budget, the marketing team took the train to the conference -------.
    (A) instead
    (B) against
    (C) despite
    (D) otherwise

121. Traffic conditions in Greenwood ------- worse and must be addressed by city officials.

(A) growing
(B) to grow
(C) had to grow
(D) have grown

122. Text message alerts about new offers are available to those ------- signed up for our reminder service.

(A) why
(B) which
(C) who
(D) when

123. ------- a post office, the Granger Building has recently been converted to a dance studio.

(A) Formerly
(B) Solely
(C) Needlessly
(D) Rarely

124. The mayor of Pacheo ------- to dedicate the fountain in Kemper Park to the city's local firefighters.

(A) declares
(B) intends
(C) refers
(D) signifies

125. A commercial license issued by the state is needed ------- operate a large moving truck legally.

(A) sometimes
(B) regarding
(C) in order to
(D) as soon as

126. The newly hired interns will require ongoing ------- until they are comfortable with their job responsibilities.

(A) supervisor
(B) supervision
(C) supervises
(D) supervised

127. Humphrey Bank is working to keep customers informed ------- eliminating unnecessary paperwork.

(A) unless
(B) while
(C) that
(D) therefore

128. New staff members are ------- to renegotiate the contract terms after the sixty-day trial period is completed.

(A) introductory
(B) familiar
(C) strict
(D) eligible

129. Despite the store owner's considerable -------, the grand opening did not have a strong turnout.

(A) optimistic
(B) optimism
(C) optimize
(D) optimistically

130. ------- the town's founding day with a parade is a tradition that goes back nearly one hundred years.

(A) Celebrate
(B) Celebrated
(C) Celebration
(D) Celebrating

PART 6

Directions: Read the texts that follow. A word, phrase, or sentence is missing in parts of each text. Four answer choices for each question are given below the text. Select the best answer to complete the text. Then mark the letter (A), (B), (C), or (D) on your answer sheet.

Questions 131-134 refer to the following e-mail.

To: Gladys Wheeler <g.wheeler@wheeler-studio.com>
From: James Blackwell <blackwell_j@hammettdept.com>
Date: January 23
Subject: Hammett Department Store

Dear Ms. Wheeler,

I'm so pleased that you have confirmed your intention to design jackets for the upcoming winter season. -------. Therefore, it is especially exciting to be working with you on this project. As a first step, I'd like to get
131.
together to brainstorm some ideas about colors and price points. Since our department store is known for its ------- clothing, we want to make sure that we follow the trends. Diana Keasler, the assistant buyer for
132.
our store, will ------- us for the meeting. We would appreciate ------- some preliminary drawings. Please let
133.   134.
me know what date would work well for you.

Sincerely,

James Blackwell

131. (A) There are several ways to make this decision.
(B) I was impressed with the items in your online catalog.
(C) Attached you will find the contract with the necessary changes.
(D) I already received several compliments on my clothing.

132. (A) fashionably
(B) fashions
(C) fashioning
(D) fashionable

133. (A) undergo
(B) join
(C) attend
(D) remind

134. (A) views
(B) to view
(C) viewing
(D) viewed

Questions 135-138 refer to the following letter.

Dear Webster City Resident,

The Webster City Library System strives ------- a comfortable environment for patrons to study, read, and
                                            135.
conduct research. In light of this, we are scheduling renovations at our Hollis Street location. The project will

consist of two phases of construction ------- a total of six months.
                                       136.

The work will begin on February 16 and will be carried out by local firm Benley Designs. Some sections

of the library will be closed, and noisy equipment will be in operation. ------- Should you need a quiet
                                                                          137.
environment, our other sites will be available during their normal opening -------.
                                                                            138.

Sincerely,

Douglas Braun
Head Administrator, Webster City Library System

---

135. (A) to be created
(B) to create
(C) created
(D) creating

136. (A) out
(B) except
(C) for
(D) beside

137. (A) Our new selection of books is very popular.
(B) Unfortunately, your card is no longer valid.
(C) The library fines should be paid right away.
(D) We regret any disturbances to patrons.

138. (A) hours
(B) statements
(C) branches
(D) sessions

Questions 139-142 refer to the following e-mail.

To: stephenshaw@bvmail.com
From: corrine@odinsalesconference.com
Date: March 28
Subject: Odin Sales Conference

Dear Mr. Shaw,

I would like to thank you for agreeing to be a presenter at the upcoming Odin Sales Conference.

As one of our featured speakers, you ------- an audience of over five thousand people in the main auditorium. There is a great deal of interest in the regulations surrounding imports and exports, so we'd like you to give a talk on the ------- agencies that affect these activities.
139.   140.

To ensure that your digital files are compatible with our system, please send us an electronic copy of your presentation ------- the conference on May 17. You should upload your handouts to our Web site rather than printing them out. -------.
141.   142.

Sincerely,

Corrine Roland

139. (A) have addressed
(B) addressed
(C) have been addressed
(D) will be addressing

140. (A) regulatorily
(B) regulatory
(C) regulating
(D) regulate

141. (A) behind
(B) until
(C) before
(D) since

142. (A) We appreciate your creative suggestions.
(B) The position should be filled as quickly as possible.
(C) Our import business has grown substantially.
(D) Participants will download the materials in advance.

Questions 143-146 refer to the following letter.

Valdez Insurance
4309 Holmes Street
Dallas, TX 75240

To Whom It May Concern:

I am writing this letter on behalf of Ana Robinson, who has recently applied for a sales position at your company. Ms. Robinson has ------- (143.) as a senior sales associate at Hampton Industrial for the past three years. As a key member of our team, she handled a number of duties, from ------- (144.) new clients to developing promotional materials. Ms. Robinson is a people person, and she has a natural talent for communication. Most of these ------- (145.) will be perfect for your position, even though the field is different.

I would be happy to discuss Ms. Robinson's work performance in greater detail. ------- (146.) My phone extension from the main switchboard, which is listed below, is 35.

Sincerely,

Maria Yokota
Sales Director, Hampton Industrial
469-555-6489

143. (A) accomplished
(B) served
(C) recognized
(D) applied

144. (A) having attracted
(B) attracted
(C) attracting
(D) attracts

145. (A) changes
(B) agreements
(C) skills
(D) concerns

146. (A) She will review the application for the job.
(B) I will invite you to the next round of interviews.
(C) She will give you an update with more precise data.
(D) Please feel free to contact me at my office.

PART 7

Directions: In this part you will read a selection of texts, such as magazine and newspaper articles, e-mails, and instant messages. Each text or set of texts is followed by several questions. Select the best answer for each question and mark the letter (A), (B), (C), or (D) on your answer sheet.

Questions 147-148 refer to the following coupon.

RDC
Ideas in Motion
15% off your visit

15% admission discount

This coupon is valid at RDC for 15% off admission for up to four people. There is no expiration date, but the coupon cannot be combined with other discounts. Visitors are permitted access to all displays, hands-on lab activities, and biology lectures (view our Web site for the lecture schedule).

Summer Hours (June–August): Mon.–Sat., 9 A.M.–7 P.M.
Standard Hours (September–May): Tues.–Sun., 11 A.M.–7 P.M.

---

147. What most likely is RDC?
(A) A movie theater
(B) A utility company
(C) A science center
(D) A department store

148. What is true about RDC in September?
(A) It has an earlier closing time.
(B) It is closed in the mornings.
(C) It is open for more days.
(D) It is open for fewer hours.

GO ON TO THE NEXT PAGE

Questions 149-150 refer to the following e-mail.

To: bruce_garmon@writersunite.com
From: reneevarney@alabasterediting.com
Date: October 3
Subject: Writers Unite Newsletter

Dear Mr. Garmon,

I have been a subscriber to the Writers Unite monthly newsletter for about three years. I look forward to receiving it every month, as it always provides an extensive index of companies that are currently hiring freelancers. In fact, it has helped me to find several projects, so I'm thankful to have such a useful resource.

I sometimes read the featured articles, but it does seem that there are several potential topics that have not been covered since I started receiving the publication. Do you accept suggestions for upcoming newsletters? If so, here's what I was thinking:

- Writing a Book Proposal
- Tips for Overcoming Writer's Block

Thanks for all the help you've given to me and other freelancers!

Sincerely,

Renée Varney

149. What aspect of the monthly newsletter does Ms. Varney praise?

(A) Its project management tips
(B) Its easy search features
(C) Its list of job opportunities
(D) Its information about discounts

150. What does Ms. Varney point out in the e-mail?

(A) Posts that she forwarded to others
(B) Subjects that she thinks need attention
(C) Articles that contained inaccuracies
(D) Policies that need to be changed

Questions 151-152 refer to the following text-message chain.

Shirley Campbell (10:33 A.M.)
I've just dropped off the boxes of the Summer Breeze perfume at the South Bend store. I have three boxes for your branch in Oakland. When does your shift end?

Chiara Feliciano (10:35 A.M.)
I've just started, so feel free to stop by anytime before we close.

Shirley Campbell (10:36 A.M.)
OK. The South Bend branch did a great job setting up the display for the perfume. They decorated the display area with beach towels, beach balls, and colorful balloons.

Chiara Feliciano (10:37 A.M.)
That sounds exactly like us. Will you need help unloading the items?

Shirley Campbell (10:38 A.M.)
Yes, so please send someone out when I arrive. I'll text you then.

151. Why did Ms. Campbell send a message to Ms. Feliciano?
    (A) To confirm a delivery of goods
    (B) To inquire about a new product
    (C) To schedule a time for a demonstration
    (D) To get directions to the South Bend store

152. At 10:37 A.M., what does Ms. Feliciano suggest when she writes, "That sounds exactly like us"?
    (A) Oakland has similar sales figures to South Bend.
    (B) Ms. Feliciano will get advice from the South Bend manager.
    (C) Some decorations have been set up in Oakland.
    (D) Ms. Campbell can purchase the towels she requested.

Questions 153-155 refer to the following report.

Houghton Construction

Customer: Cecilia Irwin
Shingle/Tile Type: Slate
Time Since Last Visit: 1 year

Address: 429 Jaksa Lane, Baltimore, MD 21202
Date of Visit: September 29
Houghton Representative: Andrew Lahti

Roof Features	Grade
Shingles	3
Tiles	0
Gutters	4
Drainpipe	1
Roof deck	2
Solar panels	0
Chimney (including seal)	3

Representative's Comments:
I recommended ordering more slate tiles for storage, as the particular version in use will be discontinued soon. Awaiting customer approval.

Grade Descriptions: 0: Not present / **1:** Excellent: No action needed / **2:** Minor deterioration: Recheck in one year / **3:** Medium deterioration: Recheck in six months / **4:** Major deterioration: Replace within three to six months / **5:** Severe deterioration: Replace immediately

---

153. What did Mr. Lahti most likely do on September 29?

(A) Placed an order
(B) Assessed a roof's condition
(C) Repaired some components
(D) Delivered a shipment

154. What feature should be replaced the soonest?

(A) Shingles
(B) Gutters
(C) Drainpipe
(D) Roof deck

155. What is implied about Ms. Irwin's roof?

(A) It was originally installed by an amateur.
(B) It will be replaced immediately.
(C) Its chimney edges were resealed in September.
(D) It is not equipped to generate energy from the sun.

Questions 156-157 refer to the following information.

Logan Community Center
4-week classes beginning the week of August 10th

DIY Marketing
Learn the basics of promoting your business without spending a lot of money to hire experts.

Enrollment #	Instructor	Day/Time	Location
839586-01	Patricia DeRosa	Mondays/6–8 P.M.	Room 103
839586-02	Stewart Crompton	Thursdays/1–3 P.M.	Room 206

Knowing Your Audience
Learn to make the most of your next speech by tailoring your comments to the audience.

Enrollment #	Instructor	Day/Time	Location
842771-01	Patricia DeRosa	Thursdays/2–4 P.M.	Room 205
842771-02	Abhinav Patel	Saturdays/9–11 A.M.	Room 102

156. What is true about Ms. DeRosa?
 (A) She teaches two days a week.
 (B) She is a financial expert.
 (C) She was hired by Mr. Crompton.
 (D) She operates her own business.

157. Why might people sign up for Mr. Patel's course?
 (A) To improve public speaking skills
 (B) To get advice on basic laws
 (C) To learn how to analyze comments
 (D) To practice making advertisements

GO ON TO THE NEXT PAGE

Questions 158-160 refer to the following e-mail.

To: Muldoon Enterprises Employees
From: Navin Kamath
Date: February 20
Subject: Please note

Dear Muldoon Enterprises Employees,

As discussed in the most recent staff meeting, the human resources department has made a change to the vacation policy. —[1]—. From now on, a maximum of three people can be absent from a department at any given time. We hope this will help us to maintain a high level of productivity and customer service. —[2]—. An up-to-date calendar of planned absences is available on our company Web site, so that should be checked first. You should also talk to your colleagues about their vacation plans. —[3]—.

As you can only request vacation time up to four months in advance, you may want to consider downloading the 159 EZ-Cal smartphone app. —[4]—. You can set it to remind you to request vacation time on a certain date.

Thank you for your cooperation.

Sincerely,

Navin Kamath
HR Director, Muldoon Enterprises

---

158. What is suggested about Muldoon Enterprises?
(A) It will no longer offer paid vacation days to employees.
(B) It will restrict the conditions for taking time off.
(C) It will give bonuses to employees who don't miss work days.
(D) It will e-mail staff members updates to the vacation calendar.

159. According to Mr. Kamath, what can the EZ-Cal smartphone application do?
(A) Share messages between employees
(B) Track the amount of time spent working
(C) Schedule meetings on short notice
(D) Send a reminder about a task

160. In which of the positions marked [1], [2], [3], and [4] does the following sentence best belong?

"Please take these measures to ensure that your application is not rejected."

(A) [1]
(B) [2]
(C) [3]
(D) [4]

Questions 161-163 refer to the following article.

Vaka Sees Business Boom

Sales at Vaka Tech have increased by over 200% compared to the same period last year, mainly driven by its popular Spirex-80 device. Earlier this year, the EU added strict regulations on bottled water, limiting the mineral content far below the previous threshold. Many beverages companies were forced to use additional finances to bring their products into compliance.

The change was announced in early March. From that point, sales of the Spirex-80—a system that effectively purifies water—skyrocketed. Offering a solution that all beverage companies need, the Spirex-80 certainly seems to be in the right place at the right time.

161. According to the article, what has increased costs for beverage companies?

(A) New government regulations
(B) A shortage of ingredients
(C) Wage payments for staff
(D) Rising fuel prices

162. The word "point" in paragraph 2, line 1, is closest in meaning to

(A) location
(B) detail
(C) instant
(D) purpose

163. What does the article indicate that Vaka Tech has done?

(A) Changed the design of the Spirex-80
(B) Moved to a country in the Europe
(C) Taken over one of its competitors
(D) Created a purification system

Questions 164-167 refer to the following online chat discussion.

Kirby Auyer (9:08 A.M.)		Hi, Deandra and Paola. Could we review the résumés for the tax compliance officer position sometime in the afternoon instead of at 10? I need to cover Mr. Hong's presentation at the board meeting.
Deandra Calteaux (9:09 A.M.)		How about 3 P.M.? We could get together in the meeting room to go over everything.
Paola Gomez (9:10 A.M.)		That works perfectly for me. I'm still working on a report that's due at 1 P.M.
Kirby Auyer (9:10 A.M.)		That'll be a problem. According to the online schedule, the IT team will be in there all day for their quarterly training.
Deandra Calteaux (9:11 A.M.)		We could meet in the employee lounge. It's usually empty.
Paola Gomez (9:12 A.M.)		OK. Should I bring my laptop so I can look at the electronic versions of the files?
Deandra Calteaux (9:13 A.M.)		That's not necessary. I'll print paper copies for everyone.
Kirby Auyer (9:14 A.M.)		See you then. Thanks for accommodating me.

164. Why is Mr. Auyer busy in the morning?
(A) He will give board members a tour.
(B) He has to give a talk in place of a colleague.
(C) He must visit another branch.
(D) He has an urgent report to complete.

165. Why does Ms. Calteaux think they should meet in the employee lounge?
(A) Because the meeting room will be in use
(B) Because food is allowed in the area
(C) Because it is nearest to Mr. Auyer's office
(D) Because it has extra space for visitors

166. At 9:13 A.M., what does Ms. Calteaux suggest when she writes, "That's not necessary"?
(A) Mr. Auyer does not have to help with a project.
(B) He has already contacted some job candidates.
(C) Ms. Gomez will not need to use a laptop.
(D) Ms. Gomez should not review the files in advance.

167. When will the writers meet today?
(A) At 10:00 A.M.
(B) At 1:00 P.M.
(C) At 3:00 P.M.
(D) At 4:00 P.M.

Questions 168-171 refer to the following letter.

Brian Streich
502 Carissa Avenue
Aberdeen, SD 57401

April 3

Dear Mr. Streich,

I recently met with a colleague of mine who is in charge of the Community Outreach Contest to promote quality-of-life improvements. Based on the ideas you presented at our last Millennial Leaders Club meeting, I believe that you would be an excellent fit for this event. Your program of relaxation techniques for reducing stress and preventing illness is sure to impress the judging panel.

If you are interested, you must provide a 300-word description of your program and how it can help others. You easily meet the entry criteria, so I believe you would definitely make it past the screening phase. After that, you would be invited to give a brief talk about your program and answer questions. The winner will receive a cash prize of $5,000, so I think it's definitely worth giving it a try.

I've taken the liberty of downloading and printing the application form, which you will find enclosed. You must complete and send it, along with your program description and a copy of your passport or driver's license for identification purposes, no later than April 30.

Warmest regards,

Elaina Urmanski

---

168. Why did Ms. Urmanski send the letter?
    (A) To suggest entering a competition
    (B) To recruit a judge for a panel
    (C) To extend an invitation to join a club
    (D) To inform Mr. Streich of a job opening

169. What most likely is Mr. Streich's field of expertise?
    (A) Investing
    (B) Technology
    (C) Health
    (D) Manufacturing

170. The word "meet" in paragraph 2, line 2, is closest in meaning to
    (A) collect
    (B) greet
    (C) sustain
    (D) fulfill

171. What should Mr. Streich do by April 30?
    (A) Download a form
    (B) Submit the required documents
    (C) Respond to questions
    (D) Renew a passport

Questions 172-175 refer to the following article.

Surabaya Herald
March 24

The number of new Internet customers in Indonesia is nearly three times that of other countries over the same one-year period. Competition among Internet service providers has heated up as more and more people, especially in rural communities, come online. —[1]—.

Lumbra Communication has been a long-time provider of Internet services, focusing mainly on major cities. It used to be the only option for Internet users in many places, but that is changing. —[2]—. As a result, most new customers are not first-time Internet users, but rather transferred customers from other companies.

With so many companies to choose from, customers no longer put up with long periods of downtime. If customers cannot rely on a stable connection, they simply change to another provider. This is what caused the downfall of Dhanas Web, which went out of business two months ago after previously holding the second highest amount of market share. —[3]—.

Lumbra Communication still leads the market, but Sandang Tech is gaining ground. —[4]—. Sandang Tech has only been in operation for eighteen months, but it is grabbing the attention of consumers through its phone and Internet packages. It works continually to provide faster Internet speeds, which is particularly important to those who use the Internet for video streaming. Sandang Tech's focus is on young professionals, and it hopes to make them lifelong customers. It also has a reputation for making same-day repairs to broken lines and routers. A smart and adaptable business model may be the key to maximizing the surge in Internet usage.

172. What is the main topic of the article?

(A) The popularity of Internet-based businesses
(B) The most common marketing methods
(C) The rapid growth of an industry
(D) The best companies to work for in Indonesia

173. What is implied about Dhanas Web?

(A) Its prices were too high.
(B) Its main business was phone packages.
(C) It was the area's longest-running business.
(D) It had unreliable service.

174. What is NOT indicated as a strategy of Sandang Tech?

(A) Offering a video streaming service
(B) Targeting young consumers
(C) Increasing its Internet speed
(D) Resolving technical issues quickly

175. In which of the positions marked [1], [2], [3], and [4] does the following sentence best belong?

"The customer pool is expected to start shrinking due to the high market saturation."

(A) [1]
(B) [2]
(C) [3]
(D) [4]

Questions 176-180 refer to the following e-mails.

To: Gregorio Dellucci <dellucci@kokomohotel.com>
From: Joyful Cleaning <c_emmerson@joyfulcleaning.com>
Date: November 19, 9:23 A.M.
Subject: Account #5872-R2003

Dear Mr. Dellucci,

Thank you for your recent order for cleaning supplies through Joyful Cleaning. We particularly hope that you get excellent results from the Lemontime Floor Cleaner, whose formula has recently been changed to make it more effective. The shipment is currently scheduled to arrive on November 24.

This order puts you into the category of "High-Volume Customer", meaning that you are now eligible to join our High-Volume Customer Rewards program (HVCR). Under this program, businesses like yours pay an annual fee of $95 for a membership card. The card allows you to get five percent off all orders for a twelve-month period. You'll also be able to sign up for next-day delivery instead of our usual five-day delivery, even without advance notice. This would apply to any of your three hotel branches. You'll also be sent free samples of new products as they come out.

To sign up, please respond to this e-mail. If you do so by 5 P.M. today, you'll be able to receive your current order one day early.

Warmest regards,

Connie Emmerson

---

e-mail

To: Joyful Cleaning <c_emmerson@joyfulcleaning.com>
From: Gregorio Dellucci <dellucci@kokomohotel.com>
Date: November 19, 1:48 P.M.
Subject: RE: Account #5872-R2003

Dear Ms. Emmerson,

I am interested in HVCR membership, so please bill my account for the $95 membership fee. Also, for the last shipment, the delivery person left the box on the reception desk while the receptionist had stepped out, so it sat there for several minutes with no one keeping an eye on it. I hope this will not happen on the new delivery date.

Thanks!

Gregorio Dellucci

176. What is one purpose of the first e-mail?

(A) To get feedback about a service
(B) To explain an opportunity for businesses
(C) To promote a cleaning product
(D) To advertise a new loyalty program

177. What is NOT indicated as a benefit of HVCR?

(A) Lower prices on products
(B) Advance notice of sales
(C) Complimentary samples
(D) Overnight shipments

178. What is suggested about Mr. Dellucci?

(A) He wrote a review for Lemontime Floor Cleaner.
(B) He wanted to add more items to his order.
(C) He oversees more than one business location.
(D) He paid for the express delivery of some items.

179. When most likely will Mr. Dellucci receive his order?

(A) On November 19
(B) On November 20
(C) On November 23
(D) On November 24

180. What problem does Mr. Dellucci tell Ms. Emmerson about?

(A) A package had the wrong items.
(B) A package was left unattended.
(C) He received some damaged items.
(D) He was overcharged for delivery.

GO ON TO THE NEXT PAGE

Questions 181-185 refer to the following letter and order form.

Kimberly Shaw
1358 Wilmington Avenue
Winnipeg, MB R3G 3P4
Canada

February 6

Dear Ms. Shaw,

Thank you for sending in your updated photo release form, which shows that we have permission to use the photo for a limited purpose once you receive payment from us. As usual, your payment for any outstanding commissions will be issued on the 20th of this month.

I'm also pleased to inform you that Kirwan Publishing will launch several new publications in the coming months, so we will be relying on freelance photography services more than ever. We're offering a fifty percent discount on all magazines to freelancers who have contributed to any of our magazines in the past month. The discount can be obtained by using the code REF561 on the online checkout page.

I look forward to continuing working with you!

Warmest regards,

Calvin Leroy

---

www.kirwanpublishing.com/checkout

Your order has been processed!

February Special: Subscribe to three or more magazines and receive a complimentary calendar.

Name: José Hudson
E-mail Address: jose@hudsonphotoshowcase.com
Order Date: February 19
Payment Method: Credit Card XXXX-XXXX-XXXX-4574
Billing Address: José Hudson, 925 Bolman Court, Vancouver, BC V6J 4A1, Canada
Shipping Address: same as above

Product Description(s)	
Outdoor Monthly 1-year subscription	$20.00
Under the Stars 1-year subscription	$15.00
Wildlife Insider 1-year subscription	$18.00
Discount Code (REF561)	-$26.50
TOTAL DUE	$26.50

You will receive the first issue of your subscription(s) on the 5th of the month following your order. Customers are sent paperwork to renew their subscriptions two months before the subscription expires.

181. Why did Mr. Leroy send the letter?

(A) To request adjustments to a photo
(B) To offer Ms. Shaw a job
(C) To acknowledge receipt of a form
(D) To apologize for a delay

182. What will be sent to Ms. Shaw later this month?

(A) A work assignment
(B) A new magazine
(C) A contract
(D) A payment

183. What is true about Kirwan Publishing?

(A) It will open a new photography department.
(B) It plans to expand its product range.
(C) It has experienced a decline in readership.
(D) It has been nominated for an award.

184. What is implied about Mr. Hudson?

(A) He provided a letter of reference for Ms. Shaw.
(B) He recently published work through Kirwan Publishing.
(C) He is a regular customer of Kirwan Publishing.
(D) He is the editor of *Outdoor Monthly*.

185. What is suggested about Mr. Hudson's order?

(A) It will be automatically renewed.
(B) It will be sent to multiple addresses.
(C) It will include a free gift.
(D) It will expire in about two months.

GO ON TO THE NEXT PAGE

Questions 186-190 refer to the following e-mail, flyer, and schedule.

To: Carolyn Dana <dana_c@ingrameden.com>
From: Matthew Wallace <wallace_m@ingrameden.com>
Date: March 8
Subject: Cultural activities

Hi Carolyn,

How are you? I hope you are getting used to the differences between the Covington branch and our branch. We're glad to have you as part of the team. As you we unable to attend the most recent team leader meeting, I wanted to let you know what happened. We mainly discussed what to do for our spring team-building activity next month. Based on the feedback we've previously received from the staff, we thought that a traditional dance show would be best.

We haven't announced the date yet, as I'm still looking into our ticketing options. On the event day, everyone will work a half day in the morning, attend the show in the afternoon, and return to the office by early evening. I'll buy group tickets for non-members so that everyone can participate. It seems like our budget of five hundred dollars will cover the tickets for all staff members with a little left over for the parking fees.

I'll provide you with more details once they are finalized.

Sincerely,

Matthew Wallace
HR Team Leader, Ingram Eden

Take a trip to the past with a traditional dance show at Horizon Theater!

The Moon Bay Dance Troupe has been sharing the joy of traditional dance with audiences all over the world. Enjoy the sights and sounds of dances that have been passed down through generations. Visit our box office to reserve your tickets. Or book online to avoid the ticket handling fee.

Group rates are available no matter how you purchase your tickets.
10 tickets: $140
20 tickets: $250
40 tickets: $480
50 tickets: $550

Box office: 806 Kent Street, (649) 555-3198
Web site: www.htheaterboxoffice.com

Horizon Theater
Moon Bay Dance Troupe Upcoming Shows

Date	Start Time	Featured Performer	Ticket Restrictions
April 2	8:00 P.M.	Salini Chetti	None
April 5	2:00 P.M.	Salini Chetti	Members only
April 9	8:00 P.M.	Ayush Kamal	Members only
April 12	2:00 P.M.	Ayush Kamal	None

For a complete list of events at Horizon Theater, visit www.htheaterboxoffice.com.

186. What is the purpose of Mr. Wallace's e-mail?
    (A) To request a feedback form
    (B) To reschedule a meeting
    (C) To report a decision
    (D) To schedule a job interview

187. What is suggested in the e-mail about Ms. Dana?
    (A) She used to work at Horizon Theater.
    (B) She recently transferred to a new branch.
    (C) She suggested attending more cultural events.
    (D) She lost some tickets to a show.

188. What benefit of making an online booking is mentioned in the flyer?
    (A) Selecting parking in advance
    (B) Having more seating options
    (C) Receiving discounts on refreshments
    (D) Avoiding a handling charge

189. How many people most likely work at Ingram Eden?
    (A) 10
    (B) 20
    (C) 40
    (D) 50

190. When will Ingram Eden employees most likely attend a performance?
    (A) April 2
    (B) April 5
    (C) April 9
    (D) April 12

Questions 191-195 refer to the following memo, schedule, and notice.

To: All Staff
From: Natalie Lantz, Office Manager
Re: Renovations

April 17

Due to renovations throughout the Perine Enterprises building beginning on May 2, the two conference rooms on the 2nd floor will be used as workspaces for employees. We understand that this is an inconvenience, but we're certain you will be able to get by with the temporary setup as necessary. Departments will use the conference rooms according to the following schedule:

    Week 1 (May 2–8): Sales and Marketing
    Week 2 (May 9–15): Accounting
    Week 3 (May 16–22): Research and Development
    Week 4 (May 23–29): Human Resources

In Week 5 (May 30–June 5), renovations will take place in the lobby. The main entrance will be closed during this time, so employees and visitors should use the door on the eastern side of the building.

Thank you for your cooperation.

O'Malley Construction
Work Schedule: Perine Enterprises, May 2–June 5
Work Order: #58305 / Contact: Natalie Lantz

WEEK	LOCATION	TASKS
Week 1	4th Floor	Repaint walls, remove carpeting, install floor tiles
Week 2	5th Floor	Repaint walls, build cupboards at end of hallway
Week 3	2nd Floor	Repaint walls, window installation x 12
Week 4	3rd Floor	Repaint walls, fix broken floor tiles
Week 5	1st Floor (Lobby)	Expand entrance, install marble flooring, rewire ceiling lights

NOTICE TO PERINE ENTERPRISES STAFF

The Saginaw Avenue entrance to our building will be closed from May 30 to June 5 as part of the renovation work. For those of you who need a security card for the Turner Street entrance, please see Security Director Li Wan. The reception area will be closed during this time, but a table will be set up near the elevators, from which the receptionists will carry out their regular duties. Please inform visitors of the change. If it is easier to see visitors at an off-site location, you may be eligible to have the expenses covered by company funds. See Eleanor Butler to get permission in advance. Questions about the progress of the renovations may be directed to Gina Lombardi.

191. In the memo, the phrase "get by" in paragraph 1, line 3, is closest in meaning to
    (A) manage
    (B) receive
    (C) approve
    (D) surpass

192. Where is the accounting department located in the Perine Enterprises Building?
    (A) On the second floor
    (B) On the third floor
    (C) On the fourth floor
    (D) On the fifth floor

193. What is NOT mentioned as part of the renovation project?
    (A) Repairing some flooring
    (B) Installing new windows
    (C) Laying some carpeting
    (D) Adding a storage area

194. What is true about Perine Enterprises?
    (A) Its building's walls will all be repainted.
    (B) Its main entrance is on Saginaw Avenue.
    (C) Its employees requested site improvements.
    (D) Its reception services will be unavailable for a week.

195. Why are employees advised to contact Ms. Butler?
    (A) To provide visitors' names
    (B) To get funding approval
    (C) To ask for a security pass
    (D) To be updated on a project

Questions 196-200 refer to the following schedule, e-mail, and article.

Gaskell Creations
Sample Order Production Run
Description: Skylark full-length dress

Date	Production Plan
Sunday, May 12	– Design finalized by Anja Rembert
Monday, May 13	– Presentation of fabric options by Stroop Supplies – Request rush order on selected items
Thursday, May 16	– Production of ten dresses – Quality control inspection (dimension check, zipper test, visual analysis)
Friday, May 17	– Production of full sample
Saturday, May 18	– Completed samples sent to Orchard Fashions

---

To: Beth Ehmann <ehmannb@orchardfashions.com>
From: Tammy Culver <culvert@orchardfashions.com>
Date: May 21
Subject: Skylark dresses

Dear Ms. Ehmann,

I have received the samples of Skylark full-length dresses from Gaskell Creations. Having reviewed the production costs and the high quality of the completed samples, I believe Gaskell Creations is the right choice for this project.

Last Thursday, I participated in the quality control inspection of the first ten dresses. The following morning, I met with the factory foreman to express my concerns about uneven hemlines. He made the appropriate adjustments to the cutting machines before resuming production. The problem did not occur in any of the dresses from the full sample.

I had a teleconference with Lily Zemanski this morning, during which I explained that the only issue with our potential partnership is that Gaskell Creations does not fit with our mission statement. Ms. Zemanski promised that the company would take measures next month to resolve that issue to our satisfaction. Therefore, I am pleased to say that we are able to move forward.

Tammy Culver

Small-Town Factory Make Big Corporate Connection

August 8 — Manufacturer Gaskell Creations, located in the southern part of Clairsville, has started a partnership with its largest client in the company's history. Gaskell is now producing clothing garments for Orchard Fashions. To secure the contract, Gaskell made several training and equipment upgrades in June to bring its safety rating up.

"We were happy to make changes to make sure this agreement went forward," said Lily Zemanski, Gaskell's executive director. "The large contract means that we can earn back our investment quickly, and the change benefits our employees greatly. For the first time ever, we're turning away job applicants because we don't have room for them."

196. What activity was completed on May 13?
 (A) Designs were advertised.
 (B) Presentations were assigned.
 (C) Fabrics were ordered.
 (D) Samples were shipped.

197. What does Ms. Culver suggest about the finished sample products?
 (A) They are suitable for her company's needs.
 (B) Their quality may affect the selling price.
 (C) They were made by inexperienced workers.
 (D) They arrived later than originally scheduled.

198. When did Ms. Culver most likely meet with a factory supervisor?
 (A) May 12
 (B) May 16
 (C) May 17
 (D) May 18

199. What did Ms. Zemanski guarantee on May 21?
 (A) That more workers would be hired right away
 (B) That the products could be produced on short notice
 (C) That environmentally friendly fabrics would be used
 (D) That Gaskell Creations would improve its safety rating

200. What does Ms. Zemanski suggest about her company?
 (A) There is a high demand for its jobs.
 (B) There are plans to open a new branch.
 (C) It is the largest employer in Clairsville.
 (D) It is currently seeking new investors.

Stop! This is the end of the test. If you finish before time is called, you may go back to Part 5, 6, and 7 and check your work.

TEST 09

PART 5 · PART 6 · PART 7

준비하기

손목시계

뭉뚝한 연필과 지우개

Answer Sheet

토익 RC는 75분 동안 진행됩니다.
반드시 75분 이내에 문제 풀이와 답안지 마킹을 완료하세요.

고난도 문제는 해설집에서 확인할 수 있습니다.
해설집 p.169

TEST 09는 **고난도 문제가 많이 포함**된 대박달 :) TEST입니다.
다른 TEST에 비해 상대적으로 **환산 점수가 높게** 나올 수 있습니다.

맞은 개수	환산 점수	맞은 개수	환산 점수
96-100	465 - **495**	41-45	145 - **215**
91-95	430 - **490**	36-40	120 - **180**
86-90	400 - **465**	31-35	100 - **145**
81-85	375 - **440**	26-30	80 - **120**
76-80	340 - **415**	21-25	65 - **95**
71-75	315 - **390**	16-20	50 - **75**
66-70	285 - **365**	11-15	35 - **55**
61-65	255 - **335**	6-10	15 - **40**
56-60	225 - **305**	1-5	5 - **30**
51-55	200 - **270**	0	5
46-50	170 - **240**		

READING TEST

In the Reading test, you will read a variety of texts and answer several different types of reading comprehension questions. The entire Reading test will last 75 minutes. There are three parts, and directions are given for each part. You are encouraged to answer as many questions as possible within the time allowed.

You must mark your answers on the separate answer sheet. Do not write your answers in your test book.

PART 5

Directions: A word or phrase is missing in each of the sentences below. Four answer choices are given below each sentence. Select the best answer to complete the sentence. Then mark the letter (A), (B), (C), or (D) on your answer sheet.

101. Traffic was rerouted while the work crew painted new lane lines ------- the downtown streets.
    (A) than
    (B) until
    (C) on
    (D) as

102. Customers interested in top-quality kitchen appliances should read ------- brochure.
    (A) ours
    (B) our
    (C) theirs
    (D) they

103. Among the articles included in this month's journal, most readers agree that Dr. Cavalcanti's piece was the most -------.
    (A) prompt
    (B) dissatisfied
    (C) informative
    (D) constant

104. The bank teller assured Ms. Reeves that the ------- of the document would be protected.
    (A) confident
    (B) confidentially
    (C) confidential
    (D) confidentiality

105. The impressive ------- of the Winchell Dance Group has resulted in rave reviews by critics.
    (A) disposal
    (B) performance
    (C) renovation
    (D) compensation

106. Employees who have recently ------- a professional seminar are asked to give feedback.
    (A) to attend
    (B) attending
    (C) attended
    (D) attend

107. The water filter's ------- design reduces the growth of mold and bacteria on the surface.
    (A) innovatively
    (B) innovating
    (C) innovative
    (D) innovations

108. The new Yao Auto commercial targets young professionals ------- than the campaign from last year.
    (A) specifically
    (B) specificity
    (C) specific
    (D) more specifically

109. Please be sure to ------- the registration form to the event planners no later than Friday.
    (A) obtain
    (B) accept
    (C) submit
    (D) praise

110. The committee will discuss each new product presented and select ------- that has the best chance of market success.
    (A) other
    (B) some
    (C) one
    (D) both

111. The sales manager requested ------- to a few of the slides in the presentation.
    (A) transfers
    (B) documents
    (C) standards
    (D) revisions

112. ------- weeks of intense negotiations, the merger between GW Sports and Poncia Inc. was finally agreed.
    (A) After
    (B) Between
    (C) Before
    (D) Even

113. ------- considering the opinions of employees is important, leaders must be capable of following their own instincts.
    (A) Meanwhile
    (B) Rather
    (C) Although
    (D) Regardless

114. Park visitors should be aware ------- the trails can become very slippery in rainy weather.
    (A) so
    (B) that
    (C) while
    (D) of

115. City officials in Nashville plan to make an infrastructure ------- as soon as the funds are released.
    (A) investing
    (B) investment
    (C) invest
    (D) investors

116. Maxwell Cleaning Supplies ------- that its dishwashing liquid dissolves grease better than any other brand.
    (A) modifies
    (B) claims
    (C) attempts
    (D) involves

117. The Lansberry Business Institute offers a broad ------- of courses for professionals in a number of fields.
    (A) method
    (B) range
    (C) parcel
    (D) surplus

118. Art collectors should highly ------- the talent demonstrated in painter Ella Padovesi's new exhibition.
    (A) valued
    (B) value
    (C) valuing
    (D) valuable

119. Those who are familiar with the brand will notice designer Paula Mazzi's clothing -------, including in rural areas.
    (A) otherwise
    (B) moreover
    (C) everywhere
    (D) mutually

120. Holding the community parade in the coldest month of the year would not be ------- for planners.
    (A) senses
    (B) sensing
    (C) sensible
    (D) sense

121. If your package does not include all of the ------- items on your invoice, please contact customer service.
    (A) listed
    (B) reassured
    (C) dominated
    (D) addressed

122. The winner of the election will be officially announced ------- all of the ballots have been counted.
    (A) ever
    (B) from
    (C) these
    (D) once

123. The hiring committee's selection meeting was short, as the members ------- voted to offer the job to Ms. Steele.
    (A) nearly
    (B) unanimously
    (C) intensively
    (D) frequently

124. Businesses usually need to get government ------- in order to import goods for commercial use.
    (A) permit
    (B) permission
    (C) permitted
    (D) permitting

125. Nametags were distributed to the workshop participants ------- everyone could get to know each other more easily.
    (A) as if
    (B) except
    (C) so that
    (D) whether

126. When fully -------, the departmental reports showed a trend toward high employee satisfaction.
    (A) compile
    (B) compiles
    (C) compiled
    (D) compiler

127. If either party wants to make contract adjustments ------- those agreed upon in this session, another meeting is needed.
    (A) into
    (B) during
    (C) beyond
    (D) until

128. On the day that Shine Dental Clinic moved into the third-floor suite, the landlord added its name to the directory -------.
    (A) downstairs
    (B) until now
    (C) throughout
    (D) all in all

129. At the start of the press conference, a company spokesperson ------- reporters on the details of the merger.
    (A) briefed
    (B) recounted
    (C) discussed
    (D) expressed

130. BT Kitchens makes the most efficient use of your space by creating completely ------- cabinets.
    (A) customizes
    (B) customized
    (C) customization
    (D) customize

PART 6

Directions: Read the texts that follow. A word, phrase, or sentence is missing in parts of each text. Four answer choices for each question are given below the text. Select the best answer to complete the text. Then mark the letter (A), (B), (C), or (D) on your answer sheet.

Questions 131-134 refer to the following e-mail.

To: Ravi Harish <harishravi@dolainteriors.com>

From: Angelina Kohl <angelina@homedecmag.com>

Date: October 3

Subject: *Home Decorating Magazine* Article

Dear Mr. Harish,

Congratulations! Dola Interiors has been chosen as a "Style Star" for this quarter. Our magazine will be ------- your firm in the November issue. The "Style Star" section of our magazine highlights the work of
131.
------- that are setting trends for interior design.
132.

Do you have time for a phone interview with one of our staff members? -------. They should outline your
133.
corporate mission as well as your design strategy. This will bring some authenticity to the article. We would need to be in touch with you ------- October 25 in order to meet our publication deadline.
134.

Sincerely,

Angelina Kohl

Assistant Editor, *Home Decorating Magazine*

---

131. (A) featuring
(B) featured
(C) features
(D) feature

132. (A) procedures
(B) enterprises
(C) materials
(D) patterns

133. (A) The committee will select the questions.
(B) Our magazine's readership has been growing.
(C) A few quotes from you would be helpful.
(D) We loved the photos of the decorated room.

134. (A) besides
(B) of
(C) by
(D) within

Questions 135-138 refer to the following e-mail.

To: Livia Castro
From: Souza Electronics
Date: August 3
Subject: Order #52490

Dear Ms. Castro,

Your order has been successfully placed through our online system. Upon ------- of the packaging process, we will e-mail you again to inform you that the items have been dispatched. -------. You may use it to check the status of your delivery.
                                135.   136.

As soon as you receive your order, we ------- you to verify the contents of the package. If there is an issue, we are ------- to solve it more easily on the delivery day.
                                                137.   138.

Sincerely,

Souza Electronics

---

135. (A) elimination
(B) completion
(C) intersection
(D) generation

136. (A) The component is currently out of stock.
(B) Your account will be credited the difference.
(C) We can assist you with assembly.
(D) You will then receive a tracking code.

137. (A) have encouraged
(B) were encouraging
(C) encouraged
(D) encourage

138. (A) able
(B) comprehensive
(C) talented
(D) acceptable

Questions 139-142 refer to the following information.

Calls to international telephone numbers can be made from any office phone. First, dial 9 and then input the entire number when you hear the dial tone. As soon as your call ------- , per-minute charges will start to accrue. As these charges can be expensive, the finance team may contact you to ------- the reason for the call. There is no formal limit to the duration of international calls. -------. If you are concerned about your amount of calling time within a given month, it is ------- that you check with your supervisor. This will help you to ensure that you are keeping within a reasonable amount.

139. (A) connecting
(B) connected
(C) to connect
(D) is connected

140. (A) adjust
(B) relocate
(C) confirm
(D) terminate

141. (A) We do ask, however, that they are kept to a minimum.
(B) Thank you for reviewing the budget carefully.
(C) Your phone can be upgraded through the IT department.
(D) Other staff members may be disturbed by the sound.

142. (A) portable
(B) significant
(C) visible
(D) advisable

Questions 143-146 refer to the following memo.

To: All Staff
From: Stella Reynell, Site Manager
Re: Entertainment Coordinator
Date: April 3

Dear Staff,

From next week, Laguna Botanical Gardens will advertise a job opening for a full-time entertainment coordinator. The -------- of the "Daisy Dance Show" we held recently demonstrated the need for more activities on site, as they attract many more visitors than usual. The management team -------- the first round of interviews for this position in the first week of May. --------. Applications from the general public will also be considered, which is why we plan to post the opening on career Web sites. Those who are -------- should pick up an application from the administrative office.

Sincerely,

Stella

---

143. (A) purpose
 (B) champion
 (C) popularity
 (D) courtesy

144. (A) was beginning
 (B) began
 (C) has begun
 (D) will begin

145. (A) Our preference is to promote a current employee.
 (B) The managers usually meet once a month.
 (C) We hope you will all enjoy the performance.
 (D) The peak season may be much busier than it was last year.

146. (A) renegotiated
 (B) qualified
 (C) enrolled
 (D) affected

PART 7

Directions: In this part you will read a selection of texts, such as magazine and newspaper articles, e-mails, and instant messages. Each text or set of texts is followed by several questions. Select the best answer for each question and mark the letter (A), (B), (C), or (D) on your answer sheet.

Questions 147-148 refer to the following invitation.

Business Builders Luncheon

Thursday, March 8
11:30 A.M. – 1:00 P.M.

Thai Garden, Private Meeting Room
1926 Lang Avenue
Bloomington, IL 61701

Speaker: Georgia Rufin
"Expanding Your Customer Base on a Budget"

Tickets are $12 per person, which includes a three-course meal.
Please RSVP by March 1 so we may prepare the catering order.
Event Planner Tyson Lee: 555-7833

---

147. What will guests learn about at the event?

(A) Creating a logo
(B) Gaining more customers
(C) Using budgeting software
(D) Expanding their staff

148. What is suggested about the event?

(A) Guests should indicate whether they plan to attend.
(B) Groups can get a discount on the admission tickets.
(C) The charge for the meal depends on what is ordered.
(D) It is held every Thursday in March.

Questions 149-150 refer to the following e-mail.

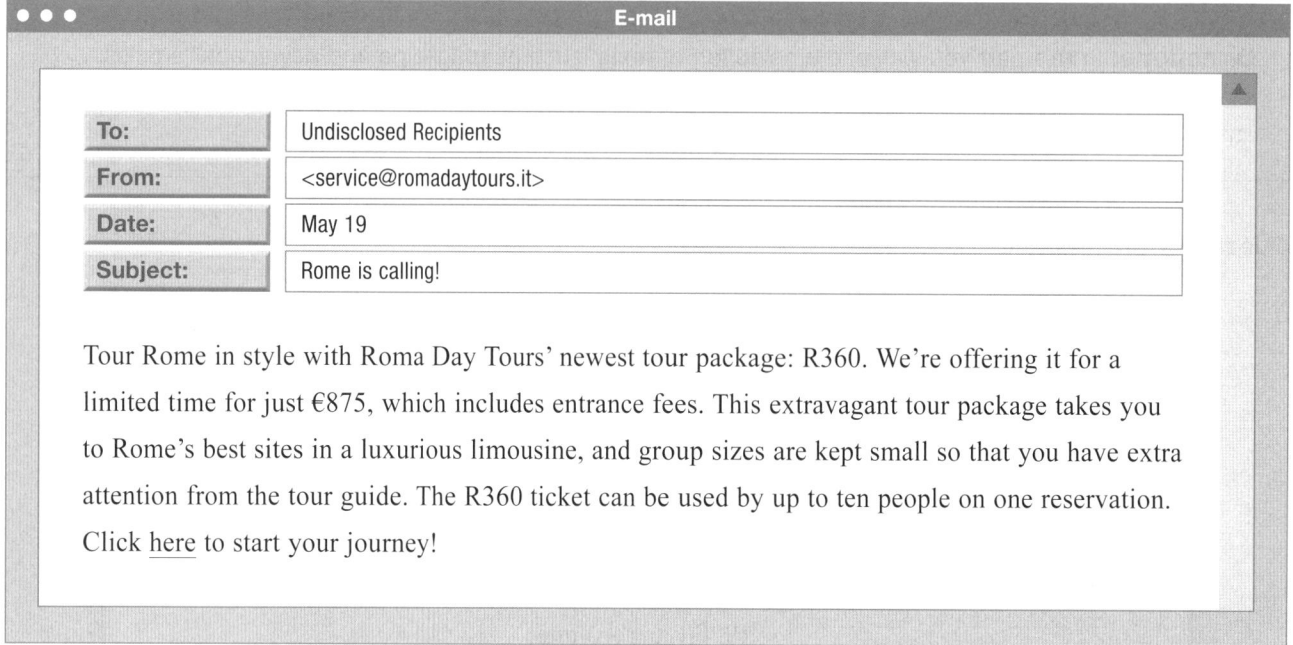

To:	Undisclosed Recipients
From:	<service@romadaytours.it>
Date:	May 19
Subject:	Rome is calling!

Tour Rome in style with Roma Day Tours' newest tour package: R360. We're offering it for a limited time for just €875, which includes entrance fees. This extravagant tour package takes you to Rome's best sites in a luxurious limousine, and group sizes are kept small so that you have extra attention from the tour guide. The R360 ticket can be used by up to ten people on one reservation. Click here to start your journey!

149. Why was the e-mail written?
    (A) To thank customers for their loyalty
    (B) To boost the sale of a luxury package
    (C) To recruit tour guides for the peak season
    (D) To publicize a schedule change

150. What is indicated about the R360 ticket?
    (A) It is for groups of people booking together.
    (B) It is limited to adults only.
    (C) It includes all meals throughout the day.
    (D) It should be ordered by phone.

Questions 151-152 refer to the following text message chain.

Isabelle Chauncy (9:03 A.M.)
Hi, Beau. I'm in the storage area of the basement getting some items for the new employee. I saw that there's a spare computer monitor in here. Didn't you say you needed a second one for your desk?

Beau Esson (9:05 A.M.)
Yes, I did, but I wasn't approved for a new purchase. I didn't know that we had a spare. I'll have to test it to see whether it's working.

Isabelle Chauncy (9:06 A.M.)
Do you want me to bring it up to you with the other items?

Beau Esson (9:07 A.M.)
It's your call. If you have too much already, I can go and get it later. Thanks.

151. Why did Ms. Chauncy contact Mr. Esson?
(A) To ask for assistance moving a desk
(B) To suggest putting more items in storage
(C) To check the arrival time of an employee
(D) To find out if he wants some equipment

152. At 9:07 A.M., what does Mr. Esson mean when he writes, "It's your call"?
(A) Ms. Chauncy should make a decision about organizing an area.
(B) Ms. Chauncy should decide whether to bring an item or not.
(C) He will wait until an order is approved by the management.
(D) He does not have time to fix Ms. Chauncy's computer.

Questions 153-154 refer to the following notice.

Aldridge Fabrics
Managing Director: Michelle Struble
Production Manager: Allen Buchanan

We hope you enjoy your time at Aldridge Fabrics. For your safety, the safety of our staff, and the quality of our products, please follow the rules below throughout your tour. Additional gear is available from the production manager. Should you have any questions about carrying Aldridge Fabrics in your store, please speak to the managing director.

Do's
- Follow your guide's instructions at all times.
- Keep your temporary ID badge visible.
- Ask questions to workers not operating machinery.
- Take photos (with the flash turned off).

Don'ts
- Distract workers operating machinery.
- Bring food or beverages into the production area.
- Get separated from your group.

153. Who most likely was the notice written for?
 (A) Fabric designers
 (B) Job recruiters
 (C) Plant visitors
 (D) Safety experts

154. According to the notice, what will Ms. Struble do?
 (A) Distribute some necessary gear
 (B) Provide product catalogs
 (C) Update the site's rules regularly
 (D) Handle inquiries regarding sales

Questions 155-157 refer to the following form.

Emerson Apartments Request Form
Building Supervisor: Diego Landeros
d.landeros@emersonapt.com / 555-4848

Tenant: Elizabeth Swanson
Tower: C
Unit: 518
Contact Number: 555-4510

Type of Request:
Tenant's Unit [✓]
Common Areas – Indoor [ ]
Common Areas – Outdoor [ ]

Description of Issue: The valve for the gas fireplace is stuck closed, so it does not turn on. The property manager, Denise Platt, said it was not a safety issue (as there is no gas odor).

Notes: Please let me know in advance when you plan to visit. I have two paintings hanging on the wall above the fireplace. I'll take these down shortly before the work begins to provide extra room for the technician.

FOR OFFICE USE ONLY
Date of Request: January 9
Ranking: Urgent [ ]   Potentially Urgent [✓]   High Priority [ ]   Standard [ ]
Received by: Jerry Tobin
Assigned to: Ryan Marrero

Instructions: Please call the tenant to inform her that you will visit today. The office can book a specialist if you determine from your inspection that it is necessary.

---

155. Why did Ms. Swanson submit the form?

(A) To tour a property
(B) To update a billing method
(C) To renew a lease
(D) To schedule a repair

156. What does Ms. Swanson mention about some paintings?

(A) They will be removed from the wall.
(B) They were received as a gift.
(C) They have an unusual odor.
(D) They were accidentally damaged.

157. Who will call Ms. Swanson on January 9?

(A) Mr. Landeros
(B) Ms. Platt
(C) Mr. Tobin
(D) Mr. Marrero

GO ON TO THE NEXT PAGE

Questions 158-160 refer to the following article.

TAIPEI (October 7)—Sampaga, a Philippines-based home furnishings store, opened its first branch in Taiwan about three months ago. The brand is known for its affordable collections of home products with bright colors and joyful patterns. Sampaga is a household name across the Philippines. —[1]—.

The new store is located in the popular Ximending neighborhood of Taipei. The store is not as large as most of the branches in the Philippines. —[2]—. However, its manager, Mei-hua Liu, has added her own idea—several small rooms set up like rooms in a house. They are decorated from top to bottom with Sampaga products. Ms. Liu believes this helps customers to visualize the products in their own homes.

—[3]—. One top-selling product is the store's line of rugs. They come in a variety of sizes and bring a pop of color to any room. These hand-woven items are becoming the trendy accessory for Taiwanese homes.

The Taipei branch may be the newest store in the Sampaga chain, but it is already the most popular. —[4]—.

158. What unique feature does the Taipei store have?

(A) Its experienced employees
(B) Its considerable size
(C) Its display rooms
(D) Its convenient location

159. What is mentioned about Sampaga's rugs?

(A) They use sustainable materials.
(B) They vary depending on the branch.
(C) They are made by hand.
(D) They are available in custom sizes.

160. In which of the positions marked [1], [2], [3], and [4] does the following sentence best belong?

"In fact, the branch broke long-standing company sales records in its first month."

(A) [1]
(B) [2]
(C) [3]
(D) [4]

Questions 161-163 refer to the following press release.

For Immediate Release
Ulyerra, PR Director Sharon Lindquist 315-555-7190

Ulyerra Helps Ryker Pharmaceuticals to Cut Energy Usage

BRISTOL (22 May)—Ryker Pharmaceuticals, has implemented a lighting system by Ulyerra to reduce energy consumption and cut the costs of utilities. Using a combination of timers and light sensors, the system is able to program the lights in all buildings in its complex to perfectly match their purpose. Electric lights can be dimmed when natural light levels are high, and lights can be set to turn off automatically in areas that aren't frequently used.

Site Manager Glenn Bradley was pleased with the results. "I was able to install the entire system myself, and it was much easier than I expected," he said.

"I looked into similar systems," reported Ryker's General Manager, Marc Coronado, "but we weren't sure whether or not we were ready for such an investment. Since Ulyerra offered a full refund if we weren't satisfied, I knew it was the right choice."

Just last month, Ryker Pharmaceuticals moved from the fourth-largest to the third-largest supplier of pharmaceuticals in the UK. Its willingness to embrace innovative technologies will certainly take it even further.

161. What is suggested about Mr. Bradley?
    (A) He invented a light-sensor system.
    (B) He prefers to work in natural light.
    (C) He performed installations at several buildings.
    (D) He has recorded a drop in energy usage.

162. Why did Mr. Coronado choose Ulyerra over its competitors?
    (A) It sold the only system of its kind.
    (B) It has the most affordable product on the market.
    (C) It was recommended by a colleague.
    (D) It came with a money-back guarantee.

163. What is indicated about Ryker Pharmaceuticals?
    (A) It was acquired by Ulyerra.
    (B) It plans to open an overseas branch.
    (C) It has recently gained market share.
    (D) It secured a contract with the government.

Questions 164-167 refer to the following information.

Feeney Accounting On-Site Refreshments

Feeney Accounting provides some refreshments to employees and visitors. These are intended to be shared, but some areas are stocked differently than others in order to help us make the best impression while keeping our costs within a reasonable range.

- A bowl of wrapped candy is positioned in the reception area and is intended for short-term visitors.
- The staff meeting room, Room 222, contains instant coffee, tea bags, and a selection of crackers and cookies. Those with allergies should check the packaging before consumption.
- Room 301 has brewed coffee and fresh pastries. These are to be served during meetings with clients only.

If you need to restock any of the non-perishable foods, you can find them in Room 335. Napkins and cups are also stored there. If we're out of any of the supplies, please inform Vernita Neilsen. However, if the budget for the month has already been spent, they may not be refilled until the following month. If you notice that an area is disorganized and you do not have time to tidy it up yourself, please contact David Haas.

164. Why was the information written?
(A) To gather food requests before an order
(B) To welcome new visitors to a building
(C) To describe a team's restructuring
(D) To outline a policy at a company

165. Where do Feeney Accounting clients most likely have meetings?
(A) In Room 222
(B) In Room 301
(C) In Room 335
(D) In the reception area

166. According to the information, why may some areas have no food?
(A) Some delicate equipment is in operation.
(B) A monthly budget has been reached.
(C) The person in charge is absent.
(D) A health code should not be violated.

167. Why should staff members contact Mr. Haas?
(A) To check on a budget
(B) To ask for more supplies
(C) To report a messy area
(D) To explain food allergies

Questions 168-171 refer to the following online chat discussion.

Liberty Hotel Online Chat Service

Wen Shao (2:14 P.M.): I took advantage of the recent offer you advertised on your Web site. It said that Liberty Rewards members who stay three nights or more at Liberty Hotel or any hotel in its network between February 1 and March 31 can receive a voucher for a free night's stay. When I checked out of Gateway Hotel, the front desk clerk said I'd get the voucher in the mail, but there's no sign of it.

Claudia McLeish (2:15 P.M.): The voucher is valid at both Liberty Hotel and our partners' hotels, and it does not have an expiration date. I'll add Jasper Rautio to this conversation, as he handles Gateway's administration. Could you give me your rewards membership number? That'll help me check into this matter.

Jasper Rautio (2:17 P.M.): I've got it here. I found Ms. Shao in our system, and her stay from February 8 to February 15 definitely makes her eligible for the voucher.

Wen Shao (2:18 P.M.): It's R389-07164.

Jasper Rautio (2:19 P.M.): The voucher will be sent the day after the promotion finishes. We have your mailing address on file. Could I help you to upgrade your Liberty Rewards account to the Premium level, which gives you more benefits?

Wen Shao (2:20 P.M.): Thanks, but I'm not interested in that. I'll wait for the voucher.

---

168. Why did Ms. Shao use the online chat service?
(A) To report that an item was not received
(B) To renew a loyalty program membership
(C) To inquire about how to use a voucher
(D) To cancel a hotel room reservation

169. At 2:17 P.M., what does Mr. Rautio suggest when he writes, "I've got it here"?
(A) He can report the invoice number.
(B) He found a lost personal item.
(C) He already looked up some information.
(D) He was able to check a balance.

170. What does Mr. Rautio offer to do?
(A) Upgrade Ms. Shao's room reservation
(B) Change Ms. Shao's membership type
(C) Send an account summary to Ms. Shao
(D) Issue a refund to Ms. Shao

171. What is NOT indicated about the Liberty Hotel voucher?
(A) It will be mailed on April 1.
(B) It can be used at sites other than Liberty Hotel.
(C) It gives the user a free stay of three nights.
(D) It does not have an expiration date.

Questions 172-175 refer to the following letter.

Sandra Duarte
1881 McCabe Drive
Oak Hill, VA 20171

Manuel Bruckner
590 Caynor Avenue
Herndon, VA 22090

Dear Mr. Bruckner,

I was searching through some old records that have now been uploaded as digital copies to the Fairfax County Web site, and they indicated that you are the current owner of the property at 559 Varner Street in Herndon. —[1]—. You are probably aware that this building is one of the oldest in Herndon, and it features some architectural elements that are rarely found in the region. —[2]—.

I'm wondering if you would like to form a partnership regarding this building. I understand that it does not meet the building codes, and, therefore, is not permitted for residential or commercial use at this time. It would be a shame if such an old building were to be abandoned or destroyed. —[3]—. If there is a way to prevent this, that would be the best-case scenario.

I propose working together to bring this building back to its former glory. I could provide capital to restore the building as part of some kind of partnership arrangement. —[4]—. I think you'll find that it would be a worthwhile project.

If you are interested in my offer, please call me so that we may discuss the matter further. My number is 703-555-7193. I hope that I will hear from you soon.

Kindest regards,

Sandra Duarte

Sandra Duarte

172. What is true about Fairfax County?
(A) It has passed stricter building regulations.
(B) It has converted some records to digital form.
(C) Its main office is in the city of Herndon.
(D) It charges a fee for registering a property.

173. What is suggested about Mr. Bruckner's Varner Street property?
(A) It cannot be used in its current condition.
(B) It is registered as a residential address.
(C) It used to be a public library.
(D) It has recently been put up for sale.

174. Why most likely does Ms. Duarte want to form a partnership?
(A) She is interested in learning about architecture.
(B) She is looking for a place to run her store.
(C) She wants to protect a historical building.
(D) She has recently entered the real estate business.

175. In which of the positions marked [1], [2], [3], and [4] does the following sentence best belong?

"You could, for example, provide me with a share of the ownership."

(A) [1]
(B) [2]
(C) [3]
(D) [4]

Questions 176-180 refer to the following e-mail and agenda.

To: Department List <departmentstaff@myraco.net>
From: Ranjan Naidu <r_naidu@myraco.net>
Date: July 18
Subject: Monthly Meeting

Dear Team,

The next departmental monthly meeting for Myra Co. will take place on Thursday, July 20, at 3 P.M. in the main conference room. I've invited Robert Sabo and his department to join us, as the speakers can benefit both teams. The agenda I sent you has one change. Mr. Sabo will take over Mr. Crawford's time slot, and Mr. Crawford's talk will be moved to next month's agenda.

For those of you who have volunteered to assist with the customer feedback questionnaire, please write down your question ideas before the meeting. We'll meet after the main meeting to discuss which ones should be included.

See you at the meeting!

Ranjan

Myra Co. Departmental Monthly Meeting Agenda
July 20, 3:00 P.M. – 6:30 P.M.

Speaker	Topic	Details
Pamela Toth	Customer Care	Tips for interacting with customers How to suggest items to accompany makeup purchases
Darrell Crawford	Social Media Strategy	Review of social media marketing plan
Maria Elliot, founder of Environment Connect	Local Outreach	Weekend volunteer opportunities for Myra Co. employees at this environmental charity
Augusta Ramos	Product Demonstration	Sample the company's new hand cream Brief feedback session regarding the item's packaging
Lori Vogel	Newsletter Launch	Information on a monthly newsletter for customers and how to contribute articles

176. What does Mr. Naidu suggest about the meeting in his e-mail?
(A) Participants will share a meal together after the meeting.
(B) More people will be in attendance than initially expected.
(C) The site of the meeting will be in a different place.
(D) Many of the speakers had to cancel their talks.

177. What topic will meeting participants hear about in August?
(A) Newsletter Launch
(B) Customer Care
(C) Social Media Strategy
(D) Product Demonstration

178. What are some employees asked to do prior to the meeting?
(A) Research the market trends
(B) Order some product samples
(C) Review the sales figures
(D) Prepare some survey questions

179. According to the agenda, what is true about Ms. Elliot?
(A) She is the newest team member of Myra Co.
(B) She started a local charity.
(C) She will arrive at the meeting late.
(D) She works in Mr. Naidu's department.

180. What type of goods does Myra Co. most likely sell?
(A) Footwear
(B) Cosmetics
(C) Office supplies
(D) Power tools

GO ON TO THE NEXT PAGE

Questions 181-185 refer to the following e-mail and policy information.

---

e-mail

To: Margaret Wenski <m_wenski@edr1.com>
From: Tae-min Lim <limtaemin@anaheimco.com>
Date: March 2
Subject: From Anaheim Co.
Attachment: anaheimstaff.dox

Dear Ms. Wenski,

Welcome to Anaheim Co. Your start date will be Monday, March 6. I understand that my colleague, Janet Baxter, figured that it would be best for you to receive the training materials in advance. However, the policy information file that she sent you is from last year. Please delete that file and refer to the attached one instead.

Monday and Tuesday will be made up of training activities, and then you'll have your first visit to a client's office on Friday. Vincent Trevisan will accompany you, so you will mainly take on an observer role.

Please note that on your first day, you will be issued your own company laptop with special software loaded onto it. If you have any questions before your first day, please feel free to e-mail me.

Warmest regards,

Tae-min Lim

Anaheim Co.
Policy Information

Parking
The northern parking lot is reserved for employees only. The pass needed for this lot can be picked up in the HR office. The southern lot is for visitors, who can purchase an hourly pass at the gate. The cost can be refunded if they show a validated ticket on the way out. The east and west parking lots are a combination of visitor and employee parking. They both require a valid pass. No overnight parking is permitted.

Electronic Equipment
Employees are responsible for taking care of the electronic equipment assigned to them. Each employee receives a desktop computer, except receptionists in the administration department, who share one computer at the desk. Graphic designers have an additional assigned laptop, one per person. This should be used when working from home due to the software installed on it. Sales team members may check out a laptop from IT if needed for off-site sales presentations. The standard maximum is three days, but this can be extended with a manager's approval.

181. Why did Mr. Lim send the e-mail?

(A) To explain topics in an orientation session
(B) To provide an updated document
(C) To inform a new employee of a schedule change
(D) To confirm changes to an employment contract

182. In the e-mail, the word "figured" in paragraph 1, line 2, is closest in meaning to

(A) appeared
(B) followed
(C) computed
(D) thought

183. What is suggested about Ms. Wenski?

(A) She will be trained by Ms. Baxter.
(B) She must provide her own computer equipment.
(C) She will meet with a client in March.
(D) She must pass a training test on her first day.

184. What department will Ms. Wenski most likely work in?

(A) Administration
(B) Graphic design
(C) IT
(D) Sales

185. According to the policy information, what is true about all Anaheim Co. parking lots?

(A) A parking pass is required.
(B) Visitors are allowed to park at no cost.
(C) They each offer the same number of spaces.
(D) Employees can park overnight if needed.

GO ON TO THE NEXT PAGE

Questions 186-190 refer to the following e-mails and memo.

To: Eugenia Arcuri <e.arcuri@cunhasoftware.com>
From: Sunder Pandya <s.pandya@cunhasoftware.com>
Date: November 3
Subject: A few suggestions

Dear Ms. Arcuri,

I continue to receive a lot of complaints about the lack of meeting spaces in our building. I've spoken to other team leaders, who have reported the same problem. Team communication is essential to our operations. Due to this, teams are regularly having to hold meetings after the office closing time, with no additional pay for employees, as it is the only way to get an empty room.

I believe that the company should reimburse the cost of drinks and food so that teams can meet at a nearby coffee shop. We should also look into renting an additional meeting room off-site to help relieve the pressure. Another option would be to limit the number of team meetings per week so that everyone has a chance to use the room. Thank you for considering my ideas.

Sincerely,

Sunder Pandya

To: Cunha Software Employees
From: Eugenia Arcuri
Date: November 24
Subject: Meeting rooms

In an effort to improve the meeting room situation at our company, we have rented a private room at Bowman Tower, which is the building next to ours. The room is available all day on Tuesdays and Thursdays. We've also ordered a Zuniga flat-screen TV for our own conference room, which will be delivered on November 27.

Some of you have been holding small meetings in the break room. Please refrain from doing so, as this is supposed to be a place of rest, and it should be kept as quiet as possible. We will remodel the storage room on the third floor to create a small meeting room that can be used by up to 6 people. I hope the above solutions help resolve the problem.

E-mail

To:	Eugenia Arcuri <e.arcuri@cunhasoftware.com>
From:	Zuniga <orders@zuniga.com>
Date:	November 25
Subject:	Zuniga Order

Dear Ms. Arcuri,

Thanks for being a Zuniga customer! We stand by the quality of our products. That's why customers may send items back to the store within 6 weeks of the delivery date. This can be done for any reason, and we will issue you a full refund. Please note that all original packaging materials should be included.

Are you hanging onto faulty or outdated electronic device because they cannot go in the regular trash? We've just started a new program to help the environment. We will pick up your old electronics and recycle them properly to prevent harmful chemicals from leaking into our ecosystem. To find out more, visit our Web site.

Regards,

Albert Mills
Zuniga Customer Service

---

186. According to Mr. Pandya, how has the lack of meeting spaces affected to employees?

(A) They have sent more information by e-mail.
(B) They have changed the size of their teams.
(C) They have had to stay late at the office.
(D) They have had to bring their own equipment.

187. Which recommendation made by Mr. Pandya did Ms. Arcuri adopt?

(A) Renting an off-site location
(B) Holding meetings by teleconference
(C) Reimbursing café spending
(D) Limiting the duration of meetings

188. In the memo, what does Mr. Arcuri mention about the break room?

(A) It is located on the third floor.
(B) It will undergo a remodeling project.
(C) Its noise levels should be kept low.
(D) Its space is suitable for small meetings.

189. What is indicated about the new monitor purchased by Cunha Software?

(A) It will be installed in Bowman Tower.
(B) It was requested by the team leaders.
(C) It was ordered on November 27.
(D) It can be returned anytime in December.

190. What service has Zuniga recently added?

(A) Extended warranties
(B) Used electronics recycling
(C) Weekend delivery
(D) Online tracking

Questions 191-195 refer to the following article, e-mail, and program.

Galway Traditional Music Festival

GALWAY (August 7)—Back by popular demand, the Galway Traditional Music Festival is scheduled for October 10–16 this year. The festival was founded by a group of fiddlers who wanted to share their music with a wider audience. Since its founding, the festival has grown in size and has made people interested in traditional Irish music again.

The festival will mainly take place at Straffan Park. Admission is free to the public, and a total of 50 musicians will put on performances on the outdoor stage. A closing ceremony on the final day of the festival will be held at the Bluebell Center, which is adjacent to the park. This is the only part of the festival that is by invitation only.

A complete list of performances is available at www.galwaymusic.ie. Visitors are encouraged to take public transportation to the event, as parking at Straffan Park is limited.

To: Calvin Vaughn
From: Adrienne Kenner
Date: August 10
Subject: RE: Music Festival Awards

Dear Mr. Vaughn,

I'm delighted to hear that you were able to adjust your schedule to accommodate the festival awards ceremony. We were ready to present your award via teleconferencing, but it's even better that you'll be there to accept it yourself. The doors at the Bluebell Center will open for guests at 6:30 P.M. Bonnie Forbes, the festival's event planner, will introduce you and present the award.

You will be sent one ticket in the mail, so please provide me with your mailing address at your earliest convenience. It is valid for yourself and a guest of your choice. Please note that tickets are available through the event committee only and are not being sold to the public.

Warmest regards,

Adrienne Kenner
Administrator, Galway Traditional Music Festival

Galway Traditional Music Festival Closing Ceremony
Order of Events

6:30 P.M.	Doors Open
7:00 P.M.	Welcome Speech by Mayor Amy McDaniel
7:10 P.M.	Musical Presentation: Irish fiddle, Darcy Byrne and the Lark Dance Troupe
8:00 P.M.	Music Awards presented by Robert Wright
8:20 P.M.	Donor Appreciation Award presented by Bonnie Forbes
8:30 P.M.	Lifetime Achievement Award presented by Aidan Quinn
8:40 P.M.	Musical Presentation: Celtic harp, Dylan Flynn
9:30 P.M.	Closing Speech by Amy McDaniel

191. What is indicated about the festival?
(A) It will increase the number of stage shows this year.
(B) It has renewed an interest in an art form.
(C) It has been running for 50 years.
(D) It offers traditional musical instruments for sale.

192. What is Ms. Kenner pleased about?
(A) Mr. Vaughn has nominated her for an award.
(B) Mr. Vaughn will make an in-person appearance.
(C) She will be able to get a last-minute ticket.
(D) She was selected to give a speech.

193. What is implied about the closing event's tickets?
(A) They should be picked up at the Bluebell Center.
(B) They will generate money to support the festival.
(C) They can be purchased online by customers.
(D) They permit two people to enter with the same ticket.

194. Who most likely is Dylan Flynn?
(A) An event planner
(B) A city official
(C) A performer
(D) A reporter

195. Why most likely is Mr. Vaughn receiving an award?
(A) He formed his own musical group.
(B) He has dedicated his life to music.
(C) He made a donation to an event.
(D) He teaches a music class.

GO ON TO THE NEXT PAGE

Questions 196-200 refer to the following e-mails and letter.

To: Sasha Juarez <sashaj@arroya.com.au>
From: Connor Walkom <c_walkom@montagu.com.au>
Date: July 19
Subject: Letter of recommendation

Dear Ms. Juarez,

Thank you for writing a reference for my application to Carnegie Publishing. I was excited about this opportunity, but ultimately I was not selected for the position. I was required to take an online screening test, which I scored very low on. I thought my experience editing instruction manuals for technical devices when I worked at Montagu would carry over well. However, the test included a lot of literary questions, because the job was for a literary magazine, and my degree and experience are not in that field. I will keep you posted on my job hunt.

Warmest regards,

Connor

Connor Walkom
708 Moruya Road
BRISBANE QLD 4001

August 5

Dear Mr. Walkom,

On behalf of Bayview Manufacturing, I would like to welcome you to our team. During the interview at our head office, you showed a thorough understanding of our needs. The sample work you provided from Montagu was a perfect fit, as you will have a very similar position here.

Enclosed you will find the orientation materials for your first day of work, August 12. Please report to work at 9 A.M. You should first go to my office, which is number 211. There you will meet Marvin Carillo, who will be your immediate supervisor. He will conduct the training for you and will introduce you to the rest of the team. At 11:30 A.M., you'll pick up your ID badge from the security department. The lunch plan has not been finalized yet, but it will most likely be in the cafeteria with your team.

See you on August 12!

Rafael Prescott

To: Sasha Juarez <sashaj@arroya.com.au>
From: Connor Walkom <c_walkom@montagu.com.au>
Date: August 7
Subject: Success!

Dear Ms. Juarez,

I've been offered a job with Bayview Manufacturing. In fact, I was given the employment contract at the close of my interview! This job is a perfect fit for me, and I appreciate your work in writing recommendation letters throughout my job search.

Warmest regards,

Connor

196. Why was Mr. Walkom not offered a job at Carnegie Publishing?
(A) He performed poorly on a test.
(B) He could not provide a copy of his degree.
(C) He arrived late for an interview.
(D) He asked for too high a salary.

197. What is implied about Mr. Walkom?
(A) He recently completed his university education.
(B) He used to work on Mr. Prescott's team.
(C) He left his job at Montagu because he moved to a new city.
(D) He will review technical manuals for Bayview Manufacturing.

198. Who most likely is Mr. Carillo?
(A) A financial specialist
(B) A senior editor
(C) A company investor
(D) An HR director

199. According to the letter, where should Mr. Walkom go at 11:30 A.M. on August 12?
(A) To a security office
(B) To a break room
(C) To a cafeteria
(D) To Mr. Prescott's office

200. How did Mr. Walkom receive his contract?
(A) By e-mail
(B) By fax
(C) In person
(D) By mail

Stop! This is the end of the test. If you finish before time is called, you may go back to Part 5, 6, and 7 and check your work.

TEST 10

PART 5 · PART 6 · PART 7

준비하기

손목시계

뭉뚝한 연필과 지우개

Answer Sheet

토익 RC는 75분 동안 진행됩니다.
반드시 75분 이내에 문제 풀이와 답안지 마킹을 완료하세요.

고난도 문제는 해설집에서 확인할 수 있습니다.
해설집 p.190

TEST 10은 **고난도 문제가 평균적으로 포함된** 평달 TEST입니다.
환산 점수가 중간값으로 나올 수 있습니다.

맞은 개수	환산 점수	맞은 개수	환산 점수
96-100	465 - 495	41-45	145 - 215
91-95	430 - 490	36-40	120 - 180
86-90	400 - 465	31-35	100 - 145
81-85	375 - 440	26-30	80 - 120
76-80	340 - 415	21-25	65 - 95
71-75	315 - 390	16-20	50 - 75
66-70	285 - 365	11-15	35 - 55
61-65	255 - 335	6-10	15 - 40
56-60	225 - 305	1-5	5 - 30
51-55	200 - 270	0	5
46-50	170 - 240		

READING TEST

In the Reading test, you will read a variety of texts and answer several different types of reading comprehension questions. The entire Reading test will last 75 minutes. There are three parts, and directions are given for each part. You are encouraged to answer as many questions as possible within the time allowed.

You must mark your answers on the separate answer sheet. Do not write your answers in your test book.

PART 5

Directions: A word or phrase is missing in each of the sentences below. Four answer choices are given below each sentence. Select the best answer to complete the sentence. Then mark the letter (A), (B), (C), or (D) on your answer sheet.

101. Ms. Floyd will ------- the information to all of her employees.
(A) forwarded
(B) forward
(C) forwards
(D) forwarding

102. ------- the recent economic crisis, Richland Manufacturing has increased its workforce by 15 percent.
(A) About
(B) Instead
(C) Very
(D) Despite

103. The HR department will throw a party to ------- Ariel Pacheco, the new chief financial officer.
(A) welcome
(B) replace
(C) transfer
(D) retire

104. Switzerland's most ------- chocolatier will soon be expanding into Germany.
(A) popularity
(B) popularly
(C) popular
(D) popularize

105. Norman Technologies' sales ------- in the last quarter even though it introduced a new product.
(A) fall
(B) falls
(C) fell
(D) fallen

106. The ------- of discount chain stores to the Akron Mall can bring in more low-budget shoppers.
(A) addition
(B) vendor
(C) service
(D) position

107. Mr. Cohen is conducting a survey to see if more serving staff members should -------.
(A) have hired
(B) be hiring
(C) hire
(D) be hired

108. When returning books ------- of library hours, please use the book drop box near the entrance.
(A) across
(B) outside
(C) until
(D) except

109. ------- customers are encouraged to join a membership of Ramsey Sporting for extra rewards points.
(A) Frequent
(B) Willing
(C) Repeated
(D) Quick

110. The ideal candidate for this job ------- would have extensive experience in marketing.
(A) open
(B) opened
(C) opens
(D) opening

111. Don't forget to confirm the shipping address ------- filing a new contract.
(A) from
(B) to
(C) when
(D) until

112. Ripley Power, Inc. has produced a new solar panel that is ------- more innovative than any other of its kind.
(A) considerable
(B) considerably
(C) considering
(D) considered

113. The CEO of Neo Producers ------- the press that his company's acquisition of Eastland Company has almost been finalized.
(A) told
(B) stated
(C) spoke
(D) mentioned

114. All inquiries regarding the new accounting software will be ------- answered by the manager of the technical support team.
(A) currently
(B) personally
(C) smoothly
(D) equally

115. Upon ------- the regular inspection yesterday, Mr. Maki wrote a report of its results to his supervisor.
(A) complete
(B) completion
(C) completing
(D) completed

116. Due to Ms. Reyes' plan to retire in September, Dorsey Industries decided to recruit her ------- from inside the company.
(A) achievement
(B) replacement
(C) ceremony
(D) organization

117. The high-speed Internet service ------- by Coyote Cable has been received favorably by customers.
(A) provide
(B) provides
(C) provided
(D) providing

118. ------- he was accepted for the position in Tokyo, Mr. Kim began preparing to move overseas.
(A) As soon as
(B) If
(C) Whereas
(D) Besides

119. Special holiday bonuses will be given to the salespeople ------- sales figures exceeded their annual goals.
(A) who
(B) which
(C) that
(D) whose

120. This handbook describes each of the ------- skills for the professional engineering license.
(A) competing
(B) essential
(C) dedicated
(D) dependent

121. BoBo Tech's new tablet ------- highly profitable, so the company decided to continue producing it.
    (A) proved
    (B) created
    (C) earned
    (D) applied

122. Mr. Gates held training sessions for all of the sales floor associates ------- before installing the new cash registers.
    (A) right
    (B) almost
    (C) often
    (D) more

123. Longwood Seniors' Community is well-known for having a ------- and safe neighborhood.
    (A) relaxation
    (B) relax
    (C) relaxed
    (D) relaxing

124. The engineer put the engine in the rear end of the car ------- make it more evenly balanced.
    (A) in addition to
    (B) as a result of
    (C) in order to
    (D) on behalf of

125. Chester Hall was ------- designed to accommodate a wide variety of musical performances.
    (A) punctually
    (B) intentionally
    (C) aggressively
    (D) enormously

126. ------- for employment at successful companies is strong, so job applicants should write impressive résumés.
    (A) Competitor
    (B) Compete
    (C) Competitive
    (D) Competition

127. Board members gathered at the Middleton branch to decide ------- they should sell the company.
    (A) whose
    (B) what
    (C) who
    (D) whether

128. Rainbow Café is always crowded with tourists thanks to its ------- to the National History Museum.
    (A) navigation
    (B) attraction
    (C) necessity
    (D) proximity

129. Hirohito Robostars has announced that its new assembly robot will be ------- at the Tokyo Expo this summer.
    (A) decreased
    (B) referred
    (C) unveiled
    (D) urged

130. Travis Barber, a sales team head, requested that he ------- one-on-one interviews with all new salespeople.
    (A) conducted
    (B) conducts
    (C) conduct
    (D) will conduct

PART 6

Directions: Read the texts that follow. A word, phrase, or sentence is missing in parts of each text. Four answer choices for each question are given below the text. Select the best answer to complete the text. Then mark the letter (A), (B), (C), or (D) on your answer sheet.

Questions 131-134 refer to the following letter.

Huiling Lee
Pasir Pajang Road
Singapore 619998

Dear Ms. Lee,

I'd like to inform you about a ------- in our quarterly catalog. We have discontinued the CTR-60 external
                                 131.
hard drive, so it should not have been included. I have enclosed the updated copy of the catalog. -------.
                                                                                                  132.
Your order for the CTR-60 has been canceled. If you place a new order ------- the next two weeks, you will
                                                                      133.
be eligible for free shipping due to our autumn sale, which runs until October 10. ------- that your order is
                                                                                   134.
received in time, we recommend placing it via our Web site, www.ophirelectronics.com.

Sincerely,

Ophir Electronics

---

131. (A) misprint
(B) collection
(C) price
(D) promotion

132. (A) We have resolved the safety issue found in earlier versions.
(B) These can be downloaded at no cost to the customer.
(C) The hard drive can store more data than ever before.
(D) It will show you exactly what we have available at this time.

133. (A) thanks to
(B) since
(C) instead of
(D) within

134. (A) Ensured
(B) To ensure
(C) Ensures
(D) Having ensured

Questions 135-138 refer to the following memo.

To: All Romani Consulting staff
From: Philip Shealey
Date: May 4
Re: Yamal Gupte

Hello Everyone,

Because so many people participated in the first two professional development skills events, we're pleased to bring you this ------- workshop led by Yamal Gupte. We have arranged for him to visit our company on May 22. Mr. Gupte ------- a number of strategies for maximizing social media for product promotion. This is the only workshop that is available to all staff members. -------. Mr. Gupte is a leading motivation speaker, so this is a fantastic opportunity to learn from him. Ms. Yates in the administration office is responsible for ------- a participant list, so please talk to her to sign up.

Thank you.

135. (A) private
 (B) weekly
 (C) initial
 (D) recent

136. (A) will introduce
 (B) introduced
 (C) will have introduced
 (D) has been introduced

137. (A) For several years, Mr. Gupte operated a small Web site.
 (B) Each activity comes with its own handbook.
 (C) The others are for management-level employees only.
 (D) You probably have at least one social media account.

138. (A) who created
 (B) creates
 (C) having created
 (D) the creation of

Questions 139-142 refer to the following e-mail.

To: Fang Jin <fangjin@grand-mail.net>
From: Noah Cole <n.cole@hartway101.net>
Date: September 16
Subject: Freelance Project

Dear Mr. Jin,

I am the editor of a Web site that posts news from the cosmetics industry. We have set a goal of ------- our
                                                                                                    139.
contents in five different languages by the end of next year. Since performing English to Chinese translation
is your -------, I think you would be perfect for this project. If you're not working in the cosmetics industry,
        140.
some of our articles may seem ------- boring, but they are useful to many companies around the world. We
                              141.
have hundreds of articles that need to be translated. To see if we can work well together, I'd like to have you
translate five articles at first. -------. Please let me know your availability.
                                142.

Thank you!

Noah Cole

---

139. (A) offers
(B) offering
(C) offer
(D) offered

140. (A) capacity
(B) requirement
(C) specialty
(D) response

141. (A) else
(B) rather
(C) soon
(D) still

142. (A) If possible, the cosmetics should be shipped quickly.
(B) Sadly, we were disappointed with the level of service.
(C) These visitors can learn a lot from the provided information.
(D) If this is successful, we'll give you a full-time contract.

Questions 143-146 refer to the following article.

Relief for Commuters on the Horizon

January 5—At a meeting held at City Hall yesterday, the Detroit Highway Association (DHA) announced plans to create a toll road to ease traffic congestion in the western part of the city. -------. Commuters who use the current road often complain about the traffic backups, especially during rush hour. -------, the city is exploring ways to relieve this pressure without putting an unnecessary burden on taxpayers. Work could begin on the new road as early as this summer. A committee has been set up to ------- bids from contractors. A ------- by committee members will be made on April 1.

143. (A) The area has seen a decrease in population.
(B) The city welcomes workers from all over the state.
(C) The road would provide an alternative to route I-94.
(D) The DHA is pleased with the final result.

144. (A) In conclusion
(B) As a result
(C) In contrast
(D) For instance

145. (A) accept
(B) insist
(C) convince
(D) launch

146. (A) decided
(B) decide
(C) decision
(D) decisive

PART 7

Directions: In this part you will read a selection of texts, such as magazine and newspaper articles, e-mails, and instant messages. Each text or set of texts is followed by several questions. Select the best answer for each question and mark the letter (A), (B), (C), or (D) on your answer sheet.

Questions 147-148 refer to the following notice.

Tony's Steakhouse

ENJOY AN APPETIZER ON THE HOUSE!

After eating at any of Tony's Steakhouse locations, go online to www.tonyssteak.com/survey to win a coupon for a FREE appetizer of your choice with the purchase of any meal!

If you are placing a takeout order on the phone and want to apply an appetizer coupon to your bill, please be sure to mention it before coming to pick up your order to ensure that your total is accurate.

---

147. What is indicated about Tony's Steakhouse?

(A) It offers reward points to diners.
(B) It has multiple locations.
(C) It has a separate takeout menu.
(D) It takes online reservations.

148. What are takeout customers asked to do to get a complimentary appetizer?

(A) Mention a coupon
(B) Call in advance
(C) Become a member
(D) Use a pick-up counter

Questions 149-150 refer to the following product review.

Armor Shell

Even though I'm not a professional photographer, I have enjoyed taking pictures of everyday moments with my high-end digital camera, DP-150. I do my best to handle it with care, but getting worn out and scratched is unavoidable in daily use. Sometimes it slips out of my hand and drops on the floor. That is why I tried the Armor Shell casing to protect my camera from cracking or breaking. Even though it has been bumped into walls and objects, there have been no signs of damage since using Armor Shell. I recommend this product to everyone with a digital camera. If you are skeptical, it offers a 100% satisfaction policy. You can always return it for a full refund if you are not happy with it.

149. What product is reviewed?

(A) An earphone set
(B) A digital camera
(C) A battery charger
(D) A camera case

150. What is mentioned about the product?

(A) It received favorable reviews from industry experts.
(B) It has a money-back guarantee.
(C) It is lighter than other similar products.
(D) It is heat and water resistant.

Questions 151-152 refer to the following text message chain.

Troy Whitlock   10:11 A.M.
The Getz Corporation representatives will be here this afternoon to present ideas for our spring ad campaign.

Lian Zou   10:12 A.M.
That's for our Angus Athletic line, right?

Troy Whitlock   10:14 A.M.
Yes. Some of the product developers will be there. Are you going?

Lian Zou   10:15 A.M.
Probably not. I was disappointed that the meeting is scheduled to take place in Conference Room C. That's too small to include many people.

Troy Whitlock   10:16 A.M.
It's been changed.

Lian Zou   10:19 A.M.
Oh, really? Where is it now?

Troy Whitlock   10:21 A.M.
In the main conference room. The first presenter will be Carol Dodson at 1 P.M.

Lian Zou   10:22 A.M.
Okay. In that case, I'll be there as long as my manager says it's okay.

---

151. At 10:16 A.M., what does Mr. Whitlock mean when he writes, "It's been changed"?
(A) A new policy was approved.
(B) A meeting will start late.
(C) Attendance is now mandatory.
(D) A problem has been resolved.

152. Who most likely is Ms. Dodson?
(A) A product developer
(B) A Getz Corporation employee
(C) Ms. Zou's manager
(D) An Angus Athletic investor

Questions 153-155 refer to the following notice.

Upcoming Events

Aurora Theater will be featuring a series of performances this summer from July 6 through August 30. Jackie Astor, who just took over as the theater's head manager last month, announced that she wants to do something new this summer. Unlike previous years, this summer will solely feature solo artists. The move was praised by Nancy Short in her article in the May edition of *Monthly Entertainment in Aurora*. Some of the upcoming solo acts include Mario Torres doing stand-up comedy, Jillian Villa playing Mozart on the piano, and Hector Fray performing monologues based on Shakespeare's original works. In Ms. Short's May article, she mentioned, "It's not every day you get to enjoy an outdoor concert solo by a recipient of a Golden Piano prize." Anyone interested can find more details regarding the event on Aurora Theater's Web site, www.auroratheater.com, or by picking up a pamphlet at the box office.

153. What is mentioned about the theater?
(A) Its stage is too small for large groups.
(B) It is being operated by new management.
(C) It only operates seasonally.
(D) It recently underwent renovations.

154. Who most likely is Ms. Short?
(A) A performer
(B) A film critic
(C) A journalist
(D) A director

155. Who has won an award?
(A) Hector Fray
(B) Nancy Short
(C) Mario Torres
(D) Jillian Villa

Questions 156-157 refer to the following contract form.

Project Adjustment Details

Contractor: Connie McCarthy – McCarthy Roofing & Siding – 444 Bronson Road, Hardenville, MO 65666
Client: Gregory Houston – 4425 Court Street, Olivette, MO 63132
Begin On: 7 August
Finish By: 16 August

This document specifies the adjustments made to the original contract signed on 28 July.

Additional / Cancelled Work: Weatherproof paint will be used on the siding instead of regular paint as per request of Mr. Houston.
Original Fee (Including Labor & Materials): $4,700
Net Fee Change: $400
Final Agreed Upon Cost: $5,100
Other Notes: 10% ($510) is due on the start date. The remainder ($4,590) is due upon completion of the specified work.

Contractor: *Connie McCarthy*
Connie McCarthy

Client: *Gregory Houston*
Gregory Houston

156. Why was the original contract altered?
(A) A different material was selected.
(B) The work date had to be postponed.
(C) Additional work was requested.
(D) The work needed to be finished earlier.

157. How much will Mr. Houston most likely owe McCarthy Roofing & Siding on 16 August?
(A) $510
(B) $4,590
(C) $4,700
(D) $5,100

GO ON TO THE NEXT PAGE

Questions 158-160 refer to the following e-mail.

To: Lorna Parnell <lornaparnell@exactagencyteam.com>
From: Asif Mustafi <asif.mustafi@miventerprises.net>
Date: August 15
Subject: Photos

Dear Ms. Parnell,

Thank you for letting me know about the watermark on the photos you downloaded from our collection for your advertising campaign. As you correctly pointed out, your photos should not have our watermark on them because you are a paid subscriber. —[1]—. It seems the problem stems from the fact that your assistant sent the purchase request from a personal e-mail account rather than from your business account. —[2]—. As we process thousands of requests for images each day, we use an automated system. The request was flagged as a "One-Time Request," which contains a watermark so the image can't be copied, when it should have been a "Paid Subscriber Request," which is the full version for corporate use. I have updated the request on our system manually. —[3]—.

In the future, as long as you process requests using the e-mail address registered on the system, you should have no further difficulties. —[4]—. Once again, please accept my apologies for any inconvenience caused.

Best regards,

Asif Mustafi
Customer Service Manager
MIV Enterprises

---

158. What type of company most likely is MIV Enterprises?

(A) An Internet provider
(B) A photo library
(C) An advertising agency
(D) A graphic design institute

159. What is NOT mentioned by Mr. Mustafi?

(A) The volume of requests processed daily
(B) The difference between account types
(C) The system upgrade requirements
(D) The preferred login method

160. In which of the positions marked [1], [2], [3] and [4] does the following sentence best belong?

"You should now be able to log in normally and download the correct version of the files you need."

(A) [1]
(B) [2]
(C) [3]
(D) [4]

Questions 161-164 refer to the following notice.

Rational Running

Rational Running is coming to Lewiston on Sunday, April 7! Find a local business that is willing to sponsor you to run in this fundraising event. The more people who run, the more will be raised!

All of the money raised by Rational Running events is used to support local food drives. The proceeds from this event will go to the Lewiston Soup Kitchen. Volunteering to participate in this event as either a runner or an assistant coordinator also counts as community service time. See a Soup Kitchen representative to get a validation signature.

The race will be held at Lewiston High School on its outdoor track. Anyone who lives nearby and is not participating in the event is encouraged to come and cheer on the runners.

A check-in booth will be set up by the north side of the bleachers. The booth will also be selling memorabilia t-shirts. Also, volunteers will hand out flyers that feature the names of each runner and all of his or her sponsors.

For more information about volunteering or making a donation to the Lewiston Soup Kitchen, please visit www.lewistonrationalrunning.org.

---

161. What is the main purpose of the notice?

(A) To encourage people to exercise regularly
(B) To announce a policy change
(C) To promote a charity event
(D) To profile a local business

162. What most likely is Lewiston Soup Kitchen?

(A) A restaurant
(B) A food bank
(C) An animal shelter
(D) A farm

163. What is mentioned about participating runners?

(A) They receive official recognition for participating.
(B) They are required to pay a registration fee.
(C) They are expected to attend an orientation.
(D) They will be given a free t-shirt.

164. Where can attendees learn more about event sponsors?

(A) From a Web site
(B) From a registration booth
(C) From an event pamphlet
(D) From a local newspaper

Questions 165-167 refer to the following letter.

Fitness Magazine
PO Box 51854
Denver, CO 80907

3 September

Jacquie Berman
1872 Berry Street
Colorado Springs, CO 80903

Dear Ms. Berman,

Congratulations on renewing your subscription to *Fitness Magazine* for another year! Your renewal also qualifies you for a free trial subscription to any other magazine run by our publisher. That's two months longer than normal four-month trial periods. Enclosed you can find a full list of our publisher's magazines.

Now that you have been reading our magazine for a year, we would like to hear from you. Please fill out the survey on the back side of this page and return it to us. For your convenience, we included a pre-addressed postage-paid envelope so that you don't have to go to the post office.

Sincerely,

Michael Boles
Customer Service Representative

---

165. How long can Ms. Berman receive a free magazine?

(A) For 3 months
(B) For 4 months
(C) For 6 months
(D) For 12 months

166. What is enclosed with the letter?

(A) A membership card
(B) A list of periodicals
(C) An order form
(D) A meal voucher

167. What is Ms. Berman asked to do?

(A) Make a payment on time
(B) Mail back a feedback form
(C) Write a comment online
(D) Update her contact information

Questions 168-171 refer to the following online chat discussion.

John Bautista [9:54 A.M.]	Are there any questions you have before this afternoon's planning meeting? I'm so pleased that Eunha Baek agreed to give a talk at our museum.
Satya Kamei [9:55 A.M.]	Me too. I've read several of her studies in journals, and I'm looking forward to hearing more about her research. The Marshall Center agreed to let us rent the hall for half off the usual rate.
Kun Quan [9:56 A.M.]	That's wonderful news!
Maura Genovesi [9:57 A.M.]	Yes, it is! I didn't think they would go for it.
Satya Kamei [9:59 A.M.]	Well, since it's a weekday, they didn't think they'd get a booking at the standard rate. Everything is coming together perfectly, isn't it?
John Bautista [10:01 A.M.]	Yes and no. I just found out that the Regional Music Association will hold a rock festival at Flynn Auditorium on the same night. People will be highly interested in that.
Kun Quan [10:02 A.M.]	That just means we need to promote our event more heavily. I can contact the editor of the *Stoneybrook Times* to see if we can get some free news coverage.
John Bautista [10:03 A.M.]	Thank you! Let's have Renee Abraham cater the refreshments again. She did a great job last time.
Maura Genovesi [10:06 A.M.]	Great idea. I'll call her before our meeting to see if she is available.

168. What event are the participants in the discussion organizing?

(A) A music festival
(B) An awards ceremony
(C) An academic lecture
(D) A museum grand opening

169. At 9:57 A.M, what does Ms. Genovesi most likely mean when she writes, "I didn't think they would go for it"?

(A) She did not think the city would allow the event to be held.
(B) She is surprised that a venue wasn't booked.
(C) She thought a committee would elect someone else.
(D) She doubted that a discount rate would be given.

170. What does Mr. Bautista think will happen?

(A) A competing event will draw a lot of people.
(B) A newspaper will be delivered early.
(C) A crowd will be difficult to handle.
(D) A promotion will be given to a coworker.

171. Who most likely will Ms. Genovesi contact today?

(A) A city official
(B) A reporter
(C) A caterer
(D) A musician

Questions 172-175 refer to the following notice.

NOTICE TO ALL HIGHTOWN LITHO CUSTOMERS:

From October 11 to 14, the largest machine (DC 10506) at the Rockford branch will be out of service due to regular maintenance and upgrades being made by the manufacturer. These adjustments will help us to improve our turnaround time on large orders by up to 15%. —[1]—. However, this will mean that the following services will be temporarily unavailable in Rockford during that time: A0 & A1 copies, banners (both cloth and vinyl), billboard posters, and plastic signage larger than A2. There will be no change to operations in Cedar Falls and Westerville. —[2]—.

We are still accepting print jobs for the above types, but they will all be processed at our Cedar Falls branch. Shipping charges usually apply when work is outsourced to another branch, but these will be waived during the maintenance work. —[3]—.

We expect normal service to resume in Rockford from October 15. —[4]—. Customers should speak to one of our representatives to see how this affects requested projects or e-mail our headquarters at customerservices@hightownlitho.com. Customers may also visit www.hightownlitho.com for more information.

172. What is the purpose of the notice?
 (A) To announce a temporary store closure
 (B) To introduce a newly available service
 (C) To announce the opening of an additional branch
 (D) To inform customers of reduced services

173. What advantage does the company hope to gain?
 (A) An increase in printing speed
 (B) An expanded customer base
 (C) A location for a new outlet
 (D) A decrease in prices

174. Where will orders for billboard posters be processed from October 11 to 14?
 (A) At the headquarters
 (B) At the Rockford branch
 (C) At the Cedar Falls branch
 (D) At the Westerville branch

175. In which of the positions marked [1], [2], [3] and [4] does the following sentence best belong?

"Please allow an additional day for deliveries in this case."

 (A) [1]
 (B) [2]
 (C) [3]
 (D) [4]

GO ON TO THE NEXT PAGE

Questions 176-180 refer to the following advertisement and e-mail.

Pearl Beach Vacation Rentals

Take a few days to escape from the stress of daily life and enjoy relaxing in a rental house located right on Pearl Beach! Choose from one of the options below. Whether you're coming with your family members or a group of friends, we have a place to match your needs, all with beachfront views.

Rental Property	Features	Daily Rate ($)
Couple Suite	1 Bedroom (2 guests) Buffet Passes	140
Honeymoon Suite	1 Bedroom (2 guests) Room service on Request	170
Family Retreat	2 Bedrooms (up to 4 guests) Barbecue Pit	260
Party House	3 Bedrooms (6 guests) Barbecue Pit	310

Although rooms can accommodate more than the suggested number of guests, there is a $20 per person per night fee. Extra beds are available for extra costs. Food menus differ based on the season.

*Any child under the age of 4 will be exempt from all extra fees.

TO: Pearl Beach Vacation Rentals <custserv@pbvr.com>
FROM: John Woodall <j.woodall@jmail.net>
DATE: 8 March
SUBJECT: Rental questions

I plan on taking a trip with my wife and son this summer, and we are interested in spending a few days at one of your properties. We have stayed at other resorts run by your parent company, Global Resorts, and really enjoyed them. There are a few questions I have about your properties before I make a reservation, though. First, are we allowed to have an extra person in the room? Our son is only 2 years old and still sleeps in the same room with us. Also, we would prefer to have our meals in private in the guest room. Finally, I would like to know if the area your resort is located in has stores and restaurants to wander around at on foot or if your resort offers a shuttle bus service. I have a tight budget and want to save some money on transportation such as renting a car or taking a taxi.

Thank you in advance.

John Woodall

176. What feature do the properties of Pearl Beach Vacation Rentals have in common?

(A) The number of bedrooms
(B) The views that they have
(C) The meal options
(D) The suggested number of guests

177. What kind of property will Mr. Woodall most likely rent?

(A) Couple Suite
(B) Honeymoon Suite
(C) Family Retreat
(D) Party House

178. What is stated about Pearl Beach Vacation Rentals?

(A) It is a subsidiary company.
(B) It normally has a wait list.
(C) It has a famous kitchen staff.
(D) It only operates during the summer.

179. What is implied about Mr. Woodall?

(A) He travels for business often.
(B) He won't pay for an extra bed.
(C) He prefers to cook meals himself.
(D) He has been to Pearl Beach before.

180. In the e-mail, what does Mr. Woodall suggest about his vacation plans?

(A) He wants to spend time on the beach.
(B) He is going to attend social events.
(C) He will reserve a morning flight.
(D) He does not intend to rent a car.

Questions 181-185 refer to the following flyer and online form.

Bristow Cultural Museum

Sign up for a membership at Bristow Cultural Museum to enjoy a variety of benefits. For a small monthly fee of $25, you can:

- Receive a copy of the museum's monthly newsletter
- Receive daily "This Day In History" text messages
- Get early access to cultural event tickets, as well as $5 off any event ticket (Normally $20)
- Enter museum exhibit areas for free (Normally $10)

Cultural events such as theatrical or musical performances are held every weekend. Visit the museum's Web site for a schedule of upcoming events. Weather permitting, events are held outdoors from April to September. All outdoor cultural events are provided to all museum visitors for free.

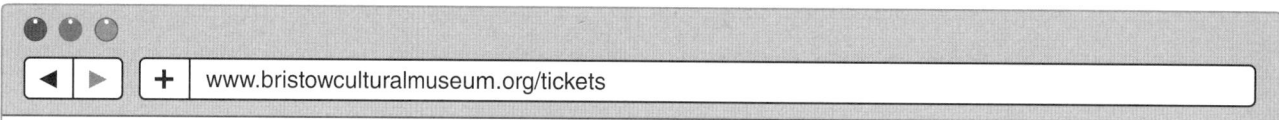

www.bristowculturalmuseum.org/tickets

Bristow Cultural Museum

Event Tickets

Event Date: 7 February
Event: Traditional Russian Dance
Ticket Price: $15.00
Number of Tickets: 2
Total Cost: $30.00

Personal Information
Name: Elias Dorsey
Address: 944 Ridge Drive, Bristow
Phone Number: 555-8592
Card Type: Visa
Name On Card: ELIAS DORSEY
Card Number: xxxx-xxxx-xxxx-7021

I agree to the terms of membership: [Yes]

181. What is the main purpose of the flyer?
    (A) To advertise a performance
    (B) To introduce a new exhibition
    (C) To recruit qualified employees
    (D) To publicize a membership program

182. What is implied about Bristow Cultural Museum?
    (A) It has an outdoor stage.
    (B) It offers free memberships.
    (C) It changes exhibits monthly.
    (D) It employs multilingual staff members.

183. What is NOT stated about cultural events?
    (A) They are held throughout the year.
    (B) Their schedules are posted online.
    (C) Members get discounted tickets for them.
    (D) All of them are musical concerts.

184. What is most likely true about Mr. Dorsey?
    (A) He is an employee of Bristow Cultural Museum.
    (B) He gets a discount when viewing exhibits.
    (C) He pays $25 every month.
    (D) He has recently been to Russia.

185. What is suggested about the event Traditional Russian Dance?
    (A) Its tickets have been sold out.
    (B) It was originally scheduled to be held outdoors.
    (C) It will be held indoors.
    (D) All of the dancers are coming from Russia.

Questions 186-190 refer to the following letters and invoice.

Eastland Sports Memorabilia
623 Stafford Road
Eastland, TX 76448

July 18

To Whom It May Concern:

I have been an avid collector of baseball cards and collectibles for approximately seven years. I was pleased to come across your shop recently while visiting some relatives in Eastland. I purchased several items at that time. However, when I got home and took a closer look at the items, I became concerned that one of them was fake. The signature on the baseball autographed by Alfonzo Deluca is quite different from those on the other signed posters and baseball cards that I have of him. Of course, if this is not his real signature on the ball, it is completely worthless to a collector like me. I would like you to look into this matter as soon as possible. I have enclosed a copy of the invoice for your convenience. I await your response.

Sincerely,

Luis Sullivan

CUSTOMER INVOICE • EASTLAND SPORTS MEMORABILIA
623 Stafford Road, Eastland, TX 76448 • 254-555-6211

Date: June 29   Customer: Luis Sullivan

Item #	Description	Price
1094	Baseball display case (empty, wooden base, glass sides)	$49.99
1722	Leather-bound baseball card binder (displays 9 cards/page)	$39.99
2948	Wildcats Championship Baseball signed by Alfonzo Deluca	$495.99
2659	Wildcats Stadium Home Plate (1994 season)	$565.99
3029	Eagles batting practice jersey worn by Alex McManus (1999 season)	$295.99
	Total	**$1,447.95**

Do you have sports memorabilia or collectible items to sell? Call us today to get a quote.

Luis Sullivan
3271 Troy Avenue
Whitestone, NY 11357

July 23

Dear Mr. Sullivan,

Regarding your most recent purchase from Eastland Sports Memorabilia, I can assure you that all of our items are certified by an independent agency, and the certificate for the item you mentioned is enclosed. For baseballs, sometimes the signature is slightly different because of the difficulty of writing on a rounded surface. If you still feel that the purchase is unsatisfactory, we would be happy to refund the full price. However, in this case I would recommend taking action quickly because we can only process returns within 45 days of the purchase date.

No matter what you decide to do, I will send you an additional baseball display case for you to keep as our gift.

Sincerely,

William Mason

---

186. What is the purpose of Mr. Sullivan's letter?
(A) To complain about a shipping problem
(B) To report some broken merchandise
(C) To request a refund for an overcharge on a bill
(D) To question a product's authenticity

187. Which item does Mr. Mason offer to refund?
(A) 1094
(B) 2948
(C) 2659
(D) 3029

188. What is implied about Eastland Sports Memorabilia?
(A) It has a branch near Mr. Sullivan's home.
(B) It offers an expedited shipping option.
(C) It purchases used items from customers.
(D) It has been open for about seven years.

189. What is indicated by Mr. Mason?
(A) A receipt should be included with a request.
(B) Returns must be made in person at the store.
(C) The price of an item has recently changed.
(D) A solution is available for a limited time.

190. What is the value of the item that will be sent to Mr. Sullivan for free?
(A) $39.99
(B) $49.99
(C) $295.99
(D) $495.99

GO ON TO THE NEXT PAGE

Questions 191-195 refer to the following memo, e-mail, and article.

To: All Balentine Labs Employees
From: Saeko Nagao
Re: Please read

March 3

A group of chemistry students from the Lavelle Institute is scheduled to visit our headquarters on Thursday, March 17. I want to make sure that you don't forget our company regulations on visitors, the same ones discussed prior to the press event last month. Employees may answer general questions about the work duties and our existing products on the market. For the sake of company privacy, you are not to discuss any current projects. It is important that we keep our trade secrets secure. During the visit, the site manager will give the students a tour, and then they will attend a question-and-answer session led by the director of the research department. Your cooperation is appreciated.

E-mail

To:	Saeko Nagao <saeko.negao@balentinelabs.com>
From:	Karen Dupree <dupreek@lavelleinstitute.edu>
Date:	March 10
Subject:	Upcoming Visit

Dear Ms. Nagao,

I regret to inform you that my class will not be able to visit your facility on the day we had planned. Unfortunately, there were some scheduling problems. We would still very much like to see your operations, if possible. We are available for any of the following: Tuesday, March 15 (9–noon), Friday, March 18 (2–5), or Saturday, March 19 (1–4). Please let me know if any of these time slots work with your schedule, and thank you for accommodating us.

Warmest regards,

Karen Dupree
Instructor, Chemistry Department, Lavelle Institute

Lavelle Institute April Newsletter–Vol. 254

Students See Laboratory Jobs in Action
By Corey Ramey

A group of undergraduates from Lavelle Institute's chemistry department, along with instructor Karen Dupree, visited Balentine Labs last month. They toured the facility, saw equipment demonstrations, and learned about the operations there. Even though it was a weekend, the facility was still as busy as ever, as it is open seven days a week to accommodate time-sensitive research. "I learned a great deal from the tour," said second-year student Cynthia Lester.

"We are particularly proud to show off our recently opened building extension," said Mira Prakash as she responded to inquiries from the group at a special session following the tour. "Thanks to the new space, we are now running trials with patients right here at our headquarters. This is saving us a lot of time and hassle because we don't need to try to find clinic space for this purpose."

191. Why did Ms. Nagao send the memo?
 (A) To announce a regulation change
 (B) To ask for volunteers for a tour
 (C) To remind employees of a policy
 (D) To introduce a job opportunity

192. In the memo, the word "secure" in paragraph 1, line 6, is closest in meaning to
 (A) confident
 (B) closed
 (C) protected
 (D) fastened

193. When did Ms. Dupree's group most likely visit Balentine Labs?
 (A) March 15
 (B) March 17
 (C) March 18
 (D) March 19

194. What is implied about Ms. Prakash?
 (A) She is the site manager for Balentine Labs.
 (B) She has been in school for two years.
 (C) She is the head of a department.
 (D) She is planning another tour soon.

195. What is suggested about Balentine Labs?
 (A) It is conducting on-site trials with patients for the first time.
 (B) It exclusively hires Lavelle Institute graduates.
 (C) It has difficulty recruiting patients for its research.
 (D) It runs a free clinic to provide medical care.

Questions 196-200 refer to the following advertisement, form, and e-mail.

Morris Fabrics

Don't replace your old furniture. Instead, why not have the worn fabric replaced by our skilled technicians at a fraction of the cost of buying new? Here at Morris Fabrics, we have been upholstering furniture with only the finest-quality materials for nearly twenty years. Our staff members are trained and managed to the highest standards, and we have an experienced crew that concentrates solely on working with chairs and sofas that are over one hundred years old.

For orders of five or more similar items, we will be offering a discount of 20% until the end of September. This is perfect for hotels and offices. Contact us at (302) 555-9898 or visit www.morrisfabrics.com for more information.

Work Order #3299

Employee: Holly Weston #145
Completion due: September 25
Customer name: David Greaves

Date: September 23
Scheduled delivery date: September 26

Details: 6 Mahogany Georgian-style chairs. Each to be stripped of all seating fabric. Replacement fabric Burgundy Felt (#13437B) to be applied using standard pinning. Ensure double seam on the underside. Re-polish worn areas on front bar and arms. Check for loose crossbars on legs. Apply transparent adhesive, if required.

To	Morris Fabrics <customerservices@morrisfabrics.com>
From	David Greaves <david.greaves@localmail.net>
Date	September 28
Subject	Additional request

To Whom It May Concern:

I was extremely pleased with the quality of work on my most recently order, and I was pleasantly surprised to receive my chairs a day earlier than scheduled. The work done on them is fantastic, especially considering the price. Having had the chance to look at the chairs in place in my entrance hall, I now realize that the new covering does not go with the curtains I currently have. I was wondering if you sell fabric. If I could get an additional 36 yards of the same fabric, I could have curtains made that would be exactly the same as the chairs.

Please e-mail me back to arrange a time for me to come in and look at the fabric again, if it's available, as well as some other complementary options.

Yours sincerely,

David Greaves

196. What is suggested about Morris Fabrics?
    (A) It has a photo gallery of finished projects online.
    (B) It accepts used furniture for recycling.
    (C) It has a team that specializes in antique pieces.
    (D) It has recently changed ownership.

197. What is true about Mr. Greaves?
    (A) He works as an interior designer.
    (B) He got a bulk discount on his order.
    (C) He is an employee at a hotel.
    (D) He selected two fabrics for a project.

198. What does Mr. Greaves ask Morris Fabrics to do?
    (A) Send a fabric sample
    (B) Set up an appointment
    (C) Recommend some product styles
    (D) Put some curtains on reserve

199. In the e-mail, the phrase "go with" in paragraph 1, line 4, is closest in meaning to
    (A) provide
    (B) match
    (C) accept
    (D) accompany

200. When did Mr. Greaves receive his goods?
    (A) On September 23
    (B) On September 25
    (C) On September 26
    (D) On September 27

Stop! This is the end of the test. If you finish before time is called, you may go back to Part 5, 6, and 7 and check your work.

ANSWER SHEET
TEST

ANSWER SHEET
TEST

– ANSWER SHEET TEST –

ANSWER SHEET
TEST ___

ANSWER SHEET
TEST

✂ 자르는 선

ANSWER SHEET

TEST ___________

수험번호		
성명	한글	
	영자	

응시일자	20 . . .
맞은 개수	/ 100
환산 점수	/ 495

Listening Comprehension (PART I ~ PART IV)

1	ⓐ ⓑ ⓒ ⓓ	26	ⓐ ⓑ ⓒ	51	ⓐ ⓑ ⓒ ⓓ	76	ⓐ ⓑ ⓒ ⓓ
2	ⓐ ⓑ ⓒ ⓓ	27	ⓐ ⓑ ⓒ	52	ⓐ ⓑ ⓒ ⓓ	77	ⓐ ⓑ ⓒ ⓓ
3	ⓐ ⓑ ⓒ ⓓ	28	ⓐ ⓑ ⓒ	53	ⓐ ⓑ ⓒ ⓓ	78	ⓐ ⓑ ⓒ ⓓ
4	ⓐ ⓑ ⓒ ⓓ	29	ⓐ ⓑ ⓒ	54	ⓐ ⓑ ⓒ ⓓ	79	ⓐ ⓑ ⓒ ⓓ
5	ⓐ ⓑ ⓒ ⓓ	30	ⓐ ⓑ ⓒ	55	ⓐ ⓑ ⓒ ⓓ	80	ⓐ ⓑ ⓒ ⓓ
6	ⓐ ⓑ ⓒ ⓓ	31	ⓐ ⓑ ⓒ	56	ⓐ ⓑ ⓒ ⓓ	81	ⓐ ⓑ ⓒ ⓓ
7	ⓐ ⓑ ⓒ	32	ⓐ ⓑ ⓒ ⓓ	57	ⓐ ⓑ ⓒ ⓓ	82	ⓐ ⓑ ⓒ ⓓ
8	ⓐ ⓑ ⓒ	33	ⓐ ⓑ ⓒ ⓓ	58	ⓐ ⓑ ⓒ ⓓ	83	ⓐ ⓑ ⓒ ⓓ
9	ⓐ ⓑ ⓒ	34	ⓐ ⓑ ⓒ ⓓ	59	ⓐ ⓑ ⓒ ⓓ	84	ⓐ ⓑ ⓒ ⓓ
10	ⓐ ⓑ ⓒ	35	ⓐ ⓑ ⓒ ⓓ	60	ⓐ ⓑ ⓒ ⓓ	85	ⓐ ⓑ ⓒ ⓓ
11	ⓐ ⓑ ⓒ	36	ⓐ ⓑ ⓒ ⓓ	61	ⓐ ⓑ ⓒ ⓓ	86	ⓐ ⓑ ⓒ ⓓ
12	ⓐ ⓑ ⓒ	37	ⓐ ⓑ ⓒ ⓓ	62	ⓐ ⓑ ⓒ ⓓ	87	ⓐ ⓑ ⓒ ⓓ
13	ⓐ ⓑ ⓒ	38	ⓐ ⓑ ⓒ ⓓ	63	ⓐ ⓑ ⓒ ⓓ	88	ⓐ ⓑ ⓒ ⓓ
14	ⓐ ⓑ ⓒ	39	ⓐ ⓑ ⓒ ⓓ	64	ⓐ ⓑ ⓒ ⓓ	89	ⓐ ⓑ ⓒ ⓓ
15	ⓐ ⓑ ⓒ	40	ⓐ ⓑ ⓒ ⓓ	65	ⓐ ⓑ ⓒ ⓓ	90	ⓐ ⓑ ⓒ ⓓ
16	ⓐ ⓑ ⓒ	41	ⓐ ⓑ ⓒ ⓓ	66	ⓐ ⓑ ⓒ ⓓ	91	ⓐ ⓑ ⓒ ⓓ
17	ⓐ ⓑ ⓒ	42	ⓐ ⓑ ⓒ ⓓ	67	ⓐ ⓑ ⓒ ⓓ	92	ⓐ ⓑ ⓒ ⓓ
18	ⓐ ⓑ ⓒ	43	ⓐ ⓑ ⓒ ⓓ	68	ⓐ ⓑ ⓒ ⓓ	93	ⓐ ⓑ ⓒ ⓓ
19	ⓐ ⓑ ⓒ	44	ⓐ ⓑ ⓒ ⓓ	69	ⓐ ⓑ ⓒ ⓓ	94	ⓐ ⓑ ⓒ ⓓ
20	ⓐ ⓑ ⓒ	45	ⓐ ⓑ ⓒ ⓓ	70	ⓐ ⓑ ⓒ ⓓ	95	ⓐ ⓑ ⓒ ⓓ
21	ⓐ ⓑ ⓒ	46	ⓐ ⓑ ⓒ ⓓ	71	ⓐ ⓑ ⓒ ⓓ	96	ⓐ ⓑ ⓒ ⓓ
22	ⓐ ⓑ ⓒ	47	ⓐ ⓑ ⓒ ⓓ	72	ⓐ ⓑ ⓒ ⓓ	97	ⓐ ⓑ ⓒ ⓓ
23	ⓐ ⓑ ⓒ	48	ⓐ ⓑ ⓒ ⓓ	73	ⓐ ⓑ ⓒ ⓓ	98	ⓐ ⓑ ⓒ ⓓ
24	ⓐ ⓑ ⓒ	49	ⓐ ⓑ ⓒ ⓓ	74	ⓐ ⓑ ⓒ ⓓ	99	ⓐ ⓑ ⓒ ⓓ
25	ⓐ ⓑ ⓒ	50	ⓐ ⓑ ⓒ ⓓ	75	ⓐ ⓑ ⓒ ⓓ	100	ⓐ ⓑ ⓒ ⓓ

Reading Comprehension (PART V ~ PART VII)

101	ⓐ ⓑ ⓒ ⓓ	126	ⓐ ⓑ ⓒ ⓓ	151	ⓐ ⓑ ⓒ ⓓ	176	ⓐ ⓑ ⓒ ⓓ
102	ⓐ ⓑ ⓒ ⓓ	127	ⓐ ⓑ ⓒ ⓓ	152	ⓐ ⓑ ⓒ ⓓ	177	ⓐ ⓑ ⓒ ⓓ
103	ⓐ ⓑ ⓒ ⓓ	128	ⓐ ⓑ ⓒ ⓓ	153	ⓐ ⓑ ⓒ ⓓ	178	ⓐ ⓑ ⓒ ⓓ
104	ⓐ ⓑ ⓒ ⓓ	129	ⓐ ⓑ ⓒ ⓓ	154	ⓐ ⓑ ⓒ ⓓ	179	ⓐ ⓑ ⓒ ⓓ
105	ⓐ ⓑ ⓒ ⓓ	130	ⓐ ⓑ ⓒ ⓓ	155	ⓐ ⓑ ⓒ ⓓ	180	ⓐ ⓑ ⓒ ⓓ
106	ⓐ ⓑ ⓒ ⓓ	131	ⓐ ⓑ ⓒ ⓓ	156	ⓐ ⓑ ⓒ ⓓ	181	ⓐ ⓑ ⓒ ⓓ
107	ⓐ ⓑ ⓒ ⓓ	132	ⓐ ⓑ ⓒ ⓓ	157	ⓐ ⓑ ⓒ ⓓ	182	ⓐ ⓑ ⓒ ⓓ
108	ⓐ ⓑ ⓒ ⓓ	133	ⓐ ⓑ ⓒ ⓓ	158	ⓐ ⓑ ⓒ ⓓ	183	ⓐ ⓑ ⓒ ⓓ
109	ⓐ ⓑ ⓒ ⓓ	134	ⓐ ⓑ ⓒ ⓓ	159	ⓐ ⓑ ⓒ ⓓ	184	ⓐ ⓑ ⓒ ⓓ
110	ⓐ ⓑ ⓒ ⓓ	135	ⓐ ⓑ ⓒ ⓓ	160	ⓐ ⓑ ⓒ ⓓ	185	ⓐ ⓑ ⓒ ⓓ
111	ⓐ ⓑ ⓒ ⓓ	136	ⓐ ⓑ ⓒ ⓓ	161	ⓐ ⓑ ⓒ ⓓ	186	ⓐ ⓑ ⓒ ⓓ
112	ⓐ ⓑ ⓒ ⓓ	137	ⓐ ⓑ ⓒ ⓓ	162	ⓐ ⓑ ⓒ ⓓ	187	ⓐ ⓑ ⓒ ⓓ
113	ⓐ ⓑ ⓒ ⓓ	138	ⓐ ⓑ ⓒ ⓓ	163	ⓐ ⓑ ⓒ ⓓ	188	ⓐ ⓑ ⓒ ⓓ
114	ⓐ ⓑ ⓒ ⓓ	139	ⓐ ⓑ ⓒ ⓓ	164	ⓐ ⓑ ⓒ ⓓ	189	ⓐ ⓑ ⓒ ⓓ
115	ⓐ ⓑ ⓒ ⓓ	140	ⓐ ⓑ ⓒ ⓓ	165	ⓐ ⓑ ⓒ ⓓ	190	ⓐ ⓑ ⓒ ⓓ
116	ⓐ ⓑ ⓒ ⓓ	141	ⓐ ⓑ ⓒ ⓓ	166	ⓐ ⓑ ⓒ ⓓ	191	ⓐ ⓑ ⓒ ⓓ
117	ⓐ ⓑ ⓒ ⓓ	142	ⓐ ⓑ ⓒ ⓓ	167	ⓐ ⓑ ⓒ ⓓ	192	ⓐ ⓑ ⓒ ⓓ
118	ⓐ ⓑ ⓒ ⓓ	143	ⓐ ⓑ ⓒ ⓓ	168	ⓐ ⓑ ⓒ ⓓ	193	ⓐ ⓑ ⓒ ⓓ
119	ⓐ ⓑ ⓒ ⓓ	144	ⓐ ⓑ ⓒ ⓓ	169	ⓐ ⓑ ⓒ ⓓ	194	ⓐ ⓑ ⓒ ⓓ
120	ⓐ ⓑ ⓒ ⓓ	145	ⓐ ⓑ ⓒ ⓓ	170	ⓐ ⓑ ⓒ ⓓ	195	ⓐ ⓑ ⓒ ⓓ
121	ⓐ ⓑ ⓒ ⓓ	146	ⓐ ⓑ ⓒ ⓓ	171	ⓐ ⓑ ⓒ ⓓ	196	ⓐ ⓑ ⓒ ⓓ
122	ⓐ ⓑ ⓒ ⓓ	147	ⓐ ⓑ ⓒ ⓓ	172	ⓐ ⓑ ⓒ ⓓ	197	ⓐ ⓑ ⓒ ⓓ
123	ⓐ ⓑ ⓒ ⓓ	148	ⓐ ⓑ ⓒ ⓓ	173	ⓐ ⓑ ⓒ ⓓ	198	ⓐ ⓑ ⓒ ⓓ
124	ⓐ ⓑ ⓒ ⓓ	149	ⓐ ⓑ ⓒ ⓓ	174	ⓐ ⓑ ⓒ ⓓ	199	ⓐ ⓑ ⓒ ⓓ
125	ⓐ ⓑ ⓒ ⓓ	150	ⓐ ⓑ ⓒ ⓓ	175	ⓐ ⓑ ⓒ ⓓ	200	ⓐ ⓑ ⓒ ⓓ

ANSWER SHEET
TEST _____

ANSWER SHEET
TEST ___

ANSWER SHEET
TEST

ANSWER SHEET
TEST

영단기
eng.conects.com

영단기
eng.conects.com

영단기
eng.conects.com

토익 실전서

해설집

영단기 토익
실전 1000제 RC

vol.1

토익 실전서

해설집

영단기 토익
실전 1000제 RC

vol.1

TEST 01

PART 5
101 (C)	102 (C)	103 (A)	104 (B)	105 (D)
106 (C)	107 (D)	108 (D)	109 (D)	110 (C)
111 (C)	112 (B)	113 (D)	114 (D)	115 (C)
116 (D)	117 (C)	118 (B)	119 (C)	120 (A)
121 (C)	122 (B)	123 (C)	124 (A)	125 (C)
126 (A)	127 (D)	128 (C)	129 (A)	130 (B)

PART 6
131 (C)	132 (B)	133 (C)	134 (B)	135 (C)
136 (B)	137 (C)	138 (A)	139 (A)	140 (B)
141 (C)	142 (D)	143 (B)	144 (C)	145 (D)
146 (B)				

PART 7
147 (D)	148 (C)	149 (C)	150 (D)	151 (B)
152 (D)	153 (C)	154 (A)	155 (C)	156 (B)
157 (A)	158 (C)	159 (B)	160 (A)	161 (A)
162 (D)	163 (C)	164 (B)	165 (D)	166 (A)
167 (A)	168 (A)	169 (C)	170 (C)	171 (D)
172 (B)	173 (D)	174 (C)	175 (A)	176 (C)
177 (A)	178 (C)	179 (C)	180 (C)	181 (C)
182 (B)	183 (D)	184 (C)	185 (D)	186 (B)
187 (B)	188 (C)	189 (C)	190 (B)	191 (D)
192 (B)	193 (C)	194 (C)	195 (C)	196 (C)
197 (B)	198 (B)	199 (A)	200 (D)	

PART 5

101. 명사 자리 - 동사의 목적어
주민들은 그 동네의 제한 속도를 낮추기 위해 시 의회에 호소했다.
| 해설 | 빈칸은 동사 made의 목적어 자리이며, 관사 an과 전치사 to 사이에 있으므로, 단수 명사가 들어갈 자리이다. 따라서 단수 명사인 (C) appeal이 정답이다. make an appeal은 '호소하다, 간청하다'라는 의미의 숙어이다.
| 어휘 | resident 주민 city council 시 의회 speed limit 제한 속도 neighborhood 동네, 이웃 appealingly 호소하듯이, 매력적으로 appeal 호소하다, 간청하다; 호소, 매력

102. 동사 어휘
실험실에 있는 모든 화학 물질은 전면에 명확한 라벨들이 부착된 밀폐 용기에 보관되어야 한다.
| 해설 | 빈칸은 앞에 있는 be와 함께 수동태 동사를 이루는 과거 분사가 들어갈 자리로, 문맥상 '모든 화학 물질은 밀폐 용기에 보관되어야 한다'라는 의미로 전개되는 것이 적절하므로 '보관하다, 저장하다'라는 뜻의 (C) stored가 정답이다.

| 어휘 | chemical 화학 물질 lab 실험실 air-tight container 밀폐 용기 serve 제공하다 estimate 추정하다, 추산하다 resolve 해결하다

103. 등위 접속사
콜럼버스 도서관에서 새 계정을 만들려면, 사진이 있는 신분증과 주소를 증명하는 서류가 필요하다.
| 해설 | 빈칸은 앞뒤의 명사구를 연결해 줄 등위 접속사가 들어갈 자리이며, 문맥상 '사진이 있는 신분증과 주소를 증명하는 서류가 필요하다'라는 의미로 전개되는 것이 적절하므로 (A) and가 정답이다.
| 어휘 | open an account 계정을 만들다 proof 증명, 증거

104. 대명사 선택
그 재고 목록은 오늘 관리자에게 제출되어야 하기 때문에 주의 깊게 재확인해 주세요.
| 해설 | 빈칸은 because가 이끄는 절의 주어 자리이므로, 주어 자리에 들어갈 수 없는 소유격 대명사인 (A) their와 목적격 대명사인 (C) her는 오답이며, 앞에 제시된 the inventory list를 가리키는 대명사가 들어가야 하므로 3인칭 단수 주격 대명사인 (B) it이 정답이다.
| 어휘 | double-check 재확인하다 inventory 재고 carefully 주의 깊게 turn in 제출하다

105. 최상급 숙어
직원들은 해외 전근을 신청하기 전에 국내 지사에서 최소 3년의 경험이 필요하다.
| 해설 | 빈칸 뒤에 있는 수사 three를 수식할 수 있는 것을 묻는 문제로, 부사절 접속사인 (A) even if와 (B) just as, (C) so that은 모두 수사를 수식하는 것이 아니므로 오답이다. 따라서 '적어도, 최소한'이라는 뜻의 숙어 (D) at least가 정답이다.
| 어휘 | transfer 전근 가다 overseas 해외로

106. 부사절 접속사
요리사가 접시에 음식을 담아내자마자, 종업원 중 한 명이 그것을 주문한 사람에게 가지고 가야 한다.
| 해설 | 빈칸 뒤로 두 개의 완전한 절이 있으므로, 빈칸은 두 절을 연결해 줄 접속사가 들어갈 자리이다. 따라서 부사절 접속사인 (C) As soon as가 정답이다. (A) For instance, (B) Still, (D) Meanwhile은 모두 접속 부사로 두 절을 연결할 수 없다.
| 어휘 | arrange 배열하다, 배치하다 plate 접시 meanwhile 그동안에

107. 명사 어휘
HR 팀은 보안 관리자 직책을 자격을 갖춘 지원자로 충원하는 데 어려움을 겪고 있다.
| 해설 | 빈칸은 앞의 명사와 함께 복합 명사를 완성해 줄 명사가 들어갈 자리로, 문맥상 충원하는 대상으로 적절한 것은 '보안 관리자 직책'이므로 '직책, 자리'라는 뜻의 (D) position이 정답이다.
| 어휘 | have difficulty -ing ~하는 데 어려움을 겪다 fill 충원하다, 채우다 security director 보안 관리자 qualified 자격을 갖춘, 자격이 있는 applicant 지원자

108. 동사 어휘
환자들에게 우수한 간호를 제공하기 위해 병원 관리자는 전체 시설의 의료 서비스들을 감독한다.
| 해설 | 빈칸은 문장의 동사가 들어갈 자리로, 문맥상 '병원 관리자가 전체 시설의 의료 서비스들을 감독한다'라는 의미로 전개되어야 하므로 '감독하다'라는 뜻의 (D) oversees가 정답이다.
| 어휘 | hospital administrator 병원 관리자 health service 의료 서비스 entire 전체의 facility 시설 patient 환자 care 간호, 돌봄 predict 예상하다

109. 전치사 어휘
기자들이 Maxwell 뮤직 페스티벌의 개막식 동안 사진을 찍었다.
| 해설 | 빈칸은 앞의 절과 뒤의 명사구를 연결해 줄 전치사가 들어갈 자리이므로 접속사인 (B) while은 오답이며, 문맥상 '개막식 동안 사진을 찍었다'라는 의미로 전개되는 것이 적절하므로 '~ 중에, ~ 동안'이라는 뜻의 (D) during이 정답이다.
| 어휘 | reporter 기자 opening ceremony 개막식

🔺 고난도
110. 복합 관계 대명사
보관실에 있는 비품들은 모두를 위한 것이니, 작업자들은 필요한 것은 무엇이든 가져갈 수 있다.
| 해설 | 빈칸에는 뒤에 있는 절(they need)을 이끌어 앞에 있는 동사 take의 목적어 역할을 할 수 있게 만들어줄 명사절 접속사가 필요한데, 빈칸 뒤의 절에 목적어 자리가 비어 있으므로, 명사절을 이끌며 그 자체로 명사절의 목적어 역할을 할 수 있는 복합 관계 대명사가 필요하다. 따라서 복합 관계 대명사인 (C) whatever가 정답이다.
| 어휘 | supplies 비품, 물품 storage room 저장실

🔺 고난도
111. 부사 자리 - 동사 수식
각 팀원의 책무들은 가능한 한 명확하게 설명되어야 한다.
| 해설 | 빈칸은 3형식 동사의 수동태 be explained를 수식하는 부사 자리이므로 '명확하게, 분명히'라는 뜻의 부사인 (C) clearly가 정답이다. 참고로 'as ~ as possible' 표현에서는 as와 as 사이에 반드시 형용사나 부사의 원급이 들어가야 하므로 나머지는 모두 답이 될 수 없다.
| 어휘 | responsibility 책무, 책임 clarity 명료성, 명확성

112. 형용사 어휘
가장 최근의 여론 조사에 따르면 상원 의원 선거전에서 주요 두 후보 어느 쪽이든 승리할 수 있다.
| 해설 | 빈칸은 the most의 수식을 받으며, 뒤에 있는 명사 poll을 수식하는 형용사가 들어갈 자리로, 문맥상 '가장 최근의 여론 조사에 따르면'이라는 의미로 전개되는 것이 적절하므로 '최근의, 최신의'라는 뜻의 형용사인 (B) recent가 정답이다.
| 어휘 | senatorial race 상원 의원 선거전 candidate 후보 poll 여론 조사 fragile 취약한, 깨지기 쉬운 entire 전체의 consecutive 연이은, 연속되는

113. 형용사 자리 - 주격 보어
수속을 마친 가방들은 흔히 쌓아 올려지기 때문에, 여행자들은 깨지기 쉬운 물품들은 (기내) 휴대용 가방에 넣는 것이 바람직하다.
| 해설 | 빈칸은 be동사의 보어 자리이므로 동사 형태인 (A) advises는 답이 될 수 없고, 문맥상 '휴대용 가방에 넣는 것이 바람직하다'라는 의미로 전개되어야 하므로 '바람직한, 권할 만한'이라는 뜻의 형용사인 (D) advisable이 정답이다.
| 어휘 | checked 수화물로 부친 stack up 쌓아 올리다 carry-on (기내) 휴대용 가방 advise 조언하다, 충고하다 advice 조언, 충고 advising 조언하는

114. 부사 어휘
실험실의 장비는 프로젝트들 사이에 교차 오염을 피하기 위해 사용 후에 항상 철저히 청소된다.
| 해설 | 빈칸은 수동태로 제시된 동사를 수식해줄 부사가 들어갈 자리로, 문맥상 '항상 철저히 청소된다'는 일반적인 사실을 나타내는 내용으로 전개되는 것이 적절하므로 '항상, 늘'이라는 뜻의 (D) always가 정답이다.
| 어휘 | laboratory 실험실 equipment 장비 thoroughly 철저히 avoid 피하다 cross-contamination 교차 오염 afterward 그 후에, 나중에 straight 똑바로, 곧장

🔺 고난도
115. 분사 구문
그 도시의 시장이 기금 모금 행사에 후한 기부를 하여, 총액이 25,000달러가 넘었다.
| 해설 | 빈칸 앞 절에 동사 made가 있고, 접속사가 없으므로 또 다른 동사 형태인 (A) brings와 (B) bring은 답이 될 수 없다. 따라서 접속사가 생략된 형태의 분사 구문을 만들어 줄 분사가 필요한데 빈칸 뒤에 목적어가 있으므로 현재 분사인 (C) bringing이 정답이다.
| 어휘 | mayor 시장 make a donation 기부를 하다 generous 후한 fundraiser 기금 모금 행사

🔺 고난도
116. 등위 접속사
그 소기업 사장은 정규직 사진사를 고용하지 않고 상업용 사진 데이터베이스를 이용하기로 결정했다.
| 해설 | 동사 decided의 목적어인 to부정사구 to use a stock photo database와 (to) hire a full-time photographer가 빈칸 앞뒤로 병치를 이루는 구조인데, 앞에 제시된 상업용 사진을 이용하는 것과 뒤에 제시된 사진사를 고용하는 것은 대조적인 내용이므로, '~보다, ~하지 않고'라는 뜻의 등위 접속사인 (D) rather than이 정답이다.
| 어휘 | stock photo 상업용 사진 photographer 사진사

117. 부사 자리 - 동사 수식
Crestline Institute의 새로운 요리 강좌들은 처음으로 혼자 생활하는 젊은이들을 특별히 겨냥하였다.
| 해설 | '~을 겨냥하다, ~을 목표로 하다'라는 뜻의 동사구 are aimed at 안에 빈칸이 있으므로 빈칸은 동사구를 수식하는 부사 자리이다. 따라서 '특별히, 특히'라는 뜻의 부사인 (C) specifically가 정답이다.

| 어휘 | be aimed at ~을 겨냥하다, ~을 목표로 하다   on one's own 혼자, 혼자 힘으로   specify 명시하다, 구체화하다   specificity 특수성, 특별함   specific 구체적인, 특정한

118. 명사 자리 - 주어 | 수 일치
그 저널 기사는 연구팀의 결과들이 약물의 효과에 대한 확증이라고 명시한다.
| 해설 | 빈칸은 앞의 소유격 표현 the research team's의 수식을 받는 that절의 주어가 들어갈 자리이므로 동사 형태인 (C) find와 (D) found는 답이 될 수 없고, 뒤에 있는 복수 동사 are과 수가 일치되는 복수 명사인 (B) findings가 정답이다.
| 어휘 | state 명시하다, 서술하다   confirmation 확증, 확인   medication 약물, 약물 치료   effectiveness 효과, 유효성

119. 형용사 자리 - 주격 보어
쇼핑 센터 프로젝트는 계획자들이 예상했던 것만큼 새로운 투자자들에게 매력적이지 않았다.
| 해설 | as ~ as 사이에 있는 빈칸은 be동사 was의 보어가 들어갈 자리이므로, 동사인 (A) attracts와 (B) attract, 부사인 (D) attractively는 모두 답이 될 수 없고, '매력적인'이라는 뜻의 형용사인 (C) attractive가 정답이다.
| 어휘 | investor 투자자   attract 끌어들이다, 유치하다   attractively 매력적으로

120. 동사 어휘 [고난도]
Ooshima 씨가 예기치 않게 싱가포르로 출장을 가서, 그녀는 자신의 업무들 중 일부를 자신의 부하 직원들에게 위임해야 했다.
| 해설 | 빈칸은 some of her tasks를 목적어로 취하는 동사가 들어갈 자리로, 문맥상 출장을 간 것과 관련 지어 '업무 중 일부를 위임해야 했다'라는 의미로 전개되는 것이 적절하므로 '위임하다'라는 뜻의 (A) delegate가 정답이다.
| 어휘 | unexpectedly 예기치 않게, 갑자기   task 일, 업무   subordinate 부하 직원, 하급자   complete 완료하다   invest 투자하다   reply 응답하다

121. 명사 자리 - 동사의 목적어 [고난도]
그 보안 요원은 Dillon 씨가 유효한 사원증을 제공할 수 없었기 때문에 그의 입장을 거부했다.
| 해설 | 빈칸은 타동사 refuse의 간접 목적어 Mr. Dillon 뒤에 직접 목적어가 들어갈 자리이므로 '입장, 들어감'이라는 뜻의 명사인 (C) admittance가 정답이다. 동사 (A) admits, 부사 (B) admittedly, 현재 분사 (D) admitting은 모두 목적어 자리에 올 수 없으므로 오답이다.
| 어휘 | security guard 보안 요원   refuse 거부하다, 거절하다   valid 유효한   admit 인정하다, 입장을 허락하다   admittedly 인정하건대

122. 부사절 접속사
Top Gardening이 자사 웹 사이트의 계산 절차를 변경한 이후로 온라인 매출이 급격하게 올랐다.
| 해설 | 빈칸 뒤로 두 개의 완전한 절이 있으므로, 빈칸은 두 절을 연결해 줄 접속사가 들어갈 자리이다. 따라서 관계 부사인 (A) Why와 부사인 (D) Still은 답이 될 수 없고, 문맥상 '변경한 이후로, 매출이 급격하게 올랐다'라는 의미로 전개되는 것이 적절하므로 부사절 접속사 (B) Since가 정답이다.
| 어휘 | checkout procedure 계산 절차   dramatically 급격하게

123. 도치 - 가정법 if 생략 [고난도]
은행 이체가 오후 5시 이후에 이루어진다면, 그것이 다음 영업일에 처리될 것으로 예상할 수 있다.
| 해설 | 빈칸 뒤에 두 개의 절이 있는데 두 절을 연결해 줄 접속사가 보이지 않고, 3인칭 단수 주어인 the bank transfer 뒤에 be동사가 원형으로 제시되어 있는 것으로 볼 때, 가정법의 접속사 if가 생략되고 동사 원형 앞의 조동사가 앞으로 도치된 구문임을 알 수 있으므로, (B) Should가 정답이다.
| 어휘 | bank transfer 은행 이체   process 처리하다   following 다음의

124. 형용사 어휘
안전성 위반에 관한 최근 항의들로, Colbert 항공사는 아마도 평소보다 승객들이 더 적을 것이다.
| 해설 | 빈칸은 뒤에 있는 명사 passengers를 수식해줄 형용사가 들어갈 자리로, 문장 끝에 비교 대상을 나타내는 than usual이 있고, 문맥상 '최근 항의들로, 평소보다 승객들이 더 적을 것이다'라는 의미로 전개되는 것이 적절하므로 비교급 형용사인 (A) fewer가 정답이다.
| 어휘 | complaint 항의, 불만   safety violation 안전성 위반   passenger 승객

125. 부사 어휘
그 파일들은 영구히 삭제될 것이니 이 작업을 선택하기 전에 그것들이 필요하지 않다는 것을 확인해 주세요.
| 해설 | 빈칸은 동사 be deleted를 수식할 부사가 들어갈 자리로, 문맥상 파일들이 삭제되는 상황과 관련 지어 '영구히 삭제될 것이니 확인해 주세요'라는 의미로 전개되는 것이 적절하므로 '영구히, 영구적으로'라는 뜻의 (C) permanently가 정답이다.
| 어휘 | confirm 확인하다   select 선택하다   action 행동, 작업   favorably 호의적으로   substantially 상당히   forcefully 힘차게, 힘 주어

126. to부정사 관용 표현
Marquee 택배 회사는 직책들을 더 빨리 충원하기 위해 배달 기사들의 시간당 임금을 인상했다.
| 해설 | 빈칸 앞에는 완전한 절이 있고, 뒤에는 동사 원형이 이어지고 있으므로 동사 원형을 받을 수 있는 to부정사 형태인 (A) in order to가 정답이다. (B) similarly, (C) moreover, (D) in any case는 모두 접속 부사로 동사 원형을 취할 수 없으므로 오답이다.
| 어휘 | increase 인상하다, 올리다   hourly wage 시간당 임금, 시급   similarly 비슷하게, 유사하게   moreover 게다가, 더욱이   in any case 어쨌든, 여하튼

127. 전치사 어휘 [고난도]
항공사 대표가 취소에 대해 사과했지만 그것은 회사의 통제 범위를 넘어서는 요인들 때문이었다고 설명했다.

| 해설 | 빈칸은 뒤의 명사구 the company's control을 목적어로 취하는 전치사가 들어갈 자리로, 문맥상 '회사의 통제 범위를 넘어서는 요인들 때문이었다'라는 의미로 전개되는 것이 적절하므로 '~을 넘어서는'이라는 뜻의 (D) beyond가 정답이다.
| 어휘 | representative 대표, 담당자   apologize 사과하다   cancellation 취소   factor 요인, 요소

고난도
128. 동사의 형태와 시제
연말까지, 주의 보건부는 식품 안전성 위반을 확인하기 위해 5천 개 이상의 레스토랑들을 점검할 것이다.
| 해설 | 빈칸은 문장의 본동사가 들어갈 자리로, 빈칸 뒤에 목적어 over five thousand restaurants가 있으므로 수동태 동사인 (C) will be inspected와 (D) has been inspected는 오답이고, 앞에 제시된 By the end of the year를 단서로, 미래 특정 시점까지 지속될 상황을 나타내는 동사가 들어가야 함을 알 수 있으므로 능동의 미래 완료 시제 동사인 (B) will have inspected가 정답이다.
| 어휘 | state 주   health department 보건부   food safety violation 식품 안전성 위반

고난도
129. 동사 어휘
기조 연설에서 Grayson 박사는 전 세계적으로 빈곤을 줄이는 데 있어서 비영리 단체들의 역할을 강조했다.
| 해설 | 빈칸은 문장의 동사가 들어갈 자리로, 문맥상 '비영리 단체들의 역할을 강조했다'라는 의미로 전개되는 것이 적절하므로 '강조했다, 역설했다'라는 뜻의 (A) emphasized가 정답이다.
| 어휘 | keynote speech 기조 연설   role 역할   nonprofit organization 비영리 단체   poverty 빈곤, 가난   worldwide 전세계적으로   assume 추정하다, 맡다   hesitate 망설이다, 주저하다   conserve 보호하다

고난도
130. 명사 어휘
Grand Villa 인근은 고급 부티크들이 그 도시에서 가장 크게 밀집되어 있는 것으로 알려져 있다.
| 해설 | 빈칸은 앞에 있는 최상급 형용사 the city's largest의 수식을 받는 명사가 들어갈 자리로, 문맥상 '고급 부티크들이 가장 크게 밀집되어 있는 것으로 알려져 있다'라는 의미로 전개되는 것이 적절하므로 '밀집, 집중'이라는 뜻의 (B) concentration이 정답이다.
| 어휘 | neighborhood 인근, 동네   be known for ~로 알려져 있다, 유명하다   high-end 고급의   mobilization 동원, 유통   recipient 수령인, 수취인   commodity 상품, 원자재

PART 6

131-134 다음 편지를 참조하시오.

11월 16일

Charron 씨 귀하,

오늘 오전에 직접 만나 뵙고 Eastway 배송의 장부 기장을 외부에 위탁하고자 하시는 귀하의 바람에 관해 더 알게 되어 기뻤습니다. ¹³¹귀하의 회계적 요구는 저희 경험 있는 팀에 의해 쉽게 처리될 수 있습니다. 귀하께서 더 이상 이런 유형의 업무를 처리하고 싶어 하지 않으시는 것을 이해합니다. 저희 믿을 수 있는 공인 회계사들이 그 ¹³²역할을 맡아줄 수 있을 것으로 확신합니다. 귀하의 질문과 용건들이 저희 미팅 중에 ¹³³다뤄졌기를 바랍니다. 그렇지 않다면, 추가 문의 사항들에 대해 555-7966으로 저에게 부담 없이 연락해 주세요. 덧붙여, 귀하께서 ¹³⁴검토하시도록 저희 서비스에 관한 안내서를 동봉했습니다.

따뜻한 안부를 전하며,

William Satterfield

| 어휘 | in person 직접   desire 바람   outsource 외부에 위탁하다   bookkeeping 장부 기장, 부기   handle 처리하다   task 일, 업무   confident 확신하는   dependable 믿을 수 있는   certified 공인된   accountant 회계사   take on 맡다   concerns 용건, 우려 사항   feel free to 부담 없이 ~하다   further 추가의   inquiry 문의 사항   enclose 동봉하다

131. 알맞은 문장 고르기
(A) 제가 10월 청구서에서 그 오류를 즉시 삭제하겠습니다.
(B) 물품들이 제때 도착하지 않으면 제 사무실로 전화해 주세요.
(C) 귀하의 회계적 요구는 저희 경험 있는 팀에 의해 쉽게 처리될 수 있습니다.
(D) 그 업체는 상품들을 전 세계 유통 센터들로 수송합니다.
| 해설 | 앞서 장부 기장을 외부에 위탁하는 것과 관련해 고객인 you와 직접 만났음을 나타낸 문장이 제시되어 있는 것으로 볼 때, 그 연장선상에서 장부 기장을 맡을 업체 입장에서 외부 위탁 업무가 가능함을 알리는 내용의 문장이 삽입되는 것이 적절하므로 (C)가 정답이다.
| 어휘 | invoice 청구서, 송장   on time 제때, 제시간에   handle 처리하다   experienced 경험 있는, 숙련된   transport 수송하다   distribution center 유통 센터

132. 명사 어휘
| 해설 | 빈칸은 take on의 목적어가 될 명사가 들어갈 자리로, 앞서 수신자가 더 이상 회계 업무를 처리하고 싶어 하지 않는 것을 이해한다고 했고, 자사의 직원들이 회계 업무를 맡아 해줄 수 있다는 의미이므로 '역할'이라는 의미의 (B) role이 정답이다.

| 어휘 | incident 사건, 일   outcome 결과   progress 진행 (상황), 진척

133. 동사의 형태와 시제
| 해설 | 빈칸은 that절의 동사가 들어갈 자리로, address는 타동사인데 빈칸 뒤에 목적어 없이 전치사구만 있으므로 수동태가 되어야 하며, 뒤에 제시된 meeting은 오늘 오전에 있었던 일이므로 과거 시제 동사가 되어야 한다. 따라서 수동태의 과거 시제 동사인 (C) were addressed가 정답이다.

134. 동사 어휘
| 해설 | 빈칸은 to부정사를 완성해줄 동사 원형이 들어갈 자리로, 문맥상 앞에 제시된 a brochure of our services는 고객인 you가 검토할 대상이 됨을 알 수 있으므로 '검토하다'라는 뜻의 (B) review가 정답이다.
| 어휘 | translate 번역하다, 해석하다   oversee 감독하다

135-138 다음 보도 자료를 참조하시오.

Mercury 패션 가을 라인

Mercury 패션은 여러분의 라이프스타일에 어울리는 고급스러운 의류를 제공합니다. 9월 1일에, 저희가 Sapphire 플라자에서 열리는 패션쇼에서 가을 패션의 새로운 라인을 135공개할 예정입니다. 저희는 최신 패션 동향을 면밀히 주시하고 있어, 여러분의 스타일이 돋보이도록 도와줄 가장 인기 있는 색상들이 두드러진 특징이 되는 의상들을 준비할 계획입니다. 이러한 최첨단 디자인들은 매우 다양한 체형들을 돋보이게 합니다. 136또한 저희는 여러분이 섞어 조합할 수 있는 스카프와 핸드백, 모자와 같은 새로운 액세서리들도 가지고 있습니다. 137여러분이 원하시는 여러분만의 수십 가지 모습들을 연출해 보세요. 미리 보시려면 www.mercuryfashions.com을 방문하세요. 이 아름다운 품목들은 패션쇼와 같은 날에 138대부분의 고급 백화점들에 있을 것입니다.

| 어휘 | luxurious 고급스러운, 호화로운   apparel 의류, 의상   fit 어울리다   runway show 패션쇼   closely 가까이, 면밀하게   follow 따르다, 지켜보다   latest 최신의   dominate 두드러지는 특징이 되다   cutting-edge 최첨단   flattering 돋보이게 하는   a wide range of 매우 다양한   sneak peek 미리 엿보기, 살짝 엿보기   high-end 고급의

135. 동사의 시제
| 해설 | 빈칸은 문장의 동사가 들어갈 자리로, '~ on the same day as the runway show'가 제시된 마지막 문장이 미래 시제인 것으로 볼 때, 패션쇼가 열릴 On September 1은 미래임을 알 수 있으며, 예정된 미래를 나타낼 때 쓰는 표현인 be going to가 사용된 (C) are going to reveal이 정답이다.

136. 접속 부사
| 해설 | 빈칸은 앞뒤의 두 문장을 자연스럽게 연결해 줄 접속 부사가 들어갈 자리로, 뒤에 제시된 문장은 앞 문장의 추가적인 내용임을 알 수 있으므로, 추가적인 사실을 연결할 때 쓰는 접속 부사인 (B) Also가 정답이다.
| 어휘 | rather 다소, 꽤   merely 단지

137. 알맞은 문장 고르기
(A) 저희의 디자인 팀은 여러분의 주문 요구에 맞추기 위해 항상 여러분 곁에 있습니다.
(B) 그것들을 입기 전에 가격표들이 제거되어야 합니다.
(C) 여러분이 원하시는 여러분만의 수십 가지 모습들을 연출해 보세요.
(D) 저희 본사는 뉴욕 시로 이전할 것입니다.
| 해설 | 앞서 섞어 조합할 수 있는 스카프와 핸드백, 모자와 같은 새로운 액세서리들도 가지고 있다고 했으므로, 그 연장선상에서 그것들을 섞어 조합하여 다양한 모습을 연출해 볼 것을 제안하는 내용의 문장이 삽입되는 것이 적절하므로 정답은 (C)이다.
| 어휘 | stand by ~의 곁을 지키다, 대기하다   tag 가격표   remove 제거하다   create 연출하다, 만들어내다   headquarters 본사   relocate 이전하다

고난도

138. 형용사 자리 - 명사 수식
| 해설 | 빈칸은 뒤에 있는 명사 high-end department stores를 수식해 줄 형용사가 들어갈 자리이므로, 관계 대명사인 (B) which와 부사인 (D) soon은 답이 될 수 없고, '대부분의 고급 백화점들'이라는 의미를 완성해 줄 형용사인 (A) most가 정답이다.

139-142 다음 편지를 참조하시오.

10월 9일

Ralph Benton
874 Everette Way
Coral Springs, FL 33065

Benton 씨 귀하,

귀하와 귀하 팀의 공동의 139노력 덕분에, Otis 대여점이 플로리다에서 최고의 렌터카 대리점이 되었습니다. 귀하의 리더십 하에 우리 시장 점유율은 불과 3년만에 15%에서 41%로 증가했습니다. 140그러한 성취는 우리 분야에서 좀처럼 볼 수 없는 것입니다.

Otis 대여점을 대표하여, 귀하께 텍사스 지점으로 옮겨 오는 것을 요청드리고 싶은데, 그곳에서 지역 관리자의 역할을 맡게 될 것입니다. 이 지역은 국내에서 가장 경쟁이 심한 곳으로 141여겨지지만, 귀하가 도전을 감당할 것이라고 생각합니다. 선호되는 시작 날짜는 11월 15일입니다. 142그러나 준비하는 데 시간이 더 필요하시다면, 저희가 어느 정도 융통성을 발휘할 수 있습니다.

진심을 담아,

최고 운영 책임자, Lucille Walsh
Otis 대여점

| 어휘 | collaborative 공동의, 협력적인   market share 시장 점유율

on behalf of ~을 대표하여, 대신하여   invite 요청하다
transfer 옮기다, 전근 가다   take on the role of ~의 역할을 맡다
competitive 경쟁력 있는, 경쟁을 하는   be up to the challenge 도전을
감당하다   preferred 선호되는   flexible 융통성 있는, 유연한
make arrangements 준비를 하다

139. 명사 어휘

| 해설 | 빈칸은 형용사 collaborative의 수식을 받는 명사가 들어갈 자리로, 문맥상 '공동의 노력 덕분에'라는 의미로 전개되는 것이 적절하므로 '노력, 수고'라는 뜻의 (A) efforts가 정답이다.

140. 알맞은 문장 고르기

(A) 저는 처음으로 플로리다로 여행을 갈 것입니다.
(B) 그러한 성취는 우리 분야에서 좀처럼 볼 수 없는 것입니다.
(C) 어떤 입사 지원자를 선호하시는지 확인해 주시기 바랍니다.
(D) 그것은 네 개의 문과 뒤쪽에 넓은 트렁크가 있었습니다.

| 해설 | 앞서 시장 점유율이 단기간에 크게 증가한 사실이 제시되어 있는 것으로 볼 때, 그 연장선상에서 그러한 성취가 좀처럼 흔한 일이 아님을 덧붙이는 문장이 연결되는 것이 적절하므로 (B)가 정답이다.

| 어휘 | accomplishment 성취, 업적   rarely 좀처럼 ~않는   confirm 확인하다, 확정하다   job candidate 입사 지원자   spacious 넓은, 널찍한

고난도

141. 동사의 형태와 시제

| 해설 | 빈칸은 문장의 동사가 들어갈 자리로, 주어인 This region이 경쟁이 심한 곳으로 '여겨지는' 것이므로 수동태가 되어야 하며, but으로 이어지는 내용이 '하지만 그 도전을 감당할 수 있을 거라고 생각한다'는 것이므로, 경쟁이 심한 것이 현재 상황임을 알 수 있다. 따라서 현재 시제 수동태인 (C) is considered가 정답이다.

142. 접속 부사

| 해설 | 빈칸은 앞뒤의 두 문장의 내용을 적절히 연결해 줄 접속 부사가 들어갈 자리로, 선호되는 시작 날짜를 제시한 앞의 문장과 어느 정도 융통성을 발휘할 수 있다고 가능성을 열어둔 뒤의 문장은 서로 대조적인 내용이므로 역접, 대조를 나타내는 '그러나, 하지만'이라는 뜻의 (D) However가 정답이다.

| 어휘 | consequently 결과적으로   besides 게다가, 더욱이

143-146 다음 기사를 참조하시오.

(10월 12일)—국내 최대의 주택 소유자 보험 제공업체들 중 하나인 Rapid 보험사가 경영진의 변화를 발표했다. Lillian Howes가 Rapid 보험사의 이사회에 의해 회사의 새로운 CEO로 선정되었다. 그녀는 13년 동안 그 직책을 맡아왔던 James Loftin의 143뒤를 잇는다.

"Loftin 씨는 자선 분야에서 일하기 위해 회사를 떠날 것이고, 저희는 그의 144향후 노력이 모두 잘되기를 바랍니다."라고 Rapid 보험사 대변인 Anna Gilley가 말했다. 투자자들은 그 변화에 기뻐하는데, Howes 씨가 Rapid 보험사의 운영에 낯선 사람이 아니기 때문이다. "Howes 씨는 3년 전에 최고 운영 책임자가 되기 전에 145앞서 회사의 전무 이사로 일했습니다."라고 Gilley 씨가 말했다. "146저희는 이 전환이 순조롭게 진행될 것이라고 생각합니다."

| 어휘 | provider 제공업체   homeowners insurance 주택 소유자 보험   executive 임원, 중역   board 이사회   charity sector 자선 분야   wish all the best 모두 잘되기를 바라다   endeavor 노력   spokesperson 대변인   investor 투자자   be no stranger to ~에 낯선 사람이 아니다, ~를 잘 알고 있다   operation 운영   managing director 전무 이사   chief operating officer 최고 운영 책임자   comment 말하다, 언급하다

143. 동사의 형태와 시제

| 해설 | 빈칸은 문장의 동사가 들어갈 자리로, 빈칸 뒤에 목적어 James Loftin이 있으므로 능동태가 되어야 하며, James Loftin의 뒤를 잇는 것은 앞으로 예정된 상황이므로 미래 시제 혹은 현재 시제로 표현이 가능하다. 따라서 능동태의 현재 시제 동사인 (B) succeeds가 정답이다.

144. 형용사 어휘

| 해설 | 빈칸은 명사 endeavors를 수식해 줄 형용사가 들어갈 자리로, 앞 절의 미래 시제 동사 will leave로 볼 때 모두 잘되기를 바라는 대상이 될 수 있는 것은 '그의 향후 노력'일 것이므로 '향후의, 미래의'라는 뜻의 (C) future가 정답이다.

| 어휘 | constant 끊임없는, 거듭되는   accurate 정확한   distant 먼, 멀리 있는

145. 부사 어휘

| 해설 | 빈칸은 동사 worked를 수식해줄 부사가 들어갈 자리로, 문맥상 이전에 회사의 전무 이사로 일했던 상황을 알리는 내용으로 전개되는 것이 적절하므로 '이전에, 앞서'라는 뜻의 (D) previously가 정답이다.

| 어휘 | authentically 진정으로, 확실하게   suddenly 갑자기, 급작스럽게   regrettably 유감스럽게, 애석하게

146. 알맞은 문장 고르기

(A) 저희는 그 문제를 주의 깊게 조사할 계획입니다.
(B) 저희는 이 전환이 순조롭게 진행될 것이라고 생각합니다.
(C) 새로운 보험 패키지가 인기를 얻게 되었습니다.
(D) 이사회가 곧 최종 결정을 내릴 것입니다.

| 해설 | 앞서 투자자들이 새로운 CEO가 선정된 변화에 기뻐하는 이유와 그녀의 이전 경력에 관해서 구체적으로 알리는 내용이 제시되어 있는 것으로 볼 때, 이와 관련 지어 CEO의 변화를 the transition으로 받아 순조롭게 진행될 것으로 생각하는 바를 전하는 내용의 문장이 이어지는 것이 적절하므로 (B)가 정답이다.

| 어휘 | look into ~을 조사하다, 살펴보다   carefully 주의 깊게, 신중하게   transition 전환, 이행   smooth 순조로운, 원활한   decision 결정

PART 7

147-148 다음 정보를 참조하시오.

흥분과 스릴이 바로 앞으로 다가왔다!

¹⁴⁷Nick Murray 감독은 최근 인터뷰에서 인기 있는 <The Warrant>의 속편이 7월 29일에 나올 것이라고 밝혔다. <The Warrant 2: Deadly Search>라는 제목의 그 영화는 Eric Jackson이 주연을 맡고 전국 극장에서 상영될 것이다.

Baxter 극장은 그 영화를 위한 특별한 프로모션을 하고 있다. ¹⁴⁸7월 20일까지 www.baxter99.com에서 티켓을 예약하면, <The Warrant 2>의 사운드트랙의 열여덟 곡 중 하나를 다운로드할 수 있는 쿠폰을 받을 것이다.

| 어휘 | excitement 흥분, 신남   around the corner 임박하여, 아주 가까운   director 감독   reveal 밝히다, 드러내다   sequel 속편   come out 나오다   nationwide 전국적으로   voucher 쿠폰, 할인권

147. 세부 사항을 묻는 문제
정보에 따르면, 7월 29일에 무슨 일이 있을 것인가?
(A) 유명인이 인터뷰를 할 것이다.
(B) 가격이 하락할 것이다.
(C) 극장이 개장할 것이다.
(D) 영화가 첫선을 보일 것이다.

| 해설 | 첫 번째 단락에 Nick Murray 감독이 최근 인터뷰에서 인기 있는 <The Warrant>의 속편이 7월 29일에 나올 것이라고 밝혔다고(Director Nick Murray revealed in a recent interview that the sequel to the popular The Warrant is coming out on July 29) 제시되어 있으므로 정답은 (D)이다.

| 어휘 | celebrity 유명인, 유명 인사   decrease 하락하다, 감소하다   debut 첫선을 보이다, 데뷔하다

| 패러프레이징 | is coming out → will debut

148. 세부 사항을 묻는 문제
무료 음악 쿠폰은 어떻게 받을 수 있는가?
(A) 단체 티켓을 구입함으로써
(B) 설문 조사를 완료함으로써
(C) 온라인 예약을 함으로써
(D) 장소에 일찍 도착함으로써

| 해설 | 두 번째 단락에 7월 20일까지 www.baxter99.com에서 티켓을 예약하면 <The Warrant 2>의 사운드트랙의 열여덟 곡 중 하나를 다운로드할 수 있는 쿠폰을 받을 것이라고(Book your ticket at www.baxter99.com by July 20, and you'll be sent a voucher to download one of the eighteen songs from The Warrant 2's soundtrack) 제시되어 있으므로 정답은 (C)이다.

| 어휘 | survey 설문 조사

| 패러프레이징 | Book your ticket at www.baxter99.com → making an online reservation

---

149-150 다음 이메일을 참조하시오.

수신: 전 직원 <staff@cahaltravel.com>
발신: Vadim Bodrova <v.bodrova@cahaltravel.com>
날짜: 12월 18일
제목: 재구매

직원 회의에서 논의했던 대로, Cahal 여행사는 우리를 통해 한 차례 이상 예약하는 고객들의 비율을 높이기 위한 방안들을 찾고 있습니다. ¹⁴⁹현재 우리는 우리를 통해 해외 여행을 예약했던 고객들에게 일 년에 한 번 연락하여 관심을 가질 만한 패키지들을 소개하고 있습니다. 다음 주부터 4개월마다 한 번씩 여행 패키지들에 관한 정보를 보내려고 합니다. ¹⁵⁰참조를 위해 실제 등재된 고객의 아래 예시를 봐 주세요.

현재	신규
이름: 고객 이름	¹⁵⁰이름: Henrik Hetland
전화: 전화 번호	전화: 649-555-3328
이메일 주소: 이메일 주소	이메일 주소: hhetland@broadmoorinc.net
목적지(들): 이전 여행 장소들	¹⁵⁰목적지(들): 일본, 도쿄; 칠레, 산티아고
연락: 선호하는 연락 방식	연락: 이메일
	마지막 연락: 12월 2일

새로운 절차에 관해 있을 수 있는 질문들에 기꺼이 답해 드리겠습니다.

감사합니다!

Vadim Bodrova
Cahal 여행사

| 어휘 | percentage 비율   currently 현재   annually 매년, 일 년에 한 번   international trip 해외 여행   introduce 소개하다   entry 기재 사항, 등재 항목   reference 참고, 참조   destination 목적지   procedure 절차, 방법

149. 세부 사항을 묻는 문제
업체는 무엇을 변경할 것인가?
(A) 여행 예약 수수료
(B) 여행 패키지 단체들의 규모
(C) 이전 고객들에게 연락하는 빈도
(D) 새로운 휴가 계획자들의 요건

| 해설 | 현재 해외 여행을 예약했던 고객들에게 일 년에 한 번 연락하여(we annually contact customers who have booked an international trip with us ~) 관심을 가질 만한 패키지들을 소개하고 있는데, 다음 주부터 4개월마다 한 번씩 여행 패키지들에 관한 정보를 보내려고 한다는(we will send them information about tour packages once every four months) 내용으로 볼 때, 연락 횟수를 변경하는 것임을 알 수 있으므로 정답은 (C)이다.

| 어휘 | processing 처리   frequency 빈도   requirement 자격, 요건

🏠 고난도

150. 추론 문제

Hetland 씨는 누구일 것 같은가?
(A) 일자리 지원자
(B) 여행사 직원
(C) 항공사 직원
(D) 해외 여행자

| 해설 | Hetland 씨는 실제 등재된 고객 예시로(an example of a real customer entry) 제시된 고객으로, 목적지(들) 항목에서 일본과 칠레를 (Destination(s): Tokyo, Japan; Santiago, Chile) 여행했던 것을 알 수 있으므로 정답은 (D)이다.

| 어휘 | candidate 지원자, 후보자

151-152 다음 온라인 채팅 토론을 참조하시오.

> **Stewart Bowser** [오전 9:24]
> 시간 좀 있어요? ¹⁵¹Joseph Harris 씨가 Pritchard 선생님에게 검진을 받을 수 있도록 시간대를 예약하려고 하는데, 문제가 있어서요. 그가 시스템에 두 차례 입력되었던 것 같은데요. 어느 파일을 사용해야 할지 모르겠네요.
>
> **Delilah Gibbs** [오전 9:25]
> 그것은 누군가 변경 사항을 제대로 저장하지 않고 새로운 환자 정보를 입력할 때 종종 발생하는 일이에요. 하지만 ¹⁵²같은 이름을 가진 두 사람이 있을 수도 있어요.
>
> **Stewart Bowser** [오전 9:26]
> 좋은 지적이에요. 그런 경우인지 어떻게 알 수 있을까요?
>
> **Delilah Gibbs** [오전 9:27]
> ¹⁵²환자의 신원을 확인하려면 생년월일을 보세요. 그러면 제대로 된 것을 가지고 있는지 아닌지 알 수 있을 거예요.
>
> **Stewart Bowser** [오전 9:28]
> 당연히 그렇겠네요! 고마워요!

| 어휘 | reserve 예약하다   time slot 시간대   have a checkup 진찰을 받다   enter 입력하다   input 입력하다   patient 환자   information 정보   properly 제대로, 적절히   case 경우   birth date 생년월일   confirm 확인하다   identity 신원

---

151. 세부 사항을 묻는 문제

Bowser 씨는 무엇을 하려고 하는가?
(A) 주소 변경하기
(B) 예약하기
(C) 환자에게 청구서 보내기
(D) 의사에게 연락하기

| 해설 | Stewart Bowser가 오전 9:24에 환자가 검진을 받을 시간대를 예약하려고 한다고(I'm trying to reserve a time slot ~) 했으므로 정답은 (B)이다.

| 어휘 | bill 청구서를 보내다   contact 연락하다

| 패러프레이징 | reserve a time slot → Make an appointment

---

152. 의도 파악 문제

오전 9:28에 Bowser 씨가 "당연히 그렇겠네요"라고 쓸 때 의미하는 것은 무엇일 것 같은가?
(A) 그는 환자를 개인적으로 알고 있다.
(B) 컴퓨터가 잘 작동하고 있다.
(C) 그는 Gibbs 씨를 도울 의향이 있다.
(D) 해결책이 확실하다.

| 해설 | 이는 앞서 Delilah Gibbs가 이름이 같은 두 사람이 있을 수도 있다며(there could also be two people with the same name), 환자의 신원을 확인하려면 생년월일을 보라고(Look at the birth date to confirm the patient's identity) 알려준 것에 대한 응답으로, 문제 상황에 대한 확실한 해결책을 제시해 준 것에 대해 당연히 그렇겠다고 호응하는 것임을 알 수 있으므로 정답은 (D)이다.

| 어휘 | personally 개인적으로   be willing to ~할 의향이 있다   solution 해결책   obvious 확실한, 분명한

153-155 다음 이메일을 참조하시오.

> 수신: Hans Edgren <h.edgren@lincoya.com>
> 발신: Amherst 은행 <accounts@amherstbank.com>
> 날짜: 12월 9일
> 제목: Amherst 은행 신용 카드
>
> Edgren 씨 귀하,
>
> ¹⁵³귀하의 Amherst 은행 신용 카드의 한도가 1,800달러에서 2,500달러로 상향되었음을 알려드리기 위해 이 글을 씁니다. ㅡ[1]ㅡ. 저희는 지난 한 해 동안 귀하의 계정에 연체가 없었기 때문에 이러한 조치를 취합니다. 귀하 계정의 금리도 2퍼센트 낮아질 것입니다. ㅡ[2]ㅡ.
>
> 이러한 조건에 만족하신다면, 귀하의 서비스 계약이 자동으로 업데이트될 것이고, 더 이상의 조치는 필요하지 않습니다. 하지만 ¹⁵⁴/¹⁵⁵이전 신용 한도와 금리로 돌아가기를 원하신다면, 1-800-555-7799로 전화하여 은행에 알려주세요. ㅡ[3]ㅡ. Amherst 은행 고객이 되어 주셔서 감사합니다. ㅡ[4]ㅡ.
>
> 진심을 담아,
>
> Benjamin Elliot
> Amherst 은행, 고객 서비스

| 어휘 | limit 한도   raise 올리다   take action 조치를 취하다   late payment 연체, 늦은 지불   interest rate 금리, 이율   lower 내리다, 낮추다   be satisfied with ~에 만족하다   automatically 자동적으로   previous 이전의

📌 고난도
153. 주제/목적 문제
Elliot 씨는 Edgren 씨에게 왜 이메일을 보냈나?
(A) 일부 비정상적인 신용 카드 이용을 확인하기 위해
(B) 그에게 신용 한도에 도달했음을 상기시키기 위해
(C) 그의 신용 카드 계정의 변경 사항에 관해 알리기 위해
(D) 그의 계정에 월 청구액을 지불하도록 요청하기 위해

| 해설 | 첫 번째 단락에 귀하의 Amherst 은행 신용 카드의 한도가 1,800달러에서 2,500달러로 상향되었음을 알리기 위해 이 글을 쓴다고(I am writing to inform you that the limit on your Amherst Bank credit card has been raised from $1,800 to $2,500) 제시되어 있으므로 정답은 (C)이다.

| 어휘 | unusual 비정상적인, 특이한   remind 상기시키다   monthly bill 월 청구액

| 패러프레이징 | inform → notify

📌 고난도
154. 세부 사항을 묻는 문제
Edgren 씨에게 하도록 요청되는 것은 무엇인가?
(A) 일부 조건을 다시 설정하기를 원하면 회사에 연락하는 것
(B) 계정에 있는 그의 청구서 주소를 업데이트하는 것
(C) 그가 최근 구매를 승인했다는 것을 확인하는 것
(D) 연체하는 것에 대한 이유를 제공하는 것

| 해설 | 두 번째 단락에 이전 신용 한도와 금리로 돌아가기를 원하면, 전화하여 은행에 알려달라고(should you wish to return to the previous credit limit and interest rate, please inform the bank ~) 제시되어 있으므로 정답은 (A)이다.

| 어휘 | reset 재설정하다   terms 조건   billing address 청구지 주소   verify 확인하다, 입증하다

| 패러프레이징 | return to the previous credit limit and interest rate → reset some terms

155. 문장 삽입 문제
[1], [2], [3], [4]로 표시된 곳 중에 다음 문장이 들어가기에 가장 적절한 곳은?
"귀하의 요청에 대한 확인서는 이메일로 보내질 것입니다."

(A) [1]
(B) [2]
(C) [3]
(D) [4]

| 해설 | 제시된 문장은 고객인 Edgren 씨의 요청에 대한 확인서가 이메일로 보내질 것이라는 내용으로, 그 요청과 관련 지어 두 번째 단락에 이전 신용 한도와 금리로 돌아가기를 원하면 전화하여 은행에 알려달라고(please inform the bank by calling) 한 후, 주어진 문장이 이어지는 것이 가장 적절하므로 정답은 (C)이다.

| 어휘 | confirmation 확인, 확인서

156-157 다음 회람을 참조하시오.

수신: Magnolia Advisors 전 직원
발신: Kwang-min Hwang
날짜: 10월 24일
제목: 금융 데이터

Magnolia Advisors는 점점 늘고 있는 저희 고객들의 민감한 금융 데이터를 책임지고 있습니다. 이 때문에, ¹⁵⁶집행 위원회가 기밀 파일들의 보호를 개선하고 무단 접근을 방지하기 위해 몇 가지 변화를 단행하기로 결정했습니다. 11월 6일에 모든 파일 보관실의 문에 카드 판독기가 설치될 것이고, 직원들에게는 키 카드가 발급될 것입니다. 카드가 없는 사람들의 출입을 거부하는 것뿐만 아니라 카드 판독기는 보관실에 들어간 사람과 시간을 기록할 것입니다. ¹⁵⁷카드 판독기가 오작동하는 경우, 유지 관리 책임자인 Jim Abbott의 사무실을 방문하세요. 변경 사항에 대해 질문이나 용건이 있으면, 부담 없이 내선 23번으로 저에게 전화하세요.

| 어휘 | financial 금융의, 재정의   be responsible for ~을 책임지고 있다   increasing 증가하는   sensitive 민감한   executive committee 집행 위원회   improve 개선하다   confidential 기밀의   prevent 방지하다, 예방하다   unauthorized access 무단 접근   install 설치하다   storage room 보관실   issue 발급하다   deny 거부하다   entry 출입, 입장   keep a record of ~을 기록해 두다   malfunction 오작동하다   concern 용건, 우려   extension 내선

156. 주제/목적 문제
회람의 목적은 무엇인가?
(A) 디지털 파일들을 보관하는 컴퓨터 소프트웨어를 설명하는 것
(B) 직원들에게 강화된 보안 조치들에 관해 알리는 것
(C) 재정적 목표를 달성한 것에 대해 직원들을 축하하는 것
(D) 고객 상호 작용에 관한 새로운 정책을 소개하는 것

| 해설 | 도입부에 집행 위원회가 기밀 파일들의 보호를 개선하고 무단 접근을 방지하기 위해 몇 가지 변화를 단행하기로 결정했다고(the executive committee has decided to make changes to improve the protection of confidential files and prevent unauthorized access) 제시되어 있으므로 정답은 (B)이다.

| 어휘 | describe 설명하다   security measure 보안 조치   policy 정책, 방침   interaction 상호 작용

| 패러프레이징 | improve the protection of confidential files and prevent unauthorized access → increased security measures

157. 세부 사항을 묻는 문제
Hwang 씨는 기기가 작동하지 않을 경우 무엇을 하라고 권하는가?
(A) 유지 관리 직원을 방문하는 것
(B) 이메일로 문제를 알리는 것
(C) 그의 사무실로 그에게 전화하는 것
(D) 일부 교체 장비를 주문하는 것

| 해설 | 후반부에 카드 판독기가 오작동하는 경우, 유지 관리 책임자인 Jim Abbott의 사무실을 방문하라고(If a card reader malfunctions, please see Maintenance Director Jim Abbott in his office) 제시되어 있으므로 정답은 (A)이다.
| 어휘 | replacement 교체, 대체
| 패러프레이징 | ·a card reader malfunctions → a device is not working
·see Maintenance Director → Visiting a maintenance employee

158-160 다음 이메일을 참조하시오.

수신: Ellie Jarvis <elliejarvis@boylestoninc.com>
발신: GTP 청소 <info@gtpcleaning.com>
날짜: 1월 19일
제목: 주문 #49025

Jarvis 씨 귀하,

GTP 청소를 대표하여, 158배송이 일정보다 늦어지게 된 귀하의 주문 (#49025)에 발생한 문제에 대해 사과를 드리고 싶습니다.

다음 제품들은 재고가 있어 오늘 발송되어 2-3일 이내에 귀하의 우편 주소로 도착할 것입니다:

Brightex 목재용 광택제, 9.7온스 통
McGraw 다목적 세제, 32온스 병
Trumbull 수세미, 6개 팩
Avery 유리 세정제, 26온스 병, 신형 무독성의 제조

다음 물품은 현재 재고가 없습니다:

159Freida Pod, 2.5온스 방향제 세트 3개 팩, 벚꽃 향

저희는 품절인 물품에 대한 대체품들을 4~6주 동안 저희 창고로 받지 못할 것입니다. 아무런 조치도 취하지 않으실 경우, 이 물품은 다시 입고 되는 대로 배송될 것입니다. 개별 배송에 대한 추가 요금은 없을 것입니다. 159카밍 라벤더와 프렌치 바닐라 같은 동일한 방향제의 다양한 향이 있음을 유념해 주세요. 160여기를 클릭하여 저희 웹 사이트에서 전체 목록을 확인해 보세요, 선호하는 것을 찾으실 수도 있으니까요. 그럴 경우, 최종 물품이 발송되기 전에 언제든 귀하의 계정에서 주문을 수정하실 수 있습니다.

애용해 주셔서 감사드립니다!

Leon Espinoza
GTP 청소

| 어휘 | on behalf of ~을 대표하여, 대신하여   behind schedule 일정 보다 늦어진   be in[out of] stock 재고가 있다[없다]   dispatch 발송

하다   canister 통, 용기   all-purpose 다목적의, 만능의   non-toxic 무독성의   formula 제조법   currently 현재   air-freshener 방향제   replacement 대체품, 대용품   warehouse 창고   take no action 아무 조치를 취하지 않다   available 구할 수 있는   additional 추가의   charge 요금   separate 개별적인, 별개의   variation 다양한 것, 변형   complete 완전한, 전체의   adjust 조정하다   patronage 애용

158. 주제/목적 문제
이메일은 왜 보내졌나?
(A) 환불을 제공하기 위해
(B) 요청을 승인하기 위해
(C) 지연을 설명하기 위해
(D) 제품을 홍보하기 위해

| 해설 | 도입부에 배송이 일정보다 늦어지게 된 문제에 대해 사과를 하고 싶다고 (I would like to apologize for an issue with your order (#49025) that has put its delivery behind schedule) 한 후, 재고에 따른 배송 상황에 관해 설명하고 있으므로 정답은 (C)이다.
| 어휘 | refund 환불   approve 승인하다   delay 지연   promote 홍보하다
| 패러프레이징 | behind schedule → a delay

고난도
159. True 문제
Freida Pod에 관해 언급된 것은 무엇인가?
(A) 단종되었다.
(B) 여러 향들로 구입이 가능하다.
(C) 무독성 재료들이 들어 있다.
(D) 가장 인기 있는 제품이다.

| 해설 | Freida Pod는 중반부에 현재 재고가 없다고 한 벚꽃 향의 방향제 세트 (air-freshener units, Cherry Blossom fragrance)로 확인된다. 이와 관련하여 아래 단락 중반부에 카밍 라벤더와 프렌치 바닐라 같은 동일한 방향제의 다양한 향이 있다고(there are variations of the same air-freshener, such as Calming Lavender and French Vanilla) 했으므로 정답은 (B)이다.
| 어휘 | discontinue (생산을) 중단하다   multiple 여러 가지의, 많은   scent 향   ingredient 재료

160. 세부 사항을 묻는 문제
Espinoza 씨가 Jarvis 씨에게 하도록 요청하는 것은 무엇인가?
(A) 온라인에서 몇몇 대체 옵션들을 보는 것
(B) 그녀의 주문량을 확인하는 것
(C) 현재 주문에 대한 대금을 다시 보내는 것
(D) 제품을 테스트한 후 피드백을 제공하는 것

| 해설 | 아래쪽 단락 후반부에 여기를 클릭하여 웹 사이트에서 전체 목록을 확인해 보라고(Please click here to check out the complete list on our Web site) 한 후 선호하는 것을 찾을 수도 있다고(as you may find something you prefer) 덧붙이고 있으므로 정답은 (A)이다.
| 어휘 | alternative 대체 가능한, 대안이 되는   quantity 양   payment 지불금, 납입

| 패러프레이징 | · check out → View
· something you prefer → alternative options
· Web site → online

161-163 다음 기사를 참조하시오.

Cantrece 쇼핑 센터가 국가적인 상을 받다

3월 22일—Cantrece 쇼핑 센터가 어젯밤 San Mateo 호텔에서 열린 시상식에서 권위 있는 Conifer 상을 받았다. ¹⁶¹그 상은 매년 그 건물이 친환경적인 관행을 따르고, 환경 파괴 없이 지속 가능한 건축 자재를 쓰고, 에너지 소비를 줄이는 회사나 기관에 수여된다. 이 쇼핑 센터는 이 모든 카테고리들의 모범적인 모델이다. 그 건물의 옥상에 있는 태양 전지판은 그 건물 수요의 80% 이상을 공급한다. 게다가 채광창들은 낮 시간 조명의 필요성을 줄이고, 빗물 수집 시스템은 화장실용 물과 청소용 물을 공급한다. ¹⁶²그 건물의 설계자인 Yolanda Knapp이 시상식에서 상을 받기 위해 참석했고, 그녀는 자신과 그 동료들이 자원을 책임 있게 사용하는 기능적인 건축물을 만들어내기 위해 계속 노력할 것이라고 말했다.

Conifer 상의 수상자를 선정하는 심사 위원단이 계속해서 그들의 기준을 충족시키는 회사들을 찾고 있다. ¹⁶³회사를 이 상에 고려되도록 추천하고 싶다면, www.coniferprize.com을 방문하면 된다.

| 어휘 | be honored with ~의 영광을 가지다   prestigious 권위 있는   ceremony 시상식, 의식   present 수여하다   annually 매년   organization 기관   follow 따르다   eco-friendly 친환경적인   practice 관행   sustainable (환경 파괴 없이) 지속 가능한   materials 재료, 자재   reduce 줄이다   consumption 소비   exemplary 모범적인, 본보기가 되는   solar panel 태양 전지판   rooftop 옥상   supply 공급하다   skylight 채광창   lighting 조명   rainwater collection 빗물 수집   flushing 물내림   colleague 동료   strive 노력하다   functional 기능적인   structure 구조물, 건축물   resources 자원   responsibly 책임 있게   judging panel 심사 위원단   continually 계속해서   meet one's criteria 기준을 충족시키다, 기준에 맞다

161. 세부 사항을 묻는 문제
Cantrece 쇼핑 센터는 무엇 때문에 상을 받았나?
(A) 환경친화적인 설계
(B) 자선 단체 기부
(C) 독특한 판매용 제품들
(D) 기록적인 고객 수
| 해설 | 도입부에 Cantrece 쇼핑 센터의 수상 사실을 알린 후, 그 상은 매년 그 건물이 친환경적인 관행을 따르고, 환경 파괴 없이 지속 가능한 건축 자재를 쓰고, 에너지 소비를 줄이는 회사나 기관에 수여되는 상이라고(~ whose building follows eco-friendly practices, uses sustainable building materials, and reduces energy consumption) 제시되어 있으므로 정답은 (A)이다.
| 어휘 | environmentally friendly 환경친화적인   contribution 기부   charity 자선 단체   unique 독특한

162. 추론 문제
Knapp 씨는 어디에서 일하는 것 같은가?
(A) 잡지사에서
(B) 쇼핑 센터에서
(C) 부동산 중개업소에서
(D) 건축 회사에서
| 해설 | 첫 번째 단락 후반부에 그 건물의 설계자인 Yolanda Knapp(The building's designer, Yolanda Knapp)이라고 제시되어 있으므로 정답은 (D)이다.
| 어휘 | magazine publisher 잡지사   real estate agency 부동산 중개업소

163. 세부 사항을 묻는 문제
기사에 따르면, 웹 사이트에서 무엇을 할 수 있나?
(A) 선정 기준 목록을 다운로드하는 것
(B) 이전 수상자들의 사진을 보는 것
(C) 회사들을 향후 상의 후보로 추천하는 것
(D) Knapp 씨와의 인터뷰를 읽는 것
| 해설 | 두 번째 단락 후반부에 회사를 이 상에 고려되도록 추천하고 싶다면 웹 사이트를 방문하라고(If you would like to recommend a company to be considered for this prize ~) 알려주고 있으므로 정답은 (C)이다.
| 어휘 | selection 선택, 선정   criteria 기준   previous 이전의   nominate 후보로 추천하다, 지명하다
| 패러프레이징 | recommend a company → Nominating companies

164-167 다음 이메일을 참조하시오.

수신: Sylvia Reid <s.reid@harringoninc.com>
발신: Chris Alexander <chris_alexander@modoccorp.com>
날짜: 2월 19일
제목: Modoc 사

Reid 씨 귀하,

샌프란시스코에서 열렸던 ¹⁶⁵최근의 화장품 소매업체 무역 박람회에서 귀하를 만나게 되어 기뻤습니다. ¹⁶⁴/¹⁶⁷약속대로 Modoc 사의 최신 카탈로그를 보내드립니다. —[1]—.

¹⁶⁵귀하가 가게의 매출을 증가시킬 방안을 찾고 계시다는 것을 알고 있고, 저희 제품들이 이 목표에 도달하도록 도와드릴 수 있을 것이라고 생각합니다. —[2]—. ¹⁶⁵저희는 다양한 얼굴 크림과 세안제, 그리고 기타 스킨케어 제품들을 가지고 있습니다. ¹⁶⁶저희 베스트셀러 중 하나는 Meridian으로, 매일 사용하는 가벼운 보습제입니다. ¹⁶⁶고객들은 향이 없기 때문에 그것을 좋아하는데, 그래서 그것이 그들의 향수나 다른 미용 제품과 어떻게 결합될 수 있을지에 관해 걱정하지 않아도 됩니다. —[3]—.

질문이 있으시면, 언제든 기꺼이 대답해 드리겠습니다. —[4]—. 이 이메일 주소나 248-555-0973으로 저에게 연락하실 수 있습니다.

따뜻한 안부를 전하며,

Chris Alexander

| 어휘 | cosmetics 화장품   retailer 소매업자, 소매업체   as promised 약속대로   boost 증가시키다   reach 도달하다   goal 목표   a variety of 다양한   lightweight 가벼운   moisturizer 보습제   intended for ~를 위한 것인, ~를 위해 의도된   fragrance-free 향이 없는   combine with ~와 결합되다   perfume 향수   beauty product 미용 제품

🔺 고난도
164. 주제/목적 문제
이메일의 목적은 무엇인가?
(A) 시연에 대해 Reid 씨에게 감사하는 것
(B) 요청을 이행하는 것
(C) 무역 박람회에 등록하는 것
(D) 업무 회의를 정하는 것

| 해설 | 첫 번째 단락에 약속대로 Modoc 사의 최신 카탈로그를 보낸다고(As promised, I'm sending you the current catalog for Modoc Corp.) 한 것에서 요청을 이행할 목적으로 보낸 이메일임을 유추할 수 있으므로 정답은 (B)이다.
| 어휘 | demonstration 시연   follow through on ~을 이행하다, 완수하다   set up 정하다

165. 추론 문제
Reid 씨에 관해 암시되는 것은 무엇인가?
(A) 무료 샘플들을 써 봤다.
(B) 샌프란시스코에 살고 있다.
(C) 새로운 향수를 개발했다.
(D) 화장품 분야에서 일한다.

| 해설 | Reid 씨는 이메일 수신자로, 최근의 화장품 소매업체 무역 박람회에서 만나 기뻤다고(It was a pleasure meeting you at the recent Cosmetics Retailers Trade Expo) 한 것과 가게의 매출을 증가시킬 방안을 찾고 있다는 것을 알고 있다고(I understand that you are looking for ways to boost sales in your shop) 한 것, 다양한 얼굴 크림과 세안제, 그리고 기타 스킨케어 제품들을 가지고 있다고(We have a variety of face creams, cleansers, and other skincare products) 한 것을 종합해 볼 때, 화장품 분야에서 일하고 있는 것으로 유추할 수 있으므로 정답은 (D)이다.
| 어휘 | develop 개발하다   field 분야

166. 세부 사항을 묻는 문제
Meridian의 이점으로 언급된 것은 무엇인가?
(A) 냄새가 없다.
(B) 환경친화적이다.
(C) 오랫동안 지속된다.
(D) 다양한 크기로 나온다.

| 해설 | 두 번째 단락 중반부에 베스트셀러들 중 하나는 Meridian으로(One of our best sellers is Meridian) 고객들은 향이 없기 때문에 그것을 좋아한다고(Customers love it because it is fragrance-free) 제시되어 있으므로 정답은 (A)이다.
| 어휘 | odor 냄새   environmentally friendly 환경친화적인   last 지속되다   various 다양한
| 패러프레이징 | is fragrance-free → does not have any odor

167. 문장 삽입 문제
[1], [2], [3], [4]로 표시된 곳 중에, 다음 문장이 들어가기에 가장 적절한 곳은?

"분명히 그 안에 귀하가 관심이 있을 많은 품목들이 있다는 것을 아시게 될 것입니다."

(A) [1]
(B) [2]
(C) [3]
(D) [4]

| 해설 | 제시된 문장에 대명사 it이 있는 것으로 볼 때, 이를 가리키는 것이 구체적으로 언급된 문장 뒤에 들어가야 함을 알 수 있는데, it이 될 수 있는 것은 첫 번째 단락의 Modoc 사의 최신 카탈로그(the current catalog for Modoc Corp.)일 것이므로, 약속대로 Modoc 사의 최신 카탈로그를 보내드린다고(As promised, I'm sending you the current catalog for Modoc Corp.) 한 문장 뒤인 (A)가 정답이다.
| 어휘 | numerous 많은, 수많은

168-171 다음 온라인 채팅 토론을 참조하시오.

Kelly Ward [오후 1:30]
안녕하세요. 제가 Esther Tsao를 이 채팅에 초대했어요, 기획하는 것을 돕겠다고 자원하셨거든요.

Esther Tsao [오후 1:31]
이 행사의 일원으로 일하게 되어 기쁩니다. [168]제가 운영했던 지붕 공사업체가 지금은 문을 닫았지만, 수년간 콘퍼런스의 저희 부스에서 많은 자재들을 항상 팔았습니다.

Kelly Ward [오후 1:32]
그렇다고 하시니 기쁘네요. 이제 다른 측면에서 참여하실 수 있을 거예요.

Herbert Inez [오후 1:34]
당신의 도움을 받게 되어 기쁩니다. [169]처음으로 둘째 날을 추가하는 것은 몇 가지 특별한 도전을 불러일으키는데요. 예를 들어, [170]10월 8일 주말에 이용 가능한 것으로 제가 찾은 유일한 장소는 Orchard 홀이에요. 전에 행사를 개최했던 Toliver 플라자만큼 편리한 위치에 있지는 않지만, [170]가격이 훨씬 더 적당해요.

Kelly Ward [오후 1:35]
딱 좋네요. 오늘 Orchard 홀에 연락해서 계약금을 걸고 그 날짜들로 잡아둘 수 있을까요?

Herbert Inez [오후 1:36]
그럼요. 그리고 그곳에서 숙박하는 콘퍼런스 참가자들을 위한 할인도 협상해 보도록 할게요.

Esther Tsao [오후 1:38]
저녁 세션의 초청 연사는 이미 선정되었나요?

Kelly Ward [오후 1:39]
171Marcel Dillon에게 요청드렸어요.

Esther Tsao [오후 1:40]
그분은 끝내줄 거예요! 171뉴욕에 있는 그가 설계한 최근 건물의 사진들을 봤는데, 그야말로 걸작이에요.

Herbert Inez [오후 1:42]
동감이에요. 분명 많은 사람들이 그분이 말하는 것을 듣는 것에 관심이 있을 거예요.

Kelly Ward [오후 1:43]
맞아요! 이번 주 중에 그분에게 확약을 받을 것으로 기대하고 있어요.

| 어휘 | volunteer 자원하다   roofing 지붕 공사   materials 자재, 재료   create 불러일으키다, 만들어내다   unique 특별한   available 이용 가능한   conveniently located 편리하게 위치해 있는   affordable (가격이) 알맞은   put down a deposit 계약금을 걸다   lock in 고정하다   negotiate 협상하다   guest speaker 초청 연사   select 선정하다   fantastic 끝내주는, 환상적인   masterpiece 걸작, 명품   be interested in ~에 관심이 있다   get confirmation 확약을 받다

168. True 문제
Tsao 씨에 관해 제시된 것은 무엇인가?
(A) 판매업체로 콘퍼런스에 참여했었다.
(B) 부스들을 장식하는 것을 책임지고 있다.
(C) 콘퍼런스에서 프레젠테이션을 할 것이다.
(D) 자신의 업체를 팔려고 내놓을 계획이다.

| 해설 | 오후 1:31에 Esther Tsao가 본인이 운영하던 지붕 공사 업체가 지금은 문을 닫았지만, 수년간 콘퍼런스의 부스에서 많은 자재들을 팔았다고(My roofing business, which has now been closed, always sold a lot of materials from our booth at the conference over the years) 한 것을 통해, 과거 판매업체로 콘퍼런스에 참여했음을 알 수 있으므로 정답은 (A)이다.

| 어휘 | participate in ~에 참여하다   vendor 판매업체   be responsible for ~을 책임지다   decorate 장식하다   put up for sale 팔려고 내놓다

| 패러프레이징 | sold a lot of materials from our booth at the conference → participated in the conference as a vendor

169. 추론 문제
올해 콘퍼런스에 관해 암시되는 것은 무엇인가?
(A) 장소가 편리한 위치에 있다.
(B) 입장료가 인상될 것이다.
(C) 이전 것들보다 더 길 것이다.
(D) 뉴욕에서 열릴 것이다.

| 해설 | 오후 1:34에 Herbert Inez가 처음으로 둘째 날을 추가하는 것은 몇 가지 특별한 도전을 불러일으킨다고(Adding a second day for the first time creates some unique challenges) 한 것을 통해, 이전보다 하루 더 길게 진행될 것임을 알 수 있으므로 정답은 (C)이다.

| 어휘 | venue 장소   admission rate 입장료   previous 이전의
| 패러프레이징 | Adding a second day → will be longer

170. 의도 파악 문제
오후 1:35에 Ward 씨가 "딱 좋네요"라고 쓸 때 의미하는 것은 무엇인가?
(A) Inez 씨가 계약서를 마무리해서 기쁘다.
(B) Inez 씨가 고른 행사 날짜가 마음에 든다.
(C) 그들이 이용할 장소가 만족스럽다.
(D) 초청 연사가 잘해줄 것이라고 생각한다.

| 해설 | 이는 앞서 오후 1:34에 Herbert Inez가 10월 8일 주말에 이용 가능한 것으로 찾은 유일한 장소는 Orchard 홀이라고(the only site I found that is available for the weekend of October 8th is Orchard Hall) 한 후, 가격이 훨씬 더 적당하다고(it's much more affordable) 알려준 말에 대한 응답으로, 뒤이어 계약금을 걸 수 있는지 묻는 것을 통해 장소에 만족스러움을 표하고자 쓴 것임을 알 수 있으므로 정답은 (C)이다.

| 어휘 | contract 계약, 계약서   be satisfied with ~이 만족스럽다

171. 추론 문제
Marcel Dillon은 누구일 것 같은가?
(A) 기자
(B) 패션 디자이너
(C) 행사 기획자
(D) 건축가

| 해설 | 오후 1:39에 Kelly Ward가 Marcel Dillon에게 요청했다고(We have invited Marcel Dillon to do it) 한 부분에서 언급되며, 뒤이어 Esther Tsao가 뉴욕에 있는 그가 설계한 최근 건물의 사진들을 봤다고(I saw photos of the latest building he designed in New York) 한 것을 통해, 건물을 설계하는 건축가임을 유추할 수 있으므로 정답은 (D)이다.

172-175 다음 웹 페이지를 참조하시오.

https://www.seymourmusichall.com

Seymour 뮤직 홀
음악을 넘어서!

봄은 Seymour 뮤직 홀을 방문하여 음악 관련 프로그램들과 활동들을 즐기기에 딱 좋은 때입니다. 매주 수요일 정오에, 저희 음악 개인 교습 프로그램에서 레슨을 받고 있는 학생들의 재능을 선보이기 위해 대중에게 무료 콘서트를 제공합니다.

172**운영 시간:**
월요일-목요일 오전 10시-오후 6시 / 금요일 오전 11시-오후 8시 / 토요일-일요일 오전 11시-오후 7시 / 주요 휴일에는 모두 휴관.

현재 전시회들:
173 (C)**음악의 역사** (영구 소장): Rio 룸
173 (A)**모던 재즈**: Amber 룸
173 (B)**전세계 악기들**: Dunbar 룸

강연들:
3월 16일, 오후 6:30
Surat 심포니 오케스트라의 지휘자인 Ranjeet Sardar가 각자의 관심과 신체적 특성들에 기반하여 여러분에게 딱 맞는 악기를 고르는 방법에 관해 이야기합니다. 이 정보는 오케스트라나 밴드에 처음으로 참여하고 있는 어린이들에게 특히 도움이 될 수 있습니다.

175**4월 20일, 오후 6:30**
17410년 넘게 앨범 표지와 콘서트 포스터의 디자인을 만들어 오고 있는 Jihee Kim이 175음악의 감정을 그림으로 옮기는 방법을 설명합니다.

5월 18일, 오후 7:30
Amber 룸에서 전시 중인 173 (A)<모던 재즈> 전시회의 큐레이터인 Archie Bouley가 자신의 연구 방법들에 관해 이야기합니다. 173 (A)그 전시에 대한 그녀의 목표는 재즈 경향이 어떻게 발전하고 변화되는지 보여주는 것이었습니다.

| **어휘** | activity 활동   public 대중   showcase 선보이다, 보여주다   talent 재능   hours of operation 운영 시간   permanent 영구적인   instrument 악기   conductor 지휘자   based on ~에 기반하여   physical attribute 신체적 특성   translate A into B A를 B로 옮기다   emotion 감정   on display 전시된, 진열된   research method 연구 방법

고난도
172. True 문제
웹 페이지에 Seymour 뮤직 홀에 관해 제시된 것은 무엇인가?
(A) 전시회들이 매달 달라진다.
(B) 무료 음악 레슨을 제공하고 있다.
(C) 현장 강연들은 티켓이 필요하다.
(D) 매일 대중에 개방된다.
| **해설** | 두 번째 단락에 운영 시간(Hours of Operation)이 월요일-목요일 오전 10시-오후 6시(Monday-Thursday 10 A.M.-6 P.M.) / 금요일 오전 11시-오후 8시(Friday 11 A.M.-8 P.M.) / 토요일-일요일 오전 11시-오후 7시(Saturday-Sunday 11 A.M.-7 P.M.)인 것으로 볼 때, 월요일부터 일요일까지 시간만 다르게 매일 대중에 개방됨을 알 수 있으므로 정답은 (D)이다.

| **어휘** | on-site 현장의   daily 매일
| **패러프레이징** | Monday-Thursday / Friday / Saturday-Sunday
→ daily

173. NOT True 문제
Seymour 뮤직 홀의 현재 전시들에서 다뤄지는 주제가 아닌 것은 무엇인가?
(A) 특정 장르의 동향들
(B) 국제적인 악기들
(C) 음악의 역사
(D) 현대적인 녹음 기술들
| **해설** | 세 번째 단락의 음악의 역사(Music Through the Ages)에서 (C), 전세계 악기들(Instruments Across the Globe)에서 (B), 마지막 단락에 현재 전시 중인 <모던 재즈> 전시회("Modern Jazz" exhibit)의 목표는 재즈 경향이 어떻게 발전하고 변화되는지 보여주는 것이었다고(Her goal for the exhibit was to show how jazz trends develop and change) 한 것에서 (A)는 모두 다뤄지는 주제로 확인된다. 따라서 정답은 (D)이다.

| **어휘** | particular 특정한
| **패러프레이징** | · Modern Jazz → a particular genre
· Instruments Across the Globe → International musical instruments

174. 추론 문제
Kim 씨는 누구일 것 같은가?
(A) 영화 제작자
(B) 음악 평론가
(C) 그래픽 디자이너
(D) 전문적인 음악가
| **해설** | Kim 씨가 제시된 후반부에서 10년 넘게 앨범 표지와 콘서트 포스터의 디자인을 만들어 오고 있는 Jihee Kim(Jihee Kim, who has been creating designs for album covers and concert posters for over a decade)이라고 했으므로 정답은 (C)이다.
| **어휘** | critic 평론가, 비평가   professional 전문적인, 직업의
| **패러프레이징** | has been creating designs for album covers and concert posters → A graphic designer

175. 세부 사항을 묻는 문제
강연 참석자들은 4월에 무엇에 관해 배울 것인가?
(A) 감정을 시각적 형태로 담아내는 것
(B) 음악 연주 기술을 향상시키는 것
(C) 유명한 음악가들을 조사하는 것
(D) 악기를 선택하는 것
| **해설** | 후반부에 4월 20일 강연에서 그래픽 디자이너인 Jihee Kim이 음악의 감정을 그림으로 옮기는 방법을 설명한다고(explains how she translates the emotions of the music into pictures) 제시되어 있으므로 정답은 (A)이다.
| **어휘** | capture 담아내다, 포착하다   visual 시각적인
| **패러프레이징** | translates the emotions of the music into pictures
→ Capturing feelings in visual form

176-180 다음 이메일과 편지를 참조하시오.

수신: Raul Wolfe <r.wolfe@wolfetiles.com>
발신: Kelly Wagner <kellywagner@anokabank.com>
날짜: 3월 19일
제목: Anoka 은행을 통한 기업 대출

Wolfe 씨 귀하,

¹⁷⁶제 이름은 Kelly Wagner입니다. 귀하의 여성복 제조업체를 위한 대출과 관련하여 3월 4일에 있었던 약속에 대한 후속 조치를 취하고자 하는데요. ¹⁷⁶원래 Constance Gauthier를 만나셨던 것으로 알고 있는데, 그분이 다른 지점으로 전근을 가셔서, 제가 그분을 대신하고 있습니다. 분명 Gauthier 씨가 설명했던 대로, 대출 금액은 귀하 업체의 재정 상황에 달려 있습니다. 귀하의 업체는 2만 5천 달러의 대출을 받으시려면 지난 2년간 각각 연간 수익이 적어도 12만 5천 달러가 되셔야 합니다. ¹⁷⁹지난 2년간 각각의 연간 수익이 20만 달러 이상이시면 4만 달러를 받으실 자격이 있습니다.

귀하의 신청을 처리하는 데 있어 다음 단계는 귀하께서 확인을 위한 서류들을 보내주시는 것입니다. ¹⁷⁷⁽ᴮ⁾귀하의 사업 계획서 사본과 ¹⁷⁷⁽ᶜ⁾직원 급여 지급을 보여주는 서류들, 귀하의 16자리 영업 허가 번호, 그리고 지난 2년간 ¹⁷⁷⁽ᴰ⁾귀하의 기업 회계 장부의 개요가 필요할 것입니다.

대출이 승인되면 우편으로 통지해 드리며, ¹⁷⁸대출 금액은 승인 날짜로부터 3일 후에 귀하의 은행 계좌에 입금될 것입니다. 자금이 입금되는 대로, 어떤 사업 목적으로든 그것을 이용하실 수 있습니다.

따뜻한 안부를 전하며,

Kelly Wagner

| 어휘 | follow up on ~에 대해 후속 조치를 하다   loan 대출   dress-making business 여성복 제조업체   originally 원래   transfer 전근 가다   take over 대신하다, 인수하다   be dependent on ~에 달려 있다   financial situation 재정 상황   annual earnings 연간 수익   be eligible to ~에 자격이 있다   process 처리하다   application 신청   verification 확인   salary payments 급여 지급   business license 영업 허가   overview 개요, 개관   account 회계 장부   approve 승인하다   deposit 입금하다   access 이용하다, 접근하다

Raul Wolfe
524 Boswell Court
San Diego, CA 92101

¹⁷⁸4월 7일

Wolfe 씨 귀하,

¹⁷⁸Anoka 은행이 오늘 오전에 귀하의 사업 대출 신청을 승인했음을 알

려 드리게 되어 기쁩니다. 대출 계약서 사본을 동봉해 드렸는데, 그것은 귀하의 기록을 위해 보관하고 계셔야 합니다. ¹⁷⁹4만 달러가 일시불로 귀하의 은행 계좌로 입금될 것이고, 납입은 5월 15일부터 시작될 것입니다. 864.79달러의 납입금은 ¹⁸⁰60개월(5년)의 기간 동안 매달 15일에 귀하의 계좌에서 자동으로 인출될 것입니다. ¹⁸⁰원하신다면 대출금을 조기에 상환하기 위해 납입금을 늘리실 수도 있습니다.

문의 사항이 있으시면, 555-7947에 내선 번호 24로 귀하의 지정 대출 담당 직원인 Kelly Wagner에게 편하게 연락해 주세요.

Anoka 은행의 고객이 되어주셔서 감사합니다!

Anoka 은행 대출 팀

| 어휘 | enclosed 동봉된   loan agreement 대출 계약서   retain 보유하다, 간직하다   lump sum 일시불   payment 납입(금), 납부(금)   automatically 자동적으로   period 기간   pay off 갚다   designated 지정된   loan officer 대출 담당 직원   extension 내선 번호

고난도
176. 추론 문제
Wagner 씨에 관해 암시되는 것은 무엇인가?
(A) 최근에 새 지점으로 전근을 갔다.
(B) Gauthier 씨의 관리자이다.
(C) Wolfe 씨를 직접 만나지 않았다.
(D) 회의 일정을 재조정하고 싶어한다.
| 해설 | 이메일 도입부에 제 이름은 Kelly Wagner라고(My name is Kelly Wagner) 소개한 Wagner 씨가 뒤이어 이메일 수신자인 Wolfe 씨에게 원래 Constance Gauthier를 만나셨던 것으로 알고 있는데, 그분이 다른 지점으로 전근을 가셔서 제가 그분을 대신하고 있다고(I understand that you originally met with Constance Gauthier, but she has transferred to another branch, so I am taking over for her) 한 것을 통해, 두 사람은 직접 만나지 않았음을 유추할 수 있으므로 정답은 (C)이다.
| 어휘 | supervisor 관리자   in person 직접   reschedule 일정을 재조정하다

177. NOT True 문제
Wolfe 씨의 신청을 위해 Wagner 씨에 의해 요청된 것이 아닌 것은?
(A) 영업 허가증 원본
(B) 사업 계획서
(C) 지급 기록
(D) 회계 장부 요약본
| 해설 | 이메일 두 번째 단락에 언급된 사업 계획서 사본(a copy of your business plan)에서 (B), 직원 급여 지급을 보여주는 서류들(documents showing the salary payments to employees)에서 (C), 기업 회계 장부의 개요(an overview of your business account)에서 (D)는 모두 요청된 자료로 확인된다. 반면 영업 허가증 원본이 아닌 16자리 영업 허가 번호(your sixteen-digit business license number)를 요청했으므로 정답은 (A)이다.

| 어휘 | original 원본의 summary 요약본, 개요
| 패러프레이징 | · documents showing the salary payments
→ Payment records
· overview of your business account → An account summary

| 어휘 | flexible 융통성 있는, 탄력적인

181-185 다음 웹 페이지와 이메일을 참조하시오.

José Acevedo는 아주 어릴 때부터 자신이 작가가 되고 싶었다는 것을 알고 있었습니다. [182]오늘날에도 여전히 살고 있는 토론토에서 성장한 어린 소년으로, 그는 자신의 가족과 친구들을 위해 짧은 이야기들을 썼습니다. 그는 <Toronto Daily Herald>에서 일하기 전에 언론학 학사 학위를 받았습니다. 그 시기에 그는 [181]McKinley 상을 수상했는데, [181]그것은 신문 형식의 최고 보도에 주어지는 것입니다. 이후 Acevedo 씨는 자신의 책들을 출간하기 시작했고, 지금까지 네 권을 보유하고 있습니다.

고난도

178. 연계 문제 – 세부 사항

Wolfe 씨는 언제 처음으로 대출 자금을 이용할 수 있을 것인가?

(A) 4월 7일에
(B) 4월 8일에
(C) 4월 10일에
(D) 4월 15일에

| 해설 | 이메일 세 번째 단락에, 대출 금액은 승인 일자 3일 후에 귀하의 은행 계좌에 입금될 것이며(the loan amount will be deposited into your bank account three days after the approval date), 자금이 입금되는 대로 어떤 사업 목적으로든 그것을 이용하실 수 있다고(As soon as the funds are deposited, you can access them for any business purpose) 제시되어 있다. 또한 편지를 보낸 날짜는 4월 7일로, 도입부에 Anoka 은행이 오늘 오전에 귀하의 사업 대출 신청을 승인했다고(Anoka Bank approved your business loan request this morning) 한 것을 통해 4월 7일에 대출 승인이 되어, 3일 후인 4월 10일에 대출 금액이 입금될 것임을 알 수 있다. 따라서 정답은 (C)이다.

<플라스틱 세계>, 2012년 출간
현대 세계의 플라스틱 중독과 그것이 야생 동물 및 환경에 미치는 영향에 관한 조사. 그 책은 플라스틱 사용과 그것의 부정적인 면들에 관한 논의를 전국으로 확산시키는 데 도움이 되었습니다.

<바람 혁명>, 2015년 출간
그 책은 풍력 발전기의 역사와 지속 가능한 에너지원으로서 점점 높아지고 있는 인기를 기술합니다. 또한 개인들이 자신들의 건물에 발전기를 이용하는 것에 어떻게 관여할 수 있는지에 관해서도 개괄하고 있습니다.

고난도

179. 연계 문제 – 추론

Wolfe 씨의 업체에 관해 암시되는 것은 무엇인가?

(A) 하나 이상의 도시에서 운영한다.
(B) 2년 전에 문을 열었다.
(C) 건축 프로젝트를 진행할 것이다.
(D) 작년에 적어도 20만 달러를 벌었다.

| 해설 | 이메일 첫 번째 단락 후반부에 지난 2년간 각각의 연간 수익이 20만 달러 이상이시면 4만 달러를 받을 자격이 있다고(If your annual earnings for each of the past two years have been $200,000 or more, then you would be eligible to receive $40,000) 제시된 것과 편지 중반부에 4만 달러가 일시불로 귀하의 은행 계좌로 입금될 것이라고(A lump sum of $40,000 will be deposited in your bank account) 한 것을 연계해 볼 때, 연간 수익이 20만 달러 이상이어서 4만 달러의 대출을 승인받은 것임을 알 수 있으므로 정답은 (D)이다.

| 어휘 | operate 운영하다 undergo 진행하다, 겪다 earn 벌다, 얻다

<따라잡기>, 2016년 출간
[182]Acevedo가 토론토 시 의회 의원들을 인터뷰하여 특히 기술 및 환경과 관련하여 대중의 변화하는 요구에 대한 법을 채택하려는 그들의 노력을 조사합니다.

[183]<텍사스 보물>, 2017년 출간
미국 텍사스 주의 석유 산업에 대한 비밀 조사. Acevedo는 근로자의 건강, 환경 보호, 그리고 기업의 탐욕과 같은 중요한 주제들을 조사합니다.

| 어휘 | university degree 학사 학위 award 수여하다 reporting 보도 format 형식 publish 출간하다, 출판하다 to date 지금까지 addiction 중독 effect 영향 wildlife 야생 동물 environment 환경 further 진전시키다, 촉진시키다 downside 불리한 면 trace 기술하다, 조사하다 wind turbine 풍력 발전기 popularity 인기 sustainable 지속 가능한 energy source 에너지원 outline 개괄하다 get involved with ~에 참여하다, 관여하다 property 건물, 부동산 investigate 조사하다 adopt 채택하다 undercover 비밀의, 비밀리에 하는 oil industry 석유 산업 examine 조사하다 essential 필수적인, 극히 중요한 environmental protection 환경 보호 corporate greed 기업의 탐욕

180. 세부 사항을 묻는 문제

편지에 따르면, 대출 계약의 어느 부분이 탄력적인가?

(A) 일시불 금액
(B) 매월 납기일
(C) 이자율
(D) 납부 기간

| 해설 | 편지 후반부에 대출 기간이 60개월(5년)(60 months (five years))으로 제시되어 있는데, 뒤이어 원한다면 대출금을 조기에 상환하기 위해 납입금을 늘릴 수도 있다고(If you prefer, you may make larger payment in order to pay the loan off early) 한 것을 통해, 납부 기간이 단축될 수 있음을 알 수 있으므로 정답은 (D)이다.

수신: José Acevedo <contact@joseacevedo.com>
발신: Namiyo Sawada <n.sawada@zlproductions.com>
[184]날짜: 8월 30일

TEST 01 **17**

제목: 다큐멘터리

Acevedo 씨 귀하,

제가 현재 다큐멘터리를 작업 중인데, ¹⁸³귀하의 최근 책에 실린 세부 사항들이 제 영화에 큰 보탬이 될 것이라고 생각합니다. 귀하의 통찰력은 저희 시청자들에게 매우 유익할 것입니다. 저는 제 북 클럽에서 귀하의 데뷔 소설을 읽었을 때 귀하의 작품에 처음 친숙하게 되었고, 그때 이후로 귀하의 이력을 계속 주시해 왔습니다. 먼저 제 소개를 하고 싶었지만, 관심이 있으시면 ¹⁸⁴내일 전화드려서 만날 시간을 정하도록 하겠습니다. 제가 당신 ¹⁸⁵쪽으로 갈 수 있으니, 멀리 오지 않으셔도 됩니다.

따뜻한 안부를 전하며,

Namiyo Sawada
ZL 제작자

| 어휘 | currently 현재 details 세부 사항 latest 최신의 addition 보탬, 추가 insight 통찰력 valuable 유익한, 귀중한 familiar with ~에 친숙한 follow 유심히 지켜보다 introduce oneself 자기소개를 하다 arrange a time 시간을 정하다

181. 세부 사항을 묻는 문제
McKinley 상의 의도된 수상자들은 누구인가?
(A) 소설가들
(B) 영화 감독들
(C) 신문 기자들
(D) 환경 운동가들
| 해설 | 웹 페이지 첫 번째 단락 후반부에 José Acevedo가 수상했다고 한 McKinley 상에 대해 그것은 신문 형식의 최고 보도에 주어지는 것이라고(which is given for top reporting in a newspaper format) 제시되어 있으므로 정답은 (C)이다.
| 어휘 | novelist 소설가 film director 영화 감독 journalist 기자 environmental activist 환경 운동가

182. 추론 문제
Acevedo 씨에 관해 암시되는 것은 무엇인가?
(A) 자신의 건물에 풍력 발전기를 설치했다.
(B) 그의 지역 정치인들과 이야기를 나누었다.
(C) 텍사스에 새로운 사무실을 열었다.
(D) 대학 과정을 가르칠 것이다.
| 해설 | 웹 페이지 첫 번째 단락에 José Acevedo에 대해, 오늘날에도 여전히 살고 있는 토론토에서 성장한 어린 소년으로(As a young boy growing up in Toronto, where he still lives today) 짧은 이야기들을 썼다고 한 것과 출간한 책 중 세 번째에 있는 <따라잡기> 설명에 Acevedo가 토론토 시 의회 의원들을 인터뷰한다고(Acevedo interviews Toronto City Council members) 한 것을 연계해 볼 때, 자신이 살고 있는 지역인 토론토의 정치인들과 이야기했음을 알 수 있으므로 정답은 (B)이다.

| 어휘 | politician 정치인 university course 대학 과정
| 패러프레이징 | · interviews → spoke with
· Toronto City Council members → local politicians

183. 연계 문제 – 세부 사항
Sawada 씨가 다큐멘터리에 특별히 포함시키고 싶어하는 것은 어떤 책인가?
(A) <플라스틱 세계>
(B) <바람 혁명>
(C) <따라잡기>
(D) <텍사스 보물>
| 해설 | Sawada 씨는 이메일 발신자로 초반부에 귀하의 최근 책에 실린 세부 사항들이 제 영화에 큰 보탬이 될 것이라고 생각한다(I believe that the details from your latest book would be a great addition to my film) 했고, 여기서 your latest book에 해당하는 것은 웹 페이지 마지막에 제시된 가장 최근에 출간된 <텍사스 보물>(Texas Treasures, published 2017)일 것이므로 정답은 (D)이다.

184. 세부 사항을 묻는 문제
Sawada 씨가 8월 31일에 하고자 희망하는 것은 무엇인가?
(A) 약속을 정하는 것
(B) 회의에 참석하는 것
(C) 비디오를 공개하는 것
(D) 북 클럽을 알리는 것
| 해설 | 이메일을 보낸 날짜가 8월 30일이고, 이메일 후반부에 내일 전화드려서 만날 시간을 정하도록 하겠다고(I will call you tomorrow to arrange a time to meet) 한 것을 통해, 내일인 8월 31일에 수신자인 Acevedo 씨와 만날 약속을 정하고 싶어함을 알 수 있으므로 정답은 (A)이다.
| 어휘 | set up 정하다 appointment 약속, 예약 release 공개하다, 출시하다
| 패러프레이징 | arrange a time to meet → Set up an appointment

고난도
185. 동의어 문제
이메일에서 첫 번째 단락 다섯 번째 줄에 있는 단어 "way"와 의미가 가장 유사한 것은
(A) 방법
(B) 스타일
(C) 특징
(D) 방향
| 해설 | 해당 단어가 들어간 문장은 '제가 당신 쪽으로 갈 수 있으니, 멀리 오지 않으셔도 됩니다'라고 해석된다. 따라서 way는 '~ 쪽'이라는 의미로 쓰인 것이므로 이와 가장 유사한 '방향'이라는 뜻의 (D)가 정답이다.

186-190 다음 이메일들과 일정표를 참조하시오.

수신: Valley 부동산 전 직원
발신: William Monahan
날짜: 9월 18일

제목: 곧 있을 소프트웨어 교육
첨부: training.docx

Valley 부동산 직원들 귀하,

직원들이 10월의 초반부에 의무적인 소프트웨어 교육을 이수해야 함을 알아두시기 바랍니다. 교육에서 다뤄질 두 가지 프로그램이 있습니다. ¹⁸⁶Investiprop-7이 모든 회사 컴퓨터에 설치되어야 하며, 모든 부동산 검색에 EstateMax 프로그램 대신에 그것을 이용하기 시작할 것입니다. 그것은 훨씬 더 사용하기 쉽고, 특정한 검색 기준을 추가하기 위한 더 많은 옵션들이 있습니다. 모든 직원들은 그 교육을 이수해야 하지만, 날짜를 선택할 수 있습니다. 다른 프로그램은 Slate Books Pro로, 그것은 청구서 발부 소프트웨어입니다. 그 프로그램은 최근에 여러 차례 업그레이드를 진행했습니다. ¹⁸⁸회계사들만 Slate Books Pro 교육을 받아야 하고, 그것은 저희 회의실에서 현장 제공될 것입니다.

감사합니다,

William Monahan
Valley 부동산, 사무실 관리자

| 어휘 | complete 이수하다, 완료하다   mandatory 의무적인   first half 초반, 전반   cover 다루다   property 부동산   search 검색   user-friendly 사용하기 쉬운   specific 특정한, 구체적인   criteria 기준   billing 청구서 발부   undergo 진행하다, 받다   accountant 회계사   on-site 현장에서   conference room 회의실

Valley 부동산 교육 일정

날짜	소프트웨어 프로그램	형식	모듈의 수	시간
10월 2일	¹⁸⁷Investiprop-7	온라인	6	오전 10:30-오후 12:30
10월 5일	Slate Books Pro	현장 워크숍	4	오후 2:00-오후 4:00
10월 6일	¹⁸⁷Investiprop-7	온라인	6	오전 10:30-오후 12:30
¹⁸⁹10월 8일	¹⁸⁷Investiprop-7	현장 워크숍	6	오후 1:00-오후 4:00
10월 10일	Slate Books Pro	현장 워크숍	4	오전 9:00-오전 11:00
10월 13일	¹⁸⁷Investiprop-7	온라인	6	오후 2:00-오후 4:00

수신: William Monahan
발신: Tabitha Foster
날짜: 9월 19일
제목: 회신: 곧 있을 소프트웨어 교육

Monahan 씨 귀하,

¹⁸⁸저는 두 소프트웨어 프로그램 교육을 모두 받아야 되는데, 유감스럽게도 약간의 일정 충돌이 있습니다. ¹⁸⁹저는 10월 1일부터 10월 7일까지 연례 휴가를 가도록 이미 승인을 받았습니다. 또한 10월 10일부터 14일까지 전국 부동산 중개인 협의회를 위해 댈러스에 있을 것이고요. ¹⁹⁰이 문제를 해결할 방법에 관해 이야기할 수 있도록 내선 번호 21로 저에게 전화해 주세요.

감사합니다!

Tabitha Foster

| 어휘 | scheduling conflict 일정 충돌, 일정상의 겹침   be approved to ~하도록 승인을 받다   annual 연례의   vacation 휴가   extension 내선 번호   resolve 해결하다   issue 문제, 사안

186. True 문제
Investiprop-7에 관해 언급된 것은 무엇인가?
(A) 고객 청구서 발부 정보를 추적할 수 있다.
(B) 다른 프로그램을 대체하도록 의도된 것이다.
(C) 최근에 그 기능들의 일부가 변경되었다.
(D) 계정과 비밀번호를 요구한다.

| 해설 | 첫 번째 이메일 초/중반부에 Investiprop-7에 대해, 모든 회사 컴퓨터에 설치되어야 하며, 모든 부동산 검색에 EstateMax 프로그램 대신에 그것을 이용하기 시작할 것이라고(Investiprop-7 ~ will start using it for all property searches instead of the EstateMax program) 제시되어 있는 것을 통해, EstateMax 프로그램을 대체하게 될 것임을 알 수 있으므로 정답은 (B)이다.

| 어휘 | track 추적하다   replace 대체하다, 대신하다   feature 기능, 특징   account 계정

| 패러프레이징 | using it for ~ instead of the EstateMax program
→ replace another program

187. 세부 사항을 묻는 문제
모든 Investiprop-7 교육 세션들에 관해 동일한 것은 무엇인가?
(A) 모두 인터넷에서 진행된다.
(B) 같은 시간 동안 지속된다.
(C) 모두 오전에 개최된다.
(D) 모두 동일한 모듈의 수를 가지고 있다.

| 해설 | 일정표에서 첫 번째, 세 번째, 네 번째, 여섯 번째에 제시되어 있는 Investiprop-7을 확인하면 온라인 또는 현장 워크숍으로 진행되고 시간대도 각기 다른 반면, 모듈의 수(Number of Modules)가 모두 6으로 동일한 것으로 확인되므로 정답은 (D)이다.

| 어휘 | last 지속되다   take place 개최되다, 열리다

🔺고난도
188. 연계 문제 – 추론
Foster 씨에 관해 암시되는 것은 무엇인가?
(A) 댈러스 지사로 전근 갈 계획이다.
(B) 새로 고용된 직원이다.
(C) 회계사로 일한다.
(D) 소프트웨어를 설치하는 데 어려움을 겪었다.

| 해설 | Foster 씨는 두 번째 이메일의 발신자로, 도입부에 두 소프트웨어 프로그램 교육을 다 받아야 된다고(I am required to undergo training for both

software programs) 했는데, 첫 번째 이메일 후반부에 회계사들만 Slate Books Pro 교육을 받아야 한다고(Only accountants need to take the Slate Books Pro training) 한 것을 연계해 볼 때, Foster 씨는 회계사이기 때문에 교육을 둘 다 받아야 하는 것으로 유추할 수 있으므로 정답은 (C)이다.

| 어휘 | transfer 전근 가다, 이전하다   have difficulty -ing ~하는 데 어려움을 겪다

189. 연계 문제 – 추론
Foster 씨는 언제 교육을 받을 것 같은가?
(A) 10월 6일에
(B) 10월 8일에
(C) 10월 10일에
(D) 10월 13일에

| 해설 | Foster 씨가 보낸 이메일에 10월 1일부터 10월 7일까지 연례 휴가를 가도록 이미 승인을 받았고(I have already been approved to take my annual vacation from October 1 to October 7), 10월 10일부터 14일까지 전국 부동산 중개인 협의회를 위해 댈러스에 있을 것이라고(I'll also be in Dallas from October 10 to 14 for the National Realtors Convention) 알렸으므로, 일정표에서 이 날을 제외하고 가능한 날짜를 찾아보면 10월 8일로 확인된다. 따라서 정답은 (B)이다.

190. 세부 사항을 묻는 문제
Monahan 씨는 왜 Foster 씨에게 전화할 것을 요청받는가?
(A) 업데이트된 일정을 제공하기 위해
(B) 문제의 해결책을 논의하기 위해
(C) 협의회 참석을 확인하기 위해
(D) 휴가 요청을 승인하기 위해

| 해설 | Foster 씨가 보낸 이메일 후반부에 문제를 해결할 방법에 관해 이야기할 수 있도록 내선 번호 21로 전화해 달라고(Please call me at extension 21 so we can talk about how to resolve this issue) 요청했으므로 정답은 (B)이다.

| 어휘 | solution 해결책   confirm 확인하다, 확정하다   attendance 참석

| 패러프레이징 | talk about how to resolve this issue
→ discuss solutions to a problem

191-195 다음 웹 페이지, 주문서, 이메일을 참조하시오.

www.hampstead4u.com

Hampstead

지난 20년 동안, Hampstead는 Culver City 지역에서 조경 자재와 장비를 공급해 왔습니다. ¹⁹¹저희는 매년 초봄부터 가을 중반까지 문을 열고, 여러분의 업체를 위해 쇼핑하시든 아니면 가정을 위해 쇼핑하시든 여러분의 꿈의 야외 공간을 조성하는 것을 도와드릴 수 있습니다.

저희는 모든 기호와 예산에 맞는 아주 다양한 옵션들을 가지고 가격 알맞은 상품들을 제공하고자 열심히 일하고 있습니다. 저희는 가능한 경우에는 언제나 Culver City와 주변의 업체들로부터 상품을 공급받고자

하는데, ¹⁹²이것이 지역 경제를 지원하고 운송으로 야기되는 오염을 줄여주기 때문입니다. 저희 제품 라인에 추가하여, 다음과 같은 서비스도 제공합니다.

· 35달러를 초과하는 모든 주문에 대해 무료 지역 배달
· 정원 설계 서비스 (장식용이든 수확용이든)
· 전화나 온라인으로 빠르고 쉬운 주문
· 여러분 지역의 조경 전문가들 추천

저희는 배송 일자로부터 30일 이내에 어떠한 이유로든 반품을 받습니다. 흙과 나무 조각 같은 포대에 든 물품들은 개봉되지 않은 상태여야 합니다. ¹⁹⁵파손된 상품이나 잘못된 물품을 받으실 경우, 저희가 반품 운송 비용을 환불해 드릴 것입니다. 그렇지 않을 경우, 그 비용은 직접 부담하셔야 합니다.

| 어휘 | supply 공급하다, 제공하다   landscaping 조경   materials 재료, 자재   annually 해마다   create 조성하다, 만들다   outdoor 야외의   affordable (가격이) 알맞은, 저렴한   a wide range of 아주 다양한   suit 맞다, 적합하다   taste 기호   budget 예산   source 공급받다   support 지원하다   reduce 줄이다   pollution 오염   transportation 수송   exceed 초과하다   ornamental 장식용의   crop 수확, 농작물   referral 추천   professional 전문가   accept 받다   return 반품   bagged 포대에 든, 봉지에 든   wood chip 나무 조각   damaged 파손된   wrong 잘못된   reimburse 환급하다   cover 부담하다

Hampstead

이름: Ray Casper   주문 날짜: 5월 24일   배송 날짜: 5월 26일
배송 주소지: 442 Emerson Road, Culver City, CA 90230

설명	제품 ID	개당 가격	수량	
태양열 LED 길 전등 (4개 팩)	NR5472	29.99달러	10	299.90달러
올림 텃밭, 목재 틀 (48′ x 96′ x 5.5′)	HL195	99.99달러	3	299.97달러
나무 부스러기 (50파운드 포대)	HL3810	8.99달러	5	44.95달러
¹⁹⁴회색 돌 (20파운드 포대)	PS024	23.49달러	5	117.45달러
금속 정원 테두리 장식 (검정, 75피트 롤)	AE638	319.49달러	1	319.49달러
주문 관련 의문 사항이나 의견에 대해서는 info@hampstead4u.com으로 이메일을 보내주세요.			소계	1,081.76달러
			세금	64.90달러
			배송	0.00달러
			총액	1,146.66달러

| 어휘 | description 설명, 기술   per unit 개당   Qty.(=quantity) 수량   path 길   raised (주변보다) 높이 올린   garden bed 상자 텃밭   frame 틀   shredded 잘게 조각난   mulch 잡초가 자라거나 땅의 수분이

감소하는 것을 막기 위해 흙의 표면을 덮어주는 자재   metal 금속의
edging 테두리 장식   comment 의견   subtotal 소계

수신: Ray Casper <r.casper@lomaxltd.com>
발신: Mara Brewer <m.brewer@lomaxltd.com>
날짜: 6월 2일
제목: 조경

안녕하세요, Ray.

저희 건물 앞에 조경 작업을 하기 위해 유지 관리 팀에게 필요한 자재를 주문해 주셔서 감사합니다. ¹⁹³제가 다양한 상점들의 상품들을 이용해 봤는데, Hampstead의 이 제품들이 이제껏 봤던 것 중에서 단연 최고네요. 오랫동안 지속될 것이라는 확신이 듭니다. 저희가 변화를 꾸준히 진척시켜 나가고 있는데, ¹⁹⁴바위가 다 떨어져 가서 제가 그것들을 더 주문했습니다. 또한 ¹⁹⁵상자 텃밭들 중 하나는 도착했을 때 금이 가 있어서, 그것을 교환해야 합니다. 원래 주문을 하셨으니, 그것에 관해 Hampstead에 연락해 주시는 게 가장 좋겠습니다.

감사합니다!

Mara

| 어휘 | maintenance team 유지 관리 팀   a variety of 다양한, 여럿의   by far the best 단연 최고인   last 지속되다   steady 꾸준한   progress 진척, 진행   run low 다 떨어져 가다, 고갈되다   crack 금, 균열   exchange 교환하다   original 원래의

191. True 문제
Hampstead에 관해 사실인 것은 무엇인가?
(A) 여러 도시에 지점을 가지고 있다.
(B) 대여 서비스를 제공한다.
(C) 가족에 의해 운영된다.
(D) 계절 사업체이다.
| 해설 | 웹 페이지 첫 번째 단락에 매년 초봄부터 가을 중반까지 문을 연다고(We're open annually from early spring to mid-fall) 제시되어 있으므로 정답은 (D)이다.
| 어휘 | branch 지점   rental 대여, 임대   operate 운영하다   seasonal 계절적인
| 패러프레이징 | open annually from early spring to mid-fall
→ seasonal business

192. 세부 사항을 묻는 문제
웹 페이지에 Hampstead에 관한 어떤 측면이 언급되어 있는가?
(A) 자체 식물들을 재배하는 것
(B) 지역 업체들을 지원하는 것
(C) 경험 있는 작업 요원들을 고용하는 것
(D) 조경 전문가들을 교육하는 것

| 해설 | 두 번째 단락에 가능한 경우에는 언제나 Culver City와 주변의 업체들로부터 상품을 공급받고자 하는데, 이것이 지역 경제를 지원하고 운송으로 야기되는 오염을 줄여주기 때문이라고(as this supports the local economy and reduces pollution caused by transportation) 제시되어 있으므로 정답은 (B)이다.
| 어휘 | cultivate 재배하다, 경작하다   experienced 경험 있는
| 패러프레이징 | supports the local economy → Supporting local businesses

193. 세부 사항을 묻는 문제
Brewer 씨가 Hampstead에 관해 좋아하는 것은 무엇인가?
(A) 제품들을 빨리 배달한다.
(B) 품질 보증 기간이 길다.
(C) 고품질 제품들을 보유하고 있다.
(D) 폭넓게 엄선된 제품들을 취급한다.
| 해설 | Brewer 씨는 이메일 발신자로, 이메일 중반부에 다양한 상점들의 상품들을 이용해 봤는데, Hampstead의 제품들이 이제껏 봤던 것 중에 단연 최고라고(I've used goods from a variety of stores, and these items from Hampstead are by far the best I've seen) 한 것을 통해, 품질에 만족한다는 것을 알 수 있으므로 정답은 (C)이다.
| 어휘 | warranty 품질 보증   high-quality 고품질의, 고급의   carry 취급하다
| 패러프레이징 | by far the best → high-quality

194. 연계 문제 – 세부 사항
Brewer 씨는 어떤 제품을 주문했나?
(A) NR5472
(B) HL195
(C) HL3810
(D) PS024
| 해설 | Brewer 씨는 이메일 중반부에 바위가 다 떨어져 가서 그것들을 더 주문했다고(we're running low on rocks, so I've ordered more of those) 했고, 주문서에서 rocks에 해당하는 것은 회색 돌(20파운드 포대)(Grey stones (20-lb bag))로 그 제품 ID는 PS024로 확인되므로 정답은 (D)이다.

195. 연계 문제 – 추론
Hampstead는 Casper 씨의 요청에 어떻게 응답할 것 같은가?
(A) 빠른 배송을 제공함으로써
(B) 무료 수리를 해 줌으로써
(C) 제품을 전액 환불해 줌으로써
(D) 운송 비용을 환급해 줌으로써
| 해설 | 웹 페이지 마지막 부분에 파손된 상품이나 잘못된 물품을 받을 경우, 반품 운송 비용을 환급해 준다고(If you receive damaged goods or the wrong item, we will reimburse you for the return shipping costs) 제시되어 있고, 이메일 후반부에 상자 텃밭들 중 하나가 도착했을 때 금이 가 있어서 그것을 교환해야 한다고(one of the garden beds had a crack in it when it arrived, so we should exchange it) 알려주고 있다. 이를 연계해 볼 때, Casper 씨가 파손된 상품의 교환을 요청하면 Hampstead가 운송 비용을 환급해줄 것임을 알 수 있으므로 정답은 (D)이다.

| 어휘 | express delivery 빠른 배송   issue a full refund 전액 환불해 주다

196-200 다음 광고, 서식, 이메일을 참조하시오.

Bryson 캠핑 봄 세일
저희 봄 세일 때 필수품들을 비축해 두세요. **196**4월 2일-8일까지 단 1주일간.

모든 Kolbert 침낭 각 29.99달러	모든 Hathaway 손전등 10% 할인	엄선된 야외용 스토브 60% 할인	모든 Forestlife 배낭 15달러 할인	모든 Benson 2인용, 3인용 텐트 30% 할인

쿠폰들은 특정한 세일 가격과 함께 사용될 수 없습니다.
자세한 사항은 저희 웹 사이트를 확인하세요.

| 어휘 | stock up on ~을 비축하다   essential goods 필수품   sleeping bag 침낭   flashlight 손전등   backpack 배낭   certain 특정한

Bryson 캠핑
고객 문의/의견 서식

고객명: Rachel Barry
회사명 (해당되는 경우): Adventure 여행사
이메일 주소: rachelb@adventuretoursltd.net
고객 카드 번호 (해당되는 경우): 7625003
파일 업로드: receipt.jpg

문의/의견: 제가 최근에 저희 고객들의 일박 캠핑 여행을 위한 용품들을 대량으로 구입했습니다. 이것에는 Renway 침낭 5개, Hathaway 손전등 20개, Benson 텐트(3인용) 8개, 그리고 **199**Forestlife 배낭 3개가 포함되어 있습니다. **196**귀사의 웹 사이트에서 이 물품들의 대부분이 봄 세일로 인해 현재 할인된 가격에 제공되고 있는 것을 보았는데요. **197**검토를 위해 제 영수증의 사본을 업로드했습니다. 제가 그 할인을 이용할 수 있도록 제 주문에 귀사의 30일 최저 가격 보장을 적용해 주시기를 바랍니다.

| 어휘 | inquiry 문의   comment 의견   loyalty card 고객[포인트 적립] 카드   supplies 용품, 물품   overnight 일박의, 하룻밤 동안의   receipt 영수증   apply 적용하다   price match 최저 가격 보장   take advantage of ~을 이용하다

수신: Rachel Barry <rachelb@adventuretoursltd.net>
발신: Bryson Camping <inquiries@brysoncamping.com>
날짜: 4월 4일
제목: Bryson 캠핑 고객 문의/의견

Barry 씨 귀하,

Bryson 캠핑에 연락해 주셔서 감사합니다. 만약 구매일로부터 30일 이내에 가격이 떨어질 경우 저희가 차액을 환불해 드리는 것은 귀하의 말씀이 맞습니다. 그런데 일부 세일 가격들은 귀하께서 이미 받으셨던 것만큼 낮지 않습니다. 예를 들어, **198**Benson 텐트는 50% 할인을 받으셨는데요, 그 제품이 시장에 새로 나온 것이라서 처음에 출시 기념 가격에 제공되었기 때문입니다. 또한 10개 이상 묶음으로 주문된 물품들은 대량 할인을 받으셨습니다. 그래서 **199**Forestlife 제품들에 대한 부분 환불만 받으실 것인데요. 그것은 5영업일 이내에 그 물품들에 대한 새로운 영수증과 함께 발송될 것입니다.

200첨부된 설문 조사를 통해 저희 문의 과정에 관해 어떻게 생각하시는지 알고 싶은데요. 그것을 다시 보내주시면, 50달러 매장 상품권이 걸린 경품 추첨에 응모될 것입니다.

Justin Dugan
Bryson 캠핑, 고객 서비스 담당자

| 어휘 | correct 맞는, 정확한   refund 환불하다   difference 차액, 차이   drop 떨어지다   get half off 50% 할인을 받다   introductory 출시 기념의, 소개의   a bulk discount 대량 할인   partial 부분적인   refund 환불   business day 영업일   process 과정, 절차   via ~를 통한   attached 첨부된   prize drawing 경품 추첨   voucher 상품권, 할인권

🔺 고난도

196. 연계 문제 – 추론
Barry 씨에 관해 암시되는 것은 무엇인가?
(A) 최근에 관광 가이드로 고용되었다.
(B) 매장 정책에 관해 잘못된 정보를 받았다.
(C) 4월 2일 이전에 구매를 했다.
(D) 30일 전에 매장을 방문했다.

| 해설 | Barry 씨는 고객 문의/의견 서식에 글을 남긴 사람으로, 최근 구매 사실을 알린 후 중반부에 귀사의 웹 사이트에서 이 물품들의 대부분이 봄 세일로 인해 현재 할인된 가격에 제공되고 있는 것을 보았다고(I saw on your Web site that most of these items are now being offered at discounted prices because of your Spring Sale) 한 것을 통해, 봄 세일 이전에 구매한 것임을 알 수 있고, 광고에서 봄 세일 기간은 4월 2일-8일까지 단 1주일(One week only— April 2–8)로 확인되므로 정답은 (C)이다.

| 어휘 | misinform 잘못된 정보를 주다

197. 세부 사항을 묻는 문제
Barry 씨는 왜 업체가 영수증을 검토하기를 원하는가?
(A) 파손된 물품들을 환불해주기 위해
(B) 가격 변경에 관한 요청을 처리하기 위해
(C) 일부 품목이 배송되지 않았음을 확인하기 위해
(D) 직원이 실수를 했는지 여부를 확인하기 위해

| 해설 | Barry 씨가 남긴 고객 문의/의견 서식 후반부에 검토를 위해 제 영수증의 사본을 업로드했다고(I have uploaded a copy of my receipt for review)

한 후, 할인을 이용할 수 있도록 30일 최저 가격 보장을 적용해 주기를 바란다고 (I hope you will apply your 30-day price match to my order so that I can take advantage of the discount) 덧붙였으므로 정답은 (B)이다.

| 어휘 | damaged 파손된 process 처리하다 confirm 확인하다 make an error 실수하다

| 패러프레이징 | apply your 30-day price match → process a request for a price change

198. 세부 사항을 묻는 문제
Dugan 씨에 따르면, Barry 씨는 왜 Benson 제품들에 대한 할인을 제공받았나?
(A) 단골 고객 클럽 프로그램에 등록했다.
(B) 제품 출시를 이용했다.
(C) 많은 물건을 샀다.
(D) 할인 쿠폰을 제시했다.

| 해설 | 이메일 첫 번째 단락 중반부에 Benson 텐트들은 50% 할인을 받았다고 한 후, 그 이유로 시장에 새로 나온 것이라서 출시 기념 가격에 제공되었기 때문이라고(because the product was first offered at an introductory rate, as it was new to the market) 제시되어 있으므로 정답은 (B)이다.

| 어휘 | sign up for ~에 등록하다 launch 출시 present 제시하다

| 패러프레이징 | the product was first offered at an introductory rate → took advantage of a product launch

199. 연계 문제 - 세부 사항
Barry 씨는 어떤 제품에 대해 새로운 영수증을 받을 것인가?
(A) 배낭
(B) 손전등
(C) 침낭
(D) 텐트

| 해설 | 이메일 첫 번째 단락 후반부에 Forestlife 제품들에 대한 부분 환불만 받을 것인데(you will only receive a partial refund for the Forestlife products) 그것은 5영업일 이내에 그 물품들에 대한 새로운 영수증과 함께 발송될 것이라고(It will be sent along with a new receipt for those items within five business days) 했고, 고객 문의/의견 서식에서 Barry 씨가 구입한 Forestlife 제품은 배낭 3개(3 Forestlife backpacks)로 확인되므로 정답은 (A)이다.

200. 세부 사항을 묻는 문제
Dugan 씨가 이메일과 함께 보낸 것은 무엇인가?
(A) 일부 조사 결과
(B) 매장 상품권
(C) 일부 할인 코드
(D) 피드백 서식

| 해설 | 이메일 두 번째 단락에 첨부된 설문 조사를 통해 문의 절차에 관해 어떻게 생각하는지 알고 싶다고(We would love to know what you think about our inquiry process via the attached survey) 제시되어 있는 것을 통해, 설문 조사지를 함께 보냈음을 알 수 있으므로 정답은 (D)이다.

| 패러프레이징 | survey → A feedback form

TEST 02

PART 5

101 (C)	102 (B)	103 (A)	104 (D)	105 (A)
106 (C)	107 (B)	108 (C)	109 (A)	110 (B)
111 (C)	112 (A)	113 (A)	114 (C)	115 (C)
116 (B)	117 (B)	118 (C)	119 (C)	120 (D)
121 (D)	122 (B)	123 (C)	124 (D)	125 (B)
126 (C)	127 (D)	128 (C)	129 (B)	130 (B)

PART 6

131 (D)	132 (C)	133 (A)	134 (C)	135 (B)
136 (D)	137 (D)	138 (B)	139 (C)	140 (B)
141 (B)	142 (C)	143 (B)	144 (B)	145 (D)
146 (C)				

PART 7

147 (C)	148 (D)	149 (C)	150 (A)	151 (C)
152 (A)	153 (C)	154 (B)	155 (A)	156 (D)
157 (C)	158 (A)	159 (B)	160 (B)	161 (C)
162 (D)	163 (C)	164 (B)	165 (A)	166 (A)
167 (C)	168 (C)	169 (A)	170 (B)	171 (D)
172 (D)	173 (A)	174 (C)	175 (A)	176 (C)
177 (D)	178 (A)	179 (B)	180 (A)	181 (B)
182 (B)	183 (B)	184 (D)	185 (A)	186 (C)
187 (D)	188 (B)	189 (D)	190 (B)	191 (A)
192 (C)	193 (A)	194 (B)	195 (D)	196 (C)
197 (A)	198 (D)	199 (C)	200 (A)	

PART 5

101. 부사 자리 – 동사 수식
전국 언론은 교량 안전과 권고 사항들에 관한 보고서를 대체로 무시했다.
| 해설 | 주어 The national media와 동사 ignored 사이에 빈칸이 있으므로, 빈칸은 동사를 수식할 부사가 들어갈 자리이다. 따라서 '보고서를 대체로 무시했다'라는 의미를 완성해줄 '대체로, 주로'라는 뜻의 부사인 (C) largely가 정답이다.
| 어휘 | national 전국적인   media 매체, 언론   ignore 무시하다   bridge 다리   safety 안전   recommendation 권고 사항

🏠 고난도
102. 명사 자리 – 동사의 목적어 | 가산 명사
새로운 보안 시스템은 창문이나 문이 열려 있을 때 전화로 경보를 제공할 수 있다.
| 해설 | 빈칸은 타동사 provide의 목적어가 들어갈 자리이므로 명사 자리이다. alert은 가산 명사인데 빈칸 앞에 관사 등 한정사가 없으므로 복수형인 (B) alerts가 정답이다.

| 어휘 | security system 보안 시스템   alertly 기민하게, 경계하여   alert 경보, 경계

103. 부사 자리 – 어휘
직원들은 출장 중에 발생된 비용을 곧 환급받게 될 것이다.
| 해설 | 빈칸은 앞의 동사를 수식해 줄 부사가 들어갈 자리이므로, 형용사이자 대명사인 (C) many와 전치사인 (D) about은 답이 될 수 없고, '곧 환급받게 될 것이다'라는 의미를 완성해 줄 미래 시제 동사와 잘 쓰이는 부사인 (A) soon이 정답이다.
| 어휘 | reimburse 환급하다   expense 경비, 비용   incur 발생하다

🏠 고난도
104. 인칭 대명사
나머지 팀원들이 교통 체증에 갇혀 있었기 때문에 Herrera 씨와 Lee 씨가 연회를 위한 중앙 장식들의 대부분을 스스로 설치했다.
| 해설 | 빈칸은 완전한 문장 뒤에 위치해 있으므로, 소유 대명사인 (A) theirs와 소유격 대명사인 (B) their과 (C) their own은 모두 답이 될 수 없고, 부사와 같은 강조 역할을 할 수 있는 강조 용법의 재귀 대명사가 들어가야 하므로 (D) themselves가 정답이다.
| 어휘 | set up 설치하다, 놓다   centerpiece 중앙 장식   banquet 연회   rest 나머지   get stuck in traffic 교통 체증에 갇히다

105. 전치사 어휘
엔지니어 직책의 지원서는 3월 31일까지만 받을 것이니, 귀하의 것을 제출하는 것을 잊지 마세요.
| 해설 | 빈칸은 부사 only의 수식을 받으며 앞의 절과 뒤의 시간 명사를 연결해 줄 전치사가 들어갈 자리로, 문맥상 '3월 31일까지만 받을 것이다'라는 의미가 되어야 하므로 '~까지'라는 뜻의 전치사인 (A) until이 정답이다.
| 어휘 | application 지원서, 신청서   position 직책   accept 수락하다, 받아들이다   submit 제출하다

106. 동사 자리
정비공은 그 차량의 타이어들이 심하게 닳았고 교체가 필요하다고 언급했다.
| 해설 | 빈칸은 문장의 주어인 The mechanic 뒤에 본동사가 들어갈 자리이므로, 준동사인 (A) noting과 (D) to note, 복수 동사인 (B) note는 모두 답이 될 수 없고, 과거 시제 동사인 (C) noted가 정답이다.
| 어휘 | mechanic 정비공   vehicle 차량   heavily 심하게   worn 닳은, 해진   be in need of ~이 필요하다   replacement 교체

107. 동사 어휘
Sheridan 해변의 놀랄 만큼 아름다운 흰 모래가 매년 수천 명의 관광객들을 끌어들인다.
| 해설 | 빈칸은 문장의 동사가 들어갈 자리로, 문맥상 '놀랄 만큼 아름다운 흰 모래가 관광객들을 끌어들인다'라는 의미로 전개되는 것이 적절하므로 '끌어들이다, 유치하다'라는 뜻의 (B) attract가 정답이다.
| 어휘 | stunning 놀랄 만큼 아름다운   exhibit 전시하다   improve 개선하다, 향상시키다   feature 특징으로 하다

108. 형용사 자리 - 주격 보어
자신의 요리에 어떤 재료들을 쓰기 전에, 요리사 Montague는 그것들이 방부제가 없는지 확인한다.
| 해설 | 빈칸은 be동사 are의 보어 자리이므로, 부사 (B) freely, 주어인 they와 동격이 될 수 없는 명사 (D) freedom은 답이 될 수 없고, '방부제가 없는'이라는 의미를 완성해 줄 '~이 없는'이라는 뜻의 형용사인 (C) free가 정답이다.
| 어휘 | ingredient 재료   free from ~이 없는   preservative 방부제   freedom 자유

109. 전치사 어휘
Elliot 씨에 의해 준비된 예산안은 환율의 변화에 대해 고려하지 않아서, 부정확한 것으로 간주되었다.
| 해설 | 빈칸 앞에 있는 동사 account와 함께 쓰이는 전치사를 묻는 문제로 정답은 (A) for이다. 'account for(설명하다, 고려하다)'를 하나의 표현으로 알아두자.
| 어휘 | budget 예산안   account for ~을 설명하다   currency rates 환율   consider 간주하다   inaccurate 부정확한

110. 명사 어휘
주 정부가 최근에 대기 오염을 예방하기 위한 전략들을 분석하기 위한 위원회를 구성했다.
| 해설 | 빈칸은 동사 formed의 목적어가 될 명사가 들어갈 자리로, 문맥상 대기 오염을 예방하기 위한 전략들을 분석하기 위해 주 정부가 구성한(formed) 대상이 될 수 있는 것으로는 '위원회'가 가장 적절하므로 (B) committee가 정답이다.
| 어휘 | state government 주 정부   form 구성하다   explore 탐사하다, 분석하다   strategy 전략   prevent 예방하다   air pollution 대기 오염   relationship 관계   barrier 장벽, 장애물   politician 정치인

111. 형용사 어휘
저희 유통업체에 약간의 문제가 있었기 때문에, 그 전화 모델은 향후 몇 주 동안 구할 수 없습니다.
| 해설 | 빈칸은 be동사 is의 보어가 될 형용사가 들어갈 자리로, 문맥상 문제가 있었던 사실과 관련 지어 '그 모델은 구할 수 없다'라는 의미로 전개되는 것이 적절하므로 '구할 수 없는, 이용할 수 없는'이라는 뜻의 (C) unavailable이 정답이다.
| 어휘 | distributor 유통업체, 배급업체   occupied 차지된, 사용 중인   rearranged 재배치된   correct 맞는, 정확한

112. 전치사 어휘
그의 조각품들을 갤러리에 전시 중인 Harvey 씨는 40년 넘게 전문적인 미술가로 일해왔다.
| 해설 | 빈칸은 앞의 절과 뒤의 기간 표현을 연결해줄 전치사가 들어갈 자리이므로, '40년 넘게'라는 의미를 완성해줄 기간 전치사인 (A) for가 정답이다.
| 어휘 | sculpture 조각품, 조각   professional 전문적인, 직업적인

고난도
113. 인칭 대명사
Mueller 씨는 경영 팀에 의해 가장 선호되는 제안이 사실은 자신의 것이었다는 것에 놀랐다.
| 해설 | 빈칸은 be동사 was의 보어가 들어갈 자리이고, 주어인 the suggestion이므로 재귀 대명사인 (B) himself와 목적격 대명사 (C) him, 주격 대명사 (D) he는 모두 답이 될 수 없고, the suggestion과 동격이 될 수 있는 '그(자신)의 것'이라는 뜻의 소유 대명사인 (A) his가 정답이다.
| 어휘 | surprised 놀란   suggestion 제안   favored 선호되는   management team 경영 팀, 관리 팀

고난도
114. 대명사 - 수 일치
기자들은 그 회사의 CEO에 의해 이루어진 발언들의 몇몇이 옳지 않았다고 지적했다.
| 해설 | 빈칸은 뒤에 있는 전치사구의 수식을 받는 that절의 주어가 들어갈 자리로, 선행사를 포함하는 관계 대명사인 (A) what과 형용사 (B) other, 부사인 (D) even은 답이 될 수 없고, '발언들의 몇몇'이라는 의미를 완성해 줄 '몇몇'이라는 뜻의 대명사인 (C) several이 정답이다.
| 어휘 | remark 발언   incorrect 옳지 않은, 틀린

115. 동명사 자리 - 동사의 목적어
많은 온라인 소매업체들이 민감한 고객 데이터가 도난당할 수 없도록 자신들의 보안 조치를 변경하는 것을 고려할지도 모른다.
| 해설 | 빈칸은 타동사 consider의 목적어 자리로, consider는 동명사를 목적어로 취하는 동사이므로 동명사인 (C) modifying이 정답이다.
| 어휘 | retailer 소매업체, 소매업자   consider 고려하다   security measures 보안 조치   sensitive 민감한   steal 훔치다

116. 형용사 자리 - 명사 수식
Carlyle 학술 도서관은 소설가 Ann Ortega에 의해 만들어진 가장 방대한 원고 수집물을 소장하고 있다.
| 해설 | 최상급 표현인 the most와 명사 collection 사이에 빈칸이 있으므로 빈칸에는 명사를 수식해줄 형용사가 들어가야 한다. 따라서 '가장 방대한 원고 수집물'이라는 의미를 완성해줄 '방대한, 폭넓은'이라는 뜻의 형용사인 (B) extensive가 정답이다.
| 어휘 | research library 학술 도서관, 연구 도서관   house 소장하다, 수용하다   collection 수집물, 컬렉션   manuscript 원고   produce 생산하다   novelist 소설가   extend 확장하다   extension 확장

117. 부사절 접속사
도시 계획가가 도로 공사를 위한 계획을 마무리 지은 후에, 더 정확한 견적이 제공될 수 있다.
| 해설 | 빈칸은 뒤에 제시된 두 절을 연결해줄 접속사가 들어갈 자리로, 두 절의 내용으로 볼 때 일의 진행 순서를 나타내줄 접속사가 들어가는 것이 적절함을 알 수 있으므로 '~ 마무리 지은 후에 ~ 제공될 수 있다'라는 의미를 완성해줄 접속사인 (B) After가 정답이다.
| 어휘 | city planner 도시 계획가   roadwork 도로 공사   accurate 정확한   estimate 견적, 견적서

118. 부사 어휘
선거 사무장은 Joan Moore의 문체가 연설문 작성자 역할의 필요에 완벽하게 딱 맞는다고 생각했다.

| 해설 | 빈칸은 동사 fit을 수식해줄 부사가 들어갈 자리로, 문맥상 fit의 정도를 나타내 '완벽하게 딱 맞는다'라는 의미로 전개되는 것이 적절하므로 '완벽하게, 더할 나위 없이'라는 뜻의 (C) perfectly가 정답이다.
| 어휘 | campaign manager 선거 사무장 writing style 문체, 작문 스타일 fit 꼭 맞다 speechwriter 연설문 작성자 routinely 일상적으로, 정기적으로 constantly 끊임없이 urgently 긴급하게, 급히

고난도
119. 명사 자리 – 동사의 목적어 | 복합 명사
회사가 그 분야의 여러 상들의 후보로 지명되었고, 이것이 증가된 투자자 열의로 이어졌다.
| 해설 | 빈칸은 동사 has led to의 목적어 자리로, investor와 함께 복합 명사를 만들어 줄 명사가 들어갈 자리이므로, 동사인 (A) enthuse와 형용사인 (B) enthusiastic, 부사인 (D) enthusiastically는 모두 답이 될 수 없고, '열의, 열정'이라는 뜻의 명사인 (C) enthusiasm이 정답이다.
| 어휘 | be nominated for ~의 후보로 지명되다 award 상 field 분야 lead to ~로 이어지다 increased 증가된 investor 투자자 enthuse 열광시키다 enthusiastic 열광적인 enthusiastically 열광적으로

120. 동사 어휘
그 데이터베이스는 암호로 보호되어 있어 그것을 사용할 권한이 있는 직원들에 의해서만 접근될 수 있다.
| 해설 | 빈칸은 employees를 수식하는 관계 대명사 who절에서 be동사 are와 함께 수동태 동사를 이루는 과거 분사가 들어갈 자리로, 문맥상 '그것을 사용할 권한이 있는 직원들에 의해서만'이라는 의미로 전개되는 것이 적절하므로 (D) authorized가 정답이다.
| 어휘 | be password protected 암호로 보호되다 access 접근하다 compile 편집하다 authorize 권한을 부여하다

121. 부사절 접속사
그 잡지는 구독을 하면 한 호당 1.95달러인 반면에 신문 가판대 가격은 그 금액의 거의 세 배이다.
| 해설 | 빈칸은 앞뒤의 두 절을 연결해 줄 접속사가 들어갈 자리이므로, 한정사이자 대명사인 (B) all, 부사인 (C) approximately는 답이 될 수 없고, 두 절이 서로 상반되는 내용이므로 '~인 반면에'라는 뜻의 역접의 부사절 접속사인 (D) whereas가 정답이다.
| 어휘 | cost 비용이 ~이다 per ~당 via ~을 통해 subscription 구독 newsstand 신문 가판대 amount 금액

고난도
122. 부정 대명사
여섯 회사들이 그 도시의 레크리에이션 센터의 건설을 위한 입찰에 참여했고, 모두 그 프로젝트에 요구되는 기준을 충족시켰다.
| 해설 | 빈칸은 접속사 and로 연결된 절의 주어가 들어갈 자리로, 앞에 제시된 사물 주어 Six companies를 가리킬 수 있는 (B) all이 정답이다. (D) everything의 경우 all thing의 의미를 가지는 대명사이다.
| 어휘 | enter a bid 입찰에 참여하다, 응찰하다 construction 건설 criteria 기준

123. 형용사 어휘
Lee 씨는 15피트 화물 트럭이 자신의 소지품과 가구를 옮기기에 충분할 것이라고 확인했다.
| 해설 | 빈칸은 be동사의 보어가 될 형용사가 들어갈 자리로, 문맥상 '15 피트 화물 트럭이 짐을 옮기기에 충분할 것'이라는 의미로 전개되는 것이 적절하므로 '충분한'이라는 뜻의 (C) sufficient가 정답이다.
| 어휘 | confirm 확인하다 cargo truck 화물 트럭 belonging 소유물, 소지품 occasional 때때로, 가끔 flexible 유연한, 탄력적인 eligible 자격이 있는

고난도
124. 부사 자리
그 지역에 있는 대부분의 사무실들은 종이와 유리 그리고 플라스틱만 재활용하지만, Logan 주식회사는 판지용 수거 용기들 역시 가지고 있다.
| 해설 | 빈칸 앞에 등위 접속사 but으로 연결된 완전한 두 절이 있고, 문장 끝에 빈칸이 있으므로 빈칸은 부사가 들어갈 자리이다. 따라서 전치사인 (A) such as와 형용사구인 (B) long enough는 오답이고, 문장 끝에 위치할 수 있으며, 문맥상으로도 적절한 '역시, 또한'이라는 뜻의 (D) as well이 정답이다.
| 어휘 | recycle 재활용하다 collection container 수거 용기 cardboard 판지

125. 부사 어휘
Santa Rosa 리조트의 방문객들은 관례적으로 객실 청소 직원에게 1박당 5달러의 팁을 준다.
| 해설 | 빈칸은 동사 tip을 수식해줄 부사가 들어갈 자리로, 문맥상 '방문객들은 관례적으로 1박당 5달러의 팁을 준다'라는 의미로 전개되는 것이 적절하므로 '관례적으로, 관습적으로'라는 뜻의 (B) customarily가 정답이다.
| 어휘 | tip 팁을 주다 housekeeping staff 객실 청소 직원 mutually 상호 간의, 서로 sharply 급격하게, 날카롭게

고난도
126. 명사 어휘
처음 매니저가 된 이들을 위한 Horace 기관의 일련의 강연들은 매우 인기가 있었다.
| 해설 | 소유격 표현 뒤에 있는 빈칸은 명사가 들어갈 자리로, 문맥상 '일련의 강연들은 매우 인기가 있었다'라는 의미가 되는 것이 자연스러우므로, '일련, 시리즈'라는 뜻의 (C) series가 정답이다.
| 어휘 | lecture 강연, 강의 extremely 매우, 극도로 behavior 행위, 행동 movement 움직임, 운동 route 경로, 노선

127. 전치사 어휘
Condor Laboratories에 의해 개발된 저울들은 유래 없이 정확하게 액체와 고체 둘 다의 무게를 잰다.
| 해설 | 빈칸은 앞의 절과 뒤의 명사를 연결해 줄 전치사가 들어갈 자리로, 문맥상 '유래 없이 정확하게 무게를 잰다'라는 의미가 되어야 하므로, 뒤에 있는 명사 precision와 함께 쓰여 부사(precisely)의 의미를 완성해 줄 전치사인 (D) with가 정답이다.
| 어휘 | scale 저울 develop 개발하다 weigh 무게를 재다 liquid 액체

solid 고체   unprecedented 전례 없는   precision 정확함

128. 동명사 자리 – 전치사의 목적어
Bonfoy 제조사에 설치된 새로운 기계는 하루에 수백 야드의 직물을 생산할 수 있다.
| 해설 | 빈칸은 전치사 of의 목적어 자리이며, 빈칸 뒤에 목적어가 있으므로 동명사인 (C) producing이 정답이다.
| 어휘 | machinery 기계   install 설치하다   be capable of ~할 수 있다   fabric 직물, 천   per day 하루에   producer 생산자, 제작자

129. 동사 어휘
사람들이 그 안으로 돌아오도록 허용하기 전에 그 구조물에 이상이 없다는 것을 확실히 하기 위해 소방서 직원이 건물을 철저하게 확인할 것이다.
| 해설 | 빈칸은 to부정사를 완성해 줄 동사가 들어갈 자리로, 문맥상 건물을 철저하게 점검하는 목적을 나타내는 것으로 '이상 없다는 것을 확실히 하기 위해'라는 의미로 전개되는 것이 적절하므로 '확실히 하다, 반드시 ~이다'라는 뜻의 (B) ensure가 정답이다.
| 어휘 | fire department 소방서   personnel 직원   thoroughly 철저하게   structure 구조물, 건물   sound 견고한, 이상 없는   allow 허용하다   calculate 계산하다   accept 수락하다   retain 보유하다

130. 부사 자리 – 동사 수식
이 새로운 내비게이션 시스템은 실시간 교통량을 고려하여 자동으로 최선의 경로를 다시 계산할 수 있다.
| 해설 | 빈칸 앞에는 동사와 목적어가 있고, 빈칸 뒤에는 전치사구가 있는데, 빈칸이 없어도 완전한 문장이 되는 것으로 볼 때, 빈칸에는 앞에 있는 동사 recalculate를 수식해줄 부사가 들어가야 함을 알 수 있다. 따라서 부사인 (B) automatically가 정답이다.
| 어휘 | navigation 내비게이션, 항법   recalculate 다시 계산하다   route 노선, 경로   factor in ~을 고려하다   real-time 실시간   traffic 교통량

PART 6

131-134 다음 편지를 참조하시오.

Daniel Vance
1749 Oxford Court
Tulsa, OK 74106

1월 7일

Vance 씨 귀하,

저는 12월 20일에 배달되기로 되어 있었지만 1월 2일까지 도착하지 않은 Montclair 스테레오 시스템에 관한 귀하의 최근 주문과 관련하여 이 글을 쓰고 있습니다. 이 물품이 ¹³¹지연된 것에 대해 깊이 사과드립니다.

그 ¹³²불편 때문에 귀하가 보상을 받을 자격이 있다는 것에 동의합니다. 첫째로, 저희가 이 상품에 대한 모든 운송 요금을 환불해 드릴 것입니다. 또한 저희 ¹³³실수로부터 발생된 모든 문제를 만회하는 것을 돕고자 귀하의 계좌에 50달러를 입금해 드릴 것입니다. ¹³⁴이 제안에 만족하시기를 바랍니다. 입금액은 1월 15일까지 귀하의 계좌에 보내질 것입니다.

진심을 담아,

Finwood 전자 고객 서비스 팀

| 어휘 | regarding ~와 관련하여   be supposed to ~하기로 되어 있다   agree 동의하다, 의견이 일치하다   be entitled to ~에 자격이 있다   compensation 보상   refund 환불하다   charge 요금   merchandise 상품, 물품   credit 입금하다; 입금액   account 계정   make up for ~을 만회하다, 보상하다   result 발생하다, 생기다

131. 동사의 형태와 시제
| 해설 | 빈칸은 that절의 동사가 들어갈 자리로, 빈칸 뒤에 delay의 목적어가 없으므로 수동태가 되어야 하고, 주어인 this item은 12월 20일에 배달되기로 되어 있었지만 1월 2일까지 도착하지 않은 Montclair 스테레오 시스템을 가리키는 것이므로, 과거 동사가 들어가야 한다. 따라서 과거 시제 수동태인 (D) was delayed가 정답이다.

132. 명사 어휘
| 해설 | 보상을 받을 자격이 있는 이유가 될 만한 것을 골라야 하는데, 앞에 배송 지연에 대해 사과하는 내용이 있으므로 이런 상황과 어울리는 '불편'이라는 뜻의 (C) inconvenience가 정답이다.
| 어휘 | absence 부재, 결근, 결석   disadvantage 불리한 점, 약점   shortage 부족

133. 전치사 어휘
| 해설 | 앞에 제시된 resulted와 연결 지어 '저희 실수로부터 발생된 모든 문제'라는 의미로 전개되는 것이 적절하므로 result from(~에서 발생하다, ~에서 기인하다) 표현을 완성해줄 출처 표현 전치사인 (A) from이 정답이다.

134. 알맞은 문장 고르기
(A) 저희 창고 팀이 그 물품을 확인할 것입니다.
(B) 판매는 공급이 지속되는 한 계속할 것입니다.
(C) 이 제안에 만족하시기를 바랍니다.
(D) 두 가지 납입금 모두 지난달의 명세서에 인쇄되어 있습니다.
| 해설 | 앞서 Firstly와 also로 업체가 배송 지연에 대한 보상으로 고객에게 제공하려고 하는 두 가지 사항이 제시되어 있는 것으로 볼 때, 그와 관련하여 고객이 업체의 제안에 만족하기를 바라는 희망을 언급하는 문장이 삽입되는 것이 가장 적절하므로 (C)가 정답이다.
| 어휘 | warehouse 창고   supply 공급(량)   last 지속되다   be satisfied with ~에 만족하다   proposal 제안   payment 지급, 납입금   statement 명세서

135-138 다음 기사를 참조하시오.

고용 보고서 발표
1월 3일

시의 노동부에 의해 수집된 수치들은 Lawton의 취업률이 증가했음을 보여준다. ¹³⁵실제로, 시의 실업률은 역대 최저이다. 이는 부분적으로 6개월 전에 Marquette 제조 시설이 문을 연 덕택이다. 거의 150명을 고용하고 있는 그 공장은 레이저 커터들을 사용하여 목재, 금속 그리고 플라스틱 같은 ¹³⁶재료들로 맞춤형 부품들을 만들어낸다. ¹³⁷그 회사의 제품에 대한 수요가 증가해 오고 있다. 따라서, 새로운 일자리들을 정기적으로 구할 수 있게 되었다. 시 공무원들은 제조 부문의 상승이 다른 현지 업체들의 성장으로 이어지게 될 것이라고 ¹³⁸생각한다.

| 어휘 | figure 수치   indicate 보여주다, 나타내다   employment rate 취업률   unemployment 실업, 실업률   partially 부분적으로   manufacturing facility 제조 시설   fashion (재료를 써서) 만들다   custom-made 맞춤의   component 부품   available 구할 수 있는   regularly 정기적으로   city official 시 공무원   upturn 상승   sector 부문   lead to ~로 이어지다   growth 성장

고난도

135. 접속 부사

| 해설 | 앞뒤 문장을 자연스럽게 연결해 줄 접속 부사를 고르는 문제로, 문맥상 앞 뒤 문장은 같은 맥락으로 뒤 문장은 앞 문장의 상황으로 나타난 실질적인 사실을 설명한 것임을 알 수 있으므로 '실제로, 사실상'이라는 뜻의 (B) In fact가 정답이다.
| 어휘 | otherwise 그렇지 않으면   nonetheless 그럼에도 불구하고   on the contrary 반대로

136. 명사 어휘

| 해설 | such as 앞에 있는 빈칸은 뒤에 있는 목재, 금속, 플라스틱을 포함하는 것이어야 하므로 '재료, 자재'라는 뜻의 (D) materials가 정답이다.
| 어휘 | production 생산   advantage 이점, 장점   expense 비용

137. 알맞은 문장 고르기

(A) 일자리 상황에 관한 보고서들은 분기별로 한 차례씩 준비된다.
(B) 공장은 직원 채용 절차에 관한 데이터를 제공했다.
(C) 각 제품에는 환불 보증이 딸려 있다.
(D) 그 회사의 제품에 대한 수요가 증가해 오고 있다.
| 해설 | 뒤이어 결과를 나타내는 접속 부사 Therefore(따라서, 그러므로)가 있는 것으로 볼 때, 새로운 일자리들을 정기적으로 구할 수 있게 된 것과 관련하여, 그것을 가능하게 한 제품 수요 증가에 관해 언급한 문장이 삽입되는 것이 가장 적절하므로 정답은 (D)이다.
| 어휘 | quarter 분기   staffing procedure 직원 채용 절차   come with ~이 딸려 있다   money-back guarantee 환불 보증   demand 수요

138. 동사의 형태

| 해설 | 빈칸은 문장의 동사 자리이므로 동사 형태가 아닌 (A) believing은 오답이며, 복수형인 주어 City officials와 수가 일치되지 않는 단수 동사인 (D) believes도 오답이다. 문맥상 주어인 시 공무원들이 '~라고 생각한다'라고 전개되는 것이 적절하므로 능동태 복수 동사인 (B) believe가 정답이다.

139-142 다음 이메일을 참조하시오.

수신: 전 직원
발신: Loni Jordan
날짜: 11월 2일
제목: 직원 상

안녕하세요, 여러분.

한 해가 빠르게 지나갔고, 또 다시 직원들에게 상을 주는 우리의 ¹³⁹연례 행사를 하는 시기가 거의 다 되었습니다. 이것은 우리 직원들의 노고와 헌신을 ¹⁴⁰인정해줄 절호의 기회입니다. 물론, 우리는 맛있는 식사와 함께 서로 어울리며 즐길 수도 있습니다. 우리의 평소 장소는 Newton 홀인데, 그곳이 12월에 이미 예약이 꽉 찬 상황입니다. 제가 100명의 사람들을 ¹⁴¹수용할 수 있는 다른 시설을 찾고 있는데, 전체 직원이 참석하고 직원들 중 일부는 자신들의 배우자들도 데리고 오는 것을 선택할 수도 있기 때문입니다. 아마도, 우리는 Violet 호텔의 연회장을 이용할 것입니다. ¹⁴²식단에 제한이 있으신 경우 저에게 알려주시기 바랍니다. 저희가 이용할 출장 음식 서비스 업체가 채식주의자와 엄격한 채식주의자 등에 맞춰줄 수 있습니다. 여러분은 행사 날짜가 다가옴에 따라 더 많은 정보를 받게 될 것입니다.

진심을 담아,

Loni Jordan
Sanders 주식회사, 행사 위원회

| 어휘 | go by 지나가다   ceremony 행사, 의식   present an award 상을 주다   opportunity 기회   hard work 노고   dedication 헌신, 전념   socialize (사람들과) 어울리다   fully booked 예약이 꽉 찬   entire 전체의   be in attendance 참석하다   spouse 배우자   ballroom 연회장   catering company 출장 음식 서비스 업체   accommodate 맞추다, 수용하다   vegetarian 채식주의자   vegan 엄격한 채식주의자   approach 다가오다

139. 형용사 자리 – 어휘

| 해설 | 빈칸은 our의 수식을 받는 명사 ceremony를 수식해줄 형용사나 복합 명사를 완성해줄 명사가 들어갈 수 있는 자리로, 명사인 (B) debut와 (D) recruitment의 경우 복합 명사를 만들기에 의미상 부적절하므로 답이 될 수 없고, 문맥상 '연례 행사'라는 의미로 전개되는 것이 적절하므로 '연례의, 매년의'라는 뜻의 형용사인 (C) annual이 정답이다.
| 어휘 | closing 마감; 마감하는   debut 데뷔   recruitment 신규 모집, 채용

140. to부정사

| 해설 | 빈칸 앞에 문장의 동사인 is가 있으므로 또 다른 동사인 (A) will recognize는 답이 될 수 없고, 빈칸 뒤에 목적어가 될 명사구가 있으며, 앞에 있는 opportunity는 to부정사와 함께 자주 쓰이는 명사이므로 to부정사인 (B) to recognize가 정답이다.

🏔 고난도

141. 명사 어휘

| 해설 | 빈칸은 facility를 수식하는 that절에서 has의 목적어가 될 명사가 들어갈 자리로, 문맥상 '100명의 사람들을 수용할 수 있는 시설'이라는 의미로 전개되는 것이 적절하므로 '수용력'이라는 뜻의 (B) capacity가 정답이다.

142. 알맞은 문장 고르기

(A) 최종 좌석 배치도는 다운로드될 수 있습니다.
(B) 이런 지연은 다시 발생하지 않을 것입니다.
(C) 계획을 돕는 것에 자원해 주셔서 감사합니다.
(D) 식단에 제한이 있으신 경우 저에게 알려주시기 바랍니다.

| 해설 | 뒤이어 출장 음식 서비스 업체의 음식 제공에 관한 내용이 제시되어 있는 것으로 볼 때, 그와 연결 지어 채식주의자나 엄격한 채식주의자 등과 같이 먹는 것에 제한이 있을 경우 미리 알려줄 것을 요청하는 내용의 문장이 삽입되는 것이 적절하므로 (D)가 정답이다.

| 어휘 | seating chart 좌석 배치도   delay 지연, 지체   volunteer 자원하다   assist with ~을 돕다   dietary restrictions 식단 제한

143-146 다음 회람을 참조하시오.

수신: Sunset 헤어 살롱 전 직원
발신: 총괄 관리자, Geneva Curtis
날짜: 5월 31일, 수요일
제목: 샴푸 구역

우리 샴푸 구역에 2개의 새로운 개수대를 설치하기 위해 고용했던 배관공이 며칠 동안 병가를 내서 이제 6월 1일이 아닌 6월 4일에 그 작업이 완료될 것입니다. 이 예기치 못한 143상황을 고려하면, 우리는 이미 예약하신 많은 수의 고객들을 쉽게 처리할 수 없을 것입니다. 수요에 맞추기 위해, 자신의 고객들의 머리를 감기는 일을 가능한 한 빨리 완료해 주세요. 특히 수납장 144가까이에 있는 고압 수도꼭지를 사용하는 경우에는요. 이것으로 여러분의 고객에게 야기될 수 있는 문제에 대해 145유감스럽게 생각하지만, 저희는 며칠 동안 이를 참아야만 합니다. 146변화는 결국 충분히 가치 있을 것입니다.

| 어휘 | hair-washing area 샴푸 구역   plumber 배관공   install 설치하다   sink 개수대   take a sick day 병가를 내다   complete 완료하다   handle 처리하다   volume 양   keep up with ~에 발맞추다, 따라가다   demand 수요   high-pressure 고압   tap 수도꼭지   storage closet 수납장   put up with ~을 참다

143. 명사 어휘

| 해설 | 빈칸 앞에 있는 this는 배관공이 병가를 내서 완료일이 미뤄진 것을 가리키는 것으로, '이 예기치 못한 상황'이라는 의미가 되는 것이 적절하므로 (B) situation이 정답이다.

| 어휘 | structure 구조, 건축물   situation 상황   treatment 처리, 시술   hesitation 주저, 망설임

🏔 고난도

144. 형용사 어휘

| 해설 | 빈칸은 the high-pressure tap을 뒤에서 수식하는 형용사가 들어갈 자리로, 문맥상 뒤에 있는 storage closet과 관련 지어 '수납장 가까이에 있는 고압 수도꼭지'라는 의미로 전개되는 것이 적절하므로 '~ 가까이에 있는(adjacent to ~)'이라는 뜻의 (B) adjacent가 정답이다.

| 어휘 | furnished 가구가 비치된   essential 필수적인   comparable 비교할 만한, 비슷한

145. 동사의 형태와 시제

| 해설 | 빈칸은 문장의 동사가 들어갈 자리이므로 준동사인 (A) to regret은 오답이고, 주어가 I이므로 3인칭 단수 동사인 (B) regrets도 오답이다. 야기될 수 있는 문제에 대해 유감스럽게 생각하는 건 과거가 아니라 현재이므로 현재 시제인 (D) regret이 정답이다.

🏔 고난도

146. 알맞은 문장 고르기

(A) 여러분이 선호하는 스타일을 저에게 알려주세요.
(B) 그들에게 곧 돌아오라고 말해 주세요.
(C) 변화는 결국 충분히 가치 있을 것입니다.
(D) 각 세션은 단지 몇 분 걸릴 것입니다.

| 해설 | 앞서 작업 지연으로 고객에게 야기될 수 있는 문제에 대해 유감스럽게 생각하지만, 며칠 동안 이를 참아야만 한다고 했으므로, 이후 그렇게 참고 일해야 하는 이유가 될 만한 것으로, 며칠만 참으면 상황이 더 나아질 것임을 언급하는 문장이 이어지는 것이 적절하므로 정답은 (C)이다.

| 어휘 | be well worth 충분히 가치 있다

PART 7

147-148 다음 명함을 참조하시오.

Elaine's 수선
529 Cambridge Avenue ◆ 555-3223
주인, Elaine Smith

정장, 드레스 등 맞춤 수선.
147빠른 단 줄임 서비스: 기다리시는 동안 바지를 줄여 드립니다!

148월-금: 오전 9시-오후 6시 / 토: 오전 10시-오후 4시

| 어휘 | business card 명함 custom 맞춤의 alteration 수선 suit 정장 hemming 단 줄임 trouser 바지 shorten 줄이다, 짧게 하다

147. 세부 사항을 묻는 문제
어떤 서비스가 짧은 시간 내에 행해질 수 있나?
(A) 찢어진 정장 재킷을 수선하는 것
(B) 옷의 잃어버린 단추를 교체하는 것
(C) 바지의 길이를 조정하는 것
(D) 맞춤 드레스를 위해 치수를 재는 것
| 해설 | 명함 내용 중반부에 빠른 단 줄임 서비스(Quick Hemming Service)로 기다리는 동안 바지를 줄여 준다고(Trousers shortened while you wait!) 제시된 것에서, 바지 길이 조정은 맡기지 않고 그 자리에서 바로 서비스됨을 알 수 있으므로 정답은 (C)이다.
| 어휘 | torn 찢어진 replace 교체하다 adjust 조정하다 length 길이 take a measurement 치수를 재다
| 패러프레이징 | shortened → Adjusting the length

148. 추론 문제
Elaine's 수선에 관해 암시되는 것은 무엇인가?
(A) 환불 보증을 제공한다.
(B) 직원이 한 명뿐이다.
(C) 다양한 직물을 판매한다.
(D) 일요일마다 문을 닫는다.
| 해설 | 명함 마지막에 운영 시간이 '월-금: 오전 9시-오후 6시 / 토: 오전 10시-오후 4시(Mon. - Fri. 9 A.M. - 6 P.M. / Sat. 10 A.M. - 4 P.M.)'로 제시된 것을 통해, 일요일은 영업하지 않음을 유추할 수 있으므로 정답은 (D)이다.
| 어휘 | a money-back guarantee 환불 보증 a variety of 다양한, 여러 가지의 fabric 직물

149-150 다음 이메일을 참조하시오.

수신: Larry Morgan <morgan.l@crescentinc.com>
발신: Celeste Ross <ross.c@crescentinc.com>
날짜: 12월 2일
제목: 월간 회의

Morgan 씨 귀하,

[149]12월 3일로 예정된 월간 관리자 회의가 30분 미뤄져 3시 30분에 시작할 것임을 알리고자 이 글을 씁니다. 이는 회의실의 일정 겹침 때문입니다. 그래도 여전히 그 회의는 약 1시간 정도 지속될 것으로 예상합니다. [150]그 회의에서 다뤄져야 한다고 생각하는 것이 있다면, 오늘 저녁까지 저에게 이메일을 보내주세요. 그렇게 하면, 제가 그것을 안건에 공식적으로 추가할 수 있습니다.

내일 봐요!

Celeste

| 어휘 | scheduled 예정된 push back 미루다 scheduling conflict 일정 겹침 conference room 회의실 last 지속되다 approximately 대략 cover 다루다 formally 공식적으로, 정식으로 agenda 안건, 의제

149. 세부 사항을 묻는 문제
회의에 관해 무엇이 변경되었나?
(A) 날짜
(B) 장소
(C) 시작 시간
(D) 지속 시간
| 해설 | 초반부에 12월 3일로 예정된 월간 관리자 회의가 30분 미뤄져서 3시 30분에 시작할 것임을(the monthly managers meeting scheduled for December 3 has been pushed back by half an hour, so it will begin at 3:30) 알리고자 이 글을 쓴다고 했으므로 정답은 (C)이다.

150. 세부 사항을 묻는 문제
Morgan 씨는 왜 Ross 씨에게 글을 써야 하는가?
(A) 논의의 주제를 제안하기 위해
(B) 자신의 회의 참석을 확정하기 위해
(C) 안건의 사본 한 부를 제공하기 위해
(D) 그녀에게 일정 문제에 관해 주의를 주기 위해
| 해설 | Ross 씨는 이메일을 보낸 사람으로, 이메일 후반부에 그 회의에서 다뤄져야 한다고 생각하는 것이 있다면, 오늘 저녁까지 이메일을 보내달라고(If there is anything you think should be covered at the meeting, please e-mail me by the end of the day) 했으므로 정답은 (A)이다.
| 어휘 | discussion 논의 warn 주의를 주다, 경고하다
| 패러프레이징 | anything you think should be covered at the meeting → a topic for discussion

151-152 다음 문자 메시지 대화를 참조하시오.

Ivan Mathiasen [오전 9:20]
제가 Seneca Hospitality를 위한 사업 제안서를 이메일로 보내드렸는데요. [151]그것을 확인해 볼 기회가 있으셨는지 궁금해서요.

Amina Behane [오전 9:23]
[152]곧 주요 고객이 제 사무실을 방문할 것이지만, 지금 잠깐은 볼 수 있어요.

Ivan Mathiasen [오전 9:24]
감사해요. 제가 모든 것을 다 다룬 것인지 확실히 하고 싶어요.

Amina Behane [오전 9:25]
몇 가지 조정이 이루어져야 할 것이 있지만, 보통 그렇죠. [151]제가 동일한 사안들에 대해 당신의 다른 팀원들을 지도해 줘야 했었거든요. 그것은 점심 식사 후에 만나 논의해 보죠.

Ivan Mathiasen [오전 9:26]
네, 저는 언제든 시간 돼요.

Amina Behane [오전 9:27]
이제 그분이 왔네요. ¹⁵²끝나면 전화할게요.

| 어휘 | business proposal 사업 제안서   have a chance to ~할 기회가 있다   major 중요한, 주된   cover 다루다   adjustment 조정   normal 보통의, 일반적인   issue 사안

151. 추론 문제
Behane 씨에 관해 암시되는 것은 무엇인가?
(A) 몇 가지 업데이트된 수치들을 요청했다.
(B) 이메일을 받는 데 어려움을 겪었다.
(C) Mathiasen 씨의 관리자이다.
(D) Seneca Hospitality에서 일했었다.

| 해설 | 오전 9:20에 Mathiasen 씨가 이메일로 보낸 사업 제안서를 확인해 볼 기회가 있었는지 궁금하다고(I'm wondering if you've had a chance to check it out) 물은 것과 오전 9:25에 Behane 씨가 동일한 사안들에 대해 다른 팀원들을 지도해 줘야 했었다고(I've had to coach your other team members on the same issues) 한 것을 통해, Behane 씨는 팀원들을 지도해 주는 위치에 있는 관리자일 것으로 유추할 수 있으므로 정답은 (C)이다.

| 어휘 | figure 수치   supervisor 상사, 관리자

152. 의도 파악 문제
오전 9:27에 Behane 씨가 "이제 그분이 왔네요"라고 쓸 때 의미하는 것은 무엇인가?
(A) 중요한 고객이 도착했다.
(B) 커리어 코치가 적극 권장된다.
(C) 동료가 질문들에 대답할 수 있다.
(D) 동료가 Behane 씨의 업무들을 대신할 것이다.

| 해설 | 오전 9:23에 Amina Behane이 곧 주요 고객이 사무실을 방문할 것이라고(I have a major customer visiting my office soon) 했는데, 이 표현에서 her가 가리키는 것은 앞서 말한 a major customer로, 주요 고객이 도착한 사실을 알린 후, 그 만남이 끝나면 연락하겠다고(I'll call you when I'm done) 덧붙인 것임을 알 수 있으므로 정답은 (A)이다.

| 어휘 | colleague 동료   coworker 동료   cover 대신하다
| 패러프레이징 | a major customer → An important client

153-154 다음 설명을 참조하시오.

Vision-HD 스마트폰 앱으로 여러분이 좋아하는 텔레비전 프로의 다른 에피소드를 다시는 놓치지 마세요. ¹⁵³Vision-HD 스마트폰 앱은 여러분의 스마트 TV가 프로그램을 녹화하도록 원격으로 프로그램을 짤 수 있도록 해 주고, 그것은 최대 7일 전에 미리 이용될 수 있습니다.

1. www.myappstore.com/visionhd를 방문하여 앱을 다운로드하세요. 이 앱은 모든 사용자들에게 무료이지만, 이용 가능한 일부 선택적인 앱 내 구매들이 있습니다.
2. ¹⁵⁴여러분의 케이블 서비스 제공업체에서 받은 여러분의 고객 번호를 입력하세요. 그 번호는 여러분의 대금 청구서 상단에서 찾으실 수 있습니다.
3. 다 됐습니다! 앱 사용을 시작하여 여러분의 일정대로 텔레비전을 즐기세요!

| 어휘 | miss 놓치다   remotely 원격으로   up to 최대 ~까지   in advance 미리   optional 선택적인   purchase 구매   available 이용 가능한   provider 제공업체   billing statement 대금 청구서

153. 세부 사항을 묻는 문제
Vision-HD 스마트폰 어플리케이션은 무엇을 하기 위해 만들어졌나?
(A) 기기가 텔레비전 프로들을 녹화하도록 설정하는 것
(B) 인기 있는 TV 프로그램들의 후기를 보여주는 것
(C) 인터넷에서 영상들이 나오게 하는 것
(D) 영상들의 이미지 품질을 개선하는 것

| 해설 | 첫 번째 단락에 Vision-HD 스마트폰 앱은 스마트 TV가 프로그램을 녹화하도록 원격으로 프로그램을 짤 수 있도록 해 준다고(The Vision-HD smartphone app allows you to remotely program your smart TV to record a program) 했으므로 정답은 (A)이다.

| 어휘 | device 기기   stream 인터넷에서 다운로드와 동시에 재생하다   improve 개선하다   quality 품질
| 패러프레이징 | smart TV → a device

154. 세부 사항을 묻는 문제
고객들이 서비스를 신청할 때 제공해야 하는 것은 무엇인가?
(A) 신분증
(B) 고객 번호
(C) 이메일 주소
(D) 계약금

| 해설 | 2번에 케이블 서비스 제공업체에서 받은 고객 번호를 입력하라고(Input your customer number from your cable service provider) 했으므로 정답은 (B)이다.

| 어휘 | down payment 계약금, 착수금

155-157 다음 후기를 참조하시오.

www.semoracityreviews.com/home_improvements/Cerritos_Flooring

업체: Cerritos Flooring   작성자: Ruben Ives

평가: 5/5

나무 바닥을 설치하는 것을 고려하고 계신 분 누구에게나 Cerritos Flooring을 적극 추천할 것입니다. ¹⁵⁵업체를 고를 때, 저는 그저 가장 저렴한 곳을 택해서, 작업의 질이 충분히 괜찮을지 여부는 확신하지 못했습니다. 하지만 기분 좋게 놀랐는데요. 예약을 잡기 위해 단 며칠만 기다리면 됐고, 작업 팀이 필요한 도구를 모두 가지고 오전에 제때 도착했습니다. 그들은 효율적으로 작업해 주었고요. ¹⁵⁶제가 정말 대단하다고 생각했던 것은 그들이 떠나기 전에 진공청소기로 청소를 하고 모든 것을 다 정리했다는 것이었습니다. 누구도 그들이 거기 있었다는 것을 짐작조차 할 수 없도록 말이죠! 그 새 마루로 2주 동안 지내봤는데, 훌륭해 보입니다. 앞으로도 몇 년 동안 새것처럼 좋아 보일 것이라고 확신합니다.

¹⁵⁷한 가지 제안할 점은 예약 전에 확실히 복도를 비우라는 것입니다. 저는 이렇게 하는 것을 잊어버려서, 그들이 지나는 길에 어떤 것도 깨뜨리지 않기 위해 아주 조심하느라, 작업자들이 물품들을 들여오는 것을 다소 힘들게 했습니다.

| 어휘 | hardwood floors 나무 바닥   install 설치하다   go for ~을 택하다   quality 질, 품질   pleasantly surprised 기분 좋게 놀란   appointment 예약   on time 제때   tool 도구, 공구   perform 행하다   efficiently 효율적으로   amazing 대단한   vacuum 진공청소기로 청소하다   fantastic 훌륭한   corridor 복도   prior to ~ 전에   supplies 물품

155. 세부 사항을 묻는 문제
Ives 씨는 왜 Cerritos Flooring을 선택했나?
(A) 가격이 가장 낮았다.
(B) 친구에 의해 추천되었다.
(C) 좋은 평판을 가지고 있었다.
(D) 그의 집에서 가장 가까웠다.
| 해설 | Ives 씨는 후기를 남긴 사람으로 초반부에 업체를 고를 때, 그저 가장 저렴한 곳을 택했다고(When choosing a company, I just went for the cheapest one) 했으므로 정답은 (A)이다.
| 어휘 | reputation 평판, 명성
| 패러프레이징 | · went for → select
· the cheapest → the lowest prices

156. 세부 사항을 묻는 문제
Ives 씨가 서비스에 관해 가장 깊은 인상을 받은 것은 무엇인가?
(A) 주문한 날에 이용이 가능했다.
(B) 작업에 보증이 딸려 있다.
(C) 일정에 앞서 완료되었다.
(D) 작업반이 지저분한 상태로 두고 가지 않았다.
| 해설 | 중반부에 정말 대단하다고 생각했던 것은 그들이 떠나기 전에 진공청소기로 청소를 하고 모든 것을 다 정리한 것이었다고(What I really thought was amazing was that they vacuumed and cleaned up everything before they left) 제시되어 있으므로 정답은 (D)이다.

| 어휘 | available 이용 가능한   come with ~이 딸려 있다   complete 완료하다   ahead of ~에 앞서   leave behind 두고 가다   mass 지저분한 상태
| 패러프레이징 | vacuumed and cleaned up everything before they left → did not leave behind a mess

157. 세부 사항을 묻는 문제
Ives 씨가 하도록 제안하는 것은 무엇인가?
(A) 오전 예약을 하는 것
(B) 2주 후에 바닥을 확인하는 것
(C) 복도에서 물품들을 치우는 것
(D) 회사에 깨진 물품들을 알리는 것
| 해설 | 두 번째 단락에 한 가지 제안할 점은 예약 전에 확실히 복도를 비우라는 것이라고(The one thing I would suggest is to make sure your corridor is empty prior to your appointment) 한 후, 자신의 경험을 덧붙이고 있으므로 정답은 (C)이다.
| 어휘 | remove 치우다   hallway 복도, 통로
| 패러프레이징 | make sure your corridor is empty → Removing items from a hallway

158-160 다음 기사를 참조하시오.

방문자 수를 높일 것으로 예상되는 웹 사이트 업그레이드

(2월 22일)—Maywood 시 정부가 더 많은 주민들에게 어필하기 위해 그 웹 사이트의 업그레이드된 버전을 출시했다. 이것은 15년 이상 만에 그 사이트의 첫 번째 큰 변화이다.

이전처럼, 사이트 방문객들은 날짜별로 활동들을 검색할 수 있고, 뿐만 아니라 지역 사회와 관련된 문서들의 데이터베이스에도 접속할 수 있다. ¹⁵⁸가장 눈에 띄는 새로운 기능은 등록된 사용자들이 지역 사회 활동들의 이미지를 업로드할 수 있는 온라인 갤러리이다. —[1]—.

시가 그 프로젝트에 2만 달러 이상을 썼기 때문에, ¹⁶⁰일부 주민들은 웹 사이트를 업그레이드하는 비용에 대해 우려를 표명했다. "우리처럼 인구가 적은데, 이미 완벽하게 작동하고 있는 것에 투자하는 것은 정당화하기 힘들죠."라고 Maywood의 한 사업주인 Joshua Quentin이 말했다. —[2]—.

시 공무원들은 새로운 웹 사이트가 Maywood의 지역 활동들에 새로운 관심을 불러일으키길 바라고 있다. —[3]—. 예를 들어, ¹⁵⁹ ⁽ᴬ⁾연례 여름 노래 경연 대회와 ¹⁵⁹ ⁽ᴰ⁾강변 쓰레기 수거의 날은 이번 달에 주민들이 함께할 수 있는 기회이다. 웹 사이트에는 또한 라이브 영상 스트림 방송을 위한 기술도 있는데, 그 시스템은 ¹⁵⁹ ⁽ᶜ⁾다음 주에 있을 주 상원 의원 후보자 토론에서 선보일 것이다. —[4]—. 그것은 또한 올해 동안 쭉 있을 지역 축제를 방송하는 데도 이용될 것이다.

| 어휘 | boost 신장시키다, 북돋우다   city government 시 정부   launch 출시하다   resident 주민   activity 활동   access 접속하다, 이용하다   noticeable 눈에 띄는, 두드러진   feature 기능   registered

등록된 express 표현하다 concern 우려 population 인구 justify 정당화하다 invest 투자하다 city official 시 공무원 create 만들다 renewed 새로워진 interest 관심 annual 연례의 litter 쓰레기 opportunity 기회 broadcast 방송하다 debut 선보이다 debate 토론, 논쟁 candidate 후보자 state senator 주 상원 의원

158. 세부 사항을 묻는 문제

시의 웹 사이트에 추가된 것은 무엇인가?

(A) 사진들 모음
(B) 쌍방향 일정표
(C) 검색 엔진
(D) 비디오 녹화 기능

| 해설 | 두 번째 단락에 가장 눈에 띄는 새로운 기능은 등록된 사용자들이 지역 사회 활동들의 이미지를 업로드할 수 있는 온라인 갤러리라고(The most noticeable new feature is an online gallery where registered users can upload images of community activities) 제시되어 있으므로 정답은 (A)이다.

| 어휘 | interactive 쌍방향의, 대화형의

| 패러프레이징 | an online gallery → A collection of photographs

159. NOT True 문제

Maywood에서 곧 있을 행사로 제시되지 않은 것은 무엇인가?

(A) 음악 경연 대회
(B) 스포츠 경기
(C) 정치 토론
(D) 청소 프로젝트

| 해설 | 마지막 단락의 연례 여름 노래 경연 대회(the annual Summer Singing Contest)에서 (A), 강변 쓰레기 수거의 날(the Riverside Litter Collection Day)에서 (D), 다음 주에 있을 주 상원 의원 후보자 토론(next week's debate among candidates for state senator)에서 (C)를 확인할 수 있으므로 정답은 (B)이다.

| 어휘 | competition 대회 race 경기 political 정치적인 cleanup 청소, 정화

| 패러프레이징 |
· the annual Summer Singing Contest → A music competition
· the Riverside Litter Collection Day → A cleanup project
· debate among candidates for state senator → A political debate

🏠 고난도

160. 문장 삽입 문제

[1], [2], [3], [4]로 표시된 곳 중에 다음 문장이 들어가기에 가장 적절한 곳은?

"그럼에도 불구하고, 대부분의 사람들은 그 사이트가 구식이고 변화가 필요하다고 생각했다."

(A) [1]
(B) [2]
(C) [3]
(D) [4]

| 해설 | 제시된 문장에 있는 역접의 접속 부사 Nonetheless로 볼 때, 웹 사이트 업그레이드에 대한 반대나 우려 의견을 나타내는 내용 뒤에 들어가야 함을 알 수 있으므로, 세 번째 단락에 일부 주민들은 웹 사이트를 업그레이드하는 비용에 대해 우려를 표명했고(Some residents expressed concern about the cost of upgrading the Web site ~) 그에 관한 인터뷰 내용이 한 예로 제시된 이후인 (B)가 정답이다.

| 어휘 | outdated 구식인 necessary 필요한

161-163 다음 이메일을 참조하시오.

¹⁶²수신: Madison Seneca <mseneca@professionaltraining.net>
발신: Davi Gomez <gomez_davi@blaine-inc.com>
날짜: 1월 29일
제목: Professional Training: 2월 행사

Seneca 씨 귀하,

아시다시피, Professional Training이 2월 12일 금요일에 다음 교육 행사를 개최할 것입니다. 저희가 귀하에게 1시간짜리 강연 일정을 두 개 잡았는데요. ¹⁶¹유감스럽게도 등록자 수가 저조해 그것들 중 하나가 일정에서 삭제되었습니다. ¹⁶²따라서 귀하는 다음과 같은 <웹의 힘을 이용하여 여러분의 업체를 광고하기>라는 강연만 하게 될 것입니다. 늦게 통지되었기 때문에 계약에 따라, 귀하는 진행되지 않을 강연에 대해 강연료의 50%를 받을 권리가 있습니다. ¹⁶³그날 다른 강연들이나 워크숍들 중 하나에 무료로 참석하시는 것을 환영하며, 그렇게 하실 것을 적극 권장합니다. ¹⁶³2월 6일까지 저에게 회신 이메일을 보내 가장 선호하는 것을 알려주시면 제가 입장권을 발급해 드리겠습니다.

진심을 담아,

Davi Gomez

| 어휘 | remove 삭제하다, 제거하다 enrollment 등록 figure 수치 following 다음의 be entitled to ~에 권리가 있다, 자격이 있다 go forward 진행되다 at no charge 무료로 issue 발급하다

161. 주제/목적 문제

Gomez 씨는 왜 이메일을 보냈는가?

(A) 등록자 수를 확인하기 위해
(B) 발표 제안을 승인하기 위해
(C) 취소를 알리기 위해
(D) 교육 행사에 등록하기 위해

| 해설 | 초반부에 유감스럽게도 낮은 등록자 수로 인해 예정되어 있는 1시간짜리 두 개의 강연 중 하나가 일정에서 삭제되었다고(Unfortunately, one of them has been removed from the schedule due to low enrollment figures) 한 후, 관련 사항에 관해 설명하고 있으므로 정답은 (C)이다.

| 어휘 | approve 승인하다 register for ~에 등록하다

| 패러프레이징 | has been removed from the schedule → a cancellation

🔺 고난도
162. 추론 문제
Seneca 씨는 무엇을 전문으로 할 것 같은가?
(A) 계약 협상
(B) 에너지 생산
(C) 기업 대출
(D) 온라인 마케팅
| 해설 | Seneca 씨는 이메일을 받는 수신자로, 예정된 강연 중 하나가 삭제된 사실을 알린 후 <웹의 힘을 이용하여 여러분의 업체를 광고하기>라는 강연만 하게 될 것이라고(Therefore, you will only be giving the following talk: "Using the Power of the Web to Advertise Your Business.") 제시되어 있으므로 (D)가 정답이다.
| 어휘 | specialize in ~을 전문으로 하다   negotiation 협상   loan 대출
| 패러프레이징 | Using the Power of the Web to Advertise Your Business → Online marketing

🔺 고난도
163. 세부 사항을 묻는 문제
Seneca 씨가 2월 6일까지 하도록 권고되는 것은 무엇인가?
(A) 발표 파일을 업로드하는 것
(B) 여행 일정을 계획하는 것
(C) 참석할 활동을 선택하는 것
(D) 참가자들 목록을 제공하는 것
| 해설 | 2월 6일이 제시된 후반부에 그날 다른 강연들이나 워크숍들 중 하나에 무료로 참석하시는 것을 환영한다고(You are welcome to attend one of the other talks or workshops on that day at no charge) 한 후, 2월 6일까지 이메일을 보내 선택한 것을 알려달라고(Please e-mail me back by February 6 to let me know your top choice ~) 제시되어 있으므로 정답은 (C)이다.
| 어휘 | participant 참가자
| 패러프레이징 | top choice → Select

164-167 다음 기사를 참조하시오.

PENNSWOOD, 1월 19일—한 독립적인 회사가 주의 경제 수치를 검토했고 ¹⁶⁴그 주의 방문객 수가 작년과 비교하여 7.3퍼센트 떨어져, 이 부문으로부터의 수익이 대략 32억 달러에 이른다고 추정했다. —[1]—.

호텔과 레스토랑 같은 다양한 업체들이 업체를 유지하는 데 관광객들의 지출에 크게 의존하기 때문에, 이런 수치에 직접적으로 영향을 받는다. —[2]—. "저희 객실들이 비어 있다면" 호텔 소유주 Mathew Ledford가 말하기를, "저희 직원들을 계속 전임으로 일하게 할 수 없습니다."

¹⁶⁵관광 국장 Kathleen Renfrow는 최근 공개된 수치를 맥락 안에 넣고 봐야 한다고 말했다. "¹⁶⁵작년은 Human Freedom Monument의 건립 100주년이었습니다." 그녀가 말했다. "그 행사가 평소보다 훨씬 더 많은 관광객들을 끌어들여서, 그것은 공정한 비교가 아닙니다. ¹⁶⁷우리가 어떻게 하고 있는지 더 잘 이해하려면 그 수치를 2년 전과 비교하는 것이 더 낫죠. —[3]—. 저희 부서는 계속해서 우리 주에 관심을 불러일으킬

방안을 찾고 있고, 보트 타기 축제와 스포츠 토너먼트 같이 저희의 인지도를 높일 다양한 활동들도 하고 있습니다."

이런 유형의 행사들을 성공시키기 위해서는 적절한 자금이 필요하다. 다행스럽게도 관광 산업이 예산 고려에 있어 최우선 사항이 될 것 같다. ¹⁶⁶이번 가을 주지사에 출마하는 세 사람인 Melvin Ramey, Ann Alvarez, 그리고 Luke Zimmer 모두 과세 소득을 창출하고 주 전역의 지역 사회들을 풍요롭게 하는 방안으로 주의 관광 산업에 투자하는 것에 공개적으로 지지를 표명했다. —[4]—.

| 어휘 | independent 독립적인   economic 경제의   figure 수치   estimate 추정하다   compared to ~와 비교하여   revenue 수입, 수익   sector 부문   approximately 대략   directly 직접적으로   be affected by ~의 영향을 받다   depend on ~에 의존하다   spending 지출   vacant 비어 있는   released 발표된, 공개된   put in context 맥락 안에 넣다   celebration 기념, 축하 행사   erection 건립   monument 기념물   fair 공정한   comparison 비교   get the picture 이해하다   generate 발생시키다   raise one's profile 인지도를 높이다   adequate 적절한   funding 자금   a top priority 최우선 사항   budgetary 예산의   consideration 고려   run for ~에 출마하다   governor 주지사   publicly 공개적으로   show support for ~에 지지를 표하다   invest 투자하다   as a way of ~의 방안으로   tax income 과세 소득   enrich 풍요롭게 하다

164. 주제/목적 문제
기사는 주로 무엇에 관한 것인가?
(A) 관광 사업에 제안된 세금
(B) 관광 산업의 감소
(C) 관광객들을 위한 광고 캠페인
(D) 새로운 관광 명소
| 해설 | 첫 번째 단락에 방문객 수가 작년과 비교하여 7.3퍼센트 떨어졌다고(the number of visitors to the state has dropped by 7.3 percent compared to last year) 한 이후, 방문객 감소로 인한 문제와 그것을 극복하기 위한 노력 등이 제시되어 있으므로 정답은 (B)이다.
| 어휘 | tax 조세, 세금   reduction 감소, 축소   ad(= advertisement) 광고   tourist attraction 관광 명소
| 패러프레이징 | the number of visitors to the state has dropped → A reduction in tourism

165. 세부 사항을 묻는 문제
Renfrow 씨에 따르면, 작년에 어떤 특별한 행사가 열렸나?
(A) 한 기념물의 기념일
(B) 음악 시상식
(C) 야외 보트 타기 축제
(D) 스포츠 토너먼트
| 해설 | Renfrow 씨는 세 번째 단락 도입부에 제시된 관광 국장으로(Tourism Director Kathleen Renfrow), 작년은 Human Freedom Monument의 건립 100주년 기념이었다고(Last year was the 100th celebration of the

erection of the Human Freedom Monument) 말한 내용이 제시되어 있으므로 정답은 (A)이다.

| 어휘 | anniversary 기념일   outdoor 야외의
| 패러프레이징 | 100th celebration → An anniversary

166. 추론 문제
Alvarez 씨는 누구일 것 같은가?
(A) 정치 후보자
(B) 호텔 소유주
(C) 재정 고문
(D) 관광 국장
| 해설 | 네 번째 단락에 Alvarez 씨가 이번 가을 주지사에 출마하는 세 사람 중 한 명으로(All three people running for governor this fall—Melvin Ramey, Ann Alvarez, and Luke Zimmer) 제시되어 있으므로 정답은 (A)이다.
| 어휘 | political 정치적인   candidate 후보자, 출마자   financial 재정의   advisor 고문, 자문가
| 패러프레이징 | running for governor → A political candidate

고난도
167. 문장 삽입 문제
[1], [2], [3], [4]로 표시된 곳 중에 다음 문장이 들어가기에 가장 적절한 곳은?
"그렇게 하면, 그것들이 거의 같다는 것을 알 수 있습니다."
(A) [1]
(B) [2]
(C) [3]
(D) [4]
| 해설 | 제시된 문장은 어떤 행위의 결과를 나타내는 것으로, 본문에서 이와 관련된 내용을 찾을 수 있는 것은 세 번째 단락이다. 중반부에 우리가 어떻게 하고 있는지 더 잘 이해하려면 그 수치를 2년 전과 비교하는 것이 더 낫다고(To get a better picture of how we are performing, it would better to compare the figures to those of two years ago) 한 문장 뒤에 그 결과로 제시된 문장이 이어지는 것이 적절하므로 정답은 (C)이다.
| 어휘 | equal 같은, 동일한

168-171 다음 온라인 채팅 토론을 참조하시오.

> **Heather Teodros** [오후 4:25]
> ¹⁶⁸Wyatt 공원에서 열린 예술 축제 첫날에 저를 대신해 줘서 고마워요, 모두들. 일은 어떻게 진행되었나요?
>
> **Arnaldo Guevara** [오후 4:26]
> 저희가 부스들과 활동들의 ¹⁶⁸사진을 많이 찍었고, 많은 미술가들과 방문객들뿐만 아니라 행사 코디네이터와도 ¹⁶⁸인터뷰를 했어요. ¹⁶⁸/¹⁶⁹신문에 인쇄할 것을 요약한 것도 이미 가지고 있고요.
>
> **Heather Teodros** [오후 4:27]
> 준비가 되면 한 부 가지고 싶네요.
>
> **Arnaldo Guevara** [오후 4:29]
> 물론이죠. 우리가 이야기했던 사람들 모두 그 행사를 아주 즐거워했어요. 추가 보너스로, ¹⁷⁰도시 외부의 사람들을 많이 불러들였고요. 그것은 늘 지역 경제를 위해 좋아요.
>
> **Ganesh Bhagat** [오후 4:31]
> 맞아요. 시 대표들이 우리 지역 사회에 더 많은 관심을 끌기 위해 노력하고 있었다는 거 알아요.
>
> **Sharon Moyer** [오후 4:32]
> 행사의 나머지 부분도 순조롭게 진행되면 좋겠어요.
>
> **Ganesh Bhagat** [오후 4:33]
> 음, 앞으로 며칠 동안 비가 올 것이라고 해서 참가자 수에 부정적으로 영향을 미칠 수도 있겠어요.
>
> **Heather Teodros** [오후 4:34]
> 다행히도 ¹⁷¹행사 장소에 있는 모든 피크닉 비 대피소들을 이용하고 있어서 부스들 대부분은 보호가 돼요.
>
> **Arnaldo Guevara** [오후 4:35]
> 일기 예보에서 산발적인 소나기가 있을 것이라고 했으니 그렇게 나쁘지는 않을 거예요.

| 어휘 | cover 대신하다   activity 활동   summary 개요, 요약   added 추가된   bring in 불러들이다   economy 경제   representative 대표자   grab attention 관심을 끌다   smoothly 순조롭게   negatively 부정적으로   affect 영향을 미치다   turnout 참가자 수   shelter 대피소   weather report 일기 예보   scattered showers 산발적인 소나기

고난도
168. 추론 문제
Teodros 씨는 누구일 것 같은가?
(A) 행사 기획자
(B) 전문 화가
(C) 기자
(D) 시 공무원
| 해설 | Teodros 씨는 대화를 시작한 사람으로 도입부에 Wyatt 공원에서 열린 예술 축제 첫날에 자신을 대신해 줘서 고맙다며(Thanks for covering the first day of the arts festival at Wyatt Park for me) 일의 진행 상황을 묻는 말에, 부스들과 활동들의 사진을 많이 찍었고(got a lot of photos), 인터뷰를 했고(had interviews with), 신문에 인쇄할 것을 요약한 것도 이미 가지고 있다고(We've already got a summary of what we're going to print in the paper) 답하고 있다. 이를 통해, Teodros 씨와 동료들은 기자일 것으로 유추할 수 있으므로 정답은 (C)이다.

169. 의도 파악 문제
오후 4:27에 Teodros 씨가 "준비가 되면 한 부 가지고 싶네요"라고 쓸 때 의미하는 것은 무엇일 것 같은가?
(A) 일부 정보에 관한 개요를 읽고 싶어 한다.
(B) 참가자들의 전체 목록을 보는 것에 관심이 있다.
(C) 행사에 대한 피드백 설문을 만들기를 원한다.
(D) VIP 방문객들에게 카드를 보낼 것이다.
| 해설 | 이는 앞서 신문에 인쇄할 것을 요약한 것도 이미 가지고 있다고(We've already got a summary of what we're going to print in the paper) 한 것에 대한 응답으로, 그것이 준비되면 한 부 가지고 싶다는 말로 요약한 것을 보고 싶다는 뜻을 전하는 것임을 알 수 있으므로 정답은 (A)이다.
| 어휘 | outline 개요   complete 전체의   participant 참가자   create 만들다
| 패러프레이징 | summary → outline

170. 세부 사항을 묻는 문제
행사에 관해 이루어진 긍정적인 언급은 무엇인가?
(A) 미술 클럽 회원들에게 할인을 제공했다.
(B) 그 지역에 거주하지 않는 방문객들을 끌어들였다.
(C) 입장료가 합리적이었다.
(D) 주차 환경이 잘 정리되어 있었다.
| 해설 | 오후 4:29에 Arnaldo Guevara 씨가 추가 보너스로, 그 도시 외부의 사람들을 많이 불러들였다고(it brought in a lot of people from out of town) 했으므로 정답은 (B)이다.
| 어휘 | attract 끌어들이다, 유치하다   non-resident (특정 장소에) 거주하지 않는   admission fee 입장료   reasonable 합리적인   well organized 잘 정리된, 잘 구성된
| 패러프레이징 | brought in a lot of people from out of town → attracted non-resident visitors

171. 추론 문제
Wyatt 공원에 관해 암시되는 것은 무엇인가?
(A) 도시에서 가장 큰 공원이다.
(B) 부정적인 평가를 받았다.
(C) 일일 보고서를 발표한다.
(D) 지붕이 덮인 구조물들이 있다.
| 해설 | Wyatt 공원은 도입부에 Teodros 씨가 Wyatt 공원에서 열린 예술 축제를(~ the arts festival at Wyatt Park ~) 언급한 부분에서 확인되는데, 오후 4:34에 Heather Teodros 씨가 행사 장소에 있는 모든 피크닉 비 대피소들을 이용하고 있어서 부스들 대부분은 비로부터 보호가 된다고(they're using all of the picnic shelters at the event site, so most of the booths are protected) 했으므로 정답은 (D)이다.
| 어휘 | negative 부정적인   release 발표하다   covered 지붕이 덮인   structure 구조물
| 패러프레이징 | picnic shelters → covered structures

172-175 다음 구인 공고를 참조하시오.

현재 고용 중: 선임 행정 보조원

Salco 지역 대학에서 정규직 선임 행정 보조원을 찾고 있습니다. ¹⁷²즉시 시작할 수 있는 지원자들에게 우선권이 제공될 것입니다.

선임 행정 보조원은 사무실이 순조롭게 운영되도록 돕는 다양한 업무들을 맡고, 이 직책은 활동을 자주 바꾸는 것을 좋아하고 압박 아래서 일할 수 있는 사람에게 이상적일 것입니다. 직무에는 ^{173 (B)}지역 사회로부터의 정보 요청에 응답하는 것과 ^{173 (D)}직원들의 출장을 위해 비행기, 호텔, 차량 렌트를 예약하는 것, 월간 소식지에 내용을 기고하는 것, 그리고 ^{173 (C)}사무실의 지출을 관찰하는 것을 포함합니다. 대략 28,000달러(협의 가능)의 연봉이 4주의 유급 휴가와 의료 보험과 함께 제공됩니다.

지원하려면, 4월 7일 또는 그 전에 hr@salcocc.edu로 이력서와 자기소개서를 보내세요. ¹⁷⁴저희 채용 위원회가 4월 8일에 지원서들을 검토할 것이고, 합격자들은 면접을 정하기 위해 다음 날 연락을 받게 될 것입니다. 면접은 4월 11일에 열릴 것 같습니다. ¹⁷⁵면접을 위해 저희 사무실로 오는 이들은 또한 컴퓨터 기반 능력 시험을 보도록 요청받을 것입니다. 채용 절차에 관한 문의들은 위에 있는 이메일 주소로 보내실 수 있습니다. 저희는 또한 정규 업무 시간 중에는 555-7931번으로 전화 문의도 받습니다.

| 어휘 | senior 선임의   administrative assistant 행정 보조원   seek 찾다   preference 우선권   candidate 지원자   immediately 즉시   be responsible for ~을 맡다   frequently 자주   under pressure 압박 아래에   vehicle rental 차량 렌트   contribute 기고하다   content 내용   expenditure 지출, 경비   annual salary 연봉   approximately 대략   negotiable 협의 가능한   paid vacation 유급 휴가   medical insurance 의료 보험   cover letter 자기소개서   hiring committee 채용 위원회   application 지원서   successful applicant 합격자   following day 다음 날   examination 시험   process 절차   inquiry 문의   regular 정기적인, 평상시의

172. 추론 문제
Salco 지역 대학에 관해 암시되는 것은 무엇인가?
(A) 정규 학생들의 수가 증가했다.
(B) 하나 이상의 캠퍼스에서 서비스를 제공한다.
(C) 예산이 최근에 증가되었다.
(D) 한 직책을 빨리 충원해야 한다.
| 해설 | 첫 번째 단락에 즉시 시작할 수 있는 지원자들에게 우선권이 제공될 것이라고(Preference will be given to candidates who can start immediately) 제시되어 있는 것을 통해, 빨리 직원을 채용하고자 하는 상황임을 알 수 있으므로 정답은 (D)이다.
| 어휘 | recently 최근에   increase 증가하다   fill a position 충원하다, 자리를 채우다
| 패러프레이징 | immediately → quickly

🔺고난도
173. NOT True 문제
직책의 직무로 언급되지 않은 것은 무엇인가?
(A) 소식지의 발행 부수를 늘리는 것

(B) 대중에게 정보를 제공하는 것
(C) 지출을 계속 파악하는 것
(D) 여행 준비를 하는 것

| 해설 | 직무 내용이 열거된 두 번째 단락에 지역 사회로부터의 정보 요청에 응답하는 것(responding to information requests from the community)에서 (B), 직원들의 출장을 위해 비행기, 호텔, 차량 렌트를 예약하는 것(booking flights, hotels, and vehicle rentals for staff members' business trips)에서 (D), 사무실의 지출을 관찰하는 것(monitoring the office's expenditures)에서 (C)는 언급된 것으로 확인되므로 정답은 (A)이다.

| 어휘 | circulation 발행 부수   keep track of ~을 계속 파악하다
travel arrangement 여행 준비

| 패러프레이징 | ·responding to information requests → Providing information
·booking flights, hotels, and vehicle rentals → Coordinating travel arrangements
·monitoring the office's expenditures → Keeping track of spending

174. 세부 사항을 묻는 문제
합격자들은 언제 처음 연락을 받을 것인가?
(A) 4월 7일
(B) 4월 8일
(C) 4월 9일
(D) 4월 11일

| 해설 | 세 번째 단락 초반부에 채용 위원회가 4월 8일에 지원서들을 검토할 것이고, 합격자들은 면접을 정하기 위해 다음 날 연락을 받게 될 것이라고(Our hiring committee will review the applications on April 8, and successful applicants will be contacted the following day to set up an interview) 제시된 것에서 4월 9일에 연락을 받을 것임을 알 수 있으므로 정답은 (C)이다.

175. 세부 사항을 묻는 문제
구인 공고에 따르면, 일부 지원자들은 무엇을 하도록 요구될 것인가?
(A) 현장에서 시험을 보는 것
(B) 추천서를 제출하는 것
(C) 작업 포트폴리오를 제시하는 것
(D) 온라인 지원을 완료하는 것

| 해설 | 세 번째 단락 후반부에 면접을 위해 사무실로 오는 이들은 컴퓨터 기반 능력 시험을 보도록 요청받을 것이라고(Those who come to our office for an interview will also be asked to take a computer-based skills examination) 제시되어 있으므로 정답은 (A)이다.

| 어휘 | on site 현장의   letters of recommendation 추천서   present 제시하다

| 패러프레이징 | take a computer-based skills examination → Take a test

176-180 다음 온라인 기사와 포럼 의견을 참조하시오.

http://www.ashevilleherald.com

<Asheville Herald>, 5월 25일, "Fresh Flow 무용단이 여름 시즌을 준비하다"

빠른 속도의 리듬과 완벽하게 동시에 움직이는 춤 동작으로, Asheville에 기반을 둔 현대 무용단인 Fresh Flow가 전국의 관객들을 놀라게 했다. Fresh Flow의 공연에 참석한 이들은 환상적인 쇼를 구경할 것이다. 176그들은 심지어 무대 위로 초대되거나 통로에서 함께 춤추기를 요청받는 자신들을 발견할 수도 있다. 무용단은 최근에 여름 일정을 발표했는데, 그것에는 6월과 7월 내내 Kiernan 극장에서의 일주일에 4차례 공연을 포함할 것이다.

Fresh Flow는 10년 전 Saldivar 예술 대학에서 공연 예술 학사 학위를 받고 졸업한 178Dario Varela에 의해 창단되었다. 그는 Asheville에서 댄스 활동들을 촉진하기 위한 방안으로 졸업 몇 년 후에 이 무용단을 시작했다.

Fresh Flow의 공연 티켓은 Fresh Flow 웹 사이트를 통해 온라인으로나 Kiernan 극장 매표소에서 구입할 수 있다. 177일요일 공연들은 특별히 어린이와 가족들에게 맞추어진다. 보다 어린이 친화적인 곡들을 추가하는 것뿐 아니라, 무용단은 시설을 조정하기도 한다. 예를 들어 공연을 라이브로 방송하는 스크린들이 로비에 설치되는데, 일부 어린이들이 음악과 동작이 너무 강렬하다고 느껴 휴식을 취해야 할 수도 있기 때문이다.

| 어휘 | fast-paced 빠른 속도의   synchronized 동시 진행되는   contemporary 현대의   amaze 놀라게 하다   performance 공연   spectacular 환상적인   urge 요구하다, 촉구하다   aisle 통로   form 창단하다, 형성하다   graduate 졸업하다   a bachelor's degree 학사 학위   promote 촉진하다   be geared toward ~에 맞추어지다   child-friendly 어린이 친화적인   tune 곡, 곡조   make adjustments 조정을 하다   set up 설치하다   overwhelming 너무 강렬한, 압도적인

http://www.ashevilleherald.com/readerforum

Fresh Flow에 관한 귀사의 최근 기사에 감사드립니다. 이 무용단은 아주 재능있고, 그 단원들은 일반 대중들에게 무용 예술을 더 흥미롭게 만들어줄 방법도 찾고 있죠. 몇 년 전에 처음으로 Fresh Flow 공연을 본 것을 기억하는데요. 무용수들의 정확성이 놀라웠고, 178그 무용단의 창단자 본인에 의해 디자인된 아름다운 의상들이 마음에 들었습니다. 그 공연 이후로, 다른 Fresh Flow 공연들에도 많이 갔었는데, 179때로 그 안무를 제가 저희 학생들에게 가르치는 동작들에 영감을 주는 것으로 이용하기도 합니다. 180무용단에 대한 저의 유일한 비평은 예약 안내가 늘 막판에 나오는 것 같다는 것인데요. 대부분의 사람들이 그저 즉흥적으로 티켓을 사는 것보다 미리 계획하는 것을 더 선호한다고 생각합니다.

—Melissa Nash

| 어휘 | appreciate 감사하다   talented 재능 있는   art of dance

무용 예술   general public 일반 대중   precision 정확, 정확성
amazing 놀라운   costume 의상   founder 창단자, 설립자
choreography 안무   inspiration 영감(을 주는 것)   criticism 비평
ahead 미리, 앞서   on a whim 즉흥적으로

176. 추론 문제
Fresh Flow에 관해 암시되는 것은 무엇인가?
(A) 4차례 주말 공연을 할 것이다.
(B) 시에서 자금을 제공받는다.
(C) 관객 참여를 장려한다.
(D) 10년 전에 창단되었다.

| 해설 | 온라인 기사 첫 번째 단락 중반부에 관객들이 심지어 무대 위로 초대되거나 통로에서 함께 춤추기를 요청받는 자신들을 발견할 수도 있다고(They may even find themselves invited onto the stage or urged to dance along in the aisles) 제시되어 있는 것에서, 무용단 단원들이 관객들에게 함께 춤추기를 요청하며 참여를 장려함을 알 수 있으므로 정답은 (C)이다.
| 어휘 | fund 자금을 제공하다   encourage 장려하다   participation 참여   found 창단하다

고난도
177. 추론 문제
일요일 공연들에 관해 암시되는 것은 무엇인가?
(A) 좌석이 선착순으로만 이용 가능하다.
(B) 티켓들이 평소보다 더 낮은 가격에 제공된다.
(C) 어린이들에 의해 공연되는 특별한 부분이 있다.
(D) 그것들의 춤과 내용은 어린이들이 보기에 적합하다.

| 해설 | 온라인 기사 세 번째 단락에, 일요일 공연은 특별히 어린이와 가족들에게 맞춰진다고(Sunday performances are geared specifically toward children and families) 제시되어 있으므로 정답은 (D)이다.
| 어휘 | seating 좌석   available 이용 가능한   on a first-come, first-served basis 선착순으로   segment 부분   content 내용물   suitable 적합한
| 패러프레이징 | are geared specifically toward children → are suitable for children to watch

178. 연계 문제 - 추론
Varela 씨에 관해 암시되는 것은 무엇인가?
(A) 의상 디자인 기술을 가지고 있다.
(B) Saldivar 예술 대학에서 일했었다.
(C) 개인 댄스 수업을 제공한다.
(D) Nash 씨의 개인적인 친구이다.

| 해설 | 온라인 기사 두 번째 단락에 Fresh Flow는 Dario Varela에 의해 창단되었다고(Fresh Flow was formed by Dario Varela) 한 것과 포럼 의견 중반부에 그 무용단의 창단자 본인에 의해 디자인된 아름다운 의상들이 마음에 들었다고(I loved the beautiful costumes designed by the group's founder himself) 한 것을 연계해 볼 때, 창단자인 Dario Varela는 의상 디자인도 할 수 있다는 것을 알 수 있으므로 정답은 (A)이다.
| 어휘 | private 사적인, 개인을 위한   personal 개인적인

179. 추론 문제
Nash 씨에 관해 사실일 것 같은 것은 무엇인가?
(A) Asheville에서 자랐다.
(B) 무용 강사로 일한다.
(C) <Asheville Herald>와 인터뷰를 했다.
(D) Kiernan 극장을 방문했다.

| 해설 | Nash 씨는 두 번째 지문인 포럼 의견을 쓴 사람으로, 중/후반부에 Fresh Flow 공연에 많이 갔는데, 때로 그 안무를 본인의 학생들에게 가르치는 동작들에 영감을 주는 것으로 이용하기도 한다고(sometimes using the choreography as inspiration for the moves that I teach to my own students) 한 것에서 무용을 가르치는 강사일 것으로 유추할 수 있으므로 정답은 (B)이다.
| 어휘 | instructor 강사
| 패러프레이징 | teach to my own students → a dance instructor

180. 추론 문제
Nash 씨가 지지할 것 같은 변화는 무엇인가?
(A) 공연들을 더 미리 홍보하는 것
(B) 관객들에게 사인을 해 주는 것
(C) 주말에 공연을 더 추가하는 것
(D) 전화로 티켓 예약을 가능하게 하는 것

| 해설 | 포럼 의견 후반부에, 무용단에 대한 유일한 비평은 예약 안내가 늘 막판에 나오는 것 같다는 것인데(My only criticism of the group is that the announcements of its bookings always seem to come at the last minute) 대부분의 사람들이 그저 즉흥적으로 티켓을 사는 것보다 미리 계획하는 것을 더 선호한다고 생각한다는(I think most people prefer to plan ahead rather than just buy tickets on a whim) 의견이 제시되어 있으므로 정답은 (A)이다.
| 어휘 | in advance 미리   autograph 사인, 서명   audience member 관객, 청중

181-185 다음 이메일과 문자 메시지를 참조하시오.

수신: Colin Vogel <vogelcolin@blevinsinc.com>
발신: Flores Air <bookings@flores-air.com>
날짜: 4월 28일
제목: Flores 항공사 항공편

Vogel 씨 귀하,

Flores 항공사의 항공편을 예약해 주셔서 감사합니다. 아래 귀하의 일정표를 확인해 주세요.

승객: Colin Vogel   편명: F950
예약 확인 번호: GS595867   좌석: 15C
출발: 5월 6일, 오후 7:32, 애틀랜타   도착: 5월 7일, 오전 8:47, 런던
[182]등급: 비즈니스

탑승은 출발 1시간 전에 시작합니다. [181]작년에 저희와 함께 최소 10만

마일을 여행하신 승객들에게 주어지는 자격인 플래티넘 회원으로서, 귀하는 이번 비행으로 2,500 보너스 상용 고객 마일리지를 받을 자격이 있습니다. 이는 비행 일자에 귀하의 계정에 자동으로 추가될 것입니다.

수하물 정보:

	기내용 1개	첫 번째 부치는 짐	182두 번째 부치는 짐	세 번째 부치는 짐
이코노미 클래스	무료	25.00달러	35.00달러	50.00달러
182비즈니스 클래스	무료	무료	25.00달러	35.00달러
퍼스트 클래스	무료	무료	무료	25.00달러

1시간에서 2시간 사이로 비행 연착이 발생하는 승객들에게는 게이트에서 무료 음료(생수, 탄산음료, 커피, 차)가 제공될 것입니다. 184 2시간 이상 연착의 경우에는 승객들에게 점심/저녁 무료 식사 쿠폰이 발행될 것인데, 그것은 공항 내에 관계 레스토랑에서 이용할 수 있습니다.

| 어휘 | itinerary 일정표   confirmation 확인   departure 출발   boarding 탑승   status 자격, 신분   granted 주어진, 승인된   be entitled to ~할 자격이 있다   frequent flyer (비행기) 상용 고객   automatically 자동으로   carry-on 기내용 가방   checked 수속된, 부친   delay 지연, 연착   complimentary 무료의   bottled water 생수   issue 발행하다, 발급하다   voucher 쿠폰   participating 관계 있는, 참여하는

수신: Colin Vogel, 793-555-0899
발신: Flores 항공사, 비공개 번호
날짜: 5월 6일, 오후 3:51

183Flores 항공사의 런던행 항공기 F950의 출발이 악천후로 인해 지연되었습니다. 184그것은 이제 원래 예정된 시간보다 3시간 늦은 오후 10시 32분에 출발할 것입니다. 이것이 오늘 런던으로 출발하는 저희의 유일한 항공편이기 때문에, 다른 항공편으로 185타실 수는 없습니다. 이것이 야기할 수 있는 불편에 대해 사과드립니다.

| 어휘 | postpone 연기하다, 미루다   severe weather 악천후   originally scheduled 원래 예정된   inconvenience 불편   cause 야기하다, 초래하다

181. True 문제
Vogel 씨에 관해 제시된 것은 무엇인가?
(A) 항공편의 비용을 회사의 계정에 청구했다.
(B) 작년에 10만 마일 이상 비행기를 탔다.
(C) 그의 사무실은 현재 애틀랜타에 본사가 있다.
(D) 그의 항공권은 부분적으로 보상 포인트로 지불되었다.
| 해설 | Vogel 씨는 이메일의 수신자로, 도표 위에 작년에 최소 10만 마일을 여행한 승객들에게 주어지는 자격인 플래티넘 회원이라고(As a Platinum Member, a status granted to passengers who traveled at least 100,000 miles with us last year) 제시되어 있으므로 정답은 (B)이다.
| 어휘 | charge 청구하다   cost 비용   account 계정   currently 현재   be based in ~에 기반을 두다, 본사를 두다   partially 부분적으로
| 패러프레이징 | traveled at least 100,000 miles → flew over one hundred thousand miles

182. 세부 사항을 묻는 문제
Vogel 씨는 두 번째 부치는 가방에 얼마를 지불할 것인가?
(A) 무료
(B) 25.00달러
(C) 35.00달러
(D) 50.00달러
| 해설 | 이메일에 따르면, Vogel 씨의 좌석 등급은 비즈니스(Class: Business)이고, 비즈니스 클래스(Business Class)가 두 번째 짐을 부치는(2nd Checked Bag) 비용은 25.00달러($25.00)이므로 정답은 (B)이다.

183. 주제/목적 문제
문자 메시지의 목적은 무엇인가?
(A) 취소 정책의 개요를 서술하는 것
(B) 항공편 지연을 알리는 것
(C) 게이트 변경을 설명하는 것
(D) 좌석 요청을 확인하는 것
| 해설 | 문자 메시지 도입부에 수신자인 Vogel 씨에게 Flores 항공사의 런던행 항공기 F950의 출발이 악천후로 인해 지연되었다고(The departure of Flores Air's flight F950 with service to London has been postponed due to severe weather) 알리고 있으므로 정답은 (B)이다.
| 어휘 | outline 개요를 서술하다   confirm 확인하다

184. 연계 문제 – 세부 사항
Vogel 씨는 무엇을 받을 자격이 있는가?
(A) 셔틀 티켓
(B) 부분 환불
(C) 좌석 업그레이드
(D) 식사 쿠폰
| 해설 | 이메일의 후반부에 2시간 이상 연착의 경우에는 승객들에게 점심/저녁 무료 식사 쿠폰이 발행될 것이라고(For delays of two hours or more, passengers will be issued a voucher for a free lunch/dinner) 제시된 내용과 문자 메시지에 Vogel 씨가 탑승할 항공편이 원래 예정된 시간보다 3시간 늦은 오후 10시 32분에 출발할 것이라고(It will now depart three hours later than originally scheduled, at 10:32 P.M.) 한 것을 연계해 볼 때, Vogel 씨는 무료 식사 쿠폰을 받을 것임을 알 수 있으므로 정답은 (D)이다.
| 어휘 | partial 부분   refund 환불
| 패러프레이징 | a voucher for a free lunch/dinner → A meal voucher

185. 동의어 문제
문자 메시지에서 첫 번째 단락 다섯 번째 줄에 있는 단어 "take"와 의미가 가장 유사한 것은

(A) 여행하다
(B) 제거하다
(C) 이해하다
(D) 수집하다

| 해설 | 해당 단어가 들어간 문장은 앞의 사실을 이유로 들어 '~ 다른 비행기를 타실 수는 없습니다'라고 해석된다. 따라서 take는 '(비행기를) 타다'라는 의미로 쓰인 것이므로 '(타고) 여행하다'라는 의미의 (A) travel on이 정답이다.

186-190 다음 광고와 이메일들을 참조하시오.

보조원 구함

Wallenberg 부동산의 Newport 지점 팀에 합류할 부동산 보조원 자리에 공석이 있습니다. 부동산 자격증은 요구되지 않는데, 이 직책은 고객들에게 자문을 해 주거나 조건을 협상하는 것은 포함하지 않기 때문입니다. 업무는 주택 공개를 위해 준비하고, 저희 웹 사이트에 새로운 목록들을 게시하고, 186정부 데이터베이스와 공공 기록에서 주택과 토지 권리에 관한 정보를 수집하는 것으로 구성됩니다. 이 직책은 파트 타임뿐이고, 188합격자는 자신의 시간을 정할 수 있을 것입니다. a.prescott@wallenbergre.com으로 Alice Prescott에게 이력서를 보내주세요.

| 어휘 | opening 공석   real estate assistant 부동산 보조원   license 자격증, 면허증   involve 포함되다   negotiate 협상하다   consist of ~로 구성되다   set up 정하다   post 게시하다   gather 모으다, 수집하다   right 권리   governmental 정부의   successful candidate 합격자

수신: Alice Prescott <a.prescott@wallenbergre.com>
발신: Candace Steiner <steinerc@hillhaven.net>
날짜: 4월 20일
제목: 부동산 보조원

Prescott 씨 귀하,

저는 <Newport Herald>의 안내 광고 섹션에 최근에 게시되었던 부동산 보조원 자리에 관심이 있습니다. 비록 부동산 회사에서 일한 적은 없지만, 187Linden 보험사의 사무실에서 접수 담당자로 3년을 보내서, 행정 업무들에 익숙합니다. 188Wallenberg의 일자리에 특히 끌렸던 것은 제가 Montford 기관에서 시간제로 강의를 듣고 있어서, 그 근로 조건이 저에게 딱 맞기 때문입니다.

저는 열심히 일하는 사람이고, 새로운 일들을 빨리 배울 수 있습니다. 190첨부된 것에서 제가 능숙한 소프트웨어 프로그램들을 상세히 열거하는 추가 파일들과 함께 저의 현재 이력서를 보시게 될 텐데요. 이러한 기량으로 인해, 시작하기 위해 저는 아주 적은 교육만 필요할 것이라고 생각합니다. 저는 향후 장기적인 직업으로 부동산 쪽을 고려하고 있어서, 직접 만나 직책에 대해 더 논의할 수 있으면 좋겠습니다.

진심을 담아,

Candace Steiner

| 어휘 | classified ads 안내 광고   receptionist 접수 담당   be used to ~에 익숙하다   administrative duty 행정 업무   particularly 특히   attract 마음을 끌다, 끌어들이다   working condition 근로 조건   current 현재의   detail 상세히 열거하다   proficient 능숙한   in person 직접   long-term 장기적인   career 직업

수신: Randall Santiago <r.santiago@wallenbergre.com>,
     Stella McCord <s.mccord@wallenbergre.com>,
     Joseph Duncan <j.duncan@wallenbergre.com>
발신: Alice Prescott <a.prescott@wallenbergre.com>
날짜: 4월 24일
제목: 부동산 보조원 공석

안녕하세요,

이번 주에 시간을 내어 면접에 참석해 주신 모두에게 감사드립니다. 입사 지원자에 대한 최종 결정을 내릴 기회를 갖지 못했기 때문에, 그것을 이메일로 할 수 있겠다고 생각했습니다. 189저는 Steiner 씨가 이 직책에 가장 적합한 사람일 것이라고 믿고 있으므로 그녀에게 일자리를 제공해야 한다고 생각합니다. 면접에서 그녀가 우호적이고 느긋하다고 생각했습니다. 190가장 중요한 것으로, 그녀가 자신의 보충 파일에 정리했던 정보가 많은 교육을 해야 하는 것을 피하기 위해 우리에게 딱 필요한 것입니다. 여러분의 생각을 알려주세요!

감사합니다!

Alice Prescott

| 어휘 | sit in on ~에 참석하다   job candidate 입사 지원자   easygoing 느긋한   organize 정리하다, 구성하다   supplemental 보충의   exactly 정확하게   avoid 피하다

186. 세부 사항을 묻는 문제
광고에서 직책의 업무로 제시된 것은 무엇인가?
(A) 계약을 수립하는 것
(B) 전화를 받는 것
(C) 부동산을 조사하는 것
(D) 웹 사이트를 디자인하는 것

| 해설 | 중반부에 부동산 보조원이 할 업무에 대해, 정부 데이터베이스와 공공 기록에서 주택과 토지 권리에 관한 정보를 수집하는 것(gathering data about homes and land rights from governmental databases and public records)이 제시되어 있으므로 정답은 (C)이다.

| 어휘 | contract 계약   property 부동산, 건물

| 패러프레이징 | gathering data about homes and land rights
→ Researching properties

187. True 문제
Steiner 씨에 관해 사실인 것은?
(A) 주택 소유자 보험을 판매하는 것에 익숙하다.
(B) 현재 부동산 중개업체에 고용되어 있다.
(C) 면허 프로그램에 등록했다.
(D) 사무실 환경을 경험해 본 적이 있다.

| 해설 | Steiner 씨는 첫 번째 이메일 발신자로, 이메일 첫 번째 단락에 부동산 회사에서 일한 적은 없었지만, Linden 보험사의 사무실에서 접수 담당자로 3년을 보냈다고(I spent three years as a receptionist at the office of Linden Insurance, ~) 제시되어 있으므로 정답은 (D)이다.

| 어휘 | be familiar with ~에 익숙하다   insurance 보험   enroll 등록하다

| 패러프레이징 | spent three years as a receptionist at the office → has experience in an office setting

188. 연계 문제 - 세부 사항
Steiner 씨에 따르면, 무엇이 그 직책에 끌리게 했는가?
(A) 직무들
(B) 탄력적인 근무 시간
(C) 편리한 위치
(D) 넉넉한 휴가 시간

| 해설 | 첫 번째 이메일의 첫 단락 후반부에 Wallenberg의 일자리에 특히 끌렸던 것은 Montford 기관에서 시간제로 강의들을 듣고 있어서, 그 근로 조건이 딱 맞기 때문이라고(I was particularly attracted to the job at Wallenberg ~, so the working conditions are perfect for me) 한 것과 광고 후반부에 합격자는 자신의 시간을 정할 수 있을 것이라고(the successful candidate will be able to set his or her own hours) 한 것을 연계시켜 볼 때, 탄력적인 근무 시간에 끌린 것임을 알 수 있으므로 정답은 (B)이다.

| 어휘 | flexible 탄력적인   convenient 편리한   generous 넉넉한, 후한

| 패러프레이징 | able to set his or her own hours → flexible working hours

189. 주제/목적 문제
Prescott 씨는 왜 이메일을 보냈는가?
(A) 일부 면접관들의 가능 여부에 대해 묻기 위해
(B) 새로 고용된 직원을 소개하기 위해
(C) 동료들에게 면접 변경에 관해 알리기 위해
(D) 직책에 지원자를 추천하기 위해

| 해설 | 이메일에 Steiner 씨가 이 직책에 가장 적합한 사람일 것이라고 믿고 있으므로, 그녀에게 일자리를 제공해야 한다고 생각한다고(I believe that Ms. Steiner would be the best person for this position, so I think we should make her a job offer) 제시되어 있으므로 정답은 (D)이다.

| 어휘 | availability 유효성, 시간 가능성   coworker 동료

고난도
190. 연계 문제 - 세부 사항
Prescott 씨가 가장 관심 있는 Steiner 씨의 특징은 무엇인가?
(A) 부동산 분야에서의 그녀의 경험
(B) 소프트웨어 프로그램에 대한 그녀의 지식
(C) 촉박한 통보에도 일할 능력

(D) 확실한 대인 관계 기술

| 해설 | 두 번째 이메일 후반부에 가장 중요한 것으로, 그녀가 자신의 보충 파일에 정리했던 정보가 우리에게 딱 필요한 것이라고(the information she organized in her supplemental file is exactly what we need ~) 했는데, 그 보충 파일은 첫 번째 이메일 두 번째 단락에서 능숙한 소프트웨어 프로그램들을 상세히 설명하는 추가 파일들로(an extra file detailing the software programs in which I am proficient) 확인되므로 정답은 (B)이다.

| 어휘 | field 분야   knowledge 지식   short notice 촉박한 통보   people skills 대인 관계 기술

| 패러프레이징 | proficient → knowledge

191-195 다음 기사, 초대장, 이메일을 참조하시오.

STAUNTON (4월 10일)—피트니스에 대한 자신의 열정과 타고난 대인 관계 능력을 결합하여, ¹⁹¹Fabio Souza가 Staunton의 근처인 Valley Lane에서 24시간 헬스장을 시작할 것이다. ¹⁹⁵Souza 씨는 10년 동안 Hillcrest에 있는 TCB 헬스장에 고용되었기 때문에, 자격증을 소지한 개인 트레이너로서 풍부한 경험을 가지고 있다. 그는 그 업체의 긍정적인 측면에 주목했고 그것들을 자신의 헬스장에 통합시켰다.

Loxley라고 불리는 그 새로운 헬스장은 최첨단 운동 기구, 단체 참여 수업, 그리고 월간 건강 세미나들이 특징이 될 것이다. Kyle Avenue에 위치한 그 건물은 매끈한 선들과 색상의 전문적 사용으로 아름답게 설계되어 있다. 사실, ¹⁹²Souza 씨는 Canton 주식회사에서 인테리어 디자이너로 경력을 시작했다. 하지만 그의 아버지가 심장 질환 진단을 받은 후에, Souza 씨는 운동의 중요성을 이해하기 시작했다.

"저는 사람들이 좋은 몸 상태를 유지하도록 돕기 위해 재미있고 도움이 되는 환경을 만들고 싶었습니다."라고 Souza 씨가 최근 인터뷰에서 말했다.

Loxley는 5월 1일에 문을 열 예정이다. ¹⁹³그 서비스는 1년에 600달러인 회원 자격을 가진 이들만 이용할 수 있게 될 것이다.

| 어휘 | bring together 결합하다, 모으다   passion 열정   natural 타고난   launch 시작하다   neighborhood 인근, 근처   a wealth of 풍부한   certified 자격증을 소지한, 공인된   take note of ~에 주목하다   positive aspect 긍정적인 측면   incorporate into ~에 통합시키다   feature 특별히 포함하다, 특징이 되다   state-of-the-art 최첨단의   workout equipment 운동 기구   engaging 참여하는, 관여하는   career 직업, 경력   be diagnosed with ~로 진단받다   heart condition 심장 질환   supportive 도움이 되는   get in shape 좋은 몸 상태를 유지하다   be set to ~할 예정이다   available 이용 가능한

저희의 대규모 개장을 축하하며!

LOXLEY
~ 24시간 내내 문을 여는 풀 서비스 헬스장 ~

¹⁹³5월 1일, 금요일
특별 활동들*: 오전 9시 – 오후 7시

*저희 시설의 투어와 무료 요가 수업들, 그리고 무료 피트니스 상담을 즐겨보세요. ¹⁹³500달러로 1년 회원에 등록하세요.

| 어휘 | celebrate 축하하다, 기념하다   around the clock 24시간 내내   consultation 상담   sign up for ~에 등록하다

수신: Fabio Souza <f.souza@loxleygym.com>
발신: ¹⁹⁵Bonnie Tolbert <bonnietolbert@bairdcorporation.net>
날짜: 4월 18일
제목: Loxley

Fabio 귀하,

당신의 헬스장의 대규모 개장 행사에 초대해 주셔서 고마워요. ¹⁹⁴당신이 꿈을 좇아가는 것을 보게 되어 아주 좋네요. 훌륭해요! 늘 자신만의 업체를 가지고 싶어했던 것으로 기억하는데요, ¹⁹⁵우리가 TCB 헬스장에서 동료였을 때조차도 말이에요.

개장 일에 제가 직접 그곳에 갈 수 있으면 좋겠는데요. 유감스럽게도, 업무 차 시외로 나가게 될 거예요. 하지만 그 후에 가능한 한 빨리 당신을 방문하고 Loxley를 확인해볼 계획이에요. ¹⁹⁴당신의 새로운 모험에서 모든 일이 잘되기를 바랄게요!

몸 건강해요,

Bonnie

| 어휘 | follow 추구하다, 따르다   coworker 동료   in person 직접   unfortunately 유감스럽게도   venture 모험

191. 주제/목적 문제
기사는 왜 작성되었나?
(A) 새로운 피트니스 시설의 개업을 홍보하기 위해
(B) 개인 트레이닝 자격증을 위한 수업들을 알리기 위해
(C) Staunton의 다양한 업무 기회들을 강조하기 위해
(D) 운동 커뮤니티의 새로운 동향을 설명하기 위해
| 해설 | 기사 첫 번째 단락에 Fabio Souza가 Staunton의 근처인 Valley Lane에서 24시간 헬스장을 시작할 것이라고(Fabio Souza is launching a 24-hour gym in the Valley Lane neighborhood of Staunton) 알린 후, 그와 관련된 내용을 구체적으로 제시하고 있으므로 정답은 (A)이다.
| 어휘 | certification 자격증   highlight 강조하다   a variety of 다양한
| 패러프레이징 | is launching a 24-hour gym → the opening of a new fitness facility

192. 세부 사항을 묻는 문제
Souza 씨가 진로를 변경하도록 동기를 부여한 것은 무엇인가?
(A) 아버지 회사의 상속
(B) 근무 중 부상
(C) 친인척의 병
(D) 일자리 시장의 침체
| 해설 | 기사의 두 번째 단락 후반부에 Souza 씨는 Canton 주식회사에서 인테리어 디자이너로 경력을 시작했지만(Mr. Souza started his career as an interior designer at Canton Inc.) 아버지가 심장 질환 진단을 받은 후에, 운동의 중요성을 이해하기 시작했다고(However, after his father was diagnosed with a heart condition, Mr. Souza started to understand the importance of exercise ~) 제시되어 있으므로 정답은 (C)이다.
| 어휘 | inheritance 상속   illness 병, 질환   relative 친척, 인척   downturn 침체
| 패러프레이징 | his father was diagnosed with a heart condition
→ The illness of a relative

193. 연계 문제 – True
5월 1일 행사에 관해 제시된 것은 무엇인가?
(A) 회원 요금 할인을 특별히 포함한다.
(B) 방문객들이 이용할 수 있는 다과가 있을 것이다.
(C) 참가자들을 위한 무료 마사지를 포함한다.
(D) 한 시간에 한 번 현장 투어를 운영할 것이다.
| 해설 | 기사 마지막 단락에 1년에 600달러인 회원 자격을 가진 이들만 이용할 수 있게 될 것이라고(Its services will be available to those with memberships only, at a cost of $600 annually) 제시되어 있는데, 초대장에 500달러로 1년 회원에 등록하라고(Sign up for a one-year membership for $500) 한 것을 연계해 볼 때, 5월 1일 행사 때는 원래 600달러인 회원 요금이 500달러로 할인될 것임을 알 수 있으므로 정답은 (A)이다.
| 어휘 | refreshments 다과   participant 참가자   run 운영하다

194. 주제/목적 문제
Tolbert 씨의 이메일의 목적은 무엇인가?
(A) 일자리 제안에 대해 Souza 씨에게 감사를 전하는 것
(B) 초대를 수락하는 것
(C) 회원에 등록하는 것
(D) Souza 씨를 축하하는 것
| 해설 | 이메일 첫 번째 단락에 당신이 꿈을 좇아가는 것을 보게 되어 아주 좋다며(It's wonderful to see that you've followed your dream) 훌륭하다고(Way to go!) 덧붙인 것과 두 번째 단락에 당신의 새로운 모험에서 모든 일이 잘되기를 바란다고(I wish you all the best on your new venture) 한 것을 통해, 새로운 헬스장 사업을 시작한 Souza 씨를 축하하기 위해 보낸 이메일임을 알 수 있으므로 정답은 (D)이다.
| 어휘 | job offer 일자리 제안   congratulate 축하하다

195. 연계 문제 – True

Tolbert 씨에 관해 사실인 것은 무엇인가?
(A) Loxley의 투자자이다.
(B) 최근에 Staunton으로 이사했다.
(C) 경험 많은 인테리어 디자이너이다.
(D) Hillcrest에서 일했었다.

| 해설 | Tolbert 씨는 이메일 발신자로, 이메일 첫 번째 단락에 Souza 씨에게 TCB 헬스장에서 동료였을 때를(even back when we were coworkers at TCB Fitness) 언급했는데, 기사의 첫 번째 단락에서 Souza 씨는 Hillcrest에 있는 TCB 헬스장에 고용되었었다고(~ he was employed by TCB Fitness in Hillcrest for ten years) 한 것을 연계해 보면, Tolbert 씨도 Hillcrest에서 일했었다는 것을 알 수 있다. 따라서 정답은 (D)이다.

| 어휘 | investor 투자자 experienced 경험 많은, 숙련된

196-200 다음 기사, 이메일, 개요를 참조하시오.

작은 변화가 큰 차이를 만들 수 있다

LONGVIEW (1월 15일)—¹⁹⁶/²⁰⁰지역의 사업가 Gwen Langston이 환경친화적인 가정용 세제를 만들고 쓰는 것에 관한 무료 워크숍을 개최하겠다고 자원했다. 그 워크숍은 모두에게 열려 있고, 1월 21일 오후 7시 30분에 Longview 커뮤니티 센터 103호에서 열릴 것이다.

Langston은 환경을 돕기 위해 일생을 헌신해오고 있다. ¹⁹⁸그녀는 시내에서 Reclaim Depot라는 작은 가게를 운영하는데, 그곳에서는 오로지 재활용되거나 폐기된 재료들로 만들어진 상품들만 판매한다. 그녀의 가게는 또한 특정 쓸모없는 물품들을 위한 수거 장소이기도 하다.

"많은 사람들이 페인트, 자동차 유동액, 유통 기한이 지난 약 등을 하수구로 흘려 버려요. 이런 해로운 화학 물질이 흔히 결국 우리의 상수도로 들어가죠. ¹⁹⁷저는 Longview 지역에 살고 있는 모두가 이런 물질들이 종국에 잘못된 장소로 들어가지 않도록 확실히 하기 위해 화학 폐기물 처리를 위해 저희 수거 장소를 이용하도록 동기 부여가 되시기를 바랍니다."라고 Langston가 말했다.

워크숍을 위해 등록할 필요는 없다. 그러나 참석자들은 좌석이 선착순으로 이용 가능하다는 것을 유념해야 한다.

| 어휘 | entrepreneur 사업가 volunteer 자원하다 put on ~을 개최하다 eco-friendly 환경친화적인 household cleaner 가정용 세제 dedicate 헌신하다, 전념하다 environment 환경 exclusively 오로지, 독점적으로 salvaged 폐기된 collection point 수거 장소 unwanted 원치 않는, 쓸모없는 dump 버리다 fluid 유동액 expired 유통 기한이 지난, 만료된 drain 하수구 harmful 유해한 chemical 화학 물질 end up in 결국 ~로 들어가다 water supply 상수도 motivate 동기를 부여하다 substance 물질 registration 등록 note 유념하다 on a first-come, first-served basis 선착순

수신: <stafflist@longviewquarterly.com>
발신: <editor@longviewquarterly.com>
날짜: 1월 17일
제목: 기회

직원 귀하,

Gwen Langston은 1월 21일에 워크숍을 주최할 것인데요. ¹⁹⁸제가 오늘 아침에 그녀의 가게에 들러 저희 출판물을 위해 간단한 인터뷰에 참여하는 것에 관심이 있는지 알아보았어요. 다행히, 이것을 할 의향이 있다고 하니, 여러분 중에 이 이야기를 다뤄줄 사람이 필요해요. 우리 독자들이 그녀의 조언에 관심이 있을 것이라고 확신해요.

Christopher Mitchem
<Longview Quarterly>, 편집장

| 어휘 | opportunity 기회 participate in ~에 참여하다 brief 간단한, 짧은 publication 출판물 cover 취재하다, 다루다

<Longview Quarterly>
봄 호

제목	기사 상세	필자
독성 물질 버리기	²⁰⁰독한 화학 물질과 독성 물질을 이용하지 않고 여러분의 가정을 청소하는 팁	Enrico Padovano
심장 건강	여전히 아주 맛이 좋으면서도 저지방과 저염분의 조리법 모음	Danielle Laprade
¹⁹⁹현금을 위해 수집하기	돈을 절약하고 환경을 돕기 위해 가정용으로 빗물을 쉽게 이용하기	Jeff Wofford
Longview의 자랑	관광객들이 우리의 작은 도시에 관심을 갖도록 지역 정치인들이 무엇을 하고 있는지 들여다보기	Victoria Fomina

| 어휘 | ditch 버리다 toxin 독성 물질 harsh 독한, 강한 low-fat 저지방의 low-sodium 저염분의 recipe 조리법 pack a punch 강력한 효과가 있다 flavorful 맛있는, 풍미 있는 harness 이용하다 rainwater 빗물 politician 정치인

196. 주제/목적 문제

기사는 주로 무엇에 관한 것인가?
(A) 자원봉사 기회
(B) 업체의 대규모 개장 행사
(C) 교육적인 행사
(D) 환경 규제

| 해설 | 첫 번째 단락 도입부에 지역의 사업가 Gwen Langston이 환경친화적인 가정용 세제를 만들고 쓰는 것에 관한 무료 워크숍을 개최하겠다고 자원했다고(~ put on a free workshop on making and using eco-friendly

household cleaners) 한 후, 그 사업가와 무료 워크숍에 관한 내용이 전개되어 있으므로 정답은 (C)이다.

| 어휘 | grand opening 대규모 개장 행사   educational 교육적인   regulation 규제

| 패러프레이징 | workshop on making and using eco-friendly household cleaners → An educational event

🔼 고난도
197. 세부 사항을 묻는 문제
기사에 따르면, Langston 씨는 주민들이 어떤 활동을 하기를 바라는가?
(A) 화학 물질을 책임감 있게 처리하는 것
(B) 자신의 업체에서 나온 제품들을 검토하는 것
(C) 에너지 효율적인 가전제품을 사용하는 것
(D) 공공장소에 있는 쓰레기를 수거하는 것

| 해설 | 세 번째 단락의 인터뷰 내용에서, Langston 씨는 Longview 지역에 살고 있는 모두가 화학 폐기물 처리를 위해 수거 장소를 이용하도록 동기 부여가 되기를 바란다고(I hope everyone living in the Longview area will be motived to use our collection point for their chemical waste ~) 했으므로 정답은 (A)이다.

| 어휘 | dispose 처리하다   responsibly 책임감 있게   energy-efficient 에너지 효율적인   household appliances 가전제품   pick up 수거하다   litter 쓰레기

| 패러프레이징 | use our collection point for their chemical waste → Dispose of chemicals responsibly

198. 연계 문제 – 추론
Mitchem 씨에 관해 암시되는 것은 무엇인가?
(A) 재활용을 위해 물건을 수집하고 있다.
(B) 오늘 아침에 면접을 실시했다.
(C) 워크숍에 동료와 동행할 것이다.
(D) Reclaim Depot를 방문했다.

| 해설 | 기사 두 번째 단락에 Langston이 시내에 Reclaim Depot라는 작은 가게를 운영한다고(She operates a small shop downtown called Reclaim Depot) 했고, 이메일에서 발신자인 Mitchem 씨가 오늘 아침에 Langston의 가게에 들렀다고(I stopped by her shop this morning) 한 것을 연계해 볼 때, her shop에 해당하는 Reclaim Depot을 방문했음을 알 수 있으므로 정답은 (D)이다.

| 어휘 | conduct 실시하다, 시행하다   accompany 동행하다, 동반하다

🔼 고난도
199. 추론 문제
자연적인 물 공급원을 이용하고자 하는 사람들에게 가장 좋은 기사는 무엇인가?
(A) 독성 물질 버리기
(B) 심장 건강
(C) 현금을 위해 수집하기
(D) Longview의 자랑

| 해설 | 세 번째 지문에 기사 상세 내용에서 자연적인 물 공급원과 관계된 것은 돈을 절약하고 환경을 돕기 위해 가정용으로 빗물을 쉽게 이용하기임을 (Harness rainwater easily for home use to save money and help the environment) 알 수 있고, 이 기사에 해당하는 제목은 현금을 위해 수집하기로 (Collecting for Cash) 확인되므로 정답은 (C)이다.

🔼 고난도
200. 연계 문제 – 추론
누가 Langston 씨를 인터뷰했을 것 같은가?
(A) Padovano 씨
(B) Laprade 씨
(C) Wofford 씨
(D) Fomina 씨

| 해설 | 첫 번째 지문인 기사에서 도입부에 Langston 씨는 환경친화적인 가정용 세제를 만들고 쓰는 것에 관한 무료 워크숍을 개최한다고(~ put on a free workshop on making and using eco-friendly household cleaners) 하였고, 세 번째 지문인 개요에서 이와 관련된 내용은 독한 화학 물질과 독성 물질을 이용하지 않고 여러분의 가정을 청소하는 팁임을(Tips for cleaning your home without the use of harsh chemicals and toxins) 알 수 있다. 그리고 이 기사를 쓴 이는 Enrico Padovano로 확인되므로 정답은 (A)이다.

TEST 03

PART 5

101 (D)	102 (C)	103 (A)	104 (C)	105 (B)
106 (B)	107 (C)	108 (B)	109 (C)	110 (A)
111 (B)	112 (B)	113 (B)	114 (D)	115 (C)
116 (B)	117 (B)	118 (C)	119 (B)	120 (C)
121 (C)	122 (C)	123 (C)	124 (B)	125 (C)
126 (D)	127 (B)	128 (B)	129 (B)	130 (D)

PART 6

131 (C)	132 (C)	133 (B)	134 (C)	135 (D)
136 (B)	137 (C)	138 (C)	139 (A)	140 (C)
141 (C)	142 (C)	143 (C)	144 (B)	145 (D)
146 (A)				

PART 7

147 (A)	148 (C)	149 (B)	150 (D)	151 (C)
152 (C)	153 (B)	154 (D)	155 (A)	156 (B)
157 (D)	158 (B)	159 (C)	160 (C)	161 (B)
162 (C)	163 (A)	164 (D)	165 (D)	166 (B)
167 (C)	168 (D)	169 (C)	170 (C)	171 (D)
172 (D)	173 (C)	174 (D)	175 (C)	176 (D)
177 (B)	178 (C)	179 (B)	180 (B)	181 (C)
182 (A)	183 (C)	184 (B)	185 (C)	186 (B)
187 (D)	188 (A)	189 (C)	190 (C)	191 (B)
192 (D)	193 (A)	194 (B)	195 (B)	196 (C)
197 (A)	198 (C)	199 (C)	200 (C)	

PART 5

101. 형용사 자리 – 비교급
영업 팀은 재무 팀보다 새로운 소프트웨어에 적응하는 데 더 힘든 시간을 보냈다.
| 해설 | 관사 a와 명사 time 사이에 빈칸이 있으므로 빈칸은 명사를 수식해줄 형용사가 들어갈 자리인데, 뒤에 비교급과 함께 쓰이는 than이 제시되어 있으므로 비교급 형용사인 (D) harder가 정답이다.
| 어휘 | adjust to ~에 적응하다　finance 재무　hardly 거의 ~ 아니다

102. 인칭 대명사
Marlowe 씨는 그것이 발견되자마자 팀에 자신의 실수를 인정했다.
| 해설 | 빈칸은 타동사 admitted의 목적어인 mistake를 한정 수식하는 자리이므로 소유격 대명사가 들어가야 한다. 따라서 (C) his가 정답이다.
| 어휘 | admit 인정하다　mistake 실수, 잘못　discover 발견하다

103. 부사 어휘
같은 사람에게 또 다른 온라인 송금을 하려면, 그저 금액을 입력한 다음 "확인" 버튼을 클릭하세요.
| 해설 | 빈칸은 동사 input을 수식하는 부사가 들어갈 자리인데, 문맥상 일반적인 사항을 알려주는 지시 사항인 것으로 볼 때 '그저 금액을 입력한 다음 "확인" 버튼을 클릭하세요'라는 의미로 전개되는 것이 적절하므로 '그저, 간단히'라는 뜻의 (A) simply가 정답이다.
| 어휘 | wire transfer 온라인 송금　input 입력하다　amount 금액　confirm 확인하다, 확정하다　closely 긴밀히

104. 전치사 어휘
Logan 제조사의 상품의 품질은 지난 20년 동안 한결같았다.
| 해설 | 빈칸 뒤에 기간을 나타내는 명사가 있고, 문맥상 '지난 20년 동안 한결같았다'라는 의미로 전개되어야 하므로 기간을 나타낼 때 쓰는 전치사인 (C) for가 정답이다.
| 어휘 | quality 품질　goods 상품　consistent 변함없는　decade 10년

105. 부사절 접속사
그 차량의 예비 테스트 과정은 과열되기 시작할 때까지 엔진을 가속하는 것을 포함한다.
| 해설 | 빈칸 앞뒤로 두 개의 절이 있으므로, 빈칸은 절과 절을 연결해줄 접속사가 들어갈 자리이다. 따라서 부사인 (A) seldom과 부사이자 전치사인 (C) besides는 오답이며, 문맥상 '과열되기 시작할 때까지 엔진을 가속하는 것'이라는 의미가 되는 것이 적절하므로 (B) until이 정답이다.
| 어휘 | vehicle 차량　preliminary 예비의　process 과정, 절차　include 포함하다　accelerate 가속하다　overheat 과열되다

106. 명사 자리 – 전치사의 목적어
두 비즈니스 파트너들은 그들의 상호 보완적인 재능과 상호간의 존중 때문에 완벽하게 함께 일한다.
| 해설 | 빈칸은 전치사 due to의 목적어 자리이자 앞에 있는 형용사 mutual의 수식을 받는 명사가 들어갈 자리이므로 명사인 (B) admiration이 정답이다. 전치사 due to의 목적어 두 개가 접속사 and로 연결된 형태이다.
| 어휘 | complementary 상호 보완적인　talent 재능　mutual 상호간의　admiration 감탄, 존경　admire 존중하다, 감탄하다

107. 부사 어휘
고대 이집트에 관한 책의 저자인 Kendra Fabiano는 이전에 로마 제국에 관한 책을 출판했다.
| 해설 | 빈칸은 동사 published를 수식하는 부사가 들어갈 자리인데, 문맥상 '이전에 로마 제국에 관한 책을 출판했다'라는 의미로 전개되는 것이 적절하므로 '이전에'라는 뜻의 (C) previously가 정답이다.
| 어휘 | author 저자, 작가　ancient 고대의　publish 출판하다, 출간하다　accordingly 그에 맞춰

🔺고난도
108. 형용사 자리 – 명사 수식
Linden 스튜디오는 인기 있는 소설 <Holding On>을 기반으로 한 영화를 제작할 독점적인 권한을 작가인 Rita Palmer에게서 받았다.
| 해설 | 빈칸은 명사 rights를 수식할 형용사가 들어갈 자리이므로 '독점적인, 전용의'라는 뜻의 형용사인 (B) exclusive가 정답이다. (A) excluding은 전치사, (C) exclude와 (D) excludes는 동사이므로 오답이다.
| 어휘 | grant 주다, 승인하다   based on ~에 기반을 둔   novel 소설   exclusive 독점적인, 전용의   exclude 제외하다, 배제하다

고난도
109. 인칭 대명사
그 자체로 아주 멋진 이 실크 커튼들은 그 뒷면에 있는 레이스 그물 세공으로 더 좋아 보인다.
| 해설 | 빈칸은 전치사 by의 목적어가 들어갈 자리이므로 주격 대명사인 (D) they는 답이 될 수 없고, 아주 멋진 대상이 되는 것은 앞에 제시된 주어인 These silk curtains이므로, 주어와 목적어의 대상이 일치할 때 쓰는 재귀 대명사인 (C) themselves가 정답이다.
| 어휘 | fabulous 아주 멋진, 기막히게 좋은   netting 그물 세공

110. 명사 어휘
신입 사원들용 유니폼의 비용은 부서별 예산에 의해 지급된다.
| 해설 | 빈칸은 문장의 주어 자리이므로 동사 is paid for와 어울리는 명사가 들어가야 한다. 따라서 '비용은 부서별 예산에 의해 지급된다'라는 의미로 전개되는 것이 적절하므로 '비용'이라는 뜻의 (A) cost가 정답이다.
| 어휘 | departmental 부서의   budget 예산   benefit 수당, 이득   contribution 기여, 공헌   value 가치, 값어치

111. 형용사 어휘
그 회사는 보도 자료들의 초안을 작성할 수 있는 재능 있는 전속 작가를 보유함으로써 자사의 이미지를 개선하기를 바란다.
| 해설 | 빈칸은 명사 writer를 수식해줄 형용사가 들어갈 자리로, 문맥상 '재능 있는 전속 작가를 보유함으로써'라는 의미가 되는 것이 적절하므로 '재능 있는'이라는 뜻의 (B) talented가 정답이다.
| 어휘 | improve 개선하다   writer on staff 전속 작가   draft 초안을 작성하다   press release 보도 자료   reluctant 마지못한, 꺼리는   compatible 호환되는, 양립할 수 있는

112. 전치사 어휘
Midnight Blue는 어린 자녀들이 있는 가정에서 가장 잘 팔리는 세탁용 세제이다.
| 해설 | 빈칸은 앞의 절과 뒤의 명사구를 연결해주며 뒤의 명사구를 목적어로 가지는 전치사가 들어갈 자리로, 문맥상 '어린 자녀들이 있는 가정들 사이에서'라는 의미가 되어야 하므로 셋 이상의 대상 앞에 쓸 수 있는 '~ 사이에, ~ 중에'라는 뜻의 (B) among이 정답이다.
| 어휘 | laundry detergent 세탁용 세제

113. 형용사 자리 - 주격 보어
Vance 교수의 책을 읽은 판매원들은 이제 자신들의 협상 능력에 더 자신감이 생겼다고 말한다.
| 해설 | 빈칸은 be동사 are의 보어가 들어갈 자리이자 비교급을 나타내는 부사 more의 수식을 받는 자리이므로 형용사인 (B) confident가 정답이다.
| 어휘 | professor 교수   negotiation skills 협상 능력   confidence 자신감, 확신   confidently 자신 있게, 확신을 갖고

114. 동사 어휘
Madison 요리 학교는 초보자들부터 전문가들에게까지 음식 준비 기술에 관해 적정한 가격의 강좌들을 제공한다.
| 해설 | 빈칸은 문장의 동사가 들어갈 자리로, 문맥상 뒤에 제시된 명사구 affordable courses를 목적어로 취해 '적정한 가격의 강좌들을 제공한다'라는 의미로 전개되는 것이 적절하므로 '제공하다'라는 뜻의 (D) offers가 정답이다.
| 어휘 | culinary institute 요리 학교   affordable 가격이 알맞은   course 강좌   preparation 준비   technique 기술, 기법   complete 완료하다, 작성하다

115. 부사 어휘
종업원은 Baker 씨가 심지어 식사를 다 끝내기도 전에 그의 후식을 가져왔다.
| 해설 | 과거 완료 시제인 had와 finished 사이에 빈칸이 있으므로 빈칸은 동사 finished를 수식하는 부사가 들어갈 자리이다. '심지어 식사를 다 끝내기도 전에'라는 의미로 전개되는 것이 적절하므로 '심지어'라는 뜻의 부사인 (C) even이 정답이다.
| 어휘 | bring out 내오다

116. 전치사 자리
좋지 않은 날씨 때문에, 지역 화가들과 조각가들을 지원하는 갤러리의 경매에 극히 적은 사람들이 나왔다.
| 해설 | 빈칸은 뒤의 명사구를 이끌어줄 전치사가 들어갈 자리이므로, 접속사인 (A) As long as, (C) Given that, (D) Even if는 모두 답이 될 수 없고, '~ 때문에'라는 뜻의 전치사인 (B) Due to가 정답이다.
| 어휘 | poor weather 좋지 않은 날씨   turn up for ~에 나오다, 나타나다   auction 경매   support 지원하다   sculptor 조각가

고난도
117. 명사 어휘
이 도표는 공공 보험안과 민간 보험안의 장단점을 이해하는 데 도움을 줄 것이다.
| 해설 | 빈칸은 앞의 명사 insurance와 함께 복합 명사를 완성해줄 명사가 들어갈 자리인데, '공공 보험안과 민간 보험안의 장단점'이라는 의미로 전개되는 것이 적절하므로 '옵션, 선택 사항'이라는 뜻의 (B) options가 정답이다.
| 어휘 | diagram 도표   pros and cons 장단점   public 공공의   private 민간의   insurance 보험   caution 주의, 경고   motivation 동기 부여   removal 제거

118. 동사의 형태와 시제
Allan 씨는 풍경 열차를 타고 전국을 여행했는데, 그러는 동안 독특한 풍경 사진을 많이 찍었다.
| 해설 | 빈칸은 3인칭 단수 주어 뒤에 본동사가 들어갈 자리이므로 수 일치가 되지 않는 (A) photograph와 준동사인 (D) to photograph는 오답이고, 앞의 절의 동사의 시제가 과거이고 주어가 사진을 찍는 능동의 의미가 되어야 하므로 '~의 사진

을 찍었다'라는 뜻의 능동의 과거 시제 동사인 (C) photographed가 정답이다.
| 어휘 | scenic 경치가 좋은   unique 독특한   landscape 풍경   feature 특징, 특색

🏠 고난도
119. 등위 접속사

창고 팀은 일주일 내내 직원이 부족할 것이어서, 요청이 처리되기까지 반드시 추가적인 시간을 허용해야 합니다.
| 해설 | 빈칸은 앞뒤의 두 절을 연결해줄 접속사가 들어갈 자리로, 내용 전개상 앞의 절이 뒤의 절의 원인이 됨을 알 수 있으므로 인과 관계를 나타낼 때 쓰는 '그래서'라는 뜻의 접속사인 (B) so가 정답이다.
| 어휘 | warehouse 창고   short-staffed 직원이 부족한, 일손이 모자란   allow 허용하다, 허락하다   additional 추가적인   process 처리하다

🏠 고난도
120. 복합 관계 대명사

Marlin 호텔의 프런트 데스크 직원들은 고객들이 무엇을 필요로 하든지 그들의 요청에 시기 적절하게 대응하기 위해 노력한다.
| 해설 | 빈칸 앞에는 완전한 절이, 빈칸 뒤에는 주어 they와 타동사 need만 있을 뿐 타동사의 목적어가 빠진 불완전한 절이 있는데, 두 절을 연결하는 접속사가 없으므로, 빈칸에는 빈칸 이하의 절을 부사절로 만들어 주는 접속사 역할과 동사 need의 목적어 역할을 동시에 할 수 있는 것이 필요하다. 따라서 이런 역할이 가능한 복합 관계 대명사인 (C) whatever가 정답이다.
| 어휘 | strive 노력하다, 애쓰다   respond to ~에 대응하다   in a timely manner 시기 적절하게

🏠 고난도
121. to부정사

최근 거래에 관한 세부 사항을 보거나 계좌에서 자금을 인출하려면, 은행의 입구 근처에 있는 ATM을 이용하세요.
| 해설 | 빈칸은 등위 접속사 or로 연결된 병치 구문을 완성하며, 뒤에 목적어 funds를 가질 수 있는 타동사를 포함한 것이 들어가야 하므로, 주어 뒤에 위치해야 하는 일반 동사 형태인 (A) withdrew와 (B) withdraws, 목적어를 가질 수 없는 명사인 (D) withdrawal은 답이 될 수 없다. 따라서 뒤에 목적어를 가질 수 있는 to부정사 형태인 (C) to withdraw가 정답이다.
| 어휘 | details 세부 사항   transaction 거래   funds 자금   account 계좌   withdrawal 인출

🏠 고난도
122. 명사 어휘

행사 기획자를 고용하는 것은 행사 장소와 공급업체들 사이의 조정을 처리하는 효과적인 방법이 될 수 있다.
| 해설 | 빈칸은 take care of의 목적어가 들어갈 자리로, 문맥상 처리의 대상이 될 수 있는 것으로 적절한 것은 '행사 장소와 공급업체들 사이의 조정'이므로 '조정'이라는 뜻의 (C) coordination이 정답이다.
| 어휘 | effective 효과적인   take care of ~을 처리하다, 돌보다   venue 장소   supplier 공급업체   appreciation 감사   indication 표시, 징후   formation 형성

123. 형용사 어휘

금융 전문가 Ken Ramsey가 진행하는 주간 팟캐스트의 인기는 그의 책 매출에 상당한 활력을 불어넣었다.
| 해설 | 빈칸은 타동사 gave의 목적어인 명사 boost를 수식해줄 형용사가 들어갈 자리로, 문맥상 '상당한 활력을 불어넣었다'라는 의미로 전개되는 것이 적절하므로, '상당한, 많은'이라는 뜻의 정도를 나타내는 형용사인 (C) considerable이 정답이다.
| 어휘 | popularity 인기   give a boost to ~에 활력을 불어넣다   financial expert 금융 전문가   sales 매출(량)   valid 유효한   successive 연속적인   frank 솔직한

124. 부사 자리 – 동사 수식

그 소유주가 소셜 미디어 광고에 투자한다면, 웹 사이트의 트래픽 양은 상당히 향상될 것이다.
| 해설 | 조동사 will과 동사 improve 사이에 빈칸이 있으므로 빈칸은 동사를 수식하는 부사 자리이다. 따라서 '상당히, 많이'라는 뜻의 부사인 (B) substantially가 정답이다.
| 어휘 | amount 양   owner 소유주, 주인   invest 투자하다   ad 광고

🏠 고난도
125. 형용사 어휘

Yorktown의 작은 지역 사회 내 공공 도서관의 개관은 주민들의 재정적 지원으로 가능하게 되었다.
| 해설 | 빈칸은 수동태로 제시된 5형식 동사 made의 목적격 보어가 될 형용사가 들어갈 자리로, 문맥상 '도서관 개관은 주민들의 재정적 지원으로 가능하게 되었다'라는 의미로 전개되는 것이 적절하므로 '가능한'이라는 뜻의 (C) possible이 정답이다.
| 어휘 | opening 개관   financial support 재정적 지원   resident 주민   generous 관대한, 후한   evident 명백한, 분명한

🏠 고난도
126. 소유격 관계 대명사

집주인은 새로운 파이프에 10년 품질 보증을 제공할 수 있는 회사의 배관공을 고용하고 싶어한다.
| 해설 | 빈칸 앞뒤에 완전한 절이 있는데, 빈칸 이하가 절의 형태로 앞의 명사 a plumber를 수식하므로 빈칸은 관계 대명사 자리이다. 빈칸 뒤에 완전한 절이 있고, 빈칸 바로 뒤에 있는 명사 company에 관사나 소유격이 없으며, a plumber whose company가 되어 '배관공의 회사'라는 의미로 해석되는 것이 문맥상 적절하므로 (D) whose가 정답이다.
| 어휘 | homeowner 집주인   plumber 배관공   guarantee 품질 보증

🏠 고난도
127. 형용사 어휘

꽃들은 온도 변화에 취약하기 때문에 온실에 보관된다.
| 해설 | 빈칸은 they(= flowers)의 상태를 설명하는 형용사가 들어갈 자리로, 문맥상 꽃들이 온실에 보관되는 이유가 나와야 하는데, '온도 변화에 취약하기 때문에'라는 의미로 전개되는 것이 적절하므로 '취약한, 연약한'이라는 뜻의 (B) vulnerable이 정답이다.

| 어휘 | greenhouse 온실   fluctuation 변동, 오르내림   temperature 온도   threatened 멸종 위기에 직면한, 위협 당한   feeble 약한, 미약한   limited 제한된, 한정된

128. 명사 자리 – 동사의 목적어
정부 보조금이 휠체어를 탄 사람들을 위해 그 시설의 접근성을 개선하도록 Arlene 극장에 제공되었다.
| 해설 | 빈칸은 동사 improve의 목적어 자리이고, 관사 the와 전치사 of 사이에 있으므로 명사 자리이다. 따라서 '접근성, 접근'이라는 뜻의 명사 (B) accessibility가 정답이다.
| 어휘 | government grant 정부 보조금   accessible 접근[이용] 가능한   accessibly 접근 가능하게

고난도
129. 동사의 시제
여행자가 추가적인 특별 항목들에 대해 돈을 내지 않으면, 유람선의 환영 꾸러미에는 두 장의 식사 카드와 두 개의 객실 열쇠가 포함될 것이다.
| 해설 | Unless로 시작하는 조건절의 내용이 '추가적인 특별 항목들에 대해 돈을 내지 않으면'이란 뜻으로 일반적인 상황을 조건으로 제시하는 것이므로 주절의 시제는 미래가 되는 것이 자연스럽다. 따라서 (B) will contain이 정답이다.
| 어휘 | feature 특징, 특매품   cruise 유람선   welcome packet 환영 꾸러미

고난도
130. 명사 어휘
그 뮤지컬은 르네상스 시대의 시를 노래 가사로 창의적으로 결합하여 비평가들로부터 찬사를 받았다.
| 해설 | 빈칸은 전치사 for의 목적어로 creative의 수식을 받아 비평가들로부터 찬사를 받은 이유가 되어야 하고, 또한 뒤에 제시된 전치사 into와 연결 지어 문맥상 '노래 가사로 창의적인 결합'이라는 의미로 전개되는 것이 적절하므로 '통합, 결합'이라는 뜻의 (D) incorporation이 정답이다.
| 어휘 | praise 칭찬하다   critic 비평가   creative 창의적인, 창조적인   poetry 시   song lyrics 노래 가사   intermission 중간 휴식 시간   method 방법

PART 6

131-134 다음 정보를 참조하시오.

자동 이체 설정하기

여러분의 공과금을 자동 이체로 납부하는 것은 연체가 발생될 일이 결코 없다는 것을 보장합니다. 게다가 많은 공익 기업들이 자동 이체 고객들에게 할인을 제공하여, 그것은 여러분의 월 비용을 ¹³¹낮출 좋은 방법입니다. 여러분의 계정에 로그인한 후, 자동 이체 버튼을 클릭하세요. 드롭 다운 메뉴에서 납부하고자 하는 회사를 선택하세요. ¹³²원하는 옵션이 거기 없을 경우, 수동으로 입력하실 수도 있습니다. 다음으로, 여러분의 고객 ID 코드를 ¹³³신중하게 입력하세요. 매달 납부가 이루어지기 원

하는 날짜를 선택하실 수 있습니다. 이는 여러분의 계정에서 ¹³⁴설정을 조정함으로써 언제든지 변경될 수 있습니다.

| 어휘 | set up 설정하다   direct debit 자동 이체   utility bill 공과금   guarantee 보장하다   additionally 게다가   utility company 공익 기업   cost 비용   sign into 로그인하다   account 계정   select 선택하다   input 입력하다   payment 납입, 지불   adjust 조정하다

131. 동사 어휘
| 해설 | 앞에 할인을 제공한다는 내용이 있으므로 이와 연계하면 '월 비용을 낮출 좋은 방법이다'라는 내용으로 이어지는 것이 자연스럽다. 따라서 '낮추다'라는 뜻의 (C) lower가 정답이다.
| 어휘 | predict 예측하다

고난도
132. 알맞은 문장 고르기
(A) 가장 좋은 금리를 받기 위해, 저희 은행 직원들 중 한 명과 이야기하세요.
(B) 분쟁의 경우에는 계량기 검침이 제공되어야 합니다.
(C) 원하는 옵션이 거기 없을 경우, 수동으로 입력하실 수도 있습니다.
(D) 그 탭을 클릭하여 저희 최신 고객 후기를 읽어보세요.
| 해설 | 자동 이체를 신청하기 위해 진행해야 하는 절차를 설명하고 있고, 바로 앞에 언급된 드롭 다운 메뉴에서 원하는 회사를 선택하는 것과 관련 지어 원하는 회사가 없을 경우에 할 수 있는 것을 알려주는 내용의 문장이 이어지는 것이 적절하므로 (C)가 정답이다.
| 어휘 | interest rate 금리, 이율   bank teller 은행 직원   meter reading 계량기 검침   dispute 분쟁   desired 원하는, 바라는   manually 수동으로

133. 부사 자리 – 동사 수식
| 해설 | 명령문으로 제시된 동사 input 앞에 빈칸이 있으므로 빈칸은 동사를 수식해 줄 부사가 들어갈 자리이다. 따라서 부사인 (B) carefully가 정답이다.
| 어휘 | careful 주의 깊은   carefulness 주의, 신중함

134. 명사 어휘
| 해설 | 빈칸은 adjusting의 목적어가 들어갈 자리로, 계정에서 조정하여 변경할 수 있는 대상으로 '설정'이 적절하므로 (C) settings가 정답이다.
| 어휘 | saving 저축, 절약된 금액   settlement 합의, 정착   specialty 전문, 특산물

135-138 다음 이메일을 참조하시오.

수신: Gilbert 주식회사 전 직원
발신: Courtney Austin
날짜: 6월 30일 월요일
제목: 긴급 수리

Putnam 건설의 일부 기술자들이 복사실의 천장 타일에 긴급한 수리를

¹³⁵실시하기 위해 우리 사무실을 방문할 것입니다. ¹³⁶이 구역은 남은 시간 동안 출입이 금지될 것입니다. 복사할 것이 있으면, 길 건너에 있는 인쇄소를 이용하거나 내일 처리해 주시기 바랍니다. 금이 간 타일 여러 개가 제거되고, 노출된 배선 문제가 해결될 것입니다. 그들이 현장에 있는 ¹³⁷동안에, 작업 팀이 시끄러운 도구를 이용할 수도 있습니다. 작업 현장 인근에 계신 분들께서는 일시적으로 다른 업무 공간으로 이동하기를 원하실 수도 있는데요. 이것이 불편한 상황임을 ¹³⁸이해합니다. 여러분의 인내에 감사드립니다.

| 어휘 | urgent 긴급한   ceiling 천장   cracked 금이 간   remove 제거하다   exposed 노출된   wiring 배선   resolve 해결하다   on site 현장에   noisy 시끄러운   workstation 업무 공간   temporarily 일시적으로, 임시로   inconvenience 불편함   patience 인내, 참을성

135. 동사 어휘

| 해설 | 기술자들의 방문 목적을 나타내는 to부정사를 완성할 동사가 들어갈 자리로, 뒤에 제시된 목적어인 urgent repairs와 관련 지어 '긴급한 수리를 실시하기 위해'라는 의미로 전개되는 것이 적절하므로 '실시하다, 수행하다'라는 뜻의 (D) perform이 정답이다.

| 어휘 | divulge 누설하다, 폭로하다   acquire 얻다, 획득하다

136. 알맞은 문장 고르기

(A) 여러분은 어떤 회사가 선정되었는지에 관해 통지를 받을 것입니다.
(B) 이 구역은 남은 시간 동안 출입이 금지될 것입니다.
(C) 사용된 종이의 양이 감소되어야 합니다.
(D) 초대장을 원하시면 저에게 알려주시기 바랍니다.

| 해설 | 앞서 복사실의 긴급한 수리 사실을 제시했고, 뒤이어 복사가 필요할 경우 취해야 할 조치에 관해 안내하고 있는 것으로 볼 때, 그 사이에는 복사실의 긴급한 수리로 인해 이용이 불가함을 알리는 내용의 문장이 삽입되는 것이 적절하므로 (B)가 정답이다.

| 어휘 | notify 통지하다   be off limits 출입이 금지되다   reduce 감소하다   invitation 초대장

137. 전치사 자리

| 해설 | 빈칸은 뒤의 명사구를 목적어로 가지는 전치사가 들어갈 자리이므로, 접속사인 (A) When, 부사인 (B) Lastly와 (D) Soon은 모두 답이 될 수 없고, '~ 동안에'라는 의미의 전치사인 (C) During이 정답이다.

138. 동사의 시제

| 해설 | 긴급 수리와 관련하여 안내한 후 이 상황이 불편한 상황임을 이해한다는 내용이므로 현재 시제가 되어야 한다. 따라서 현재 시제인 (C) understand가 정답이다. 동사 understand는 진행형으로 사용하지 않으므로 (B)는 오답이다.

139-142 다음 공지를 참조하시오.

Bellshire 백화점의 직원들은 Cobblestone 주식회사의 ¹³⁹조리 기구에 대한 브랜드 인지도를 높이는 것을 목표로 하는 판촉 활동들에 관해 알고 있어야 합니다.

시연 구역이 2층에 설치될 것이고, 쇼핑객들은 그곳에서 설명회에 참석할 수 있습니다. ¹⁴⁰각각은 Cobblestone 주식회사의 직원에 의해 진행될 것인데, 그분이 주철 프라이팬들 같은 제품들의 장점들을 보여줄 것입니다. 설명회는 하루에 몇 차례 개최되고 ¹⁴¹대략 30분간 지속될 것입니다.

Cobblestone 주식회사의 수프 냄비들과 기타 상품에 대한 질문들을 받을 수도 있으니 제품 설명들을 검토해 주시기 바랍니다. ¹⁴²시연될 제품들의 매출이 증가할 것으로 예상됩니다. Cobblestone 주식회사가 부족을 막기 위해 저희에게 제품들을 추가로 공급해 줄 것입니다.

| 어휘 | be aware of ~에 관해 알다   promotional activity 판촉 활동   aimed at ~을 목표로 하는   raise 높이다   brand awareness 브랜드 인지도   demonstration 시연   set up 설치하다   information session 설명회   conduct 시행하다   benefit 장점, 이점   cast-iron 주철로 만든   merchandise 제품   description 설명   supply 공급하다   shortage 부족

🔺 고난도
139. 명사 어휘

| 해설 | 빈칸에는 Cobblestone 주식회사가 취급하는 제품이 들어가야 함을 알 수 있는데, 이후 단락들에 제시된 주철 프라이팬들(cast-iron frying pans)과 수프 냄비들(soup pots)을 단서로 조리 기구를 만드는 회사임을 알 수 있으므로 (A) cookware가 정답이다.

| 어휘 | electronics 전자 제품   apparel 의류

140. 부정 대명사

| 해설 | 빈칸은 문장의 주어 자리로, 문맥상 '각각의 설명회가 Cobblestone 주식회사 직원에 의해 진행될 것이다'라는 의미로 전개되어야 하므로 '각각'이라는 뜻의 부정 대명사인 (C) Each가 정답이다.

141. 부사 자리

| 해설 | 빈칸이 없어도 '30분간 지속될 것이다'라는 완전한 문장이 되므로, 빈칸에는 뒤의 시간 표현 half an hour를 수식해 줄 부사가 들어가야 함을 알 수 있다. 따라서 '대략, 거의'라는 뜻의 부사인 (C) roughly가 정답이다.

| 어휘 | rough 개략적인, 거친   roughness 거칢, 난폭함

🔺 고난도
142. 알맞은 문장 고르기

(A) 일부 고객들이 파손된 제품들을 반품했습니다.
(B) 직원들은 미리 각자의 프레젠테이션을 연습해야 합니다.
(C) 시연될 제품들의 매출이 증가할 것으로 예상됩니다.
(D) 저희는 여러분이 그것들 모두에 대한 명확한 설명을 써 주시기를 바랍니다.

| 해설 | 뒤이어 Cobblestone 주식회사가 부족을 막기 위해 제품들을 추가로 공

급해 줄 것이라는 문장이 제시되어 있는 것으로 볼 때, 부족이 나타날 수 있는 상황과 관련하여 그 앞에는 매출 증가를 예상한다는 내용의 문장이 삽입되는 것이 가장 적절하므로 정답은 (C)이다.

| 어휘 | damaged 파손된, 손상된   practice 연습하다   in advance 미리   increase 증가하다   explanation 설명

143-146 다음 웹 페이지를 참조하시오.

방문객 정보

Skyway 식물원은 유리 온실들 내의 습기를 143**모니터링함**으로써 식물들과 꽃들의 건강을 유지합니다. 저희가 소장하고 있는 많은 종들은 건조한 환경에서는 생존할 수 없습니다. 144**이런 이유로,** 스프링클러들이 간헐적으로 작동합니다. 방문객들의 안전을 위해, 물을 주고 있는 구역들은 일시적으로 문을 닫습니다. 그 구역들은 방문객들이 145**축축한**, 아마도 미끄러운, 길들을 걷지 않도록 스프링클러가 꺼진 후에도 일정 시간 동안 닫힌 채로 있을 수 있습니다. 146**게다가 방문객들은 식물들을 만지는 것이 허용되지 않습니다.** 이러한 규정이 엄격하게 보일 수도 있지만, 그것이 피해를 예방하고 식물원을 더 아름답게 만듭니다.

| 어휘 | botanical garden 식물원   maintain 유지하다   moisture 습기, 수분   glass greenhouse 유리 온실   species 종   house 소장하다, 수용하다   survive 생존하다, 살아남다   dry 건조한   be in operation 작동 중이다   intermittently 간헐적으로   safety 안전   section 구역   water 물을 주다   turn off 끄다   possibly 아마도   slippery 미끄러운   path 길   rule 규정   strict 엄격한   prevent 예방하다, 막다   damage 피해, 손상

143. 동사 어휘
| 해설 | 빈칸은 전치사 by의 목적어가 될 동명사가 들어갈 자리로, 문맥상 식물과 꽃들의 건강을 지키는 방안이 되도록 '습기를 모니터링함으로써'라는 의미로 전개되는 것이 적절하므로 (C) monitoring이 정답이다.
| 어휘 | defend 방어하다, 지키다   eliminate 제거하다   acquire 얻다, 획득하다

144. 접속 부사
| 해설 | 빈칸은 앞뒤의 두 문장을 연결해줄 접속 부사가 들어갈 자리로, 내용 전개상 앞에 제시된 내용이 빈칸 뒤 문장의 이유가 됨을 알 수 있으므로, '이런 이유로'라는 의미의 (B) For this reason이 정답이다.
| 어휘 | in contrast 그에 반해서

🔺고난도
145. 형용사 자리 - 명사 수식
| 해설 | 빈칸은 slippery와 함께 전치사 on의 목적어로 쓰인 명사 paths를 수식해줄 형용사가 들어갈 자리이므로 형용사인 (D) damp가 정답이다.
| 어휘 | damply 축축하게   dampness 축축함   dampen 축축하게 하다

146. 알맞은 문장 고르기
(A) 게다가, 방문객들은 식물들을 만지는 것이 허용되지 않습니다.
(B) 경험 있는 저희 가이드들은 각각의 꽃을 식별할 수 있습니다.
(C) 플래시 사용 여부와 관계없이 언제든지 사진을 촬영할 수 있습니다.
(D) 따라서, 운영 시간이 여름에는 연장될 것입니다.
| 해설 | 뒤이어 이러한 규정이 엄격하게 보일 수도 있다고 제시되어 있는 것을 통해, 그 앞에는 엄격하다고 생각할 만한 규정을 알리는 내용의 문장이 삽입되는 것이 적절하므로 (A)가 정답이다.
| 어휘 | be permitted to ~하도록 허용되다   touch 만지다, 손대다   experienced 경험 있는, 숙련된   identify 확인하다, 식별하다   hours of operation 운영 시간   extend 연장하다

PART 7

147-148 다음 영수증을 참조하시오.

Tabor's

2월 28일, 오전 11:41	정비사: John Prieto
주문: 04976	모델: 4도어 Crestin

147**오일 교환**   29.99달러
– 합성 오일 1리터 포함

147**타이어 펑크 수리**   12.99달러

147/148**브레이크 테스트**   5.99달러

147**타이어 압력 점검**   3.99달러

소계   52.96달러
세금   4.38달러
총계   **57.34달러**

Tabor's에서의 여러분의 경험에 관해 듣고 싶습니다! 저희 웹 사이트를 방문하여 위의 주문 번호를 제출하고 설문 조사를 작성하세요. 완료하신 후에, 다른 서비스 구매 시 148**무료 브레이크 테스트를 받을 수 있는 쿠폰을 다운로드할 수 있습니다.**

| 어휘 | mechanic 정비사   synthetic 합성   puncture (타이어에 난) 펑크   pressure 압력   subtotal 소계   experience 경험   submit 제출하다   voucher 쿠폰, 할인권

147. 추론 문제
Tabor's는 어떤 종류의 업체일 것 같은가?
(A) 차량 정비소
(B) 자동차 영업소

(C) 렌터카 대리점
(D) 운전 학원

| 해설 | 세부 항목으로 제시된 오일 교환(Oil Change), 타이어 펑크 수리(Tire Puncture Repair), 브레이크 테스트(Brake Test), 타이어 압력 점검(Tire Pressure Check) 등으로 볼 때, 자동차 정비소에서 발행한 영수증인 것으로 유추할 수 있으므로 정답은 (A)이다.

| 어휘 | dealership 영업소   institute 학원, 교육원

148. 세부 사항을 묻는 문제
설문 조사 응답자들은 쿠폰으로 얼마를 절약할 수 있나?
(A) 3.99달러
(B) 4.38달러
(C) 5.99달러
(D) 12.99달러

| 해설 | 영수증 하단에서 설문 조사를 완료한 후에, 무료 브레이크 테스트 쿠폰을 다운로드할 수 있다고(you can download a voucher for a free brake test) 제시되어 있고, 중반부에 브레이크 테스트(Brake Test)의 가격은 5.99달러로 확인되므로 정답은 (C)이다.

149-150 다음 이메일을 참조하시오.

수신: Marion Knox
발신: Fernando Lugo
날짜: 3월 19일
제목: 테이크아웃 컵

Marion 귀하,

¹⁴⁹저희 프로젝트를 맡아주실 수 있을 것이라니 기쁩니다. 전화상으로 말씀드렸듯이, 저희 커피숍에서 차가운 음료들의 새로운 조리법을 개발했고, 그것들을 특별한 컵에 담아 제공하고자 합니다. 다음 제안 사항들을 유념해 주시기 바랍니다:

¹⁴⁹문구: Bueno 카페에서 즐거운 여름을!
이미지: Bueno 카페 로고와 더불어 여름과 관련된 이미지 2-3개
크기: 2 x 3인치의 인쇄 영역

¹⁵⁰저희 로고는 보통 네이비 블루로 인쇄되지만, 이번 프로젝트에서는 다른 아이디어들도 받아들일 준비가 되어 있는 상황입니다. 귀하가 제시하는 것을 보고 싶은데요. 고객 자문단에게 선보일 몇 가지 시제품을 4월 3일까지 실물 크기 모형으로 만들어야 하니, 3월 31일까지 ¹⁴⁹저에게 초안을 보내주시기 바랍니다. 정말 감사합니다!

Fernando

| 어휘 | take on 맡다, 떠맡다   recipe 조리법, 요리법   keep in mind 염두에 두다   following 다음의   suggestion 제안 사항   associated with ~와 관련된   come up with 제시하다, 내놓다   first draft 초안   prototype 시제품   mock up 실물 크기 모형으로 만들다   consumer

feedback panel 고객 자문단

149. 추론 문제
Knox 씨는 무엇을 전문으로 할 것 같은가?
(A) 시장 분석
(B) 그래픽 디자인
(C) 요리법 개발
(D) 금융 관리

| 해설 | Knox 씨는 이메일의 수신자로, 도입부에 프로젝트를 맡아줄 수 있을 것이라니 기쁘다고(I'm glad that you will be able to take on our project) 한 것, 이후 디자인 관련 세부 제안 사항들(Text: / Images: / Size:)을 명시한 것, 두 번째 단락에 3월 31일까지 초안을 보내달라고(Please send your first drafts to me) 요청한 것을 통해, Knox 씨는 컵 등을 디자인하는 그래픽 디자이너일 것으로 유추할 수 있으므로 정답은 (B)이다.

| 어휘 | analysis 분석   finance 금융, 재정

🔺고난도
150. True 문제
새로운 컵에 관해 사실인 것은 무엇인가?
(A) 다른 음료용 컵들보다 더 작을 것이다.
(B) 3월 31일에 고객들에게 선보여질 것이다.
(C) 재료는 재활용할 수 있는 것이어야 한다.
(D) 색채 배합이 아직 결정되지 않았다.

| 해설 | 두 번째 단락에 저희 로고는 보통 네이비 블루로 인쇄되지만, 이번 프로젝트에서는 다른 아이디어들도 받아들일 준비가 되어 있는 상황이라며(Our logo is usually printed in navy blue, but for this project, we're open to other ideas) 수신자가 제시하는 것을 보고 싶다고 한 것을 통해, 아직 로고를 인쇄할 색상을 결정하지 않았음을 알 수 있으므로 정답은 (D)이다.

| 어휘 | material 재료, 소재   recyclable 재활용할 수 있는   color scheme 색채 배합

151-152 다음 광고를 참조하시오.

<Move 월간 매거진>

건강에 좋을 뿐만 아니라 즐거운 취미를 찾고 계신가요? <Move 월간 매거진>은 여러분이 멋진 달리기의 세계를 탐험할 수 있게 도와드릴 수 있습니다! ¹⁵¹저희 독자들 대부분이 장거리 경주에 참가한 것은 고사하고 러닝머신에 발을 올려본 적도 없으셨다는 것을 알고 있습니다. 그것은 문제가 되지 않습니다! 저희 기사들이 여러분에게 동기를 부여하고 여러분에게 맞는 달리기 운동을 찾도록 도와드릴 것입니다. 많게는 50퍼센트까지 광고로 가득 차 있는 다른 많은 스포츠 잡지들과 달리, 저희는 여러분에게 광고가 없는 경험을 제공합니다. ¹⁵²매월 호는 전문 운동선수들과 코치들에 의해 특별히 고안된 운동 일과들을 제공합니다. 여러분의 수준을 찾고, 단계들을 따르며, 여러분의 달리기 시간이 나아지는 모습을 지켜보세요. 구독하시려면 www.movemonthlymag.com을 방문하세요.

| 어휘 | enjoyable 즐거운   navigate 항해하다, 길을 찾다   set foot 발을 들여놓다   treadmill 러닝머신   let alone ~는 고사하고, 말할 것도 없이   long-distance 장거리   race 경주   get motivated 동기가 부여되다   workout 운동   be filled with ~로 가득 차다   ad-free 광고가 없는   issue (잡지 등의) 호   routine 일과   athlete 운동선수   follow 따르다, 따라 하다   subscribe 구독하다

151. 추론 문제
잡지의 의도된 독자는 누구일 것 같은가?
(A) 운동복 디자이너들
(B) 전문 운동선수들
(C) 달리기 초보자들
(D) 신발 판매원들

| 해설 | 잡지 광고로, 초반부에 독자들 대부분이 장거리 경주에 참가한 것은 고사하고 러닝머신에 발을 올려본 적도 없다는 것을 알고 있다고(We understand that most of our readers have never set foot on a treadmill, let alone entered a long-distance race) 제시되어 있는 것을 통해, 달리기 초보자들을 위한 잡지임을 알 수 있으므로 정답은 (C)이다.

| 어휘 | sportswear 운동복

152. 세부 사항을 묻는 문제
광고에 따르면, 잡지에서 찾아볼 수 있는 것은 무엇인가?
(A) 추천 경로
(B) 스포츠 광고
(C) 훈련 일정
(D) 제품 후기

| 해설 | 후반부에 매월 호는 전문 운동선수들과 코치들에 의해 특별히 고안된 운동 일과들을 제공한다고(Each issue offers workout routines specially designed by professional athletes and coaches) 제시되어 있으므로 정답은 (C)이다.

| 어휘 | route 경로, 노선

| 패러프레이징 | workout routines → Training schedules

153-154 다음 문자 메시지 대화를 참조하시오.

Nella Lettiere [오전 7:52]
제가 막 토론토 공항에 도착했는데, ¹⁵³렌터카 대리점에서 제 예약을 분실했어요. 이용 가능한 차량들이 없고, ¹⁵⁴Vance 플라자까지 택시를 타면 아주 비쌀 텐데. 어떻게 해야 할까요?

Kwangseok Jang [오전 7:55]
알겠어요. 학회로 곧장 가는 대신에 ¹⁵⁴5번 출구에서 Eldridge 호텔로 가는 무료 셔틀버스를 타세요.

Nella Lettiere [오전 7:56]
고마워요! 그런 선택지가 있는 줄 몰랐어요.

Kwangseok Jang [오전 7:57]
첫 번째 프레젠테이션이 몇 시죠?

Nella Lettiere [오전 7:58]
10시예요. ¹⁵⁴그래서 제 가방들을 내려놓고 나서 걸어서 갈 시간이 될 거예요.

| 어휘 | lose 분실하다, 잃어버리다   reservation 예약   available 이용 가능한   expensive 비싼   go straight 곧장 가다   exit 출구   drop off 내려놓다   head over 향하다   on foot 걸어서

153. 의도 파악 문제
오전 7:55에 Jang 씨가 "알겠어요"라고 쓸 때 의미하는 것은 무엇일 것 같은가?
(A) 그는 메시지를 전달하는 것을 처리할 것이다.
(B) 그는 문제를 해결할 방안을 생각했다.
(C) 그는 Lettiere 씨가 필요한 서류를 가지고 있다.
(D) 그는 Lettiere 씨에게 확인 번호를 보낼 수 있다.

| 해설 | 이는 앞서 렌터카 대리점에서 예약을 분실(the car rental agency lost my reservation) 이용 가능한 차량들이 없고, Vance 플라자까지 택시를 타면 아주 비쌀 것이라며(There are no vehicles available, and a cab to Vance Plaza would be very expensive) 어떻게 해야 할지(What can I do) 물은 것에 대한 응답으로, 뒤이어 대신 무료 셔틀버스를 타라(take the free shuttle)는 해결책을 제시하고 있다. 이를 통해 Lettiere 씨의 상황을 알고 해결 방안을 생각했음을 알리고자 이 말을 한 것임을 알 수 있으므로 정답은 (B)이다.

| 어휘 | pass along 전달하다   confirmation 확인

🔺고난도
154. 추론 문제
Eldridge 호텔에 관해 암시된 것은 무엇인가?
(A) 교통 서비스에 요금을 부과한다.
(B) Lettiere 씨의 예약을 올바르게 처리하지 않았다.
(C) 업계 학회를 주최하고 있다.
(D) Vance 플라자까지 걸어갈 수 있는 거리에 있다.

| 해설 | 도입부에 Vance 플라자까지 택시를 타면 아주 비쌀 것이라는(a cab to Vance Plaza would be very expensive) Lettiere 씨의 말에 Kwangseok Jang이 5번 출구에서 Eldridge 호텔로 가는 무료 셔틀버스를 타라고(take the free shuttle from exit 5 to the Eldridge Hotel) 제안하고 있다. 이를 마지막에 Nella Lettiere가 가방들을 내려놓고 나서 걸어서 갈 시간이 있을 것이라고(That'll give me time to drop off my bags and then head over on foot) 한 것과 연계해 볼 때, Eldridge 호텔에서 Vance 플라자까지 걸어서 갈 수 있다는 것을 유추할 수 있으므로 정답은 (D)이다.

| 어휘 | charge 부과하다, 청구하다   fee 요금   transportation 교통, 운송   process 처리하다   correctly 올바르게, 정확하게   host 주최하다   within walking distance 걸어갈 수 있는 거리에

| 패러프레이징 | on foot → within walking distance

155-157 다음 회람을 참조하시오.

수신: 모든 고객 서비스 담당자
발신: 유통 관리자, Kenneth Greer
날짜: 1월 15일
주제: 긴급

주말 동안 IT 팀이 모든 컴퓨터에 새로운 청구서 발송 소프트웨어를 설치했습니다. ─[1]─. 그 소프트웨어는 고객들의 전기와 가스 월 사용량을 보다 쉽게 추적할 수 있도록 고안된 것입니다. [155]소프트웨어가 설치되었을 때, 정확한 설치 날짜 대신 기본 날짜인 1월 1일이 사용되었습니다. ─[2]─. [155]이로 인해 고객들에게 1월 청구서가 자동으로 다시 발송되었습니다. ─[3]─.

[157]저희는 이 문제가 해결됐을 것으로 생각하지만, 다음 청구서들이 발송될 때까지는 확실히 알 수 없을 것입니다. ─[4]─. 청구서를 또 받는 것은 고객을 화나고 혼란스럽게 할 수 있으니, [156]향후 며칠 내에 많은 사람들이 저희에게 연락할 것으로 예상하고 있습니다. 여러분에게 전달되는 모든 전화에 확실히 응답해 주시기 바랍니다.

| 어휘 | urgent 긴급한   install 설치하다   billing software 청구서 발송 소프트웨어   track 추적하다   monthly usage 월 사용량   electricity 전기   default date 기본 날짜   correct 정확한   automatically 자동으로   upset 화나게 하다   confuse 혼란스럽게 하다   forward to ~에게 전달하다

155. 주제/목적 문제
회람은 주로 무엇에 관한 것인가?
(A) 왜 일부 청구서 발송 오류가 발생했는지
(B) 왜 어떤 서비스가 더 비싸지게 되었는지
(C) 새로운 소프트웨어를 어떻게 설치하는지
(D) 에너지 사용량을 어떻게 확인하는지
| 해설 | 첫 번째 단락 후반부에 소프트웨어가 설치되었을 때, 정확한 설치 날짜 대신 기본 날짜인 1월 1일이 사용되었다고(When the software was installed, the default date—January 1—was used instead of the correct installation date) 한 후, 이로 인해 고객들에게 1월 청구서가 자동으로 다시 발송되었다고(This caused the bills for January to be automatically sent out to customers again) 문제 사실을 알리고 있으므로 정답은 (A)이다.
| 어휘 | occur 발생하다

156. 세부 사항을 묻는 문제
Greer 씨가 직원들이 하기를 원하는 것은 무엇인가?
(A) IT 부서에 문제를 알리는 것
(B) 고객 불만을 처리하는 것
(C) 자신들의 컴퓨터에 있는 정보를 백업하는 것
(D) 정보 회의에 참석하는 것
| 해설 | 두 번째 단락 후반부에 많은 사람들이 연락할 것으로 예상하고 있다고(we are expecting a lot of people to contact us ~) 한 후, 전달되는 모든 전화에 확실히 응답해 주시기 바란다고(Please make sure you answer any calls forwarded to you) 했으므로 정답은 (B)이다.
| 어휘 | handle 처리하다   complaint 불만   informational 정보의, 정보를 제공하는

🔼 고난도
157. 문장 삽입 문제
[1], [2], [3], [4]로 표시된 곳 중에 다음 문장이 들어가기에 가장 적절한 곳은?
"유감스럽게도, 그것은 앞으로 몇 주 동안 일어나지 않을 것입니다."
(A) [1]
(B) [2]
(C) [3]
(D) [4]
| 해설 | 제시된 문장은 주어인 that이 가리키는 것이 명시된 문장 뒤에 들어가야 함을 알 수 있는데, 몇 주 동안 일어나지 않을 것은 두 번째 단락 초반부에 언급된 다음 청구서들이 발송되는 것이므로, 이 문제가 해결됐을 것으로 생각하지만, 다음 청구서들이 발송될 때까지 확실히 알 수 없을 것이라고(We believe the issue has been resolved, but we won't know for certain until the next series of bills is sent out) 한 문장 뒤인 (D)가 정답이다.

158-160 다음 서식을 참조하시오.

Sunshine 커튼

서비스 개요

고객:	Jason Elsner
커튼 유형:	연필 모양 주름
직물:	핑크 가든 플라워 (#298)
상세:	커튼 교체 ([160]요금 면제; 아래 참조)
[158]주문을 받은 사람:	Denise Cowen
주문에 배정된 사람:	Rose Navarro

크기 (길이 x 너비): 152cm x 165cm
솔기: 섹션 1 (상부 10cm), 섹션 2 (좌측 5cm), [159]섹션 3 (우측 5cm), 섹션 4 (하부 10cm)

섹션 1: 5cm마다 갈고리 모양 고리가 있는 연필 모양 주름
섹션 2: 연한 분홍색 술 장식 (색상 P21)
[159]섹션 3: 보강용으로 안감을 댈 추가 천 조각
섹션 4: 특별한 지시 사항 없음

주석: [160]이 커튼은 세트 중 직물에 찢어진 곳이 있는 것을 교체한 것입니다.

| 어휘 | overview 개요   pencil pleat 연필 모양 주름   fabric 직물   description 상세, 설명   replacement 교체, 대체   waived 면제된   assigned 배정된   seam 솔기   hook 갈고리   loop 고리   pale pink 연분홍   fringe 술 장식   strip 길고 가느다란 조각   reinforcement 보강, 강화   instructions 지시 사항, 설명   comment 주석, 의견   tear 찢어진 곳

158. 추론 문제
Cowen 씨는 누구일 것 같은가?
(A) 직물 디자이너
(B) 판매 사원
(C) 실내 장식가
(D) 재봉사
| 해설 | Cowen 씨는 서비스 개요 중반부에 주문을 받은 사람으로(Order taken by) 확인되므로 정답은 (B)이다.

고난도

159. 세부 사항을 묻는 문제
고객이 추가 직물을 원하는 곳은 어디인가?
(A) 상부에
(B) 하부에
(C) 우측에
(D) 좌측에
| 해설 | 섹션별 설명에서 섹션 3: 보강용으로 안감을 댈 추가 천 조각(Section 3: Extra strip of lining for reinforcement)이 확인되고, 그 위에 섹션 3은 우측 5cm(right-hand side 5 cm)로 확인되므로 정답은 (C)이다.
| 패러프레이징 | Extra strip of lining → additional fabric

160. 세부 사항을 묻는 문제
Elsner 씨에게 왜 무료로 서비스가 제공될 것인가?
(A) 직원이 잘못된 수치를 적어 두었다.
(B) 구매 시에 쿠폰이 사용되었다.
(C) 제품이 일부 손상되었다.
(D) 프로젝트에 잘못된 직물이 사용되었다.
| 해설 | 서비스 개요 중반부에 요금 면제; 아래 참조(fee waived; see below) 사항이 확인되고, 아래 주석에 이 커튼은 세트 중 직물에 찢어진 곳이 있는 것을 교체한 것이라고(This panel replaces one in a set that had a tear in the fabric) 제시되어 있으므로 정답은 (C)이다.
| 어휘 | note 적어 두다 measurement 수치, 치수 sustain (피해 등을) 입다 damage 손상
| 패러프레이징 | had a tear in the fabric → sustained some damage

161-163 다음 고객 후기를 참조하시오.

Ezell 의류 후기
Sherry Kaplar 작성, 3일 전

저는 Ezell 의류의 단골 쇼핑객으로, 그곳에서 쇼핑할 때마다 항상 아주 좋은 경험을 합니다. 161최근에 너무 긴 것을 빼면 저에게 딱 맞는 리넨 바지를 샀는데요. 그 매장의 현장 서비스를 이용하여 이 문제를 바로잡을 수 있었습니다. 일요일에 구매를 했고, 직원이 제 치수를 쟀습니다. 162월요일 오후에 매장의 누군가가 저에게 전화해서 바지가 준비되었다고 알려줬는데요. 제가 매장을 다시 방문하는 대신 소정의 비용을 지불하고 저희 집까지 배달되도록 부탁했고, 162그것은 바로 다음 날 도착했습니다. 서비스는 처음부터 끝까지 흠잡을 데 없었습니다.

저는 주로 평상복을 구입하지만, 많은 사람들이 Ezell 의류에 대규모의 비즈니스 의류 코너가 있다는 것을 모르더군요. 제 친구들 중 한 명이 최근에 일을 시작했고, 자신의 옷장을 163새롭게 해야 했는데요. 그녀는 한 곳에서 필요했던 것을 모두 찾을 수 있었답니다.

| 어휘 | regular shopper 단골 쇼핑객 recently 최근에 trouser 바지 fit perfectly 딱 맞다 on-site 현장의, 현지의 rectify 바로잡다, 수정하다 take measurements 치수를 재다 fee 요금 impeccable 흠잡을 데 없는 casual clothing 평상복 realize 알다, 알아차리다 extensive 대규모의, 폭넓은 section 코너, 구역 wardrobe 옷장

고난도

161. 추론 문제
Ezell 의류에 관해 암시된 것은 무엇인가?
(A) 관대한 반품 정책을 제공한다.
(B) 수선 서비스를 제공한다.
(C) 하나 이상의 지점을 가지고 있다.
(D) 정기적으로 판촉 행사를 한다.
| 해설 | 초반부에 너무 긴 것을 빼면 딱 맞는 리넨 바지를 샀는데(I purchased some linen trousers that fit me perfectly except for being too long) 현장 서비스를 이용하여 문제를 바로잡을 수 있었다고(I was able to use the shop's on-site service to rectify this problem) 한 것에서 수선 서비스를 제공한다는 것을 유추할 수 있으므로 정답은 (B)이다.
| 어휘 | generous 관대한, 후한 alteration 수선, 변경 branch 지점 promotion 프로모션, 판촉 행사 regularly 정기적으로

162. 세부 사항을 묻는 문제
Kaplar 씨의 제품은 언제 배달되었나?
(A) 일요일에
(B) 월요일에
(C) 화요일에
(D) 수요일에
| 해설 | 첫 번째 단락 중반부에 월요일 오후에 바지가 준비되었다고 전화로 알려줬는데(Someone from the store called me on Monday afternoon to let me know the trousers were ready) 배달을 부탁했고, 바로 다음 날 도착했다고(they arrived the very next day) 했으므로 정답은 (C)이다.

고난도

163. 동의어 문제
두 번째 단락 두 번째 줄에 있는 단어 "update"와 의미가 가장 유사한 것은
(A) 현대화하다, 최신식으로 하다
(B) 알리다, 통지하다
(C) 개조하다
(D) 평가하다
| 해설 | 해당 단어가 들어간 문장은 '제 친구들 중 한 명이 최근에 일을 시작했고, 자신의 옷장을 새롭게 해야 했는데요'라고 해석된다. 따라서 update는 '새롭게 하다, 최신식으로 하다'라는 의미로 쓰인 것이므로 이와 가장 유사한 '현대화하다, 최

신식으로 하다'라는 뜻의 (A) modernize가 정답이다.

164-167 다음 회사 소식지의 기사를 참조하시오.

직원 코너
Neil Reece 작성

이번 달, ¹⁶⁴Dennis Kennedy가 올해 50번째 신규 고객과 계약하게 된 것을 축하하고 싶습니다. Kennedy 씨는 이러한 인상적인 대기록을 달성한 최초의 홍보 이사인 만큼, 그가 매우 자랑스럽습니다. 향후에 Kennedy 씨로부터 더 많은 훌륭한 것들을 기대하고 있습니다.

¹⁶⁵고객들이 Kennedy 씨의 창의적인 광고 캠페인에 끌리는 것은 놀라운 일이 아닙니다. 그는 또한 자신의 팀이 ¹⁶⁶민감한 고객 정보를 보호하는 관행을 취하도록 도왔습니다. 각고의 노력을 통해, 그는 회사가 우수성과 신뢰성에 대한 평판을 발전시켜 나가도록 도왔습니다. 이로 인해, ¹⁶⁷현재 고객들이 우리 업체를 친구들과 지인들에게 추천하여, 저희 고객 기반을 꾸준히 구축해 나가는 데 도움을 주고 있습니다.

| 어휘 | congratulate 축하하다   sign up ~와 계약하다   advertising executive 홍보 이사   reach 도달하다   impressive 인상적인   milestone 획기적인 사건   proud 자랑스러운   be drawn to ~에 끌리다   inventive 독창적인, 창의적인   assist 돕다   adopt 취하다, 채택하다   practice 관행, 관례   sensitive 민감한   reputation 평판, 명성   reliability 신뢰성   acquaintance 지인   customer base 고객 기반   steadily 꾸준히, 지속적으로

고난도

164. 주제/목적 문제

기사는 왜 작성되었나?
(A) 귀중한 고객을 소개하기 위해
(B) 수상자를 축하하기 위해
(C) 승진을 발표하기 위해
(D) 직원의 성취를 인정하기 위해

| 해설 | 첫 번째 단락 도입부에 Dennis Kennedy가 올해 50번째 신규 고객과 계약하게 된 것을 축하하고 싶다고(we'd like to congratulate Dennis Kennedy on signing up his 50th new client of the year) 제시된 것을 통해, 한 직원의 성취를 축하하기 위해 쓴 기사임을 알 수 있으므로 정답은 (D)이다.
| 어휘 | valued 귀중한, 소중한   job promotion 승진   recognize 인정하다   achievement 성취, 업적

165. True 문제

Reece 씨가 Kennedy 씨에 관해 언급한 것은 무엇인가?
(A) 그는 자신의 사업을 시작하고 싶어한다.
(B) 그는 자신의 분야의 자격증을 가지고 있다.
(C) 그는 새로운 팀으로 변경될 것이다.
(D) 그는 창의적인 아이디어들을 가지고 있다.

| 해설 | 두 번째 단락 초반부에 고객들이 Kennedy 씨의 창의적인 광고 캠페인에 끌리는 것은 놀라운 일이 아니라고(It's no surprise that clients are drawn to Mr. Kennedy's inventive ad campaigns) 한 것을 통해, Kennedy 씨가 창의적인 아이디어들을 가지고 있음을 알 수 있으므로 정답은 (D)이다.
| 어휘 | certified 자격증을 소지한   field 분야   creative 창의적인
| 패러프레이징 | inventive → creative

고난도

166. 동의어 문제

두 번째 단락 두 번째 줄에 있는 단어 "sensitive"와 의미가 가장 유사한 것은
(A) 깨지기 쉬운, 취약한
(B) 기밀의, 비밀의
(C) 사려 깊은
(D) 미묘한

| 해설 | 해당 단어가 들어간 문장은 '그는 자신의 팀이 민감한 고객 정보를 보호하는 관행을 취하도록 도왔다'라고 해석된다. 따라서 sensitive는 '민감한, 신중을 요하는'이라는 의미로 이와 가장 유사한 '기밀의, 비밀의'라는 뜻의 (B) confidential이 정답이다.

고난도

167. 추론 문제

업체에 관해 암시된 것은 무엇인가?
(A) 업계의 선두주자이다.
(B) 고객 감사 행사들을 개최한다.
(C) 입소문으로 성장해 왔다.
(D) 새 지점을 열 계획이다.

| 해설 | 두 번째 단락 후반부에 현재 고객들이 업체를 친구들과 지인들에게 추천하여, 고객 기반을 구축해 나가는 데 도움을 주고 있다고(current clients have recommended our business to their friends and acquaintances, helping us to build our customer base steadily) 한 것을 통해, 고객들의 입소문을 통해 성장하고 있다는 것을 알 수 있으므로 정답은 (C)이다.
| 어휘 | leader 선두주자   word of mouth 입소문
| 패러프레이징 | current clients have recommended our business to their friends and acquaintances → word of mouth

168-171 다음 온라인 채팅 토론을 참조하시오.

Patrick Kincaid [오전 9:31]
안녕하세요. 저는 Meridian Enterprises의 Patrick입니다. ¹⁶⁸귀하께서 지붕에 대해 손해 배상 청구를 하셨네요.

Alicia Tidwell [오전 9:33]
네, 맞아요. 최근 폭풍으로 인한 강풍으로 지붕널들의 일부가 날아가고 다른 것들은 느슨해졌어요.

Patrick Kincaid [오전 9:34]
오늘 오후에 피해를 평가하고 ¹⁶⁸저희가 귀하에게 판매했던 보험 증서에 따라 보상되는 것을 알아볼 시간 괜찮으실까요?

Alicia Tidwell [오전 9:35]
그럼요. 몇 시에 오시는 것으로 예상하면 될까요?

Patrick Kincaid [오전 9:36]
제가 오후 1시에 Rosebank에서 청구 건을 평가해야 하는데, ¹⁶⁹Hadley로 돌아오는 것은 교통량에 따라 1시간에서 2시간 반 정도 걸릴 수 있어요.

Alicia Tidwell [오전 9:37]
제 쪽에서 그것은 크게 상관없어요. ¹⁷⁰저는 재택 근무를 하고 있어서, 특별히 뭔가 준비해야 할 게 없거든요.

Patrick Kincaid [오전 9:38]
그러시다니 다행이네요. ¹⁷¹보통 작업은 저 혼자 하는데, 새로운 직원 한 명과 같이 가도록 할게요. 그녀 역시 피해를 산정하여 제가 그 정확성을 확인할 수 있도록 할 거예요.

Alicia Tidwell [오전 9:39]
그것은 문제없어요.

| 어휘 | make a claim for damages 손해 배상 청구를 하다 correct 맞는 high winds 강풍 shingle 지붕널 loosen 느슨하게 하다 assess 평가하다, 산정하다 cover 보장하다 policy 보험 증서 depending on ~에 따라 traffic 교통, 교통량 on one's end ~의 쪽에서, 입장에서 arrangement 준비 normally 보통, 일반적으로 carry out 시행하다, 수행하다 accuracy 정확성, 정확도

🔺고난도
168. 추론 문제
Kincaid 씨는 어디에서 일할 것 같은가?
(A) 인테리어 디자인 스튜디오에서
(B) 정비소에서
(C) 건설 회사에서
(D) 보험 대리점에서

| 해설 | 9:31에 Patrick Kincaid가 상대가 지붕에 대해 손해 배상 청구를 했다고(You made a claim for damages to your roof) 한 것과 9:34에 오늘 오후 피해를 산정하고 판매했던 보험 증서에 따라 보상되는 것을 알아볼(see what is covered under the policy we sold you) 시간이 괜찮을지 묻는 것을 통해, Kincaid 씨는 보험 대리점 직원인 것으로 유추할 수 있으므로 정답은 (D)이다.

🔺고난도
169. 추론 문제
Kincaid 씨에 관해 암시된 것은 무엇인가?
(A) 일부 서류 작업을 기다리고 있다.
(B) 평가가 2시간 넘게 걸릴 수 있다고 생각한다.
(C) 도착 시간을 장담할 수 없다.
(D) 1시에 Tidwell 씨에게 다시 연락할 것이다.

| 해설 | 9:36에 Patrick Kincaid가 오후 1시에 Rosebank에서 청구 건을 평

가해야 하는데, Hadley로 돌아오는 것은 교통 상황에 따라 1시간에서 2시간 반 정도 걸릴 수 있다고(~ but getting back to Hadley could take anywhere between one to two-and-a-half hours, depending on traffic) 한 것을 통해, Tidwell 씨의 집에 도착할 정확한 시간을 장담할 수 없는 상황임을 알 수 있으므로 정답은 (C)이다.

| 어휘 | paperwork 서류 작업 assessment 평가 guarantee 장담하다, 보장하다

170. 의도 파악 문제
오전 9:37에 Tidwell 씨가 "제 쪽에서 그것은 크게 상관없어요"라고 쓸 때 의미하는 것은 무엇인가?
(A) 그녀는 회의를 다른 날로 연기할 수 있다.
(B) 그녀는 다른 장소에서 만나는 것을 꺼리지 않는다.
(C) 그녀는 오후 내내 집에 있을 계획이다.
(D) 그녀는 작업을 위해 충분한 자금을 준비했다.

| 해설 | 이는 도착 시간을 장담할 수 없다는 Kincaid 씨의 메시지에 대한 응답으로, 뒤이어 집에서 일하고 있어서 특별히 뭔가 준비해야 할 게 없다고(I'm working from home, so I don't have to make any special arrangements) 덧붙인 것을 통해, 계속 집에 있을 것이어서 도착 시간이 크게 상관없다고 한 것임을 알 수 있으므로 정답은 (C)이다.

| 어휘 | postpone 연기하다 funds 자금

171. 세부 사항을 묻는 문제
Kincaid 씨가 방문에 대해 평소와 다르다고 말하는 것은?
(A) 약속이 더 오래 지속될 것이다.
(B) 몇몇 특별한 도구들이 필요할 것이다.
(C) 그것이 추가 요금을 발생시킬 것이다.
(D) 한 명 이상의 직원이 참석할 것이다.

| 해설 | 9:38에 Patrick Kincaid가 보통 작업은 혼자 하는데, 새로운 직원 한 명과 같이 가겠다며(Normally, the work would be carried out only by me, but I'll have a new employee with me) 평소와 다른 사실을 알리고 있으므로 정답은 (D)이다.

| 어휘 | appointment 약속 last 지속되다 incur 발생시키다 charge 요금 present 참석한

172-175 다음 이메일을 참조하시오.

수신: Finn Carmichael <f_carmichael@victoriainbox.com>
발신: Myrna Kerr <myrna@becketthistory.org>
날짜: 7월 10일
제목: ¹⁷³Beckett County 역사 박물관

¹⁷³Carmichael 씨 귀하,

Beckett County 역사 박물관을 대표하여, ¹⁷²박물관이 서비스를 개선하는 것을 돕기 위해 수년 동안 재정적 기부를 해주신 것에 대해 감사드리고 싶습니다. 대중의 아낌없는 후원이 없다면 매년 박물관을 방문하는 수천 명의 사람들에게 서비스를 제공할 수 없을 것입니다. ―[1]―.

작년 기금 모금 행사를 통해, 저희는 가장 오래되고 가장 손상되기 쉬운 문서들을 보호하기 위한 온도 조절 진열장을 구입할 수 있었습니다. ―[2]―. 그 전년에는 쌍방향 비디오 투어를 포함하여, 박물관에 대한 정보가 담긴 웹 사이트를 개설했고요.

앞으로는 저희 시설에 구조적인 변경을 진행할 계획인데요. **174휠체어를 사용하는 방문객들을 수용할 수 있도록 양쪽 입구에 경사로를 추가하고 출입구들의 일부를 넓힐 것입니다. 175이것은 매우 야심 찬 프로젝트인데요.** ―[3]―. 저희가 정부 보조금을 신청했고, 시에서 시 예산으로 자금을 보태줄 것입니다. 하지만 여전히 부족분이 있습니다. **173귀하와 같은 지역 주민들이 저희가 차액을 메우도록 도와줄 것이라고 믿습니다.** 공유해 주실 수 있는 어떤 것도 대단히 감사할 것입니다. ―[4]―.

진심을 담아,

Myrna Kerr
Beckett County 역사 박물관 관장

| 어휘 | on behalf of ~을 대표하여, 대신하여   financial 재정적인   contribution 기부   generosity 관대함, 후함   annually 매년   fundraiser 기금 모금 행사   display case 진열장   fragile 손상되기 쉬운, 취약한   launch 개설하다, 출시하다   including ~을 포함하여   interactive 쌍방향의, 대화형의   undergo 진행하다   structural 구조적인   ramp 경사로   entrance 입구   widen 넓히다   doorway 출입구   accommodate 수용하다   ambitious 야심 찬   apply for ~을 신청하다   government grants 정부 보조금   chip in (돈을) 보태다   municipal budget 시의 예산   shortfall 부족분   rely on ~을 믿다, 의존하다   locals 주민   make up the difference 차액을 메우다

172. 주제/목적 문제
Carmichael 씨는 왜 이 이메일을 받고 있나?
(A) 그가 박물관에서 일한 경험이 있기 때문에
(B) 그가 시 의회 의원이기 때문에
(C) 그가 역사 전문가이기 때문에
(D) 그가 박물관에 돈을 기부했기 때문에
| 해설 | 첫 번째 단락 도입부에 박물관이 서비스를 개선하는 것을 돕기 위해 수년 동안 재정적 기부를 해준 것에 대해 감사드리고 싶다고(I would like to thank you for your financial contributions throughout the years to help the museum improve its services) 했으므로 정답은 (D)이다.
| 어휘 | city council 시 의회   donate 기부하다, 기증하다
| 패러프레이징 | your financial contributions → donated funds

🏠 고난도
173. 추론 문제
Carmichael 씨에 관해 암시된 것은 무엇인가?
(A) 박물관 회원을 신청했다.
(B) 박물관에 몇몇 문서들을 기증했다.
(C) 현재 Beckett County에 살고 있다.

(D) 박물관에서 기꺼이 강연을 할 것이다.
| 해설 | Carmichael 씨는 이메일을 받는 수신자로, 제목에 Beckett County 역사 박물관이 제시되어 있고, 마지막 단락에 귀하와 같은 지역 주민들이 저희가 차액을 메우도록 도와줄 것이라고 믿는다고(We rely on locals like you to help us make up the difference) 한 것을 연계해 볼 때, Beckett County에 살고 있는 주민으로 유추할 수 있으므로 정답은 (C)이다.
| 어휘 | sign up for ~을 신청하다, 등록하다   currently 현재   reside 살다, 거주하다   be willing to 기꺼이 ~하다

174. 세부 사항을 묻는 문제
박물관에서 곧 어떤 프로젝트가 시작될 것인가?
(A) 정보를 제공하는 웹 사이트를 개설하는 것
(B) 온도 조절 진열장을 설치하는 것
(C) 소장품에 물품들을 추가하는 것
(D) 건물의 접근성을 개선하는 것
| 해설 | 세 번째 단락에 휠체어를 사용하는 방문객들을 수용할 수 있도록 건물 양쪽 입구에 경사로를 추가하고 출입구들의 일부를 넓힐 것이라고(We will add ramps at both entrances and widen some of the doorways to accommodate visitors who use wheelchairs) 제시되어 있으므로 정답은 (D)이다.
| 어휘 | collection 소장품, 수집품
| 패러프레이징 | add ramps at both entrances and widen some of the doorways → Improving accessibility

175. 문장 삽입 문제
[1], [2], [3], [4]로 표시된 곳 중에 다음 문장이 들어가기에 가장 적절한 곳은?

"그것은 상당한 비용은 말할 것도 없고, 3주간의 시설 폐쇄를 수반합니다."

(A) [1]
(B) [2]
(C) [3]
(D) [4]
| 해설 | 제시된 문장은 주어인 It이 가리키는 것이 명시된 문장 뒤에 들어가야 함을 알 수 있는데, 상당한 비용과 시설 폐쇄가 필요한 것은 앞으로 박물관에서 진행할 프로젝트이므로, 세 번째 단락에 프로젝트에 관해 설명한 후, 이것은 매우 야심 찬 프로젝트라고(This is a very ambitious project) 한 문장 뒤인 (C)가 정답이다.
| 어휘 | entail 수반하다, 필요로 하다   closure 폐쇄   not to mention ~는 말할 것도 없이   considerable 상당한, 많은

176-180 다음 기사와 편지를 참조하시오.

지역 사회 최신 소식
Adrienne Morton 작성

WOODHILL (3월 13일)―**176Lynn 극장이 마침내 건물을 원래 상태로 복원하는 야심 찬 프로젝트를 시작할 준비가 되어 있다고**, Fred Lloyd 전무 이사가 확인해 주었다. 건물 외부는 수십 년간 축적된 오염물을 제거하기 위해 고압 세척될 것이다. 그러나 변화의 대부분은 내부에서 일어나게 될 것이다. [180]인테리어 디자이너인 Zeming Jiang은 이전의 웅장함을 되살리기 위한 노력으로 극장의 옛날 사진들을 보았다. 총 1,000개가 조금 넘는 극장의 모든 좌석들은 관객의 편안함을 극대화하고 화재 안전 규정을 준수하기 위해 교체될 것이다. 메인 강당의 벽면들은 일부분 금박을 바르고, 다시 페인트칠되며, 손상된 목조 부분은 모두 수리될 것이다. [179]극장의 로비 구역도 극적인 탈바꿈을 진행하기로 예정되어 있다. 현재의 선물 가게는 이전 규모로 축소될 것이다. 약 15년 전, 로비의 일부가 선물 가게를 확장하기 위해 분할되었지만, 이 변경 사항이 되돌려질 것이다.

그 공사는 개인 시민들뿐 아니라 Woodhill에 있는 업체들의 후한 기부로 가능하게 되었다. [177]기금 모금 캠페인을 담당했던 Glen Bowers 재무 이사는 그 목표가 1년 내에 도달될 것이라고 예상했다. 그러나 지역 경제의 침체와 다른 자선 프로젝트들과의 경쟁으로 인해, [177]2년 반의 계속되는 노력이 필요했다. 극장은 공사를 위해 폐쇄될 것이지만, Woodhill 지역 사회 극장 공연단은 여전히 Mercer 고등학교에서 임시적으로 연극을 공연할 것이다.

| 어휘 | ambitious 야심 찬   restore 복원하다   exterior 외부   pressure wash 고압 세척하다   pollution 오염   buildup 축적   majority 대부분   in an effort to ~하려는 노력으로   recreate 되살리다, 재현하다   magnificence 웅장함, 장엄   replace 교체하다   maximize 극대화하다   comfort 편안함   comply with ~을 따르다, 준수하다   fire safety regulation 화재 안전 규정   gold leaf 금박   apply 바르다   woodwork 목재 부분, 목공예   be set to ~하기로 예정되어 있다   undergo 진행하다   spectacular 극적인, 장관의   transformation 탈바꿈, 변화   be sectioned off 분할되다   extend 확장하다   reverse 되돌리다   generous 후한   donation 기부   be in charge of ~을 담당하다, 맡다   fundraising 기금 모금   downturn 침체, 하락   competition 경쟁   charity 자선, 자선 단체   ongoing 계속되는, 지속적인

<Woodhill Herald>의 편집자에게:

[178]Lynn 극장에 관한 귀사의 최근 기사에 독자들이 가장 관심이 있을 구체적인 내용들 중 하나—그 장소가 얼마 동안 이용할 수 없을지—가 없는 것 같았습니다. Woodhill 지역 사회 극장 공연단은 그저 그 시설을 이용하는 많은 그룹들 중 하나입니다. 예를 들어, Indira Vaknis와 제가 시티 밴드를 시작해서, 그 극장에서 자주 콘서트를 여는데, 기사에 앞서 어떤 변화에 대해서도 통보받지 못했습니다.

극장이 보수에 들어간다는 점은 기쁘게 생각하지만, [179]로비에 제안된 변화는, 제 의견으로는 잘못된 것입니다. 이는 추가 수익을 창출하는 극장의 역량을 상당히 저해할 것입니다. [180]독자들이 그 프로젝트의 인테리어 디자이너에게 직접 연락하여 대체 방안들을 제안하면 좋겠습니다.

진심을 담아,

Francesco Lund

| 어휘 | lack ~이 없다, 부족하다   unavailable 이용 불가능한   make use of ~을 이용하다   in advance of ~에 앞서   revamp 개조하다   opinion 의견   significantly 상당히, 크게   hinder 저해하다, 방해하다   generate 창출하다   revenue 수익   directly 직접, 곧장   alternative plan 대체 방안

176. 주제/목적 문제

기사의 목적은 무엇인가?
(A) 지역 사회 극장 공연을 홍보하는 것
(B) 모금 행사에 기부하는 방법을 설명하는 것
(C) 극단 회원들을 모집하는 것
(D) 복원 프로젝트를 발표하는 것

| 해설 | 도입부에 Lynn 극장이 마침내 건물을 원래 상태로 복원하는 야심 찬 프로젝트를 시작할 준비가 되어 있다고(Lynn Theater is finally ready to begin an ambitious project to restore the building to its original condition) 제시되어 있으므로 정답은 (D)이다.
| 어휘 | donate 기부하다   fundraiser 모금 행사   acting troupe 극단   restoration 복원
| 패러프레이징 | an ambitious project to restore the building → a restoration project

177. True 문제

기금 모금 캠페인에 관해 제시된 것은 무엇인가?
(A) 극장의 관리자에 의해 감독되었다.
(B) 예상보다 오래 진행되었다.
(C) 다른 자선 단체들을 위한 기금을 모았다.
(D) 업체들에 의해서만 후원을 받았다.

| 해설 | 기사 두 번째 단락에 기금 모금 캠페인을 담당했던 재무 이사는 그 목표가 1년 내에 도달될 것이라고 예상했지만(~ who was in charge of the fundraising campaign, expected the goal to be reached within one year) 지역 경제의 침체와 다른 자선 프로젝트들과의 경쟁으로 인해, 2년 반의 계속되는 노력이 필요했다고(it took two-and-a-half years of ongoing efforts) 제시되어 있으므로 정답은 (B)이다.
| 어휘 | oversee 감독하다   director 관리자, 책임자   gather 모으다

178. 세부 사항을 묻는 문제

Lund 씨는 기사에 어떤 정보가 포함되어 있어야 했다고 생각하는가?
(A) 필요한 기금의 총액
(B) 극장 티켓을 구입하는 절차
(C) 폐쇄 기간
(D) 부지에서 이루어질 변화들

| 해설 | Lund 씨가 보낸 편지 도입부에 Lynn 극장에 관한 귀사의 최근 기사에 독자들이 가장 관심이 있을 구체적인 내용들 중 하나—그 장소가 얼마 동안 이용할 수 없을지—가 없는 것 같았다고(Your recent article on Lynn Theater seemed to lack one of the details that readers would be most interested in—how long the site will be unavailable) 제시되어 있으므로 정답은 (C)이다.

| 어휘 | process 절차, 과정   duration 기간
| 패러프레이징 | how long the site will be unavailable → The duration of the closure

고난도
179. 연계 문제 – True
Lund 씨가 그의 편지에 제시한 것은 무엇인가?
(A) 좌석들이 불편해질 것을 우려하고 있다.
(B) 선물 가게를 더 작게 만들어서는 안 된다고 생각한다.
(C) 로비에 금박을 사용하는 것을 좋아하지 않는다.
(D) 극장의 옛날 사진들이 보관되기를 원한다.
| 해설 | 먼저 기사 첫 단락에 극장의 로비 구역 변화를 언급하며 현재의 선물 가게가 이전 규모로 축소될 것이라고(The current gift shop will be reduced to its former size) 했는데, 편지 두 번째 단락에 로비에 제안된 변화는 잘못된 것이라며 추가 수익을 창출하는 극장의 역량을 상당히 저해할 것이라고(the proposed changes to the lobby are a mistake, in my opinion. This will significantly hinder the theater's ability to generate additional revenue) 제시되어 있으므로 정답은 (B)이다.
| 어휘 | concerned 우려하는   uncomfortable 불편한

180. 연계 문제 – 세부 사항
Lund 씨는 독자들이 누구에게 연락하도록 권장하는가?
(A) Lloyd 씨
(B) Jiang 씨
(C) Bowers 씨
(D) Vaknis 씨
| 해설 | 먼저 Lund 씨가 보낸 편지의 후반부에 독자들이 그 프로젝트의 인테리어 디자이너에게 직접 연락하여 대체 방안들을 제안하면 좋겠다고(I hope readers will contact the interior designer of the project directly to suggest alternative plans) 했는데, 인테리어 디자이너는 기사 첫 번째 단락 중반부에서 Zeming Jiang(Interior designer Zeming Jiang)으로 확인되므로 정답은 (B)이다.

181-185 다음 웹 페이지와 서식을 참조하시오.

www.francisdelorenzo.com

Francis Delorenzo는 커리어 코칭 서비스의 선두적인 제공자입니다. Delorenzo 씨는 비즈니스 세계에서 풍부한 경험을 가지고 있고, 181 (D) 하급 회계사 그리고 후에 Magnolia 주식회사에서 181 (B) 수석 재정 컨설턴트로 일했습니다. 그곳에 재직하는 동안, 그는 상담에 대한 관심을 발전시켜 나갔고 그 분야의 석사 학위를 따기 위해 Anaheim 대학교로 돌아갔습니다. 그는 그 분야에 대한 통찰력을 얻기 위해 자신의 공부를 하면서 파트타임으로 Diana Whitlam 박사의 181 (A) 행정 보조원으로 일했습니다. 석사 학위를 받자마자, 그는 다른 사람들이 잠재력을 최대한 발휘하고 보수가 좋은 진로를 찾도록 돕기 위해 자신의 상담 사업을 시작했습니다.

새로운 분야로 전환하는 것에 관해 생각하고 계시거나, 현재 자신의 분야의 최고로 이동해갈 최선의 방법을 찾고 싶다면, Delorenzo 씨가 도와드릴 수 있습니다. 전국의 고객들이 Delorenzo 씨의 서비스를 이용하여 도움을 받아 왔는데, 182그는 그 서비스에서 오로지 각 고객의 특정한 필요와 목표만을 위해 설계된 프로그램을 만듭니다. 183이전 고객들이 그 서비스에 관해 말한 것을 읽어보시려면, 여기를 클릭하여 링크를 따라가세요.

Delorenzo 씨의 서비스를 예약하는 것에 관심이 있으시면, 647-555-8703으로 전화하세요. Delorenzo 씨는 또한 인터뷰와 공개 석상 출연도 가능합니다. 예약 서식을 요청하시려면 info@francisdelorenzo.com으로 이메일을 보내세요. 서식을 작성하여 제출하신 후에, 미디어 담당관 Sheila Tanner(TV와 라디오 출연) 또는 184언론 담당관 Satoya Kouno(강연과 인쇄 매체 인터뷰)의 연락을 받게 되실 것입니다.

| 어휘 | leading 선두적인   provider 제공자   junior accountant 하급 회계사   master's degree 석사 학위   field 분야   administrative assistant 행정 보조   insight 통찰력   reach one's full potential 잠재력을 최대한 발휘하다   rewarding 보람 있는, 보수가 좋은   transition 전환하다   benefit from ~의 도움을 받다   solely 단지   specific 특정한   public appearance 공개 석상 출연   booking form 예약 서식   lecture 강연   print media 인쇄 매체

Francis Delorenzo 예약 서식

이름: Violet Richardson
이메일 주소: vrichardson@molinopublishing.com
회사/기관: Boyar 주식회사   전화번호: 497-555-8217
행사 유형: 사생활과 직장 생활을 체계화하는 것에 관한 팁을 제공하는 출판물인 184<Take Control> 잡지 인터뷰
제안된 날짜: 인터뷰는 8월 중 언제든 전화로 진행될 수 있음
의견: 제가 직업을 바꾸려고 했을 때, 185동료가 저에게 Delorenzo 씨의 서비스를 소개해 주었습니다. 그 이후로 여러 강연들에 참석했고 그것들이 매우 유용하다는 것을 알게 되었습니다. 저희 독자들이 Delorenzo 씨로부터 많은 것을 배울 수 있을 것으로 알고 있습니다.

| 어휘 | publication 출판물, 출간   organize 체계화하다, 정리하다   personal 개인적인   switch 바꾸다   career 직업, 경력   introduce 소개하다   invaluable 매우 유용한, 귀중한

181. NOT True 문제
Delorenzo 씨가 가졌던 직업으로 언급되지 않은 것은 무엇인가?
(A) 보조원
(B) 재정 고문
(C) 대학 교수
(D) 회계사
| 해설 | 웹 페이지의 첫 단락에 제시된 하급 회계사(a junior accountant)에서

(D), 수석 재정 컨설턴트(a lead financial consultant)에서 (B), 행정 보조원(an administrative assistant)에서 (A)는 모두 Delorenzo 씨가 가졌던 직업으로 확인되므로, 정답은 (C)이다.

| 패러프레이징 | a lead financial consultant → Financial advisor

182. True 문제
웹 페이지에서 Delorenzo 씨의 서비스에 관해 제시한 것은 무엇인가?
(A) 각각의 개인 고객들에게 맞춰진다.
(B) 첫 상담 이후에 이용 가능하다.
(C) 금융 전문가들에 의한 수요가 많다.
(D) 파트 타임 직원들에게 추천된다.

| 해설 | 웹 페이지 두 번째 단락 중반부에, Delorenzo 씨의 서비스에 대해, 오로지 각 고객의 특정한 필요와 목표만을 위해 설계된 프로그램을 만든다고(he creates a program designed solely for each client's specific needs and goals) 제시되어 있으므로 정답은 (A)이다.

| 어휘 | be tailored to ~에게 맞춰지다   initial 처음의, 최초의   be in high demand 수요가 많다   financial professional 금융 전문가

| 패러프레이징 | designed solely for each client's specific needs and goals → tailored to each individual client

고난도
183. 세부 사항을 묻는 문제
방문객들은 링크를 클릭함으로써 무엇을 할 수 있나?
(A) 직업에 관한 조언 읽기
(B) 예약 서식 요청하기
(C) 고객 추천 글 보기
(D) 상담 신청하기

| 해설 | 웹 페이지의 두 번째 단락 후반부에, 이전 고객들이 그 서비스에 관해 말한 것을 읽어보려면, 여기를 클릭하여 링크를 따라가라고(To read what past clients said about the service, click here to follow the link) 알려주고 있으므로 정답은 (C)이다.

| 어휘 | career advice 직업에 관한 조언   testimonial 추천 글

| 패러프레이징 | read what past clients said about the service → View customer testimonials

고난도
184. 연계 문제 - True
Richardson 씨에 관해 사실인 것은 무엇인가?
(A) 8월에 Delorenzo 씨를 방문하기를 원한다.
(B) Kouno 씨의 연락을 받을 것이다.
(C) Delorenzo 씨와 함께 일했었다.
(D) Boyar 주식회사의 설립자이다.

| 해설 | Richardson 씨는 두 번째 지문인 예약 서식의 작성자로, 행사 유형(Type of Event)에서 잡지 인터뷰(Interview for *Take Control* magazine)를 선택한 것을 알 수 있고, 웹 페이지 세 번째 단락 후반부에서 서식을 작성해서 제출한 후에 강연과 인쇄 매체 인터뷰의 경우 언론 담당관 Satoya Kouno가 연락할 것이라고(After completing and submitting the form, you will be contacted by ~ Press Officer Satoya Kouno (for lectures and print media interviews)) 했다. 이를 연계해 볼 때, 잡지 인터뷰를 예약한 Richardson 씨는 Satoya Kouno의 연락을 받을 것임을 알 수 있으므로 정답은 (B)이다.

| 어휘 | founder 설립자

185. 세부 사항을 묻는 문제
Richardson 씨는 처음에 어떻게 Delorenzo 씨에 관해 듣게 되었나?
(A) 잡지 기사를 읽음으로써
(B) 강연에 참석함으로써
(C) TV 프로그램을 시청함으로써
(D) 동료의 추천을 받음으로써

| 해설 | 두 번째 지문인 예약 서식의 Comments에서, 직업을 바꾸려고 했을 때 동료가 Delorenzo 씨의 서비스를 소개해 주었다고(a coworker introduced me to Mr. Delorenzo's services) 제시되어 있으므로 정답은 (D)이다.

| 어휘 | colleague 동료   recommendation 추천

| 패러프레이징 | a coworker → a colleague

186-190 다음 온라인 메시지 보드, 이메일, 웹 페이지를 참조하시오.

http://www.eventplanningworld.com

홈 >> Woodbridge >> 장소 >> 회원 질문

질문
일반 / 특정: __Charleston 플라자__
회원: Devin Hume [10월 3일]
질문: Charleston 플라자는 높은 예약 수수료를 낼 가치가 있나요?

답변
회원: Harold Vela [10월 4일]
저희 보험 회사가 최근에 투자자들을 위한 저희 연례 감사 연회를 위해 Charleston 플라자를 이용했습니다. 그 시설은 현대적이고 세련되어, 손님들에게 좋은 인상을 줄 필요가 있을 때 더할 나위 없이 좋아요. 행사 일에 잠시 정전이 발생해서 프레젠테이션 시작 시간이 지연되었어요. 비록 그것이 Charleston 플라자의 잘못은 아니었지만, ¹⁸⁶그 장소에서 사과의 의미로 저희에게 무료 쿠키와 머핀을 제공해 주었습니다. 며칠 후에 ¹⁸⁷제 사무실에서 손으로 쓴 카드를 받았는데요. 그것은 Maria Martin으로부터 온 것이었고, 그녀는 제 예약에 대해 저에게 감사했고 불편에 대해 다시 한 번 사과했어요. 이런 개인적인 접촉에 아주 깊은 인상을 받았습니다.

| 어휘 | appreciation banquet 감사 연회   investor 투자자   sophisticated 세련된   make a good impression 좋은 인상을 주다   brief 짧은, 잠깐의   power outage 정전   delay 지연시키다   fault 잘못   venue 장소   complimentary 무료의   apology 사과   personal touch 개인적인 접촉

수신: 전 임원진
^{187/189}발신: Maria Martin
날짜: 10월 28일

제목: 환대(서비스) 콘퍼런스

임원진 귀하,

[187]Charleston 플라자의 부지배인으로서, 저는 대중을 대하는 것에 대해 많이 배워왔습니다. [188]다가오는 지역 호텔 콘퍼런스에 참석하도록 저를 선정해 주셔서 대단히 감사합니다. 이는 제가 비슷한 역할을 하는 사람들과 인맥을 형성하고 저희 고객들의 경험을 향상시키는 것에 관해 더 많이 배울 좋은 방법이 될 것입니다. [189]제 직속 상사인 Ayaan Tavada가 작년에 그 행사가 특히 유익했다고 생각했다는 것을 알고 있습니다. 실제로 이 행사에서의 인맥 형성 덕택에, 그는 Woodbridge 관광청의 일자리를 제안받았습니다.

저는 그 콘퍼런스에서 제 시간을 최대한 활용하여 제 전문성 개발을 강화하기 위해 이용할 것입니다.

따뜻한 안부를 전하며,

Maria Martin

| 어휘 | assistant manager 부지배인 deal with ~을 대하다, 다루다 upcoming 다가오는, 곧 있을 network 인맥을 형성하다 role 역할 immediate supervisor 직속 상사 particularly 특히, 특별히 informative 유익한 make the most of ~을 최대한 활용하다 enhance 강화하다, 향상시키다 professional development 전문성 개발

---

www.woodbridge.gov/tourism

Woodbridge 관광청 위원회 책임자들 확정

재무 및 회계 감사 위원회: Siddhi Vadekar, Randolph 호텔
국제 봉사 위원회: [190]Tai Lian, Dalroy 호텔
[189]환대(서비스) 사업 개발 위원회: Ayaan Tavada, Charleston 플라자
행사 및 활동 위원회: [190]Riet Maat, Dalroy 호텔

Woodbridge 관광청은 지역 업체들을 지원하고, 활동들을 주최하고, 시외 방문객들에게 광고함으로써 Woodbridge의 관광 산업을 증진시키기 위해 애쓰고 있습니다. 회의는 매달 첫 번째 월요일 저녁에 열리고 일반인에게 개방됩니다. 회의 시간과 장소를 위해, 555-4997로 전화하세요.

| 어휘 | head 책임자 seek to ~하려고 애쓰다 promote 증진하다, 촉진하다 tourism industry 관광 산업 local business 지역 업체 host 주최하다 advertise 광고하다 out-of-town 시외의 location 장소

---

186. True 문제

Vela 씨가 Charleston 플라자에 대해 언급한 것은 무엇인가?
(A) 1년에 한 번씩 그의 회사에 의해 이용된다.
(B) 그의 단체에 무료 음식을 제공했다.
(C) 장비가 제대로 설치되지 않았다
(D) 웹 사이트가 현대적인 디자인이다.

| 해설 | Vela 씨는 첫 번째 지문인 온라인 메시지 보드에서 답변을 작성한 사람으로 짧은 정전 상황을 언급한 후, 그것이 Charleston 플라자의 잘못은 아니었지만, 그 장소에서 사과의 의미로 무료 쿠키와 머핀을 제공해 주었다고(the venue provided us with complimentary cookies and muffins by way of apology) 했으므로 정답은 (B)이다.

| 어휘 | equipment 장비 properly 제대로

| 패러프레이징 | ·provided → served
·complimentary cookies and muffins → some free food

187. 연계 문제 – True

Vela 씨에 관해 제시된 것은 무엇인가?
(A) 지역에서 가장 큰 보험 회사들 중 한 곳에서 일한다.
(B) 행사 당일에 자신의 손님들에게 프레젠테이션을 할 수 없었다.
(C) Charleston 플라자의 도움으로 새로운 투자자들을 유치했다.
(D) 부지배인으로부터 손으로 쓴 메시지를 받았다.

| 해설 | 온라인 메시지 보드의 답변에 Vela 씨가 사무실에서 손으로 쓴 카드를 받았는데(I received a card written by hand at my office) 그것은 Maria Martin에게서 온 것이라고(It was from Maria Martin ~) 한 것과 이메일에 발신자인 Maria Martin이 첫 단락에 자신이 Charleston 플라자의 부지배인이라고(As the assistant manager of Charleston Plaza) 한 것을 연계해볼 때, Vela 씨는 Charleston 플라자의 부지배인으로부터 손으로 쓴 카드를 받았음을 알 수 있으므로 정답은 (D)이다.

| 어휘 | region 지역 attract 유치하다, 끌다

| 패러프레이징 | a card written by hand → a hand-written message

188. 주제/목적 문제

이메일의 목적은 무엇인가?
(A) 기회에 대한 감사를 표하는 것
(B) 직원들에게 행사에 참여하도록 장려하는 것
(C) 전문성 개발을 위한 자금 제공을 요청하는 것
(D) 콘퍼런스에서 일할 자원봉사자들을 모집하는 것

| 해설 | 첫 번째 단락 초반부에 다가오는 지역 호텔 콘퍼런스에 참석하도록 선택해 줘서 대단히 감사하다고(I am so thankful that you have selected me to attend the upcoming Regional Conference of Hotels) 한 후에, 그것이 많은 도움이 될 것임을 덧붙이고 있으므로 정답은 (A)이다.

| 어휘 | show appreciation 감사를 표하다 funding 자금 제공 recruit 모집하다 volunteer 자원봉사자

189. 연계 문제 – 세부 사항

어느 위원회를 Martin 씨의 상사가 이끄는가?
(A) 재무 및 회계 감사
(B) 국제 봉사

(C) 환대(서비스) 사업 개발
(D) 행사 및 활동

| 해설 | Martin 씨가 이메일 첫 번째 단락 중반부에, 직속 상사인 Ayaan Tavada를(my immediate supervisor, Ayaan Tavada) 언급했고, Ayaan Tavada는 세 번째 지문인 웹 페이지에 환대(서비스) 사업 개발 위원회(Hospitality Business Development Committee)의 책임자로 확인되므로 정답은 (C)이다.

🔺고난도

190. 추론 문제
웹 페이지에서 암시된 것은 무엇인가?
(A) 위원회 책임자들은 일반인에 의해 선출된다.
(B) 대부분의 이사진들은 업체 소유주들이다.
(C) Lian 씨와 Maat 씨는 동료이다.
(D) 단체는 매주 월요일 저녁에 만난다.

| 해설 | 웹 페이지에 위원회 책임자들의 선출 및 이사진의 직업에 관한 (A)와 (B) 내용은 언급되어 있지 않고, 아래 단락에 회의는 매달 첫 번째 월요일 저녁에 열린다고(Meetings are held on the first Monday evening of every month) 제시되어 있으므로 (D)는 답이 될 수 없다. 반면 Tai Lian과 Riet Maat의 소속이 모두 Dalroy 호텔로 확인되는 것으로 볼 때, 두 사람은 같은 업체에서 일하는 동료임을 유추할 수 있으므로 정답은 (C)이다.

| 어휘 | elect 선출하다, 뽑다

191-195 다음 웹 페이지, 이메일, 일정표를 참조하시오.

http://www.icno.org/overview

| 홈 | 개요 | 지난 이벤트 | 티켓 예약 | 연락처 |

비영리 단체들의 국제 학회 (ICNO)
6월 18일, 토요일 ◆ Beacon 컨벤션 센터

ICNO는 비영리 단체들이 그들의 효과를 극대화하고 진정으로 차이를 만들어내도록 돕기 위해 ¹⁹¹ ⁽ᴬ⁾매년 열립니다. ¹⁹¹ ⁽ᶜ⁾런던에서 열렸던 작년 행사에 기록적인 수가 참석한 후, 저희는 올해 베를린에서 열리는 학회에서 더한 성공을 고대하고 있습니다. 지원 서비스가 제공되는 유익한 부스들, 다양한 강연들, 그리고 ¹⁹¹ ⁽ᴰ⁾그 분야의 다른 사람들과 만나 이야기할 수 있는 선택 가능한 저녁 식사가 있을 것입니다.

또한 처음으로 질의응답 세션들을 포함시키게 되어 대단히 기쁩니다. 어느 것을 ¹⁹²택하더라도, 분명 많이 배우게 될 것입니다.

Q&A 세션 (Creston 룸)
자원봉사자 모집 / 오전 9:30-오전 10:30
¹⁹⁴소셜 미디어 마케팅 / 오전 11:00-정오 12:00
기업 기부 / 오후 1:30-오후 2:30
간접비 줄이기 / 오후 3:00-오후 4:00

| 어휘 | annually 매년, 연례의 nonprofit organization 비영리 단체 maximize 극대화하다 effect 영향, 효과 truly 정말로, 진심으로 record 기록적인 attendance 참석자 수 informative 유익한 a wide range of 다양한, 광범위한 lecture 강연 optional 선택적인 field 분야 recruitment 채용, 모집 corporate 기업, 회사 donation 기부 overhead expense 간접비

수신: Lucy Thurman
발신: Conrad Riley
날짜: 6월 9일
제목: ICNO

Lucy 씨 귀하,

ICNO 행사 기획자가 저에게 그들의 다가오는 행사에서 질의응답 세션을 진행해 달라고 요청했어요. ¹⁹³저를 위해 6월 18일 편도 티켓을 예약해 주시면 좋겠어요. 휴가를 위해 베를린에서 며칠 더 머물고 제가 직접 준비할 것이어서 돌아오는 티켓은 필요하지 않아요. 비록 제가 Balanitis역과 Rehbach역 근처에 살고 있지만, 시설이 더 낫기 때문에 ¹⁹⁵Balanitis역에서 출발하고 싶어요. ¹⁹⁴저의 11시 세션을 위해 학회 장소로 갈 충분할 시간이 있도록 ¹⁹⁵오전 9시 30분과 10시 사이에 도착해야 해요. ¹⁹⁵예산 한도는 30유로라는 것을 염두에 두세요.

고마워요!

Conrad

| 어휘 | upcoming 다가오는, 곧 있을 one-way ticket 편도 티켓 vacation 휴가 make an arrangement 준비하다 depart 출발하다 venue 장소 keep in mind 염두에 두다 budget limit 예산 한도

www.eztraintickets.de

티켓 검색 결과: 성인 1, 편도, 라이프치히에서 베를린, 6월 18일

출발 역	출발 시간	도착 시간	가격	운행사
Balanitis	오전 7:56	오전 9:36	34.00유로	Breite
¹⁹⁵Balanitis	오전 8:01	오전 9:41	29.00유로	TRX
Rehbach	오전 7:55	오전 9:48	27.00유로	Schwartz
Rehbach	오전 8:12	오전 10:05	28.00유로	Davoser

191. NOT True 문제
ICNO에 관해 제시되지 않은 것은 무엇인가?
(A) 1년에 한 번 열린다.
(B) 발표자들이 상을 받을 수 있다.
(C) 행사 장소가 달라진다.
(D) 인맥 형성 기회가 있다.

| 해설 | 도입부에 ICNO는 매년 열린다고(ICNO is held annually) 한 것에서 (A), 작년 행사는 런던에서(last year's event in London) 열렸고, 올해는 베를린

에서(in Berlin this year) 열린다고 한 것에서 (C), 단락 마지막에 다른 사람들과 만나 이야기할 수 있다고(you can meet and talk to others in the field) 한 것에서 (D)를 확인할 수 있다. 따라서 정답은 (B)이다.

| 패러프레이징 |
· annually → once a year
· meet and talk to others → networking

192. 동의어 문제
웹 페이지에서 두 번째 단락 첫 번째 줄에 있는 어구 "go for"와 의미가 가장 유사한 것은
(A) 작동하다
(B) 출발하다
(C) 수송하다
(D) 선택하다

| 해설 | 해당 단어가 들어간 문장은 '어느 것을 택하더라도, 분명 많이 배우게 될 것이다'라고 해석된다. 따라서 go for는 '~을 택하다'라는 의미로 쓰인 것이므로 이와 가장 유사한 '선택하다, 고르다'라는 뜻의 (D) choose가 정답이다.

고난도
193. 추론 문제
Riley 씨는 누구에게 이메일을 보낸 것 같은가?
(A) 개인 비서
(B) 기차 회사 직원
(C) 이벤트 기획자
(D) 회의 장소 소유주

| 해설 | 이메일 도입부에 질의응답 세션의 진행을 요청받은 사실을 알리고, 6월 18일 편도 티켓을 예약해 주면 좋겠다고(I would like you to book a one-way ticket for me ~) 한 후, 티켓 예약에 필요한 사항을 구체적으로 알려주고 있으므로, 이런 업무를 진행해 줄 수 있는 사람에 해당하는 (A)가 정답이다.

| 어휘 | assistant 비서, 보조

194. 연계 문제 – 세부 사항
Riley 씨는 학회에서 어떤 주제를 다룰 것인가?
(A) 자원봉사자 모집
(B) 소셜 미디어 마케팅
(C) 기업 기부금
(D) 간접비 줄이기

| 해설 | 이메일 후반부에 본인의 세션이 11시라고(my eleven o'clock session) 하였고, 웹 페이지의 질의응답 세션에서(Q&A Sessions) 오전 11시에(11:00 A.M.–12:00 noon) 예정되어 있는 것은 소셜 미디어 마케팅으로 확인되므로 정답은 (B)이다.

195. 연계 문제 – 추론
Riley 씨는 6월 18일에 어떤 회사를 이용할 것 같은가?
(A) Breite
(B) TRX
(C) Davoser
(D) Schwartz

| 해설 | 이메일에서 Balanitis 역에서 출발하고 싶고(I'd like to depart from Balanitis Station ~), 오전 9:30과 10시 사이에 도착해야 하고(I should arrive between 9:30 and 10 in the morning ~), 예산 한도가 30유로라고(budget limit is €30) 했는데, 이를 바탕으로 시각 자료를 보면 Balanitis 역에서 출발하여 9:30분과 10시 사이에 도착하고 30유로를 넘지 않는 열차의 운행사는 TRX로 확인되므로 정답은 (B)이다.

196-200 다음 광고, 편지, 상품권을 참조하시오.

Keystone 가전의 메가 세일을 놓치지 마세요!

¹⁹⁶Keystone 가전이 Gaviota 브랜드의 가전 제품을 출시하게 되어 기쁩니다. 이 제품들은 오직 Keystone 가전에서만 구입할 수 있습니다! ¹⁹⁶저희는 여러분께 이 제품들의 모든 특징들을 보여드리고 싶은 마음이 간절해, 1월 8일 토요일에 Artesia 지점에서 특별한 행사를 열 것입니다. 하루 종일, 고객들은 무료 다과와 Gaviota 제품들뿐만 아니라 매장 전체에 있는 다른 제품들에 대한 놀라운 할인을 즐기실 수 있습니다. Keystone 로열티 클럽 회원들은 구매에 대해 5% 추가 할인을 받으실 것입니다. 게다가 ¹⁹⁸저희 직원들이 Gaviota 제품의 기능을 시연하는 것을 보시는 분들에게는 경품 추첨 참가 신청서가 제공될 것입니다.

Gaviota의 이 놀라운 신제품들을 볼 기회를 놓치지 마세요!
  G60: 스타일과 기능성을 위한 크롬 전자레인지
  H103: 자동 정지를 위한 수분 센서가 있는 에너지 효율이 높은 드라이어
  ¹⁹⁹K24: 급속 냉동™ 설정을 특징으로 하는 스마트 냉장고
  T990: 내부 공간이 넓고 거의 소음이 안 나는 식기 세척기

1월 8일부터 Keystone 가전에서 이 신제품들과 그 외 것들을 구입하세요!

| 어휘 | appliance 가전 제품 available 구입 가능한 exclusively 오로지, 독점적으로 complimentary 무료의 refreshment 다과 demonstrate 시연하다 feature 기능, 특징 entry form 참가 신청서 prize drawing 경품 추첨 functionality 기능성 energy-efficient 에너지 효율이 높은 moisture 수분 automatic shutoff 자동 정지 refrigerator 냉장고 setting 설정 silent 소음이 안 나는 dishwasher 식기 세척기 spacious 넓은

Carol Cortez
989 Mill Street
San Jose, CA 95136

Cortez 씨 귀하,

축하합니다! ¹⁹⁸귀하는 Keystone 가전 고객들을 대상으로 한 1월 8일 추첨의 대상 당첨자이십니다. 귀하의 경품인 500달러 상품권을 동봉합니다. Keystone 가전에서 저희는 고객들께 긍정적인 경험을 만들어 드리기 위해 최선을 다하고 있습니다. 이런 관점에서, ¹⁹⁷저희 팀에 배달 기

사들을 더 추가했으며, 이는 귀하께서 이전보다 더 빨리 제품을 받으실 수 있음을 의미합니다. 상품권을 즐겁게 사용하시기를 바라며, 곧 귀하에게 서비스를 제공하기를 고대합니다!

진심을 담아,

Sydney Hansen
Keystone 가전 [Artesia 지점], 매장 관리자

| 어휘 | winner 당첨자   grand prize 대상, 1등   enclosed 동봉된   voucher 상품권   create 만들어내다   positive 긍정적인   in light of ~의 관점에서, ~에 비추어   look forward to -ing ~하기를 고대하다

Keystone 가전 상품권

발행일: 1월 8일   상세: 경품 추첨
금액: 500달러

²⁰⁰이 상품권은 모든 Keystone 가전 소매점에서 직접 사용될 수 있습니다. 전액 사용되지 않을 경우, 소지자는 남은 잔액의 새로운 상품권을 발행받게 될 것입니다. ¹⁹⁹상품권은 Gaviota의 K24 구매에는 유효하지 않음을 유념해 주시기 바랍니다. 유효 기간: 10월 31일.

| 어휘 | in person 직접   retail location 소매점   full amount 전액   holder 소지자   issue 발행하다   remaining balance 남은 잔액   valid 유효한   expiration date 유효 기간, 만료일

196. 세부 사항을 묻는 문제
1월 8일 행사의 목적은 무엇이었나?
(A) 국경일을 인정하는 것
(B) 기념일을 축하하는 것
(C) 새로운 브랜드를 소개하는 것
(D) 매장 이전을 준비하는 것

| 해설 | 광고의 첫 번째 단락 초반부에 Keystone 가전이 Gaviota 브랜드의 가전 제품을 출시하게 되어 기쁘다고(Keystone Appliances is pleased to launch the Gaviota brand of appliances) 한 후, 이 제품들의 모든 특징들을 보여주고 싶은 마음이 간절해 1월 8일에 특별한 행사를 열 것이라고(We are excited to show you all the features of these products, so we are holding a special event at the Artesia Branch on Saturday, January 8) 제시되어 있다. 이를 통해, 신제품 출시에 관한 특별 행사임을 알 수 있으므로 정답은 (C)이다.

| 어휘 | national holiday 국경일   celebrate 축하하다, 기념하다   anniversary 기념일   relocation 이전

197. 세부 사항을 묻는 문제
Keystone 가전은 최근에 무엇을 했나?
(A) 배달 직원들을 늘렸음
(B) 배달 요금을 낮췄음
(C) 배달 차량들을 더 구입했음

(D) 배달 구역을 넓혔음

| 해설 | 편지 중반부에 배달 기사들을 더 추가했다고(we have just added more delivery drivers to our team) 제시되어 있으므로 정답은 (A)이다.
| 어휘 | expand 늘리다, 확장하다   lower 낮추다   widen 넓히다
| 패러프레이징 | added more delivery drivers → Expanded its delivery staff

198. 연계 문제 - 추론
Cortez 씨에 관해 암시된 것은 무엇인가?
(A) 1월 8일에 가전 제품을 구입했다.
(B) 로열티 프로그램에 등록했다.
(C) 제품 시연을 보았다.
(D) 구매한 것에 대해 항의를 제기했다.

| 해설 | Cortez 씨는 편지를 받은 수신인으로, 편지 도입부에 축하 인사를 건넨 후 Keystone 가전 고객들을 대상으로 한 1월 8일 추첨의 대상 당첨자라고(You are the winner of the grand prize in the January 8 drawing for Keystone Appliances customers) 알려줬고, 광고 첫 번째 단락 후반부에 직원들이 Gaviota 제품의 기능을 시연하는 것을 보는 사람들에게는 경품 추첨 참가 신청서가 제공될 것이라고(those who watch our employees demonstrate the features of any Gaviota product will be given an entry form for our prize drawing) 제시되어 있다. 이를 연계해 볼 때 Cortez 씨는 시연을 보고 경품 추첨에 참가하여 당첨자가 된 것임을 알 수 있으므로 정답은 (C)이다.
| 어휘 | sign up for ~에 등록하다, ~을 신청하다   make a complaint 항의를 제기하다

199. 연계 문제 - 세부 사항
상품권으로 구입될 수 없는 신제품은 무엇인가?
(A) 전자레인지
(B) 드라이어
(C) 냉장고
(D) 식기 세척기

| 해설 | 상품권 이용과 관련하여 마지막 지문 후반부에 Gaviota의 K24 구매에는 유효하지 않음을 유념하라고(Please note that the voucher is not valid toward the purchase of Gaviota's K24) 제시되어 있는데, 광고에서 K24는 스마트 냉장고(K24: A smart refrigerator)로 확인되므로 정답은 (C)이다.

200. True 문제 [고난도]
상품권에 관해 사실인 것은 무엇인가?
(A) 현금으로 받기 위해 제조사에 반납될 수 있다.
(B) 연말까지 유효하다.
(C) 온라인에서는 이용할 수 없다.
(D) 그 금액은 한 번의 구매에 소비되어야 한다.

| 해설 | 세 번째 지문 도입부에 이 상품권은 모든 Keystone 가전 소매점에서 직접 사용될 수 있다고(This voucher can be used in person at any Keystone Appliances retail location) 제시된 것을 통해, 온라인이 아닌 매장에 직접 방문할 경우 사용이 가능함을 알 수 있으므로 정답은 (C)이다.
| 어휘 | manufacturer 제조사   cash 현금   value 액면 금액

TEST 04

PART 5

101 (C)	102 (B)	103 (D)	104 (D)	105 (D)
106 (C)	107 (B)	108 (B)	109 (A)	110 (C)
111 (B)	112 (B)	113 (D)	114 (C)	115 (C)
116 (B)	117 (B)	118 (C)	119 (C)	120 (C)
121 (D)	122 (B)	123 (B)	124 (C)	125 (C)
126 (B)	127 (C)	128 (D)	129 (C)	130 (C)

PART 6

131 (C)	132 (B)	133 (C)	134 (D)	135 (C)
136 (B)	137 (B)	138 (D)	139 (B)	140 (A)
141 (B)	142 (D)	143 (C)	144 (B)	145 (B)
146 (C)				

PART 7

147 (C)	148 (A)	149 (A)	150 (D)	151 (C)
152 (B)	153 (C)	154 (C)	155 (A)	156 (A)
157 (A)	158 (C)	159 (B)	160 (C)	161 (B)
162 (A)	163 (B)	164 (C)	165 (D)	166 (C)
167 (C)	168 (C)	169 (D)	170 (A)	171 (C)
172 (D)	173 (B)	174 (C)	175 (A)	176 (B)
177 (A)	178 (B)	179 (C)	180 (A)	181 (D)
182 (B)	183 (B)	184 (C)	185 (A)	186 (A)
187 (C)	188 (D)	189 (D)	190 (B)	191 (A)
192 (D)	193 (A)	194 (C)	195 (B)	196 (B)
197 (D)	198 (A)	199 (B)	200 (C)	

PART 5

101. 동사 어휘
Hobbs 제조는 그곳의 모든 직원들에게 연례 장비 운용 강좌를 수강할 것을 요구한다.

| 해설 | 문장의 동사가 들어갈 자리로, 문맥상 '직원들에게 강좌를 수강할 것을 요구한다'라는 의미로 전개되는 것이 적절하므로 '요구하다, 필요로 하다'라는 뜻의 (C) requires가 정답이다.

| 어휘 | annual 연례의   equipment 장비   operation 조작, 운용   course 강의, 강좌   recover 회복하다   appear 나타나다   claim 주장하다

102. 인칭 대명사
그의 보너스 수표는 12월 급여 지급과 같은 날에 발행될 것이다.

| 해설 | 명사 bonus check 앞에 빈칸이 있으므로 명사 앞에 쓸 수 있는 소유격 대명사인 (B) His가 정답이다.

| 어휘 | check 수표   issue 발행하다   salary payment 급여 지급

103. 전치사 어휘
이사회 회원으로서, Lessing 씨는 기업에 영향을 미치는 많은 사안들에 대해 투표할 자격이 있다.

| 해설 | 빈칸은 뒤의 명사구 a board member를 목적어로 받는 전치사가 들어갈 자리인데, 문맥상 '이사회 회원으로서'라는 의미로 자격을 나타내는 전치사가 들어가야 하므로 '~로(서)'라는 뜻의 (D) As가 정답이다.

| 어휘 | be eligible to ~할 자격이 있다   vote 투표하다   issue 사안   affect 영향을 미치다   corporation 기업

🔥 고난도

104. 명사 자리 – 동사의 목적어 | 가산 명사
Plympton 화물의 트럭들은 무거운 짐들을 전국으로 운반한다.

| 해설 | 빈칸은 동사 carry의 목적어 자리이자 형용사 heavy의 수식을 받는 명사가 들어갈 자리이므로 동사 형태인 (C) loaded는 오답이고, '짐 싣는 사람'도 heavy의 수식을 받기에 의미상 어색하므로 (A) loader도 오답이다. load는 가산 명사인데 빈칸 앞에 관사나 소유격 등 한정사가 없으므로 복수형이 되어야 한다. 따라서 복수형인 (D) loads가 정답이다.

| 어휘 | freight 화물 (운송)   loader 짐 싣는 사람   load 짐; 싣다

105. 부사 어휘
몇몇 이사진들은 그 프로젝트에 추가 자금 제공이 필요하다고 완전히 확신하진 않았다.

| 해설 | 빈칸은 convinced를 수식하는 부사 자리로, 문맥상 '완전히 확신하진 않았다'라는 의미로 전개되는 것이 적절하므로 '전적으로, 완전히'라는 뜻의 (D) completely가 정답이다.

| 어휘 | convince 확신시키다, 납득시키다   further 추가의   funding 자금 제공   necessary 필요한   occasionally 때때로   preferably 가급적이면, 오히려   equally 동등하게

106. 동사의 형태와 시제
Miller 씨가 병가로 사무실을 떠나 있는 동안 Romero 씨가 그의 교육 업무를 처리할 것이다.

| 해설 | 빈칸은 문장의 본동사가 들어갈 자리이므로 준동사인 (D) to handle은 오답이고, 뒤에 목적어가 있으므로 수동태인 (B) is handled도 오답이다. 또한 while로 시작되는 시간 부사절의 동사 is가 현재 시제이므로 시제가 맞지 않는 (A) handled도 오답이다. 시간/조건 부사절의 현재 시제는 미래 시제를 대신하는 것이므로, 이와 시제가 일치되는 미래 시제 동사인 (C) will handle이 정답이다.

| 어휘 | duties 업무, 의무   medical leave 병가

107. 형용사 자리 – 명사 수식
Sweet Story 베이커리의 직원들은 항상 금요일에 더 활기찬 태도를 가지는 것처럼 보인다.

| 해설 | 명사 attitude와 비교급 부사 more 사이에 빈칸이 있으므로, 빈칸은 명사를 수식하는 형용사 자리이다. 따라서 '활기찬, 쾌활한'이라는 뜻의 형용사인 (B) cheerful이 정답이다.

| 어휘 | attitude 태도, 자세   cheerfully 활기차게   cheerful 활기찬   cheer 환호; 환호하다

108. 부사 자리 – 형용사 수식
두 작가의 문체가 대체로 비슷해서, 사람들이 종종 그들을 혼동한다.
| 해설 | be동사 are와 형용사 similar 사이에 빈칸이 있으므로 빈칸은 형용사를 수식하는 부사 자리이다. 따라서 '대체로, 대략적으로'라는 뜻의 부사인 (C) broadly가 정답이다.
| 어휘 | writing style 문체   author 작가   confuse 혼동하다   broaden 넓히다   broad 넓은   broadly 대체로, 대략적으로   broadness 넓음

고난도
109. 형용사 어휘
그 블로그는 소비자들에게 항상 이용 가능한 최고의 거래를 찾기 위한 팁과 요령들을 제공한다고 주장한다.
| 해설 | 빈칸은 동명사 finding의 목적어 the best deal 뒤 목적격 보어가 들어갈 자리로, 문맥상 '이용 가능한 최고의 거래를 찾기 위한'이라는 의미로 전개되는 것이 적절하므로 '이용 가능한, 유효한'이라는 뜻의 (A) available이 정답이다.
| 어휘 | claim 주장하다   consumer 고객, 소비자   available 이용 가능한, 유효한   straight 곧은, 똑바른   durable 내구성 있는

고난도
110. 부사 어휘 – 문법
달리 명시되지 않는 한 회사의 안내서에 열거된 방침들은 전 직원에게 적용된다.
| 해설 | unless가 이끄는 절에 주어와 동사(it is)가 생략되고 과거 분사 specified만 남은 분사 구문의 의미를 완성해 줄 부사가 들어갈 자리이므로, 형용사이자 대명사인 (D) few는 답이 될 수 없고, 문맥상 '달리 명시되지 않는 한'이라는 의미로 전개되는 것이 적절하므로 '달리'라는 뜻의 (C) otherwise가 정답이다.
| 어휘 | policy 방침, 정책   listed 열거된   handbook 안내서, 편람   apply 적용하다   specified 명시된

111. 관계 대명사
공원에서 자신의 개의 뒤처리를 깨끗이 하지 않는 이들에게 벌금이 부과될 수 있다.
| 해설 | 빈칸은 뒤에 오는 불완전한 절(do not clean ~ the park)의 주어 자리이며, 빈칸 이하가 앞에 있는 대명사 those를 수식하고 있다. 따라서 빈칸에는 불완전한 절의 주어 역할을 하면서 두 절을 이어주는 접속사가 들어가야 하므로 주격 관계 대명사인 (B) who가 정답이다. (A) when, (C) why, (D) where는 모두 접속 부사로 뒤에 완전한 절이 온다.
| 어휘 | fine 벌금   impose 부과하다   clean up after ~의 뒤를 깨끗이 청소하다

112. 현재 분사 vs. 과거 분사
대부분의 고객들은 그 제품의 품질에 실망하지 않았지만, 몇몇 사람들이 그것을 반품했다.
| 해설 | be동사 were 뒤에 빈칸이 있으므로 동사 원형인 (C) disappoint는 오답이고, 주어인 Most customers와 동격이 될 수 없는 명사인 (D) disappointment도 오답이다. 문맥상 고객들이 실망을 느끼는 것이므로 과거 분사인 (B) disappointed가 정답이다. (A) disappointing은 고객들이 실망을 시킨다는 의미이므로 오답이다.
| 어휘 | quality 품질   disappoint 실망시키다   disappointment 실망, 낙담

고난도
113. 명사 어휘
지배인이 부재중일 때는 부지배인이 주간 일정을 세우고 모든 고객 불만을 처리할 것이다.
| 해설 | 전치사 in의 목적어이자 the manager's의 수식을 받는 명사가 들어갈 자리로, 문맥상 '지배인이 부재중일 때는 부지배인이 처리할 것이다'라는 의미가 되는 것이 적절하므로, in one's absence(~가 부재중일 때)라는 표현을 완성하는 (D) absence가 정답이다.
| 어휘 | assistant manager 부지배인   create 만들다   handle 처리하다   complaint 불만   instance 사례, 경우   ability 능력   possession 소유, 보유   absence 부재, 결근

114. 동사의 형태와 시제
문제가 계속되면 실험실 정문에 있는 키패드 잠금 장치가 교체되어야 할 수도 있다.
| 해설 | 빈칸은 부사절 접속사 if절의 3인칭 단수 주어 the problem 뒤에 동사가 들어갈 자리이므로 준동사인 (B) persisting와 주어에 수 일치가 되지 않는 (A) persist는 오답이다. 주절의 동사가 가능성을 나타내는 may need인 것으로 볼 때, 조건 부사절의 동사는 미래 시제를 대신하는 현재 시제 동사가 되어야 하므로 (C) persists가 정답이다.
| 어휘 | lock 잠금 장치   laboratory 실험실   replace 교체하다   persist 계속되다

115. 부사 어휘
합병이 마무리되자마자, Vertox Tech의 직원들은 좋은 소식을 신속히 퍼뜨렸다.
| 해설 | 빈칸은 앞의 동사 spread를 수식해줄 부사가 들어갈 자리로, 문맥상 '좋은 소식을 신속히 퍼뜨렸다'라는 의미로 전개되는 것이 적절하므로 '신속히, 빨리'라는 뜻의 (C) swiftly가 정답이다.
| 어휘 | merger 합병   spread 퍼뜨리다   rigidly 엄격하게, 완고하게   swiftly 신속히, 빨리   logically 논리적으로

116. 전치사 어휘
기계적 결함이 발견된 이래로 안전 검사관이 다음 주에 세 번째로 공장을 검사할 것이다.
| 해설 | 빈칸은 뒤에 있는 명사 the discovery를 목적어로 취하는 전치사가 들어갈 자리로, 문맥상 '기계 결함이 발견된 이래로'라는 의미가 되는 것이 적절하므로 (B) since가 정답이다.
| 어휘 | safety inspector 안전 검사관   examine 검사하다, 조사하다   discovery 발견   mechanical 기계적인

117. 형용사 자리 – 명사 수식
그 자선 단체의 기금 모금 부서의 서로 협력하는 성향이 그곳을 모든 자원봉사자들이 일하기에 즐거운 곳으로 만든다.
| 해설 | 관사 The와 명사 nature 사이에 빈칸이 있으므로 빈칸은 명사를 수식하는 형용사 자리이다. 따라서 '협력적인, 협동하는'이라는 뜻의 형용사인 (B) cooperative가 정답이다. 명사 앞에 명사가 와서 복합 명사가 되기도 하지만 의미상 적절치 않으므로 (A) cooperation은 오답이다.

| 어휘 | nature 특성, 성향   charity 자선 단체   fundraising 기금 모금   pleasant 즐거운   volunteer 자원봉사자   cooperation 협력, 협동   cooperatively 협조적으로, 협력하여

고난도
118. 전치사 어휘
이사진들은 주식 공모에 들어가기 직전에 경영 팀에 변화를 주는 것은 위험할 것이라고 생각한다.
| 해설 | 빈칸은 앞에 있는 heading과 함께 쓰여 뒤에 있는 명사구를 목적어로 가지는 전치사가 들어갈 자리로, 문맥상 '주식 공모에 들어가기 직전에'라는 의미로 전개되는 것이 적절하므로 head into(~로 들어가다) 표현을 완성해줄 (C) into가 정답이다.
| 어휘 | board members 이사진   risky 위험한   management 경영   initial public offering 주식 공모

119. 전치사 어휘
앞으로 3일에 걸쳐, Carson 거리에 있는 버려진 부지가 아름다운 정원으로 변모될 것이다.
| 해설 | 빈칸 뒤에 시간 표현 명사구가 제시되어 있으므로 '~에 걸쳐서, ~ 동안'이라는 뜻의 기간을 나타낼 때 쓰는 전치사인 (C) Over가 정답이다.
| 어휘 | abandoned 버려진   lot 부지   be transformed into ~로 변모되다, 변화되다   sustaining 지탱하는, 유지하는   given ~을 고려해 볼 때

120. 부사 자리 - 부정사 수식
코치의 도움 덕택에, Vincent Salinas는 경쟁력 있게 마라톤에 참가할 준비가 되어 있다.
| 해설 | 문장 끝에 빈칸이 있고 빈칸이 없어도 완전한 문장이 되므로, 빈칸에는 부사가 들어가야 함을 알 수 있다. 따라서 participate를 수식하는 '경쟁력 있게, 경쟁적으로'라는 뜻의 부사인 (C) competitively가 정답이다.
| 어휘 | participate in ~에 참가하다   compete 경쟁하다   competitively 경쟁력 있게, 경쟁적으로   competitive 경쟁적인, 경쟁의

121. 명사 자리 - 동명사의 목적어
풍부한 세부 사항을 포함시킴으로써, 작가는 독자가 쉽게 상상할 수 있는 독특한 세상을 만들어낸다.
| 해설 | 빈칸은 동명사 including의 목적어 자리이며, 형용사 rich의 수식을 받는 명사가 들어갈 자리이고, 문맥상 '풍부한 세부 사항을 포함시킴으로써'라는 의미로 전개되는 것이 적절하므로 '세부 사항, 자세한 정보'라는 뜻의 (D) details가 정답이다.
| 어휘 | include 포함시키다   create 만들어내다   unique 독특한   detailing 세부 장식   detailed 상세한   detailer 판촉 사원, 판매점 지원 담당자

고난도
122. 동사 어휘
여름 인턴십 프로그램에 참여하는 동안, Pineda 씨는 시장 내 잠재적인 틈새를 발견하는 것에 탁월했다.
| 해설 | 빈칸 뒤에 전치사 at이 있으므로 자동사가 들어가야 하고, 문맥상 '발견하는 것에 탁월했다'라는 의미로 전개되는 것이 적절하므로 '탁월했다, 뛰어났다'라는 뜻의 자동사인 (B) excelled가 정답이다.
| 어휘 | participation 참여, 참가   identify 알아보다, 발견하다   potential 잠재적인   gap 틈, 간격   excel 탁월하다, 뛰어나다   instruct 지시하다, 가르치다   guarantee 보증하다, 보장하다

123. 명사 자리 - 동명사의 목적어 | 복합 명사
Belmont 회사는 해외에서 일하고 있는 직원들을 위해 언어 교육과 문화 연구 프로그램을 제공하는 것을 고려하고 있다.
| 해설 | 빈칸은 동명사 providing의 목적어 자리이자, 앞의 명사 language와 함께 복합 명사를 완성해줄 명사가 들어갈 자리로, 문맥상 해외에서 일하는 직원들을 위해 제공하는 것으로는 '언어 교육'이 적절하므로 '교육, 가르침'이라는 뜻의 (B) instruction이 정답이다. (A) instructor도 명사이지만 의미상 적절치 않고, 가산 명사이기 때문에 단수로 쓸 때는 관사나 소유격과 함께 써야 하므로 오답이다.
| 어휘 | consider 고려하다   language 언어   cultural studies 문화 연구   overseas 해외에서   instructor 강사   instruction 교육, 가르침

고난도
124. 전치사 자리
기금 모금 만찬 중에 받는 돈의 액수에 따라 박물관 직원이 기업 기부자들에게 연락을 취할 수도 있다.
| 해설 | 빈칸은 뒤에 명사구를 목적어로 가질 전치사가 들어갈 자리이므로, 접속사인 (B) Whether와 (C) Because는 오답이고, 문맥상 '돈의 액수에 따라 연락을 취할 수도 있다'라는 의미로 전개되는 것이 적절하므로 '~에 따라'라는 뜻의 전치사구인 (D) Depending on이 정답이다.
| 어휘 | fundraising dinner 기금 모금 만찬   reach out to ~에게 연락을 취하다   corporate donor 기업 기부자

고난도
125. 분사 자리
Liveta 의류는 매 시즌 말에 팔리지 않은 모든 옷을 재활용하거나 기부하기로 약속했다.
| 해설 | 빈칸이 has와 to부정사 to recycle 사이에 있으므로, 뒤에 있는 to부정사를 목적어로 취할 수 있도록 has와 함께 현재 완료 시제 동사를 완성해줄 과거 분사가 들어가야 함을 알 수 있다. 따라서 (C) promised가 정답이다.
| 어휘 | recycle 재활용하다   donate 기부하다   unsold 팔리지 않은   promptly 지체 없이   prior 앞서, 전의

126. 부사 어휘
누구를 고용할 것인지에 관해 결정하는 것을 연기한 후에, 그 관리자는 결국 최고 대학 출신의 지원자를 선택했다.
| 해설 | 빈칸은 뒤에 있는 동사 selected를 수식해줄 부사가 들어갈 자리로, 앞에 제시된 결정을 연기한 것과 관련 지어 '결국 선택했다'라는 의미로 전개되는 것이 적절하므로 '결국, 마침내'라는 뜻의 (B) eventually가 정답이다.
| 어휘 | put off 연기하다, 미루다   select 선택하다   candidate 지원자   steadily 꾸준히   eventually 결국, 마침내   thoroughly 철저히   formerly 이전에, 예전에

127. 명사 자리 – 전치사의 목적어
비용이 1천만 달러가 넘기 때문에 유권자들은 제안된 예배당 복원에 관해 엇갈린 견해를 가지고 있다.

| 해설 | 빈칸은 전치사 about의 목적어 자리이며, proposed의 수식을 받는 명사가 들어갈 자리이므로 '복원, 복구'라는 뜻의 명사인 (C) restoration이 정답이다.

| 어휘 | voter 유권자, 투표자 mixed 엇갈린 opinion 견해, 의견 proposed 제안된 chapel 예배당 cost 비용 restore 복원하다 restorable 복원할 수 있는 restoration 복원, 복구

128. 부사 자리 – 동사 수식
간식과 배터리 같은 막판 구매 품목들은 판매를 높이기 위해 전략적으로 계산대 복도 근처에 놓여진다.

| 해설 | be동사 are와 분사 placed 사이에 빈칸이 있으므로, 빈칸은 동사를 수식하는 부사 자리이다. 따라서 '전략적으로'라는 뜻의 부사인 (D) strategically가 정답이다.

| 어휘 | last-minute purchase 막판 구매 checkout 계산대 aisle 통로 increase 늘리다 strategize 전략을 세우다 strategic 전략적인 strategy 전략 strategically 전략적으로

고난도

129. 동사 어휘
아주 유사한 가방이 남겨져 있었기 때문에 Roth 씨의 여행 가방은 다른 승객이 실수로 가져간 것 같다.

| 해설 | 빈칸은 문장의 동사가 들어갈 자리로, 문맥상 '비슷한 가방이 남겨져 있으니 다른 승객이 가방을 잘못 가져간 것 같다'라는 의미로 전개되는 것이 적절하므로 (C) appears가 정답이다.

| 어휘 | suitcase 여행 가방 passenger 승객 by mistake 실수로, 잘못해서 leave behind 뒤에 남겨두다, 두고 가다 vacate 비우다 relieve 완화시키다, 안도하다 appear ~인 것 같다 arrange 마련하다, 준비하다

고난도

130. 명사 어휘
Kim Welsh 책의 인기 때문에 Avalon 영화사는 영화 판권을 취득할 가능성에 즐거워하고 있다.

| 해설 | 빈칸은 Avalon 영화사가 즐거워하는 이유가 될 명사가 들어갈 자리로, 문맥상 '영화 판권을 취득할 가능성에 즐거워하다'라는 의미로 전개되는 것이 적절하므로 '가능성, 전망'이라는 뜻의 (C) prospect가 정답이다.

| 어휘 | popularity 인기 be delighted with ~에 기뻐하다 acquire 취득하다 movie right 영화 판권 preference 선호 distress 괴로움 prospect 가능성, 전망 summary 요약, 개요

PART 6

131-134 다음 회람을 참조하시오.

발신: Theo Jaworski

수신: 전 직원들
날짜: 9월 22일
주제: 주 출입구

¹³¹기다리는 시간을 줄이기 위한 시도로, 주 출입구에서의 보안 점검 구성이 변경될 것입니다. 새로운 시스템은 10월 4일 월요일에 ¹³²시작될 것입니다. 그날 아침부터 직원들은 건물에 들어갈 때 고속 라인을 이용할 것이고, 그저 자신들의 사원증만 보여주면 될 것입니다. ¹³³방문객들은 일반 라인을 이용할 것이고 질문을 받을 수도 있습니다.

출입 절차에 관한 ¹³⁴모든 불만 사항은 보안 사무실로 보내져야 합니다. 여러분의 의견은 향후 변경에 고려될 것입니다.

| 어휘 | entrance 출입구 in an attempt to ~하려는 시도로 reduce 줄이다 configuration 구성, 배치 security check 보안 점검 express 고속의, 급행의 regarding ~ 관한 entry 출입 process 절차, 과정 direct 보내다 security office 보안 사무실 comment 의견, 논평 take into consideration 고려하다, 참작하다

131. 명사 자리 – 동사의 목적어
| 해설 | 빈칸은 reduce의 목적어가 들어갈 자리이므로 명사 자리이다. 따라서 동사인 (A) wait와 (B) waited는 오답이고, 문맥상 '기다리는 시간을 줄이기 위한 시도로'라는 의미로 전개되는 것이 적절하므로 '대기, 기다림'이라는 뜻의 명사 (C) waiting이 정답이다.

고난도

132. 동사 어휘
| 해설 | 빈칸 뒤에 날짜가 제시되어 있고, 바로 뒤 문장에는 그날 아침부터 달라지게 되는 것을 구체적으로 말하고 있다. 따라서 빈칸이 포함된 문장은 주어진 날짜부터 새로운 시스템이 시작된다는 내용으로 전개되는 것이 적절하므로 '시작하다, 실시하다'라는 뜻의 (B) instituted가 정답이다.

| 어휘 | institute 시작하다, 실시하다 overturn 뒤집히다 persuade 설득하다

133. 알맞은 문장 고르기
(A) 사내의 자료들은 항상 그곳에 보관되어야 합니다.
(B) 일부 직원들에 의해 제출된 사진들이 충분히 최신 것이 아니었습니다.
(C) 방문객들은 일반 라인을 이용할 것이고 질문을 받을 수도 있습니다.
(D) 그 지연은 우리 보안 소프트웨어의 오류에 의해 야기되었습니다.

| 해설 | 앞서 직원들이 이용할 라인과 필요한 절차가 제시되어 있는 것으로 볼 때, 그 연장선상에서 방문객들이 이용할 라인과 필요한 절차를 설명하는 내용이 이어지는 것이 가장 적절하므로 (C)가 정답이다.

| 어휘 | in-house 사내의, 내부의 material 자료 submit 제출하다 recent 최근의 standard 일반적인, 보통의 delay 지연 cause 야기하다

고난도

134. 부정 형용사
| 해설 | 빈칸은 뒤에 있는 명사 complaints를 수식할 형용사가 들어갈 자리로, 문

맥상 '모든 불만 사항은'이라는 의미로 전개되는 것이 적절하므로 '모든'이라는 의미로 쓸 수 있는 (D) Any가 정답이다.

| 어휘 | former 이전의, 예전의   further 더 추가된, 더 먼

135-138 다음 기사를 참조하시오.

토론토 (4월 10일)— 캐나다 회사인 Arrington 주식회사의 새로운 음악 스트리밍 서비스인 Melody Mix의 제품 135테스터들뿐만 아니라 회사 직원들도 그 서비스에 대해 엇갈린 반응을 보였다. 예비 사용자들은 그 서비스의 추천 기능이 계획대로 작동하지 않는다고 말한다. 예를 들어, 하드 록을 자주 듣는 사용자가 클래식 음악을 제안받기도 한다는 것이다. 업계 전문가들은 그 회사가 이러한 문제를 바로잡기 위해 서비스의 출시를 연기할 것이라고 136추측했다. Arrington 주식회사는 자사의 현재 음악 서비스의 1,500만 사용자들에 의해 입증되었듯이, 고객들에게 137즐거운 경험을 창출해내는 것으로 유명하다. 138Melody Mix가 그 수치를 3배가 되게 할 것으로 예상된다.

| 어휘 | mixed reaction 엇갈린 반응   preliminary 예비의   state 말하다   recommendation 추천   function 기능   regularly 자주, 정기적으로   suggestion 제안   industry expert 업계 전문가   delay 연기하다, 미루다   release 출시   rectify 바로잡다, 고치다   have a reputation for ~로 유명하다, ~에 명성을 가지고 있다   create 창출하다   demonstrate 입증하다, 보여주다   current 현재의

135. 상관 접속사

| 해설 | 빈칸 앞뒤로 두 개의 명사구가 있고, 그 뒤로 문장의 동사 have provided 가 이어지는 구조이므로, 빈칸에는 두 명사구를 연결해줄 것이 들어가야 함을 알 수 있다. 따라서 '~뿐만 아니라, 게다가'라는 뜻의 상관 접속사인 (C) as well as가 정답이다.

| 어휘 | whereas 반면에

[고난도]
136. 동사 어휘

| 해설 | Industry experts가 주어이고 that절을 목적어로 받는 동사가 들어갈 자리로, 앞서 추천 기능이 제대로 작동하지 않는 것을 언급했으므로, '업계 전문가들이 서비스 출시를 연기할 것이라고 추측했다'고 전개되는 것이 적절하므로 '추측했다, 짐작했다'라는 뜻의 (C) speculated가 정답이다.

| 어휘 | analyze 분석하다   demand 요구하다   argue 주장하다

137. 형용사 자리 - 명사 수식

| 해설 | 관사 an과 명사 experience 사이에 빈칸이 있으므로 빈칸은 명사를 수식하는 형용사 자리이다. 따라서 '즐거운, 재미있는'이라는 뜻의 형용사인 (B) enjoyable이 정답이다.

[고난도]
138. 알맞은 문장 고르기

(A) 웹 사이트를 방문하여 이 로열티 프로그램에 등록하면 된다.

(B) Arrington 주식회사가 곧 본사를 이전할 수도 있다.
(C) 회사 판매원들은 그 상을 탄 것을 기뻐했다.
(D) Melody Mix가 그 수치를 3배가 되게 할 것으로 예상된다.

| 해설 | 앞서 Arrington 주식회사의 현재 음악 서비스를 이용하는 사용자 수가 구체적으로 제시되어 있는 것으로 볼 때, 새로운 음악 스트리밍 서비스인 Melody Mix와 연결 지어 그 서비스 출시로 예상하는 바를 언급하는 문장으로 기사가 마무리되는 것이 적절하므로 (D)가 정답이다.

| 어휘 | sign up for ~에 등록하다   relocate 이전하다   headquarters 본사   win the award 상을 받다   be projected to ~할 것으로 예상되다   triple 3배가 되다   figure 수치

139-142 다음 이메일을 참조하시오.

수신: 사진 촬영 팀
발신: Ermanno Mancini
날짜: 8월 10일
제목: 곧 있을 사진 촬영

사진 촬영 팀 귀하,

Navagio 비치웨어 라인을 위한 다음 사진 촬영이 8월 13일 목요일에 있을 것입니다. 모델들이 9시까지 준비되고 채비되어 있을 것입니다. 139가능하면, 모든 사진 작가들이 7시까지 도착하여 장소들을 살펴보고 장비를 설치하는 것을 도와야 합니다. 사진들은 남성들만으로, 여성들만으로, 또는 140혼합하여 촬영될 것입니다.

사진 촬영은 4시간 정도 걸릴 것으로 예상합니다. 141하지만 하루 종일 현장에 있는 것으로 계획하셔야 합니다. 이것이 필요시에 저희에게 추가 시간을 허용할 것입니다. 갈매기들을 유인할 수 있기 때문에 모든 음식물은 사진 촬영 장소에서 멀리하는 것의 중요성을 142강조해야 합니다.

| 어휘 | take place 개최되다   prep 준비하다   scout 정찰하다, 살펴보다   set up 설치하다   equipment 장비   allow 허용하다, 허락하다   additional 추가의   importance 중요성   keep away from ~에서 멀리하다   attract 유인하다, 끌어들이다   seagull 갈매기

139. 접속 부사

| 해설 | 빈칸은 앞뒤 문장의 의미를 자연스럽게 연결해줄 접속 부사가 들어갈 자리로, 문맥상 '가능하다면 모든 사진 작가들이 7시까지 도착해야 한다'라는 의미로 전개되는 것이 적절하므로 '가능하면'이라는 뜻의 (B) If possible이 정답이다.

| 어휘 | likewise 마찬가지로, 똑같이   on the other hand 다른 한편으로

140. 명사 자리 - 전치사의 목적어

| 해설 | 전치사 with 뒤에 명사가 병렬로 이어진 형태이고, 관사 a 뒤에 빈칸이 있으므로 명사 자리이다. 따라서 '조합, 혼합'이라는 뜻의 명사인 (A) combination이 정답이다.

| 어휘 | combination 조합, 결합   combine 조합되다, 결합시키다

141. 알맞은 문장 고르기

(A) 새로운 장비는 우리가 더 효율적으로 되도록 도와줍니다.
(B) 하지만 하루 종일 현장에 있는 것으로 계획하셔야 합니다.
(C) 저희가 날짜를 정하기 위해 일기 예보를 확인할 것입니다.
(D) 다행히도, 고객이 사진의 모습을 좋아했습니다.

| 해설 | 앞서 사진 촬영 예상 시간을 언급하였고, 뒤이어 이렇게 하면 추가 시간을 가질 수 있다는 내용을 언급한 것을 볼 때, 그 사이에는 예상 시간이 맞지 않고 추가 시간이 필요한 경우를 대비하는 것과 관련된 문장이 삽입되는 것이 적절하므로 역접의 접속 부사 However를 이용해 이를 나타낸 (B)가 정답이다.

| 어휘 | efficient 효율적인   weather report 일기 예보   decide 정하다
fortunately 다행히

142. 동사 어휘

| 해설 | 문장의 동사가 들어갈 자리로, 갈매기를 유인할 수 있으니 음식물을 촬영장에서 멀리해야 한다고 주의를 주는 내용이다. 따라서 '강조하다'라는 뜻의 (D) stress가 정답이다.

| 어휘 | avoid 피하다   appreciate 알아주다, 고마워하다   stress 강조하다

143-146 다음 기사를 참조하시오.

12월 10일—어제 저녁 뉴욕의 한 행사에서 디자이너 Claudia Larmon이 새로운 보석 라인을 143출시했다. Eternal Sparkle로 알려진 그 컬렉션은 격식을 차린 행사와 차리지 않은 다양한 행사들 모두에 적합한 세련되고 현대적인 목걸이와 반지 그리고 귀걸이를 포함한다. 그 보석은 공정 거래를 하는 144공급자들의 원석만 사용한다. 145이는 몇 달에 걸친 Larmon 씨 측의 조사를 통해 이루어졌다. Larmon 씨는 "원석들이 진짜이고 공정한 노동 행위로 생산된 것임을 확실히 하기 위해 146공인된 보석 전문가들을 통해 구입하세요."라고 말하며, 모두에게 책임감 있는 소비자들이 되기를 권장한다.

| 어휘 | jewelry 보석류   fashionable 멋있는, 유행을 따르는   necklace 목걸이   earring 귀걸이   suitable 적합한   a variety of 다양한   occasion 행사, 때   formal 격식을 차린   gemstone 원석   fair-trade 공정 거래   source 출처, 공급자   encourage 권장하다   responsible 책임감 있는   ensure 확실히 하다   authentic 진짜인   labor practice 노동 행위, 노동 관행

143. 동사 어휘

| 해설 | 문장의 동사가 들어갈 자리로, 빈칸 뒤에 있는 목적어 '새로운 보석 라인'과 연계하여 생각해 볼 때, 디자이너가 '새로운 보석 라인을 출시했다'라는 의미로 전개되는 것이 적절하므로 '출시했다'라는 뜻의 (C) launched가 정답이다.

144. 전치사 어휘

| 해설 | 빈칸은 앞의 절과 뒤의 명사구를 연결해 줄 전치사가 들어갈 자리로, 문맥상 '공정 거래를 하는 공급자들의 원석만 사용한다'라는 의미로 전개되는 것이 적절

하므로 출처, 기원 등을 나타낼 때 쓰는 전치사인 (D) from이 정답이다.

145. 알맞은 문장 고르기

(A) 다른 회사들은 새로운 규정에 세심한 주의를 기울이고 있다.
(B) 이는 몇 달에 걸친 Larmon 씨 측의 조사를 통해 이루어졌다.
(C) 고객들은 종종 가격보다 색상에 기반하여 원석들을 선택한다.
(D) 패션 업계에서는 보석이 더 단순화되는 추세가 있어져 왔다.

| 해설 | 앞서 보석 제작에 공정 거래를 하는 공급자들의 원석만 사용한다는 문장이 제시되어 있으므로, Larmon 씨가 그렇게 할 수 있었던 이유를 나타내는 내용의 문장이 이어지는 것이 가장 적절하므로 (B)가 정답이다.

| 어휘 | pay attention to ~에 주목하다   accomplish 이루다, 해내다
based on ~에 기반하여   simplified 단순화된

146. 형용사 자리 - 명사 수식

| 해설 | 빈칸은 뒤에 있는 명사 jewelry experts를 수식해 줄 형용사가 들어갈 자리이므로, '공인된'이라는 뜻의 과거 분사형 형용사인 (C) certified가 정답이다.

| 어휘 | certify 자격증을 교부하다, 증명하다   certified 공인된   certificate 증명서, 자격증

PART 7

147-148 다음 공지를 참조하시오.

Spadaro 고객들에게 알리는 공지:

147Spadaro는 25년 넘게 이 지역에서 골동품 식탁들과 책꽂이 그리고 기타 가구들을 판매하는 유일한 업체인 것이 자랑스럽습니다. 저희 고객들의 편의를 위해, 저희는 남서 지역 어디에든 배달 서비스를 제공하고 있습니다. 저희 물품들은 모두 100년이 넘은 것이기 때문에, 세심한 취급을 요하는 물품들을 다루는 데 익숙한 고도로 숙련된 배달 기사들이 필요합니다. 이것은 높은 임금을 지불해야만 가능합니다. 그래서 148저희가 최근에 배달 요금을 15% 인상했습니다. 이 서비스를 이용하시는 분들께는 저희가 귀하의 물품들의 안전한 운송을 보장하기 위해 노력하고 있음을 이해해 주시기 바랍니다.

| 어휘 | antique 골동품인; 골동품   convenience 편의, 편리   region 지역   highly skilled 고도로 숙련된   be used to -ing ~하는 데 익숙하다   handle 다루다, 취급하다   delicate 세심한 취급을 요하는, 깨지기 쉬운   accomplish 완수하다, 해내다   premium 아주 높은, 고급의   wage 임금   increase 인상하다   ensure 보장하다, 확실히 하다   transport 운송

147. 세부 사항을 묻는 문제

Spadaro는 무엇을 판매하는가?

(A) 식품
(B) 전자 제품

(C) 가구
(D) 도서

| 해설 | 도입부에 Spadaro는 골동품 식탁들과 책꽂이 그리고 기타 가구들을 판매하는 업체라고(Spadaro has been proud to be the area's only seller of antique dining tables, bookcases, and other furnishings ~) 하였으므로 (C)가 정답이다.

| 어휘 | electronics 전자 제품

| 패러프레이징 | antique dining tables, bookcases, and other furnishings → Furniture

148. 세부 사항을 묻는 문제
공지에서 알려진 것은 무엇인가?
(A) 배송 요금 변경
(B) 더 넓은 배송 구역
(C) 지연된 배송 일정
(D) 새로운 배송 방법

| 해설 | 중후반부에 최근에 배달 요금을 15% 인상했다고(we have recently increased the delivery charges by fifteen percent) 알리는 내용이 제시되어 있으므로 정답은 (A)이다.

| 어휘 | method 방법

| 패러프레이징 | increased the delivery charges by fifteen percent → A change in delivery fees

---

149-150 다음 문자 메시지 대화를 참조하시오.

> **Helen Montoya** [오전 10:06]
> 안녕하세요, Cameron. ¹⁴⁹제가 막 Strasburg에서 돌아오는 제 열차가 취소되었다는 것을 알게 되었어요.
>
> **Cameron Reagan** [오전 10:08]
> 사무실로 돌아오지 않을 것이라는 뜻인가요?
>
> **Helen Montoya** [오전 10:09]
> 그곳에 갈 것인데, ¹⁴⁹대신 버스를 타야 해요. 그것은 제가 공석을 위한 단체 면접에 45분 정도 늦을 것이라는 뜻이에요. 그리고 일정을 다시 잡기에는 너무 늦은 상황이고요.
>
> **Cameron Reagan** [오전 10:10]
> 걱정 말아요. ¹⁵⁰지원자들이 컴퓨터 기반 인성 검사를 먼저 받도록 할게요. 그것은 적어도 30분은 걸릴 거예요. 그리고 나서 면접을 시작하기 전에 잠깐 쉬어야 할 것이고요.
>
> **Helen Montoya** [오전 10:11]
> 그러면 되겠네요. 정말 고마워요! 더 가까이 가면 문자 보낼게요.

| 어휘 | find out 알게 되다   open position 일자리 공석   reschedule 일정을 다시 잡다   candidate 지원자   computer-based 컴퓨터 기반의   personality test 인성 검사   text 문자를 보내다

149. 세부 사항을 묻는 문제
Montoya 씨가 가지고 있는 문제는 무엇인가?
(A) 이동 계획을 변경해야 한다.
(B) 면접 세션을 취소해야 한다.
(C) 장소에 가는 방법을 모른다.
(D) 일부 회의록들을 잘못 두었다.

| 해설 | 오전 10:06에 Helen Montoya가 본인의 열차가 취소된 것을 막 알게 되었다고(I just found out that my train back from Strasburg has been canceled) 하였고, 이후 오전 10:09에 대신 버스를 타야 한다고(I have to take the bus instead) 했으므로 정답은 (A)이다.

| 어휘 | get to ~에 도착하다   misplace 잘못 두다

| 패러프레이징 | have to take the bus instead → has to change her travel plans

🔺고난도
150. 의도 파악 문제
오전 10:11에 Montoya 씨가 "그러면 되겠네요"라고 쓸 때 의미하는 것은 무엇인가?
(A) 컴퓨터 프로그램이 충분히 좋다.
(B) 지원자가 빨리 선정되어야 한다.
(C) 활동을 위한 충분한 물품이 있다.
(D) Reagan 씨의 제안이 효과가 있을 것이다.

| 해설 | 이는 앞서 오전 10:10에 Cameron Reagan이 지원자들이 컴퓨터 기반 인성 검사를 먼저 받도록 할 것이고(I'll have the candidates take the computer-based personality test first. ~) 그리고 나서 면접을 시작하기 전에 잠깐 쉬어야 할 것이라고(Then we'll just need to have a short break before beginning the interviews) 한 것에 대한 응답으로, Reagan 씨의 제안이 효과가 있을 것이라는 의미임을 알 수 있으므로 정답은 (D)이다.

| 어휘 | sufficient 충분한   supplies 물품   activity 활동

151-153 다음 일자리 광고를 참조하시오.

> **Finesse 어학 센터**
> finesselanguage.com ◆ 349-555-3165
>
> 4월 1일부터 Finesse 어학 센터가 증가하는 수업의 수요에 맞추기 위해 더 많은 수업들을 추가하여 두 시간 더 늦게까지 문을 열 것입니다. 결과적으로 ¹⁵¹추가 운영 시간을 감당하는 것을 도와줄 시간제 접수 담당자를 찾고 있습니다. 교대 근무 시간은 국경일을 제외하고 매주 월요일부터 토요일까지 4시간에서 6시간 사이일 것입니다.
>
> 이상적인 지원자는 저희 학생들에게 최상의 서비스를 제공하기 위해 ¹⁵² ⁽ᴰ⁾영어와 스페인어 둘 다 유창해야 합니다. 게다가, 저희는 접수 담당자에게 ¹⁵² ⁽ᴬ⁾컴퓨터 사용에 익숙하고 ¹⁵² ⁽ᶜ⁾문서들과 일정을 잘 정리할 것을 요구합니다. ¹⁵³이 직책에 지원하고 싶으시면, 이력서와 과거 또는 현재 고용주의 추천서를 준비하여 그것들을 저희 웹 사이트에 업로드해 주시기 바랍니다.

| 어휘 | keep up with ~에 맞추다, 따라잡다   growing 증가하는   demand 수요   seek 찾다, 구하다   receptionist 접수 담당자   assist 돕다   cover 다루다, 감당하다   shift 교대 근무   range from A to B A에서 B까지의 범위에 있다   national holiday 국경일   ideal candidate 이상적인 지원자   fluent 유창한, 능통한   have a familiarity with ~에 익숙하다, 잘 알고 있다   well organized 잘 정리된   apply for ~에 지원하다   résumé 이력서   letter of recommendation 추천서

151. 세부 사항을 묻는 문제
어학 센터는 왜 접수 담당자를 찾고 있나?
(A) 업체의 새로운 지점이 문을 열 것이다.
(B) 경험 많은 직원이 곧 은퇴할 것이다.
(C) 그곳의 운영 시간이 연장될 것이다.
(D) 걸려오는 전화의 수가 증가했다.

| 해설 | 첫 번째 단락 도입부에 2시간 더 문을 열 것이라는 내용을 전한 후 추가 운영 시간을 감당하는 것을 도와줄 시간제 접수 담당자를 찾고 있다고(we are seeking a part-time receptionist to assist in covering the additional opening times) 제시되어 있으므로 정답은 (C)이다.

| 어휘 | branch 지점   experienced 경험 있는   retire 은퇴하다, 퇴직하다   extend 연장하다   incoming call 걸려오는 전화

| 패러프레이징 | the additional opening times → business hours will be extended

152. NOT True 문제
직책의 요건이 아닌 것은 무엇인가?
(A) 기본적인 컴퓨터 지식
(B) 휴일 근무 기꺼이 하기
(C) 정리 능력
(D) 두 가지 언어를 할 수 있는 능력

| 해설 | 두 번째 단락에 이상적인 지원자는 영어와 스페인어 둘 다 유창해야 한다고(must be fluent in both English and Spanish) 한 것에서 (D), 컴퓨터 사용에 익숙해야 한다고(have a familiarity with using computers) 한 것에서 (A), 문서들과 일정을 잘 정리할 수 있어야 한다고(be able to keep documents and schedules well organized) 한 것에서 (C)는 모두 제시된 요건으로 확인되므로 정답은 (B)이다.

| 어휘 | knowledge 지식   willingness 기꺼이 하기, 기꺼이 하는 마음   organizational 조직적인, 조직의

| 패러프레이징 |
· fluent in both English and Spanish → Ability to speak two languages
· have a familiarity with using computers → Basic computer knowledge
· be able to keep documents and schedules well organized → Organizational skills

153. 세부 사항을 묻는 문제
사람들은 어떻게 그 일자리에 관심을 보일 수 있나?
(A) 전화를 걸어서

(B) 이력서를 이메일로 보내서
(C) 온라인으로 지원해서
(D) 센터를 방문해서

| 해설 | 두 번째 단락 후반부에 이 직책에 지원하고 싶으면, 이력서와 과거 또는 현재 고용주의 추천서를 준비하여 웹 사이트에 업로드하라고(If you would like to apply for the position, ~ upload them on our Web site) 제시되어 있으므로 정답은 (C)이다.

| 어휘 | apply 지원하다

| 패러프레이징 | Web site → online

154-155 다음 이메일을 참조하시오.

수신: Christie Layton <layton.c@bridge-post.com>
발신: Video View Direct <support@videoviewdirect.com>
날짜: 8월 31일
제목: 회신: 계정 #49762

Layton 씨 귀하,

154귀하의 문의와 관련하여, 저희 시스템은 비밀번호가 세 차례 부정확하게 입력되면 고객들이 자신의 비디오 스트리밍 계정에 접속하지 못하게 자동으로 잠깁니다. 이것이 귀하에게 발생한 상황인 것 같습니다. 귀하의 계정을 재설정하려면, 아래 단계를 따르세요.

1. 이곳을 클릭하여 저희 웹 사이트의 올바른 페이지로 연결되는 링크를 따라가세요.
2. 귀하의 계정 번호(#49762)와 임시 비밀번호 9B770QW를 입력하세요. "재설정"을 클릭하여 새로운 비밀번호를 선택하고, 그것을 두 번 입력하세요.
3. 155그런 다음 어떤 영화와 장르를 좋아하는지에 관한 선택할 수 있는 설문지를 보게 될 것입니다. 이 정보를 제공해주실 것을 권고하는데, 그것이 저희 시스템이 귀하에게 더 나은 영화 추천을 하도록 도와줄 것이기 때문입니다.
4. 귀하가 계정을 성공적으로 재설정하셨다는 확인서를 이메일로 보내 드릴 것입니다.

귀하의 애용에 감사드립니다!

Video View Direct 고객 서비스 팀

| 어휘 | inquiry 문의   automatically 자동으로   lock out of 잠가서 못 들어가게 하다   enter 입력하다   incorrectly 부정확하게   case 경우   reset 재설정하다   follow 따르다   correct 정확한   temporary 임시의, 일시적인   optional 선택적인   questionnaire 설문지   urge 권고하다   confirmation 확인서   successfully 성공적으로   patronage 애용

154. 추론 문제
이메일에서 Layton 씨에 관해 암시되는 것은 무엇인가?
(A) Video View Direct의 새로운 고객이다.
(B) 월간 서비스를 업그레이드하고 싶어한다.
(C) 자신의 계정에 접속하는 데 어려움을 겪었다.
(D) 현재 영화 감독으로 일하고 있다.

| 해설 | 첫 번째 단락에 비밀번호가 세 차례 부정확하게 입력되면 계정에 접속하지 못하게 자동으로 잠긴다는(~ our system automatically locks customers out of their video streaming accounts after a password is entered incorrectly three times) 사실을 알린 후, 이것이 귀하에게 발생한 상황인 것 같다고(We believe this is what happened in your case) 한 것을 통해, Layton 씨는 비밀번호 입력 오류로 계정에 접속하지 못했던 것으로 유추할 수 있으므로 정답은 (C)이다.

| 어휘 | have difficulty -ing ~하는데 어려움을 겪다   access 접속하다, 이용하다   currently 현재   film director 영화 감독

155. 세부 사항을 묻는 문제
Layton 씨가 하도록 권장되는 것은 무엇인가?
(A) 온라인으로 선호하는 것을 나타내는 것
(B) 고객 서비스 팀에게 다시 이메일을 보내는 것
(C) 계정 비밀번호를 정기적으로 변경하는 것
(D) 다른 이들에게 그 업체를 추천하는 것

| 해설 | 고객이 따라야 할 단계 3에 어떤 영화와 장르를 좋아하는지에 관한 설문지를 보게 될 것이라며(You will then see an optional questionnaire about which movies and genres you like), 이 정보를 제공할 것을 권고한다고(We urge you to provide this information) 했으므로 정답은 (A)이다.

| 어휘 | indicate 나타내다   preference 선호 사항   regularly 정기적으로

| 패러프레이징 | which movies and genres you like / provide this information → Indicate her preferences online

---

156-158 다음 이메일을 참조하시오.

수신: Sandra Huynh <shuynh@cmai.com>
발신: Trifon Glazkov <tglazkov@kenzieco.com>
날짜: 5월 24일
제목: 예약

Huynh 씨 귀하,

아시다시피, 제가 휴가 시간도 가지고 주요 회사들을 둘러보기 위해 한국으로 여행을 가는 동안 거의 6월 내내 사무실을 비우게 될 거예요. —[1]—. ¹⁵⁶현재 개발 중인 우리의 컴퓨터 프로그램들과 각각을 작업 중인 개별 프로그래머의 연락처 목록을 보내드릴 것입니다. 이것은 그저 참조용일 뿐인데요, 제가 없는 동안 Ruben Fletcher가 제 모든 정규 업무들을 처리할 것이기 때문입니다.

¹⁵⁷Fletcher 씨는 2년 동안 우리 팀의 2인자로 일해 왔고, 모든 직원들과 좋은 업무 관계를 유지하고 있습니다. —[2]—. ¹⁵⁷그가 일주일에 두 번 각 팀장과 만나 진행 상황을 관찰할 것입니다. 저희가 어제 몇 시간 동안 앉아서 ¹⁵⁸얼마간의 만일의 사태에 대비하기 위한 상세한 계획을 세웠습니다. —[3]—. 하지만 현재 상태로는, 모든 것이 순조롭게 진행될 것이라고 전적으로 확신합니다. 부재중일 동안 드물게 제 이메일을 확인할 것이지만, rfletcher@kenzieco.com으로 Fletcher 씨에게 연락하실 수 있습니다. —[4]—.

진심으로,

Trifon Glazkov

| 어휘 | in development 개발 중인   contact information 연락처   individual 개개의   reference 참고, 참조   regular duty 정규 업무   second-in-command 2인자, 부사령관   relationship 관계   progress 진행 상황, 진척   detailed 상세한   contingency 만일의 사태, 우발 사건   confident 확신하는, 자신감 있는   smoothly 순조롭게   somewhat 다소   infrequently 어쩌다, 드물게

156. 추론 문제
Glazkov 씨는 어떤 종류의 업체에서 일하는 것 같은가?
(A) 소프트웨어 회사
(B) 금융 기관
(C) 여행 업체
(D) 잡지사

| 해설 | 첫 번째 단락에 현재 개발 중인 컴퓨터 프로그램들과 각각을 작업 중인 프로그래머의 연락처 목록을 보내줄 것이라고(I will send you a list of our computer programs currently in development ~ the individual programmers working on each one) 제시되어 있는 것을 통해, 소프트웨어 회사의 직원일 것으로 유추할 수 있으므로 정답은 (A)이다.

| 어휘 | financial institution 금융 기관

| 패러프레이징 | computer programs → software

157. 세부 사항을 묻는 문제
Glazkov 씨에 따르면, Fletcher 씨는 무엇을 할 것인가?
(A) 정기 회의들을 여는 것
(B) 상세한 계획을 만들어내는 것
(C) 목록을 이메일로 보내는 것
(D) 새로운 지점을 운영하는 것

| 해설 | 두 번째 단락에 Fletcher 씨에 대해 그가 일주일에 두 번 각 팀장과 만나 진행 상황을 관찰할 것이라고(He will get together twice a week with each team leader to monitor progress) 제시되어 있으므로 정답은 (A)이다.

| 어휘 | regular 정기적인   create 만들어내다   run 운영하다

| 패러프레이징 | get together twice a week with each team leader → Hold regular meetings

158. 문장 삽입 문제 [고난도]
[1], [2], [3], [4]로 표시된 곳 중에 아래 문장이 들어가기에 가장 적절한 곳은?

"그것이 없다면, 이런 오랜 부재에 관해 걱정하게 될 것입니다."

(A) [1]
(B) [2]
(C) [3]
(D) [4]

| 해설 | 제시된 문장은 대명사 it이 있는 것으로 볼 때, 이를 가리키는 것이 구체적으로 언급된 문장 뒤에 들어가야 함을 알 수 있는데, it이 될 수 있는 것은 두 번째 단락 중반부에 있는 상세한 계획(a detailed plan)일 것이므로, 어제 몇 시간 동안 앉아서 얼마간의 만일의 사태에 대비하기 위한 상세한 계획을 세웠다고(made a detailed plan to prepare for a number of contingencies) 한 문장 뒤인 (C)가 정답이다.

| 어휘 | be concerned about ~에 대해 걱정하다   absence 부재

159-160 다음 안내서를 참조하시오.

Enterprise 주식회사

자랑스럽게 Wilmington과 주변 지역에 서비스합니다.

서비스의 개요:
- 회사 문서들의 파쇄 및 처리
- 여러분의 편의를 위한 수거 서비스
- 여러분의 폐기물에 대한 가능한 한 많은 재활용

가격은 양을 기반으로 하니, 견적을 위해 555-0387로 저희에게 전화해 주세요. ¹⁵⁹저희는 수년 동안 기밀 문서들을 처리해왔고 항상 여러분의 자료가 안전하도록 보장할 수 있습니다.

고객 추천 글들:
"제 치과 업무를 디지털 기록으로 바꿀 때, Enterprise 주식회사에 저희 오래된 문서들의 수거를 맡겨 아주 편리했습니다. 그리고 직원이 친절하고 도움이 되었습니다."
— Lauren Tedesco, 5번가 치과

"제 업체를 이전하기 전에, 불필요한 종이 파일들을 없애고 싶었습니다. ¹⁶⁰제가 Enterprise 주식회사에 전화했고, 그들이 바로 당일에 트럭을 보내줄 수 있었습니다. 확실히 향후에 그들을 이용할 것입니다!"
— ¹⁶⁰Charles Merrill, Merrill 회계소

| 어휘 | proudly 자랑스럽게 surrounding 주변의 overview 개요 shredding 파쇄, 파기 disposal 처리, 처분 convenience 편의, 편리 volume 양 estimate 견적 confidential 기밀의 secure 안전한 testimonial 추천 글 dental practice 치과 업무, 치과 운영 switch over to ~로 바꾸다 convenient 편리한 relocate 이전하다 get rid of ~을 없애다, 제거하다 unneeded 불필요한 definitely 확실하게, 분명히

159. True 문제

Enterprise 주식회사에 관해 제시된 것은 무엇인가?
(A) 인터넷 보안에 대한 조언을 제공한다.
(B) 비공개 정보를 취급한 경험이 있다.
(C) 모든 종류의 폐기물을 재활용한다.
(D) 10년 넘게 영업해 오고 있다.

| 해설 | 서비스 개요 아래 단락에 수년 동안 기밀 문서들을 처리해왔다고(We have been disposing of confidential documents for years) 제시되어 있으므로 정답은 (B)이다.

| 어휘 | advice 조언   private 개인의, 비공개의   decade 10년

| 패러프레이징 | have been disposing of confidential documents → has experience handling private information

160. 세부 사항을 묻는 문제

Merrill 씨가 언급하는 서비스의 이점은 무엇인가?
(A) 편리한 위치
(B) 낮은 가격
(C) 빠른 대응
(D) 친절한 직원

| 해설 | Merrill 씨는 두 번째 고객 추천 글 작성자로 전화한 당일에 Enterprise 주식회사가 트럭을 보내줬다고(I called Enterprise Inc., and they were able to send a truck the very same day) 했으므로 정답은 (C)이다.

| 어휘 | convenient 편리한   response 대응, 응답

| 패러프레이징 | send a truck the very same day → The fast response

161-163 다음 기사를 참조하시오.

Business Corner
Diana Keith 작성

BLACKWELL (5월 23일)—Blackwell의 지역 경제가 호황을 누리고 있으며, 전문가들은 이러한 추세가 계속될 것이라고 높은 ¹⁶¹정도의 확신을 가지고 있다. 업체들은 부분적으로 ¹⁶²Blackwell로 숙련된 근로자들을 끌어들이기 위해 지방 정부에 의해 진행된 광고 캠페인들 덕분에, 지난 3년 동안 매 분기 꾸준한 증가를 보여왔다. 기술 분야는 이러한 관행으로부터 특히 혜택을 받아 왔고, 다양한 산업에서의 인상적인 성장이 주목을 받고 있다. "긍정적인 성장 추세 때문에 ¹⁶³제 투자를 위해 Blackwell을 살펴보기 시작했고, 이곳의 업체들이 지역 사회 지원을 잘 받는다는 것도 알고 있습니다."라고 Burnley 사의 ¹⁶³Paul Crawford 가 말했다.

전 경제학 교수이자 현 시 의회 의원인 Gabrielle Velez에 따르면, "더 많은 돈이 Blackwell로 유입되는 것이 사업 확장과 더 많은 일자리들 그리고 더 많은 지출을 야기하고, 그것은 계속 상승할 수 있는 사이클입니다."

| 어휘 | local economy 지역 경제   booming 호황인   degree 수준, 정도   confidence 확신   trend 추세, 동향   steady 꾸준한   quarter 분기   municipal government 지방 정부   skilled 숙련된   sector

분야　particularly 특히　benefit from ~로부터 혜택을 받다　practice 관행　impressive 인상적인　growth 성장　various 다양한　get attention 주목[관심]을 받다　investment 투자　positive 긍정적인　support 지원, 지지　former 이전의　economics 경제학　professor 교수　city council member 시 의회 의원　flow 유입, 흐름　expansion 확장, 확대　spending 지출　go upwards 상승하다

161. 동의어 문제
첫 번째 단락 첫 번째 줄에 있는 단어 "degree"와 의미가 가장 유사한 것은
(A) 온도
(B) 양
(C) 순서
(D) 척도

| 해설 | 해당 단어가 들어간 문장은 '~ 전문가들은 이러한 추세가 계속될 것이라는 높은 정도의 확신을 가지고 있다'라고 해석된다. 따라서 degree는 '정도'라는 의미로 쓰인 것이므로 이와 가장 유사한 '양'이라는 뜻의 (B) amount가 정답이다.

162. True 문제
기사에서 Blackwell의 지방 정부에 관해 언급하는 것은 무엇인가?
(A) 그 도시를 홍보하기 위해 일해오고 있다.
(B) 지역 업체들의 주식을 매입한다.
(C) 최근에 기술을 업그레이드했다.
(D) 회사들에게 더 많은 세금 우대 조치를 제공할 계획이다.

| 해설 | 첫 번째 단락 중반부에 Blackwell로 숙련된 근로자들을 끌어들이기 위해 지방 정부에 의해 진행된 광고 캠페인들(ad campaigns run by the municipal government to attract skilled workers to Blackwell) 덕분에 업체들이 꾸준한 증가를 보여왔다고 제시되어 있으므로 정답은 (A)이다.
| 어휘 | promote 홍보하다　share 주식　tax break 세금 우대 조치
| 패러프레이징 | · municipal government → local government
· ad campaigns → promote

163. 추론 문제
Crawford 씨는 누구일 것 같은가?
(A) 시 의회 의원
(B) 사업 투자자
(C) 대학 교수
(D) 새로운 Blackwell 주민

| 해설 | Crawford 씨는 첫 번째 단락 후반부에 제시된 Paul Crawford로, 투자를 위해 Blackwell을 살펴보기 시작했다고(I started looking at Blackwell for my investments ~) 한 것을 통해, 투자자인 것으로 유추할 수 있으므로 정답은 (B)이다.
| 어휘 | investor 투자자　resident 주민, 거주자

164-167 다음 기사를 참조하시오.

수십 년 동안 사업을 해 온 회사들은 자신들의 오랜 역사와 미래 비전 사이에 균형을 유지할 방법을 찾아야 한다. ―[1]―. 그러한 회사의 하나인 Winthrop 커뮤니케이션이 더 젊은 소비자들에게 모험을 시도하고 있다. 그 회사는 일반 전화 서비스 제공에 기반한 비즈니스 모델로 70년대 초에 설립되었지만, 이제 휴대 전화 기술에 새로운 초점을 맞추고 있다. 그 결과, 164Winthrop은 보다 현대적인 모습을 위해 로고의 이미지와 색상을 조정할 계획이다. "칙칙한 회색과 구식의 이미지들을 버리고 더욱 경쾌하고 쉽게 알아볼 수 있는 것을 만들어야 할 때입니다."라고 Winthrop 대변인 Melanie Myers가 말했다.

"브랜드 이미지를 새롭게 하는 것은 늘 위험이 따르죠."라고 업계 분석가인 Malcolm Collins가 말했다. "하지만 일반 전화에서 모바일 네트워크로 Winthrop이 전환하는 것은 165시기가 좋습니다. 이런 유형의 전환은 최상의 기회의 창을 제공하니, 유사한 조치를 고려하는 회사들은 그것을 염두에 두어야 합니다. ―[2]―."

Winthrop의 야심적인 마케팅 캠페인으로 인해 소비자들은 분명 새로운 로고에 많이 노출된다. Karen Ramirez가 그 캠페인을 담당했다. 166Ramirez는 20년의 경력 동안 기술 관련 마케팅을 중점적으로 해왔고, 167소비자들이 소셜 미디어에서 이야기하고 공유하는 기발한 광고들을 만들어 명성을 쌓아왔다. ―[3]―.

소비자들이 Winthrop을 현대성 및 진보와 관련 짓기 시작하는 데 시간이 걸릴 수 있지만, Winthrop의 CEO인 Jamie Beck은 그것이 노력과 비용을 들일 가치가 있다고 믿는다. ―[4]―. "저희는 창립했을 때와 같은 회사가 아니고, 이를 저희 브랜드 이미지에 반영하기 시작해야 합니다."라고 Beck이 언급했다. Winthrop의 곧 출시될 스마트폰의 성과는 분명 회사가 새로운 통신 세계에서 경쟁할 준비가 되어 있는지 여부에 관한 지표를 제공할 것이다.

| 어휘 | strike a balance 균형을 유지하다　take a chance on ~에 모험을 시도하다　landline telephone 일반 전화　focus on ~에 초점을 맞추다　adjust 조정하다　appearance 겉모습　abandon 버리다　dull 칙칙한　outdated 구식인　upbeat 경쾌한　recognizable (쉽게) 인식 가능한　spokesperson 대변인　analyst 분석가　shift 이동, 전환　favorable 유리한, 좋은　changeover 전환　action 조치　exposure 노출　on account of ~ 때문에　ambitious 야심적인　put in charge of ~의 책임을 맡다　reputation 명성　quirky 기발한, 독특한　associate 관련 짓다　progress 진보, 진척　worth 가치 있는　reflect 반영하다　performance 성과, 실적　indication 지표, 표시

164. 주제/목적 문제
기사는 주로 무엇에 관한 것인가?
(A) 한 회사의 로고 변경
(B) 스마트폰 시장이 직면한 도전
(C) 새롭게 소개된 제품
(D) 소비자 구매 동향

| 해설 | 첫 번째 단락에 Winthrop이 보다 현대적인 모습을 위해 로고의 이미지와 색상을 조정할 계획이라고(~ is planning to adjust the image and color of

its logo for a more modern appearance) 한 후, 그 로고 변경과 관련된 내용이 제시되어 있으므로 정답은 (A)이다.
| 어휘 | face 직면하다   introduced 소개된
| 패러프레이징 | adjust the image and color of its logo → A change in a company's logo

165. 세부 사항을 묻는 문제
Collins 씨가 하도록 권고하는 것은 무엇인가?
(A) 더 많은 이동 전화 기지국을 건설하는 것
(B) 광고들을 더 다채롭게 만드는 것
(C) 대상 시장들을 주의 깊게 조사하는 것
(D) 전환기를 활용하는 것
| 해설 | Collins 씨는 두 번째 단락에 제시된 업계 분석가로, Winthrop의 경우 시기가 좋다며(the timing is favorable), 이런 유형의 전환은 최상의 기회의 창을 제공하니, 유사한 조치를 고려하는 회사들은 그것을 염두에 두어야 한다고(This kind of changeover offers the best window of opportunity, and companies considering similar action should keep that in mind) 했으므로 정답은 (D)이다.
| 어휘 | cell phone tower 이동 전화 기지국   colorful 다채로운   take advantage of ~을 이용하다   transition period 전환기

166. True 문제
Ramirez 씨에 관해 언급된 것은 무엇인가?
(A) 광고로 상을 받았다.
(B) 새로운 스마트폰을 디자인하는 것을 도왔다.
(C) 기술 브랜드 홍보를 전문으로 한다.
(D) 회사의 이름을 줄이는 것을 제안했다.
| 해설 | Ramirez 씨는 세 번째 단락에 제시되었고, 20년의 경력 동안 기술 관련 마케팅을 중점적으로 해왔다고(Ramirez has focused her-twenty-year career on tech-related marketing) 했으므로 정답은 (C)이다.
| 어휘 | specialize in ~을 전문으로 하다   shorten 짧게 하다
| 패러프레이징 | focused ~ on tech-related marketing → specializes in promoting technology brands

167. 문장 삽입 문제
[1], [2], [3], [4]로 표시된 곳 중에 다음 문장이 들어가기에 가장 적절한 곳은?
"회사는 입으로 전달된 소개로부터 힘을 얻기를 바라고 있다."
(A) [1]
(B) [2]
(C) [3]
(D) [4]
| 해설 | 세 번째 단락 후반부에 Ramirez 씨가 소셜 미디어에서 이야기하고 공유하는 기발한 광고들을 만들어 명성을 쌓아왔다고(she has built a reputation for creating quirky ads that consumers talk about and share on social media) 했는데, 소비자들의 이런 행위가 word-of-mouth referrals에 해당함을 알 수 있으므로 그 문장 바로 뒤인 (C)가 정답이다.

| 어휘 | get a boost from ~로부터 힘을 얻다   word-of-mouth 입소문   referral 소개, 추천

168-171 다음 온라인 채팅 토론을 참조하시오.

Alem Semere (오전 10:10)
168화재 안전 인증을 받는 절차에 관해 우리가 할 수 있는 개선에 관한 여러분의 생각을 듣고 싶어요. 171위원회 회의가 목요일에 있어요.

Itsuka Mitani (오전 10:11)
업체들이 그들의 정보를 온라인으로 작성하도록 하는 게 어떨까요? 그것이 보고서들을 완료하는 시간을 절약해줄 거예요.

Philip Kowal (오전 10:12)
현재 조사관들 전용으로 설정되어 있기 때문에, 우리의 온라인 시스템을 완전히 점검해야 할 거예요.

Alem Semere (오전 10:13)
맞아요. 그것은 예산의 상당 부분을 필요로 할 거예요. 169하지만 우리 부서는 분기 말까지 밀린 일을 해결할 방안을 찾아야 해요.

Philip Kowal (오전 10:14)
음, 조사관들을 더 채용할 형편은 안 돼요.

Itsuka Mitani (오전 10:15)
170조사관들을 둘씩 보내는 대신 혼자 보낼 수 있고, 그들이 2차 소견이 필요한 경우 사진을 찍을 수 있어요.

Philip Kowal (오전 10:16)
맞아요! 분명 직원들이 건물들을 혼자 방문하는 것을 꺼리지는 않을 거예요.

Alem Semere (오전 10:17)
좋아요! 171제가 회의에서 이야기할 때 세부 사항을 설명할게요.

| 어휘 | thought 생각   improvement 개선, 향상   fire safety certification 화재 안전 인증   committee 위원회   fill out 작성하다   complete 완료하다   overhaul 점검하다   set up 설정하다   inspector 조사관   portion 부분   budget 예산   backlog 밀린 일   can't afford to ~할 여유가 없다   in pairs 둘씩 짝을 지어   property 건물, 부동산   details 세부 사항

168. 주제/목적 문제
무엇에 관한 논의인가?
(A) 더 많은 업체들을 모집하는 것
(B) 신입 조사관들을 교육하는 것
(C) 인증 절차를 조정하는 것
(D) 온라인 청구 시스템을 시행하는 것

| 해설 | 오전 10:10에 Alem Semere가 화재 안전 인증을 받는 절차에 관해 우리가 할 수 있는 개선에 관한 생각을 듣고 싶다고(I'd like to hear your thoughts on improvements we can make to the process of receiving fire safety certification) 논의의 주제를 제시했으므로 정답은 (C)이다.
| 어휘 | recruit 모집하다, 뽑다 procedure 절차, 방법 implement 시행하다
| 패러프레이징 | improvements we can make to the process of receiving fire safety certification → Adjusting a certification procedure

🏔고난도
169. 추론 문제
글쓴이들에 관해 암시되는 것은 무엇인가?
(A) 연수생 그룹을 감독한다.
(B) 분기마다 한 번씩 회의를 연다.
(C) 화재 안전 수업들을 가르친다.
(D) 업무 일정이 뒤처진 상태이다.

| 해설 | 오전 10:13에 Alem Semere가 분기 말까지 밀린 일을 해결할 방안을 찾아야 한다고(But our department has to find some way to clear the backlog by the end of the quarter) 한 것으로 볼 때, 밀린 일이 있는 상황임을 알 수 있으므로 정답은 (D)이다.
| 어휘 | oversee 감독하다 behind schedule 일정에 뒤처진
| 패러프레이징 | the backlog → behind schedule on their work

170. 의도 파악 문제
오전 10:16에 Kowal 씨가 "맞아요"라고 쓸 때 의미하는 것은 무엇일 것 같은가?
(A) 그는 Mitani 씨의 전략이 도움이 될 것이라는 데 동의한다.
(B) 그는 Mitani 씨가 프로젝트를 처리할 능력이 있다고 생각한다.
(C) 그는 일정에 관한 정보가 더 필요하다.
(D) 그는 Mitani 씨에게 보내진 최신 사진들을 원한다.

| 해설 | 이는 앞서 Itsuka Mitani가 조사관들을 둘씩 보내는 대신 혼자 보낼 수 있고, 그들이 2차 소견이 필요한 경우 사진을 찍을 수 있다고(We could send inspectors alone instead of in pairs, and they could take photos if they needed a second opinion) 한 것에 대한 응답으로, 그 의견에 동의하는 의미로 맞다고(Right) 맞장구친 것임을 알 수 있으므로 정답은 (A)이다.
| 어휘 | strategy 전략 capable of ~할 수 있는

🏔고난도
171. 세부 사항을 묻는 문제
Semere 씨가 목요일에 하려고 계획하는 것은 무엇인가?
(A) 일부 화재 안전 규정들을 검토하는 것
(B) 새 온라인 서식을 업로드하는 것
(C) 위원회 구성원들에게 계획을 발표하는 것
(D) 업무를 위해 더 많은 조사관들을 고용하는 것

| 해설 | 오전 10:10에 Alem Semere가 위원회 회의가 목요일에 있다고(The committee meeting is on Thursday) 한 것과 마지막 오전 10:17에 회의에서 이야기할 때 세부 사항을 설명하겠다고(I'll explain the details when I speak at the meeting) 한 것을 통해, 목요일 위원회 회의에서 세부 사항 즉, 계획을 발표할 것임을 알 수 있으므로 정답은 (C)이다.
| 어휘 | regulation 규정 present 발표하다, 제시하다 task 업무, 일

| 패러프레이징 | explain the details → Present a plan

172-175 다음 공지를 참조하시오.

"동작과 빛"
12월 9일, 오후 7시-오후 10시

¹⁷²Sparkle 스튜디오가 다시 한번 Anaheim 강당에서 연말 댄스 공연을 개최할 것입니다. 무대에서 공연될 정해진 춤 동작들은 안무가 Maria Osborne에 의해 개발되었습니다. 예리한 관찰자는 모든 춤에서 공통적인 남아메리카의 영향을 알아차릴 텐데요, ¹⁷³Osborne 씨가 미국에 있는 자신의 고향인 애틀랜타로 돌아오기 전에 3년 동안 베네수엘라와 칠레에서 문화적 전통을 연구했기 때문입니다. 공연에 이어, Osborne 씨와 몇몇 무용수들과 함께하는 ¹⁷⁵⁽ᶜ⁾질의응답 시간이 있을 것입니다.

행사 입장료는 무료이지만, ¹⁷⁵ ⁽ᴮ⁾저희 프로그램들을 지원하도록 도와줄 금전적인 기부를 받습니다. 직원들이 이를 모금하기 위해 문에 있을 것입니다. 저희는 댄스의 즐거움을 전파하는 데 전념하는 비영리 단체이니, 여러분께서 주실 수 있는 어떤 지원도 매우 감사할 것입니다. ¹⁷⁴저희 웹사이트 www.sparklestudio.org를 방문하시면 저희 스튜디오에 관해 더 알아보시고 ¹⁷⁴작년 공연 클립들을 보실 수 있습니다. 방문객들은 Anaheim 강당의 메인 주차장에 주차하도록 권장되는데, ¹⁷⁵⁽ᴰ⁾그곳은 그날 저녁 오후 5시 이후에는 5달러의 평상시 주차 요금을 부과하지 않을 것입니다.

| 어휘 | host 주최하다 auditorium 강당 routine 정해진 춤 동작 perform 공연하다 develop 개발하다 choreographer 안무가 keen 예리한, 날카로운 observer 관찰자 influence 영향(력) common 공통적인 cultural tradition 문화적 전통 hometown 고향 following ~에 뒤이어 admission 입장(료) financial 재정적인 contribution 기부금 be positioned at ~에 위치해 있다 collect 모금하다, 수집하다 non-profit organization 비영리 단체 dedicated to ~에 전념하는, 헌신하는 spread 퍼뜨리다 impose 부과하다 charge 요금

🏔고난도
172. 주제/목적 문제
공지는 왜 작성되었나?
(A) 자원봉사자들로부터 피드백을 요청하기 위해
(B) 댄스 수업을 광고하기 위해
(C) 스튜디오 이전을 발표하기 위해
(D) 연례 공연을 홍보하기 위해

| 해설 | 첫 번째 단락 도입부에 Sparkle 스튜디오가 다시 한번 Anaheim 강당에서 연말 댄스 공연을 개최할 것이라고(Sparkle Studio is once again hosting its year-end dance show at Anaheim Auditorium) 한 후에, 그 공연에 대해서 구체적으로 알리고 있으므로 정답은 (D)이다.
| 어휘 | solicit 요청하다 volunteer 자원봉사자 relocation 이전
| 패러프레이징 | its year-end dance show → an annual performance

173. True 문제
Osborne 씨에 관해 제시된 것은 무엇인가?
(A) 12월 9일에 댄스 강습을 할 것이다.
(B) 해외에 살았었다.
(C) Sparkle 스튜디오의 설립자이다.
(D) 전에 Anaheim 강당에서 공연을 했었다.

| 해설 | 첫 번째 단락 후반부에 안무가인 Osborne 씨에 대해 미국에 있는 자신의 고향인 애틀랜타로 돌아오기 전에 3년 동안 베네수엘라와 칠레에서 문화적 전통을 연구했다고(Ms. Osborne studied cultural traditions in Venezuela and Chile for three years ~ her U.S. hometown of Atlanta) 제시되어 있는 것을 통해, 3년 동안 해외에서 살았음을 알 수 있으므로 정답은 (B)이다.

| 어휘 | overseas 해외에   founder 설립자

174. True 문제
Sparkle 스튜디오의 웹 사이트에 관해 언급된 것은 무엇인가?
(A) 운전 경로를 제공한다.
(B) 최근에 업그레이드되었다.
(C) 비디오 클립들을 특별히 포함하고 있다.
(D) 등록 서식들이 있다.

| 해설 | 두 번째 단락 중반부에 웹 사이트를 방문하면(You can visit our Web site ~) 작년 공연 클립들을 볼 수 있다고(~ view clips from last year's show) 제시되어 있으므로 정답은 (C)이다.

| 어휘 | driving directions 운전 경로   feature 특별히 포함하다

175. NOT True 문제
행사에 관해 사실이 아닌 것은 무엇인가?
(A) 온라인으로 방송될 것이다.
(B) 기부금이 현장에서 모금될 것이다.
(C) 관객들이 질문을 할 수 있다.
(D) 주차 요금이 면제될 것이다.

| 해설 | 첫 번째 단락 후반부에 공연에 이어, 질의응답 시간이 있을 것이라고(there will be a question-and-answer session) 한 것에서 (C), 두 번째 단락에 프로그램들을 지원하도록 도와줄 금전적인 기부를 받으며(we do accept financial contributions to help support our programs) 직원들이 이를 모금하기 위해 문에 있을 것이라고(Staff members will be positioned at the door to collect these) 한 것에서 (B), 그날 저녁 5시 이후에는 주차 요금을 부과하지 않을 것이라고(~ will not impose the usual $5.00 parking charge on that evening after 5 P.M.) 한 것에서 (D)는 모두 확인되므로 정답은 (A)이다.

| 어휘 | broadcast 방송하다   donation 기부, 기부금   audience member 관객   waive 면제하다

| 패러프레이징 |
· there will be a question-and-answer session → Audience members can ask questions
· accept financial contributions / Staff members will be positioned at the door to collect these → Donations will be collected on-site
· will not impose the usual $5.00 parking charge → The parking fee will be waived

---

176-180 다음 안내와 이메일을 참조하시오.

Lorelei 전자가 세 종의 디지털 카메라 L57, EZ-Shoot, P990에 딸린 약 250,000개의 콘센트 충전기들을 리콜하고 있습니다. 그 카메라들은 올해 2월과 7월 사이에 미국과 캐나다, 그리고 멕시코의 소매점에서 판매되었습니다. [176]충전기들이 깨지기 쉬운 플라스틱으로 만들어져서 심지어 아주 낮은 높이에서 떨어졌을 때도 내부 배선이 노출되면서 쪼개질 수 있습니다.

[177]한 Lorelei 소매점의 판매원이 그 문제를 발견한 직후에 Lorelei 경영진은 자발적인 리콜을 지시하기로 결정했습니다. 그 기기와 관련하여 어떤 상해도 보고되지는 않았습니다.

이 충전기들 중 하나를 소유하고 계신 고객들은 즉시 그것의 사용을 중단하도록 권고됩니다. 결함 있는 기기들은 더 내구성 있는 소재로 만들어진 새 것으로 무료로 교체될 것입니다. 미국과 멕시코에 있는 고객들은 백화점을 포함하여 Lorelei 제품들을 [178]취급하는 어느 매장으로든 그 제품을 가지고 오셔야 합니다. 교체품이 바로 재고가 없을 경우, 그것은 고객이 제공한 주소로 배송될 것입니다. [179]캐나다에 살고 있는 고객들은 우편으로 제품을 돌려보내셔야 합니다. 더 많은 정보를 위해, www.loreleielectronics.com을 방문하세요.

| 어휘 | approximately 대략   wall-plug charger 콘센트 충전기   accompanied 딸린, 동반된   retail store 소매점   fragile 깨지기 쉬운, 취약한   split 쪼개지다, 분리되다   height 높이   expose 노출시키다, 드러내다   internal wiring 내부 배선   executives 경영진   voluntary 자발적인   immediately 바로, 즉시   injury 상해, 부상   in relation to ~와 관련하여   device 기기   be advised to ~하도록 권고되다   faulty 결함 있는   at no charge 무료로   durable 내구성 있는   carry 취급하다   replacement 교체품   be in stock 재고가 있다

수신: [179]Ralph Lindquist <lindquistr@ashworthco.net>
발신: Lorelei 전자 고객 서비스 <service@loreleielectronics.com>
날짜: [180]10월 15일
제목: 회신: 문의
첨부: label.docx

Lindquist 씨 귀하,

저희 카메라 충전기의 리콜에 관한 귀하의 문의를 감사드립니다. 귀하가 저에게 주셨던 정보에 기반하면, [179]귀하는 기기를 우편으로 돌려보내셔야 하는데요. 우편 요금을 지불하지 않도록 인쇄되어 완충재가 들어 있는 봉투에 부착될 수 있는 주소 라벨을 첨부 파일에서 찾아보실 수 있습니다. 현재 저희는 리콜을 처리하는 사람들이 많이 있어, [180]그 제품을 향후 2주 이내에 보내실 경우, 7일 이내에 교체품을 받게 될 것임을 유념해 주세요. 하지만 11월이나 그 이후까지 기다리신다면, 감원으로 귀하의 요청을 처리하는 데 최대 4주까지 걸릴 수 있습니다.

진심으로,

Megan Jeffries
Lorelei 전자, 고객 서비스 직원

| 어휘 | inquiry 문의   based on ~에 기반하여   attach 부착하다   padded 완충재가 들어 있는   envelope 봉투   pay postage 우편 요금을 지불하다   deal with ~을 처리하다   up to ~까지   process 처리하다   reduction in staff 감원

176. 세부 사항 문제
제품이 왜 리콜되고 있나?
(A) 잘못된 배선이 이용되었다.
(B) 제품이 쉽게 깨질 수 있다.
(C) 기기가 플러그를 꽂았을 때 과열된다.
(D) 플라스틱이 화학 물질을 방출할 수 있다.

| 해설 | 첫 번째 단락 후반부에 리콜하는 이유로, 충전기들이 깨지기 쉬운 플라스틱으로 만들어져서 심지어 아주 낮은 높이에서 떨어졌을 때도 내부 배선이 노출되면서 쪼개질 수 있다고(The chargers were made of fragile plastic that can split when dropped even from a very low height, exposing the internal wiring) 제시되어 있으므로 정답은 (B)이다.

| 어휘 | crack 깨지다, 금이 가다   overheat 과열되다   emit 방출하다   chemicals 화학 물질

| 패러프레이징 | split → crack

177. 세부 사항을 묻는 문제
Lorelei 전자는 문제에 관해 어떻게 알게 되었나?
(A) 한 직원에게 정보를 받음으로써
(B) 부상을 당한 고객에게 항의를 받음으로써
(C) 정기 점검을 시행함으로써
(D) 제품 디자이너로부터 주의를 받음으로써

| 해설 | 두 번째 단락에 한 소매점의 판매원이 그 문제를 발견한 직후에 Lorelei 경영진은 자발적인 리콜을 지시하기로 결정했다고(Lorelei executives decided to order the voluntary recall immediately after a salesperson at a Lorelei retail shop discovered the issue) 제시되어 있으므로 정답은 (A)이다.

| 어휘 | complaint 항의   carry out 시행하다   routine inspection 정기 점검   warning 주의

| 패러프레이징 | a salesperson → an employee

178. 동의어 문제
안내에서 세 번째 단락 네 번째 줄에 있는 단어 "carries"와 의미가 가장 유사한 것은
(A) 광고하다, 지지하다
(B) 판매하다
(C) 수송하다

(D) 달성하다

| 해설 | 해당 단어가 들어간 문장은 '~ 고객들은 ~ Lorelei 제품들을 취급하는 어느 매장으로든 그 제품을 가지고 오셔야 합니다'라고 해석되는데, 매장에서 '취급하다'라는 의미는 '판매하다'라는 의미와 가장 유사하므로 정답은 (B) sells이다.

179. 연계 문제 - 추론
Lindquist 씨에 관해 암시되는 것은 무엇인가?
(A) 카메라를 반품하기를 원한다.
(B) 하나 이상의 기기를 구입했다.
(C) 온라인으로 구입을 했다.
(D) 캐나다에 살고 있다.

| 해설 | Lindquist 씨는 두 번째 지문인 이메일 수신자로, 이메일 초반부에 기기를 우편으로 돌려보내야 한다고(~ you should return the device by mail) 했고, 이와 관련하여 첫 번째 지문의 세 번째 단락 후반부에 캐나다에 살고 있는 고객들은 우편으로 제품을 돌려보내야 한다고(Customers living in Canada should return the item by mail) 제시되어 있다. 이를 연계해 볼 때 Lindquist 씨는 캐나다에 살고 있음을 알 수 있으므로 정답은 (D)이다.

180. 세부 사항 문제
반품이 10월에 이루어지면 교환을 받는 데 얼마나 걸릴 것인가?
(A) 1주
(B) 2주
(C) 3주
(D) 4주

| 해설 | 이메일을 보낸 날짜가 10월 15일(October 15)이고 이메일 후반부에 제품을 향후 2주 이내에 보내실 경우, 7일 이내에 교체품을 받게 될 것이라고(if you send in the item within the next two weeks, you will receive the replacement in seven days) 제시되어 있다. 이를 연계해 볼 때, 10월 내에 제품을 보내면 1주 내에 교체품을 받을 것임을 알 수 있으므로 정답은 (A)이다.

| 패러프레이징 | seven days → One week

181-185 다음 구인 광고와 이메일을 참조하시오.

Commonwealth 태양열 회사 공석들

[181]Commonwealth 태양열 회사(CSC)는 지속 가능한 에너지 분야에서 주택용 태양 전지판의 공급과 설치에 대한 믿을 수 있는 서비스로 유명합니다. 원래 뉴캐슬에 본사가 있었지만, 저희의 빠른 성장에 대응하기 위해 [185]2년 전에 시드니로 사업의 기반을 옮겼습니다. 또한 퍼스에도 지점이 있고, 저희의 모든 제품은 멜버른에 있는 Bladin 제조사에 의해 공급됩니다. 저희가 1월 20일까지 퍼스에 있는 직책들의 지원서를 받을 것이고, 그 시간 이후에 면접에 관한 [182]대략적인 일정을 계획할 것입니다.

유통 관리자: [183]물품들이 목표 일자까지 공급되도록 확실히 하며, 제품의 보관과 유통을 관리합니다. 확실한 문제 해결 능력과 기본적인 컴퓨터 활용 능력이 필수입니다.

사업 개발 관리자: 영업 리드(잠재 고객)를 식별하여 고객 기반을 확대합니다. [183]마감 일자까지 정확한 보고서들을 파일로 정리합니다. 비즈니

스 분야의 대학 학위가 요구됩니다. 뛰어난 의사소통 능력과 컴퓨터 능력은 필수입니다.
설치 기술자: 모든 안전 기준에 따라, [183]엄격한 시간 제한 내에 고객들의 가정에 설치 프로젝트를 완료합니다. 유효한 운전 면허증이 요구됩니다.

관심 있는 지원자들은 www.commonwealthsol.com.au에서 [184 (B)]웹에 기반한 지원서를 작성해야 합니다. 자격 요건을 충족시키는 이들은 [184 (D)]단체 면접에 초청될 것이고, 그곳에서 그분들은 [184 (A)]현재 또는 이전 관리자의 추천서 두 통을 제출해야 합니다. 2차 면접에 참석하는 지원자들은 면접 다음에 컴퓨터 기반의 인성 검사를 하도록 요청받을 것입니다.

| 어휘 | solar 태양의, 태양열을 이용한   sustainable 지속 가능한   dependable 믿을 수 있는   supply 공급하다   residential 주거의   panel 판   originally 원래, 본래   headquartered 본사가 있는   base 기반   operation 사업, 운영   accommodate 부응하다, 맞추다   rapid 빠른   application 지원서   devise 고안하다, 계획하다   rough 대략적인   storage 보관   distribution 유통   target date 목표 일자   essential 필수적인, 필수의   proficiency 능숙, 숙달   identify 식별하다, 확인하다   sales lead 영업 리드(잠재 고객)   accurate 정확한   due date 마감 일자   strict 엄격한, 철저한   limit 제한   safety standard 안전 기준   valid 유효한   meet the qualifications 자격 요건을 충족시키다   turn in 제출하다   reference 추천서   supervisor 관리자   personality test 인성 검사

수신: Milla Jacobs <m.jacobs@commonwealthsol.com.au>
발신: Ira Braun <braunira@quickinbox.com.au>
날짜: 2월 8일
제목: 면접

Jacobs 씨 귀하,

사업 개발 관리자 직책을 위한 [184 (D)]2차 면접에 저를 불러 주셔서 감사합니다. 저의 능력과 이력에 관해 더 상세히 이야기 나누는 것을 기대하고 있습니다. 아시다시피, 저는 현재 번버리에 살고 있지만, 알맞은 일자리 기회를 위해 이전할 의향이 있습니다. 또한, [185]제가 귀하 본사에서 일부 직원들과 만나보는 것이 도움이 될 것 같다면, 제가 다음 주에 같은 지역에 있는 친구를 방문할 것이어서 기꺼이 잠시 들르겠습니다. 이것이 귀하의 의사 결정 과정에 도움이 될지 알려주시기 바랍니다.

좋은 일만 가득하기를,

Ira Braun

| 어휘 | look forward to -ing ~하는 것을 기대하다   career history 이력   in detail 상세히   be willing to ~할 의향이 있다   relocate 이전하다   neighborhood 지역, 동네   stop by 잠시 들르다   decision-making process 의사 결정 과정

181. True 문제
CSC에 관해 제시된 것은 무엇인가?
(A) 여러 지점들에 일자리 공석이 있다.
(B) 제조 시설을 운영하고 있다.
(C) 2년 전에 설립되었다.
(D) 신뢰성으로 유명하다.
| 해설 | 구인 광고 첫 단락에 Commonwealth 태양열 회사(CSC)는 지속 가능한 에너지 분야에서 믿을 수 있는 서비스로 유명하다고(~ is known across the sustainable energy sector for its dependable service ~) 제시되어 있으므로 정답은 (D)이다.
| 어휘 | operate 운영하다   found 설립하다   reliability 신뢰성, 믿을 수 있음
| 패러프레이징 | is known ~ for its dependable service → has a reputation of reliability

182. 동의어 문제
구인 광고에서 첫 번째 단락 여섯 번째 줄에 있는 단어 "rough"와 의미가 가장 유사한 것은
(A) 불쾌한
(B) 대략적인
(C) 고르지 않은
(D) 도전적인
| 해설 | 해당 단어가 들어간 문장은 '~ 면접에 관한 대략적인 일정을 계획할 것입니다'라고 해석된다. 따라서 rough는 '대략적인'이라는 의미로 쓰인 것이므로 이와 가장 유사한 '대략적인'이라는 뜻의 (B) approximate가 정답이다.

고난도
183. 세부 사항을 묻는 문제
모든 직책들에 필요한 능력으로 언급된 것은 무엇인가?
(A) 확실한 의사소통 능력
(B) 마감 기한을 맞추는 능력
(C) 대학교에서 받은 학위
(D) 컴퓨터 작업 경험
| 해설 | 구인 광고에서 유통 관리자 직책에 물품들이 목표 일자까지 공급되도록 확실히 해야 한다고(ensuring that items are supplied by the target date) 제시되어 있고, 사업 개발 관리자 직책에 마감 일자까지 정확한 보고서들을 파일로 정리해야 한다고(Files accurate reports by due dates) 나와 있다. 또한 설치 기술자 직책에 엄격한 시간 제한 내에 고객들의 가정에 설치 프로젝트를 완료해야 한다고(Complete installation projects at customers' homes within a strict time limit) 제시되어 있으므로 이를 포괄하는 (B)가 정답이다.
| 어휘 | meet a deadline 마감 기한을 맞추다   degree 학위
| 패러프레이징 | by target date / by due dates / within a strict time limit → deadlines

고난도
184. 연계 문제 - NOT True
Braun 씨가 했을 것 같지 않은 것은 무엇인가?
(A) 직업적인 추천서를 제출하는 것
(B) 온라인 서식을 작성하는 것
(C) 인성 검사를 받는 것

(D) 단체 면접에 참석하는 것

| 해설 | Braun 씨는 이메일 발신자로 이메일 도입부에 2차 면접에 불러 줘서 감사하다고(Thank you for inviting me to the second round of interviews ~) 한 것을 통해, 1차 면접을 통과한 사람임을 알 수 있다. 구인 광고 마지막 단락에 지원자들은 웹에 기반한 지원서를 작성해야 한다고(should fill out the Web-based application) 한 것에서 (B), 자격 요건을 충족시키는 이들은 단체 면접에 초청될 것이라고(will be invited to a group interview) 한 것에서 (D), 단체 면접 시 현재 또는 이전 관리자의 추천서 두 통을 제출해야 한다고(should turn in two letters of reference from a current or former supervisor) 한 것에서 (A)를 확인할 수 있으며, 따라서 이 세 가지는 Braun 씨가 이미 했을 것임을 알 수 있다. 하지만 인성 검사는 2차 면접 시 진행할 것이라고 했으므로 (C)가 정답이다.

| 패러프레이징 |
· fill out the Web-based application → Completed an online form
· invited to a group interview → Attended a group interview
· turn in two letters of reference from a current or former supervisor → Submitted professional references

185. 연계 문제 - 세부 사항
Braun 씨가 친구를 방문하려고 계획하는 곳은 어디인가?
(A) 시드니
(B) 뉴캐슬
(C) 번버리
(D) 퍼스

| 해설 | 이메일에 중반부에 Braun 씨가 다음 주에 본사와 같은 지역에 있는 친구를 방문할 것이어서 기꺼이 잠시 들르겠다고(~ your headquarters, I will be visiting a friend in that same neighborhood next week and would be happy to stop by) 했고, 구인 광고 첫 번째 단락에 2년 전에 시드니로 사업의 기반을 옮겼다고(we moved our base of operations to Sydney two years ago ~) 제시되어 있다. 이를 연계해 볼 때, 시드니를 방문할 계획인 것을 알 수 있으므로 정답은 (A)이다.

186-190 다음 회람, 이메일, 정보를 참조하시오.

수신: Sutter 지점 전 직원
발신: [187]Silva Corporation, Sutter 지점장, Isabelle Pearce
날짜: 2월 26일
주제: 지점 폐쇄

이사회가 3월 9일에 [188]Lindbergh 지점을 폐쇄하기로 의결했습니다. [188]운영 책임자인 Scott Harley를 포함하여, 그 지점의 직원들은 우리 지점으로 새로 발령이 날 것입니다. [186]그들이 처음 업무를 하는 날은 3월 13일 화요일이 될 것입니다. 여러분이 그들을 알게 되는 기회를 가질 수 있게 그날 환영회를 열 것입니다.

비록 지점 폐쇄를 겪는 것은 늘 실망스럽기는 하지만, 이것은 간접비를 줄임으로써 회사를 계속 운영해 나갈 최선의 방법입니다. 게다가, [187]Lindbergh에 있는 사무실 건물이 매각될 것이어서, 그것이 우리에게 추가 자금을 제공할 것입니다. 이로 인해, 우리 지사는 특별한 일회성 프로젝트를 시행할 수 있을 것입니다. 우리는 직원들에게서 개선을 위한 제안들을 받고 있습니다. 공유하고 싶은 아이디어가 있다면, j_ingram@silva-corp.com으로 인사 관리자인 Jade Ingram에게 이메일을 보내주세요. 제출은 3월 20일까지 받을 것이니 보고서는 3월 22일까지 준비될 수 있습니다.

| 어휘 | the board of directors 이사회   vote 투표하다, 의결하다   shut down 폐쇄하다, 문을 닫다   reassign 새로 발령하다   disappointing 실망스러운   suffer 겪다   closure 폐쇄   keep in operation 계속 운영하다   reduce 줄이다   overhead expenses 간접비   additional capital 추가 자본   submission 제출

수신: Mariette Plante <m_plante@silva-corp.com>
발신: Jade Ingram <j_ingram@silva-corp.com>
날짜: 3월 23일
제목: 요약 보고서

Plante 씨 귀하,

아시다시피, 제가 여기 Sutter 지점에서 이루어질 수 있는 가능성 있는 개선 사항들에 관한 직원들의 제안들을 요약하도록 요청을 받았고, 그것을 첨부된 보고서에 개괄해 놓았습니다. [188]이것은 이전 Lindbergh 운영 책임자의 도움으로 가능했습니다. Pearce 씨가 어제 결과들을 검토했습니다. 그녀는 가장 인기 있는 옵션인 주차장 확장이 우리 건물의 공간 제한 때문에 실현될 수 없을 것이라고 판단했습니다. 하지만 [190]구내 카페테리아에 대한 표들도 많이 있어서, 그녀가 그 옵션을 진행시키기를 원합니다. Pearce 씨의 [189]견해로는, 그것이 회사의 사기를 높이고 점심 식사에서 늦게 돌아오는 직원들의 수를 줄이는 것을 포함하여, 많은 이점들이 있을 실용적인 프로젝트입니다. 추가적인 진전이 나타나는 대로 계속 소식을 전해드릴 것입니다.

진심을 담아,

Jade Ingram

| 어휘 | summarize 요약하다   outline 개괄하다   attached 첨부된   determine 결정하다   expansion 확장   feasible 실현 가능한   space limitation 공간 제한   on-site 구내의, 현장의   go forward with ~을 진행시키다   view 견해, 의견   practical 실용적인   numerous 수많은   benefit 이점, 혜택   raise 높이다   morale 사기   keep A updated A에게 최신 소식을 계속 전하다   development 진전, 발전   arise 나타나다, 일어나다

직원 설문 조사 결과 / Jade Ingram 수집 / 3월 22일 제출
주제: 지점 개선을 위한 제안들
총 응답자 수: 218

최소 30번 이상 제안되었던 주제들이 아래 열거되어 있습니다. 전체 리

스트는 이 보고서의 두 번째 페이지에 포함되어 있습니다.

주차 구역 확장	87
¹⁹⁰구내 카페테리아 추가	62
컴퓨터와 기타 사무기기 업그레이드	38
직원들을 위한 회사 야유회 주최	31

| 어휘 | compile 수집하다, 편집하다   respondent 응답자   complete 전체의, 완전한   retreat 야유회

186. 세부 사항을 묻는 문제
회람에 따르면, 3월 13일에 무슨 일이 있을 것인가?
(A) 직원들이 새로운 동료들을 만날 것이다.
(B) 한 지점이 문을 닫을 것이다.
(C) 새로운 서비스가 이용 가능하게 될 것이다.
(D) 설문 조사 결과가 발표될 것이다.
| 해설 | 회람의 첫 번째 단락에 새로 발령받은 이들이 처음 업무를 하는 날이 3월 13일 화요일이 될 것이고(Their first day of work will be Tuesday, March 13) 그들을 알게 되는 기회를 가질 수 있게 그날 환영회를 열 것이라고(We will hold a welcome reception on that day so that you have a chance to get to know them) 했으므로 정답은 (A)이다.
| 어휘 | coworker 동료

187. 세부 사항을 묻는 문제
회람에 따르면, 무엇이 Silva Corporation이 잉여 자금을 갖도록 할 것인가?
(A) 제품의 인기
(B) 정부 보조금
(C) 건물의 매각
(D) 세금 환급
| 해설 | Silva Corporation은 회람을 보낸 Isabelle Pearce가 속한 회사로, 회람의 두 번째 단락 초반부에 Lindbergh에 있는 사무실 건물이 매각될 것이어서, 그것이 추가 자금을 제공할 것이라고(the office building in Lindbergh will be sold, which will provide us with additional capital) 제시되어 있으므로 정답은 (C)이다.
| 어휘 | popularity 인기   grant 보조금   tax refund 세금 환급
| 패러프레이징 | the office building will be sold → The sale of building

188. 연계 문제 - 추론
Ingram 씨의 임무에 관해 암시되는 것은 무엇인가?
(A) 그것을 Lindbergh 팀의 일원에게 위임할 계획이다.
(B) 작업의 원래 마감 기한을 놓쳤다.
(C) 그것을 완료하기 위해 Plante 씨의 정보가 필요하다.
(D) Harley 씨의 도움을 받았다.
| 해설 | Ingram 씨는 두 번째 지문인 이메일의 발신자로, 이메일 초반부에 이것은 이전 Lindbergh 운영 책임자의 도움으로 가능했다고(This was made possible by the help of the former Lindbergh Director of Operations) 했는데, 첫 번째 지문의 첫 단락에 Scott Harley가 Lindbergh 지점의 운영 책임자고(Director of Operations Scott Harley) 제시되어 있으므로 정답은 (D)이다.
| 어휘 | delegate 위임하다   original 원래의   deadline 마감 기한

189. 동의어 문제
이메일에서 첫 번째 단락 여섯 번째 줄에 있는 단어 "view"와 의미가 가장 유사한 것은
(A) 경관, 장면
(B) 조사, 검사
(C) 비전, 시야
(D) 의견
| 해설 | 해당 단어가 들어간 문장은 'Pearce 씨의 견해로는, 그것이 ~ 많은 이점들이 있을 실용적인 프로젝트입니다'라고 해석된다. 따라서 view는 '견해, 의견'이라는 의미로 쓰인 것이므로 정답은 (D) opinion이다.

190. 연계 문제 - 세부 사항
Pearce 씨가 승인한 프로젝트는 몇 명의 사람들이 제안했나?
(A) 87
(B) 62
(C) 38
(D) 31
| 해설 | Pearce 씨가 승인한 프로젝트에 관해 이메일 중반부에, 구내 카페테리아에 대한 표들도 많이 있어서, 그녀가 그 옵션을 진행시키기를 원한다고(there were also plenty of votes for an on-site cafeteria, so she wants to go forward with that option) 제시되어 있고, 이와 관련하여 마지막 지문의 도표에 '구내 카페테리아 추가(Add an on-site cafeteria)'를 제안한 인원은 62명으로 확인되므로 정답은 (B)이다.

191-195 다음 제안서들과 회람을 참조하시오.

¹⁹¹**Gem 인테리어: 프로젝트 제안서**
날짜: 3월 4일
고객: Lawrence 컨설팅, 597 Duncan Avenue, Cincinnati, OH 45229

작업 상세 설명:
상업용 건물에 카펫 설치. 자재에 발포 고무 밑깔개와 나일론 카펫(제품: Azar 3535)이 포함됩니다. ¹⁹⁵Gem 인테리어는 고객들이 낡은 타일이나 카펫을 철거하고 폐기하는 등의 준비 작업을 직접 하도록 함으로써 가격을 낮게 유지합니다.

결제 정보:
이 프로젝트의 총 요금은 28,350달러가 될 것입니다. ¹⁹³저희는 이 견적을 30일 동안 유효로 인정할 것이고, 그 이후에는 가격이 변동될 수 있습니다. 착수금 10%는 처음 설치하는 날에 지불해야 하고, 나머지는 작업이 완료된 후 일주일 안에 지불해야 합니다.

기술자: Brian Harmon　　고객 서명: _____
191승인자: Edwin Prichard　　날짜: _____

| 어휘 | installation 설치　commercial 상업의　foam 발포 고무
underlay (카펫의) 밑깔개　preparation work 준비 작업　dispose of
~을 폐기하다, 처리하다　charge 요금　honor ~을 유효로 인정하다
quote 견적(액)　deposit 착수금, 보증금　due (돈을) 지불해야 하는
remainder 나머지　complete 완료하다

Carpetland 제안서
날짜: 3월 4일

고객: Lawrence 컨설팅
연락 담당자: Chad Theisen, 555-4633
작업이 시행될 장소: 597 Duncan Avenue, Cincinnati, OH 45229

Carpetland는 위 건물에 총 32,500달러에 카펫[5,500평방피트]을 설치할 것을 제안합니다. 이 금액에는 자재와 인건비, 그리고 현재 바닥재의 철거/폐기가 포함됩니다.

192착수금 4천 달러는 작업 날짜를 예약할 때 치러져야 합니다. 남은 잔액은 작업이 시작되는 날에 지불되어야 합니다. 193이 견적은 이 서식에 있는 날짜로부터 2주 동안 유효합니다.

| 어휘 | propose 제안하다　property 부동산, 건물　amount 금액
labor 노동, 근로　removal 제거　disposal 폐기, 처분　current 현재의
flooring 바닥재　reserve 예약하다　remaining balance 남은 잔액
valid 유효한

수신: Lawrence 컨설팅 전 직원
발신: Chad Theisen 지점장
날짜: 3월 7일
제목: 새로운 카펫 설치

3월 10일부터 3층 사무실들의 카펫이 교체될 것입니다. 이 프로젝트는 3일 정도 걸릴 것입니다. 이러한 변화로 더 많은 음파가 흡수됨으로써, 소음의 감소 덕분에 업무 환경이 더 쾌적해지기를 바랍니다. 그 준비로, 3월 8일에 퇴근하기 전에 1943층에 있는 모든 직원들은 자신들의 개인 물품을 정리하여 그것들을 자신의 이름이 적힌 상자에 넣어야 합니다. 임시 사무실 공간이 5층에 마련될 것입니다. 195저희 자체 유지 보수 팀이 기존의 타일들을 뜯기 위해 3월 9일에 그 층에서 작업을 진행할 것임을 유념해 주시기 바랍니다.

여러분의 협조에 감사드립니다!

| 어휘 | pleasant 쾌적한, 유쾌한　noise reduction 소음 감소
sound wave 음파　absorb 흡수하다　personal item 개인 물품
temporary 임시의, 일시적인　be set up 마련되다　maintenance

team 유지 보수 팀　pull up 잡아당기다, 뜯다　existing 기존의

191. 추론 문제
Prichard 씨는 누구일 것 같은가?
(A) Gem 인테리어의 관리자
(B) 카펫 디자이너
(C) 건설 인부 감독관
(D) 안전 조사관

| 해설 | Prichard 씨는 첫 번째 지문 아래쪽에 승인자(Approved by)로 제시된 사람으로, Gem 인테리어의 제안서를 승인한 사람인 것으로 볼 때, 그 업체의 관리자일 것으로 유추할 수 있으므로 정답은 (A)이다.
| 어휘 | supervisor 관리자

192. 세부 사항을 묻는 문제
고객들은 언제 Carpetland에 첫 번째 대금을 지불해야 하는가?
(A) 청구서 발송 2주 후에
(B) 프로젝트 완료 일주일 이내에
(C) 작업이 시작되는 날에
(D) 예약이 이루어지는 때

| 해설 | Carpetland의 제안서인 두 번째 지문 세 번째 단락에 착수금 4천 달러는 작업 날짜를 예약할 때 치러져야 한다고(A $4,000 deposit must be made at the time of reserving a work date) 제시되어 있으므로 정답은 (D)이다.
| 어휘 | bill 청구서　completion 완료, 완공　booking 예약
| 패러프레이징 | at the time of reserving a work date → When a booking is made

고난도
193. 연계 문제 – True
두 카펫 회사들에 관해 사실인 것은 무엇인가?
(A) 그들의 제안은 한정된 시간 동안 유효하다.
(B) 그들의 작업반원들은 경험이 많다.
(C) 추천을 하면 할인을 제공한다.
(D) 고객의 서명을 요구한다.

| 해설 | Gem 인테리어의 프로젝트 제안서 두 번째 단락의 결제 정보에 이 견적을 30일 동안 유효로 인정할 것이고, 그 이후에는 가격이 변동될 수 있다고(We will honor this quote for 30 days, after which time the price may change) 했고, Carpetland 제안서 마지막 단락에 이 견적은 이 서식에 있는 날짜로부터 2주 동안 유효하다고(This quote is valid for 2 weeks from the date on this form) 제시되어 있으므로 정답은 (A)이다.
| 어휘 | crew 작업반　give a referral 추천을 해주다　signature 서명

194. 세부 사항을 묻는 문제
3층에서 일하는 직원들이 하도록 요청되는 것은 무엇인가?
(A) 재택 근무를 원하는지 여부를 정하는 것
(B) 그들의 사무실 가구를 다른 방으로 옮기는 것
(C) 그들의 소지품을 라벨이 붙은 용기에 넣는 것
(D) 카펫 색상들에 관하여 추천하는 것

| 해설 | 세 번째 지문인 회람 중반부에 3층에 있는 모든 직원들은 자신의 개인 물품을 정리하여 자신의 이름이 적힌 상자에 넣어야 한다고(all third-floor employees should clear their personal items and put them in a box with their name on it) 제시되어 있으므로 정답은 (C)이다.

| 어휘 | designate 선정하다, 지정하다   belongings 소지품   labeled 라벨이 붙은   container 용기

| 패러프레이징 | · personal items → belongings
· put ~ in a box with their name on it → Place ~ in labeled containers

🔺 고난도
195. 연계 문제 - 추론
Lawrence 컨설팅에 관해 암시된 것은 무엇인가?
(A) 그 유지 보수 팀은 3월 10일에 쉴 것이다.
(B) 카펫들을 Gem 인테리어에 의해 설치되도록 할 것이다.
(C) 3월에 3일 동안 문을 닫을 것이다.
(D) 과거에 Carpetland를 이용했었다.

| 해설 | 회람 후반부에 자체 유지 보수 팀이 기존의 타일들을 뜯기 위해 3월 9일에 그 층에서 작업을 진행할 것이라고(~ our own maintenance team will be working ~ pull up the existing tiles) 한 것과 첫 번째 지문 첫 번째 단락에 Gem 인테리어는 고객들이 낡은 타일이나 카펫을 철거하고 폐기하는 등의 준비 작업을 직접 하도록 함으로써 가격을 낮게 유지한다고(Gem Interiors ~ such as removing and disposing of old tiles or carpets, themselves) 한 것을 연계해 볼 때, Lawrence 컨설팅은 Gem 인테리어에 작업을 의뢰해 자체 준비 작업을 하는 것임을 알 수 있으므로 정답은 (B)이다.

| 어휘 | take ~ off 쉬다

196-200 다음 문자 메시지, 기사, 후기를 참조하시오.

발신: Bumati Kapil, 894-555-2009 (오전 10:25)
수신: Jerome Quinn, 468-555-1373

안녕하세요, Jerome. 제가 TJ Glass의 담당자인 Clarence Wells 와 함께 ¹⁹⁷이곳 전에 Ritter 예배당이었던 곳에 있는데요. 스테인드글라스 창문들의 수리가 우리가 생각했던 것보다 더 복잡할 것 같아요. ¹⁹⁶Wells 씨는 그들의 회사는 이런 유형의 프로젝트를 처리할 만큼 경험이 충분하지 않아서 우리가 스테인드글라스 복원을 전문으로 하는 사람을 찾아야 할 것이라고 말해요. ¹⁹⁷당신이 지금 이곳에 와서 이것을 더 상의하고 곧 여기에 올 전기 기술자를 만날 수 있을까요?

| 어휘 | former 이전의, 옛날의   chapel 예배당   representative 담당자, 대표   complicated 복잡한   experienced 경험이 있는   deal with ~을 처리하다, 다루다   specialize in ~을 전문으로 하다   restoration 복원   electrician 전기 기술자

예상치 못한 장소에서 거처를 찾은 Timor 카페

COVINGTON (6월 9일)—¹⁹⁷Timor 카페가 한때 Ritter 예배당이었던 건물을 거처로 지정했고, ²⁰⁰7월 12일로 예정된 카페의 대규모 개장

을 위해 그 장소를 준비하는 수리 작업이 진행 중이다. ¹⁹⁹카페의 소유주인 Jerome Quinn이 올해 초에 그 건물을 매입했고, 그 건축물은 가능한 한 역사적으로 정확하게 복원되고 있다. ¹⁹⁹약 10년 전에 예배당에서 예배가 종료된 후에, 그 건물은 시에 매각되었다. 시 공무원들은 그곳을 공립 도서관으로 이용할 계획이었지만, 예산 삭감이 개조 작업을 중단시켜, 몇 년 동안 시의 매입물이 유휴 상태로 남아 있었다. ¹⁹⁸Jerome Quinn이 Covington에 있는 자신의 점포들 포트폴리오에 커피숍을 추가할 계획으로 이 장소를 매입했다.

그 카페는 신선한 빵과 함께 프리미엄 수제 커피 음료를 판매할 것이다. Quinn 씨는 고객들이 그 독특한 분위기를 즐기게 될 것이라고 생각하는데, 그것에는 인상적인 석조물과 아주 멋진 스테인드글라스 창문들이 포함된다. 더 알아보려면, www.timorcafe.net을 방문하면 된다.

| 어휘 | designate A as B A를 B로 지정하다   renovation 수리, 개조   underway 진행 중인   structure 구조물   restore 복원하다   historically 역사적으로   accurate 정확하게   service 예배   terminate 종료하다, 끝나다   decade 10년   city official 시 공무원   budget cut 예산 삭감   halt 중단시키다, 멈추다   acquisition 매입물, 취득물   idle 유휴의, 사용되지 않는   establishment 점포, 시설물   hand-crafted 수제의   unique 독특한   atmosphere 분위기   impressive 인상적인   stonework 석조물   gorgeous 아주 멋진

www.aroundcovington.com/visitorreviews

| 홈 | 행사 | 볼거리 | 후기 |

레스토랑과 식사 공간 >> 커피숍 >> Timor 카페

후기 작성자 Sabrina Lin

²⁰⁰저는 8월 3일에 Timor 카페의 대규모 개장 행사에 갔었고, 그곳에서 저의 전반적인 경험에 아주 깊은 인상을 받았습니다. 바리스타들이 커피 원두에 대해 아주 아는 것이 많았고, 그 카페가 보유하고 있던 각각의 종류의 미묘한 맛의 차이도 설명해 주었습니다. 제 커피는 아주 훌륭했고, 맛있는 블루베리 머핀도 곁들였습니다. 카페가 무선 인터넷을 제공하지 않아 다소 실망하기는 했지만, 독특한 예배당 실내 장식이 그곳을 방문할 가치가 충분하게 만들었습니다.

| 어휘 | overall 전반적인   knowledgeable 아는 것이 많은, 박식한   subtle 미묘한   flavor 맛, 풍미   superb 아주 훌륭한, 최고의   accompany 곁들이다, 동반하다   distinct 독특한   décor 실내 장식, 인테리어   well worth ~할 가치가 충분한

196. 주제/목적 문제
문자 메시지의 목적은 무엇인가?
(A) 예산 증액을 요청하는 것
(B) 업체가 일을 할 수 없는 이유를 설명하는 것
(C) 유리 회사에 대한 참고 자료를 얻는 것

(D) Quinn 씨에게 건축 자재를 고르도록 부탁하는 것

| 해설 | 메시지 중반부에 TJ Glass의 담당자인 Wells 씨가 그들의 회사는 이런 유형의 프로젝트를 처리할 만큼 경험이 충분하지 않아서 스테인드글라스 복원을 전문으로 하는 사람을 찾아야 할 것이라고 말한다고(~ their company is not experienced enough to deal with this kind of project and that we'll have to find someone that specializes in stained-glass restoration) 했으므로 정답은 (B)이다.

| 어휘 | task 일, 업무　reference 참고　select 고르다　building materials 건축 자재

고난도
197. 연계 문제 – 세부 사항
문자 메시지를 보냈을 때 Kapil 씨는 Quinn 씨를 어디에서 만나기를 원했나?
(A) 건축 자재 공급 매장에서
(B) 유리 제조업체의 사무실에서
(C) 부동산 회사에서
(D) 커피숍으로 제안된 장소에서

| 해설 | 문자 메시지 도입부에 Kapil 씨가 전에 Ritter 예배당이었던 곳에 있다고(I'm here at the former Ritter Chapel) 했는데, 후반부에 지금 이곳에 올 수 있냐고(Can you come here now ~) 물은 것과, 기사 도입부에 Timor 카페가 한때 Ritter 예배당이었던 건물을 거처로 지정했다고(Timor Café has designated the building that was once Ritter Chapel as its home) 한 것을 연계해 볼 때, 예전에 Ritter 예배당이었으나 Timor 카페가 될 곳에서 만나기를 원했음을 알 수 있으므로 정답은 (D)이다.

| 어휘 | supply store 공급 매장　glass maker 유리 제조업체　real estate 부동산　proposed 제안된

198. 추론 문제
기사가 Quinn 씨에 관해 암시하는 것은 무엇인가?
(A) 그 지역에 여러 업체들을 소유하고 있다.
(B) 역사 연구를 한 이력을 가지고 있다.
(C) 시 공무원으로 일하고 있다.
(D) 카페의 인테리어를 직접 디자인했다.

| 해설 | 기사 첫 번째 단락 후반부에 Jerome Quinn이 Covington에 있는 자신의 점포들 포트폴리오에 커피숍을 추가할 계획으로 이 장소를 매입했다고(Jerome Quinn purchased the site with the plan to add a coffee shop to his portfolio of establishments in Covington) 제시된 것을 통해, Quinn 씨는 그 지역에 여러 점포들을 가지고 있음을 알 수 있으므로 정답은 (A)이다.

| 어휘 | background 경력, 배경

| 패러프레이징 | add a coffee shop to his portfolio of establishments in Covington → owns several businesses in the area

고난도
199. True 문제
기사에서 Ritter 예배당에 관해 언급된 것은 무엇인가?
(A) 도서관으로 개조되었다.
(B) 이전에 시의 소유였다.
(C) 시청 근처에 위치해 있다.
(D) 안전하지 못한 것으로 간주되었다.

| 해설 | 기사 첫 번째 단락 초/중반부에, 카페의 소유주인 Jerome Quinn이 올해 초에 그 건물을 매입했다고(The café's owner, Jerome Quinn, purchased the building earlier this year) 언급되어 있고, 중/후반부에 약 10년 전에 예배당에서 예배가 종료된 후에, 그 건물은 시에 매각되었다고(the building was sold to the city) 제시되어 있다. 이를 통해 Ritter 예배당은 Jerome Quinn이 매입하기 전에 시의 소유였음을 알 수 있으므로 정답은 (B)이다.

| 어휘 | be converted to ~로 전환되다, 개조되다　previously 이전에　located 위치한　consider 간주하다, 고려하다　unsafe 안전하지 않은

| 패러프레이징 | was sold to the city → was previously owned by the city

고난도
200. 연계 문제 – 추론
Lin 씨의 후기에서 카페에 관해 암시된 것은 무엇인가?
(A) 인터넷이 너무 느렸다.
(B) 직원들이 바빴다.
(C) 개장이 지연되었다.
(D) 좌석들이 편안했다.

| 해설 | 후기 도입부에 Lin 씨가 8월 3일에 Timor 카페의 대규모 개장 행사에 갔었다고(I went to Timor Café's grand opening on August 3) 한 것과 기사 첫 번째 단락 초반부에 대규모 개장이 7월 12일로 예정되어 있다고(the café's grand opening scheduled for July 12) 한 것을 연계해 볼 때, 카페의 개장이 지연되었음을 유추할 수 있으므로 정답은 (C)이다.

| 어휘 | delay 지연시키다　comfortable 편안한

TEST 05

PART 5
101 (C)	102 (B)	103 (D)	104 (B)	105 (C)
106 (D)	107 (B)	108 (B)	109 (C)	110 (B)
111 (C)	112 (C)	113 (C)	114 (B)	115 (D)
116 (C)	117 (C)	118 (A)	119 (C)	120 (B)
121 (D)	122 (B)	123 (C)	124 (B)	125 (D)
126 (A)	127 (C)	128 (B)	129 (C)	130 (C)

PART 6
131 (B)	132 (C)	133 (D)	134 (A)	135 (A)
136 (B)	137 (C)	138 (B)	139 (D)	140 (D)
141 (B)	142 (A)	143 (B)	144 (C)	145 (D)
146 (A)				

PART 7
147 (C)	148 (A)	149 (C)	150 (B)	151 (C)
152 (D)	153 (D)	154 (A)	155 (D)	156 (C)
157 (A)	158 (C)	159 (B)	160 (D)	161 (C)
162 (C)	163 (B)	164 (B)	165 (C)	166 (C)
167 (C)	168 (B)	169 (C)	170 (A)	171 (C)
172 (B)	173 (C)	174 (C)	175 (C)	176 (C)
177 (B)	178 (B)	179 (C)	180 (A)	181 (D)
182 (C)	183 (C)	184 (C)	185 (C)	186 (B)
187 (B)	188 (A)	189 (C)	190 (C)	191 (C)
192 (A)	193 (B)	194 (C)	195 (C)	196 (D)
197 (C)	198 (D)	199 (D)	200 (B)	

PART 5

고난도
101. 형용사 자리 – 주격 보어
Moray Lab 장비는 위험 물질을 다룰 때 효과적인 것으로 입증되었다.
| 해설 | 2형식 동사 proven 뒤에 있는 빈칸은 보어가 들어갈 자리이므로 부사인 (D) effectively는 오답이고, 주어와 동격이 되기에는 부적절한 명사 (A) effect, 의미상 어울리지 않는 과거 분사형 형용사인 (B) effected도 오답이다. 따라서 '효과적인'이라는 뜻의 형용사인 (C) effective가 정답이다.
| 어휘 | lab(= laboratory) 실험실 equipment 장비 prove 입증되다, 판명되다 handle 다루다, 처리하다 hazardous 위험한 material 물질 effect 효과, 영향 effective 효과적인 effectively 효과적으로

102. 동사 어휘
Becker 씨는 자신의 요리를 위해 가장 좋은 유기농 재료들만 쓴다.
| 해설 | 빈칸은 문장의 동사가 들어갈 자리로, 뒤에 제시된 명사구 목적어와 관련지어 '요리를 위해 가장 좋은 유기농 재료들만 쓴다'라는 의미로 전개되는 것이 적절하므로 '사용하다'라는 뜻의 (B) uses가 정답이다.
| 어휘 | organic 유기농의 ingredient 재료

고난도
103. 전치사 어휘
그 광고의 마감일이 새로운 고객 요청 때문에 다음 주까지 연기되었다.
| 해설 | 뒤에 있는 시간 표현 명사구를 목적어로 가지는 전치사가 들어갈 자리로, 문맥상 '다음 주까지 연기되었다'라는 의미로 전개되는 것이 적절하므로 (D) until이 정답이다. by와 until은 둘 다 '~까지'라는 뜻이지만, by는 동사가 완료적인 의미일 때 쓰고, until은 동사가 계속적인 의미일 때 쓴다.
| 어휘 | deadline 마감(일) postpone 연기하다 request 요청

104. 인칭 대명사
Porter 씨의 도표는 그의 학생들이 화학의 기본 개념을 배우는 것을 더 쉽게 만든다.
| 해설 | 전치사 for의 목적어인 명사 students 앞에 빈칸이 있으므로, 명사를 수식/한정해 줄 수 있는 소유격 대명사가 들어가야 한다. 따라서 (B) his가 정답이다.
| 어휘 | diagram 도표, 도형 basic concept 기본 개념 chemistry 화학

105. 분사 구문
해외에 지점들을 개설하기 전에, Tinker 주식회사는 시카고와 디트로이트에 있는 자사의 국내 시설들을 업그레이드하기로 결정했다.
| 해설 | 접속사 Before와 명사구 사이에 빈칸이 있으므로, 접속사 뒤에 바로 연결될 수 없는 명사이자 동사 형태인 (A) launch와 (D) launches는 오답이다. 따라서 '부사절 접속사 Before + 분사 구문'의 형태인데, 빈칸 뒤에 목적어가 있으므로 목적어로 가질 수 있는 현재 분사인 (C) launching이 정답이다.
| 어휘 | overseas 해외에 domestic 국내의 facility 시설 launch 개설하다, 시작하다

106. 부사절 접속사
그 공연이 계속 매진된다면, 그것은 추가로 한 주 더 상연될 것이다.
| 해설 | 빈칸 뒤에 완전한 두 개의 절이 있으므로 빈칸에는 두 절을 연결해 줄 부사절 접속사가 들어가야 한다. 따라서 부사절 접속사인 (D) If가 정답이다.
| 어휘 | performance 공연 sell out 매진되다 run 상연되다

고난도
107. 최상급
<Tungsten Review>는 전문 화학자들 사이에서 두 번째로 가장 크게 인정받는 저널이다.
| 해설 | 빈칸은 뒤에 있는 established를 수식해줄 부사가 들어갈 자리이므로 명사인 (C) height는 답이 될 수 없고, 앞에 있는 the second는 뒤에 최상급이 연결되어 '두 번째로 가장 ~한'이라는 의미를 쓰이므로 이를 완성해줄 최상급 표현인 (B) most highly가 정답이다.
| 어휘 | established 인정받는, 확실히 자리를 잡은 chemist 화학자, 약사

108. 동사 어휘
Heavy Hack 제조사의 새로운 전동 공구는 테스트에서 산업 안전 기준을 초과했다.

| 해설 | 빈칸은 문장의 동사가 들어갈 자리로, 문맥상 '새로운 전동 공구는 산업 안전 기준을 초과했다'라는 의미로 전개되는 것이 적절하므로 '초과했다'라는 뜻의 (B) exceeded가 정답이다.
| 어휘 | power tool 전동 공구   industrial 산업의   safety 안전   standard 표준, 기준   relate 관련시키다   exceed 넘다, 초과하다   manage 처리하다, 운영하다   respond 응답하다

109. 등위 접속사
그 대사관은 일주일에 5일 문을 열지만, 방문객들은 예약 없이 서비스를 받을 수 없다.
| 해설 | 빈칸 앞뒤로 두 개의 완전한 절이 있으므로, 빈칸은 두 절을 연결해줄 접속사가 들어갈 자리이다. 따라서 뒤에 불완전한 절을 이끄는 명사절 접속사인 (B) what은 오답이고, 문맥상 앞의 절과 뒤의 절이 대조적인 내용이므로 (C) but이 정답이다.
| 어휘 | embassy 대사관   obtain 받다, 얻다   appointment 약속, 예약

110. 명사 자리 - 동사의 목적어
회람에 따르면, 경영진이 직원의 가족 구성원들에게 초대장을 보냈다.
| 해설 | 빈칸은 동사 extended의 목적어 자리이고, 관사 the 뒤에 있으므로 명사 자리이다. 따라서 '초대장'이라는 뜻의 명사인 (B) invitations가 정답이다. (C) invitational은 형용사와 명사로 모두 쓰이지만 명사로 쓰일 때는 '초청 경기'라는 뜻으로 문맥상 맞지 않는다.
| 어휘 | management 경영진   extend 주다, 연장하다   invitational 초대받은 사람만 참가하는; 초청 경기

111. 형용사 어휘
세일 중인 품목들의 구매 가능 여부는 지점마다 다를 것 같다.
| 해설 | 빈칸은 be동사 is의 보어가 들어갈 자리로, 문맥상 '구매 가능 여부는 지점들마다 다를 것 같다'라는 의미로 전개되는 것이 적절하므로 'be likely to(~할 것 같다)' 표현을 완성해줄 (C) likely가 정답이다.
| 어휘 | availability 이용 가능성, 입수 가능성   vary 다르다   upcoming 다가오는, 곧 있을   obvious 분명한, 명백한

🔼고난도
112. 대명사 선택
Austin 제약 회사의 새로운 멀티 비타민은 직장에서 만성 피로에 시달리는 이들을 위해 의도된 것이다.
| 해설 | 빈칸은 전치사 for의 목적어이자 뒤에 있는 분사구의 수식을 받는 대명사가 들어갈 자리이므로, 분사의 수식을 받을 수 있는 '~한 사람들'이란 뜻의 대명사 (C) those가 정답이다.
| 어휘 | pharmaceuticals 제약 회사   be meant for ~를 위해 의도되다   suffer from ~로 고통받다   chronic fatigue 만성 피로

113. 부사 자리 - 동사 수식
Bennington 사에서 Heisman 씨는 웹 디자이너로서 독립적으로 일해오고 있을 뿐만 아니라 그룹의 일원으로서도 잘해오고 있다.
| 해설 | 빈칸 앞에 있는 현재 분사 working은 has been working에서 has been이 생략된 것인데, 동사 work는 1형식 자동사로 뒤에 목적어나 보어가 올 수 없으므로 빈칸에는 working을 수식하는 부사가 들어가야 한다. 따라서 (D) independently가 정답이다.
| 어휘 | do well 잘하다   independency 독립성   independence 독립, 자립   independent 독립적인

🔼고난도
114. 형용사 어휘
Main 가의 주요 시내 번화가에 새로 연 지점이 회사에 막대한 이익을 가져다 줄 것으로 예상된다.
| 해설 | 빈칸은 뒤에 있는 명사 profit을 수식해줄 형용사가 들어갈 자리로, 문맥상 '막대한 이익'이라는 의미로 전개되는 것이 적절하므로 '막대한'이라는 뜻의 (B) massive가 정답이다.
| 어휘 | strip 번화가   earn 올리다, 벌다   profit 수익, 이익   repetitive 반복되는   massive 막대한   sturdy 견고한   reliant 의존하는

115. 명사 자리 - 주어
최근 Duluth 자동차 인수가 Border 자동차의 생산 능력을 상당히 증가시켰다.
| 해설 | 빈칸은 주어 자리이자 형용사 recent의 수식을 받는 자리이므로 명사 자리이다. 따라서 '인수'라는 뜻의 명사인 (D) acquisition이 정답이다.
| 어휘 | significantly 상당히, 크게   increase 증가시키다, 늘리다   production capacity 생산 능력   acquire 인수하다, 습득하다   acquisition 인수

116. to부정사
새로운 모바일 앱은 운전자들이 중앙 경기장 인근에 비어 있는 주차 공간의 위치를 찾을 수 있게 해준다.
| 해설 | 동사 enable은 'enable+목적어+to부정사'의 구조로 쓰이는 동사이므로, 빈칸 앞에 있는 to는 to부정사의 to이다. 따라서 to부정사를 완성해줄 동사 원형인 (C) locate가 정답이다.
| 어휘 | enable A to A가 ~할 수 있게 하다   motorist 운전자   vacant 비어 있는   location 장소, 위치   locate ~의 위치를 찾다

117. 부사절 접속사
저희가 귀하의 주문을 받자마자 귀하의 등록된 주소로 확인 이메일이 발송될 것입니다.
| 해설 | 빈칸 앞뒤로 각각 완전한 절이 있으므로 빈칸은 두 절을 연결해줄 접속사가 들어갈 자리이다. 따라서 전치사인 (B) during과 전치사이자 부사인 (D) above는 오답이고, 문맥상 '주문을 받자마자 이메일이 발송될 것이다'라는 의미로 전개되는 것이 적절하므로 '~하자마자'라는 뜻의 부사절 접속사인 (C) once가 정답이다.
| 어휘 | confirmation 확인   registered 등록된

🔼고난도
118. 명사 어휘
회사의 모든 인턴들의 의무에는 그들의 사무실 프린터에 종이와 토너를 다시 채우는 일이 포함된다.
| 해설 | 빈칸은 of 이하 전치사구의 수식을 받는 문장의 주어가 될 명사가 들어갈 자리로, 문맥상 '인턴들의 의무에는 ~이 포함된다'라는 의미로 전개되는 것이 적절

하므로 '의무'라는 뜻의 (A) Obligations가 정답이다.
| 어휘 | include 포함하다   restock 다시 채우다, 보충하다   obligation 의무   allowance 수당, 용돈   procedure 절차   donation 기부

119. 동사의 형태
Schenectady의 시 의회 의원들이 새로운 도시 미화 프로젝트를 위한 여러 제안서들을 검토하고 있다.
| 해설 | be동사 are와 명사구 several proposals 사이에 빈칸이 있으므로, 동사나 명사로 쓰이는 (A) review와 (B) reviews는 오답이다. (D) reviewed가 쓰이면 수동태가 되는데 빈칸 뒤에 명사구가 있으므로 역시 오답이다. 따라서 현재 진행 능동태 동사를 완성해줄 현재 분사인 (C) reviewing이 정답이다.
| 어휘 | city council member 시 의회 의원   proposal 제안(서)   beautification 미화

120. 전치사 어휘
비만 아동의 증가로 인해, 많은 공립 학교들이 탄산음료를 제공하는 것을 중단했다.
| 해설 | 빈칸 뒤에 있는 명사구를 목적어로 받을 전치사가 들어갈 자리로, 내용 전개상 명사구가 뒤에 있는 절의 이유가 됨을 알 수 있으므로 '~로 인해'라는 의미의 (B) Due to가 정답이다.
| 어휘 | rise 증가   obese children 비만 아동   discontinue 중단하다   soft drink 탄산음료

121. 명사 어휘
새로운 공립 미술관의 건축이 관광업을 증가시킨 주된 요인이었다.
| 해설 | 앞에 있는 형용사 major의 수식을 받으며 주어인 The construction과 동격이 될 명사가 들어갈 자리로, 문맥상 '미술관 건축이 관광업을 증가시킨 주된 요인이었다'라는 의미로 전개되는 것이 적절하므로 '요인'이라는 의미의 (D) factor가 정답이다.
| 어휘 | construction 건설, 건축   tourism 관광업   duty 의무, 임무   choice 선택   factor 요인, 요소

122. 동사의 형태
마감일 이후에 제출된 모든 지원서는 예비 학생들을 위한 학자금 지원의 대상으로 고려되지 않는다.
| 해설 | be동사 are 뒤에 빈칸이 있으므로, 일반 동사 형태인 (A) consider와 (D) considers는 오답이고, (C) considering이 되면 능동태가 되어 목적어가 필요한데 전치사구가 이어지고 있으므로 오답이다. 따라서 수동태를 만드는 과거 분사인 (B) considered가 정답이다.
| 어휘 | application 지원서, 신청서   financial aid 재정적 지원, 학자금 지원   prospective student 입학 희망자, 예비 학생

123. 전치사 어휘
저희의 새로운 언어 프로그램에 관한 모든 문의는 지도 교수인 Simpson 씨에게 보내주세요.
| 해설 | 빈칸은 뒤의 명사구를 목적어로 가지는 전치사가 들어갈 자리로, '새로운 언어 프로그램에 관한 모든 문의'라는 의미로 전개되는 것이 적절하므로 '~에 관한'이라는 뜻의 (C) concerning이 정답이다.

| 어휘 | direct 보내다   inquiry 문의   academic advisor 지도 교수   following ~ 후에, 그다음에   concerning ~에 관한

124. 전치사 자리
재무 분석가는 잘 계획된 예산 덕분에 그 벤처 사업이 성공적이었다고 결론 내렸다.
| 해설 | 빈칸 앞에는 완전한 절이 있고 빈칸 뒤에는 명사구가 있으므로, 빈칸에는 절 뒤에 명사구를 연결해줄 전치사가 필요하다. 따라서 '~ 덕분에'라는 의미의 전치사인 (B) thanks to가 정답이다. (A) totally는 부사, (C) even though와 (D) as long as은 접속사이므로 오답이다.
| 어휘 | finance analyst 재무 분석가   conclude 결론 내리다   business venture 벤처 사업   success 성공   budget 예산

🔼 고난도

125. 형용사 자리 - 목적격 보어
Saunders 씨는 계좌 정보를 비밀로 유지하는 책임을 인계받을 것이다.
| 해설 | 빈칸은 5형식 동사 keeping의 목적어인 the account information 뒤 목적격 보어가 들어갈 자리이므로, 보어 자리에 올 수 없는 동사인 (A) confide와 부사인 (C) confidentially는 오답이고, 문맥상 '계좌 정보를 비밀로 유지하는'이라는 의미를 전개되는 것이 적절하므로 '비밀의'라는 뜻의 형용사인 (B) confidential이 정답이다.
| 어휘 | take over 인계받다   responsibility 책임   account information 계좌 정보   confide 비밀을 털어놓다   confidential 비밀의   confidentially 은밀하게, 기밀로서

126. 동사 어휘
지난 학기, Darcey 대학은 외국에서 공부하는 것에 관심이 있던 학생들을 위해 6개월 집중 외국어 강좌들을 마련했다.
| 해설 | 빈칸은 문장의 동사가 들어갈 자리로, 뒤에 제시된 목적어와 연결 지어 '강좌들을 마련했다'라는 의미로 전개되는 것이 적절하므로 '마련했다, 시행했다'라는 뜻의 (A) instituted가 정답이다.
| 어휘 | semester 학기   intensive 집중적인   abroad 외국에서   institute 마련하다, 실시하다   demonstrate 시연하다, 입증하다   apply 쓰다, 적용하다   identify 확인하다, 발견하다

🔼 고난도

127. 부사 자리
그 사무실에서는 드물게, Bae 씨는 현재 자신의 집에서 원격으로 일하는 정규직 프로그래머로 근무하고 있다.
| 해설 | 빈칸 뒤에 장소의 전치사구가 제시되어 있는 것으로 볼 때, 빈칸에는 전치사구를 수식해줄 수 있는 부사가 들어가야 함을 알 수 있으므로, 비교급 형용사인 (A) Fewer와 동사이자 형용사인 (D) Close는 오답이고, '그 사무실에서는 드물게'라는 의미를 완성해줄 '드물게'라는 뜻의 부사인 (C) Rarely가 정답이다.
| 어휘 | serve as ~로 근무하다   fulltime 정규직   remotely 멀리서, 원격으로

🔼 고난도

128. 부사 자리 - 동사 수식
비록 그녀는 단지 6개월 전에 Jordan 기업에 고용되었지만, 그럼에도 불구하고

Bishop 씨는 매장 관리자로 승진했다.

| 해설 | 주어 Ms. Bishop과 동사 got 사이에 빈칸이 있으며, 빈칸이 없어도 완전한 문장이므로, 빈칸에는 문장 구조에 영향을 미치지 않는 부사가 들어가야 한다. 따라서 명사절 접속사인 (A) whomever와 부사절 접속사인 (C) while은 오답이다. 문맥상 '단지 6개월 전에 고용되었지만 그럼에도 불구하고 승진했다'라는 의미로 전개되는 것이 자연스러우므로, '그럼에도 불구하고'라는 뜻의 부사인 (B) nevertheless가 정답이다.

| 어휘 | get the promotion to ~로 승진하다   additionally 추가적으로, 게다가

고난도
129. 형용사 어휘
지금까지는 Marshal 거리에 있는 상업용 부동산이 우리의 요구를 수용하기에 적당한 유일한 것이다.

| 해설 | 빈칸은 앞의 대명사 one을 뒤에서 수식하는 형용사가 들어갈 자리인데, 문맥상 '우리의 요구를 수용하기에 적당한 유일한 것'이라는 의미로 전개되는 것이 적절하므로 '적당한'이라는 뜻의 (C) adequate가 정답이다.

| 어휘 | commercial property 상업용 부동산, 상업 용지   accommodate 수용하다   tentative 잠정적인   excessive 과도한   adequate 적당한   provisional 임시의, 일시적인

고난도
130. 부사 어휘
Bryce 사는 새로운 정부 기준에 맞출 때까지 폐기물 생산을 점진적으로 줄이는 계획을 발표했다.

| 해설 | 빈칸은 앞의 동사 decrease를 수식하는 부사가 들어갈 자리인데, decrease는 정도를 나타내는 부사와 자주 쓰이며, 문맥상 '점진적으로 줄이는 계획을 발표했다'라는 의미로 전개되는 것이 적절하므로 '점진적으로'라는 (C) incrementally가 정답이다.

| 어휘 | decrease 줄이다   waste production 폐기물 생산   government standard 정부 기준   supportively 지지하여   voluntarily 자발적으로   incrementally 점진적으로   alternatively 그 대신에, 그렇지 않으면

PART 6

131-134 다음 기사를 참조하시오.

Ashmore가 KC 항공에서 한 단계 올라서다

METRO VALLEY, 11월 10일—KC 항공의 대변인이 CEO인 Oliver Norris가 건강상의 이유로 그의 직책에서 ¹³¹사임했다는 것을 확인해 주었다. 이사회 회장인 David Ashmore가 후임자를 구하는 동안 임시로 그 역할을 인계받을 것이다. ¹³²Ashmore 씨는 전에 회사를 경영한 경험이 있다. 그는 KC 항공 팀의 일원이 되기 전에 6년 동안 항공사 Freize 의 CEO였다. ¹³³게다가, 그는 또한 90년대에 여러 해 동안 수출입 업체의 사장으로도 일했다. 이사회는 그 직책을 위해 내부와 외부의 지원자

들을 모두 고려하고 있다. 전문가들은 회사의 역대 최대 인수를 ¹³⁴협상했던 고위 관료인 Melissa Hargrove가 그 자리를 제안받을 가능성이 가장 높다고 예측한다.

| 어휘 | spokesperson 대변인   confirm 확인하다, 확정하다   take over 인계받다   temporarily 임시적으로   replacement 후임자   seek 찾다   import-export business 수출입 업체   internal 내부의   external 외부의   applicant 지원자   predict 예측하다   senior official 고위 관료   acquisition 인수

131. 동사 어휘
| 해설 | that절의 동사가 들어갈 자리로, 문맥상 뒤에 제시된 '건강상의 이유'와 연결시켜 'CEO가 사임했다'라는 의미로 전개되는 것이 적절하므로 '사임했다'라는 의미의 (B) resigned가 정답이다.

| 어휘 | decline 줄어들다, 거절하다   resign 사임하다   emerge 드러나다   refrain 자제하다

132. 알맞은 문장 고르기
(A) 경쟁적인 시장이 그 문제의 원인이 되어 왔다.
(B) KC 항공은 국내 최대의 항공 운송업체 중 하나다.
(C) Ashmore 씨는 전에 회사를 경영한 경험이 있다.
(D) 이사회 회원들은 만장일치로 로고를 변경하는 것에 투표했다.

| 해설 | 앞서 후임자를 구하는 동안 이사회 회장인 David Ashmore가 임시로 그 역할을 인계받을 것이라는 문장이 제시되어 있고, 뒤이어 그가 과거 CEO였던 경력을 구체적으로 설명하고 있다. 따라서 그 사이에는 David Ashmore와 관련된 내용으로, 구체적인 설명 전에 회사 경영 경력이 있음을 언급한 문장이 삽입되는 것이 가장 적절하므로 정답은 (C)이다.

| 어휘 | competitive 경쟁적인   contribute to ~의 원인이 되다   domestic 국내의   air carrier 항공 운송업체   previous 이전의   vote 투표하다   unanimously 만장일치로

133. 접속 부사
| 해설 | 빈칸은 앞뒤 두 문장의 의미를 부드럽게 연결해줄 접속 부사가 들어갈 자리로, 앞에 David Ashmore의 한 가지 경력이 제시되어 있고, 뒤이어 또 다른 경력이 제시되어 있으므로 추가의 의미를 지닌 부사가 들어가야 함을 알 수 있다. 따라서 '게다가'라는 뜻의 (D) Furthermore가 정답이다. (A) Consequently는 결과, (B) Rather는 양보, (C) Otherwise는 반대 가정을 나타낼 때 쓴다.

| 어휘 | consequently 결과적으로   furthermore 게다가, 더욱이

고난도
134. 관계 대명사
| 해설 | 빈칸은 앞에 있는 주어인 명사 a senior official과 뒤에 있는 동사의 목적어 역할을 하는 명사구 the company's largest ever acquisition을 연결해 줄 접속사와 동사가 들어갈 자리이며, 회사의 역대 최대 인수를 협상한 것은 고위 관료인 Melissa Hargrove의 과거 업적일 것이므로, 사람을 선행사로 받는 관계 대명사와 과거 동사로 이루어진 (A) who negotiated이 정답이다.

| 어휘 | negotiate 협상하다   negotiation 협상

135-138 다음 이메일을 참조하시오.

수신: Amy Davis
발신: Paul Kane
날짜: 1월 18일
제목: Carson 갤러리 방문에 관한 후속 조치

Davis 씨 귀하,

Carson 갤러리에 관한 조언에 감사드립니다. 귀하의 의견에 기반하여, 기념품점 입구 근처에 바구니 더미를 135추가했습니다. 지적하셨던 대로, 쇼핑객들이 그들의 모든 상품을 카운터로 가져가는 것이 136다소 어려웠습니다. 이제 사람들은 더 많은 상품들을 가지고 다닐 수 있습니다. 더하여, 특별 전시를 위한 대기선의 경로를 변경하자는 귀하의 제안이 훌륭한 아이디어라고 생각합니다. 다음 달부터 대기선은 게시판을 따라 늘어설 것입니다. 137이것이 고객들이 다가오는 행사에 관한 우리의 포스터를 읽도록 장려할 것입니다.

다음 달, 우리는 현장에 더 많은 방문객들을 유치하는 138일에 전념할 계획입니다.

안부를 전하며,

Paul Kane

| 어휘 | advice 조언, 충고   regarding ~에 관한   based on ~을 기반으로   comment 의견, 지적   a stack of 한 더미, 한 꾸러미   entrance 입구   point out 지적하다   reroute 경로를 변경하다   exhibit 전시   alongside ~와 나란히   bulletin board 게시판   concentrate 집중하다, 전념하다   attract 끌어모으다, 유치하다

135. 동사의 시제

| 해설 | 빈칸은 문장의 본동사가 들어갈 자리로, 뒤에 이제 사람들이 더 많은 물품을 가져올 수 있게 되었다는 내용이 있으므로 바구니 더미를 '추가했다'는 과거 의미로 전개되는 것이 적절하다. 따라서 과거 시제인 (A) added가 정답이다.

고난도
136. 부사 어휘

| 해설 | 빈칸은 뒤에 있는 형용사 difficult를 수식하는 부사가 들어갈 자리로, 내용 전개상 쇼핑객들이 물품을 모두 카운터로 가져가는 것이 '다소' 어려웠기 때문에, 입구에 바구니를 추가한 것임을 알 수 있다. 따라서 '다소'라는 의미의 (B) somewhat이 정답이다.

137. 알맞은 문장 고르기

(A) 그것이 이번에 저희가 시행할 수 있었던 유일한 변화였습니다.
(B) 기념품점이 우리가 원했던 물품들을 포함시키기에는 너무 작았습니다.
(C) 이것이 고객들이 다가오는 행사에 관한 우리의 포스터를 읽도록 장려할 것입니다.
(D) 저희는 지역 예술가들이 저희 갤러리와 함께 일하는 것을 고려하길 바랍니다.

| 해설 | 앞서 다음 달부터 특별 전시의 대기선이 게시판을 따라 늘어설 것임을 알리는 문장이 제시되어 있으므로, 그것의 결과로 특별 전시를 보는 고객들이 행사를 알리는 게시판 내용도 읽게 될 것이라는 내용의 문장이 삽입되는 것이 가장 적절하다. 따라서 정답은 (C)이다. 앞서 의견을 반영해 바구니를 추가한 것 역시 이번에 시행한 변화이므로 (A)는 답이 될 수 없음에 유의하자.

| 어휘 | implement 시행하다   include 포함시키다   encourage 장려하다   patron 고객   upcoming 다가오는, 곧 있을

138. 전치사 어휘

| 해설 | 동사 concentrate와 어울리는 전치사를 묻는 문제인데, concentrate는 자동사로 쓰일 때 보통 전치사 on와 함께 쓰이므로 정답은 (B) on이다.

139-142 다음 정보를 참조하시오.

귀하께서 Stockton 주방 도구에서 구매하신 것이 동봉되어 있는 것을 보실 것입니다. 저희는 모든 수준의 요리사들이 139탁월해지도록 돕는 최고 품질의 주방 도구들을 제공하고자 노력합니다. 저희는 모든 제품에 대해 환불 보장을 제공하므로 고객님들은 본인의 기준을 충족시키지 못하는 제품을 반품할 수 있습니다. 환불이나 교환 요청은 원래 구매일로부터 60일 이내에 140받아져야만 한다는 것을 유념해 주시기 바랍니다. 141이는 우편으로 또는 소매점에서 이루어질 수 있습니다. 환불은 원래 구매가 어떻게 이루어졌느냐에 따라 신용 카드로 지급되거나 현금으로 이루어질 것입니다. 여러분의 애용에 감사드립니다. 저희와 함께 142요리해 주셔서 감사합니다!

| 어휘 | enclosed 동봉된   strive to ~하려고 노력하다   top-quality 최고 품질의   kitchen tool 주방 도구   chef 요리사   money-back guarantee 환불 보장   return 반품하다   meet one's standards 기준을 충족시키다   refund 환불   exchange 교환   issue 지급하다   depending on ~에 따라   patronage 애용

고난도
139. 형용사 자리 - 주격 보어

| 해설 | 빈칸은 'help + 목적어 + 동사 원형' 구조에서 동사 원형인 be동사의 보어가 들어갈 자리이므로 보어 자리에 올 수 없는 동사인 (A) inspires와 (C) inspire는 오답이며, 또한 명사 (B) inspiration도 chefs와 동격이 되는 것은 의미상 부적절하므로 오답이다. 따라서 '모든 수준의 요리사들이 탁월해지도록 돕다'라는 의미를 완성해 줄 과거 분사형 형용사인 (D) inspired가 정답이다.

140. 동사의 형태와 시제

| 해설 | 빈칸은 that절의 동사가 들어갈 자리로, receive는 타동사인데 빈칸 뒤에 목적어 없이 전치사구가 이어지고 있으므로, 능동태인 (A) will receive와 (B) are receiving은 오답이고, '환불이나 교환 요청이 구매일로부터 60일 이내에 받아져야 한다'는 의미가 되어야 하므로 (D) must be received가 정답이다.

141. 알맞은 문장 고르기

(A) 영수증이 여러분께 총액을 제공해 드립니다.
(B) 이는 우편으로 또는 소매점에서 이루어질 수 있습니다.
(C) 저희는 국내에서 1위로 평가받습니다.
(D) 귀하께서 요청하신 물품은 단종되어 유감입니다.

| 해설 | 앞서 환불이나 교환 요청이 가능한 기간을 명시한 문장이, 뒤이어 환불 지급 방식에 관해 알리는 문장이 제시되어 있는 것으로 볼 때, 그 사이에는 환불 요청 방법을 나타내는 문장이 삽입되는 것이 적절하므로 정답은 (B)이다.

| 어휘 | receipt 영수증   total price 총액   retail store 소매점   rate 평가하다   discontinue 단종하다

142. 동사 어휘

| 해설 | Thank you for 뒤에 빈칸이 있으므로 빈칸은 감사의 이유가 되어야 하며, 빈칸 뒤에 명사가 아닌 전치사구가 있으므로 자동사가 들어가야 한다. 또한 전체적인 내용으로 볼 때, 주방 도구를 판매하는 업체임을 알 수 있는데, 이들이 감사하는 것으로 어울리는 것은 업체의 주방 도구를 이용해 '요리하는' 것이므로 (A) cooking이 정답이다.

143-146 다음 기사를 참조하시오.

평소 구두로 하는 광고에 의존하는 것과 대조적으로, Fresh-Berry가 자사의 새로운 유제품이 함유되지 않은 디저트의 마케팅에 ¹⁴³공격적인 접근법을 취하고 있다. ¹⁴⁴이 업체는 이미 아침 식사용 스무디로 알려져 있다. 홍보 담당 이사인 Christopher Diehl은 회사가 디저트를 시작으로 자사의 제품 라인에 적어도 세 개의 라인을 더 추가할 것이라고 발표했다. 이것은 7년 전에 설립된 이후, Fresh-Berry 제품의 첫 변화이다. ¹⁴⁵따라서 회사 간부들은 광고에 크게 투자함으로써 그것을 성공시키는 일에 전념하고 있다. 그 디저트는 내년 초에 시판될 것으로 예상된다. Fresh-Berry 팀은 아직 디저트 요리법에 공을 들이고 있는데, 그것은 가장 인기 있는 ¹⁴⁶맛을 포함시킬 것으로 예상된다.

| 어휘 | in contrast to ~와 대조되는   dependence on ~에의 의존   word-of-mouth advertising 구두로 하는 광고   approach 접근   dairy-free 유제품이 함유되지 않은   public relations director 홍보 담당 이사   founding 설립   company official 회사 간부   intent on ~에 전념하는   invest 투자하다   hit the shelves 시판되다   recipe 요리법

143. 형용사 어휘

| 해설 | 빈칸은 뒤에 있는 명사 approach를 수식하는 형용사가 들어갈 자리로, 앞에 제시된 구두로 하는 광고에 의존하는 것과 대조적인 마케팅 접근법이 되어야 하므로 '공격적인, 적극적인'이라는 뜻의 (D) aggressive가 정답이다.

| 어휘 | outstanding 뛰어난, 두드러진   entire 전체의   immediate 즉각적인   aggressive 공격적인, 적극적인

🔺고난도
144. 알맞은 문장 고르기

(A) 그 계획은 지난 몇 년 동안 잘되어 왔다.
(B) 점점 더 많은 업체들이 그 붐비는 시장으로 진입하고 있다.
(C) 이 업체는 이미 아침 식사용 스무디로 알려져 있다.
(D) 그 재료들은 유기 농장들로부터 오는 것으로 보증된다.

| 해설 | 앞서 Fresh-Berry라는 업체의 신제품 마케팅에 관해 언급되었고, 뒤이어 제품 라인 확대에 대한 내용이 제시되어 있는 것으로 볼 때, 그 사이에는 그 업체의 기존 제품에 관해 설명하는 문장이 삽입되는 것이 적절하므로 정답은 (C)이다.

| 어휘 | enter 들어오다, 진입하다   crowded 붐비는, 혼잡한   ingredient 재료   certify 증명하다, 보증하다   organic farm 유기 농장

145. 접속 부사

| 해설 | 빈칸은 앞뒤 두 문장의 의미를 부드럽게 연결해줄 접속 부사가 들어갈 자리로, 문맥상 '7년 전에 설립된 이후 Fresh-Berry 제품의 첫 변화'라는 앞 문장과 '회사 간부들이 그것을 성공시키는 일에 전념하고 있다'라는 뒤 문장은, 첫 변화이기 때문에 성공시키고자 전념한다는 인과 관계로 연결되는 것이 적절하므로, '따라서, 그러므로'라는 뜻의 접속 부사인 (D) Therefore가 정답이다.

146. 명사 어휘

| 해설 | 빈칸은 타동사 include의 목적어로, the most popular의 수식을 받는 명사가 들어갈 자리로, 앞에 제시된 디저트 요리법을 단서로 이러한 요리법에 포함될 것으로 예상되는 것은 '가장 인기 있는 맛'임을 알 수 있으므로 '맛, 풍미'라는 뜻의 (A) flavors가 정답이다.

| 어휘 | flavor 맛, 풍미   portion 몫, 부분

PART 7

147-148 다음 웹 페이지를 참조하시오.

http://www.stockchase.net

¹⁴⁸Stock Chase는 주가와 동향에 관한 최신 소식을 제공하여, ¹⁴⁷은행가들이 가장 수익성 있는 투자 선택을 할 수 있게 돕습니다. 실시간 갱신되는 저희의 조언은 여러분이 시장에서 한 발 앞서도록 해 드릴 수 있습니다. 회원이 되는 것은 빠르고, 쉬우며, 가장 중요한 것으로, 무료입니다! ¹⁴⁸그저 여러분의 이름과 전화번호를 입력하고 업무 시간 동안 문자를 받아보기 시작하세요.

¹⁴⁸이름: Lily Shaw
전화: 619-734-1912

[신청하기]

| 어휘 | stock price 주가   banker 은행가   profitable 수익성 있는   investment 투자   step ahead 한 발 앞서다   enter 입력하다   business hours 업무 시간

147. 추론 문제
웹 페이지는 누구를 위해 의도된 것 같은가?
(A) 트럭 운전사들
(B) 상점 소유주들
(C) 투자 은행가들
(D) 보안 요원들
| 해설 | 초반부에 은행가들이 가장 수익성 있는 투자 선택을 할 수 있게 돕는다고(helping bankers make the most profitable investment choices possible) 한 것에서, 투자 선택을 하는 은행가를 겨냥한 웹 페이지인 것으로 유추할 수 있으므로 정답은 (C)이다.
| 어휘 | owner 소유주, 주인   security guard 보안 요원

148. 추론 문제
Shaw 씨에 관해 추론될 수 있는 것은 무엇인가?
(A) Stock Chase로부터 최신 소식을 받을 것이다.
(B) 그녀의 이름이 웹 사이트에 게재될 것이다.
(C) 그녀의 투자는 매우 수익성이 있다.
(D) Stock Chase의 직원이다.
| 해설 | 도입부에 Stock Chase는 주가와 동향에 관한 최신 소식을 제공한다고(Stock Chase gives the latest updates) 하였고, 후반부에 이름과 전화번호를 입력하고 문자를 받아보기 시작하라는(Simply enter your name and phone number and begin receiving texts ~) 내용이 있는데, 그 밑에서 Shaw 씨의 이름(Lily Shaw)과 전화번호(619-734-1912)를 확인할 수 있다. 이를 통해 Shaw 씨는 Stock Chase로부터 주가에 관한 최신 소식을 문자로 받을 것임을 유추할 수 있으므로 정답은 (A)이다.
| 어휘 | post 게시하다, 붙이다

149-150 다음 영수증을 참조하시오.

영수증 #4385-0118

고객 서비스 문제를 위해 이 번호를 참조하세요

¹⁵⁰고객: Jonathan Hurst
신용 카드: Visa xxxx-xxxx-xxxx-6201
¹⁴⁹공연 날짜: 10월 13일 (금요일) 7:30
공연 제목: Life of Byron (코미디 / 뮤지컬)
좌석: D-19, D-20

¹⁵⁰극장에 일찍 오는 것이 가장 좋습니다. 늦게 도착하는 손님들은 입장하기 위해 중간 휴식 시간까지 기다려야 할 것입니다. 이 규정에 예외는 없습니다.

| 어휘 | refer 참조하다   intermission 중간 휴식 시간   exception 예외   rule 규정

149. 세부 사항을 묻는 문제
10월 13일에 무슨 행사가 예정되어 있는가?

(A) 박물관 개관식
(B) 책 사인회
(C) 극장 공연
(D) 경주 대회
| 해설 | 중반부에 공연 날짜 항목(Show Date: 13 October (Friday) 7:30)과 공연 제목 항목(Show Title: Life of Byron (Comedy / Musical))을 통해, 10월 13일에 코미디 뮤지컬 공연이 예정되어 있음을 알 수 있으므로 정답은 (C)이다.
| 어휘 | theatrical 연극의, 극장의   competition 대회, 경쟁
| 패러프레이징 | Comedy / Musical → A theatrical performance

150. 세부 정보를 묻는 문제
Hurst 씨가 하도록 권장되는 것은 무엇인가?
(A) 피드백 서식을 작성하는 것
(B) 장소에 일찍 도착하는 것
(C) 기념품 가게를 방문하는 것
(D) 중간 휴식 시간을 기다리는 것
| 해설 | Hurst 씨는 공연 예약 고객으로, 영수증 마지막 부분 *에 극장에 일찍 오는 것이 가장 좋다고(It is best to come to the theater early) 제시되어 있으므로 정답은 (B)이다.
| 어휘 | complete 작성하다, 완료하다   venue 장소   souvenir shop 기념품 가게
| 패러프레이징 | come to the theater early → Arrive to the venue early

151-152 다음 문자 메시지 대화를 참조하시오.

Evelyn Berger <오후 3:38>
전화 못 받아서 미안해요. 회의에서 발표하는 중이었거든요. 무슨 일이에요?

Randy Avalos <오후 3:41>
그저 ¹⁵¹제가 우리 온라인 쇼핑 페이지의 문제를 해결했다는 걸 알려 드리고 싶었어요.

Evelyn Berger <오후 3:42>
잘됐네요. 그럼 이제 링크들이 모두 작동되나요?

Randy Avalos <오후 3:42>
네. 링크를 클릭하면, 제품 설명으로 가게 돼요. 가격의 폰트 크기도 더 크게 해서 더 읽기 쉬워요.

Evelyn Berger <오후 3:44>
완벽하네요. 고마워요. 연결이 끊어진 링크에 관해 ¹⁵²고객들로부터 부정적인 의견이 있을 수 있어 걱정을 했거든요.

Randy Avalos <오후 3:47>
전혀 받지 않았어요.

Evelyn Berger <오후 3:48>
네. 그것 다행이에요. 그렇게 빨리 처리해 줘서 고마워요.

| 어휘 | miss 놓치다   fix 해결하다   active 작동되는, 활동적인
description 설명   negative 부정적인   comment 의견   relief 안심,
안도   take care of ~을 처리하다

151. 세부 사항을 묻는 문제
Avalos 씨가 했다고 말하는 것은 무엇인가?
(A) 온라인으로 주문을 했다.
(B) 제품 가격을 인상했다.
(C) 웹 사이트에 변화를 주었다.
(D) 몇몇 제품 설명을 작성했다.
| 해설 | 오후 3:41에 Randy Avalos가 온라인 쇼핑 페이지의 문제를 해결했다고 (I've fixed the problem with our online shopping page) 하였으므로 정답은 (C)이다.
| 어휘 | place an order 주문을 하다   raise 인상하다, 올리다
| 패러프레이징 | fixed the problem with our online shopping page
→ Made changes to a Web site

고난도
152. 의도 파악 문제
오후 3:47에 Avalos 씨가 "전혀 받지 않았어요"라고 쓸 때 암시하는 것은 무엇인가?
(A) 그는 승인을 기다리고 있다.
(B) 수송품이 늦게 도착할 것이다.
(C) 그는 서비스에 불만족스러워 한다.
(D) 문제가 알려지지 않았다.
| 해설 | 이는 앞서 오후 3:44에 Evelyn Berger가 고객들로부터 부정적인 의견이 있을 수 있어 걱정을 했다고(I was worried that there might be some negative comments from customers ~) 한 것에 대한 응답으로, 부정적인 의견을 전혀 받지 않았다는 말은 문제가 알려지지 않았음을 암시하는 것이므로 정답은 (D)이다.

153-154 다음 회람을 참조하시오.

수신: Palmore 백화점 직원들
발신: Jeffrey Dye
날짜: 9월 6일
주제: 휴식 규정

모든 직원들은 교대 근무 중에 휴식 시간을 가질 자격이 있지만, ¹⁵³따라야 하는 몇 가지 규정이 있습니다. 최근에 항의가 있어서, ¹⁵³모든 것을 명확히 하고 싶습니다.

여러분이 휴식 시간에 매장 건물 내에 머무르는 경우, 고객들은 여러분이 그들을 돕기 위해 그곳에 있다고 생각할 수 있다는 것을 알고 계셔야 합니다. 어떠한 오해도 피하기 위해, ¹⁵⁴휴식 중에는 직원 휴게실 중 한 곳을 이용해 주세요. 여러분의 협조와 이해에 감사드립니다. 이와 관련하여 질문이 있을 경우, 그것들은 여러분의 직속 상사에게 보내주세요.

| 어휘 | rule 규정   be entitled to ~할 자격이 있다   break time 휴식 시간   shift 교대 근무   follow 따르다   complaint 항의, 불만   property 구내, 부동산   aware 알고 있는   assist 돕다   avoid 피하다   misunderstanding 오해   appreciate 감사하다, 고마워하다   cooperation 협조   understanding 이해   immediate supervisor 직속 상사

153. 주제/목적 문제
회람의 주된 목적은 무엇인가?
(A) 일시적인 상점 폐장을 알리는 것
(B) 피드백을 요청하는 것
(C) 새로운 복장 규정을 소개하는 것
(D) 한 가지 정책을 명확하게 하는 것
| 해설 | 첫 번째 단락에 휴식 시간을 갖는 것과 관련하여 따라야 하는 규정이 있다며(there are some rules that are expected to be followed), 모든 것을 명확하게 하고 싶다고(I want to make sure that everything is clear) 했으므로 정답은 (D)이다.
| 어휘 | temporary 일시적인, 임시의   introduce 소개하다, 도입하다   dress code 복장 규정   policy 정책, 방침
| 패러프레이징 | · rules → a policy
· make sure that everything is clear → clarify

154. 세부 사항을 묻는 문제
직원들이 하도록 상기받는 것은 무엇인가?
(A) 지정된 구역에서 휴식을 취하는 것
(B) 그들의 집에서 원격으로 일하는 것
(C) 그들의 유니폼을 단정하고 깨끗하게 유지하는 것
(D) 상세한 고객 의견을 수집하는 것
| 해설 | 두 번째 단락에 휴식 중에는 직원 휴게실을 이용해 달라고(please use one of the employee break rooms while on break) 했으므로 정답은 (A)이다.
| 어휘 | designated 지정된   tidy 단정한, 깔끔한   collect 수집하다   detailed 상세한   opinion 의견
| 패러프레이징 | use one of the employee break rooms while on break
→ Take a break in designated areas

155-157 다음 광고를 참조하시오.

남태평양 탐험대 - 지상에 있는 천국을 찾아서!

¹⁵⁵저희의 멋진 배들 중 하나에 탑승하여 휴식하면서 남태평양의 바다를 탐험해 보세요. 저희의 모든 배에는 휴가 중에 여러분이 원할 수 있는 모든 시설이 완벽하게 갖춰져 있습니다. 바다에서 모험을 하는 동안 그레이트 배리어 리프(대보초)와 돌고래, 그리고 고래들 같은 광경에 경이로움을 느껴보세요. 배가 고파질 때면 낮이나 밤이나 언제든 저희의 24시

간 뷔페로 식사를 즐길 수 있습니다. 낮에는 앞 갑판에 있는 풀장 옆에서 일광욕을 해 보세요. 실내에서 수영하는 것을 더 좋아하실 경우, 저희 배 안에는 실내 운동 수영장도 있습니다. 매일 밤 저희 무도회장에서는 오후 8시부터 자정까지 여러분과 여러분에게 중요한 사람이 춤출 수 있게 라이브 음악을 특별히 연주합니다. 아이들을 데리고 오실 경우, 156<Parenting on Vacation Magazine>이 "가장 재미있는 어린이 오락거리"라고 이름 붙인 동화 인형극들 중 하나를 즐겨보세요. 그것들은 오전 10시부터 오후 6시까지 매시간 열립니다. 프라이버시를 원하실 경우, 바다를 향한 창문이 있고 방음이 되는 여러분의 침실로 언제든 돌아가실 수 있습니다. 157Creon 섬에서 머무르는 4시간 동안, 적은 요금으로 해양 레저 활동들을 즐기실 수 있습니다. 여러분의 객실 도우미에게 물어봄으로써 가격 정보를 얻고 자리를 예약하세요.

| 어휘 | aboard 탑승한, 승선한   explore 탐험하다   be fully equipped with ~이 완벽하게 갖춰져 있다   marvel 경이로워하다, 경탄하다   sight 경관   adventure 모험   poolside 풀장 옆   sunbathing 일광욕   forward deck 앞 갑판   indoors 실내의   ballroom 무도회장   feature 특별히 포함하다   midnight 자정   significant other 중요한 타인(배우자, 연인)   fairy tale 동화   puppet show 인형극   sound-proofed 방음이 되는   marine leisure activity 해양 레저 활동   nominal 소정의, 아주 적은   assistant 도우미, 보조

155. 주제/목적 문제
무엇이 광고되고 있나?
(A) 투어 그룹
(B) 여행사
(C) 휴양 리조트
(D) 해양 유람선
| 해설 | 도입부에 멋진 배에 탑승하여 휴식하며 남태평양 바다를 탐험해 보라고(Step aboard any one of our fine ships and relax while exploring the waters of the Southern Pacific Ocean) 제시된 것을 통해, 해양 유람선 광고임을 알 수 있으므로 정답은 (D)이다.

🔺고난도
156. True 문제
남태평양 탐험대에 관해 명시된 것은 무엇인가?
(A) 인명 구조원들을 24시간 고용한다.
(B) 배에 따라 다른 시설들을 가지고 있다.
(C) 상을 받은 오락거리를 제공한다.
(D) 경쟁사들보다 고객 만족 점수가 더 높다.
| 해설 | 중반부에 아이들을 데리고 올 경우, <Parenting on Vacation Magazine>이 "가장 재미있는 어린이 오락거리"라고 이름 붙인 동화 인형극을 즐겨보라고(enjoy one of the fairy tale puppet shows that have been named "Most Fun Child Entertainment" by Parenting on Vacation Magazine) 제시되어 있으므로 정답은 (C)이다. 잡지나 신문 등에서 타이틀을 준 것도 award-winning으로 표현할 수 있다.

| 어휘 | lifeguard 인명 구조원   depending on ~에 따라   award-winning 상을 받은   outscore 점수가 더 높다   competitor 경쟁사, 경쟁자

satisfaction 만족

| 패러프레이징 | the fairy tale puppet shows that have been named "Most Fun Child Entertainment" → award-winning entertainment

157. 세부 사항을 묻는 문제
추가 요금으로 구입될 수 있는 것은 무엇인가?
(A) 해양 활동들
(B) 아기 돌봄 서비스
(C) 라이브 극장 티켓
(D) 디지털 영화 스트리밍
| 해설 | 후반부에 적은 요금으로 해양 레저 활동들을 즐길 수 있다고(you can enjoy the marine leisure activities with nominal fees) 제시되어 있으므로 정답은 (A)이다.

158-160 다음 이메일을 참조하시오.

수신: Rachel Medrano <rachelm@center-post.com>
발신: Amil Sankar <amilsankar@llk1.com>
날짜: 9월 1일
제목: 응답 요망

Medrano 씨 귀하,

분기별 세입자 회의에서 논의된 대로, Atlas 아파트의 소유주가 시설의 보안을 업그레이드하려고 합니다. 각 호에 비디오 인터컴 시스템이 갖춰질 것이고, 그러면 버저를 눌러 사람을 들어오게 하기 전에 입구에 서 있는 사람을 볼 수 있을 것입니다. ㅡ [1] ㅡ. 158기기는 9월 7일 오전 9시와 정오 사이에 기술자에 의해 귀하의 집 안에 설치될 것입니다. 159그 작업을 하는 동안 댁에 안 계셔도, 문제가 되지 않습니다. ㅡ [2] ㅡ. 건물 관리자가 모든 세입자들의 열쇠 복사본을 가지고 있어 기술자를 들어가게 해줄 수 있습니다. 하지만 이 경우에, 159저희가 귀하의 아파트에 들어가도록 첨부된 동의서를 작성해 주셔야 할 것입니다. 그저 그것을 이 주소의 이메일로 저에게 다시 보내주세요.

비디오 인터컴 시스템은 Atlas 아파트의 보안을 개선하려는 더 큰 계획의 일부입니다. ㅡ [3] ㅡ. 저희는 모든 엘리베이터와 복도에 보안 카메라를 설치하고, 주차장에 동작 센서 조명을 놓고, 늘 두 명이 근무하고 있도록 또 다른 보안 요원도 고용할 것입니다. ㅡ [4] ㅡ. 160그것은 작년에 시행되었던 임대료 인상으로 비용이 지불될 것이기 때문입니다.

이 변화에 관해 의문 사항이 있으시면, 이메일을 주시거나 555-8330로 임대 사무실로 전화하여 편하게 저에게 연락해 주시기 바랍니다.

진심으로,

Amil Sankar
Atlas 아파트, 세입자 연락 담당자

| 어휘 | quarterly 분기별의   tenant 세입자   security 보안   buzz in 버저를 눌러 들어오게 하다   present 있는   fill out 작성하다   attached 첨부된   consent form 동의서   improve 개선하다   corridor 복도   be on duty 근무하다   rent 임대료   go into effect 시행되다, 효력이 발생되다   rental office 임대 사무실   liaison 연락 담당자

158. 주제/목적 문제
Sankar 씨는 왜 Medrano 씨에게 이메일을 보냈나?
(A) 그녀를 세입자 회의에 초대하기 위해
(B) 그녀가 가능한 시간에 관한 정보를 요청하기 위해
(C) 그녀에게 설치 계획에 관해 알리기 위해
(D) 보안 조치에 관한 피드백을 요청하기 위해

| 해설 | 첫 번째 단락에 보안을 업그레이드하려고 한다고 알린 후, 기기가 9월 7일 오전 9시와 정오 사이에 기술자에 의해 집 안에 설치될 것이라고(The device will be installed inside your home by a technician on September 7 between 9 A.M. and noon) 덧붙인 것을 통해, 기기 설치 일정을 알리기 위한 목적으로 보낸 이메일임을 알 수 있으므로 정답은 (C)이다.

| 어휘 | availability 이용 가능성, 유효성   installation 설치   measures 조치, 방안

159. 세부 사항을 묻는 문제
9월 7일에 집에 없을 경우 Medrano 씨가 해야 하는 것은 무엇인가?
(A) 다른 날로 방문 일정을 다시 잡는 것
(B) Sankar 씨에게 작성된 문서를 다시 보내는 것
(C) 자신의 열쇠를 건물 관리자에게 맡기는 것
(D) 이웃에게 일을 하도록 부탁하는 것

| 해설 | 첫 번째 단락 중반부에 작업을 하는 동안 집에 없어도 문제가 되지 않는다며, 이런 경우에는 동의서를 작성해서 이메일로 다시 보내 달라고(you will need to fill out the attached consent form for us to enter your apartment. Simply e-mail it back to me) 했으므로 정답은 (B)이다.

| 어휘 | reschedule 일정을 다시 잡다   neighbor 이웃
| 패러프레이징 | fill out the attached consent form → a completed document

160. 문장 삽입 문제
[1], [2], [3], [4]로 표시된 곳 중에 다음 문장이 들어가기에 가장 적절한 곳은?
"이 업그레이드로 인해 세입자들에게 직접적으로 부과되는 비용은 없습니다."
(A) [1]
(B) [2]
(C) [3]
(D) [4]

| 해설 | 제시된 문장은 세입자들에게 부과되는 비용이 없다는 것으로, 이는 후반부에 그것은 작년에 시행되었던 임대료 인상으로 비용이 지불될 것이기 때문이라고(That's because they are being paid for by the rent increases that went into effect last year) 덧붙인 문장 앞에 삽입되는 것이 가장 적절하므로 (D)가 정답이다. 뒤에 언급된 That's because ~가 제시된 문장의 이유로 연결되므로 정답을 찾는 단서가 된다.

161-163 다음 이메일을 참조하시오.

발신: Pamela Robbins <custserv@atlantacabs.net>
수신: Stephen Reynolds <s.reynolds@qmail.net>
[161]제목: 문의 #20149 답변
날짜: 5월 17일

Reynolds 씨 귀하,

[161]저희 운전사 중 한 명이 귀하께서 분실하셨다고 신고하신 배낭의 설명과 일치하는 것을 제출했습니다. 내리실 때 그것을 택시 안에 두고 가신 것 같습니다.

안전상의 이유로, 저희 차량에 남겨져 있는 어떤 물품도 열어보지 않는 것이 저희 회사의 방침입니다. [163]저희 본사로 오셔서 귀하의 가방을 확인하고 찾아가시길 요청드립니다. 저희의 정규 영업시간은 월요일부터 토요일까지, 오전 8시부터 오후 6시까지입니다. 일요일에는 사무실이 문을 열지 않습니다. 가방을 찾으러 오시면, 양도 서식에 서명하도록 부탁드릴 것입니다. 이는 일반적인 보안 절차입니다. [162]저희가 또한 귀하의 신분증도 복사할 것입니다.

저희가 회수한 물품은 2주 동안만 보관하니, [163]다음 달까지는 귀하의 가방을 찾아가셔야 한다는 것을 유념해 주시기 바랍니다. 추가적인 질문이 있으시면 555-2867로 저희에게 편하게 전화해 주세요.

Pamela Robbins

Atlanta 택시, 고객 서비스 담당자

| 어휘 | turn in 건네주다, 제출하다   match 일치하다   description 설명   missing 분실된, 없어진   get out 내리다   safety 안전   identify 확인하다   claim (자기 권리나 재산이라고 여겨) 요구하다   regular 정규의   release form 양도 서식, 양도 계약서   security procedure 보안 절차   recovered 되찾은   retrieve 회수하다, 되찾다

161. 추론 문제
Reynolds 씨는 무엇에 관해 물었을 것 같은가?
(A) 탑승 가능성
(B) 추가 요금
(C) 잃어버린 개인 물품
(D) 영업시간

| 해설 | 이메일의 제목이 문의 #20149 답변이고, 첫 번째 단락에 분실했다고 신고한 배낭의 설명과 일치하는 것을 찾았다고(One of our drivers has turned in a backpack that matches the description of the one you reported missing) 한 것에서 분실물에 관해 문의했을 것으로 유추할 수 있으므로 정답은 (C)이다.

| 어휘 | extra 추가의   fee 요금
| 패러프레이징 | · missing → lost
· a backpack → a personal item

162. 세부 사항을 묻는 문제
이메일에 따르면, Reynolds 씨가 제공해야 할 것은 무엇인가?
(A) 근무 일정
(B) 개인 소지품
(C) 신분증
(D) 영수증

| 해설 | 두 번째 단락 끝에 가방을 찾으러 오면 신분증을 복사할 것이라고(We will also make a photocopy of your ID) 했으므로 신분증을 제공해야 함을 알 수 있다. 따라서 정답은 (C)이다.

| 어휘 | belonging 소지품

| 패러프레이징 | ID → identification

163. 세부 사항을 묻는 문제
Reynolds 씨가 하도록 요청받는 것은 무엇인가?
(A) 더 많은 정보를 모으는 것
(B) 곧 Robbins 씨의 사무실을 방문하는 것
(C) 배달 주소를 제공하는 것
(D) 운전사에게 연락하는 것

| 해설 | 두 번째 단락 초반부에 본사로 와서 가방을 확인하고 찾아가라고(We ask that you come to our main office to identify and claim your bag) 하였고, 마지막 단락에 다음 달까지는 가방을 찾아가야 한다고(you have until next month to retrieve your bag) 한 것을 연계해 볼 때, 빠른 시일 내에 Robbins 씨의 본사 사무실을 방문해 가방을 찾아갈 것을 요청받은 것임을 알 수 있으므로 정답은 (B)이다.

| 어휘 | gather 모으다, 수집하다   information 정보

| 패러프레이징 | come to our main office → Visit Ms. Robbins' office

164-167 다음 온라인 채팅 토론을 참조하시오.

Clara Mills [오전 9:09]	안녕하세요, 여러분. 우리가 논의해야 할 사안이 있어요. ¹⁶⁴제가 생산 작업장에서 막 왔는데, Seneca 패션을 위한 우리 주문을 보류해야겠어요.
Thao Phan [오전 9:10]	무슨 일인데요? 그 회사가 모델들과의 사진 촬영이 있어서 금요일까지 ¹⁶⁴그 드레스 샘플들을 보내기로 되어 있잖아요.
Clara Mills [오전 9:11]	제가 도착한 천을 살펴보고, 색깔이 잘못된 것을 발견했어요. 그 라인의 다른 것들보다 약간 더 어두워요. 직물 제조업체에 연락했고 화요일까지 제대로 된 천을 보내줄 수 있대요.
Hedra Penhale [오전 9:11]	그것은 Seneca 패션의 주문을 처리하는 것이 늦을 것이라는 의미잖아요. ¹⁶⁵그 소유주인 Lin 씨가 무척 화낼 텐데요.
Kenny Carini [오전 9:12]	하지만 전에 결코 그런 적 없잖아요.
Thao Phan [오전 9:13]	¹⁶⁵맞아요. 그것이 우리 명성에 그렇게 많은 영향을 미치지는 않을 거예요. 저희는 믿을 만하다고 오랜 정평이 나 있잖아요.
Clara Mills [오전 9:13]	¹⁶⁶그리고 초과 근무를 할 의향이 있는 사람들을 찾을 수 있다면 단 며칠만 늦어질 거예요.
Thao Phan [오전 9:14]	¹⁶⁶그것은 제가 처리할 수 있어요.
Clara Mills [오전 9:15]	고마워요. 저에게 결정된 것을 알려주시면 제가 휴게실에 업데이트된 일정을 게시할게요.
Hedra Penhale [오전 9:16]	그리고 ¹⁶⁷Clara, 색상 문제를 발견해줘서 고마워요. 아주 대가가 큰 실수가 될 수도 있었어요!

| 어휘 | production floor 생산 작업장   put on hold ~을 보류하다, 연기하다   be supposed to ~하기로 되어 있다   fabric 직물, 천   slightly 약간, 조금   manufacturer 제조업체   fulfill 이행하다   upset 화난   affect 영향을 미치다   reputation 명성, 평판   have a long track record of ~에 오랜 정평이 나 있다   reliable 믿을 만한   be willing to 기꺼이 ~하다, ~할 의향이 있다   post 게시하다   spot 발견하다   costly mistake 대가가 큰 실수

164. 추론 문제 [고난도]
글쓴이들은 어디에서 일하는 것 같은가?
(A) 모델 에이전시에서
(B) 의류 공장에서
(C) 패션 잡지사에서
(D) 직물 제조업체에서

| 해설 | 오전 9:09에 Clara Mills가 방금 생산 작업장에서 왔다고(I just came from the production floor) 한 것과 오전 9:10에 Thao Phan이 드레스 샘플을 보내기로 되어 있다고(We're supposed to send the samples for those dresses) 한 것을 통해, 의류 공장에서 일하는 것임을 유추할 수 있으므로 정답은 (B)이다.

165. 의도 파악 문제 [고난도]
오전 9:12에 Carini 씨가 "전에 결코 그런 적 없잖아요"라고 쓸 때 의미하는 것은 무엇일 것 같은가?
(A) 그는 문제가 발생했다는 것에 놀랐다.
(B) 그는 실수를 책임지는 것을 거부한다.
(C) 그는 고객이 이해해 줄 것이라고 생각한다.
(D) 그는 문제를 어떻게 해결해야 할지 모른다.

| 해설 | 이는 앞서 오전 9:11에 Hedra Penhale이 주문 처리가 늦어지는 것에 대해 고객 업체 소유주가 무척 화를 낼 거라고(The owner, Ms. Lin, is going to be so upset) 쓴 것에 대한 응답으로, 뒤이어 오전 9:13에 Thao Phan이 동의하며 명성에 그렇게 많은 영향을 미치지는 않을 거라고(Right. I don't think it will affect our reputation that much) 덧붙인 것을 통해, 고객이 화를 낼 수는 있겠지만 전에 결코 없었던 일인 만큼 이해해 줄 것이라는 의도로 쓴 것임을 추론할 수 있으므로 정답은 (C)이다.

| 어휘 | occur 발생하다, 일어나다   refuse 거절하다, 거부하다

take responsibility for ~을 책임지다   resolve 해결하다

166. 세부 사항을 묻는 문제
Phan 씨가 할 것이라고 말하는 것은 무엇인가?
(A) 업데이트된 일정을 게시하는 것
(B) 일부 제품들을 신중히 검사하는 것
(C) 초과 근무를 할 직원들을 모집하는 것
(D) Lin 씨와의 미팅을 여는 것
| 해설 | 후반부 오전 9:14에 Thao Phan이 그것을 처리할 수 있다고(I can take care of that) 했는데, 그것은 바로 위 오전 9:13에 Clara Mills가 말한 초과 근무를 할 사람을 찾는 것임을(if we can find people who are willing to put in extra hours) 알 수 있으므로 정답은 (C)이다.
| 어휘 | inspect 점검하다, 검사하다   carefully 신중히
| 패러프레이징 | find people who are willing to put in extra hours
→ Recruit employees to work overtime

167. 추론 문제
Mills 씨에 관해 암시된 것은 무엇인가?
(A) 제품들이 더 어둡게 되는 것을 선호한다.
(B) 몇 가지 새로운 색상을 고를 것이다.
(C) 회사의 많은 돈을 절약했다.
(D) Penhale 씨가 프로젝트를 끝내도록 도왔다.
| 해설 | 마지막 오전 9:16에 Hedra Penhale이 Clara에게 색상 문제를 발견한 것에 대해 감사를(thank you, Clara, for spotting the problem with the colors) 표한 후, 아주 대가가 큰 실수가 될 수 있었다고(That could have been a very costly mistake) 한 것을 통해, 색상 문제를 발견해 회사의 많은 돈을 절약한 것으로 유추할 수 있으므로 정답은 (C)이다.
| 어휘 | save 아끼다, 절약하다
| 패러프레이징 | costly → a lot of money

168-171 다음 기사를 참조하시오.

TOPEKA (12월 19일) – 바로 이곳 Topeka에서 새해 전야에 ¹⁶⁸자선 콘서트가 계획되고 있다. 곧 있을 그 콘서트 <음악의 마법>은 아이들에게 음악과 예술을 통한 자기 표현 같은 것들을 가르치는 지역의 방과 후 프로그램들을 위한 기금을 모을 것이다. 콘서트에 몇몇 지역 밴드들과 여러 유명 밴드들이 특별히 출연할 것이다. 티켓은 행사의 웹 사이트인 www.magicofmusic.com에서 미리 구입될 수 있고, 성인은 30달러, 어린이는 20달러이다.

그 콘서트의 조직자인 Kate Dickerson은 자선 단체들을 후원하는 행사를 조직하는 일에 폭넓은 경험을 가지고 있다. ¹⁶⁹얼마 전에 그녀는 암 연구를 위한 돈을 모으기 위해 아마추어 축구 토너먼트인 <치료를 위한 발길질>을 기획했다. 그 행사의 성공에 관한 인터뷰에서 ¹⁷⁰Dickerson 씨는 성공적인 모금 행사를 기획하기 위해서는 누구든 티켓을 사는 사람들이 스스로에 대해 좋은 기분을 느끼게 만들어야 한다고 했다. "대의를 후원하는 것에 대해 사람들을 칭찬하는 것이 중요합니다." 그녀가 말했다.

¹⁷¹<음악의 마법>을 위해 왜 Topeka를 선택했는지 질문을 받았을 때, Dickerson 씨는 그곳이 연주를 자원한 밴드들의 중앙에 위치한 곳이라고 말했다. "아티스트들이 공연하러 와준다는 것에 정말 감사해요. ¹⁷¹그들이 이곳에 오기 위해 보내야 하는 이동 시간을 최소화하고 싶었어요." 그녀가 그 행사를 홍보하는 기자 회견에서 기자들에게 말했다. Dickerson 씨에 의해 계획된 대부분의 행사들처럼, <음악의 마법>은 이미 대중의 많은 관심을 끌었다.

| 어휘 | charity concert 자선 콘서트   raise 모으다   fund 기금, 돈
self-expression 자기 표현   feature 특별히 출연하다, 특징으로 하다
in advance 미리   organizer 조직자, 주최자   extensive 폭넓은
sponsor 후원하다   cancer 암   indicate 나타내다, 표하다
fundraiser 기금 모금 행사   compliment 칭찬하다   cause 대의명분
volunteer 자원하다   grateful 고마워하는   perform 공연하다
minimize 최소화하다   press conference 기자 회견   draw 끌다
attention 관심

168. 주제/목적 문제
기사의 주된 초점은 무엇인가?
(A) 환경 단체
(B) 기금 모금 행사
(C) 스포츠 대회
(D) 방과 후 프로그램
| 해설 | 도입부에 자선 콘서트가 계획되고 있다고(A charity concert is being planned) 한 후, 방과 후 프로그램을 위한 기금을 모을 것이라고 구체적으로 알리고 있으므로 정답은 (B)이다.
| 어휘 | organization 단체, 조직   competition 대회
| 패러프레이징 | A charity concert → A fundraising event

169. 세부 사항을 묻는 문제
기사에 따르면, Dickerson 씨는 최근에 무엇을 했나?
(A) 방과후 프로그램을 시작했다.
(B) 무대에서 공연했다.
(C) 축구 팀에 들어갔다.
(D) 스포츠 행사를 조직했다.
| 해설 | Dickerson 씨가 언급된 두 번째 단락에서 얼마 전에 아마추어 축구 토너먼트를 기획했다고(Not long ago, she planned the amateur soccer tournament) 했으므로 정답은 (D)이다.
| 어휘 | organize 조직하다
| 패러프레이징 | planned the amateur soccer tournament → organized a sports event

🔺고난도
170. 세부 사항을 묻는 문제
Dickerson 씨는 행사들을 조직하는 것에서 가장 중요한 부분은 무엇이라고 말하는가?
(A) 참가자들을 인정하는 것

(B) 티켓을 저렴하게 만드는 것
(C) 모든 수익금을 기부하는 것
(D) 유명 게스트들을 초대하는 것

| 해설 | 두 번째 단락 중반부에 Dickerson 씨는 성공적인 모금 행사를 기획하기 위해서는 티켓을 사는 사람들이 스스로에 대해 좋은 기분을 느끼게 만들어야 한다고 했으며(Ms. Dickerson indicated that in order to plan a successful fundraiser you have to make whoever buys a ticket to feel good about themselves), 대의를 후원하는 것에 대해 사람들을 칭찬하는 것이 중요하다고(It's important to compliment people for supporting the cause) 말한 것을 덧붙인 것에서, 참가자들을 칭찬하고 인정해 주는 것이 중요하다고 말한 것을 확인할 수 있으므로 정답은 (A)이다.

| 어휘 | recognize 인정하다 participant 참가자 affordable (가격이) 저렴한, 알맞은 donate 기부하다 proceed 수익금 celebrity 유명인

| 패러프레이징 | ·whoever buys a ticket → participants
·compliment → Recognizing

171. 세부 사항을 묻는 문제

Dickerson 씨는 왜 콘서트 장소로 Topeka를 선택했나?
(A) 그 도시에 많은 인맥을 가지고 있다.
(B) 공립 학교 교사들로부터 도움을 요청받았다.
(C) 공연하는 사람들이 편하게 이동하길 원한다.
(D) 더 유명한 장소를 감당할 수 없었다.

| 해설 | 마지막 단락에 Topeka를 선택한 이유를 묻는 질문을 받았을 때, 그곳이 밴드들의 중앙에 위치한 곳이라고 말하며(Ms. Dickerson said that it was a central location for the bands who volunteered to play), 그들의 이동 시간을 최소화하고 싶었다고(I wanted to minimize the amount of time they have to spend travelling to get here) 제시되어 있으므로 정답은 (C)이다.

| 어휘 | personal connections 인맥 public school 공립 학교 convenient 편한, 편리한 cannot afford ~에 형편이 안 되다, 여유가 없다

| 패러프레이징 | minimize the amount of time they have to spend travelling to get here → make travel convenient for performers

172-175 다음 기사를 참조하시오.

지역 단체가 장학금 기회를 발표하다

10월 8일—텍사스 농업 협회(TAA)가 각 5,000달러씩 다섯 개의 장학금을 제공할 계획이라고 발표했다. ¹⁷²이 단체의 사명은 농업에 종사하는 사람들에게 도움을 제공하는 것이다. — [1] —. 이는 회원들과의 네트워킹과 보호 법률을 통과시키려는 노력, 그리고 시장을 면밀히 감시하는 것을 통해 이루어진다.

— [2] —. 장학금 신청은 10월 15일부터 11월 1일까지 받을 것이다. ¹⁷³ ⁽ᴮ⁾/¹⁷⁵신청자들은 텍사스 주 내에 거주해야 하고, 학부 과정을 이수하고 ¹⁷³ ⁽ᴬ⁾석사 학위를 위해 노력하고 있어야 한다. — [3] —. 모든 합격자는 장점에 근거하여 선정될 것이다. ¹⁷³ ⁽ᴰ⁾장학금은 캠퍼스 내 대학생들과 원격 교육 학생들 모두에게 이용될 수 있다.

신청서는 http://www.texasagrassoc.org/scholarship에서 온라인으로 작성될 수 있다. — [4] —. ¹⁷⁴그것들에는 신청자의 학업과 직업 목표에 관해 설명하는 짧은 글이 동반되어야 한다. 여덟 명의 TAA 회원들로 구성된 위원회가 만나 장학금 대상자들을 선정할 것이다. 장학금에 관한 질문들은 r.hatcher@texasagrassoc.org로 Robin Hatcher에게 보내져야 한다.

| 어휘 | organization 단체, 기관 scholarship 장학금 assistance 지원, 도움 protective legislation 보호 법률 closely 면밀히 application 신청, 지원 undergraduate program 학부 과정 graduate degree 석사 학위 successful candidate 합격자 based on ~에 근거하여 merit 뛰어남, 장점 distance education 원격 교육 be accompanied by ~이 동반되다 educational 교육의, 교육적인 career goal 직업적 목표 committee 위원회 winner 수상자, 대상자 be directed to ~에게 보내지다

172. 세부 사항을 묻는 문제

기사에 따르면, TAA의 주된 목표는 무엇인가?
(A) 환경친화적인 식량을 재배하는 것
(B) 농업 근로자들을 지원하는 것
(C) 사람들에게 농업에 관해 가르치는 것
(D) 농업 기술을 개발하는 것

| 해설 | 텍사스 농업 협회(TAA)가 언급된 첫 번째 단락에 이 단체의 미션은 농업에 종사하는 사람들에게 도움을 제공하는 것이라고(The mission of this organization is to provide assistance to those working in the farm industry) 제시되어 있으므로 정답은 (B)이다.

| 어휘 | environmentally friendly 환경친화적인 agriculture 농업 develop 개발하다

| 패러프레이징 | ·provide assistance → support
·those working in the farm industry → farm workers

고난도

173. NOT True 문제

장학금에 관해 제시되지 않은 것은 무엇인가?
(A) 대학원 과정의 학생들을 위해 의도된 것이다.
(B) 특정 지역의 학생들에게만 주어진다.
(C) 11월 1일에 수여될 것이다.
(D) 전통적인 교육이나 온라인 교육을 위해 이용될 수 있다.

| 해설 | 두 번째 단락에 텍사스 주 내에 거주해야 한다고(Applicants must live in the state of Texas) 한 것에서 (B), 학부 과정을 이수하고 석사 학위를 위해 노력하고 있어야 한다고(~ be working toward a graduate degree) 한 것에서 (A), 캠퍼스 내 대학생들과 원격 교육 학생들 모두에게 이용될 수 있다고(~ can be used for both on-campus university students and distance education students) 한 것에서 (D)를 확인할 수 있다. 반면, 11월 1일은 신청을 받는 날짜로 제시된 것이므로 정답은 (C)이다.

| 어휘 | be intended for ~를 위해 의도되다 certain 특정한 award 주다, 수여하다 traditional 전통적인

| 패러프레이징 | ·the state of Texas → a certain location

- graduate degree → graduate-level
- on-campus university ~ and distance education → traditional or online education

174. 세부 사항을 묻는 문제
기사에 따르면, 지원서와 함께 포함되어야 하는 것은 무엇인가?
(A) 신청 요금
(B) 대학 성적 증명서
(C) 개인 에세이
(D) 추천서
| 해설 | 세 번째 단락에 신청자의 학업과 직업 목표에 관해 설명하는 짧은 글이 동반되어야 한다고(They should be accompanied by a short piece of writing explaining the applicant's educational and career goals) 제시되어 있으므로 정답은 (C)이다.
| 패러프레이징 | a short piece of writing → essay

175. 문장 삽입 문제
[1], [2], [3], [4]로 표시된 곳 중에 다음 문장이 들어가기에 가장 적절한 곳은?
"그들은 신청을 하기 위해 TAA 회원이 될 필요는 없다."
(A) [1]
(B) [2]
(C) [3]
(D) [4]
| 해설 | 제시된 문장은 신청 자격과 관련된 내용이므로, They는 신청자들을 말하는 것임을 알 수 있다. 따라서 신청자와 신청 자격이 언급된 문장(Applicants must live in the state of Texas and must have completed an undergraduate program and be working toward a graduate degree) 뒤에 들어가는 것이 적절하므로 (C)가 정답이다.
| 어휘 | apply 지원하다, 신청하다

176-180 다음 이메일과 영수증을 참조하시오.

수신: VIP 고객 메일 목록
발신: Annie's 의류점
날짜: 10월 4일
제목: 마지막 기회! 폐점 세일!

¹⁷⁶50년 동안 영업해온 후, Annie's 의류점이 영원히 문을 닫을 것입니다. 그 시간 동안의 저희 단골 고객님들 모두에게 감사드리고 싶습니다. 여러분에게 마지막 감사 인사이자 작별 인사로, 저희가 폐점 세일을 열 것이며, 모두 처분해야 합니다!

폐점 세일은 다음 주에 공식적으로 발표될 것이지만, 여러분은 저희의 VIP 고객이기 때문에, 다른 누구보다 먼저 50% 할인되는 최종 재고 정리 세일 가격을 즐기실 수 있습니다. 저희 매장에서의 마지막 한바탕 쇼핑을 위해 여러분을 뵙기를 바랍니다. 저희의 영업 마지막 날은 10월 25일이라는 것을 유념해 주세요. 그때까지 ¹⁷⁹소계가 100달러 이상인

모든 구매는 무료 선물 포장 자격을 얻게 됩니다. ¹⁷⁷이전 구매 후에 설문 조사를 완료하여 15달러 할인 쿠폰을 가지고 계시다면, 이번이 그것을 이용할 마지막 기회입니다!

Annie Cosenza
Annie's 의류점, 주인

| 어휘 | decade 10년 for good 영원히 loyal customer 단골 고객 farewell 작별 officially 공식적으로, 정식으로 clearance sale 재고 정리 세일 shopping spree 한바탕 쇼핑 subtotal 소계 qualify for ~의 자격을 얻다 wrapping 포장 previous 이전의

날짜: 10월 12일		시간: 16:42
물품 상세	정가 (달러)	귀하의 가격 (달러)
진주 귀걸이	30.00	¹⁷⁸/¹⁸⁰ ⁽ᴰ⁾15.00
가을 재킷 (가죽, 사이즈 M)	80.00	¹⁷⁸/¹⁸⁰ ⁽ᴰ⁾40.00
루비 팔찌	20.00	¹⁷⁸/¹⁸⁰ ⁽ᴰ⁾10.00
하이힐 (실버, 사이즈 6)	50.00	¹⁷⁸/¹⁸⁰ ⁽ᴰ⁾25.00
¹⁷⁹소계:		90.00
세금:		9.00
¹⁷⁹선물 포장:	2.00 (x4)	8.00
¹⁷⁷/¹⁸⁰ ⁽ᴰ⁾기타:		-15.00
총계:		$92.00

지불: 신용 카드 (xxxx-xxxx-xxxx-4913)
¹⁷⁷카드상의 이름: Samantha Henson
Annie's 의류점에서 쇼핑해 주셔서 감사합니다!
¹⁸⁰ ⁽ᴮ⁾제품 후기는 www.anniesoutfitters.com에서 찾아보실 수 있습니다!
¹⁷⁸/¹⁸⁰ ⁽ᶜ⁾재고 정리 세일 가격에 구입된 물품들은 반품이나 교환이 불가합니다

| 어휘 | earring 귀걸이 leather 가죽 bracelet 팔찌 tender 지불하다, 제출하다 review 후기

176. 주제/목적 문제
왜 이메일이 보내졌는가?
(A) 새로운 월간 회원권을 소개하기 위해
(B) 설문 조사 참가자들에게 감사를 표하기 위해
(C) 매장 폐점을 알리기 위해
(D) 계절 할인 행사를 홍보하기 위해
| 해설 | 이메일 도입부에 50년 동안 영업해온 후, 의류점이 영원히 문을 닫는다고(After being in business for five decades, Annie's Outfitters will be closing its doors for good) 제시되어 있으므로 정답은 (C)이다.
| 어휘 | introduce 소개하다 express 표현하다 participant 참가자 closure 폐쇄, 폐점

177. 연계 문제 - 추론
Henson 씨에 관해 사실일 것 같은 것은 무엇인가?
(A) 매장 신용 카드로 지불했다.
(B) 고객 설문지를 작성했다.
(C) Annie's 의류점에서 일했었다.
(D) 온라인으로 제품 후기를 확인했다.

| 해설 | Henson 씨는 영수증 하단의 카드상의 이름에서(Name on Card: Samantha Henson) 확인되는 구매 고객으로 기타 항목에서(Other:) 15달러를 할인받았음을 알 수 있고, 이메일 두 번째 단락 후반부에 이전 구매 후에 설문 조사를 완료하여 15달러 할인 쿠폰을 가지고 있다면 그것을 이용할 마지막 기회라고 (If you have a $15 discount coupon from completing a survey form after a previous purchase, this is a final chance to use it) 한 것을 연계해볼 때, 설문 작성으로 받은 15달러 할인 쿠폰을 이용했음을 추론할 수 있으므로 정답은 (B)이다.

| 패러프레이징 | completing a survey → filled out a customer survey

🔺 고난도

178. True 문제
영수증에 있는 품목들에 관해 제시된 것은 무엇인가?
(A) 다양한 주소들로 보내졌다.
(B) 환불될 수 없다.
(C) 긍정적인 고객 후기가 있다.
(D) 온라인으로 주문되었다.

| 해설 | 영수증에 있는 품목들 모두 50% 할인을 받은 것으로 확인되는데, 영수증 마지막에 재고 정리 세일 가격에 구입된 물품들은 반품이나 교환이 불가하다고(No returns or exchanges for items purchased at clearance sale price) 제시되어 있으므로 정답은 (B)이다.

| 어휘 | positive 긍정적인

179. 연계 문제 - 추론
Henson 씨는 어떻게 추가 요금이 면제되도록 할 수 있었을까?
(A) 세일이 시작되기를 기다림으로써
(B) 회원에 가입함으로써
(C) 쿠폰을 사용함으로써
(D) 더 많은 물품들을 구매함으로써

| 해설 | 영수증에 소계가(Subtotal) 90달러이고, 선물 포장이(Gift Wrapping) 8.00달러로 확인되는데, 이를 이메일 두 번째 단락 후반부에 소계가 100달러 이상인 모든 구매는 무료 선물 포장 자격을 얻게 된다고(all purchases with a subtotal of $100 or more qualify for free gift wrapping) 한 것과 연계하면, 물품을 더 구매하여 100달러 이상이 되면 선물 포장 요금이 면제될 수 있었음을 알 수 있으므로 정답은 (D)이다.

| 패러프레이징 | all purchases with a subtotal of $100 or more → purchasing more items

180. NOT True 문제
Annie's 의류점에 관해 언급되지 않은 것은 무엇인가?
(A) 빠른 배송 옵션을 제공한다.
(B) 제품 후기를 온라인으로 보여준다.
(C) 더 이상 반품된 상품을 받지 않을 것이다.
(D) 쿠폰과 세일 가격을 결합하도록 허용한다.

| 해설 | 영수증 하단에 제품 후기를 인터넷으로 볼 수 있다고(Product reviews can be found at www.anniesoutfitters.com) 한 것에서 (B), 재고 정리 세일 가격에 구입된 물품들은 반품이나 교환이 불가하다고(No returns or exchanges for items purchased at clearance sale price) 한 것에서 (C), 50% 재고 정리 할인과 15달러 기타 할인이 같이 적용되어 있는 것에서 (D)가 확인되므로 정답은 (A)이다.

| 어휘 | display 보여주다   accept 받다, 수락하다   combine with ~와 결합하다

| 패러프레이징 | ·www.anniesoutfitters.com → online
· No returns → will no longer accept returned merchandise

181-185 다음 공지와 이메일을 참조하시오.

Empire Country 클럽 회원

회원	[182]표준	[184]프린스	엠페러
요금 (월간)	500달러	950달러	1,600달러
골프 코스 이용	O	O	O
[182]기본 스파 이용 (온수 욕조, 증기 욕실)	O	O	O
개인 주차 공간*	X	O	O
전신 마사지	X	O	O
낚시 부두 이용	X	X	O

[181]모든 예약되지 않은 방문은 수락되지 않습니다. 미리 예약해 주세요.

*주차 공간은 일반 크기의 차량용만 있습니다. [185]리무진 같은 대형 차량들은 일반 주차장에서 떨어진 곳에 주차되어야 합니다.

회원들은 클럽에 오실 때 최대 3명까지 손님을 데려오는 것이 허용됩니다. 그 이상에 대해서는 추가 1인당 100달러의 방문 요금이 있습니다.

| 어휘 | access 이용, 접속   hot tub 온수 욕조   full body 전신   walk-in visit 예약되지 않은 방문   accept 수락하다, 받아들이다   make a reservation 예약하다   regular-sized 일반 크기   separately 별도로   bring 데려오다   up to 최대 ~까지   per 각, ~당

발신: Sadie Long <slong@empirecc.net>
수신: Lindsay Alexander <l.alexander@cmail.net>
제목: 회신: 고객들 방문
날짜: 9월 3일
첨부: 회원 세부 사항

Alexander 씨 귀하,

친구들을 접대하고자 하는 귀하의 요청에 대한 회신으로, 물론 그러실 수 있습니다. 귀하의 회원권은 추가 비용 없이 최대 3명까지 데려오시는 것을 허용합니다. 하지만 그 이상은 추가 요금을 [183]발생시키게 됩니다. 귀하가 데려오는 각각의 분들은 귀하와 동일한 이용권을 갖게 될 것이며, [184]이는 저희의 낚시 시설들 외에 모든 것을 즐기도록 허용됨을 의미합니다.

귀하의 교통편에 관해서는, 일반 주차장이 귀하의 교통편을 수용할 만큼 충분히 크지 않습니다. [185]귀하의 운전자에게 클럽하우스에서 귀하를 내려주고 서쪽 주차장에 주차하도록 하셔야 하는데요, 그곳은 보통 직원들에 의해 이용되는 곳입니다.

참고를 위해 귀하의 회원권 세부 사항을 첨부했습니다. 그래도 어떤 질문이나 의견이 있으면, 이메일이나 전화로 저에게 편하게 연락해 주세요.

진심으로,

Sadie Long
Empire Country 클럽, 회원 코디네이터

| 어휘 | in response to ~에 대한 회신으로, ~에 응하여   host 접대하다   incur 발생시키다   all but ~을 제외하고 모두   as for ~에 관해서는   transportation 교통편   accommodate 수용하다   drop A off A를 내려주다   normally 보통   attach 첨부하다   details 세부 사항   reference 참고, 참조   comment 의견

고난도

181. True 문제
Empire Country 클럽에 관해 제시된 것은 무엇인가?
(A) 무료 발렛 서비스를 제공한다.
(B) 시내에 편리하게 위치해 있다.
(C) 최근에 개조되었다.
(D) 예약에 의해서만 이용이 가능하다.
| 해설 | 공지의 도표 아래 모든 예약되지 않은 방문은 수락되지 않는다고(Any walk-in visits are not accepted) 제시되어 있으므로 정답은 (D)이다.
| 어휘 | complimentary 무료의   conveniently 편리하게   renovate 개조하다, 수리하다   available 이용 가능한   appointment 약속, 예약
| 패러프레이징 | Any walk-in visits are not accepted → It is available by appointment only

182. 세부 사항을 묻는 문제
표준 회원권에 포함되는 것은 무엇인가?
(A) 지정된 주차 장소
(B) 요청 시 마사지
(C) 스파 시설 출입
(D) 낚시할 기회
| 해설 | 공지의 도표에 표준(Standard)에 O 표시가 된 것은 골프 코스 이용과(Golf Course Access) 기본 스파 이용으로(Basic Spa Access) 확인되므로 이에 해당하는 (C)가 정답이다.
| 어휘 | reserved 지정된   entry 출입   opportunity 기회
| 패러프레이징 | Basic Spa Access → Entry into a spa facility

183. 동의어 문제
이메일에서 첫 번째 단락 두 번째 줄에 있는 단어 "incur"와 의미가 가장 유사한 것은
(A) 나아가다, 전진하다
(B) 진행하다
(C) 발생시키다, 만들어내다
(D) 요청하다
| 해설 | 해당 단어가 들어간 문장은 '하지만 그 이상은 추가 요금을 발생시키게 됩니다'라고 해석된다. 따라서 '발생시키다'라는 뜻의 (C) generate가 정답이다.

184. 연계 문제 – 추론
Alexander 씨에 관해 유추할 수 있는 것은 무엇인가?
(A) 단체 마사지 일정을 잡았다.
(B) 950달러의 월간 요금을 지불한다.
(C) 추가 100달러를 청구받을 것이다.
(D) 자신의 회원 계약서를 읽지 않았다.
| 해설 | Alexander 씨에게 보낸 이메일 첫 번째 단락 후반부에 데려오는 사람도 동일한 이용권을 갖게 되는데 이는 낚시 시설 외에 모든 것을 즐기도록 허용됨을 의미한다고(meaning that you are all allowed to enjoy all but our fishing facilities) 했고, 공지의 도표에 낚시 부두 이용을(Fishing Pier Access) 제외하고 모두 O 표시된 프린스의(Prince) 가격이 월 950달러로 확인되므로 정답은 (B)이다.
| 어휘 | monthly fee 월간 요금   contract 계약서

185. 연계 문제 – 추론
Alexander 씨의 단체에 관해 암시되는 것은 무엇인가?
(A) 큰 차량으로 클럽하우스까지 이동할 계획이다.
(B) 주말에 Empire Country 클럽을 방문할 것이다.
(C) 별도의 입장료를 지불해야 할 것이다.
(D) 회원 가입을 하고 싶어한다.
| 해설 | 공지의 도표 아래 리무진 같은 대형 차량은 일반 주차장에서 떨어진 곳에 주차되어야 한다고(Large vehicles such as limousines must be parked separately from the regular parking lot) 제시된 것과 이메일 두 번째 단락에 운전자에게 클럽하우스에서 내려주고 서쪽 주차장에 주차하도록 해야 한다고(You have to ask your driver to drop you off at the clubhouse and park in the West lot) 한 것을 연계해볼 때, Alexander 씨의 일행은 큰 차를 타고 클럽하우스에 올 것으로 유추할 수 있으므로 정답은 (A)이다.
| 어휘 | separate 별도의   entry fee 입장료   sign up for ~에 가입하다, ~에 등록하다

186-190 다음 광고, 설명서, 후기를 참조하시오.

모든 Web Access 아카데미 회원을 위한 특가 제공! 엄선된 강좌들 40% 할인!*

• 304: PhotoMaster 레벨 3 / 사진 수정 소프트웨어 이용하기 –

Stevie Dawson이 온라인용 이미지들을 다루는 고급 기술들을 익히도록 돕습니다.

- [186]115: Essentials 레벨 1 / 컴퓨터 언어 기초 – Gary Marlow가 컴퓨터 프로그래밍이 처음인 사람들을 위해 저희의 베스트셀러 프로그램을 지도합니다.
- 346: [190]Find Yourself 레벨 3 / 검색 엔진 최적화 (SEO) – 저희의 일류 강사인 [190]Harry Miles가 모든 주요 검색 엔진에서 여러분의 웹 사이트가 상위에 등재되도록 상세히 살펴봐 줍니다.
- 108: 상업적 기술들 / 자신만의 웹 사이트 템플릿 만들기 – Janet Sedley가 다양한 웹 사이트들에서 여러분의 시간을 절약해 줄 템플릿을 만드는 방법을 가르쳐 줍니다.

강좌들에 소프트웨어 다운로드가 필요할 수 있음을 유념해 주세요.

여기서 등록하고 결제하세요.

*8월 강좌들에만 적용됩니다. Web Access 아카데미에서 적어도 한 강좌를 완료하셨어야만 합니다.

| 어휘 | special offer 특가 제공   selected 엄선된   manipulation 조작   take A through B A가 B를 익히도록 돕다   advanced 상급의, 고급의   technique 기술   manipulate 조작하다, 다루다   conduct 진행하다, 이끌다   optimization 최적화   top-rated 일류의, 가장 인기 있는   instructor 강사   list 열거하다, 등재하다   commercial 상업적인   create 만들다   multiple 많은, 다양한   enroll 등록하다   apply to ~에 적용되다

축하합니다! 이제 등록이 되셨습니다. 아래 설명을 따라주시기 바랍니다:

1) www.webwizard.org/downloads로 가서 박스에 [187 (C)] "WEBAA33"을 입력하세요.*
2) 다운로드가 끝나면 설치를 누르고 [187 (A)]프로그램을 설치하는 것을 기다리세요. 끝나면 자동으로 열릴 것입니다.**
3) [187 (D)]여기에서 다음 문서를 다운로드하고 자신의 첫 비디오 세션이 시작될 때까지 반드시 읽도록 하세요.

어떤 어려움이 있다면, 도움을 위해 저희 강좌 포럼을 확인해 주세요. 많은 질문들이 이미 답변이 되었지만, 여러분도 질문을 올릴 수 있습니다.

*[189]이 프로그램은 7월 31일 이전에만 다운로드가 무료임을 유념해 주시기 바랍니다.
**오래된 컴퓨터들은 일부 프로그램을 작동시키는 데 어려움이 있을 수 있습니다. 여기에서 장비 요건들을 읽으세요.

| 어휘 | be signed up 등록되다   instruction 설명, 지시   input 입력하다   automatically 자동적으로   post 게시하다   have difficulty -ing ~하는 데 어려움이 있다   equipment 장비   requirement 요건

www.webaccessacademy.com/reviews

이름: David Murray
날짜: 9월 3일

의견: [190]저는 Find Yourself 강좌를 들었고 그것에 관한 제 경험에 기반하여 이 강좌를 적극 추천하고 싶습니다. 강좌 단위가 작기 때문에, 일을 하고 있는 사람들에게 최적입니다. [188]Web Wizard 프로그램을 제대로 작동시키는 데 어려움이 있었는데요. 포럼에서 제 질문에 답변을 받지 못한 후에, [190]강사에게 직접 이메일을 보냈는데 얼마나 빨리 답변을 받았는지 아주 기뻤습니다. 제공된 정보는 문제를 완전히 해결하는 데 도움이 되었습니다. 또 언급하고 싶은 것은 강좌의 일부로 [189]Web Wizard를 무료로 받았는데, 보통 청구하는 120달러를 지불해야 하는 것인지 여부를 잘 모르겠다는 것입니다. 그렇지 않다면, 저는 충분히 만족합니다. 감사합니다!

| 어휘 | run 작동하다   properly 제대로   instructor 강사   directly 직접   solve 해결하다   completely 완전히   note 언급하다   be fully satisfied 충분히 만족하다

186. 추론 문제
어느 강좌가 컴퓨터 프로그래밍 초보자들에게 가장 좋을 것인가?
(A) 304
(B) 115
(C) 346
(D) 108

| 해설 | 광고에서 두 번째에 있는 컴퓨터 언어 기초에(Computer language basics) 컴퓨터 프로그래밍이 처음인 사람들을 위해 베스트셀러 프로그램을 지도한다고(conducts our best-selling program for those who are new to computer programming) 제시되어 있고 이에 해당하는 강좌 번호는 115이므로 정답은 (B)이다.

187. NOT True 문제
설명서에서 하나의 단계로 언급되지 않은 것은?
(A) 컴퓨터 프로그램을 설치하는 것
(B) 신용 카드로 지불하는 것
(C) 코드를 입력하는 것
(D) 문서를 읽는 것

| 해설 | 설명서 1)에 웹 사이트로 가서 WEBAA33을 입력하라고(input "WEBAA33") 한 것에서 (C), 2)에 프로그램 설치를 기다리라고(wait for the program to install) 한 것에서 (A), 3)에 문서를 다운로드하여 읽으라고(make sure you have read ~) 한 것에서 (D)는 언급된 내용으로 확인되므로 정답은 (B)이다.

| 패러프레이징 | input → Entering

188. 세부 사항을 묻는 문제
Murray 씨가 언급하는 문제는 무엇인가?

(A) 컴퓨터 프로그램이 올바르게 작동하지 않았다.
(B) 포럼들이 이해하기가 어려웠다.
(C) 강좌 일정이 형편없게 짜여 있었다.
(D) 강사 지원이 예상보다 더 느렸다.

| 해설 | Murray 씨는 세 번째 지문인 후기 작성자로, 프로그램을 제대로 작동시키는 데 어려움이 있었다고(I did have difficulty getting the Web Wizard program to run properly) 했으므로 정답은 (A)이다.

| 어휘 | correctly 올바르게, 제대로   poorly 부실하게, 형편없게   organize 준비하다, 정리하다   tutor 강사

| 패러프레이징 | run properly → working correctly

고난도
189. 연계 문제 – 추론
Murray 씨에 관해 유추할 수 있는 것은?
(A) 그의 등록은 8월 1일 이후에 완료되었다.
(B) 그는 아주 경험 많은 프로그래머이다.
(C) 그는 7월 31일 전에 프로그램을 다운로드했다.
(D) 그의 컴퓨터는 업그레이드될 필요가 있다.

| 해설 | Murray 씨는 후기 작성자로, 후반부에 Web Wizard를 무료로 받았다고(I got Web Wizard for free) 했고, 이를 설명서 후반부 *표시에 이 프로그램은 7월 31일 이전에만 다운로드가 무료임을 유념하라고(Please note that this program is only free for download before July 31) 제시된 것과 연계해 보면, 7월 31일 이전에 프로그램을 다운받았을 것으로 유추할 수 있으므로 정답은 (C)이다.

| 어휘 | registration 등록   highly experienced 아주 경험 많은

190. 연계 문제 – 세부 사항
Murray 씨는 누구에게 연락했나?
(A) Stevie Dawson
(B) Gary Marlow
(C) Harry Miles
(D) Janet Sedley

| 해설 | 먼저 후기 도입부에 Murray 씨가 Find Yourself 강좌를 들었다고(I took the Find Yourself course) 한 후, 문제가 있어 강사에게 직접 이메일을 보냈다고(I e-mailed the instructor directly) 언급되어 있는데, 광고에서 Find Yourself 강좌의 강사는 Harry Miles로 확인되므로 정답은 (C)이다.

191-195 다음 이메일, 기사, 문자 메시지를 참조하시오.

수신: Sherman 도서관 이사회 <board@sherman-library.org>
발신: Katherine Milford <milfordk@sherman-library.org>
날짜: 7월 2일
제목: 다가오는 미팅

이사진들에게,

다음 도서관 이사회 회의가 7월 16일 목요일 오후 7시에 있을 것임을 상기시켜 드리고자 이 글을 씁니다. ¹⁹¹제 출장 일정에 맞추어 회의를 일주

일 미루도록 융통성을 보여 주신 여러분 모두에게 감사를 드립니다. 안건의 주된 화제는 저희 잉여 자금으로 무엇을 할지를 결정하는 것이 될 것입니다. 여러분 모두 아시다시피, 지역 사회의 일원이 도서관에 후한 재정적 지원을 해 주셨습니다. 지난달 회의에서 그 돈이 쓰일 수 있는 잠재적인 프로젝트 두 개를 선정했는데요— ¹⁹³저희 지점들 일부에 셀프서비스 대출대를 추가하거나 온라인 예약 시스템을 시행하는 것입니다. 이것들이 각각 셀프서비스와 예약 시스템으로 투표 용지들에 열거될 것입니다. ¹⁹³이 프로젝트들 중 하나를 추진하고 다른 하나를 버리기 위해서는 과반수의 이사진이 찬성 투표를 하셔야 합니다. 그렇게 되지 못할 경우, 8월 회의에서 두 프로젝트에 관해 다시 논의할 것이고, 그것은 현재 8월 15일로 예정되어 있습니다. 그러나 저는 이번 달에 합의에 도달할 수 있기를 바랍니다.

모두들 7월 16일에 뵙기를 고대하고 있겠습니다!

진심으로,

Katherine Milford
Sherman 도서관 이사회, 의장

| 어휘 | flexibility 유연성, 융통성   accommodate 수용하다, (환경 등에) 맞추다   surplus funds 잉여 자금   generous 후한   financial 재정적인   donation 기부   potential 잠재적인   checkout station 대출대   implement 시행하다   reservation 예약   voting ballot 투표 용지   respectively 각각   move forward 추진하다, 앞으로 나아가다   abandon 버리다   majority 다수, 과반수   vote in favor of ~에 찬성하는 것에 투표하다   currently 현재   reach an agreement 합의에 도달하다

새로운 서비스를 제공하는 Sherman 도서관

7월 20일—Sherman 도서관과 그 직원들은 예산 삭감과 직원 채용 문제, 그리고 심지어 자연 재해를 포함한 많은 도전들에 직면해 왔다. 직원들은 도서관에 가해지는 지속적인 압박감에 관해 우려했고 다수는 그것을 더 이상 ¹⁹²참을 수 없다고도 말했다. 그러나 이제 도서관은 특별한 프로젝트들을 위한 최근의 기부로 많이 필요했던 안도감을 얻고 있다. ¹⁹³이사회는 지난주에 투표를 하여 고객들을 위한 온라인 예약 시스템을 시행하기로 결정했다. 이것으로 지역에서 발행된 도서관 카드를 가진 이들은 누구나 온라인으로 책들을 예약하고 준비가 되면 문자 메시지를 통해 통지를 받을 수 있을 것이다.

¹⁹⁴고객들은 시스템의 시험 버전을 신청할 수 있고, 참여하는 사람들은 시스템을 개선시키기 위해 그들의 경험에 관한 상세한 설문 조사를 완료하도록 기대될 것이다. 시험 기간은 9월 한 달 동안이 될 것이고, 그 시스템은 아마도 11월 중순에 회원들 모두에게 공개가 될 것이다.

| 어휘 | face 직면하다   budget cut 예산 삭감   natural disaster 자연 재해   be concerned about ~을 우려하다   constant 지속적인, 거듭

되는   pressure 압력, 압박감   relief 안도   patron 고객   locally 지역적으로   issued 발행된   participate 참여하다   trial period 시험 기간, 체험 기간   roll out 공개하다, 출시하다

수신: [194]Josephine Kuhn 433-555-6780
발신: Sherman 도서관 433-555-1025
수신됨: [194/195]9월 6일 수요일 오전 10:52

예약 알림: 요청하신 책 3권 중 2권이 이용 가능함
대출자 이름: Josephine Kuhn
도서관 카드 번호: 89578542134758
다음 항목들은 현재 Sherman 도서관에서 가져가실 수 있습니다:
소설: 209578   <삼나무 거리 아래로>   Posner, Sarah
소설: 249503   <수사관>   Wetzel, Richard

[195]귀하의 품목은 9월 12일 화요일까지 보유될 것입니다. 가져가시지 않는다면, 그것들은 일반 대출을 위해 다시 선반으로 돌려보내질 것입니다. 귀하의 다른 항목은 3일 이내에 준비될 것으로 예상됩니다.

| 어휘 | notification 알림, 통지   borrower 대출자   pickup 가지러 감   hold 맡다, 보유하다   collect 가지러 가다

191. 세부 사항을 묻는 문제

Milford 씨는 왜 이메일 수신자들에게 감사하는가?
(A) 요청된 프로젝트를 일찍 완료했다.
(B) 유용한 제안을 제공했다.
(C) 회의 날짜를 변경하는 것에 동의했다.
(D) 도서관에 돈을 기부했다.

| 해설 | 이메일 도입부에서 회의 일자를 알리며, 출장 일정에 맞추어 회의를 미루도록 융통성을 보여줘서 감사하다고(I appreciate everyone's flexibility in moving the meeting back by a week) 했으므로 정답은 (C)이다.
| 어휘 | suggestion 제안
| 패러프레이징 | moving the meeting back by a week → change a meeting date

192. 동의어 문제

기사에서 첫 번째 단락 세 번째 줄에 있는 단어 "take"와 의미가 가장 유사한 것은
(A) 참다, 견디다
(B) 이동하다
(C) 필요하다, 요구하다
(D) 이용하다

| 해설 | 해당 단어가 들어간 문장은 '다수는 그것을 더 이상 참을 수 없다고 말했다'라고 해석된다. 따라서 take는 '참다, 받아들이다'라는 의미로 사용된 것이므로 이와 유사한 (A) endure가 정답이다.

193. 연계 문제 – 추론 (고난도)

셀프서비스 프로젝트에 관해 암시되는 것은 무엇인가?
(A) 그것은 8월 회의에서 논의될 것이다.
(B) 이사회의 절반 미만이 그것에 표를 던졌다.
(C) 처음 계획되었던 것보다 더 비쌌다.
(D) 도서관 고객들 대다수가 그것에 반대했다.

| 해설 | 먼저 이메일 중반부에 셀프서비스 대출대 추가와 온라인 예약 시스템 시행을(adding self-service checkout stations to some of our branches or implementing an online reservation system) 언급한 뒤, 하나를 선택하기 위해 과반수의 이사진이 찬성 투표를 해야 한다고(a majority of the board members must vote in favor of it) 했는데, 이를 기사 첫 번째 단락 후반부에 이사회가 투표하여 온라인 예약 시스템을 시행하기로 결정했다고(Board members voted last week to implement an online reservation system for patrons) 제시되어 있는 것과 연계해볼 때, 선택되지 않은 셀프서비스 프로젝트는 이사회에서 절반 미만의 표를 받은 것으로 유추할 수 있으므로 정답은 (B)이다.
| 어휘 | less than half of 절반 미만의   initially 원래의, 처음의

194. 연계 문제 – 추론 (고난도)

Kuhn 씨에 관해 암시된 것은 무엇인가?
(A) 이사회의 일원이다.
(B) 피드백을 주도록 요청받을 것이다.
(C) 현재 세 권의 책을 대출했다.
(D) 최근에 도서관 카드를 신청했다.

| 해설 | Kuhn 씨는 온라인 예약 시스템을 이용해 문자 메시지를 받는 수신자로, 문자가 수신된 날짜가 9월 6일이고(September 6), 이를 기사 두 번째 단락에 고객들은 시험 버전을 신청할 수 있고, 참여하는 사람들은 그들의 경험에 관해 상세한 설문 조사를 완료하도록 기대될 것이고(Patrons may sign up for a trial of the system, and those who participate will be expected to complete a detailed survey about their experience), 기간은 9월 한 달 동안이라고(The trial period will run for the entire month of September) 제시된 것을 연계해볼 때, 9월 중에 온라인 예약 시스템을 이용한 Kuhn 씨는 설문 조사를 완료해 피드백을 주도록 요청받을 것임을 유추할 수 있으므로 정답은 (B)이다.
| 어휘 | apply for ~을 신청하다
| 패러프레이징 | complete a detailed survey about their experience → give feedback

195. 세부 사항을 묻는 문제

Kuhn 씨의 항목들은 얼마 동안 보유될 것인가?
(A) 2일
(B) 3일
(C) 1주일
(D) 2주일

| 해설 | 문자 메시지가 수신된 날짜가 9월 6일이고(September 6), 문자 메시지 끝 단락에 9월 12일 화요일까지 보유될 것이라고(Your items will be held until Tuesday, September 12) 알린 것을 연계해볼 때, Kuhn 씨가 예약한 것들은 9월 6일 수요일부터 9월 12일 화요일까지 일주일 동안 보유될 것임을 알 수 있으므로 정답은 (C)이다.

196-200 다음 공지, 이메일, 티켓을 참조하시오.

JD 교통 승객 공지

JD 교통은 ¹⁹⁶ ⁽ᴮ⁾ **2월 1일부로 시행되는** 다음과 같은 저희의 서비스 변경에 관해 알리게 되어 기쁩니다:

- 새로운 노선 추가:
  - Lincoln City ↔ Deleon / ¹⁹⁶ ⁽ᴬ⁾ **모든 평일 오전** 정기 운행
  - Lincoln City ↔ Clementon / 월-목, 하루 다섯 차례 급행 서비스
  - Lincoln City ↔ Hargis Valley / 월요일 오전과 목요일 저녁, 급행 서비스

- 버스 업그레이드: ²⁰⁰ **모든 급행 버스들에는 무료 Wi-Fi가 특별히 포함될 것입니다.** Deleon를 오가는 노선들에는 무료 다과가 제공될 것입니다. ¹⁹⁶ ⁽ᶜ⁾ **일부 버스들은 텔레비전을 갖추고 있을 것입니다.**

- 요금 변경: ¹⁹⁶ ⁽ᴮ⁾ **이 변화가 발생하는 것과 동시에, 저희 요금을 약 5% 올릴 것입니다.** 이는 5년 만에 처음 있는 요금 변경으로, 저희는 요금을 낮게 유지하고자 전념하고 있습니다. 사용하지 않은 티켓을 환불하는 것은 여전히 무료입니다.

| 어휘 | effective 시행되는, 효력 있는   route 노선   regular service 정기 운행   refreshments 다과   fare 요금   occur 일어나다, 발생하다   raise 인상하다   approximately 대략   be committed to ~에 전념하다, 헌신하다   refund 환불하다   unused 사용하지 않은

수신: Yemane Girma <ygirma@ecvmail.com>
발신: Eunyoung Jang <jangeunyoung@broaddusinc.net>
날짜: 2월 10일
제목: 귀하의 Broaddus 사 방문

Girma 씨 귀하,

이곳 Broaddus 사의 모두가 2월 28일 귀하의 방문을 고대하고 있습니다. ¹⁹⁷**귀하의 워크숍이 유익하고 보람 있는 것임을 저희 직원들이 알게 될 것이라고 생각합니다.** 제가 준비해 드려야 할 어떤 특별한 자료가 있다면 알려주시기 바랍니다.

제가 귀하를 위해 필요한 여행 준비를 해 놓았습니다. 귀하는 Lincoln City의 지역 공항에 도착할 텐데요. 누군가 그곳에 모시러 나가는 것이 아니라, 버스를 타실 것을 부탁드립니다. 교통 체증을 피할 버스 전용 차선이 있기 때문에 그것이 훨씬 더 빠를 것입니다. 버스 터미널이 공항과 연결되어 있어, 카운터에서 첨부된 확인증만 보여주시고 티켓을 받으시면 됩니다. 귀하의 비행기가 버스가 출발하기 1시간 전에 도착하니, 버스를 잡아 타기에 충분한 시간이 있을 것입니다. ¹⁹⁹**그 여정은 약 2시간이 걸리고, 저는 최종 목적지에 도착하면 뵙도록 하겠습니다.** 버스에 어떠한 수하물 규정도 ¹⁹⁸**따르실 필요가 없으니**, 비행기로 무엇을 가져오셨든지 괜찮을 것입니다.

이번 주 후반에 귀하의 호텔 예약에 관한 세부 사항에 관해 보내드리

겠습니다.

진심으로,

Eunyoung Jang

| 어휘 | look forward to ~을 고대하다   informative 유익한   rewarding 보람 있는   material 자료   arrangement 준비, 마련   regional 지역의   rather than ~보다는, ~ 대신에   designated 지정된   avoid 피하다   heavy traffic 교통 체증   be connected to ~와 연결되다   confirmation 확인(증)   catch 잡아 타다   follow 따르다, 준수하다   luggage 수하물   restriction 제한

티켓 예약 확인증

승객 이름: Yemane Girma   **이동 날짜:** 2월 28일 화요일
여정: Lincoln City에서 Clementon, ²⁰⁰**급행 버스 #282**
¹⁹⁹**출발 시간: 오후 2시**
좌석: 12A
지불 상태: 지불됨

출발 시간 10분 전까지 찾아가지 않는 티켓들은 대기 승객들에게 주어질 수 있습니다. 더 많은 정보를 위해서는 저희 웹 사이트를 방문하세요.

| 어휘 | payment 지불   status 상태   departure 출발   standby passenger 대기 승객

---

196. NOT True 문제
JD 교통에 관해 제시되지 않은 것은?
(A) 노선 중 일부는 오전에만 이용이 가능하다.
(B) 티켓 가격이 2월에 인상될 것이다.
(C) 버스 중 일부는 TV 스크린이 있을 것이다.
(D) 주말에 더 많은 버스들을 제공할 것이다.
| 해설 | 공지에 서비스 변경에 관해 2월 1일부로 시행된다고(effective February 1) 했고, 변경과 동시에 요금을 올릴 것이라고(At the same time as these changes occur, we will raise our fares by approximately 5%) 한 것에서 (B), 첫 번째 노선에서 모든 평일 오전 정기 운행이라고(every weekday morning) 한 것에서 (A), 일부 버스들은 텔레비전을 갖추고 있을 것이라고(Some buses will be equipped with televisions) 한 것에서 (C)는 확인된다. 따라서 정답은 (D)이다.
| 어휘 | increase 오르다, 인상되다
| 패러프레이징 | raise → increase

197. 세부 사항을 묻는 문제
Girma 씨가 Broaddus 사를 방문하는 목적은 무엇인가?
(A) 상을 받는 것
(B) 구직 면접에 참석하는 것
(C) 직원들을 교육하는 것

(D) 시설을 점검하는 것

| 해설 | 두 번째 지문인 Girma 씨에게 보내는 이메일의 첫 번째 단락에 귀하의 워크숍이 유익하고 보람 있는 것임을 직원들이 알게 될 것이라고 생각한다고(We believe that our staff will find your workshop to be informative and rewarding) 한 것에서 워크숍 즉, 교육을 진행하기 위해 방문할 것임을 알 수 있으므로 정답은 (C)이다.

| 패러프레이징 | workshop → train

198. 동의어 문제
이메일에서 두 번째 단락 일곱 번째 줄에 있는 단어 "follow"와 의미가 가장 유사한 것은

(A) 이해하다

(B) 뒤따르다

(C) 복사하다

(D) 고수하다, 지키다

| 해설 | 해당 단어가 들어간 문장은 '버스에 어떠한 수하물 규정도 따르실 필요가 없습니다'라고 해석된다. 따라서 제한(규제)을 '따르다, 지키다'라는 뜻의 (D) adhere to가 정답이다.

199. 연계 문제 – 추론
Jang 씨는 2월 28일에 언제 Girma 씨를 만날 예정인가?

(A) 오후 1시에

(B) 오후 2시에

(C) 오후 3시에

(D) 오후 4시에

| 해설 | 세 번째 지문인 티켓에서 출발 시간이 오후 2시로(Departure Time: 2 P.M.) 확인되는데, 이를 이메일의 두 번째 단락 후반부에 여정이 약 2시간 걸린다며 최종 목적지에 도착하면 보자고(The journey is about two hours, and I will meet you when you arrive at the final stop) 한 것과 연계해 볼 때, 오후 4시에 만날 것으로 유추할 수 있으므로 정답은 (D)이다.

200. 연계 문제 – 추론
Girma 씨에 관해 암시되는 것은 무엇인가?

(A) 창가 쪽 좌석을 요청했다.

(B) 여정 중에 인터넷에 접속할 수 있을 것이다.

(C) 티켓을 찾아올 때 비용을 지불할 것이다.

(D) 여행 중에 무료 간식을 받을 자격이 된다.

| 해설 | 세 번째 지문인 티켓의 여정 항목에서 급행 버스로(Express Bus #282) 확인되는데, 이를 첫 번째 지문에 모든 급행 버스에는 무료 Wi-Fi가 특별히 포함될 것이라고(All Express buses will feature free Wi-Fi) 제시된 것과 연계해 볼 때, Girma 씨는 인터넷을 이용할 수 있을 것으로 유추할 수 있으므로 정답은 (B)이다.

| 어휘 | access 접속 be eligible to ~에 자격이 되다

| 패러프레이징 | Wi-Fi → Internet access

TEST 06

문제 본책 p. 158

PART 5
101 (C)	102 (C)	103 (D)	104 (C)	105 (D)
106 (B)	107 (D)	108 (C)	109 (B)	110 (C)
111 (B)	112 (A)	113 (D)	114 (A)	115 (C)
116 (A)	117 (D)	118 (B)	119 (C)	120 (D)
121 (C)	122 (A)	123 (B)	124 (A)	125 (C)
126 (C)	127 (D)	128 (C)	129 (B)	130 (D)

PART 6
131 (B)	132 (C)	133 (A)	134 (D)	135 (D)
136 (D)	137 (C)	138 (C)	139 (C)	140 (C)
141 (B)	142 (B)	143 (C)	144 (B)	145 (B)
146 (A)				

PART 7
147 (A)	148 (D)	149 (C)	150 (C)	151 (B)
152 (A)	153 (B)	154 (B)	155 (C)	156 (A)
157 (D)	158 (D)	159 (B)	160 (D)	161 (B)
162 (D)	163 (C)	164 (A)	165 (B)	166 (C)
167 (A)	168 (A)	169 (B)	170 (C)	171 (D)
172 (B)	173 (D)	174 (A)	175 (C)	176 (A)
177 (C)	178 (A)	179 (D)	180 (C)	181 (C)
182 (A)	183 (C)	184 (B)	185 (B)	186 (D)
187 (B)	188 (C)	189 (B)	190 (D)	191 (A)
192 (D)	193 (B)	194 (C)	195 (A)	196 (B)
197 (C)	198 (A)	199 (D)	200 (B)	

PART 5

101. 인칭 대명사
수건이나 기타 물품들이 더 필요하시면, 프런트 데스크가 아닌 객실 관리 사무소로 전화해 주세요.
| 해설 | 알맞은 인칭 대명사를 고르는 문제로, 빈칸은 if절의 주어가 들어갈 자리이므로 주격인 (C) you가 정답이다.
| 어휘 | housekeeping 객실 관리   supplies 물품, 용품

102. 동사의 시제
대변인은 어제 기자 회견에서 간단한 답변들로 대응했다.
| 해설 | 빈칸은 문장의 동사가 들어갈 자리이므로 준동사인 (D) to respond는 오답이고, 뒤에 과거 시점을 나타내는 부사 yesterday가 있으므로 과거 시제인 (C) responded가 정답이다.
| 어휘 | spokesperson 대변인   brief 간단한, 짧은   press conference 기자 회견

103. 부사 자리 - 동사 수식
심지어 단골 방문객들도 호텔 로비가 수리된 이후 그것을 거의 알아차릴 수 없었다.
| 해설 | 조동사 could와 동사 recognize 사이에 빈칸이 있으므로, 빈칸은 동사를 수식하는 부사 자리이다. 따라서 '거의 ~않다'라는 뜻의 부사인 (D) scarcely가 정답이다.
| 어휘 | regular (어떤 곳에) 고정적으로 다니는   recognize 알아보다, 인식하다   renovate 개조하다, 수리하다   scarce 드문, 부족한

104. 동사 어휘
강의 참석자들은 초청 연사와 연구 방법들에 관해 논의하기 위해 강연 후에 늦게까지 머무를 수도 있다.
| 해설 | 빈칸 뒤에 있는 research methods를 목적어로 받는 to부정사를 완성할 동사 원형이 들어갈 자리로, 문맥상 '연구 방법들에 관해 논의하기 위해'라는 의미로 전개되는 것이 적절하므로 '논의하다, 토의하다'라는 뜻의 (C) discuss가 정답이다.
| 어휘 | lecture 강연   attendee 참석자   method 방법   guest speaker 초청 연사   focus 집중하다, 초점을 맞추다   dictate 지시하다, 받아쓰게 하다   fund 자금을 제공하다

105. 동사 어휘
전체 주소가 없는 건축 허가 요청은 더 이상 수락되지 않을 것이다.
| 해설 | 수동태 동사를 완성할 과거 분사가 들어갈 자리로, 주어인 Building permit requests와 연결 지어 '건축 허가 요청은 수락되지 않을 것이다'라는 의미로 전개되는 것이 적절하므로 (D) accepted가 정답이다.
| 어휘 | building permit 건축 허가   intend 의도하다   earn 얻다, (돈을) 벌다   perceive 인지하다, 지각하다

106. 명사 자리 - 동사의 목적어
이사들은 그 계약서의 일부 조건들의 의미를 이해하지 못했다.
| 해설 | 빈칸은 동사 understand의 목적어 자리이며, 관사 the와 전치사 of 사이에 있으므로 명사 자리이다. 따라서 '의미'라는 뜻의 명사인 (B) meaning이 정답이다.
| 어휘 | board member 이사   terms 조건   contract 계약서   meanly 비열하게, 초라하게   mean 의미하다, 뜻하다; 인색한

107. 부사 자리 - 형용사 수식
그 이브닝드레스들은 두 곳의 다른 의상실에서 만들어진 것임에도 불구하고 몹시 유사한 디자인을 가지고 있다.
| 해설 | 형용사 similar를 수식하는 자리에 빈칸이 있으므로 빈칸은 부사 자리이다. 따라서 '몹시, 현저하게'라는 뜻의 부사인 (D) remarkably가 정답이다.
| 어휘 | evening gown 이브닝드레스   create 만들어내다, 제작하다   fashion house 의상실   remark 발언, 주목; 말하다, 주목하다

108. 명사 자리 - 어휘
국제 정상 회담 중에 통역사를 쓰는 것은 당사자들의 의사소통 문제를 피하는 좋은 방법이다.
| 해설 | 빈칸은 동명사 Using의 목적어 자리이자, 관사 an 뒤에 있으므로 명사 자리이다. 따라서 명사인 (A) interpretation과 (C) interpreter 중에, 문맥상 '통역

사를 쓰는 것은 좋은 방법이다'라는 의미로 전개되는 것이 적절하므로 '통역사'라는 뜻의 (C) interpreter가 정답이다.
| 어휘 | international 국제적인   summit 정상 회담   avoid 피하다   communication issue 의사소통 문제   party 당사자   interpretation 통역, 해석   interpret 통역하다, 해석하다

109. 전치사 어휘
신형 Mahlon 스마트폰의 배터리는 시판 중인 대부분의 다른 것들보다 더 오래 지속된다.
| 해설 | 빈칸은 앞의 절에 뒤의 명사구를 연결해줄 전치사가 들어갈 자리로, 앞에 비교를 나타내는 부사의 비교급 longer가 제시되어 있으므로 '~보다'라는 뜻으로 비교급과 함께 쓰이는 전치사인 (B) than이 정답이다.
| 어휘 | last 지속되다   on the market 시판 중인, 시장에 나와 있는

110. 형용사 어휘
고객 수요를 따라가기 위해, 그 카페는 온종일 갓 구운 빵의 꾸준한 공급을 필요로 한다.
| 해설 | 빈칸은 명사 supply를 수식해줄 형용사가 들어갈 자리로, 문맥상 '고객 수요를 따라가기 위해 꾸준한 공급이 필요하다'라는 의미로 전개되는 것이 적절하므로 '꾸준한, 안정된'이라는 뜻의 (C) steady가 정답이다.
| 어휘 | keep up with ~에 뒤지지 않다   demand 요구, 수요   supply 공급   freshly baked 갓 구운   rigorous 엄격한, 철저한

111. 부사 어휘
비록 날씨가 추울 것이라고 하지만, 행사 기획자들은 그래도 많은 군중을 예상한다.
| 해설 | 빈칸은 뒤의 동사 expect를 수식해줄 부사가 들어갈 자리로, 문맥상 '날씨가 추울 것이라고 하지만 그래도 많은 군중을 예상한다'라는 의미로 전개되는 것이 적절하므로 '그래도, 여전히'라는 뜻의 부사인 (B) still이 정답이다.
| 어휘 | be supposed to ~하기로 되어 있다   expect 예상하다, 기대하다   crowd 군중

112. 부사 자리 - 동사 수식
Anderson 씨의 사퇴 후에, 이사회에 의해 새로운 CEO가 즉시 임명되었다.
| 해설 | be동사 was와 과거 분사 appointed 사이에 빈칸이 있으므로 빈칸은 동사를 수식하는 부사 자리이다. 따라서 '즉시, 즉각'이라는 뜻의 부사인 (A) promptly가 정답이다.
| 어휘 | following ~ 후에   resignation 사퇴, 사임   appoint 임명하다, 지명하다   board 이사회   prompt 즉각적인; 촉구하다   prompter 프롬프터(대사를 알려주는 장치), 격려자

고난도

113. 동사의 형태와 시제
지금까지 Fleming 디자인 사는 지역 사회 프로젝트들에 5만 달러 이상 기부해 왔다.
| 해설 | 빈칸은 문장의 동사 자리인데, 빈칸 뒤에 목적어가 있으므로 능동태가 되어야 하며, 문두에 과거부터 현재까지의 상황을 나타내며 주로 현재 완료 시제 동사와 함께 쓰이는 부사인 So far가 있으므로 능동태의 현재 완료 시제 동사인 (D) has contributed가 정답이다.

| 어휘 | so far 지금까지   local community 지역 사회   contribute 기부하다, 기여하다

114. 명사 어휘
Cameron 극장은 곧 있을 연극을 위해 오디션을 열었는데, 그것은 6월에 공연될 것이다.
| 해설 | 빈칸은 타동사 held의 목적어가 들어갈 자리로, 뒤에 있는 전치사구와 관련 지어 문맥상 '곧 있을 연극을 위해 오디션을 열었는데'라는 의미로 전개되는 것이 적절하므로 (A) auditions가 정답이다.
| 어휘 | hold 열다, 개최하다   upcoming 곧 있을, 다가오는   play 연극   perform 공연하다   position 자리, 직책   examination 시험, 검토   interest 관심, 이자

115. 현재 분사 vs. 과거 분사
지역 내 강한 관광객 활기에도 불구하고, 놀랄 만한 수의 레스토랑들이 영업을 계속하는 데 어려움을 겪고 있다.
| 해설 | 관사 a와 명사 number 사이에 빈칸이 있으므로 빈칸은 명사를 수식하는 형용사 자리이다. (A) surprised는 '놀란'이란 뜻이고, (C) surprising은 '놀라운, 놀랄 만한'이란 뜻인데, '놀랄 만한 수의 레스토랑'이라는 의미가 되어야 하므로 현재 분사형 형용사인 (C) surprising이 정답이다.
| 어휘 | have trouble -ing ~하는데 어려움을 겪다   stay in business 영업을 계속하다, 사업을 유지하다   surprisingly 놀랍게도   surprise 놀라게 하다; 놀라움

116. 부사 어휘
Cobre 은행의 많은 고객들이 금리가 역사적으로 이전 어느 때보다 낮기 때문에 융자를 받고 있다.
| 해설 | 빈칸은 형용사의 비교급인 lower를 수식해줄 부사가 들어갈 자리로, 문맥상 '역사적으로 이전 어느 때보다 낮기 때문에'라는 의미로 전개되는 것이 적절하므로, '역사적으로, 역사상'이라는 뜻의 (A) historically가 정답이다.
| 어휘 | take out a mortgage 융자를 받다   interest rate 이율, 금리   urgently 긴급하게   actively 활동적으로   repeatedly 반복적으로

고난도

117. 형용사 자리 - 명사 수식
Platinum Pass는 콘서트에 자주 가는 사람들에게 공연 전후에 무대 뒤 라운지 구역에 독점적인 출입을 허용한다.
| 해설 | 빈칸은 4형식 동사 gives의 직접 목적어인 명사 access를 수식해줄 형용사가 들어갈 자리이므로 '독점적인, 전용의'라는 뜻의 형용사인 (D) exclusive가 정답이다.
| 어휘 | give access to ~에 출입[접근]을 허용하다   concertgoer 콘서트에 자주 가는 사람   backstage 무대 뒤의   excluding ~을 제외하고   exclusively 독점적으로, 오로지   exclusion 제외, 배제

고난도

118. 인칭 대명사
비록 직원들 자신들은 대회에 참가하는 것이 금지되어 있지만, 그 가족 구성원들은 자격이 있다.
| 해설 | 빈칸이 없어도 주어 employees 뒤에 수동태 동사 are prohibited가 연

결되는 완전한 문장이 되므로, 빈칸에는 문장 구조에 지장을 주지 않고 앞의 명사의 의미를 강조하는 강조 용법의 재귀 대명사가 들어가야 함을 알 수 있다. 따라서 (B) themselves가 정답이다.

| 어휘 | prohibit ~하지 못하게 하다, 금하다   enter 참가하다   contest 대회   eligible 자격이 있는

119. 부사 어휘
다락방은 진공 청소기가 손에 쉽게 닿을 수 없으니, 대신에 그것을 아래층 벽장에 보관해 주세요.

| 해설 | 빈칸은 문장 전체를 수식해줄 부사가 들어갈 자리로, 쉽게 도달할 수 없는 상황이 이유로 제시된 것으로 볼 때 문맥상 '대신에 아래층 벽장에 보관해 주세요'라는 의미로 전개되는 것이 적절하므로 '대신에'라는 의미로 문장 끝에 쓸 수 있는 부사인 (C) instead가 정답이다.

| 어휘 | vacuum 진공 청소기   reach 닿다, 도달하다   attic 다락, 다락방   store 보관하다   downstairs 아래층; 아래층의   closet 벽장   likewise 똑같이, 비슷하게   particularly 특히

120. 명사 어휘
팀원들이 회사의 정체성을 반영하는 스타일에 합의할 수 없었기 때문에 새로운 로고에 관한 논의가 교착 상태에 빠졌다.

| 해설 | 빈칸은 전치사 on의 목적어가 들어갈 자리로, 뒤에 있는 that절의 수식을 받으며 합의에 이룰 수 없었던 대상이 될 수 있는 것으로는 '회사의 정체성을 반영하는 스타일'이 가장 적절하므로 '스타일, 모양'이라는 뜻의 (D) style이 정답이다.

| 어휘 | stall 교착 상태에 빠지다   agree on ~에 합의하다   reflect 반영하다   identity 정체성, 신원   degree 도(온도의 단위), 등급   belief 믿음, 신념   route 노선, 경로

121. 부사절 접속사
저희는 일단 계약이 마무리되면 부사장 직책을 맡게 될 사람의 이름을 발표할 것입니다.

| 해설 | 빈칸 앞뒤에 완전한 절이 있으므로 빈칸에는 두 절을 연결해줄 접속사가 들어가야 한다. 따라서 부사절 접속사인 (C) once가 정답이다.

| 어휘 | take over 인계받다, 떠맡다   vice president 부사장   position 직책   contract 계약

122. 동사 어휘
Willow Inn에 숙박하는 사람들의 손님들은 단기 주차권을 얻기 위해 프런트 데스크를 방문해야 한다.

| 해설 | 빈칸은 뒤에 있는 명사구 a short-term parking pass를 목적어로 받는 to부정사를 완성해줄 동사 원형이 들어갈 자리로, 문맥상 '단기 주차권을 얻기 위해'라는 의미로 전개되는 것이 적절하므로 '얻다, 손에 넣다'라는 뜻의 (A) obtain이 정답이다.

| 어휘 | short-term 단기의   attach 첨부하다   gather 모으다

고난도

123. 분사 자리 – 명사 후치 수식
바리케이드로 막힌 시의 도로들은 마라톤 경주 직후에 대중에게 개방될 것이다.

| 해설 | 이 문장의 주어는 City roads이고, 동사는 will be이다. 따라서 빈칸에서 barricades까지가 주어 City roads를 뒤에서 수식하는 구조임을 알 수 있는데, '바리케이드로 막힌 시의 도로들'이라는 의미가 되어야 하므로 수동/완료의 의미를 지닌 과거 분사 (C) blocked가 정답이다.

| 어휘 | race 경주

124. 형용사 어휘
장마철 동안 모일 수 있는 넘치는 양의 물을 제거하기 위해 펌프 시스템이 지하에 설치될 것이다.

| 해설 | 빈칸은 뒤에 있는 명사 water를 수식해줄 형용사가 들어갈 자리로, 문맥상 제거할 대상이 되는 것은 '장마철 동안 모일 수 있는 넘치는 양의 물'이 적절하므로 '초과된, 여분의'이라는 뜻의 (A) excess가 정답이다.

| 어휘 | install 설치하다   basement 지하 층, 지하실   get rid of ~을 제거하다   collect 모이다   rainy season 장마철, 우기   valid 유효한   adequate 적절한, 충분한   distilled 증류한, 정제된

고난도

125. 명사 자리 – 어휘
회의에 있는 협상자들 어느 누구도 라이선스 계약의 가격 조건을 먼저 제시하는 것을 원하지 않았다.

| 해설 | 정관사 the 뒤에는 명사가 와야 하므로, 형용사인 (B)는 오답이고, 나머지 (A), (C), (D)는 모두 명사인데, 문맥상 '협상자들 어느 누구도 원하지 않았다'라는 의미로 전개되어야 하므로 '협상자, 교섭자'라는 뜻의 (C) negotiators가 정답이다. 또한 neither of 뒤에는 복수 명사가 와야 하므로 단수 명사인 (A), (D)는 답이 될 수 없다.

| 어휘 | be the first to 맨 먼저 ~하다, 솔선하여 ~하다   pricing terms 가격 조건   licensing agreement 라이선스 계약   negotiability 협상 가능성   negotiable 협상할 수 있는, 절충 가능한   negotiation 협상

126. 전치사 어휘
새로 설치된 포장 기계로, 그 공장은 생산량을 10퍼센트까지 늘릴 수 있을 것이다.

| 해설 | 빈칸은 뒤에 있는 명사구 the newly installed packaging machinery를 목적어로 받는 전치사가 들어갈 자리로, 빈칸 뒤에 있는 명사구가 공장이 생산량을 늘릴 수 있는 도구가 됨을 알 수 있으므로, 소유나 수단을 나타낼 때 쓰는 전치사인 (C) With가 정답이다.

| 어휘 | packaging machinery 포장 기계   increase 늘리다   output 생산량

고난도

127. to부정사 – 동사의 목적어
영업 팀은 고객 기반에 더 많은 고객들을 추가함으로써 이번 달에 이전 기록을 깨뜨리기를 바란다.

| 해설 | 빈칸은 타동사 hopes의 목적어가 들어갈 자리로, hope는 to부정사를 목적어로 취하는 동사이므로 동명사인 (B) having broken과 (C) breaking은 오답이고, 빈칸 뒤에 목적어인 its previous record가 있으므로 능동태인 (D) to break가 정답이다.

| 어휘 | previous 이전의   add 추가하다   client 고객   customer base 고객 기반, 고객층

128. 전치사 어휘

정비공들은 수리 견적을 제공하기 전에 교체 부품들의 현재 가격을 확인하도록 권고된다.

| 해설 | 빈칸은 앞의 절과 뒤의 동명사구를 연결해줄 전치사가 들어갈 자리로, 문맥상 '견적을 제공하기 전에 가격을 확인하도록 권고된다'라는 의미로 전개되는 것이 적절하므로 '~ 전에, 앞서'라는 뜻의 (C) prior to가 정답이다.

| 어휘 | mechanic 정비공   be advised to ~하도록 권고되다   current 현재의   replacement 교체   estimate 견적, 견적서   aside from ~을 제외하고, ~이외에   as of ~부로, ~부터

고난도
129. 명사절 접속사

창고 관리자는 왜 배송 상자들의 일부가 운송 중에 파손되었는지 아직 알아내지 못했다.

| 해설 | 빈칸 이하가 타동사 learned의 목적어 역할을 하는 구조이므로, 빈칸에는 명사절 접속사가 와야 하며, 빈칸 이하에 완전한 절이 왔으므로 뒤에 완전한 절이 오는 명사절 접속사인 (B) why가 정답이다. (A) what과 (C) whom은 명사절 접속사이지만, 뒤에 불완전한 절이 오고, (D) whenever는 부사절 접속사이다.

| 어휘 | warehouse 창고   crate 나무 상자   damaged 파손된   in transit 운송 중에

고난도
130. 명사 어휘

GTR 의류에서 만들어진 모든 자전거용 반바지의 솔기는 내구성을 향상시키기 위해 이중 박음질이 된다.

| 해설 | 빈칸은 improve의 목적어가 될 명사가 들어갈 자리로, 앞에 이중 박음질이 된다는 것과 연결 지어 문맥상 '내구성을 향상시키기 위해'라는 의미로 전개되는 것이 적절하므로 '내구성, 내구력'이라는 뜻의 (D) durability가 정답이다.

| 어휘 | seam 솔기, 이음매   double stitch 이중 박음질하다   improve 향상시키다, 개선하다   preference 선호   familiarity 익숙함, 친근함   attempt 시도

PART 6

131-134 다음 정보를 참조하시오.

> **지역 사회 미술 대회 정보**
>
> 심사 위원단으로 선발된 사람들은 가족들을 대회에 참가시킬 수 없습니다. 이는 심사 위원들이 편견이 ¹³¹없도록 확실하게 해 줄 것입니다. 모든 출품작은 출품을 위한 요건을 충족시켜야 합니다. ¹³²세부적인 지침들은 웹 사이트에서 제공됩니다. 출품작은 2월 6일 토요일에 Dubois 센터에서 받을 것입니다. 참가자들을 수거 지점으로 안내하는 노란 표지판을 ¹³³찾아보세요. 화가들은 각자의 캔버스를 포장한 상태로 두도록 허용됩니다. 심사를 위한 시간이 되면, 그 그림들은 손상을 피하기 위해 저희 직원들에 의해 ¹³⁴천천히 포장이 벗겨질 것입니다.

| 어휘 | judging panel 심사 위원단   ensure 확실히 하다   bias 편견   submission 제출(물)   meet the requirements 요건을 충족시키다   entry 출품물, 참가   accept 수락하다, 받아들이다   direct 안내하다   collection 수거, 수집   be permitted to ~하도록 허용되다   wrap 포장하다   unwrap 포장을 풀다   damage 손상

131. 형용사 어휘

| 해설 | be동사의 주격 보어로 쓰일 형용사가 들어갈 자리로, 심사 위원단은 가족들을 대회에 참가시킬 수 없다는 앞 문장과 연결시켜 볼 때, '편견이 없다, 편견에서 자유롭다'라는 의미로 전개되는 것이 적절하므로 '~이 없는'이라는 뜻의 (B) free가 정답이다.

| 어휘 | unlike 서로 다른   obvious 분명한

132. 알맞은 문장 고르기

(A) 미술에 대한 관심이 지역 사회 내에서 증가해 오고 있습니다.
(B) 주제를 선정하는 것이 행사 기획자들에게는 어려웠습니다.
(C) 세부적인 지침들은 웹 사이트에서 제공됩니다.
(D) 귀하의 작품이 거절되어 유감입니다.

| 해설 | 앞서 모든 출품작은 출품을 위한 요건을 충족시켜야 한다는 문장이 제시되어 있는 것으로 볼 때, 그 연장선상에서 충족시켜야 하는 요건과 관련하여 세부적인 지침을 확인할 수 있는 내용의 문장이 삽입되는 것이 가장 적절하므로 정답은 (C)이다.

| 어휘 | interest 관심   theme 주제   detailed 상세한, 세부적인   reject 거절하다, 거부하다

133. 동사 어휘

| 해설 | 문장의 동사가 들어갈 자리로, 앞 문장에 작품을 제출하는 날짜와 장소를 언급하였고, 참가자들에게 그 장소(수거 지점)로 안내하는 노란 표지판을 찾아보라는 의미로 전개되는 것이 적절하므로 빈칸 뒤에 있는 for와 함께 '찾다'라는 의미를 완성하는 (A) Look이 정답이다.

| 어휘 | account 간주하다, 설명하다

134. 부사 자리 - 동사 수식

| 해설 | be동사와 과거 분사 unwrapped 사이에 빈칸이 있으므로 빈칸은 동사를 수식하는 부사 자리이다. 따라서 '천천히'라는 뜻의 부사인 (D) slowly가 정답이다.

135-138 다음 회람을 참조하시오.

> 발신: Roberta Galvan
> 수신: Celestine 보험 전 직원
> 날짜: 7월 13일
> 주제: 수리
>
> 우리 건물 3층의 카펫과 벽지의 ¹³⁵좋지 않은 상태로 인해 그곳을 일부 수리할 회사를 고용했습니다. 그 작업은 7월 28일부터 8월 1일까지

예정되어 있습니다. 그 프로젝트의 첫날에, 3층에서 일하는 직원들은 건물의 다른 구역에 있는 업무 공간으로 ¹³⁶이동될 것입니다. 작업이 실시되는 ¹³⁷동안, 회의실은 출입이 금지될 것입니다. 따라서 팀장들은 가능하면 회의를 연기하도록 노력해야 합니다. ¹³⁸그렇지 않으면 외부에서 장소를 찾아야 할 것입니다.

| 어휘 | carry out 시행하다, 수행하다   renovation 수리, 개조   condition 상태   wallpaper 벽지   workspace 업무 공간, 작업 공간   perform 실시하다, 수행하다   conference room 회의실   off limits 출입 금지인   postpone 연기하다, 미루다

135. 형용사 어휘

| 해설 | 명사 condition을 수식해줄 형용사가 들어갈 자리로, due to는 이유를 나타내는 전치사구이므로 빈칸은 수리의 이유를 나타내야 한다. 따라서 '좋지 않은'이라는 뜻의 (D) poor가 정답이다.

| 어휘 | stable 안정된, 안정적인   sufficient 충분한

고난도
136. 동사의 시제

| 해설 | who work on the third floor는 주어인 명사 employees를 수식하는 형용사절이고, 빈칸은 문장의 동사가 들어갈 자리이다. 회람 발송 날짜가 7월 13일인 것과 작업이 7월 28일부터 8월 1일까지 예정되어 있다고 한 것을 연계해 볼 때, 직원들이 이동될 프로젝트의 첫날도 미래임을 알 수 있으므로 미래 시제 동사인 (D) will be moved가 정답이다.

137. 부사절 접속사

| 해설 | 빈칸 뒤로 두 개의 절이 제시되어 있으므로, 빈칸은 두 절을 연결해줄 접속사가 들어갈 자리이다. 따라서 '~하는 동안에'라는 뜻의 부사절 접속사인 (C) While이 정답이다. (A) During은 전치사, (B) Occasionally는 부사, (D) For the moment는 전치사구이므로 두 절을 연결할 수 없다.

| 어휘 | occasionally 때때로   for the moment 당장은, 우선은

138. 알맞은 문장 고르기

(A) 장비는 저희가 예상했던 것보다 더 시끄러웠습니다.
(B) 작업반원들은 그들의 전문성으로 알려져 있습니다.
(C) 그렇지 않으면 외부에서 장소를 찾아야 할 것입니다.
(D) 각 층은 다른 장식 스타일을 가지고 있습니다.

| 해설 | 앞서 회의실이 출입 금지될 것이라서 팀장들이 가능하면 회의를 연기하도록 노력해야 한다는 내용이 제시되어 있는 것으로 볼 때, 회의실 이용과 관련 지어 회의를 연기하지 않을 경우의 상황을 추가적으로 알려주는 내용의 문장이 이어지는 것이 적절하므로 (C)가 정답이다.

| 어휘 | equipment 장비   noisy 시끄러운   be known for ~로 알려져 있다   professionalism 전문성, 프로 정신   off-site 외부에서   decorative 장식의, 장식적인

139-142 다음 이메일을 참조하시오.

수신: Jay Williamson
발신: Kristie Aldridge
날짜: 11월 4일
제목: Broadway 헬스클럽

Williamson 씨 귀하,

Broadway 헬스클럽의 회원으로 등록해 주셔서 감사합니다. 귀하의 애용에 대해 감사를 표하기 위해, 영양사와의 한 차례 무료 ¹³⁹상담 시간을 제공하여 귀하의 피트니스 목표에 맞는 식단을 계획하실 수 있도록 하려고 합니다. 일단 운동을 하기 시작하시면, 저희가 많은 건강 지표에 있어 귀하의 추이를 ¹⁴⁰추적할 것입니다.

귀하께서 필라테스 수업에 등록하시는 것에 관심이 있으셨다는 것을 아는데, 유감스럽게도 그것은 이미 수용 인원이 꽉 찼습니다. ¹⁴¹이런 이유로, 귀하는 대기자 명단에 올려져 있습니다. 귀하의 관심사에 맞을 수도 있는 다른 많은 강좌들이 있는데요. ¹⁴²관심이 있으실 경우에 대비하여, 제가 전체 목록을 첨부했습니다.

따뜻한 안부를 전하며,

Kristie Aldridge
회원 코디네이터

| 어휘 | sign up for ~에 등록하다, 신청하다   appreciation 감사   patronage 애용, 후원   complimentary 무료의   nutritionist 영양사   diet 식단   match 맞다, 어울리다   work out 운동하다   progress 추이, 진척 상황   health indicator 건강 지표   unfortunately 유감스럽게도   be at full capacity 수용 인원이 꽉 차다   waiting list 대기자 명단   suit 적합하다

139. 명사 어휘

| 해설 | 빈칸은 offer의 직접 목적어인 명사가 들어갈 자리로, 문맥상 식단 계획을 세울 수 있도록 영양사와 함께 하는 것으로 적당한 것은 '(특정한 활동을 위한) 시간 [기간]'일 것이므로 (C) session이 정답이다.

| 어휘 | license 면허, 허가   invoice 송장, 청구서

140. 동사의 시제

| 해설 | 빈칸은 주절의 동사가 들어갈 자리로, 회원으로 등록한 사람에게 보내는 이메일로 아직 운동을 시작하지 않은 상황에서 운동을 시작하면 제공할 서비스를 안내하는 것이므로 빈칸은 미래 시제가 되어야 한다. 따라서 미래 시제 동사인 (C) will track이 정답이다.

141. 부사구

| 해설 | 빈칸은 앞뒤의 두 문장을 의미적으로 자연스럽게 연결해 줄 부사구가 들어갈 자리로, 앞에 제시된 문장 뒤에 나오는 문장의 이유가 됨을 알 수 있으므로, 이유를 나타내는 (B) For this reason이 정답이다.

| 어휘 | on the other hand 다른 한편으로   all things considered 모든 것을 고려하여

142. 알맞은 문장 고르기

(A) 저희 탈의실은 최근에 수리되었습니다.
(B) 관심이 있으실 경우에 대비하여, 제가 전체 목록을 첨부했습니다.
(C) 그럼에도 불구하고 강사들은 많은 경험을 가지고 있습니다.
(D) 필라테스 수업에 대한 귀하의 피드백에 감사할 것입니다.

| 해설 | 앞서 관심사에 맞을 수 있는 다른 강좌들이 많이 있다고 알려줬으므로, 그와 관련 지어 다른 많은 강좌들을 볼 수 있는 전체 목록을 첨부했다는 문장이 이어지는 것이 적절하므로 정답은 (B)이다.

| 어휘 | locker room 탈의실   renovate 개조하다, 보수하다   in case ~인 경우에 대비하여   attach 첨부하다   complete 전체의, 완전한   instructor 강사   a great deal of 많은   appreciate 감사하다

143-146 다음 회람을 참조하시오.

수신: Viridian 매트리스 전 직원
발신: 인사부 관리자, Damon Boswell
날짜: 11월 6일
주제: Mavis Ferguson

제가 지난주 직원 회의에서 알려드렸던 것과 같이, 저희 지역 영업 부장인 Mavis Ferguson이 1월 초에 리스본에 있는 해외 지점으로 ¹⁴³전근을 가게 될 것입니다. 그녀의 목표는 Viridian 매트리스를 포르투갈 내 일등 매트리스 브랜드로 만드는 것인데요. ¹⁴⁴저희는 그녀가 그것을 달성할 능력이 있다고 확신합니다. 그녀는 재능과 결단력 그리고 경험의 완벽한 조합을 가지고 있죠.

Dwight Wolcott가 Ferguson 씨의 역할을 ¹⁴⁵물려받을 것입니다. 그는 수년 간 영업 차장으로 일해왔기 때문에, 순조로운 이행이 될 것 같습니다.

그녀의 ¹⁴⁶발군의 공훈에 감사하기 위해 Ferguson 씨를 위한 송별회가 12월 14일에 열릴 것입니다. 이 행사의 초대장은 다음 달에 발송될 것입니다. 모두들 거기서 뵙기를 바랍니다.

Damon

| 어휘 | sales director 영업 부장   overseas 해외의   goal 목표   combination 조합   talent 재능   determination 결단력   assistant 보조의, 보좌의   smooth 순조로운, 원활한   transition 이행, 전환   farewell party 송별회

143. 동사의 시제

| 해설 | 빈칸은 문장의 동사가 들어갈 자리로, 회람을 보낸 날짜는 11월 6일이고, Mavis Ferguson이 전근을 갈 날짜는 1월 초라고 제시되어 있으므로, 미래 시제 동사인 (C) will be transferring이 정답이다.

144. 알맞은 문장 고르기

(A) 귀하가 공석에 지원하는 것을 환영합니다.
(B) 여러 주요 고객들이 그곳으로 옮기는 것에 관해 생각하고 있습니다.
(C) 축하 연회는 A회의실에서 열릴 것입니다.
(D) 저희는 그녀가 그것을 달성할 능력이 있다고 확신합니다.

| 해설 | 앞서 Mavis Ferguson의 목표가 제시되어 있는 것으로 볼 때, 그 목표와 관련 지어 앞 문장의 주어인 Her goal을 대명사 it으로 받아 그것을 달성하는 것에 관한 생각을 제시한 문장이 이어지는 것이 적절하므로 (D)가 정답이다.

| 어휘 | apply for ~에 지원하다   job opening 일자리, 공석   reception 축하[환영] 연회   have the ability to ~할 능력이 있다   achieve 달성하다, 성취하다

고난도
145. 동사 어휘

| 해설 | 빈칸은 문장의 동사가 들어갈 자리로, 다음 문장 끝에 순조로운 이행이 될 것 같다고 한 내용으로 볼 때, Dwight Wolcott가 Ferguson 씨의 뒤를 이을 것이라는 의미로 전개되는 것이 적절하므로 '물려받다, 승계하다'라는 뜻의 (B) succeed가 정답이다.

| 어휘 | accomplish 성취하다, 달성하다   restore 회복시키다, 복원하다

고난도
146. 형용사 어휘

| 해설 | 빈칸은 service를 수식해줄 형용사가 들어갈 자리로, 위에 제시된 내용으로 볼 때 송별회에서 감사하고자 하는 것은 Ferguson 씨가 회사에 근무하면서 세웠던 공로일 것이므로 distinguished service(발군의 공훈[공로])라는 의미를 완성해줄 '발군의, 탁월한'이라는 뜻의 (A) distinguished가 정답이다.

| 어휘 | impressed 감명받은, 인상 깊게 생각하는   apparent 분명한, 명백한   promising 유망한, 촉망되는

PART 7

147-148 다음 제품 설명을 참조하시오.

Lawson 농장 레몬 커드

저희 레몬 커드는 토스트와 다른 구운 제품들에 펴 바르거나 요거트에 섞기에 안성맞춤입니다. 저희는 진짜 버터와 잘 익은 레몬을 써서 여러분께 신선한 풍미를 북돋아 드립니다. ¹⁴⁷개봉 전에 그 제품은 서늘하고 건조한 곳에 보관되어야 합니다. 개봉 후에는 금속 뚜껑을 단단히 밀봉하여 5°C 이하에서 제품을 냉장 보관하세요.

알레르기 조언: 라벨에 열거된 어떠한 재료에라도 알레르기가 있다면, 이 제품을 먹지 마세요.

스페인에서 제조
용량: 350 ml

포장재 유의 사항: 플라스틱 병은 재활용될 수 있습니다. ¹⁴⁸저희는 이제 동일한 용량을 30% 적은 플라스틱으로 만든 병에 제공합니다. 수출용이 아닙니다.

| 어휘 | spread 빵에 발라 먹는 식품; 펴 바르다   baked goods 구운 제품   mix 섞다   ripe 잘 익은, 숙성된   boost 북돋움   flavor 풍미, 맛   refrigerate 냉장 보관하다, 냉장하다   lid 뚜껑   tightly 단단히   seal 밀봉하다   allergen 알레르기 유발 물질   allergic 알레르기가 있는   ingredient 재료   consume 먹다, 마시다   pot 병, 단지   recycle 재활용하다   volume 용량   export 수출

고난도
147. 세부 사항을 묻는 문제
제품 설명에 어떤 정보가 제공되어 있나?
(A) 어떻게 제품을 보관하는지
(B) 어디에서 포장재를 재활용하는지
(C) 어떤 재료가 알레르기에 영향을 미칠 수 있는지
(D) 얼마나 오래 제품이 지속되는지
| 해설 | 첫 번째 단락 후반부에 개봉 전에는 서늘하고 건조한 곳에 보관하고(Before opening, the product should be kept in a cool, dry place) 개봉 후에는 금속 뚜껑을 단단히 밀봉하여 5°C 이하에서 제품을 냉장 보관하라고(After opening, refrigerate the product at or below 5°C with the metal lid tightly sealed) 보관 방법을 알리고 있으므로 정답은 (A)이다.
| 어휘 | store 보관하다   affect 영향을 미치다   last 지속되다
| 패러프레이징 | be kept, refrigerate → store

고난도
148. 추론 문제
Lawson 농장 레몬 커드에 관해 암시되는 것은 무엇인가?
(A) 국내외에서 유통된다.
(B) 현재 전보다 30% 더 크다.
(C) 뚜껑은 플라스틱으로 만들어진다.
(D) 포장이 최근에 달라졌다.
| 해설 | 세 번째 단락에 이제 동일한 용량을 30% 적은 플라스틱으로 만든 병에 제공한다고(We now offer the same volume but with a pot made from 30% less plastic) 제시되어 있는 것을 통해, 포장이 달라졌음을 알 수 있으므로 정답은 (D)이다.
| 어휘 | distribute 유통하다   domestically 국내에서   internationally 국제적으로   be made of ~로 만들어지다   recently 최근에
| 패러프레이징 | with a pot made from 30% less plastic → Its packaging has recently changed

149-150 다음 이메일을 참조하시오.

수신: Joyce Farley <jfarley@dawsonmail.com>
발신: Centennial 화장품 <orders@centennialcosmetics.net>
날짜: 8월 30일
제목: 주문 #9258

Farley 씨 귀하,

Centennial 화장품에서 제품을 구매해 주셔서 감사합니다. 저희 연구 팀은 고객들이 젊고 건강해 보이는 피부를 유지하도록 돕기 위해 끊임없이 제품들을 개선해 나가고 있습니다. ¹⁴⁹그래서 전문 모델들이 저희 제품들을 그들의 일상적인 피부 관리 일과의 일부가 되게 하고 그것들의 사용을 옹호하는 것은 놀라운 일이 아니죠. 귀하의 피부 타입이 어떻든 간에, 어떤 성분에도 민감하지 않다는 것을 확실히 하기 위해 먼저 작은 부분에 제품을 테스트해볼 것을 권장합니다.

Centennial 화장품 소식을 하나라도 놓치지 않으시길 바라는데요! 제품 정보와 특가 상품 그리고 스타일 팁들이 담겨 있는 ¹⁵⁰저희 월간 소식지에 등록해 주세요. 저희 홈페이지에서 "소식"을 클릭함으로써 그렇게 하실 수 있습니다.

진심을 담아,

Zachary Mosquera
Centennial 화장품, 고객 서비스 관리자

| 어휘 | continually 끊임없이, 계속해서   improvement 개선, 향상   routine 일과   advocate 옹호하다, 지지하다   sensitive 민감한, 예민한   ingredient 성분, 재료   miss 놓치다   register for ~에 등록하다   monthly newsletter 월간 소식지   special deal 특가 상품

149. True 문제
회사의 제품들에 관해 언급된 것은 무엇인가?
(A) 젊은 소비자들을 위해 특별히 고안된 것이다.
(B) 천연 성분으로 만들어진다.
(C) 전문가들에 의해 추천된다.
(D) 환불 보증이 딸려 있다.
| 해설 | 첫 번째 단락 초반부에 연구 팀이 끊임없이 제품들을 개선해 나가고 있음을 알린 후, 그래서 전문 모델들이 그것들의 사용을 옹호하는 것은 놀라운 일이 아니라고(~ professional models make our products part of their daily skincare routines and advocate using them) 덧붙였으므로 정답은 (C)이다.
| 어휘 | designed 고안된, 설계된   specifically 특별히   come with ~이 딸려 있다   money-back guarantee 환불 보증
| 패러프레이징 | advocate → are recommended

150. 세부 사항을 묻는 문제
Mosquera 씨가 Farley 씨에게 하도록 요청하는 것은 무엇인가?
(A) 제품 후기를 작성하는 것
(B) 영수증을 제공하는 것
(C) 메일링 리스트에 가입하는 것
(D) 배송 주소를 확인해 주는 것

| 해설 | 두 번째 단락에 제품 정보와 특가 상품 그리고 스타일 팁들이 담겨 있는 월간 소식지에 등록해 달라고(Please register for our monthly newsletter ~) 요청했으므로 정답은 (C)이다.
| 어휘 | receipt 영수증   mailing list 우편물 수신자 명단   confirm 확인해 주다, 확인하다
| 패러프레이징 | register for our monthly newsletter → Join a mailing list

151-152 다음 설명서를 참조하시오.

Colton 전화 시스템에 착신 전화 설정하는 방법

여러분이 사무실 전화로부터 멀리 떨어져 있게 될 때 이 옵션을 이용하세요. 전화가 여러분의 휴대전화나 동료의 전화기로 전송되게 할 수 있습니다.

1. 첫째, 수화기를 드세요. 발신음이 들리면 ¹⁵²⁽ᶜ⁾착신 전환 명령 코드를 입력하는데, 그것은 *72입니다. 그런 다음 이 시스템을 설정하기 위해 여러분이 전화하고 있는 전화번호를 입력하세요.
2. 둘째, ¹⁵¹/¹⁵²⁽ᴰ⁾일련의 삐 소리를 듣고 나서 10자리 착신지 번호(전화가 전송되기를 바라는 곳)를 입력해야 합니다. 그 번호가 수락되지 않을 경우, 한 차례 긴 신호음을 듣게 될 것입니다.
3. 착신지 번호에서 사람이나 음성 사서함 둘 중 하나로 전화를 받을 때까지 끊지 말고 기다리세요.
4. 전화를 끊으세요. ¹⁵² ⁽ᴮ⁾약 30초 이내에 자동으로 다시 전화가 걸려오고 녹음된 메시지에 의해 4자리 취소 코드를 받게 될 것입니다. 참고를 위해 여기에 적어둘 것을 권장합니다.   4258
5. 언제든 착신 전환을 취소하려면, *72로 전화를 건 다음 취소 코드를 입력하세요.

| 어휘 | call forwarding 착신 전화   take advantage of ~을 이용하다   route 보내다, 전송하다   coworker 동료   dial tone 발신음   command 명령   input 입력하다   a series of 일련의   beep 삐 소리, 신호음   ten-digit 10자리   destination 도착지   accept 수락하다, 받아들이다   stay on the line (전화를) 끊지 않고 기다리다   voicemail 음성 사서함   hang up the phone 전화를 끊다   automatically 자동으로   cancellation 취소   reference 참고, 참조

151. 세부 사항을 묻는 문제
일련의 삐 소리는 무엇을 나타내는가?
(A) 착신지 번호가 수락되었다는 것
(B) 사용자가 착신지 번호를 입력해야 한다는 것
(C) 발신지 번호가 이미 사용 중이라는 것
(D) 발신지 번호의 전화들이 전송되리라는 것
| 해설 | 2번에서 일련의 삐 소리를 듣고 나서 10자리 착신지 번호(전화가 전송되기를 바라는 곳)를 입력해야 한다고(listen for a series of beeps, after which you should type in the ten-digit destination number ~) 제시되어 있으므로 정답은 (B)이다.

| 패러프레이징 | type in the ten-digit destination number → input the destination number

152. NOT True 문제
착신 전환 서비스를 설정하기 위해 요구되는 것이 아닌 것은?
(A) 고객 계정 번호를 입력하는 것
(B) 회신 전화를 기다리는 것
(C) 명령 코드를 입력하는 것
(D) 착신지 전화번호를 입력하는 것
| 해설 | 1번에 착신 전환 명령 코드를 입력하라고(type in the call forwarding command code) 한 것에서 (C), 2번에 10자리 착신지 번호를 입력하라고(you should type in the ten-digit destination number) 한 것에서 (D), 4번에 약 30초 이내에 자동으로 다시 전화가 걸려오게 될 것이라고(You will be automatically called back within about thirty seconds) 한 것에서 (B)를 확인할 수 있다. 따라서 (A)가 정답이다.
| 어휘 | enter 입력하다   account 계정
| 패러프레이징 | · called back → a return call
· type in → Input

153-154 다음 문자 메시지 대화를 참조하시오.

Sumati Chopade [오후 3:22]
IT 팀 전체가 오늘 학회에 가느라 부재중이라는 것을 방금 알았어요. ¹⁵³/¹⁵⁴급히 프로젝터를 고쳐줄 수 있는 수리 회사를 알고 있나요? 제가 Blitz 주식회사를 위한 영업 프레젠테이션을 준비하고 있거든요.

Luke Patton [오후 3:23]
그건 안 될 거예요! ¹⁵⁴그 프레젠테이션은 4시에 예정되어 있잖아요. 아마 건물 관리자가 그것을 봐줄 수 있을 거예요. IT에 대해 교육을 받지는 않았지만, 기계에 꽤 능숙하거든요.

Sumati Chopade [오후 3:29]
좋은 생각이네요! 지금 바로 전화해보는 게 좋겠어요.

| 어휘 | entire 전체의   fix 고치다   on short notice 촉박한 통지에, 촉박하게   take a look at ~을 보다   be good with ~에 능숙하다

153. 주제/목적 문제
Chopade 씨는 왜 Patton 씨에게 연락하고 있나?
(A) 그를 학회에 초대하기 위해
(B) 전문가 추천을 부탁하기 위해
(C) 매출 수치를 요청하기 위해
(D) 실수에 대한 사과하기 위해
| 해설 | 오후 3:22에 Chopade 씨가 IT 팀이 부재중이라며 급히 프로젝터를 고쳐줄 수 있는 수리 회사를 알고 있는지(Do you know of any repair companies that can fix a projector on short notice) 물었으므로 정답은

(B)이다.

| 어휘 | referral 소개, 추천 sales figures 매출 수치 apologize for ~에 대해 사과하다

고난도
154. 의도 파악 문제

오후 3:23에 Patton 씨가 "그건 안 될 거예요"라고 쓸 때 의미하는 것은 무엇일 것 같은가?

(A) 그는 교체 부품을 주문하는 것을 잊어버렸다.
(B) 그는 문제를 해결할 충분한 시간이 없다고 생각한다.
(C) 그는 프레젠테이션이 잘되지 않은 것을 걱정한다.
(D) 그는 방이 너무 작은 것을 우려한다.

| 해설 | 이는 앞서 Chopade 씨가 급하게 프로젝터를 고쳐줄 수 있는 수리 회사를 아냐고(Do you know of any repair companies that can fix a projector on short notice) 물으며, Blitz 주식회사를 위한 영업 프레젠테이션을 준비하고 있다고(I'm getting ready for the sales presentation for Blitz Inc.) 한 것에 대한 응답으로, 뒤이어 그 프레젠테이션은 4시에 예정되어 있다고(That presentation is scheduled for four) 말한 것을 통해 문제를 해결할 시간이 충분하지 않다고 생각하여 쓴 것임을 알 수 있다. 따라서 (B)가 정답이다.

| 어휘 | replacement part 교체 부품 resolve 해결하다 go well 잘되다 concerned 우려하는

155-157 다음 초대장을 참조하시오.

> 새크라멘토 역사 박물관이 여러분을 정중히 초대합니다
> **시간을 통한 여정**
> 12월 9일, 토요일
> 오후 7:30, 메인 로비와 강당
>
> 새크라멘토 역사 박물관은 이 지역의 문화와 역사를 형성해온 역사적인 문헌과 유물을 보존하기 위해 노력하고 있습니다. ¹⁵⁵박물관의 유지를 위해 기금을 기부해 주신 모든 분들께 감사를 표하기 위한 방안으로 이번 행사를 주최하게 되어 기쁩니다. 행사는 라이브 음악과 다과, 강당에서 열리는 Monica Sheenan의 프레젠테이션을 특별히 포함할 것인데, 그분은 박물관의 일일 운영을 ¹⁵⁶총괄하고 계십니다. 지역의 화가인 Todd Leday가 모든 참석자들을 대상으로 하는 경품 추첨에 이용될 그림 한 점을 후하게 제공해 주셨습니다. 이 초대장은 3명까지 유효하고, 행사일에 입구에서 제시되어야만 합니다. 미리 여러분의 참석을 확정하실 필요는 없습니다. 그러나 저희가 각 초대장을 이용하실 손님들의 수를 예측할 수 없기 때문에, ¹⁵⁷강당의 자리를 확보하기 위해 일찍 도착하시기를 권장합니다.

| 어휘 | strive to ~하려고 노력하다 preserve 보존하다 artifact 유물 shape 형성하다 culture 문화 host 주최하다 donate 기부하다 fund 기금 upkeep 유지 feature 특별히 포함하다 refreshments 다과 direct 총괄하다, 관리하다 operation 운영 generously 후하게, 관대하게 prize drawing 경품 추첨 attendee 참석자 valid 유효한 up to ~까지 present 제시하다 entrance 입구 confirm 확정하다, 확인하다 predict 예측하다 guarantee 확보하다, 보장하다 spot 자리

155. 추론 문제

누가 이 초대장을 받을 것 같은가?
(A) 골동품 수집가들
(B) 역사학 교수들
(C) 재정적 후원자들
(D) 미술 강사들

| 해설 | 초반부에 행사의 목적에 대해, 박물관의 유지를 위해 기금을 기부해 준 사람들에게 감사를 표하기 위한 방안으로(as a way to show our appreciation to everyone who has donated funds for the museum's upkeep) 이번 행사를 주최하게 되어 기쁘다고 제시되어 있으므로 정답은 (C)이다.

| 어휘 | antique 골동품 collector 수집가 professor 교수 supporter 후원자 instructor 강사

| 패러프레이징 | everyone who has donated funds → Financial supporters

156. 동의어 문제

다섯 번째 줄에 있는 단어 "directs"와 의미가 가장 유사한 것은
(A) 관리하다
(B) 보여주다
(C) 집중하다
(D) 목표로 하다

| 해설 | 해당 단어가 들어간 문장은 '그분은 박물관의 일일 운영을 총괄하고 계십니다'라고 해석된다. 따라서 directs는 '총괄하다, 관리하다'라는 의미로 쓰인 것이므로 이와 유사한 의미로 대체해 쓸 수 있는 (A) manages가 정답이다.

고난도
157. 추론 문제

행사에 관해 암시되는 것은 무엇인가?
(A) 그것은 박물관의 수집품을 위한 기금 모금 행사로 이용될 것이다.
(B) 각 손님은 자신만의 초대장을 각자 지참하도록 요구된다.
(C) 오락거리로 그림 시연을 포함할 것이다.
(D) 좌석이 한정되어 있다.

| 해설 | 후반부에 자리를 확보하기 위해 일찍 도착하시기를 권장한다고(we do recommend arriving early to guarantee a spot in the lecture room) 한 것에서 좌석이 한정되어 있음을 유추할 수 있으므로 정답은 (D)이다.

| 어휘 | fundraiser 기금 모금 행사 collection 수집품, 소장품 include 포함하다 demonstration 시연, 설명 entertainment 오락거리 limited 제한된, 한정된

158-160 다음 공지를 참조하시오.

> **Kettler 호텔 투숙객 여러분께 드리는 공지**
>
> 건물의 서쪽에 위치한 수영장 구역이 10월 20일부터 24일까지 문을 닫

을 것입니다. —[1]—. ¹⁵⁸저희가 단지 여름뿐만 아니라 모든 계절에 이용할 수 있도록 수영장에 난방 시스템을 설치하고 있습니다. 비록 이것은 일시적으로 불편을 야기하지만, 최종 결과는 저희 투숙객들이 마음껏 즐기게 될 하나의 특징이 될 것임을 알고 있습니다. —[2]—.

이 작업으로 야기될 수 있는 모든 불편에 대해 사과드립니다. 건강 혹은 휴양 목적이든 체류하시는 동안 수영장을 이용할 계획이셨다면, 호텔의 프런트 데스크로 와 주세요. —[3]—. ¹⁵⁹그곳에서 Clarkdale 지역 문화 센터의 수영장을 이용하실 수 있는 무료 입장권을 발급받게 되실 것입니다(하루에 투숙객당 한 차례로 제한). 저희 투숙객들의 계획에 지장을 최소화하기 위해 이 절충안을 마련했습니다. ¹⁶⁰그 시설은 근처에 있어, 약 20분 이내에 걸어서 그곳에 가실 수 있습니다. —[4]—.

이 변경 사항에 관해 어떤 우려 사항이 있으시면, 근무 중인 호텔 지배인에게 말씀해 주세요. 여러분의 이해에 감사드립니다.

| 어휘 | swimming pool 수영장 located on ~에 위치한 heating 난방 temporary 일시적인 inconvenience 불편, 불편함 feature 특징 immensely 엄청나게, 대단히 apologize for ~에 대해 사과하다 cause 야기하다 limit 제한하다 compromise 절충안 minimize 최소화하다 disruption 방해 neighborhood 근처, 인근 on foot 걸어서 concern 우려 사항 on duty 근무 중인

158. 세부 사항을 묻는 문제

Kettler 호텔은 왜 변화를 주고 있나?
(A) 야외 지역의 경관을 제공하기 위해
(B) 수영장의 규모를 확장하기 위해
(C) 객실의 수를 늘리기 위해
(D) 편의 시설을 연중 이용이 가능하게 하기 위해

| 해설 | 첫 번째 단락에 수영장이 며칠간 문을 닫는 이유로, 수영장을 여름뿐만 아니라 모든 계절에 이용할 수 있도록 난방 시스템을 설치하고 있다고(We are installing a heating system in the pool so that it may be used in all seasons, not just summer) 제시되어 있으므로 정답은 (D)이다.

| 어휘 | view 경관 expand 확장하다 increase 늘리다 amenity 편의 시설

| 패러프레이징 | may be used in all seasons → available year-round

159. 세부 사항을 묻는 문제

공지에 따르면, 투숙객들은 프런트 데스크에서 무엇을 받을 수 있나?
(A) 공사 일정
(B) 입장권
(C) 음식 쿠폰
(D) 부분 환불

| 해설 | 두 번째 단락 초반부에 호텔의 프런트 데스크로 와 달라고 한 후, 그 이유로 그곳에서 Clarkdale 지역 문화 센터의 수영장을 이용할 수 있는 무료 입장권을 발급받게 될 것이라고(There you will be issued a free pass to use the swimming pool at the Clarkdale Community Center) 제시되어 있으므로 정답은 (B)이다.

160. 문장 삽입 문제

[1], [2], [3], [4]로 표시된 곳 중 아래 문장이 들어가기에 가장 적절한 곳은?

"또는 호텔 셔틀이 매시간 정시에 운행됩니다."

(A) [1]
(B) [2]
(C) [3]
(D) [4]

| 해설 | 제시된 문장은 호텔 셔틀 운영에 관해 알리는 내용으로, 접속 부사 Alternatively를 단서로 앞서 셔틀버스를 타는 것 외의 다른 옵션이 제시되어 있어야 함을 알 수 있다. 따라서 두 번째 단락 마지막에 약 20분 이내에 걸어서 그곳에 갈 수 있다고(The facility is in our neighborhood, and you can get there on foot within about twenty minutes) 알려주는 것 바로 뒤인 (D)가 정답이다.

| 어휘 | alternatively 대안으로 at the top of each hour 매시간 정시에

161-163 다음 게시글을 참조하시오.

http://www.householdbargains.com/customerforum

파손된 물품
이틀 전에 Angie Dodd에 의해 게시됨

지난주에 저는 Household Bargains 웹 사이트를 이용해 ¹⁶¹ ⁽ᴰ⁾ Elite Tableware에서 만들어진 도자기 접시 세트를 주문했습니다. 그것들이 ¹⁶¹ ⁽ᶜ⁾ Cordova 택배 회사에 의해 오늘 오전에 배달되었고요. 유감스럽게도, 제가 그 제품을 곧장 확인해보지 않았는데요. 오늘 오후에 그 상자를 열었을 때, 세트에서 접시 두 개에 금이 간 것을 발견했습니다. ¹⁶¹ ⁽ᶜ⁾/⁽ᴰ⁾ Cordova와 제조업체 둘 다에 전화해 봤지만, 해결할 어떤 정보도 얻을 수 없었습니다. 이 웹 사이트의 고객 서비스 번호를 제가 찾을 수 없기 때문에 ¹⁶² 다음에 어떻게 해야 할지에 관한 여러분의 생각을 듣고 싶은데요. ¹⁶¹ ⁽ᴬ⁾ 인터넷 검색을 통해, 그 회사는 특정 조건하에서만 반품을 받아줄 것이라는 것을 알게 되었는데요. 그 정책이 제 특수한 경우에도 ¹⁶³ 적용될지 궁금합니다.

| 어휘 | ceramic dish 도자기 접시 courier service 택배 회사 unfortunately 유감스럽게도 discover 발견하다 plate 접시, 그릇 cracked 금이 간 manufacturer 제조업체 resolution 해결 under certain conditions 특정 조건에서 policy 정책, 방침 apply 적용되다 particular 특수한, 특정한

고난도

161. NOT True 문제

Dodd 씨에 의해 취해진 조치로 언급되지 않은 것은 무엇인가?
(A) 온라인으로 정책을 조사하는 것
(B) 주문한 물품을 반품하는 것
(C) 택배 서비스에 전화하는 것
(D) Elite Tableware에 연락하는 것

| 해설 | 초반부에 Elite Tableware에서 만들어진(made by Elite Tableware)

도자기 접시 세트를 주문했다고 한 것과 Cordova 택배 회사(Cordova courier service)에 의해 오늘 오전에 배달되었다고 한 것 이후 Cordova와 제조업체 둘 다에 전화해 봤다고(I called both Cordova and the manufacturer) 한 것에서 (C)와 (D), 후반부에 인터넷 검색을 통해(From my Internet search) 알게 된 것을 언급한 것에서 (A)는 모두 확인되므로 정답은 (B)이다.

162. 주제/목적 문제
Dodd 씨는 왜 게시글을 썼는가?
(A) 제품 추천을 부탁하기 위해
(B) 상품에 관한 이전 후기를 업데이트하기 위해
(C) 도자기 접시들을 관리하는 것에 관한 조언을 제공하기 위해
(D) 다른 고객들로부터 제안을 받기 위해

| 해설 | 앞서 주문한 제품에 관해 발생한 상황을 설명한 후, 중반부에 다음에 어떻게 해야 할지에 관한 여러분의 생각을 듣고 싶다고(I'd love to hear your ideas on what to do next ~) 제시되어 있으므로 정답은 (D)이다.

| 어휘 | merchandise 상품, 물품   advice 조언   care for ~을 관리하다

| 패러프레이징 | hear your ideas → get suggestions from other customers

163. 동의어 문제
일곱 번째 줄에 있는 단어 "applies"와 의미가 가장 유사한 것은
(A) 활용하다
(B) 제출하다
(C) 적용되다
(D) 만들다

| 해설 | 해당 단어가 들어간 문장은 '그 정책이 제 특수한 경우에도 적용될지 궁금합니다'라고 해석된다. 따라서 applies는 '적용되다'라는 의미로 쓰인 것이므로 이와 유사한 의미로 대체해 쓸 수 있는 (C) refers가 정답이다.

164-167 다음 기사를 참조하시오.

Derosa에 있는 경기장, 여전히 이름 없어
Mark Graham 작성

(3월 25일)—Derosa의 야구 경기장 건설은 완공까지 쭉 순조롭게 진행되었지만, 그 시설은 아직 한 가지 핵심 요소인 이름이 없다. 그 경기장은 원래 Yancey 자동차와 명명권 계약을 체결한 후 Yancey 스타디움이라고 명명되기로 되어 있었다. —[1]—. 167그래서 시 공무원들은 상업적 파트너들로부터 새로운 입찰을 받고 있다.

164/166이해 당사자들은 시의 웹 사이트에서 지원 서류를 다운로드해야 한다. 입찰과 제안된 이름은 4월 19일 이전에 언제든 제출될 수 있다. —[2]—. 시 의회 의원들과 Derosa 주민들로 구성된 위원회가 입찰들을 검토하고 다섯 곳의 최종 후보자 명단을 선정할 것이다. 이들 다섯 기업들은 또 다시 같은 문제를 겪는 것을 막기 위해 자금 조달 증명을 제시해야만 한다. 명명권은 최고 입찰자에게 주어질 것이다. —[3]—.

경기장의 법적 이름을 마무리하는 데는 몇 달이 걸릴 수 있다. —[4]—.

그 경기장이 시즌 첫 토너먼트인 지역 야구 개막전을 개최하기로 예정되어 있기 때문에, 165그동안 그 시설은 공식적으로 Derosa 스타디움으로 알려지게 될 것이다.

기업들은 (입찰에) 고려되기 위해 Derosa에 본사가 있어야 하는 것은 아니다. 예를 들어, 166Marais 음료는 이미 Marais 스타디움이라는 제안된 이름으로 지원서를 제출했다. 이것이나 다른 경기장 문제들에 관한 문의는 oliver_shaw@derosacity.gov로 Oliver Shaw에게 보내면 된다.

| 어휘 | nameless 이름이 없는   construction 건설   smoothly 순조롭게   completion 완공   lack ~이 없다, 부족하다   component 요소   naming rights 명명권, 명칭 사용권   reach an agreement 합의에 도달하다   city official 시 공무원   accept bids 입찰을 받다   commercial 상업적인   interested parties 이해 관계자, 이해 당사자   application materials 지원 서류   committee 위원회   made up of ~로 구성된   city council member 시 의회 의원   short list 최종 후보자 명단   proof 증명   financing 자금 조달   prevent 막다, 예방하다   be granted to ~에게 주어지다   bidder 입찰자   legal 법적인   be set to ~하도록 예정되어 있다   officially 공식적으로   be based in ~에 기반을 두다, ~에 본사가 있다   be referred to ~에게 보내지다

164. 주제/목적 문제
기사의 목적은 무엇인가?
(A) 입찰 과정을 설명하는 것
(B) 야구 선수들을 모집하는 것
(C) 새로운 회사를 소개하는 것
(D) 건설 결정을 발표하는 것

| 해설 | 첫 번째 단락에 시 공무원들이 새로운 입찰을 받고 있는 상황임을 알린 후, 두 번째 단락에 이해 당사자들은 시의 웹 사이트에서 지원 서류를 다운로드해야 하며(Interested parties should download the application materials from the city's Web site) 입찰과 제안된 이름은 4월 19일 이전에 언제든 제출될 수 있다고(Bids and the proposed name can be submitted anytime before April 19) 했고, 이후 입찰과 관련하여 진행될 상황이 구체적으로 제시되어 있으므로 정답은 (A)이다.

| 어휘 | process 과정, 절차   recruit 모집하다   decision 결정

165. True 문제
기사가 경기장에 관해 언급하는 것은 무엇인가?
(A) 공사가 지연을 겪었다.
(B) 임시 이름이 부여되었다.
(C) 일부 자금이 Yancey 자동차에 의해 제공되었다.
(D) 지역 토너먼트를 개최할 수 없다.

| 해설 | 세 번째 단락 후반부에 그 경기장이 시즌 첫 토너먼트인 지역 야구 개막전을 개최하기로 예정되어 있기 때문에, 그동안 그 시설은 공식적으로 Derosa 스타디움으로 알려지게 될 것이라고(the facility will be officially known as Derosa Stadium in the meantime) 제시되어 있으므로 정답은 (B)이다.

| 어휘 | suffer from ~을 겪다   delay 지연   assign 부여하다, 할당하다

partially 부분적으로   fund 자금을 제공하다

166. 추론 문제
Marais 음료에 관해 암시되는 것은 무엇인가?
(A) 경기장에서 음료를 판매할 것이다.
(B) 현재 Derosa 시에 본사가 있다.
(C) 웹 사이트에서 몇 가지 서식을 받았다.
(D) 일부 계약 조건을 변경하기를 원했다.

| 해설 | 마지막 단락에 Marais 음료는 이미 Marais 스타디움이라는 제안된 이름으로 지원서를 제출했다고(Marais Beverages has already submitted an application) 했는데, 이를 두 번째 단락에 이해 당사자들은 시의 웹 사이트에서 지원 서류를 다운로드해야 한다고(Interested parties should download the application materials from the city's Web site) 한 것과 연계해 볼 때, 웹 사이트에서 지원 서류를 다운받아 지원서를 제출했을 것임을 추론할 수 있으므로 정답은 (C)이다.

| 어휘 | currently 현재   obtain 받다, 얻다   contract terms 계약 조건
| 패러프레이징 | download the application materials from the city's Web site → obtained some forms from a Web site

고난도
167. 문장 삽입 문제
[1], [2], [3], [4]로 표시된 곳 중에 아래 문장이 들어가기에 가장 적절한 곳은?

"자금 조달 오류로 인해, 그 시도를 위한 자금 제공이 실현되지 못했다."

(A) [1]
(B) [2]
(C) [3]
(D) [4]

| 해설 | 제시된 문장은 특정한 시도가 실패로 돌아간 사실을 알리는 내용이므로, 앞서 뭔가 예정되어 있던 일이 언급되고, 뒤이어 그것이 실패로 돌아갔기 때문에 후속 조치로 진행될 일을 알리는 내용의 문장 사이에 들어가야 함을 알 수 있다. 따라서 이를 모두 충족하는 것으로 첫 번째 단락에 그래서 시 공무원들이 상업적 파트너들로부터 새로운 입찰을 받고 있다고(City officials are, therefore, accepting new bids from commercial partners) 한 문장 앞인 (A)가 정답이다.

| 어휘 | funding 자금 제공   endeavor 시도, 노력   fall through 실패하다, 실현되지 못하다

168-171 다음 문자 메시지 대화를 참조하시오.

Nazario Boni [오후 12:23]
기술자가 오늘 오전에 들러서 고장 난 도자기 오븐을 살펴봤어요.

Taylor Johnson [오후 12:25]
일찍 와서 그를 작업실에 들어가게 해 줘서 고마워요. 그가 다시 작동되게 해 줄 수 있었나요?

Nazario Boni [오후 12:26]
유감스럽게도, 아니요. 그가 할 수 있다고 말했는데, 약속대로 오늘은 안 된다고 했어요. ¹⁶⁸새로운 부품을 주문해야 하고, 그 배송이 며칠 걸릴 수 있대요.

Taylor Johnson [오후 12:27]
그것 정말 유감이네요.

Nazario Boni [오후 12:28]
¹⁶⁹당신 도자기 수업에 문제가 있나요? 그래도 당신 학생들이 작업을 할 수 있을까요?

Taylor Johnson [오후 12:29]
걱정 말아요. 제가 수업 후에 그들의 작품들을 더 작은 오븐에 구울 수 있어요. 그들이 다음 날 다시 와서 그것들을 찾아갈 수 있고요.

Nazario Boni [오후 12:31]
그 수업은 단 하루만 예정되어 있잖아요. ¹⁷⁰그들이 작업실로 다시 오는 게 번거롭지 않을까요?

Taylor Johnson [오후 12:33]
그들은 지역 내에 있어요.

Nazario Boni [오후 12:34]
그래요, 잘됐네요. 누구든 직접 다시 올 수 없는 이들에게는 우편으로 최종 작품들을 배송해 줄 수 있을 거예요.

Taylor Johnson [오후 12:35]
맞아요.

Nazario Boni [오후 12:36]
학생들에게 이것에 관해 알리는 것이 좋겠어요. ¹⁷¹제가 우리 홈페이지에 메모를 올릴 수 있어요.

Taylor Johnson [오후 12:38]
고마워요, 그게 도움이 되겠어요.

| 어휘 | stop by 들르다   examine 살펴보다   pottery 도자기   studio 작업실   as promised 약속대로   component 부품   bake 굽다   pick up 찾아가다   hassle 번거로운 일, 귀찮은 상황   in person 직접

168. 세부 사항을 묻는 문제
무엇이 지연을 야기시켰나?
(A) 부품이 주문되어야 한다.
(B) 제품이 단종되었다.
(C) 수송품이 분실되었다.
(D) 예산 요청이 거절되었다.

| 해설 | 오후 12:26에 Nazario Boni가 기술자가 새로운 부품을 주문해야 하고, 그 배송이 며칠 걸릴 수 있다고(He needs to order a new component, and the delivery could take a few days) 했으므로 정답은 (A)이다.

| 어휘 | discontinue (생산을) 중단하다   shipment 수송품   lose 분실하다
budget request 예산 요청   reject 거절하다
| 패러프레이징 | a new component → A part

169. 추론 문제
Johnson 씨는 누구일 것 같은가?
(A) 음악 교사
(B) 미술 강사
(C) 수리 기술자
(D) 판매원
| 해설 | 오후 12:28에 Nazario Boni가 대화 상대인 Taylor Johnson에게 당신 도자기 수업에 문제가 있는지(Is it a problem for your pottery class), 그래도 당신 학생들이 작업을 할 수 있을지(Will your students still be able to do their work) 묻는 것을 통해, Johnson 씨는 도자기 수업을 진행하는 강사임을 알 수 있으므로 정답은 (B)이다.

고난도
170. 의도 파악 문제
오후 12:33에 Johnson 씨가 "그들은 지역 내에 있어요"라고 썼을 때 의미하는 것은 무엇일 것 같은가?
(A) 그녀는 수송품을 곧 받을 것으로 예상하고 있다.
(B) 그녀는 배송료가 낮을 것이라고 생각한다.
(C) 그녀는 변화가 불편하지 않을 것이라고 생각한다.
(D) 그녀는 몇몇 고객들을 방문할 시간이 충분하다.
| 해설 | 이는 앞서 오후 12:31에 Nazario Boni가 그들이 작업실로 다시 오는 것이 번거롭지 않을지(Wouldn't it be a hassle for them to return to the studio) 묻는 말에 대한 응답으로, 학생들이 그 지역 내에 있어 다시 오는 일에 별 문제(불편함)가 없을 것이라는 의미로 한 말임을 알 수 있으므로 정답은 (C)이다.
| 어휘 | fee 요금   inconvenient 불편한

171. 세부 사항을 묻는 문제
Boni 씨가 한다고 제안하는 것은 무엇인가?
(A) 부분 환불을 제공하는 것
(B) 초과 근무를 하는 것
(C) 새로운 장비를 구입하는 것
(D) 온라인에 메시지를 게시하는 것
| 해설 | 오후 12:36에 Nazario Boni가 학생들에게 알리는 것이 좋겠다며 홈페이지에 메모를 올릴 수 있다고(I can put a note on our homepage) 제안하고 있으므로 정답은 (D)이다.
| 어휘 | partial refund 부분 환불   additional 추가의   equipment 장비
| 패러프레이징 | put a note on our homepage → Post a message online

172-175 다음 이메일을 참조하시오.

수신: Danielle Kaye <d_kaye@rothinsurance.com>
발신: Samuel Barbosa <samuel@alfrescodesigns.com>

날짜: 2월 7일
제목: Flanigan 건물

Kaye 씨 귀하,

Flanigan 건물의 옥상 정원 프로젝트를 위해 Alfresco 디자인을 선택해 주셔서 다시 한 번 감사드립니다. 172정원의 주된 꽃으로 원래 제비꽃을 요청하셨던 것으로 아는데요. 그런데 이것들은 그늘에서 가장 잘 자라지만, 그 구역은 대부분 햇빛이 가득할 것이에요. 그래서 172대신에 원추리를 이용하는 것을 권하고자 합니다. 173귀하의 후임자가 인계받기 전에 그 프로젝트가 완전히 마무리되기를 원하셨던 것으로 알고 있어서, 저희가 세부 사항을 계속 진행하는 것을 확인하고 싶습니다.

또한 174옥상의 북쪽 절반에 잔디밭이 설치되는 것을 원하는지 여부를 결정해 주셔야 하는데요. 이것은 아주 매력적인 모습이고 건물을 단열하는 데 도움이 될 수 있지만, 174그 계획은 추가 중량으로 인해 면허가 있는 구조 공학자의 조언이 필요할 것입니다. 귀하의 결정을 저에게 더 빨리 알려주실수록, 제가 더 빨리 누군가에게 연락할 수 있습니다.

이 프로젝트에 추가하고 싶으실 수도 있는 175야외 의자와 탁자들의 카탈로그를 첨부했습니다. 선택 사항들을 검토해 보시고 175저희 다음 회의 전에 가장 마음에 드는 것을 골라주세요. 그런 식으로, 저희가 예산상으로 어떻게 진행하고 있는지 보실 수 있습니다. 1752월 13일에 뵙기를 기대합니다.

진심을 담아,

Samuel Barbosa
Alfresco 디자인, 프로젝트 관리자

| 어휘 | rooftop garden 옥상 정원   originally 원래   violet 제비꽃
daylily 원추리   completely 완전히   successor 후임자   take over 인계받다   move ahead with ~을 계속 진행하다   details 세부 사항
grassy 풀로 덮인   attractive 매력적인, 멋진   appearance 모습, 외관
insulate 단열하다   licensed 면허가 있는   structural engineer 구조 공학자   weight 하중, 무게   attach 첨부하다   outdoor 야외의

172. 주제/목적 문제
Barbosa 씨가 이메일을 보낸 한 가지 이유는 무엇인가?
(A) 건물을 둘러볼 약속을 정하기 위해
(B) 프로젝트에 약간의 변경을 제안하기 위해
(C) 주문 상태를 확인하기 위해
(D) 지역 공급업체를 추천하기 위해
| 해설 | 첫 번째 단락에 정원에 주된 꽃으로 원래 제비꽃을 요청한 것으로 안다고(I know that you had originally requested violets as the main flower in the garden) 한 후에, 대신에 원추리를 이용하는 것을 권하고자 한다고(I would recommend using daylilies instead) 제시되어 있으므로 정답은 (B)이다.
| 어휘 | set up an appointment 약속을 정하다   propose 제안하다

status 상태   supplier 공급업체

고난도
173. 추론 문제
Kaye 씨에 관해 암시되는 것은 무엇인가?
(A) 원추리의 모습을 좋아한다.
(B) Flanigan 건물에 살고 있다.
(C) 예산을 늘릴 수 있다.
(D) 곧 일을 그만둘 계획이다.
| 해설 | 첫 번째 단락 후반부에 귀하의 후임자가 인계받기 전에(before your successor takes over) 프로젝트가 마무리되기를 원했다는 것을 알고 있다고 한 것에서, Kaye 씨는 후임자에게 인계하고 일을 그만둘 것임을 추론할 수 있으므로 정답은 (D)이다.
| 어휘 | increase 늘리다

고난도
174. 세부 사항을 묻는 문제
Barbosa 씨는 왜 잔디밭에 관해 문의하는가?
(A) 전문가에게 상담을 받아야 하는지 여부를 결정하기 위해
(B) 작업 일수를 확정하기 위해
(C) 단열재를 구입해야 하는 필요성을 표명하기 위해
(D) 그것을 옥상의 다른 부분으로 옮기도록 제안하기 위해
| 해설 | 두 번째 단락에 옥상의 북쪽 절반에 잔디밭이 설치되는 것을 원하는지 여부를 결정해 줘야 한다며(I still need you to decide whether you want to have a grassy area installed in the northern half of the rooftop) 그 이유로, 그 계획은 추가 중량으로 인해 면허가 있는 구조 공학자의 조언이 필요할 것이라고(the planning will require the advice of a licensed structural engineer due to the additional weight) 했으므로 정답은 (A)이다.
| 어휘 | determine 결정하다   express 표명하다, 나타내다   insulation materials 단열재
| 패러프레이징 | a licensed structural engineer → a professional

175. 세부 사항을 묻는 문제
Kaye 씨가 2월 13일까지 해야 하는 것은 무엇인가?
(A) 카탈로그를 요청하는 것
(B) 서명된 계약서를 보내는 것
(C) 가구를 선택하는 것
(D) 예산을 마무리하는 것
| 해설 | 마지막 단락에 야외 의자와 탁자들의 카탈로그를 첨부했다며(I have attached a catalog of outdoor chairs and tables ~) 다음 회의 전에 가장 마음에 드는 것을 골라달라고(Please look over the options and choose the ones you like best prior to our next meeting) 요청했고, 마지막에 2월 13일에 뵙기를 기대한다고(I look forward to meeting with you on February 13) 했으므로 이를 종합해 볼 때, 2월 13일 회의 전까지 가구를 선택해야 함을 알 수 있으므로 정답은 (C)이다.
| 어휘 | contract 계약서
| 패러프레이징 | ·outdoor chairs and tables → some furniture
·choose → Select

176-180 다음 회람과 서식을 참조하시오.

수신: 전 직원
발신: 인사 관리자, Marcel Bélair
날짜: 1월 10일
주제: 창의적이 됩시다!

[177]Carolina Enterprises 인사 팀은 늘 업무 환경을 더 재미있고 즐겁게 만들 방안들을 찾고 있습니다. 이러한 관점에서, [176]매월 마지막 수요일에 월간 공예 수업들을 열 계획입니다. [177]이것은 오후 4시에 이곳 우리 건물의 회의실에서 열릴 것입니다. 수업이 여러분의 정규 업무 시간과 겹칠 것이기 때문에, [180]여러분의 직속 상사가 참가 서식에 서명함으로써 여러분의 참가를 승인해야만 합니다.

각 수업에서 여러분은 MK 미술 연구소의 Leona Haigh에게 새로운 공예품을 만드는 방법을 배우게 될 것입니다. [178]첫 번째 수업은 1월 30일 수요일에 열릴 것이고, 첫 4개월 동안의 공예품들은 이미 계획되어 있습니다. 그것들은—순서대로—털실 인형, 구슬로 장식된 액자, 미니 그림, 그리고 무봉제 토트백입니다.

[179]봉급을 받든 시급을 받든 정규 직원들은 무료로 참가할 수 있습니다. 다른 이들은 재료비를 충당하는 데 도움이 되도록 약간의 요금을 지불하도록 요청될 것입니다. 인사부 사무실에서 구할 수 있는 서식을 작성함으로써 미리 신청하세요.

| 어휘 | in light of ~의 관점에서, ~을 고려하여   craft 공예, 공예품   overlap 겹치다   regular working hours 정규 업무 시간   immediate supervisor 직속 상사   approve 승인하다   participation 참가   yarn doll 털실 인형   beaded 구슬로 장식된   picture frame 액자   no-sew 무봉제   salaried 봉급을 받는   fee 요금   cover 충당하다, 부담하다   materials 재료   in advance 미리   complete 작성하다, 완료하다   available 이용 가능한

월간 공예 수업 신청서

이름: Jeremy Steele
부서: 마케팅
[180]팀장: Kylie Knight
참가 날짜(들) (해당되는 것 모두 체크): 1월 30일 [✓]
2월 27일 [✓]   3월 27일 [✓]   4월 24일 [ ]
[179]참가비: 지불 [✓]   해당 없음 [ ]
처리자: 인사부 직원 Thomas Malloy

| 어휘 | sign-up form 신청서   not applicable 해당 없음   processed 처리된

176. 주제/목적 문제
Bélair 씨는 왜 회람을 보냈나?
(A) 직원들을 위한 활동을 소개하기 위해

(B) 안전 예방책을 따르도록 장려하기 위해
(C) 직원들로부터 창의적인 피드백을 요청하기 위해
(D) 의무적인 교육 행사를 알리기 위해

| 해설 | 첫 번째 단락 초반부에 매월 마지막 수요일에 월간 공예 수업들을 열 계획이라고(we plan to hold monthly craft sessions on the last Wednesday of every month) 한 후, 그에 관해 구체적으로 알리고 있으므로 정답은 (A)이다.

| 어휘 | activity 활동   follow 따르다, 준수하다   safety precaution 안전 예방책   solicit 요구하다, 간청하다   creative 창의적인   mandatory 의무적인

| 패러프레이징 | monthly craft sessions → an activity

177. 세부 사항을 묻는 문제
수업은 어디에서 열릴 것인가?
(A) 컨벤션 센터에서
(B) 미술관에서
(C) Carolina Enterprises에서
(D) MK 미술 연구소에서

| 해설 | 첫 번째 단락 도입부에 Carolina Enterprises 인사 팀이라고 한 것과 오후 4시에 이곳 우리 건물의 회의실에서 열릴 것이라고(These will take place here in our building's conference room at 4 P.M.) 한 것을 연계해 볼 때, our building은 Carolina Enterprises의 건물을 가리키는 것임을 알 수 있으므로 정답은 (C)이다.

| 어휘 | art gallery 미술관, 화랑

🔺고난도
178. 세부 사항을 묻는 문제
참가자들은 1월 30일에 무엇에 관해 배울 것인가?
(A) 털실 인형
(B) 액자
(C) 미니 그림
(D) 토트백

| 해설 | 두 번째 단락 초반부에 첫 번째 수업은 1월 30일 수요일에 열릴 것이고, 첫 4개월 동안의 공예품들은 이미 계획되어 있다고(The first session will be held on Wednesday, January 30, and the crafts for the first four months are already planned) 한 후, 그것들은―순서대로―털실 인형(They are—in order—a yarn doll ~)이라고 알린 것을 통해, 1월 30일에는 털실 인형(a yarn doll) 만드는 것을 배울 것임을 알 수 있으므로 정답은 (A)이다.

🔺고난도
179. 연계 문제 - 세부 사항
Steele 씨는 왜 요금이 청구되었나?
(A) 회사 자료를 잃어버렸다.
(B) 한 개 이상의 수업에 등록했다.
(C) 봉급을 받는 직원이다.
(D) 회사에서 정규직으로 일하지 않는다.

| 해설 | Steele 씨는 두 번째 지문인 신청서 작성자로, 참가비(Participation Fee)가 지불(Paid)에 표시되어 있는데, 이를 회람 세 번째 단락에 봉급을 받든 시급을 받든 정규 직원들은 무료로 참여할 수 있고(Full-time employees, whether salaried or paid by the hour, can participate for free) 다른 이들은 약간의 요금을 지불하도록 요청될 것이라고(Others will be asked to pay a small fee ~) 한 것을 연계해 보면, 정규 직원이 아니기 때문에 요금을 지불한 것임을 알 수 있으므로 정답은 (D)이다.

| 어휘 | lose 잃어버리다, 분실하다

180. 연계 문제 - 세부 사항
Steele 씨의 신청서에 누가 서명해야 하는가?
(A) Bélair 씨
(B) Haigh 씨
(C) Knight 씨
(D) Malloy 씨

| 해설 | 회람 첫 번째 단락 후반부에 직속 상사가 참가 서식에 서명함으로써 참가를 승인해야 한다고(your immediate supervisor must approve your participation by signing the participation form) 했고, 신청서에서 Steele 씨의 팀장(Team Leader)은 Kylie Knight로 확인되므로 정답은 (C)이다.

181-185 다음 이메일과 광고를 참조하시오.

수신: Earl Pierce <e.pierce@evanston.com>
발신: Jaqueline Fleming <j.fleming@evanston.com>
날짜: 5월 19일
제목: 팀 교육

Pierce 씨 귀하,

[181]귀하가 제안했던 팀 교육 아이디어들을 따르는 비즈니스 교육 옵션들을 조사해 봤습니다. 첨부된 것에서 제가 귀하의 요구에 가장 적합할 것이라고 생각하는 강의를 보시게 될 텐데요. 그 강의는 그 분야의 전문가에 의해 [182]운영되고, 그 기관이 우리 사무실에서 겨우 차로 2시간 거리에 있어서, 귀하의 팀이 숙박을 할 필요가 없을 것입니다. [184]강의는 오전 10시에 시작하여 오후 5시까지 계속됩니다. 회사로부터 점심 식사비로 1인당 20달러를 받으실 것이고, 휘발유는 법인 카드로 구입하실 수 있습니다. [183]귀하와 귀하의 팀이 하나의 그룹을 채우기에 딱 맞는 규모여서, 소규모 그룹 수업이 특히 도움이 될 것이라고 생각합니다.

[181]이 교육을 진행시키도록 공식적으로 승인해 드리려고 하니, 귀하에게 적합한 날짜에 팀을 등록해 주시기 바랍니다. 그렇게 하는 데 어떤 어려움이 있으면, 저에게 알려주세요.

진심을 담아,

Jaqueline Fleming

| 어휘 | attached 첨부된   be suited for ~에 적합하다   field 분야   institute 기관   stay overnight 하루 숙박하다   last 계속되다, 지속되다   particularly 특히   fill 채우다   official 공식적인   approval 승인   go forward with ~을 진행시키다   register 등록하다

Alder 기관의 비즈니스 워크숍: 커뮤니케이션 향상시키기

780 Holgate 거리, 오클랜드, 캘리포니아 94703에 소재한 Alder 기관에서 현장 개최되는 1일 워크숍들
가능한 날짜들: 6월 4일, 6월 7일, 6월 12일, 6월 18일, 6월 21일, 6월 26일, 7월 8일

[185]다국적 기업 Lander Solutions의 이전 인사부 책임자였던 Rosina Owen이 가르치는 이 워크숍은 다른 이들의 커뮤니케이션 스타일을 확인하는 것뿐만 아니라 커뮤니케이션 능력을 발전시키는 데 도움이 될 것입니다. [185]강사는 실천적인 접근법을 이용하여 참가자들에게 역할극 활동 등을 통하여 스스로 기술들을 시도해 보도록 촉구합니다. [183]6명으로 구성된 소규모 그룹 수업들은 추가적인 토론을 용이하게 하고 아이디어들을 공고히 하는 데 도움이 됩니다. 개인들이나 너무 작은 그룹들은 결합되어 6명 그룹을 만들 것입니다.

[184]워크숍은 위에 열거된 날짜에 오전 10시부터 오후 4시까지 진행되고, 1인당 80달러의 참가비가 있습니다. www.alderinst.com에서 등록하세요.

| 어휘 | available 가능한, 이용할 수 있는   former 이전의   head 책임자, 수석   multinational firm 다국적 기업   develop 발전시키다   identify 확인하다   instructor 강사   hands-on 실천적인, 직접 해 보는   approach 접근법   urge 촉구하다   technique 기법, 기술   facilitate 용이하게 하다   solidify 공고히 하다, 확고히 하다   combine 결합하다   form 만들다, 형성하다   participation fee 참가비

🔺고난도

181. 주제/목적 문제
이메일은 왜 보내졌나?
(A) 예산 증액을 요청하기 위해
(B) 일정 변경을 보고하기 위해
(C) 제안을 수락하기 위해
(D) 등록을 확인하기 위해
| 해설 | 첫 번째 단락 도입부에 귀하가 제안했던 팀 교육 아이디어들을 따르는 비즈니스 교육 옵션들을 조사해 봤다고(I have researched some businesses training options following the team training idea that you proposed) 한 후, 적합하다고 생각하는 강의에 관해 설명하고, 두 번째 단락에 이 교육을 진행시키도록 공식적으로 승인해 주려고 한다고(I am giving my official approval to go forward with this training) 제시되어 있으므로 정답은 (C)이다.
| 어휘 | budget increase 예산 증액   confirm 확인하다, 확정하다   registration 등록
| 패러프레이징 | giving my official approval → accept

182. 동의어 문제
이메일의 첫 번째 단락, 두 번째 줄에 있는 단어 "run"과 의미가 가장 유사한 것은
(A) 실시되는
(B) 서둘러 하는
(C) 경쟁하는
(D) 흐른
| 해설 | 해당 단어가 들어간 문장은 '그 과정은 그 분야의 전문가에 의해 운영되고 ~'라고 해석된다. 따라서 run은 '운영되는'이라는 의미로 쓰인 것이므로 이와 가장 유사한 '실시되는, 시행되는'이라는 뜻의 (A) conducted가 정답이다.

🔺고난도

183. 연계 문제 – 추론
Pierce 씨에 관해 암시되는 것은 무엇인가?
(A) Alder 기관에서 일했었다.
(B) 그의 자리는 인사부에 있다.
(C) 다섯 명을 감독한다.
(D) 그의 사무실은 오클랜드에 기반을 두고 있다.
| 해설 | Pierce 씨는 이메일의 수신자로 첫 번째 단락 후반부에 귀하와 귀하의 팀이 하나의 그룹을 채우기에 딱 맞는 규모여서, 소규모 그룹 수업이 특히 도움이 될 것이라고 생각한다고(I think the mini group session would be particularly helpful ~) 한 것과 광고 후반부에 소규모 그룹 수업이 6명으로 구성된다는(Mini group sessions with six people) 것을 연계시켜 볼 때, 자신을 포함하여 6명의 팀을 구성할 수 있는 Pierce 씨는 5명의 팀원을 이끌고 있는 것으로 유추할 수 있으므로 정답은 (C)이다.
| 어휘 | oversee 감독하다   be based in ~에 기반을 두다

184. 연계 문제 – 세부 사항
Fleming 씨에 의해 제공된 워크숍에 관해 옳지 않은 정보는 무엇인가?
(A) 가능한 날짜들
(B) 참가비
(C) 다루는 주제들
(D) 종료 시간
| 해설 | 이메일 첫 번째 단락에 강의는 오전 10시에 시작하여 오후 5시까지 계속된다고(The course begins at 10 A.M., and it lasts until 5 P.M.) 한 것과 광고 마지막에 워크숍은 위에 열거된 날짜에 오전 10시부터 오후 4시까지 진행된다고(The workshop is from 10 A.M. to 4 P.M. on the dates listed above) 한 것을 연계해 볼 때, 워크숍이 끝나는 시간이 옳지 않음을 알 수 있으므로 정답은 (D)이다.
| 어휘 | cover 다루다   ending 종료

🔺고난도

185. True 문제
Owen 씨에 관해 제시된 것은 무엇인가?
(A) 커뮤니케이션 학사 학위를 소지하고 있다.
(B) 참석자들이 적극적으로 참여하도록 장려한다.
(C) Alder 기관의 신입 사원이다.
(D) Lander Solutions의 설립자였다.
| 해설 | Owen 씨는 광고 두 번째 단락에 제시된 워크숍을 진행할 강사로, 실천적인 접근법을 이용하여 참가자들에게 역할극 활동 등을 통하여 스스로 기술을 시도해 보도록 촉구한다고(The instructor uses a hands-on approach, urging participants to try the techniques for themselves through role-play activities and more) 제시되어 있으므로 정답은 (B)이다.

| 어휘 | degree 학위   encourage 장려하다   actively 적극적으로   founder 설립자

| 패러프레이징 | urging participants to try the techniques for themselves → encourages attendees to participate actively

186-190 다음 엽서, 서식, 이메일을 참조하시오.

Titan 피트니스 센터
~ 10월 부스트 ~

¹⁸⁷10월 15일에 저희 환영 투어에 오실 2명 이상의 친구들을 추천해 주시면, 아래 감사 선물 중 하나를 받으시게 됩니다:

선택 A: 무료 Titan 피트니스 센터 티셔츠
(4개 사이즈 가능)

¹⁸⁹선택 B: 시설 내 주스 바 60% 할인 쿠폰
(유효 기간 없음)

선택 C: 무료 사물함 업그레이드
(소진 시까지)

선택 D: 단체 피트니스 강좌들 중 하나에 반값으로 참여

¹⁸⁶저희와 최소 5년 동안 함께해 오신 장기 고객님들께 감사를 표현하고자 이 제안을 하는 것입니다.

---

¹⁸⁶ **Cynthia Avila**
702 Kessla Way
Charleston,
SC 29403

| 어휘 | available 이용 가능한   on-site 현장의, 현지의   expiration date 유효 기간   pending ~이 있을 때까지   entry 참여, 참석   appreciation 감사

Titan 피트니스 센터
고객 의견 서식

저희는 여러분께 가능한 최고의 운동 경험을 제공해 드리기 위해 전념하고 있습니다. 저희 서비스를 더 개선할 수 있도록 여러분의 의견을 공유해 주세요.

오늘 날짜: 11월 5일   지점 (해당되는 경우): 시내
이름: Cynthia Avila   이메일 주소: cynthia.avila@alhambra.com

의견 유형: [ ] 제안   [ ] 문의   [ ] 칭찬   [X] 불만

¹⁸⁸이 의견에 관해 전에 저희에게 연락하신 적이 있으신가요? 그랬다면, 언제, 어떻게 하셨나요? 네, 11월 2일에 전화로

세부 내용: ¹⁸⁷제가 지난달에 10월 부스트 프로모션 조건을 충족시켰습니다. 감사 선물로 강좌들 중 하나를 반값으로 참여하는 것을 요청했고, 접수 데스크의 직원이 그것이 자동으로 공제될 것이라고 했습니다.

그래서 11월 1일에 월 청구서를 받았을 때 제가 들었던 줌바 수업에 전액이 청구된 것을 보고 놀랐습니다. 이 문제를 확인해 주시기 바랍니다. 감사합니다!

| 어휘 | be dedicated to ~하는 데 전념하다, 헌신하다   workout 운동   improve 개선하다, 향상시키다   condition 조건   reception desk 접수 데스크   deduct 공제하다   automatically 자동으로   full charge 전액 청구   bill 청구서

수신: Cynthia Avila <cynthia.avila@alhambra.com>
발신: Titan 피트니스 센터 <support@titanfitcent.com>
날짜: 11월 6일
제목: 귀하의 의견 서식

Avila 씨 귀하,

저희 10월 부스트 프로모션에 참여하신 것에 대해 제대로 공제를 받지 못하셨다니 정말 죄송합니다. 저희 기록에 보면 귀하는 강좌 옵션을 고르셨는데, 어떤 이유에서인지 ¹⁸⁹귀하에게 주스 바 쿠폰이 대신 발송되었네요. 제가 지금 귀하의 계좌에 15.50달러(강습료의 반액)의 금액을 입금해 드렸으니, 이것은 귀하의 다음 청구서에 나타날 것입니다. 더불어 ¹⁹⁰사과의 방식으로 저희 Titan 피트니스 센터의 티셔츠 하나를 우편으로 보내드리겠습니다. 그리고 물론 아직 가지고 계시다면 쿠폰도 마음껏 이용하시기 바랍니다.

이해해 주셔서 감사드립니다.

Ryan Lapira
Titan 피트니스 센터 (시내 지점), 매니저

| 어휘 | reimburse 환급하다   properly 제대로, 적절히   select 고르다, 선택하다   issue a credit 입금을 해주다   account 계좌   appear 나타나다   apology 사과   feel free to 마음껏 ~하다

---

186. 주제/목적 문제
Avila 씨에게 왜 엽서가 발송되었을 것 같은가?
(A) 개인 트레이너에게 강습을 예약했다.
(B) 고객 설문지를 작성했다.
(C) 업체가 티셔츠를 디자인하는 것을 도왔다.
(D) 헬스클럽의 장기 회원이다.

| 해설 | Avila 씨는 엽서를 받는 사람으로, 엽서 내용 후반부에 최소 5년 동안 함께한 장기 고객들에게 감사를 표하고자 이 제안을 하는 것이라고(We are making this offer to show appreciation to our longest-attending customers, those who have been with us for at least five years) 제시된 것을 통해, 피트니스 센터의 장기 고객임을 알 수 있으므로 정답은 (D)이다.

| 어휘 | personal 개인의   questionnaire 설문지   long-term 장기적인

| 패러프레이징 | our longest-attending customers → a long-term member

🔺 고난도

187. 연계 문제 - 추론
Avila 씨는 10월에 무엇을 했을 것 같은가?
(A) 건강 상담을 받는 것
(B) 투어를 할 친구들을 모집하는 것
(C) 자신의 회원권을 갱신하는 것
(D) 다른 사물함으로 변경하는 것

| 해설 | 10월 부스트를 홍보하는 엽서 도입부에 10월 15일에 환영 투어에 올 2명 이상의 친구를 추천하면(Recommend 2 or more friends to take our welcome tour on October 15) 감사 선물을 받는다는 내용이 있고, 서식 상세 내용에 작성자인 Avila 씨가 지난달에 10월 부스트 프로모션 조건을 충족시켰다고(I met the conditions for your October Boost promotion last month) 한 것을 연계시켜 볼 때, Avila 씨는 10월에 환영 투어에 참석할 친구들을 모아 추천했을 것임을 알 수 있으므로 정답은 (B)이다.

| 어휘 | undergo 겪다, 받다   consultation 상담   recruit 모집하다   renew 갱신하다

188. 세부 사항을 묻는 문제
Avila 씨는 언제 처음으로 문제에 관해 업체에 알렸는가?
(A) 10월 15일
(B) 11월 1일
(C) 11월 2일
(D) 11월 5일

| 해설 | 서식 중반부에 이 의견에 관해 전에 연락한 적이 있는지, 그랬다면 언제, 어떻게 그랬는지(Have you contacted us before about this comment? If so, when and how) 묻는 질문에 그렇다면, 11월 2일에 전화로(Yes, by phone on November 2) 했다고 답하고 있다. 이를 통해, 11월 2일에 처음 문제에 관해 알렸음을 알 수 있으므로 정답은 (C)이다.

189. 연계 문제 - 세부 사항
Avila 씨에게 실수로 무엇이 지급되었나?
(A) 옵션 A
(B) 옵션 B
(C) 옵션 C
(D) 옵션 D

| 해설 | Avila 씨에게 보낸 이메일 중반부에 기록에 보면 강좌를 선택했는데, 어떤 이유에서인지 주스 바 쿠폰이 대신 발송되었다고(you were sent a juice bar coupon instead) 한 것에서 실수로 주스 바 쿠폰이 지급되었음을 알 수 있는데, 엽서에서 시설 내 주스 바 60% 할인 쿠폰(Coupon for 60% off at our on-site juice bar ~)은 옵션 B로 확인되므로 정답은 (B)이다.

190. 세부 사항을 묻는 문제
Lapira 씨가 하겠다고 말하는 것은 무엇인가?
(A) Avila 씨에게 새로운 프로모션들을 알려주는 것
(B) 줌바 수업의 일정을 이메일로 보내는 것
(C) 동료에게 더 많은 정보를 물어보는 것
(D) 무료 옷 한 벌을 보내는 것

| 해설 | Lapira 씨가 보낸 이메일 후반부에 사과의 방식으로 Titan 피트니스 센터의 티셔츠 하나를 우편으로 보내주겠다고(I'll mail you one of our Titan Fitness Center T-shirts by way of apology) 했으므로 정답은 (D)이다.

| 어휘 | coworker 동료

| 패러프레이징 | · mail → send
· T-shirts → clothing

191-195 다음 광고, 일정표, 이메일을 참조하시오.

Willmore 포크 축제의 음악과 즐거움을 놓치지 마세요!
6월 17일 토요일 - 6월 18일 일요일

191 (B)제5회 연례 Willmore 포크 축제는 포크 음악에 관한 지역 사회 행사입니다. 이 인기 있는 행사는 전국에서 방문객들을 끌어들이는데, 191 (D)입장료는 없습니다. 191 (C)지난 행사들은 Terrace 공원에서 개최되었습니다. 하지만 이 행사의 급격한 성장 덕택에, 191 (C)올해 축제는 더 많은 연주자들을 수용하기 위해 Ridgewood 공원으로 옮겨졌습니다.

올해 일정에는 McDowell Brothers Band뿐만 아니라 포크 음악 스타인 Martin Hancock도 포함되어 있습니다. 행사 기획자들은 또한 아직 지역 그룹들을 찾고 있는데, 193오전 공연들은 바로 이곳 Willmore 출신의 음악가들을 위해 남겨둔 상태이기 때문입니다. 프로와 아마추어 밴드들 모두 환영합니다. 더 많은 정보를 위해 555-3316으로 Zan Tian에게 연락하세요.

행사는 양일간 오전 10시에 시작되어 오후 8시까지 진행됩니다. 방문객들은 구내 매점의 물품이 턱없이 부족할 것이라는 점을 유념하셔서 192간식이나 도시락을 가져오는 것이 권장됩니다. 매일 업데이트되는 연주할 밴드들의 전체 목록을 보시려면, www.willmorefolk.org를 방문하세요.

| 어휘 | community 지역 사회   celebration 축하 행사   draw 끌어들이다   entrance fee 입장료   take place 개최되다   dramatic growth 급격한 성장   accommodate 수용하다   performer 연주자, 공연자   reserved for ~를 위해 남겨둔   concession stand 구내 매점   supplies 물품   severely 심하게   limited 제한된, 한정된   packed lunch 도시락   complete 전체의, 완전한

Willmore 포크 축제
6월 17일 토요일 일정 [최종]

시작 시간	공연자	장소
193오전 10:00	The Butterfly Crew	동쪽 무대
오전 11:00	John Ramos	자유 무대
오후 1:00	Sandra and the Strummers	남쪽 무대
오후 2:30	195Maria Noyola	동쪽 무대
오후 4:30	The McDowell Brothers Band	남쪽 무대
오후 6:30	Kyle Crabtree	자유 무대

벤치들은 주 무대에서만 이용 가능합니다. 다른 무대들의 경우, 관객들은 서 있거나 각자 준비해 온 담요에 앉을 수 있습니다. 모든 좌석들은 선착순으로 이용 가능합니다.

| 어휘 | available 이용 가능한   audience member 관객   blanket 담요   on a first come, first served basis 선착순으로

수신: Zan Tian <tian.z@verdurapost.com>
발신: Maria Noyola <marianoyola@ezmail.com>
날짜: 6월 3일
제목: Willmore 포크 축제

Tian 씨 귀하,

Willmore 포크 축제에서 공연하도록 저를 초청해 주신 것에 다시 한 번 감사드리고 싶습니다. **194**무대에서 저는 기타 스탠드가 세 개 필요할 텐데요, 제가 연주하는 노래에 따라 자주 악기를 바꾸기 때문입니다. **194**또한 무대에 두 개의 마이크를 놓아주세요, 하나는 보컬용이고 다른 하나는 제 어쿠스틱 기타용으로요. 가능하다면, 공연하는 동안 앉거나 설 수 있게 **194**등받이 없는 의자가 있었으면 좋겠습니다. **195**제 공연 45분 전에 지정된 공연 구역으로 제 악기들을 가져오려고 하니, 거기서 저를 만나주세요. Ridgewood 공원이 아주 익숙하지 않아서, 정문에서부터 얼마나 걸어야 할지도 알려주실 수 있을까요?

감사합니다!

Maria

| 어휘 | invite 초청하다, 초대하다   perform 공연하다   switch 바꾸다   instrument 악기   depending on ~에 따라   stool 등받이 없는 의자   assigned 지정된   be very familiar with ~에 아주 익숙하다, 아주 잘 알다   main entrance 정문

191. NOT True 문제
Willmore 포크 축제에 관해 제시되지 않은 것은 무엇인가?
(A) 해외 연주자들을 포함하고 있다.
(B) 전에 네 차례 개최되었다.
(C) 올해 새로운 장소에서 열릴 것이다.
(D) 입장료를 청구하지 않는다.

| 해설 | 광고의 첫 번째 단락의 제5회 연례 Willmore 포크 축제라고(The 5th Annual Willmore Folk Festival) 한 것에서 (B), 입장료는 없다고(there is no entrance fee) 한 것에서 (D), 지난 행사들은 Terrace 공원에서 열렸지만(Past events have taken place at Terrace Park) 올해 축제는 Ridgewood 공원으로 옮겨졌다고(this year the festival has been moved to Ridgewood Park) 한 것에서 (C)는 모두 확인된다. 따라서 정답은 (A)이다.

| 어휘 | international 국제적으로 활동하는   location 장소   admission 입장
| 패러프레이징 | · The 5th → has been held four times before
· there is no entrance fee → does not charge for admission
· has been moved to → a new location

192. 세부 사항을 묻는 문제
행사 참석자들에게 권고되는 것은 무엇인가?
(A) 문자 알림에 등록하는 것
(B) 대중교통을 이용하는 것
(C) 좌석을 미리 예약하는 것
(D) 각자의 음식을 가져오는 것

| 해설 | 광고의 세 번째 단락에 방문객들은 구내 매점의 물품이 부족할 것이니, 간식이나 도시락을 가져오는 것이 권장된다고(bringing snacks or a packed lunch is suggested) 알리고 있으므로 정답은 (D)이다.

| 어휘 | sign up for ~에 등록하다   public transportation 대중교통   in advance 미리
| 패러프레이징 | snacks or a packed lunch → food

🔺고난도

193. 연계 문제 – 추론
Butterfly Crew에 관해 암시되는 것은 무엇인가?
(A) 행사의 둘째 날에 공연할 것이다.
(B) 멤버들이 Willmore에 살고 있다.
(C) 작년에 공연을 했다.
(D) 공연이 2시간 동안 지속될 것이다.

| 해설 | Butterfly Crew는 두 번째 지문인 일정표에서 오전 10시에 공연하는 연주자로 확인되는데, 첫 번째 지문 두 번째 단락 중반부에 오전 공연들은 바로 이곳 Willmore 출신의 음악가들을 위해 남겨둔 상태라고(morning performances are reserved for musicians from right here in Willmore) 알리고 있다. 이 둘을 연계해 볼 때, 오전 공연에 배정된 Butterfly Crew는 Willmore 출신 음악가들일 것으로 유추할 수 있으므로 정답은 (B)이다.

| 패러프레이징 | musicians from right here in Willmore → members live in Willmore

194. 주제/목적 문제
이메일의 목적은 무엇인가?
(A) 일정 변경을 요청하는 것
(B) 음악가를 행사에 초청하는 것
(C) (무대) 설치 지침을 제공하는 것
(D) 음악 CD를 홍보하는 것

| 해설 | 이메일에서 먼저 초청에 감사를 표한 후, 무대에서 기타 스탠드 세 개가 필요할 것이라고(On the stage, I will need three guitar stands) 한 뒤, 또한 무대에 마이크 두 개를 놓아달라고(Please also place two microphones on the stage) 요청하고, 등받이 없는 의자가 있었으면 좋겠다고(I would like to have a stool) 덧붙이고 있다. 이를 통해 무대 설치에 필요한 것을 알려주기 위한 목적으로 보낸 이메일임을 알 수 있으므로 정답은 (C)이다.

| 어휘 | instruction 지침, 설명   promote 홍보하다

195. 연계 문제 – 세부 사항
Noyola 씨는 6월 17일에 Tian 씨를 어디서 만나고 싶어하는가?
(A) 동쪽 무대에서

125

(B) 자유 무대에서
(C) 남쪽 무대에서
(D) 정문에서

| 해설 | 이메일 후반부에 공연 45분 전에 본인에게 지정된 공연 구역으로 악기들을 가져가려고 하니, 거기서 만나달라고(I will bring my instruments to my assigned performance area 45 minutes before my show, so please meet me there) 요청했고, 일정표에서 Maria Noyola가 공연할 장소는 동쪽 무대(East Stage)로 확인된다. 따라서 정답은 (A)이다.

196-200 다음 광고, 이메일, 청구서를 참조하시오.

칠레의 아름다운 Valparaíso에 있는 Portillo 스파에서 휴식하고 재충전하세요!

Portillo 스파의 럭셔리 패키지로 정신없이 바쁜 현대 생활의 속도에서 벗어나 휴식을 취하세요. 토요일 오전에 스파에 도착하여 일요일 저녁에 떠날 때까지 저희 친절한 직원들의 극진한 접대를 받으시게 됩니다. 패키지에는 ¹⁹⁶ ⁽ᶜ⁾저희 5성 호텔 객실에서의 1박과 ¹⁹⁶ ⁽ᴬ⁾하루 세 끼 식사, 그리고 다양한 마사지와 미용 관리들이 포함됩니다. ¹⁹⁶ ⁽ᴰ⁾저희 공항 왕복 셔틀을 타셔야 한다면, 이 패키지는 무료로 그것을 제공합니다. 추가 요금으로 제공되는 ¹⁹⁷산악 요가 체험 옵션도 있습니다. 높은 고도에서의 요가와 환상적인 경관을 위해 산 중턱까지 이동하게 될 것입니다. ¹⁹⁷약간 낮은 산소 수치로 인해 이 활동에 참가하시려면 의사의 소견을 제공하셔야 합니다. 1-800-555-9771로 전화하여 오늘 여러분의 럭셔리 패키지를 예약하세요. 10명 이상의 단체들은 최소 3주 전에 예약하셔야 함을 유념해 주세요.

| 어휘 | refresh 재충전하다 hectic 정신없이 바쁜 get pampered 극진한 접대를 받다 attentive 친절한, 세심한 a variety of 다양한 beauty treatment 미용 관리 optional 선택적인 additional fee 추가 요금 transport 이동시키다, 수송하다 high-altitude 높은 고도의 fantastic 환상적인 note 소견, 메모 physician 의사 slightly 약간 oxygen level 산소 수치 make a reservation 예약을 하다

수신: Javiera Yanez <javierayanez@portillo-spa.com>
발신: Matias Alvarado <matias@alvaradoltd.com>
날짜: 3월 2일
제목: 청구서

Yanez 씨 귀하,

저희 회사에 위탁하신 ¹⁹⁷산악 요가 체험 활동에 대한 2월 청구서를 보내 드립니다. 추운 날씨로 인해 지난 몇 개월간 참가자들 수가 적었지만, 그것은 곧 ¹⁹⁸지나갈 것입니다. 참가자들이 저희에게 긍정적인 피드백을 많이 주었습니다. 실제로, ¹⁹⁷Ivonne Sousa 씨는 그것이 자신의 주말의 하이라이트였다고 말했습니다. ²⁰⁰단체 규모가 예상했던 것보다 커서 저희 승합차를 이용할 수 없어 막판에 버스를 대여해야 했기 때문에 2월 12일 단체에 발생된 추가 요금에 유념해 주세요. 청구서에 있는 다른 모든 요금들은 이전에 승인이 되었습니다. 더 많은 사람들이 참여할 수 있도록 하기 위해 사람들이 특별 활동 시간을 더 많이 갖도록 ¹⁹⁹2일 패키지를 3일로 변경하는 것을 고려하시면 좋을 것 같습니다.

진심을 담아,

Matias

| 어휘 | invoice 청구서 outsource 외부에 위탁하다 participation 참가, 참여 pass 지나가다, 끝나다 participant 참가자 positive 긍정적인 extra charge 추가 요금 incur 발생시키다 at the last minute 막판에, 마지막 순간에 previously 이전에 approve 승인하다 involve 관여시키다, 참여시키다

Alvarado Ltd.
Laguna Verde 본사 전화번호: 22864-8430

고객: Portillo 스파   청구 월: 2월
발행 날짜: 3월 2일   지불 계정: Porvenir 은행, 64870459

월간 요금		총액:
운전기사/교통편	54,000페소	174,930페소
난방기 대여	23,000페소	
요가 강사	30,000페소	기한:
²⁰⁰추가 비용	40,000페소	3월 31일
부가세	27,930페소	

| 어휘 | headquarters 본사 issue 발행, 발급 payment 지불, 지급 transportation 교통편 instructor 강사

196. NOT True 문제
럭셔리 패키지의 일부로 언급되지 않은 것은 무엇인가?

(A) 숙박 동안 모든 식사
(B) 집으로 가져갈 미용 제품들
(C) 하룻밤 호텔 숙박
(D) 공항에서부터의 교통편

| 해설 | 패키지에 포함되는 사항이 제시된 광고 중반부의 5성 호텔 객실에서의 1박(a one-night stay in a room at our five-star hotel)에서 (C), 하루 세 끼 식사(three meals a day)에서 (A), 공항 왕복 셔틀(If you need to ride our shuttle to and from the airport, this package allows you to do so for free)에서 (D)는 모두 확인된다. 따라서 정답은 (B)이다.

| 어휘 | beauty product 미용 제품 accommodation 숙소, 숙박 시설

| 패러프레이징 | ·a one-night stay in a room at our five-star hotel
→ Overnight hotel accommodations
·three meals a day → All meals during the stay
·shuttle to and from the airport → Transportation from the airport

🔼 고난도

197. 연계 문제 – 추론

Sousa 씨에 관해 암시되는 것은 무엇인가?
(A) 최소 3주 전에 자신의 객실을 예약했다.
(B) 2월 12일에 특별 행사에 참석했다.
(C) 스파에 의사의 소견을 제공했다.
(D) 최근에 처음으로 Valparaíso를 방문했다.

| 해설 | 이메일 중반부에 Sousa 씨가 산악 요가 체험이 자신의 주말의 하이라이트였다고 말했다고(Ms. Ivonne Sousa said that it was the highlight of her weekend) 한 것과, 광고에서 이 활동에 참가하려면 의사의 소견을 제공해야 한다고(You must provide a note from your physician to participate in this activity ~) 한 것을 연계해 볼 때, Sousa 씨는 의사의 소견을 제공하고 활동에 참가했을 것임을 유추할 수 있으므로 정답은 (C)이다.

| 어휘 | reserve 예약하다   recently 최근에

| 패러프레이징 | a note from your physician → a physician's note

198. 동의어 문제

이메일에서 첫 번째 단락 세 번째 줄에 있는 단어 "pass"와 의미가 가장 유사한 것은
(A) 끝나다
(B) 성공하다
(C) 파견하다
(D) 초과하다

| 해설 | 해당 단어가 들어간 문장은 '추운 날씨로 인해 지난 몇 개월간 참가자들 수가 적었지만, 그것은 곧 지나갈 것이다'라고 해석된다. 따라서 pass는 '지나가다, 끝나다'라는 의미로 쓰인 것이므로 '끝나다'라는 뜻의 (A) end가 정답이다.

199. 세부 사항을 묻는 문제

Alvarado 씨가 하도록 권하는 것은 무엇인가?
(A) 요가 강사를 추가로 고용하는 것
(B) 더 많은 외부 활동들을 추가하는 것
(C) 추운 날씨에는 행사들을 취소하는 것
(D) 패키지의 기간을 연장하는 것

| 해설 | 이메일 후반부에 더 많은 사람들이 참여할 수 있도록 2일 패키지를 3일로 변경하는 것을 고려하면 좋을 것 같다고(you might want to consider changing the two-day package to three days) 했으므로 정답은 (D)이다.

| 어휘 | off-site 외부의   extend 연장하다   duration 기간

| 패러프레이징 | changing the two-day package to three days → Extending the duration of a package

200. 연계 문제 – 세부 사항

Portillo 스파는 왜 4만 페소를 청구받았는가?
(A) Alvarado 씨가 Sousa 씨에게 추가 교통편을 제공했다.
(B) Alvarado 씨가 특별한 차량을 대여해야 했다.
(C) Alvarado 씨가 2월에 추가 단체를 접대했다.
(D) Alvarado 씨가 파손된 난방기에 대해 돈을 지불해야 했다.

| 해설 | 4만 페소(40,000 CLP)는 청구서에 추가 비용(Additional Expenses)으로 확인되는데, 이와 관련하여 두 번째 지문에 막판에 버스를 대여해야 했기에 때문에(we had to rent a bus at the last minute) 추가 요금이 발생되었다고(extra charge that was incurred) 제시되어 있으므로 정답은 (B)이다.

| 어휘 | extra 추가의, 여분의   vehicle 탈것, 차량

| 패러프레이징 | a bus → a special vehicle

TEST 07

PART 5

101 (D)	102 (C)	103 (C)	104 (C)	105 (C)
106 (A)	107 (B)	108 (A)	109 (C)	110 (C)
111 (C)	112 (C)	113 (D)	114 (B)	115 (A)
116 (D)	117 (C)	118 (D)	119 (B)	120 (B)
121 (A)	122 (B)	123 (C)	124 (D)	125 (C)
126 (A)	127 (A)	128 (D)	129 (C)	130 (A)

PART 6

131 (B)	132 (D)	133 (A)	134 (C)	135 (D)
136 (C)	137 (C)	138 (B)	139 (A)	140 (B)
141 (B)	142 (D)	143 (D)	144 (A)	145 (C)
146 (A)				

PART 7

147 (D)	148 (C)	149 (A)	150 (B)	151 (C)
152 (B)	153 (A)	154 (C)	155 (B)	156 (C)
157 (A)	158 (B)	159 (B)	160 (D)	161 (B)
162 (A)	163 (D)	164 (C)	165 (C)	166 (B)
167 (A)	168 (B)	169 (D)	170 (A)	171 (B)
172 (D)	173 (D)	174 (B)	175 (A)	176 (B)
177 (C)	178 (C)	179 (C)	180 (B)	181 (C)
182 (A)	183 (D)	184 (C)	185 (D)	186 (B)
187 (D)	188 (A)	189 (C)	190 (C)	191 (A)
192 (D)	193 (C)	194 (C)	195 (B)	196 (C)
197 (A)	198 (D)	199 (B)	200 (B)	

PART 5

고난도

101. 부사 자리 – 분사 수식
Richard's 자동차 대리점의 모든 구매자들은 그들의 정비 일정에 기반하여 자신들의 자동차를 정기적으로 점검받을 수 있다.
| 해설 | 'have+목적어+과거 분사' 형태에서 과거 분사 앞에 빈칸이 있으므로 빈칸은 과거 분사를 수식하는 부사 자리이다. 따라서 '정기적으로, 규칙적으로'라는 뜻의 부사인 (D) regularly가 정답이다.
| 어휘 | inspect 점검하다   based on ~에 기반하여   maintenance 정비   regular 정기적인, 규칙적인   regularity 정기적임, 규칙적임   regulation 규정

102. 인칭 대명사
이 다이어트 프로그램은 여러분이 건강한 생활을 하도록 돕고 장려합니다.
| 해설 | 접속사 and로 연결된 두 동사 assists와 encourages의 목적어 자리에 빈칸이 있으므로 빈칸에는 목적격 인칭 대명사가 와야 한다. 따라서 (C) you가 정답이다.
| 어휘 | assist 돕다   encourage 장려하다   lead 생활을 하다, 살다   healthy 건강한

103. 전치사 자리
폭우와 홍수 경보 때문에 강변 도로의 출입이 통제되었다.
| 해설 | 빈칸은 앞의 절에 뒤의 명사구를 연결하는 전치사가 들어갈 자리이므로, 접속사인 (A) though와 (B) wherever는 오답이고, 폭우와 홍수 경보는 통제의 이유가 될 수 있으므로 이유를 나타내는 전치사구인 (C) because of가 정답이다.
| 어휘 | access to ~에 출입, 이용   restrict 통제하다, 제한하다   heavy rain 폭우   flood warning 홍수 경보

104. 명사 자리 – 주어
이번 야구 시즌이 끝난 후에, Cooperstown 야구장의 좌석 교체가 시작될 것이다.
| 해설 | 빈칸은 동사 will begin의 주어 자리이며, 정관사 the와 전치사 of 사이에 있으므로 명사가 들어갈 자리이다. 따라서 '교체'라는 뜻의 명사인 (C) replacement가 정답이다.
| 어휘 | replace 교체하다, 대체하다   replaceable 교체 가능한, 대신할 수 있는

105. 형용사 자리 – 주격 보어
주민들은 Hayden 공원을 업그레이드하는 일에 시 자금을 쓰는 계획을 지지했다.
| 해설 | 빈칸은 be동사 were의 보어가 들어갈 자리이므로, 부사인 (B) supportively는 오답이고, support가 Residents와 동격이 될 수 없으므로 (A)도 오답이다. 문맥상 '계획을 지지했다'라는 의미로 전개되어야 하므로 '지지하는'이라는 뜻의 (C) supportive가 정답이다.
| 어휘 | resident 주민, 거주민   fund 자금, 기금   support 지원, 지지; 지지하다, 지원하다   supportively 지지하여   be supportive of ~을 지지하다   supporting 조연의, 뒷받침하는

106. 명사 어휘
Bedford 축제의 모든 행사들은 사전 공지 없이 변경될 수 있다.
| 해설 | 빈칸은 전치사 without의 목적어로, 형용사 prior의 수식을 받는 명사가 들어갈 자리로, '사전 공지 없이 변경될 수 있다'라는 의미로 전개되는 것이 적절하므로 '공지, 통지'라는 뜻의 (A) notice가 정답이다.
| 어휘 | be subject to ~하기 쉽다, ~을 받아야 한다   prior 사전의   belief 믿음, 신념

107. 형용사 자리 – 명사 수식
개막식이 예상했던 것보다 더 늦게까지 진행되고 있어, 예정된 오전 행사들이 20분 지연될 것이다.
| 해설 | 정관사 the와 복합 명사 morning sessions 사이에 빈칸이 있으므로, 빈칸은 명사를 수식하는 형용사 자리이다. 따라서 '예정된 오전 행사들'이라는 의미를 완성해줄 과거 분사형 형용사인 (B) scheduled가 정답이다. 또 다른 복합 명사를 이루는 명사가 들어갈 수도 있지만 schedule은 morning sessions와 복합 명사를 만들기에 부적절하다.

| 어휘 | opening ceremony 개막식   delay 지연시키다   schedule 일정; 일정을 잡다, 예정하다

108. 동사 어휘
Reader's House에서 발간된 원예 안내서인 <Fields of Friends>가 내년에 여러 언어들로 번역될 것이다.
| 해설 | 빈칸은 수동태 동사를 완성해줄 과거 분사가 들어갈 자리로, '여러 언어로 번역될 것이다'라는 의미로 전개되는 것이 적절하므로 (A) translated가 정답이다.
| 어휘 | gardening 원예   multiple 많은, 다수의   language 언어   translate 번역하다   organize 조직하다   involve 수반하다

109. 형용사 어휘
보안을 위해 여러분의 컴퓨터 로그인 비밀번호를 3개월마다 변경하는 것은 의무입니다.
| 해설 | 빈칸은 be동사 is의 보어인 형용사가 들어갈 자리로, '비밀번호 변경은 의무이다'라는 의미로 전개되는 것이 적절하므로 '의무적인'이라는 뜻의 (C) mandatory가 정답이다.
| 어휘 | for security purposes 보안을 위해   impressed 감명 깊은   reluctant 마지못한, 꺼리는   bountiful 풍부한

110. 부사 자리 – 동사 수식
그 종업원은 식사 손님들 중 한 명이 해산물에 알레르기가 있다는 것을 들었을 때 그들의 요청을 주방에 신속하게 전달해야 했다.
| 해설 | 빈칸이 없어도 빈칸 앞의 주절과 뒤의 when절이 모두 완전한 문장이므로, 빈칸에는 문장 구조에 지장을 주지 않으며 수식 역할을 하는 부사가 들어가야 함을 알 수 있다. 따라서 '신속히'라는 뜻의 부사인 (C) swiftly가 정답이다.
| 어휘 | relay 전달하다   diner 식사 손님   allergic to ~에 알레르기가 있는   swift 빠른, 신속한

111. 명사 어휘
귀하의 보증 조건에 따라, 모든 발생 비용과 요금들이 보장될 것입니다.
| 해설 | 빈칸은 of 이하 전치사구의 수식을 받는 명사가 들어갈 자리로, '보증 조건에 따라'라는 의미로 전개되는 것이 적절하므로 '조건'이라는 뜻의 (C) terms가 정답이다.
| 어휘 | according to ~에 따라   warranty (품질) 보증   incurred expenses 발생 비용   cover 부담하다, 보장하다   comment 의견

🔺고난도
112. 명사 어휘
Allison Barr는 Harman's 신발에서의 견습 기간을 통해 신발을 주문 제작하는 전문적인 기술을 얻었다.
| 해설 | 빈칸은 타동사 gained의 목적어로 형용사 professional의 수식을 받는 명사가 들어갈 자리로, 견습 기간을 통해 얻을 수 있는 것은 '전문적인 기술'일 것이므로 '전문 기술[지식]'을 의미하는 (C) expertise가 정답이다.
| 어휘 | customize 맞춤 제작하다   apprenticeship 견습 기간   responsibility 책임   foundation 토대, 기반

113. 전치사 어휘
Jenkins 제조사의 이사회는 3년 이내에 배기가스를 20%까지 줄인다는 계획을 발표했다.
| 해설 | 빈칸은 뒤에 있는 시간 명사를 목적어로 가지는 전치사가 들어갈 자리로 '3년 이내에'라는 의미로 전개되는 것이 적절하므로 기간 표현 앞에 '~ 이내에'라는 의미로 쓰이는 (D) within이 정답이다.
| 어휘 | board 이사회   reduce 줄이다   emission 배기가스, 배출물

114. 인칭 대명사
금융 위기로 인해, 우리 경영진은 회사를 Geyser 사에 매각하기로 결정했습니다.
| 해설 | 명사 management 앞에 빈칸이 있는데, 명사 앞에 올 수 있는 인칭 대명사는 소유격 대명사이므로 (B) our가 정답이다.
| 어휘 | due to ~로 인해   financial crisis 금융 위기   management 경영진, 관리진

115. 동사 어휘
Bentley 화학의 모든 직원은 그들이 회사에서 만 1년 근무를 끝내자마자 완전한 보험 혜택을 받을 자격이 있게 된다.
| 해설 | 빈칸은 one full year를 목적어로 취하는 현재 완료 시제 동사를 완성해줄 과거 분사가 들어갈 자리로, 문맥상 '1년을 마치자마자 보험 혜택을 받을 자격이 있게 된다'라는 의미로 전개되는 것이 적절하므로 (A) completed가 정답이다.
| 어휘 | be eligible for ~을 받을 자격이 있다   insurance benefits 보험 혜택   complete 완료하다, 끝마치다   expire 만료되다   predict 예측하다   permit 허용하다

🔺고난도
116. 부사 어휘
우리 회사는 해마다 직원 업무 평가를 하는데, 그 기간 중에 직원들은 자신의 관리자들과 솔직히 이야기할 수 있다.
| 해설 | 빈칸은 동사 conducts를 수식해줄 부사가 들어갈 자리로, '해마다 직원 업무 평가를 한다'라는 의미로 전개되는 것이 적절하므로 '해마다, 매년'이라는 뜻의 (D) annually가 정답이다.
| 어휘 | conduct 실시하다   employee performance review 직원 업무 평가, 인사 고과   openly 터놓고, 솔직하게   supervisor 관리자   boldly 대담하게

🔺고난도
117. 동사의 형태
많은 사람들이 여전히 주식과 금을 선호한다는 사실에도 불구하고 디지털 투자 시장이 부상하고 있다.
| 해설 | be동사 뒤에 빈칸이 있으므로 본동사의 형태인 (A) emerge와 (D) emerges는 오답이고, emerge는 자동사로 수동태가 될 수 없으므로 (B) emerged도 오답이다. 따라서 현재 진행 시제를 만드는 현재 분사인 (C) emerging이 정답이다.
| 어휘 | investment 투자   prefer 선호하다   stocks 주식   emerge 부상하다, 드러나다

🔺고난도
118. 형용사 어휘

Amherst 중고차에 있는 소책자는 자동차 브랜드 목록과 지불 방법이나 자동차 리스에 관련된 정보를 담고 있다.

| 해설 | 빈칸은 앞에 있는 information을 수식하는 that절의 be동사 is의 보어가 될 형용사가 들어갈 자리로, 뒤에 있는 전치사구와 연결 지어 '지불 방법과 자동차 리스에 관련된 정보'라는 의미로 전개되는 것이 적절하므로 '적절한, 관련된'이라는 뜻의 (D) relevant가 정답이다.

| 어휘 | booklet 소책자   contain ~이 들어 있다   comparable 비교할 만한, 필적하는   directed 유도된, 지시받은   skilled 숙련된, 노련한

119. 전치사 어휘

익스트림 스포츠 마니아들을 위해 개발된 이 손목시계는 심지어 수심 100미터 아래에서도 내수성이 있다.

| 해설 | 빈칸은 뒤에 있는 명사구 100 meters deep을 목적어로 가지는 전치사가 들어갈 자리로, 뒤에 제시된 명사구와 연결 지어 '수심 100미터 아래에서도'라는 의미로 전개되는 것이 적절하므로 (B) under가 정답이다.

| 어휘 | wrist watch 손목시계   developed 개발된   enthusiast 마니아, 열성 팬   resistant against water 내수성 있는

120. 동사의 형태

귀하의 주차증은 지정된 주차 구역에 들어갈 때마다 확인되어야 되어야 합니다.

| 해설 | be동사 뒤에 빈칸이 있으므로 동사 원형인 (A) verify는 오답이고, 주어인 Your parking permit과 동격이 될 수 없으므로 명사인 (C) verification도 오답이다. 동사 verify는 타동사인데 빈칸 뒤에 목적어가 없으며, '주차증이 확인되어야 한다'는 의미로 전개되어야 하므로 수동태를 만드는 과거 분사인 (B) verified가 정답이다.

| 어휘 | parking permit 주차증   reserved 지정된   parking area 주차 구역   verify 확인하다   verification 확인, 조회

121. 형용사 자리 - 명사 수식

이 건물에 있는 모든 자판기는 정확한 잔돈을 필요로 한다는 것을 유념해 주세요.

| 해설 | 명사 change 앞에 빈칸이 있으므로 빈칸은 명사를 수식하는 형용사 자리이다. 따라서 '꼭 맞는, 정확한'이라는 뜻의 형용사인 (A) exact가 정답이다. 명사 앞에 명사도 올 수 있지만 (D) exactness는 change와 복합 명사를 만들기에 부적절하므로 오답이다.

| 어휘 | vending machine 자판기, 자동 판매기   throughout 전역에, 도처에   require 요구하다, 필요로 하다   change 잔돈   exactly 정확하게   exactness 정확함

🔺고난도
122. 명사 어휘

영업 부장은 분기별 판매 할당량을 조기에 충족시킨 것을 축하하는 부서 오찬을 열 것이다.

| 해설 | 빈칸은 전치사 in의 목적어이자 뒤에 있는 전치사구의 수식을 받는 명사가 들어갈 자리로, '축하하는 오찬을 열 것이다'라는 의미로 전개되는 것이 적절하므로 in celebration of(~을 축하하는)라는 표현을 완성해줄 (B) celebration이 정답이다.

| 어휘 | luncheon 오찬   meet one's sales quota 판매 할당량을 충족시키다   deliverance 구조, 구제   perspective 관점, 시각   competence 능숙함, 능력

123. 부사절 접속사

지연 없이 환급받을 수 있도록 매달 20일까지 경비 보고서를 반드시 제출하세요.

| 해설 | 빈칸 앞뒤에 완전한 절이 있으므로 빈칸에는 두 절을 연결해줄 접속사가 들어가야 한다. 따라서 전치사인 (A) due to와 접속 부사인 (D) in addition은 오답이고, '지연 없이 환급받을 수 있도록 20일까지 제출하라'라는 의미가 되는 것이 적절하므로 부사절 접속사인 (C) so that이 정답이다.

| 어휘 | expense report 경비 보고서   reimburse 환급하다   delay 지연, 지체

🔺고난도
124. 동사 어휘

Danielle's 아울렛은 근무 중에 맞닥뜨릴 수 있는 비상 사태에 대비하여 직원들을 교육시킨다.

| 해설 | 빈칸은 조동사 뒤에 동사 원형이 들어갈 자리로, 뒤에 제시된 목적어와 연결 지어 '근무 중에 맞닥뜨릴 수 있는 비상 사태'라는 의미로 전개되는 것이 적절하므로 '맞닥뜨리다, 마주치다'라는 뜻의 (D) encounter가 정답이다.

| 어휘 | in case of ~에 대비하여   emergency 비상 사태   depend 의존하다   conclude 결론 내리다   evaluate 평가하다

🔺고난도
125. 동사의 형태

Hawthorn 씨는 잘못된 곳에 놓여 있던 그녀의 배지를 찾아가라는 연락을 받았다.

| 해설 | 빈칸은 앞에 있는 명사 badge를 수식하는 관계 대명사 that절의 동사가 들어갈 자리로, misplace는 타동사인데 빈칸 뒤에 목적어가 없으며, '배지가 잘못된 곳에 놓여 있었다'는 의미로 수동의 의미로 전개되어야 하므로 수동태인 (C) was misplaced가 정답이다.

| 어휘 | pick up 찾아가다   misplace 제자리에 두지 않다

126. 부사 자리 - 동사 수식

공급 관리자의 책무는 모든 사무실 물품들이 생산적으로 이용되도록 확실히 하는 것이다.

| 해설 | be동사 are와 과거 분사 used 사이에 빈칸이 있으므로 빈칸은 동사를 수식하는 부사 자리이다. 따라서 '생산적으로'라는 뜻의 부사인 (A) productively가 정답이다.

| 어휘 | supply manager 공급 관리자   responsibility 책무, 책임   make sure 확실히 하다   production 생산, 제작   productive 생산적인

127. 부사 어휘

비록 German Tech 회사가 자사의 세탁기 가격을 인상했음에도, 고객들은 여전히 그것들이 가장 가격이 알맞은 것이라고 생각한다.

| 해설 | 빈칸은 뒤의 동사를 수식해줄 부사가 들어갈 자리로, 앞에 양보의 부사절 접속사 Even though가 있으므로 '가격을 인상했음에도 여전히 가장 알맞은 가격이라고 생각한다'라는 의미로 전개되는 것이 적절하다. 따라서 (A) still이 정답이다.

| 어휘 | increase 인상하다, 올리다   laundry machine 세탁기   affordable 가격이 알맞은

128. 부사절 접속사
졸업을 위해 필요한 학점을 받지 못했다면, 여러분의 학업 지도 교수를 만나야 합니다.
| 해설 | 빈칸 뒤로 두 개의 완전한 절이 나란히 제시되어 있으므로 빈칸에는 두 절을 연결해줄 접속사가 들어가야 한다. 또한 앞의 절이 뒤의 절의 조건이 됨을 알 수 있으므로 조건절을 이끌어줄 부사절 접속사인 (D) If가 정답이다.
| 어휘 | earn 받다, 얻다   credit 학점   graduation 졸업   academic 학업의   supervisor 지도 교수, 관리자

고난도

129. 명사절 접속사
다가오는 이번 금요일 저녁은 Min 씨의 퇴직 기념 파티가 열리기로 예정되어 있는 때이다.
| 해설 | 빈칸은 be동사 is의 보어가 들어갈 자리로, 앞뒤에 두 개의 동사 is와 is scheduled가 제시되어 있는 것으로 볼 때, 빈칸에는 be동사의 보어가 되는 뒤의 절을 이끌어줄 명사절 접속사가 들어가야 함을 알 수 있으므로 (A) it's와 전치사인 (C) on은 답이 될 수 없고, 뒤의 절이 시점을 나타내는 주어와 동격으로 전개되어야 하므로 (D) when이 정답이다.
| 어휘 | coming 다가오는   retirement party 퇴직 기념 파티

130. 형용사 어휘
즉각적인 처리가 필요한 문제가 아니라면 휴가 중인 사람에게 연락하는 것을 피하세요.
| 해설 | 빈칸은 명사 attention을 수식해줄 형용사가 들어갈 자리로, '즉각적인 처리가 필요한 문제가 아니라면'이라는 의미로 전개되는 것이 적절하므로 '즉각적인'이라는 뜻의 (A) immediate가 정답이다.
| 어휘 | avoid 피하다   issue 사안, 문제   attention 주의   insufficient 불충분한   careless 부주의한   customary 관습적인

PART 6

131-134 다음 공지를 참조하시오.

전 직원에게 공지

여러분은 이제 생산 작업장의 작업 구역으로 들어가고 있습니다. 여러분의 131**안전**을 위해, 이 구역에서는 항상 보호 장비를 착용해야만 합니다. 여기에는 안전모와 장갑, 그리고 안경류가 포함됩니다. 규정을 준수하지 132**못하면** 회사 벌금뿐만 아니라 개인의 부상을 초래할 수 있습니다. 필요한 장비를 가지고 있지 않다면, 귀하의 직속 상사에게 133**이야기해** 주시기 바랍니다. 여러분은 또한 자신의 장비 상태도 확인하여 훼손된 것을 찾아야 합니다. 134**만약 그렇다면, 그것은 가능한 한 빨리 교체되어야 합니다.** 여러분의 협조에 감사드립니다.

| 어휘 | active area 작업 구역   production floor 생산 작업장   protective gear 보호 장비   hard hat 안전모   eyewear 안경류   comply with ~을 따르다, 준수하다   regulation 규정   result in ~를 야기하다   personal injury 개인적인 부상   fine 벌금   necessary 필요한   immediate supervisor 직속 상사   damage 훼손   cooperation 협조

131. 명사 자리 - 전치사의 목적어
| 해설 | 빈칸은 전치사 For의 목적어 자리이며, 소유격 인칭 대명사 your 뒤에 있으므로 명사 자리이다. 따라서 '안전'이라는 뜻의 명사인 (B) safety가 정답이다. (D) safe는 명사로 쓰이면 '금고'라는 뜻으로 문맥상 적절하지 않다.

132. 명사 어휘
| 해설 | 빈칸은 뒤에 있는 to부정사의 수식을 받는 명사가 들어갈 자리로, '규정을 준수하지 못하면 개인적 부상을 초래할 수 있다'라는 의미로 전개되는 것이 적절하므로 '실패, 하지 못함'이라는 뜻의 (D) Failure가 정답이다.
| 어휘 | closure 폐쇄, 마감   precaution 예방책, 예방 조치   disruption 붕괴, 분열

133. 동사의 형태
| 해설 | 빈칸은 정중한 부탁의 표현인 please 뒤에 있는데, please 뒤에는 동사원형이 오므로, '말하다, 이야기하다'라는 뜻의 동사 원형인 (A) speak가 정답이다.

134. 알맞은 문장 고르기
(A) 예상대로, 그것은 예비 테스트에서 잘 견뎌냈습니다.
(B) 각 직원은 일을 시작할 때 하나를 받았습니다.
(C) 만약 그렇다면, 그것은 가능한 한 빨리 교체되어야 합니다.
(D) 필요하다면 추가로 쓸 수 있는 시간이 있습니다.
| 해설 | 앞서 장비의 상태를 확인해 훼손된 것을 찾아야 한다는 문장이 제시되어 있으므로, 그 연장선상에서 훼손된 것을 발견 시 취해야 할 조치에 관해 알리는 문장이 이어지는 것이 가장 적절하므로 정답은 (C)이다.
| 어휘 | hold up well 잘 견딘다   preliminary test 예비 테스트

135-138 다음 이메일을 참조하시오.

수신: Ivy Acuna <acunai@woodlandinteriors.com>
발신: Frank Dotson <dotsonf@woodlandinteriors.com>
날짜: 4월 6일
제목: 우리 회의

오늘 아침에 예정되었던 회의를 놓친 것에 대해 135**사과드리고** 싶습니다. 바쁘시다는 것을 알고 있고, 분명 이로 인해 매우 불편하셨을 것입니다. 136**유감스럽게도**, 밴쿠버에서 돌아오는 제 비행기가 연착이 되어서, 원래 예상했던 것보다 훨씬 늦게 도시로 돌아왔습니다. 우리는 아직 Carter 거리에 있는 건물의 인테리어 디자인에 관해 검토해야 하는데요. 137**이는 직접 만나서 하는 것이 훨씬 수월할 것이에요.** 제가 내일 오후 3시경에 귀하의 사무실에 들를 수 있습니다. 그것을 138**수용하실** 수 있기를 바랍니다. 그렇지 않으면, 다른 가능한 시간을 찾을 수 있을 거예요.

진심을 담아,

Frank Dotson

| 어휘 | miss 놓치다   scheduled 예정된   inconvenience 불편, 불편함   go over 검토하다   property 건물, 부동산   drop by 들르다

135. to부정사 – 동사의 목적어
| 해설 | 빈칸 앞에 있는 would like는 to부정사를 목적어로 취하는 동사이므로 to부정사 형태인 (D) to apologize가 정답이다.

136. 부사 어휘
| 해설 | 앞뒤 문장의 내용을 자연스럽게 이어줄 부사가 들어갈 자리로, 앞서 회의를 놓친 것을 사과했고, 뒤이어 비행기 연착이라는 그 이유를 제시하고 있으므로, 보통 좋지 않은 소식을 전할 때 쓰는 '유감스럽게도, 안타깝게도'라는 뜻의 부사인 (C) Unfortunately가 정답이다.

| 어휘 | namely 즉, 다시 말해   moreover 게다가   nonetheless 그럼에도 불구하고

137. 알맞은 문장 고르기
(A) 그가 보낸 첨부 파일이 열리지 않았습니다.
(B) 당신은 밴쿠버 사무실에 연락해야 합니다.
(C) 이는 직접 만나서 하는 것이 훨씬 수월할 것이에요.
(D) 저희 프로젝트는 가장 높은 평가를 받았습니다.

| 해설 | 앞서 검토해야 할 사항이 있음을 제시한 후, 뒤이어 사무실에 들르는 일정을 제안하고 있는데, 그 사이에는 사무실에 들르는 이유를 알리는 문장이 제시되는 것이 자연스러우므로 직접 만나서 하는 것이 더 수월하다고 말하는 (C)가 정답이다.

| 어휘 | attachment 첨부 파일   rating 순위, 평가

138. 형용사 자리 – 목적격 보어 〈고난도〉
| 해설 | 빈칸은 'find+목적어(that)+목적 보어' 구조에서 목적 보어가 들어갈 자리이므로 부사인 (C) acceptably는 오답이고, 명사 (D) acceptance는 목적어 that(3시경에 들르는 것)과 동격이 되기에 부적절하므로 오답이다. 문맥상 '3시경에 방문하는 것을 수용할 수 있길 바란다'는 내용으로 전개되는 것이 적절하므로 '수용할 수 있는'이라는 뜻의 (B) acceptable이 정답이다.

139-142 다음 광고를 참조하시오.

자원봉사자 구함:

Helpful Hearts가 현재 노인을 돕는 프로그램을 위해 자원봉사자를 찾고 있습니다. 업무들은 그들의 가정을 방문하여 허드레 가사일을 돕는 139것에서부터 약속 장소까지 차를 태워주는 것에 이릅니다. 분명 여러분의 일정과 관심에 맞는 것을 찾으실 것입니다. Helpful Hearts와 함께 자원봉사를 함으로써, 다른 사람의 삶에 진정으로 140변화를 줄 수 있습니다. 141저희는 많은 시간의 헌신을 요구하지 않습니다. 일주일에 단 2시간만이라도 충분합니다. 이것이 매력적으로 들린다면, 한번 해보시는 게 어떤가요? 저희 웹 사이트 www.helpfulhearts1.org를 방문하시면 저희에 관해 더 많이 알아보고 저희 자원봉사자들과 참가자들의 추천 글도 142훑어보실 수 있습니다.

| 어휘 | seek 찾다   volunteer 자원봉사자   the elderly 노인들   task 일   household chores 허드레 가사일   appointment 약속   suit 맞다, 적합하다   truly 진정으로   sufficient 충분한   appealing 매력적인, 마음을 끄는   give it a try 한번 해보다   testimonial 추천 글

139. 전치사 어휘
| 해설 | 빈칸은 뒤에 있는 동명사구를 목적어로 가지는 전치사가 들어갈 자리로, range는 전치사 from, to와 함께 '범위가 A부터 B까지 이른다(range from A to B)'라는 의미로 쓰이는 동사이므로 (A) from이 정답이다.

140. 명사 어휘
| 해설 | 빈칸은 타동사 make의 목적어가 들어갈 자리로, '자원봉사를 함으로써, 다른 사람의 삶에 진정으로 변화를 만들 수 있다'라는 의미로 전개되는 것이 적절하므로, '차이, 변화'라는 뜻의 (B) difference가 정답이다. make a difference in은 '~에 차이를 만들다, 변화를 만들다'라는 의미로 쓰이는 표현이다.

| 어휘 | prediction 예측, 예견

141. 알맞은 문장 고르기
(A) 저희를 위해 일하고 있는 다양한 규모의 단체들이 있습니다.
(B) 저희는 많은 시간의 헌신을 요구하지 않습니다.
(C) 요청되는 경우 새로 오신 분들께 교육이 제공됩니다.
(D) 자원봉사를 하기 위해 특별한 기술은 필요하지 않습니다.

| 해설 | 뒤이어 일주일에 단 2시간만이라도 충분하다고 제시된 내용을 단서로, 그 앞에는 자원봉사를 진행하는 것과 관련하여 요구하는 시간에 관해 언급된 문장이 삽입되는 것이 가장 적절함을 알 수 있으므로 정답은 (B)이다.

| 어휘 | various 다양한   commitment 전념, 몰두   newcomer 신입자, 신참

142. 동사의 형태 – 병치
| 해설 | 등위 접속사 and의 앞뒤는 서로 병렬 구조가 되어야 하므로, 빈칸은 병치를 이루는 to learn과 동일한 형태가 되어야 한다. 하지만 to부정사는 and로 연결될 때 to가 생략될 수 있으므로 to가 생략된 형태인 (D) browse가 정답이다.

| 어휘 | browse 훑어보다, 검색하다

143-146 다음 이메일을 참조하시오.

수신: Quinn Gleason <gleasonq@camdencslting.com>
발신: Christina Cruz <cruzc@camdencslting.com>
날짜: 12월 17일
제목: 워크숍

제가 지난주 귀하의 조직 기술 워크숍에 참가했던 직원들로부터 수집했던 정보를 ¹⁴³분석했습니다. ¹⁴⁴전반적으로 피드백은 아주 긍정적이었어요. 예를 들어, 참석자들의 대다수가 향후에 귀하의 워크숍들 중 하나에 참가하고 싶다고 말했고, 그들 모두 그 정보가 도움이 된다고 생각했다고 말했습니다. 주된 불만은 비디오를 보여주는 데 사용하셨던 장비에 관한 것이었어요. 사람들은 오디오 트랙을 ¹⁴⁵거의 들을 수 없었다고 말했습니다. 이 문제 때문에, 말하는 ¹⁴⁶것을 이해할 수 없었다고 합니다. 다음을 위해 이 문제를 염두에 두도록 합시다.

진심을 담아,

Christina

| 어휘 | gather 모으다 organizational 조직의 majority 대다수 attendee 참석자 future 미래 complaint 불만, 불평 equipment 장비 audio track 오디오 트랙 keep ~ in mind ~을 염두에 두다, 명심하다

143. 동사 어휘

| 해설 | 빈칸은 현재 완료 시제 동사를 완성해줄 과거 분사가 들어갈 자리로, 뒤이어 직원들에게서 수집한 정보에 관한 내용이 구체적으로 제시되어 있으므로, '수집한 정보를 분석해' 그 결과를 제시하는 문맥으로 전개되는 것이 적절하다. 따라서 (D) analyzed가 정답이다.

| 어휘 | authorize 승인하다, 인가하다 emphasize 강조하다 strategize 전략을 짜다 analyze 분석하다

144. 알맞은 문장 고르기

(A) 애석하게도 참석률이 그 어느 때보다 낮았어요.
(B) 제가 기꺼이 당신을 위해 자료를 준비할게요.
(C) 전반적으로 피드백은 아주 긍정적이었어요.
(D) 이것은 올해 마지막 수업이 될 것입니다.

| 해설 | 앞에서 정보를 분석했다고 말했고, 빈칸 뒤에는 긍정적인 피드백의 예들이 제시되어 있으므로 빈칸에는 피드백이 긍정적이었음을 언급하는 문장이 삽입되는 것이 적절하다. 따라서 정답은 (C)이다.

| 어휘 | sadly 유감스럽게도 attendance 참석률, 참석자 수 materials 자료 overall 전반적으로 positive 긍정적인

145. 부사 자리 - 동사 수식

| 해설 | 조동사 could와 동사 원형 hear 사이에 빈칸이 있으므로 빈칸은 동사를 수식하는 부사 자리이다. 따라서 '거의 ~ 없이'라는 뜻의 부사인 (C) barely가 정답이다.

| 어휘 | bare 헐벗은, 노골적인; 노출하다, 드러내다

고난도
146. 명사절 접속사

| 해설 | 목적어가 필요한 타동사 understand 뒤에 빈칸과 불완전한 절이 이어지고 있으므로, 빈칸에는 불완전한 절을 이끌어 명사절로 만들어 줄 수 있는 명사절 접속사가 필요하다. 따라서 명사절 접속사인 (A) what이 정답이다.

PART 7

147-148 다음 문자 메시지를 참조하시오.

발신자: Chelsea Ware, 3월 10일 목요일, 오후 1:42

Vicky, 제가 정비 요청에 응하기 위해 Gulfport 식당에 있는데요. ¹⁴⁷처음에는 그들이 우리가 에어컨을 수리해 주기를 원해서, 그것을 위한 공구를 가져왔어요. 그런데 그들이 저에게 보일러 수리도 부탁했거든요. 그것에 필요한 것은 가지고 있지 않아서요. ¹⁴⁸부탁인데 저희 매장에서 다른 공구 세트를 가져다줄 수 있을까요? 제가 그동안 에어컨을 작업하고 있을게요. 그러면 오늘 이곳 작업을 모두 끝낼 수 있을 거예요. 도움 고마워요.

| 어휘 | respond to ~에 응하다, 응답하다 maintenance call 정비 요청 initially 처음에 fix 수리하다 air conditioning 에어컨 tool kit 공구 세트

147. 세부 사항을 묻는 문제

Ware 씨가 말하는 문제는 무엇인가?
(A) 시스템에 익숙하지 않다.
(B) 장소를 찾을 수 없다.
(C) 일이 너무 많다.
(D) 현장에서 또 다른 요청을 받았다.

| 해설 | 초반부에 그들이 에어컨을 수리해 주기를 원해서 그것을 위한 공구를 가져왔는데, 보일러 수리도 부탁했다고(Initially they wanted us to fix their air conditioning, ~ they also asked me to work on their boiler) 했으므로 정답은 (D)이다.

| 어휘 | be unfamiliar with ~에 익숙하지 않다 location 위치, 장소 site 현장

| 패러프레이징 | also asked me to work on their boiler → received another request

148. 세부 사항을 묻는 문제

Ware 씨가 Vicky 씨에게 하도록 부탁하는 것은 무엇인가?
(A) 지시를 내리는 것
(B) 교체 부품을 주문하는 것
(C) 공구를 가져다주는 것
(D) 주간 회의에 참석하는 것

| 해설 | 중반부에 매장에서 다른 공구 세트를 가져다줄 수 있을지(Could you do me a favor and bring me the other tool kit from our shop) 부탁했으므로 정답은 (C)이다.

| 어휘 | give instructions 지시를 하다 replacement part 교체 부품

149-150 다음 영수증을 참조하시오.

¹⁴⁹**도쿄 공항**

¹⁴⁹**전용 휴게 구역**

¹⁴⁹고객 이름: Yun Zhen Li

객실 유형: 싱글 베드, 샤워실

첫 시간: 1,500엔(이후 500엔/30분)

¹⁴⁹체크인 시간: 5월 16일, 0620

체크아웃 시간: 5월 16일, 0850

총 청구액: 2,700엔*

*(¹⁵⁰Air VIP 회원 할인 적용됨)
저희 시설에 머물러 주셔서 감사합니다! 다음에 또 방문해 주세요!

| 어휘 | private 전용의, 개인의   shower 샤워실   charge 청구액   apply 적용하다

149. 세부 사항을 묻는 문제
Li 씨는 5월 16일에 무엇을 했나?
(A) 공항 시설을 이용했다.
(B) 호텔에 숙박했다.
(C) 도쿄에서 출발했다.
(D) 회원권을 취소했다.
| 해설 | Li 씨는 고객 이름으로 확인되고, 영수증 상단에 있는 도쿄 공항(Tokyo Airport)과 전용 휴게 구역(Private Resting Area), 그리고 중반부에 있는 체크인 시간(Check-in Time: May 16, 0620) 등을 종합해 볼 때, 5월 16일에 도쿄 공항에 있는 휴게 시설을 이용했음을 알 수 있으므로 정답은 (A)이다.
| 어휘 | facility 시설   depart 출발하다
| 패러프레이징 | Tokyo Airport / Private Resting Area → an airport facility

150. 추론 문제
Li 씨에 관해 암시되는 것은 무엇인가?
(A) 일등석 비행기 업그레이드를 받았다.
(B) Air VIP 회원이다.
(C) 시내로 가는 셔틀을 예약했다.
(D) 체류 기간을 연장하고 싶어했다.
| 해설 | 후반부의 별표(*)에 Air VIP 회원 할인이 적용되었다고(Air VIP Member Discount Applied) 제시된 것에서, Air VIP 회원인 것으로 유추할 수 있으므로 정답은 (B)이다.
| 어휘 | downtown 시내   extend 연장하다

151-152 다음 문자 메시지 대화를 참조하시오.

Jacob Perkins [오후 1:03]
Waycross 컨벤션 센터에 벌써 도착한 거예요? ¹⁵¹버스를 놓칠까 봐 걱정했던 것으로 아는데요.

Sarama Bisrat [오후 1:06]
¹⁵¹다행히 그것을 탈 수 있었어요. 곧 센터에 도착할 거예요. 막 Crystal 몰을 지났어요.

Jacob Perkins [오후 1:07]
잘됐네요. 사무실을 떠나 있는 동안 기다리는 소포가 있나요?

Sarama Bisrat [오후 1:08]
Braxton 제조사에서 받을 게 딱 하나 있어요. 시간에 민감한 것은 들어 있진 않아요.

Jacob Perkins [오후 1:09]
알겠어요. ¹⁵²보통 사람들이 자리에 없을 때 제가 그들을 대신해 소포들을 열어봐요. 하지만 그것은 그냥 당신 책상 위에 둘게요.

Sarama Bisrat [오후 1:10]
저한테는 그게 가장 좋겠네요.

| 어휘 | miss 놓치다   catch 잡아타다   expect 기대하다, 기다리다   time-sensitive 시간에 민감한, 분초를 다투는

151. 추론 문제
Bisrat 씨는 어디에서 메시지를 보내는 것 같은가?
(A) 사무실에서
(B) 학회 장소에서
(C) 버스에서
(D) 쇼핑몰에서
| 해설 | 오후 1:03에 컨벤션 센터에 벌써 도착했냐며, 버스를 놓치는 걸 걱정했던 것으로 안다고(I know you were worried about missing the bus) 한 Jacob Perkins의 말에, Bisrat 씨가 다행히 그것을 탈 수 있었다며(Fortunately, I was able to catch it), 곧 도착할 거라고(I should be at the center soon) 했으므로, Bistat 씨는 컨벤션 센터로 가는 버스 안에서 문자를 보내고 있음을 추론할 수 있다. 따라서 정답은 (C)이다.

152. 의도 파악 문제
오후 1:10에 Bisrat 씨가 "저한테는 그게 가장 좋겠네요"라고 쓸 때 의미하는 것은 무엇인가?
(A) 그녀는 긴급한 일을 완료하기 위해 사무실로 돌아올 계획이다.
(B) 그녀는 Perkins 씨가 소포를 여는 것을 원치 않는다.
(C) 그녀는 Braxton 제조사에 연락하는 것이 좋은 아이디어라고 생각한다.
(D) 그녀는 배송품이 Perkins 씨의 사무실에 보관되기를 원한다.
| 해설 | 이는 앞서 보통 사람들이 자리에 없을 때 그들을 대신해 소포를 열어보지만 그것은 그냥 당신 책상 위에 두겠다고(Usually I open packages for people when they're gone. But I'll just leave it on your desk) 한 것에 대한 응답으로, 소포를 열어보지 않고 책상 위에 두는 것이 가장 좋다는 의향을 전하고자 한 말임을 알 수 있으므로 정답은 (B)이다.
| 어휘 | complete 끝내다, 완료하다   urgent 긴급한   store 보관하다

153-154 다음 정보를 참조하시오.

Timberland 마케팅 비용 환급 정책

- ¹⁵³모든 환급 요청은 회사 서식 AC232를 통해 이루어져야만 합니다.
- 가능한 환급 대상에는 고객들을 위한 식사, 출장, 사무용품, 그리고 기타 사전에 승인된 것들이 포함됩니다.
- 원본 영수증들은 가능하면 언제든 포함되어야만 합니다.
- 해당 달의 첫 2주 이내에 요청서가 제출된다면, 환급금은 다음 달 1일에 입금될 것입니다.

¹⁵⁴각 팀은 자체 예산이 있습니다. 환급될 것으로 기대하는 구매나 청구를 하기 전에 여러분의 팀장에게 확인하시기 바랍니다.

| 어휘 | expense reimbursement 비용 환급 acceptable 수락 가능한, 받아들일 수 있는 include 포함하다 office supplies 사무용품 approved 승인된 in advance 미리 original receipt 원본 영수증 deposit 예금하다, 예치하다 provided that ~라면 budget 예산 make a charge 청구하다

153. 세부 사항을 묻는 문제
모든 환급 요청에 요구되는 것은 무엇인가?
(A) 공식적인 서식
(B) 예산 보고서
(C) 팀장의 서명
(D) 여행 일정

| 해설 | 환급 정책 첫 번째에 모든 환급 요청은 회사 서식 AC232를 통해 이루어져야만 한다고(All reimbursement requests must be made via company form AC232) 제시되어 있으므로 정답은 (A)이다.

| 어휘 | official 공식적인, 정식의 signature 서명 travel itinerary 여행 일정

| 패러프레이징 | company form → An official form

154. True 문제
Timberland 마케팅에 대해 언급된 것은 무엇인가?
(A) 비용을 2주 후에 환급해 준다.
(B) 직원들에게 격주로 급여를 지급한다.
(C) 개별 팀 예산을 배정한다.
(D) 직원들에게 회사 신용카드를 발급해 준다.

| 해설 | 아래쪽 별표(*)에 각 팀은 자체 예산이 있다고(Each team has its own budget) 제시되어 있으므로 정답은 (C)이다.

| 어휘 | assign 배정하다 issue 발급하다, 발행하다

| 패러프레이징 | Each team has its own budget. → It assigns individual team budgets.

155-157 다음 청구서를 참조하시오.

Jacobson's Warehouse
449 Victoria Court
Standish, ME 04084

청구서 정보	배송 정보
Debra Collins	동일
73 Hawthorne Lane	
Standish, ME 04084	

¹⁵⁶예상 도착일: 4월 7일 (오후 1시 이후)

코드	품목	가격
¹⁵⁷*1612-0938	¹⁵⁵제습기	69.00달러
8704-9225	¹⁵⁵선풍기	21.00달러
7000-1643	¹⁵⁵토스터 (2구)	16.00달러
2099-5815	¹⁵⁵디지털 시계	8.00달러
0000-0000	할인 쿠폰	-15.00달러

¹⁵⁷*커다란 크기로 인해 이 품목은 별도로 배송될 것입니다. 배송에 하루에서 이틀 더 감안해 주세요.

| 어휘 | billing 청구서 발송 arrival 도착 dehumidifier 제습기 electric fan 선풍기 slot 홈, 구멍 separately 별도로, 따로 allow 고려하다, 계산에 넣다

155. 세부 사항을 묻는 문제
Jacobson's Warehouse는 어떤 종류의 업체인가?
(A) 레스토랑
(B) 택배 회사
(C) 가전제품 매장
(D) 가구 제조업체

| 해설 | 영수증 가운데 품목(Item)에 제습기(Dehumidifier), 선풍기(Electric Fan), 토스터(Toaster), 디지털 시계(Digital Clock)가 제시된 것을 통해 가전제품을 판매하는 업체임을 알 수 있으므로 정답은 (C)이다.

| 어휘 | courier 택배 manufacturer 제조업체

| 패러프레이징 | Dehumidifier / Electric Fan / Toaster / Digital Clock → appliance

156. 세부 사항을 묻는 문제
4월 7일에 무엇이 예정되어 있나?
(A) 재고가 확인될 것이다.
(B) 할인 쿠폰이 만료될 것이다.
(C) 일부 주문품이 배달될 것이다.
(D) 가전제품이 조립될 것이다.

| 해설 | 청구서 정보에 예상 도착일이 4월 7일로(Expected Arrival: 7 April) 제시되어 있으므로, 4월 7일에 별표(*) 된 것을 제외한 주문품이 배달될 것임을 알 수 있다. 따라서 정답은 (C)이다.

| 어휘 | inventory 재고 expire 만료되다 partial 부분의 assemble 조립하다

157. True 문제
제습기에 관해 제시된 것은 무엇인가?
(A) 나중에 도착할 것이다.
(B) 공장에서 직접 배송된다.
(C) 연장된 보증 기간이 포함된다.
(D) 무료 배송을 받을 수 없다.

| 해설 | 제습기(Dehumidifier)의 코드에 별표(*)가 있고, 마지막에 그 별표에 관해 커다란 크기로 인해 별도로 배송될 것이라며(Due to its large size, this item will be shipped separately) 배송에 하루에서 이틀 더 감안해 달라고(Please allow an extra 1-2 days for delivery) 제시되어 있으므로 정답은 (A)이다.

| 어휘 | directly 직접 extended 연장된 warranty 보증 (기간)
be eligible for ~에 자격이 있다

| 패러프레이징 | allow an extra 1-2 days for delivery → arrive at a later date

158-160 다음 기사를 참조하시오.

<국제 비즈니스 신문>: 비즈니스 브리핑, 11월 9일
Ansel Routhier 작성

158어젯밤 늦게 주주 총회 후에 오랫동안 예상되었던 Tanty Technologies와 Invert Solutions의 합병이 확정되었다. 새로 임명된 CEO인 Daniel Hardwick은 이 합의가 "Tanty Solutions"라는 이름으로 사업을 할 새롭게 형성된 기업이 중요한 동남아시아 국가 연합(ASEAN) 지역에 접근할 수 있게 할 것이라고 말했다. — [1] —.

많은 업계 관측통들은 작년만큼 오래 전에 그 움직임을 예측했지만, 159Invert Solutions의 뱅킹 소프트웨어와 관련된 저작권 문제로 협상이 일시적으로 지연되었었다. — [2] —. 지난달 Invert Solutions에 유리하게 법정 소송 사건이 해결되어, 합병에 대한 최종 장벽이 제거되었다. — [3] —.

동일한 관측통은 160Tanty Technologies의 탄탄한 재무 예측 컴퓨터 프로그램들을 Invert Solutions의 아시아 고객층에 판매하여, 그 신생 기업의 수익이 즉시 증가할 것으로 예측했다. 160게다가 Tanty Technologies의 많은 유럽 및 미국 고객들은 Invert Solutions 제품들의 유연성에 강한 관심을 표했다. — [4] —. 업계의 나머지들은 그 변화가 시장 거대 기업의 입지를 확고하게 할지 아니면 신생 기업들이 기반을 다질 여지를 남겨 둘지 여부를 주의 깊게 지켜보고 있다.

| 어휘 | long-expected 오랫동안 예상된, 대망의 union 연합, 합병 confirm 확정하다 following ~에 뒤이어, ~ 후에 shareholder 주주 appointed 임명된 arrangement 합의, 주선 newly-formed 새롭게 형성된 corporation 기업, 법인 trade 사업을 하다 access 접근하다 observer 관측통 predict 예측하다 negotiation 협상 temporarily 일시적으로 stall 지연되다 copyright 저작권 court case 법정 소송 사건 resolve 해결하다 in favor of ~에 찬성하여, ~의 이익이 되도록 barrier 장벽, 장애물 revenue 수익, 수입 robust 확고한, 탄탄한

customer base 고객층 express 표하다 interest 관심 flexibility 유연성 transition 변화, 변천 solidify 굳히다, 확고히 하다 start-up 신생 기업 gain ground 기반을 다지다, 전진하다

158. 주제/목적 문제
기사는 왜 작성되었나?
(A) 기업 인수를 발표하기 위해
(B) 업체 합병을 알리기 위해
(C) 주주 정책을 설명하기 위해
(D) 최근 소프트웨어 동향을 개괄하기 위해

| 해설 | 첫 번째 단락 도입부에 오랫동안 예상되었던 두 회사의 합병이 확정되었다며(The long-expected union of Tanty Technologies and Invert Solutions has been confirmed ~) 그와 관련된 내용이 이어지고 있으므로 정답은 (B)이다.

| 어휘 | buyout 매수, 인수 merger 합병 describe 설명하다, 서술하다 policy 정책, 방침 outline 개괄하다

| 패러프레이징 | union of Tanty Technologies and Invert Solutions → a business merger

159. 추론 문제
Invert Solutions는 어떤 유형의 회사일 것 같은가?
(A) 기업 컨설팅 회사
(B) 소프트웨어 개발사
(C) 컴퓨터 제조사
(D) 인터넷 보안 회사

| 해설 | 두 번째 단락 초반부에 Invert Solutions의 뱅킹 소프트웨어(Invert Solutions' banking software)라고 제시된 것을 단서로, 뱅킹 소프트웨어를 개발한 소프트웨어 개발사일 것으로 유추할 수 있으므로 정답은 (B)이다.

🔺 고난도

160. 문장 삽입 문제
[1], [2], [3], [4]로 표시된 곳 중에 다음 문장이 들어가기에 가장 적절한 곳은?

"이런 요소들은 어떻게 각 회사의 장점들이 성공의 견인차가 될지를 보여주는 예들이다."

(A) [1]
(B) [2]
(C) [3]
(D) [4]

| 해설 | 제시된 문장은 주어인 These factors가 구체적으로 나타나 있는 문장 뒤에 들어가야 함을 알 수 있는데, 이에 해당하는 것은 마지막 단락에 Tanty Technologies의 탄탄한 재무 예측 컴퓨터 프로그램들을 Invert Solutions의 아시아 고객층에 판매하는(the sale of Tanty Technologies' robust financial prediction computer programs to Invert Solutions' Asian customer base) 것과 Tanty Technologies의 많은 유럽 및 미국 고객들이 Invert Solutions 제품들의 유연성에 강한 관심을 표했다는(many European and American customers of Tanty Technologies have expressed strong interest in the flexibility of Invert Solutions' products) 것이므로 그것이 제

시된 문장 뒤인 (D)가 정답이다.

| 어휘 | factor 요인, 요소   strength 장점, 강점   success 성공

161-164 다음 웹 사이트를 참조하시오.

국립 인구 조사국

국가 인구 조사는 우리 나라의 다양한 인구 통계에 대한 ¹⁶¹일반적인 이해를 얻기 위해 매년 실시됩니다. ¹⁶² ⁽ᴰ⁾질문들은 연령, 성별, 인종, 소득, 가족 규모, 혼인 여부 및 기타 주제들을 비롯하여 폭넓은 범위를 다룹니다. ¹⁶² ⁽ᴮ⁾사람들이 솔직하게 그리고 자신들의 능력과 지식이 미치는 데까지 질문에 대답하는 것이 중요합니다. ¹⁶² ⁽ᶜ⁾의무적인 것은 아니지만, 저희 질문지에 응답해 주시는 분들께 감사를 드립니다.

인구 조사 데이터는 많은 유형의 사회적 연구와 과학적 연구에 도움이 되고, ¹⁶³많은 출판물들에 인용되어 왔습니다. 저희 인구 조사국에서 수집해온 어떤 통계 자료라도 이용하는 데 관심이 있으면, 먼저 허가를 받아야 합니다. ¹⁶⁴admin@ncb.gov로 저희에게 연락해 주시고 반드시 여러분의 이름과 저희 데이터의 사용 목적 및 그것을 사용하려고 하시는 출판물의 이름을 포함시켜 주세요. 대부분의 요청은 2영업일 이내에 응답됩니다. 일단 허가를 받게 되면 인구 조사 데이터를 사용하는 것은 무료입니다.

| 어휘 | national census 국가 인구 조사   conduct 실시하다   annually 매년, 해마다   general 일반적인   demographics 인구 통계   cover 다루다   broad 폭넓은   spectrum 범위   including ~을 포함하는   gender 성별   race 인종   income 소득   marital status 혼인 여부   honestly 솔직하게   to the best of ~이 미치는 한   ability 능력   mandatory 의무적인   questionnaire 질문지, 설문지   social 사회적인   scientific 과학적인   cite 인용하다   publication 출판물   statistics 통계 자료   collect 수집하다   obtain 얻다   permission 허가   intended use 사용 목적   charge 요금   grant 주다

---

161. 동의어 문제

첫 번째 단락, 첫 번째 줄에 있는 단어 "general"과 의미가 가장 유사한 것은
(A) 조직된
(B) 기본적인
(C) 선두적인
(D) 간단한

| 해설 | 해당 단어가 들어간 문장은 '국가 인구 조사는 우리 나라의 다양한 인구 통계에 대한 일반적인 이해를 얻기 위해 매년 실시됩니다'라고 해석된다. 따라서 '일반적인'이라는 의미와 유사하게 대체해 쓸 수 있는 '기본적인'이라는 뜻의 (B) basic이 정답이다.

⚠고난도

162. NOT True 문제

인구 조사 참가자들에 관해 제시되지 않은 것은 무엇인가?
(A) 모두 미국 시민권을 가지고 있어야 한다.
(B) 솔직할 것을 요청받는다.
(C) 설문 조사를 할 의향이 있다.
(D) 다양한 그룹들에 속한다.

| 해설 | 첫 번째 단락에 질문들은 연령, 성별, 인종, 소득, 가족 규모, 혼인 여부 및 기타 주제들을 비롯한 폭넓은 범위를 다룬다고(The questions cover a broad spectrum including age, gender, race, income, family size, marital status, and other topics) 한 것에서 (D), 사람들이 솔직하게 질문에 대답하는 것이 중요하다고(It is important that people answer the questions honestly) 한 것에서 (B), 의무적인 것은 아니라고(Although it is not mandatory) 한 것에서 자발적으로 한 것임을 알 수 있으므로 (C)는 확인된다. 따라서 정답은 (A)이다.

| 어휘 | citizenship 시민권   be willing to ~할 의향이 있다   varied 다양한
| 패러프레이징 | · answer the questions honestly → are asked to be honest
· it is not mandatory → They are willing to take a survey.

163. True 문제

국립 인구 조사국에 관해 명시된 것은 무엇인가?
(A) 정부에 의해 자금을 제공받는다.
(B) 대규모 연구 팀을 고용한다.
(C) 데이터 사용에 요금을 부과한다.
(D) 많은 출판물들에 자료를 제공해 왔다.

| 해설 | 두 번째 단락 도입부에 인구 조사국에서 수집한 인구 조사 데이터가 많은 출판물들에 인용되어 왔다고(~ has been cited in many publications) 제시되어 있으므로 정답은 (D)이다.

| 어휘 | fund 자금을 제공하다   charge 부과하다, 청구하다
| 패러프레이징 | has been cited in many publications → has supplied data to multiple publications

164. 세부 사항을 묻는 문제

수집된 데이터를 인용하려면 어떻게 허가를 받을 수 있나?
(A) 연구를 진행함으로써
(B) 소정의 요금을 지불함으로써
(C) 이메일로 신청서를 보냄으로써
(D) 서식을 작성함으로써

| 해설 | 두 번째 단락 중반부에 수집된 통계 자료를 이용하는 데 관심이 있으면, 허가를 받아야 한다고 알리는 내용 뒤에, admin@ncb.gov로 연락하라고(Please contact us at admin@ncb.gov ~) 제시되어 있으므로 정답은 (C)이다.

| 어휘 | fill out ~을 작성하다
| 패러프레이징 | contact us at admin@ncb.gov → sending a request by e-mail

165-167 다음 기사를 참조하시오.

SANTEE, CA (11월 3일)—¹⁶⁵주요 간식 생산업체인 Finley 식품이 특별한 콘테스트를 발표했다. 먼저, 사람들은 새로운 감자 칩 맛에 대한 자신들의 아이디어를 제출하도록 요청받을 것이다. 회사는 다섯 가지 맛을 골라 소형 샘플 팩 크기로 판매하기 시작할 것이다. 그런 다음, 한 달

뒤 ¹⁶⁶어떤 맛들이 브랜드에 영구적으로 추가되어야 할지를 결정하기 위한 온라인 투표를 실시할 것이다. ¹⁶⁷가장 인기 있는 새로운 맛을 제출한 1등 수상자는 Finley 식품의 생산 및 포장 현장들 중 한 곳의 선임 맛 전문가 직책을 제안받게 될 것이다. 다른 모든 상위 제출물들은 그 맛이 얼마나 잘 팔렸는지에 기반하여 현금 보너스를 받게 될 것이다.

| 어휘 | producer 생산업체 flavor 맛 select 고르다, 선정하다 poll 투표 determine 결정하다 permanent 영구적인 addition 추가물, 부가물 first place winner 1등 수상자 senior 선임의 submission 제출물, 제출품 based on ~에 기반하여

165. 주제/목적 문제
기사의 주된 목적은 무엇인가?
(A) 일자리 공석을 광고하는 것
(B) 간식을 만드는 브랜드를 홍보하는 것
(C) 대회를 알리는 것
(D) 지도부의 변화를 발표하는 것
| 해설 | 도입부에 주요 간식 생산업체인 Finley 식품이 특별한 콘테스트를 발표했다고(Finley Foods, a major snack producer, has announced a special contest) 한 후, 그 콘테스트에 관해 구체적으로 알리고 있으므로 정답은 (C)이다.
| 어휘 | advertise 광고하다 promote 홍보하다 publicize 알리다, 홍보하다 competition 대회
| 패러프레이징 | a special contest → a competition

166. 세부 사항을 묻는 문제
누가 가장 인기 있는 맛을 선택할 것인가?
(A) Finley 식품의 CEO
(B) 투표를 하는 사람들
(C) Finley 식품의 담당자들
(D) 요리사 그룹
| 해설 | 중반부에 어떤 맛들이 브랜드에 영구적으로 추가되어야 할지를 결정하기 위한 온라인 투표를 실시할 것이라고(it will hold an online poll to determine which flavors should stay as a permanent addition to the brand) 제시되어 있으므로 정답은 (B)이다.
| 어휘 | cast votes 투표하다, 표를 던지다 representative 담당자, 대표

167. True 문제
1등 수상자에 관해 명시된 것은 무엇인가?
(A) 가장 많은 액수의 현금이 수여될 것이다.
(B) 지역 신문이 수상자를 특집으로 다룰 것이다.
(C) 수상자가 공장 투어에 초대될 것이다.
(D) 고용 기회가 주어질 것이다.
| 해설 | 후반부에 가장 인기 있는 새로운 맛을 제출한 1등 수상자는 Finley 식품의 생산 및 포장 현장들 중 한 곳의 선임 맛 전문가 직책을 제안받게 될 것이라고 (The first place winner ~ will be offered a position as a senior flavor specialist at one of Finley Foods' production and packaging sites) 제시되어 있으므로 정답은 (D)이다.

| 어휘 | amount 액수 award 수여하다, 주다 feature 특집으로 다루다 employment opportunity 고용 기회
| 패러프레이징 | will be offered a position → An employment opportunity will be given

168-171 다음 온라인 채팅 토론을 참조하시오.

Aruna Jadhav [오전 9:03]
IT 부서의 Chris Edwards가 그의 팀이 우리 컴퓨터 네트워크에 침범했던 바이러스를 성공적으로 제거했다고 막 확인해 줬어요. ¹⁶⁸그래도 그 과정에서 우리 디자인 파일들 일부를 잃어버렸잖아요, 그렇죠?

Gustave Tanguay [오전 9:04]
맞아요. 유감스럽게도, ¹⁶⁸/¹⁶⁹이전 버전의 백업 파일만 가지고 있었기 때문에 새로 만든 로고를 Valmeyer 제조사에 보내는 게 늦었어요.

Camilla Calvacante [오전 9:06]
그것 유감이네요.

Riley Eldershaw [오전 9:07]
네, 그것이 우리의 명성에 부정적인 영향을 미칠 수 있어요. 직원들에게 그들의 작업을 백업하게 하는 것에 관해 우리가 더 엄격해져야 해요.

Aruna Jadhav [오전 9:08]
동의해요. ¹⁷⁰현재 할 수 있는 것은 보상의 방안으로 Valmeyer 제조사 계좌에 일부 환불금을 지급하는 것이에요. 그것을 누가 벌써 했나요?

Camilla Calvacante [오전 9:10]
¹⁷⁰제가 오늘 할 계획인데, 얼마가 적당할지 알고 싶었어요. Valmeyer 제조사는 단골 고객이니, ¹⁷¹저는 250달러 정도 생각하고 있었고요.

Gustave Tanguay [오전 9:11]
적정한 것 같은데요. Aruna, 우리 그만큼 있나요?

Aruna Jadhav [오전 9:12]
네. ¹⁷¹우리 회사 은행 계좌에 그것을 충당할 만큼은 충분해요.

| 어휘 | confirm 확인해 주다 successfully 성공적으로 remove 제거하다 affect 침범하다, 영향을 미치다 process 과정, 절차 shame 애석한 일, 유감 negatively 부정적으로 reputation 명성, 평판 strict 엄격한 partial 부분적인, 일부분의 refund 환불 account 계좌, 계정 compensation 보상, 보상금 appropriate 적절한, 적당한 regular client 단골 고객 reasonable 합리적인, 적당한 corporate 기업의, 회사의 cover 충당하다

🔺 고난도

168. 추론 문제
글쓴이들은 어디에서 일할 것 같은가?

(A) 회계 사무소에서
(B) 생산 시설에서
(C) 컴퓨터 소매점에서
(D) 그래픽 디자인 회사에서

| 해설 | 오전 9:03에 Aruna Jadhav가 바이러스 제거 소식을 전한 뒤, 그 과정에서 우리 디자인 파일들 일부를 잃어버렸다고(We did lose some of our design files in the process) 덧붙인 것과 이후 새로 만든 로고(newly created logo) 등을 언급한 것으로 볼 때, 글쓴이들은 디자인 관련 회사에서 일하는 것으로 유추할 수 있으므로 정답은 (D)이다.

169. 세부 사항을 묻는 문제
토론에서 언급되는 문제는 무엇인가?
(A) 비용이 증가되었다.
(B) 직원이 결근했다.
(C) 수송품이 파손되었다.
(D) 마감을 놓쳤다.

| 해설 | 오전 9:04에 Gustave Tanguay가 이전 버전의 백업 파일만 가지고 있었기 때문에 새로 만든 로고를 Valmeyer 제조사에 보내는 게 늦었다고(we were late getting the newly created logo to Valmeyer Manufacturing because we only had an earlier version of the file backed up) 쓴 것으로 볼 때, 마감을 맞추지 못하고 일정이 늦춰졌음을 알 수 있으므로 정답은 (D)이다.

| 어휘 | absent 결근한, 부재한   shipment 수송품
| 패러프레이징 | were late → was missed

170. 추론 문제 [고난도]
Calvacante 씨가 오늘 할 것 같은 일은 무엇인가?
(A) 고객에게 사과의 편지를 보내는 것
(B) 직원들을 위한 회의를 이끄는 것
(C) 고객 계좌에 환불을 해 주는 것
(D) 온라인 가격 리스트를 업데이트하는 것

| 해설 | 오전 9:08에 Aruna Jadhav가 현재 할 수 있는 것은 보상의 방안으로 Valmeyer 제조사 계좌에 일부 환불금을 지급하는 것이라고(All we can do now is provide a partial refund to the Valmeyer Manufacturing account by way of compensation) 한 후 그것을 누가 벌써 했는지 묻는 말에 Camilla Calvacante가 자신이 오늘 할 계획이라고(I plan to do that today) 했으므로 정답은 (C)이다.

| 어휘 | letter of apology 사과 편지   issue a refund 환불을 해 주다
| 패러프레이징 | provide a partial refund → Issue a refund

171. 의도 파악 문제
오전 9:11에 Tanguay 씨가 "우리 그만큼 있나요"라고 쓸 때 의미하는 것은 무엇인가?
(A) 그는 누락된 서류를 찾으려 노력하고 있다.
(B) 그는 충분한 자금이 있는지 궁금하다.
(C) 그는 고객의 연락처가 필요하다.
(D) 그는 계좌 번호를 확인하기를 원한다.

| 해설 | 이는 고객 계좌에 지급할 환불 액수에 대해, 오전 9:10에 Camilla Calvacante가 250달러 정도 생각하고 있었다고(I was thinking around $250) 한 말에 대해 적정한 것 같다며(That sounds reasonable) 그만큼 가지고 있는지 물은 것으로, 고객에게 줄 자금이 충분히 있는지 확인하기 위해 물은 것임을 알 수 있으므로 정답은 (B)이다.

| 어휘 | missing 누락된, 빠뜨린   funds 자금   contact information 연락처

172-175 다음 광고를 참조하시오.

Rashid 맞춤 신사복의 봄 세일

[173 (A)]현 CEO이자 Rashid 맞춤 신사복의 창립자의 아들인 J. Rashid 씨는 [172]수석 재단사 Joseph McPherson이 매장을 방문해 4월 4일까지 현장에서 일을 할 것임을 알리게 되어 기쁩니다. 파리 패션 지구에서 30년 넘게 보낸 McPherson 씨는 완벽한 바느질과 꼭 맞는 옷을 제공하는 것으로 세계적으로 유명합니다. — [1] —. [175]그래서 이번이 이런 특별한 제품을 구매할 수 있는 흔하지 않은 기회입니다.

그 행사를 축하하기 위해, [173 (B)]Rashid 맞춤 신사복은 맞춤 양복을 두 벌 주문하면 드레스 셔츠 3벌 세트를 무료로 제공해 드릴 것입니다. — [2] —. 이 셔츠들은 [173 (C)]우리가 60년 넘게 제작해 온 모든 양복들과 마찬가지로, 고객의 요구 조건에 수작업으로 맞춰지고, 다양한 색상과 스타일로 이용할 수 있을 것입니다. — [3] —. 4월 4일부터 계속, Rashid 맞춤 신사복은 우리 역사상 처음으로 완전한 셔츠 제작 서비스를 제공할 것이고, 이 품목들은 주문 제작 또는 기성복에서 선택하여 이용할 수 있을 것입니다. — [4] —.

이미 파일에 치수가 있는 저희 해외 고객들도 이 기회를 이용하실 수 있습니다. [174]그저 www.rashidgtailors.com에 로그인해 해당란에 MCP1022 코드를 넣어서 귀하의 온라인 계정을 통해 주문하세요.

| 어휘 | founder 설립자, 창립자   be known for ~로 알려져 있다   worldwide 세계적으로   stitching 바느질   rare 드문   opportunity 기회   one-of-a-kind 특별한   celebrate 축하하다   complimentary 무료의   custom-made 맞춤의, 주문 제작의   specification 요구 조건, 사양   decade 10년   a wide range of 다양한, 폭넓은   onwards 계속, 앞으로   made-to-order 주문 제작된, 맞춤의   off-the-rack 기성품인   overseas 해외의   measurement 치수   take advantage of ~를 이용하다   appropriate 적절한, 알맞은

172. 추론 문제
McPherson 씨는 누구일 것 같은가?
(A) 의류 유통업자
(B) 회사의 CEO
(C) 재단 작업 인턴
(D) 초청된 전문가

| 해설 | McPherson 씨는 첫 번째 단락 초반부에 제시되어 있는데, 수석 재단사 Joseph McPherson이 매장을 방문해 4월 4일까지 현장에서 일을 할 것이라고(Master Tailor Joseph McPherson will be visiting the business and working on site until April 4) 한 것에서, McPherson 씨는 초청을 받아 매장

을 방문하는 전문 재단사임을 알 수 있으므로 정답은 (D)이다.

🔺고난도
173. NOT True 문제
Rashid 맞춤 신사복에 대해 암시되는 것이 아닌 것은 무엇인가?
(A) 가족 소유의 업체이다.
(B) 프로모션에 무료 제품이 포함될 것이다.
(C) 60년 넘게 영업을 해 오고 있다.
(D) 현재 정장 셔츠를 만든다.
| 해설 | 첫 번째 단락 도입부에 현 CEO이자 Rashid 맞춤 신사복의 창립자의 아들인 J. Rashid 씨라고(Mr. J. Rashid, current CEO and son of Rashid Gentlemen's Tailors' founder) 한 것에서 (A), 두 번째 단락 도입부에 양복을 두 벌 주문하면 무료 드레스 셔츠 3벌 세트가 포함된다고(~ will be including a set of three complimentary dress shirts with any order of two custom-made suits) 한 것에서 (B), 60년 넘게 제작해 온 모든 양복들이라고(~ all the suits we have produced for over six decades) 한 것에서 (C)는 확인된다. 따라서 정답은 (D)이다. 셔츠 제작 서비스는 4월 4일부터 제공할 것이라고 했으므로 현재 셔츠를 만든다는 것은 오답이다.
| 어휘 | family-owned 가족 소유의   promotion 홍보, 프로모션   currently 현재   formal 격식을 차린
| 패러프레이징 | ・complimentary dress shirts → free items
・six decades → 60 years

174. 세부 사항을 묻는 문제
해외 구매자들에게 권장되는 것은 무엇인가?
(A) 미리 약속을 예약하는 것
(B) 웹 사이트를 통해 주문하는 것
(C) 이메일로 그들의 치수를 보내는 것
(D) 그들의 양복을 일찍 주문하는 것
| 해설 | 마지막 단락에 해외 고객도 이 기회를 이용할 수 있다며, 그저 로그인해서 온라인 계정을 통해 주문하라고(Simply log in and place an order through your online account) 제시하고 있으므로 정답은 (B)이다.
| 패러프레이징 | ・overseas customers → foreign buyers
・place an order through your online account → ordering through a Web site

🔺고난도
175. 문장 삽입 문제
[1], [2], [3], [4]로 표시된 곳 중에 다음 문장이 들어가기에 가장 적절한 곳은?
"그는 대개 유명인들과 고위급 정치인들에게만 서비스를 제공합니다."
(A) [1]
(B) [2]
(C) [3]
(D) [4]
| 해설 | 제시된 문장은 앞의 대상을 He로 받아 그가 하는 일을 설명한 것으로, He가 가리키는 것은 첫 단락에 언급된 수석 재단사 Joseph McPherson일 것으로 파악할 수 있다. 이에 따라 대개 유명인들과 고위급 정치인들에게만 서비스를 제공하며, 그래서 이번에 이런 특별한 제품을 구매할 수 있는 흔하지 않은 기회라는(So, this is a rare opportunity to purchase these one-of-a-kind goods) 문맥으로 연결되는 것이 적절하므로 정답은 (A)이다.
| 어휘 | cater 서비스를 제공하다   exclusively 독점적으로, 오로지   celebrity 유명인   high-level politician 고위급 정치인

176-180 다음 회람과 일정표를 참조하시오.

수신: 전 직원
제목: 1월 9일 – 13일 주
날짜: 1월 2일 월요일

[176]우리 사무실에 페인트를 다시 칠하기 위한 일정이 확정되었습니다. 첨부된 것은 그 작업이 진행될 일정표입니다. [177/179]여러분의 예정일 전날 저녁에 모든 가구를 벽면에서 떨어뜨려 중앙으로 당겨 주시고 주어진 천으로 그것들을 덮어서 도장공들이 장애물 없이 작업할 수 있도록 해주세요. 페인트는 하루 후에 마를 테지만, 금요일에 진행될 페인트 작업을 제외하고, 여러분의 사무실을 이틀 동안 떠나 있도록 계획하는 것이 가장 좋습니다.

[176]여러분의 사무실에 페인트칠을 하는 동안, [178]우리의 주 회의실인 716호실을 임시 사무실로 이용해 주세요. 다음 주에 그 회의실을 이용할 계획이라면, 누구든 그곳에서 임시적으로 일하게 될 이들과 반드시 조정하세요. [178]그곳은 우리 사무실에서 마이크와 스피커가 있는 유일한 회의실이기 때문에, 그곳에서 회의를 여는 것은 그곳을 임시 사무실 공간으로 이용하는 사람들의 주의를 아주 산만하게 할 수 있습니다. 이 문제에 관하여 어떤 질문이 있으면 관리진에게 연락해 주세요.

| 어휘 | repaint 페인트를 다시 칠하다   attached 첨부된   take place 진행되다   pull 당기다   cover 덮다   cloth 천   obstruction 방해, 장애물   temporary 임시의, 일시적인   coordinate with ~와 조정하다   distracting 산만하게 하는, 마음을 산란시키는   management 경영진, 관리진

사무실 페인트칠 일정표 (1월 9일 – 13일)

1월 9일 월요일	704호 (Michelle Cox)
1월 10일 화요일	714호 (Teddy Boyle)
1월 11일 수요일	705호 (Jessica Ramsey)
[179]1월 12일 목요일	715호 (John Hack)
1월 13일 금요일	706호 ([180]James Holder & Danielle Atchison)

176. 주제/목적 문제
회람의 주된 목적은 무엇인가?
(A) 새로운 사무실 장소로 가는 길을 안내하는 것
(B) 일시적인 업무 공간의 변경을 알리는 것
(C) 근무 환경에 대한 피드백을 수집하는 것
(D) 진행되어야 할 작업을 명시하는 것
| 해설 | 첫 번째 단락에 사무실에 페인트를 다시 칠하기 위한 일정이 확정되었다고

(The schedule for repainting our offices has been finalized) 알린 것과 두 번째 단락에 사무실에 페인트칠을 하는 동안, 주 회의실인 716호를 임시 사무실로 이용해 달라고(During the time your offices are being painted, please use Room 716, our main meeting room, as a temporary office) 한 것을 통해, 페인트칠 작업으로 인해 임시적으로 업무 공간을 변경한다는 것을 알리기 위해 보낸 회람임을 알 수 있으므로 정답은 (B)이다.

| 어휘 | give directions 길 안내를 해주다   gather 모으다, 수집하다   specify 명시하다

177. 세부 사항을 묻는 문제
직원들이 예정된 작업을 위해 하도록 요청받는 것은 무엇인가?
(A) 자신들의 개인 소지품들을 포장하는 것
(B) 자신들의 붓을 가져오는 것
(C) 자신들의 책상을 덮는 것
(D) 작업자들을 감독하는 것

| 해설 | 첫 번째 단락에 모든 가구를 벽면에서부터 떨어뜨려 중앙으로 당기고 천으로 그것들을 덮어 달라고(Please pull all furniture away from the walls to the center and cover them with given cloths) 요청했으므로 정답은 (C)이다.

| 어휘 | personal belongings 개인 소지품   brush 붓   oversee 감독하다

| 패러프레이징 | all furniture → their desks

178. True 문제
716호실에 관해 언급된 것은 무엇인가?
(A) 그 건물에서 가장 큰 방이다.
(B) 수리될 것이다.
(C) 음향 시스템을 갖추고 있다.
(D) 회사의 웹 사이트를 통해 예약될 수 있다.

| 해설 | 두 번째 단락에 사무실에 페인트칠을 하는 동안, 주 회의실인 716호실을 임시 사무실로 이용해 달라고(~ please use Room 716, our main meeting room, as a temporary office) 했고, 그곳이 마이크와 스피커가 있는 유일한 회의실이라고(Since it is the only room in our office with a microphone and speakers ~) 했으므로 정답은 (C)이다.

| 어휘 | undergo 진행하다   renovation 개조, 수리   be equipped with ~을 갖추고 있다   reserve 예약하다

| 패러프레이징 | with a microphone and speakers → equipped with a sound system

고난도

179. 연계 문제 - 추론
Hack 씨는 언제 가구를 옮길 것 같은가?
(A) 1월 9일 월요일에
(B) 1월 10일 화요일에
(C) 1월 11일 수요일에
(D) 1월 12일 목요일에

| 해설 | 회람 첫 번째 단락에 예정일 전날 저녁에 모든 가구를 벽면에서 떨어뜨려 중앙으로 당기라고(Please pull all furniture away from the walls to the center ~ on the evening of the day before your scheduled date) 했고, 일정표에서 Hack 씨가 있는 715호(Room 715)의 작업 예정일이 1월 12일 목요일(Thursday, January 12)로 확인되므로, 그 전날인 (C)가 정답이다.

180. 추론 문제
Atchison 씨에 관해 암시되는 것은 무엇인가?
(A) 다른 회사의 직책을 수락했다.
(B) 동료와 사무실을 같이 쓴다.
(C) 새로운 사무실로 이사할 것이다.
(D) 최근에 경영진으로 승진되었다.

| 해설 | Atchison 씨는 일정표 마지막에 706호실 사용자로, 사용자 이름이 두 명(James Holder & Danielle Atchison) 표시되어 있는 것으로 볼 때, 두 사람이 함께 사무실을 이용하고 있음을 유추할 수 있으므로 정답은 (B)이다.

| 어휘 | accept 수락하다   share 같이 쓰다, 공유하다   recently 최근에   be promoted to ~로 승진되다

181-185 다음 팸플릿과 이메일을 참조하시오.

Byron 마케팅
www.byronmarketing.net

브랜드 인지도는 성공적인 업체를 **181 운영하는** 열쇠입니다. Byron 마케팅이 여러분의 업체가 알려지도록 도와드리겠습니다. 저희 서비스에 포함되는 것은:

182 (D)인쇄물 - 전통적인 옵션인 이것은 포스터와 전단, 그리고 신문 광고를 포함합니다. **182 (C)**저희 담당자들 중 한 명과 상담하여 여러분 업체에 적당한 인쇄물 양을 추천받으세요.

182 (D)라디오 - 대부분의 사람들이 자동차나 사무실에 있는 동안 라디오를 듣기 때문에, 이것은 여러분의 광고 타깃이 일하는 연령인 경우 이상적인 선택입니다. **182 (C)**여러분 회사의 광고를 방송할 방송국을 선택할 수 있습니다.

182 (D)/184 텔레비전 - 이것은 어린이들과 같은 어린 시청자들에게 도달하기 위한 아주 좋은 옵션입니다. 흥미로운 시청각의 조합이 그들의 관심을 끌고 유지할 수 있습니다.

182 (D)인터넷 - 저희 그래픽 디자이너들 중 한 명과 협력하여 여러분의 마케팅 요구에 가장 적합한 창 크기를 결정하세요. 그런 다음 **182 (C)**광고하고 싶은 사이트를 선택하세요.

저희는 무료 초기 상담을 제공하는데 상담 중에 여러분은 저희가 어떤 서비스를 제공해 주길 원하는지 선택할 수 있습니다. 후속 상담들은 관련된 서비스의 기간과 수에 기반하여 비용이 청구될 것입니다. **182 (B)**저희 모든 광고 아이디어들은 최종안이 제작되기 전에 승인을 위해 제시될 것입니다. custserv@byronmarketing.net으로 저희에게 이메일을 보내거나 555-3189로 저희에게 전화해 회의 일정을 잡으세요.

| 어휘 | recognition 인지도   run 운영하다   include 포함하다

| 어휘 | traditional 전통적인   flyer 전단   recommendation 권고, 추천   appropriate 적당한, 적절한   ideal 이상적인   target audience 광고 타깃[대상자]   station 방송국   broadcast 방송하다   commercial 광고   reach 닿다, 이르다   combination 조합   visual 시각 자료   grab 사로잡다   attention 관심   dimension 크기, 규모   suit 적합하다, 어울리다   initial 초기의   follow-up 후속의   based on ~에 기반하여   duration 기간   involved 관련된   approval 승인   final draft 최종안   produce 제작하다

¹⁸⁵수신: Byron 마케팅 고객 서비스
<custserv@byronmarketing.net>
발신: Genevieve Wagner <gwagner@wagner.net>
제목: 광고 캠페인
¹⁸³날짜: 1월 6일

안녕하세요, 저는 Wagner 인형의 사장입니다. ¹⁸³제 사업을 시작한 지 한 달 조금 넘었는데, 이곳에서 그것을 홍보하기 위한 광고 캠페인을 진행해야 할 것 같아요. ¹⁸⁴이 지역의 아이들이 제가 파는 수제 인형들을 아주 잘 가지고 놀 것 같습니다. 그런데 제 제품들에 관해 입소문을 낼 방법을 찾아야 해요. ¹⁸⁵귀사에서 제작한 광고가 Lil' Truckers' 장난감 가게를 유명하게 만들어서 제 업체를 위해서도 똑같이 해주실 수 있기를 바랍니다. 오늘부터 일주일 후에 귀사의 담당자를 만나서 귀사가 제공해줄 수 있는 것에 관해 논의하고 싶습니다. 감사합니다.

진심을 담아,

Genevieve Wagner
Wagner 인형 사장

| 어휘 | owner 소유주, 주인   handmade doll 수제 인형   get the word out 말을 퍼뜨리다, 입소문을 내다   famous 유명한

181. 동의어 문제
팸플릿에서 첫 번째 단락 첫 번째 줄에 있는 단어 "running"과 의미가 가장 유사한 것은
(A) 서두르는
(B) 이동하는
(C) 운영하는
(D) 방송하는
| 해설 | 해당 단어가 들어간 문장은 '브랜드 인지도는 성공적인 업체를 운영하는 열쇠입니다'라고 해석된다. 따라서 '운영하는'이라는 의미를 대체해 쓸 수 있는 (C) operating이 정답이다.

182. NOT True 문제
Byron 마케팅에 관해 암시되지 않은 것은 무엇인가?
(A) 온라인 상담을 제공한다.
(B) 고객들에게 초안을 보여준다.
(C) 맞춤 서비스 플랜을 개발한다.
(D) 여러 플랫폼용의 광고들을 만든다.
| 해설 | 서비스에 포함되는 것으로 인쇄물(Print), 라디오(Radio), 텔레비전(Television), 인터넷(Internet) 네 개의 플랫폼이 제시되어 있는 것에서 (D), 인쇄물 항목에 담당자와 상담하여 적당한 양을 추천받으라고(Consult with one of our representatives for recommendations ~) 한 것과 라디오 항목에 광고를 방송할 방송국을 선택할 수 있다고(You can choose which stations to broadcast your company's commercial on) 한 것, 인터넷 항목에 광고하고 싶은 사이트를 선택하라고(select the sites you want to advertise on) 한 것에서 (C), 마지막 단락에 모든 광고 아이디어들은 최종안이 제작되기 전에 승인을 위해 제시될 것이라고(All of our ad ideas will be presented for approval before final drafts are produced) 한 것에서 (B)를 확인할 수 있다. 따라서 정답은 (A)이다.
| 어휘 | rough draft 초안   develop 개발하다   custom 맞춤의   create 만들어내다
| 패러프레이징 | ·Print / Radio / Television / Internet → multiple platforms
·All of our ad ideas will be presented for approval → shows its customers rough drafts

183. True 문제
Wagner 인형에 관해 제시된 것은 무엇인가?
(A) 이전에 Byron 마케팅과 거래를 했었다.
(B) 수입품들을 전문으로 한다.
(C) 작년에 영업을 시작했다.
(D) 요청에 따라 맞춤형 디자인을 만든다.
| 해설 | 이메일의 날짜가 1월 6일인데(Date: January 6) 이메일 초반부에 사업을 시작한 지 한 달 조금 넘었다고(Just over a month ago I started my business ~) 제시되어 있으므로 정답은 (C)이다.
| 어휘 | do business with ~와 거래하다   specialize in ~을 전문으로 하다   imported goods 수입품   on request 요청에 따라
| 패러프레이징 | started my business → It opened for business

🏠 고난도
184. 연계 문제 – 추론
Wagner 씨는 어떤 옵션에 가장 관심이 있겠는가?
(A) 인쇄물
(B) 라디오
(C) 텔레비전
(D) 인터넷
| 해설 | Wagner 씨가 보낸 이메일에서 자신이 판매하는 수제 인형을 아이들이 아주 잘 가지고 놀 것 같다고(I think that kids in the area would really enjoy the handmade dolls that I sell) 했고, 팸플릿에서 텔레비전 항목에 어린이들과 같은 어린 시청자들에 도달하기 위한 아주 좋은 옵션이라고(This is a great option for reaching young audiences such as children) 했으므로 정답은 (C)이다.

185. 추론 문제
Lil' Truckers' 장난감 가게에 관해 추론할 수 있는 것은 무엇인가?
(A) 손으로 만든 장난감들을 판매한다.

(B) 그 지역에서 가장 성공한 장난감 가게이다.
(C) 사업을 대부분 온라인으로 진행한다.
(D) Byron 마케팅과 계약을 맺고 있다.
| 해설 | 이메일 수신자가 Byron 마케팅 고객 서비스이고(Byron Marketing Customer Service) 이메일 중반부에 귀사에서 제작한 광고가 Lil' Truckers' 장난감 가게를 유명하게 만들었다고(Commercials produced by your company have made Lil' Truckers' Toy Shop famous) 제시되어 있는 것에서 Lil' Truckers' 장난감 가게가 Byron 마케팅과 계약을 맺고 있음을 유추할 수 있으므로 정답은 (D)이다.
| 어휘 | region 지역   have a contract with ~와 계약을 맺고 있다

186-190 다음 광고, 서식, 이메일을 참조하시오.

Hometown 가전제품 · 451 Pine Street
여러분 가정에 필요한 모든 것을 한 번에 한 곳에서!

Hometown 가전제품은 주방과 세탁실 등에서 쓰이는 가전제품을 이 지역 최대 규모로 보유하고 있습니다. [186]저희 두 번째 기념일을 축하하기 위해, 2월 한 달 내내 고객들에게 두 가지 특별한 혜택을 제공합니다. [188]주문서에 NYT1030 코드를 입력하여 무료 배송을 요청하세요. NRL2997 코드를 이용하면 설치비를 50% 할인받을 수도 있습니다. 저희 소식지를 신청한 고객들은 또한 EverShine 가정용 세제 무료 샘플을 받을 것입니다. 등록하려면, www.hometownappliances.com을 방문하세요.

| 어휘 | selection 선택 가능한 것들   appliance 가전제품   laundry room 세탁실   in celebration of ~을 축하하며   anniversary 기념일   special deal 특별 거래, 특가 제품   throughout 내내   claim 요청하다   installation fee 설치비   sign up for ~에 등록하다, 신청하다   cleaner 세제   register 등록하다

Hometown 가전제품 주문 확인 #860175

[187]이름: Johnathan Holt
청구 주소: 317 Terra Cotta Street, Ulen, MN 56585
주문 날짜: 2월 3일   배송 주소: 위와 동일
물품:
 1) MaxHome 커피 머신 $499.00
 2) EasyClean 진공청소기 $120.00
 3) [189]Durham 제빵 기계 $140.00
 4) Kessler 손에 들고 쓰는 푸드 믹서 $69.99

소계: $828.99
[188]판촉 코드 (해당되는 경우):   NYT1030
총액 (배송, 설치 그리고 세금 포함): $878.73

[187]결제: 신용 카드 ***********6767
설치 유형: 없음

주문이 처리되도록 하기 위해 모든 은행 계좌 이체에는 자신의 참조 번호가 표시되어야 함을 유념해 주시기 바랍니다.

교체 보증 Hometown 가전제품을 통해 주문된 제품에 결함이 있을 경우, 무료로 교체해 드릴 것입니다. 환불 정책에 관한 정보는 저희 고객 서비스 팀에 연락해 주세요.

| 어휘 | confirmation 확인   vacuum cleaner 진공청소기   bread-making machine 제빵 기계   handheld 손에 들고 쓰는   food mixer 조리용 믹서   promo code 판촉 코드   applicable 적용되는, 적용 가능한   mark 표시하다   reference number 참조 번호   process 처리하다   replacement 교체, 대체   guarantee 보증   defective 결함이 있는   free of charge 무료로   refund 환불

수신: Hometown 가전제품 <customerservice@hometownappliances.com>
발신: Johnathan Holt <j.holt@readymail.com>
날짜: 2월 10일
제목: 주문 #860175

관계자 귀하:

[189]지난주에 귀사에서 주문한 Durham 제품의 문제를 알리고자 합니다. 전력 케이블이 하부에 제대로 부착되어 있지 않습니다. 플러그를 꽂아 보려고도 하지 않았어요, 그렇게 하는 것이 안전해 보이지 않아서요. [190]이것이 교체 보증에 해당되는지 아니면 그저 환불 대상인지 잘 모르겠습니다. 가능하다면 전자를 선호하는데, 바로 이 기기의 특징들이 마음에 들기 때문입니다. 이것이 우편으로 환불 수표를 받는 것보다 저에게는 훨씬 더 나은 선택입니다. 과거에 수 차례 아무런 문제 없이 Hometown 가전제품을 이용한 적이 있으니, 이 사소한 문제가 귀사의 평소 품질 수준을 손상시키는 것은 아님을 확신합니다.

진심을 담아,

Johnathan Holt

| 어휘 | properly 적절하게   attached to ~에 부착된   plug in 플러그를 꽂다   fall under ~에 해당되다, ~의 책임이다   be subject to ~의 대상이다   refund 환불   the former 전자   feature 특징   particular 특정한   refund check 환불 수표   minor 사소한   be a reflection on ~의 불명예가 되다   level of quality 품질 수준

186. True 문제
Hometown 가전제품에 관해 사실인 것은 무엇인가?
(A) 웹 사이트를 업그레이드했다.
(B) 1년 넘게 영업해 오고 있다.
(C) 신제품들을 출시했다.
(D) 새로운 장소로 이사했다.

| 해설 | 첫 번째 지문 초반부에 두 번째 기념일을 축하하기 위해(In celebration of our second anniversary ~) 특별한 혜택을 제공한다고 했으므로 정답은 (B)이다.
| 어휘 | launch 출시하다

187. 세부 사항을 묻는 문제
Holt 씨는 물건 대금을 어떻게 지불했나?
(A) 매장 적립금으로
(B) 은행 이체로
(C) 수표로
(D) 신용 카드로
| 해설 | 두 번째 지문인 주문 확인서에서 Holt 씨가 주문한 사람인 것을 확인할 수 있고, 결제(Payment) 항목에서 신용 카드로(Credit Card) 결제했음을 알 수 있으므로 정답은 (D)이다.

고난도
188. 연계 문제 - 추론
Holt 씨의 주문에 관해 암시되는 것은?
(A) 무료로 배송이 되었다.
(B) 틀린 가격이 있었다.
(C) 설치비를 할인받았다.
(D) 세금에 적용이 되지 않았다.
| 해설 | Holt 씨의 주문 확인서에서 판촉 코드(Promo code): NYT1030이 확인되는데, 이것을 첫 번째 지문에서 주문서에 NYT1030 코드를 입력하여 무료 배송을 요청하라고(Enter code NYT1030 on your order form to claim free delivery) 제시된 것과 연계하면, Holt 씨는 무료 배송을 받았을 것임을 추론할 수 있으므로 정답은 (A)이다.
| 어휘 | incorrect 옳지 않은, 틀린   discounted 할인된   applicable 적용되는, 적용할 수 있는

189. 연계 문제 - 세부 사항
Holt 씨에 따르면, 어떤 물품에 문제가 있나?
(A) 커피 머신
(B) 진공 청소기
(C) 제빵 기계
(D) 손에 들고 쓰는 푸드 믹서
| 해설 | Holt 씨가 보낸 이메일 도입부에 Durham 제품의 문제를 알리고자 한다고(I would like to report an issue with the Durham product) 제시되어 있고, 주문 확인서에서 Durham 제품은 제빵 기계(Durham bread-making machine)로 확인되므로 정답은 (C)이다.

고난도
190. 세부 사항을 묻는 문제
Holt 씨는 Hometown 가전제품이 무엇을 해주기를 원하는가?
(A) 자신의 온라인 계정에 적립해주는 것
(B) 자신의 우편 주소를 변경하는 것
(C) 교체 제품을 보내주는 것
(D) 기존 주문을 업그레이드하는 것
| 해설 | 이메일에서 제품의 문제를 알린 후, 중반부에 이것이 교체 보증에 해당되는지 아니면 환불 대상인지 잘 모르겠다며, 전자를 선호한다고(I am not sure if this falls under your Replacement Guarantee or if it is just subject to a refund. I would prefer the former,) 한 것에서, Holt 씨는 교체 보증을 원하는 것임을 알 수 있으므로 정답은 (C)이다.
| 어휘 | credit 적립해 주다   existing 기존의
| 패러프레이징 | Replacement Guarantee → Send a replacement product

191-195 다음 이메일, 서식, 기사를 참조하시오.

수신: Goodwin Solutions 직원들
발신: Joanne Pruett
날짜: 9월 12일
제목: 커뮤니케이션 워크숍
첨부: 신청서.docx

¹⁹³Goodwin Solutions가 최소 12개월 이상 회사를 위해 일해온 정규직 직원과 파트 타임 직원들을 위해 10월에 한 달간 커뮤니케이션 워크숍을 개최할 것입니다. 이용 가능한 자리의 수가 제한되어 있으므로, ¹⁹¹워크숍의 어떤 부분도 빠지지 않을 것을 약속할 수 있을 경우에만 등록해 주세요. 그것은 10월의 매주 목요일 오후 6시부터 8시까지 실시될 것이어서, 여러분의 관리자에 의해 배정된 어떤 업무 의무에도 지장을 주지 않을 것입니다. 다양한 주제들이 경험 있는 강사들에 의해 다뤄질 것입니다.

관심이 있으면 첨부된 신청서를 작성하여 r.vaughn@goodwinsol.com으로 Rafael Vaughn에게 늦어도 9월 19일까지 제출해 주세요. ¹⁹²Vaughn 씨가 그 서식들을 평가하여 9월 22일에 합격자들을 선발할 것입니다.

| 어휘 | host 주최하다   spot 자리   sign up 등록하다   miss 빠뜨리다   conduct 실시하다   interfere with ~을 방해하다   obligation 의무   assign 배정하다, 맡기다   supervisor 관리자   a variety of 다양한   lecturer 강사   completed 작성된, 완료된   attached 첨부된   request form 신청서   no later than 늦어도 ~까지   evaluate 평가하다   successful applicant 합격자

커뮤니케이션 워크숍 등록 신청

¹⁹³이름: Tony Henning
부서: 홍보
업무 이메일: t.henning@goodwinsol.com

왜 이 워크숍에 관심이 있나요? ¹⁹⁴제 일의 주된 어려움은 제 국제 고객들과의 의사소통 간극을 처리하는 것인데, 제가 취해야 하는 접근법이 문화에 따라 다르기 때문입니다. 저는 이것에 관해 더 배우고 싶습니다.

워크숍 수업들과 일정이 겹치나요? 아니요

| 어휘 | public relations 홍보　navigate 처리하다, 다루다　gap 간극, 틈　international client 국제 고객　approach 접근법　vary 다르다, 달라지다　depending on ~에 따라　scheduling conflict 일정 충돌, 일정 겹침

Goodwin Solutions 회사 소식
11월 호

워크숍, 대성공으로 여겨지다

직원들의 요청에 응하여, Goodwin Solutions가 커뮤니케이션에 관한 한 달간의 워크숍을 주최했다. Goodwin Solutions의 고참 직원들의 발표와 함께, 4주간의 강의에서 다양한 커뮤니케이션 주제들이 다뤄졌다. "이 프로젝트의 발표자가 되어 영광이었습니다." Kevin Terrell이 말했다. "제 전문 지식을 다른 사람들과 공유할 기회를 주었을 뿐만 아니라, ¹⁹⁵저는 또한 몇몇 직원들을 더 잘 알게 되었습니다."

프로그램 참가자들은 전원이 다른 이들에게 그것을 추천하겠다고 말하며, 워크숍 이후 피드백 설문 조사에서 압도적으로 긍정적인 반응을 보였다. "저는 아주 많이 배웠어요." 홍보 부서에서 일하는 Tony Henning이 말했다. "¹⁹⁴저는 특히 Kristie Fultz의 강연이 좋았는데, 그것이 제 일의 가장 큰 난제에 도움을 주었기 때문이에요, 훨씬 더 자신감을 갖게 되었어요. 게다가 ¹⁹⁵다른 직원들과 인맥을 쌓고 그들과 더 친밀한 관계를 발전시킬 수 있었습니다."

새로운 워크숍을 위한 계획들이 이미 진행 중이고, 세부 사항은 다음 소식지에 발표될 것이다.

| 어휘 | deem 여기다　in response to ~에 응하여　various 다양한　senior 고위의, 상급의　honored 영광스러운　opportunity 기회　expertise 전문 지식　be acquainted with ~를 알게 되다　participant 참가자　overwhelmingly 압도적으로　positive 긍정적인　PR department 홍보 부서　challenge 난제, 도전　confident 자신감 있는　underway 진행 중인

191. True 문제
워크숍에 관해 사실인 것은 무엇인가?
(A) 참가자들은 모든 수업에 참석할 것을 약속해야 한다.
(B) 참가자들은 자신들의 관리자로부터 승인을 받아야 한다.
(C) 회사에서 1년에 한 번 열린다.
(D) 홍보 직원들만을 대상으로 한다.
| 해설 | 이메일 첫 번째 단락에 워크숍의 어떤 부분도 빠지지 않을 것을 약속할 수 있을 경우에만 등록해 달라고(please only sign up if you can promise that you will not miss any parts of the workshop) 제시되어 있으므로 정답은 (A)이다.
| 어휘 | commit 약속하다　get approval from ~로부터 승인을 받다　be intended for ~를 위해 의도되다
| 패러프레이징 | promise that you will not miss any parts of the workshop → commit to attending all sessions

192. 세부 사항을 묻는 문제
프로그램 참가자들은 어떻게 결정될 것인가?
(A) 패널에게 프레젠테이션을 함으로써
(B) 온라인 테스트를 통과함으로써
(C) 그룹 인터뷰에 참석함으로써
(D) Vaughn 씨에 의해 평가됨으로써
| 해설 | 이메일 마지막에 Vaughn 씨가 신청서를 평가하여 합격자들을 선발할 것이라고(Mr. Vaughn will evaluate the forms and choose the successful applicants ~) 제시되어 있으므로 정답은 (D)이다.
| 어휘 | pass 통과하다　assess 평가하다, 사정하다
| 패러프레이징 | Mr. Vaughn will evaluate the forms → being assessed by Mr. Vaughn

🔺고난도
193. 연계 문제 – 추론
Henning 씨에 관해 암시되는 것은 무엇인가?
(A) 승진이 고려되고 있다.
(B) 현재 파트 타임 직원으로 고용되어 있다.
(C) Goodwin Solutions를 위해 1년 이상 일했다.
(D) 최근에 자신의 고객들 중 일부를 잃었다.
| 해설 | Henning 씨는 두 번째 지문인 서식에 나타난 신청자인데, 워크숍 신청과 관련하여 이메일 도입부에 Goodwin Solutions가 최소 12개월 이상 회사를 위해 일해온 직원들을 위해 커뮤니케이션 워크숍을 개최할 것이라고(Goodwin Solutions will host a month-long communication workshop ~ employees who have worked for the company for at least twelve months) 제시되어 있으므로 정답은 (C)이다.
| 어휘 | consider 고려하다　promotion 승진
| 패러프레이징 | have worked for the company for at least twelve months → has worked for Goodwin Solutions for more than a year

🔺고난도
194. 연계 문제 – 추론
Fultz 씨에 관해 암시되는 것은 무엇인가?
(A) 다음 워크숍을 위한 일정표를 만들 것이다.
(B) Terrell 씨의 직무들 중 일부를 대신했다.
(C) 문화적 차이에 대해 발표를 했다.
(D) 마케팅 방법들에 관한 많은 경험을 가지고 있다.
| 해설 | 기사에서 Tony Henning이 특히 Fultz 씨의 강연이 일의 가장 큰 난제에 도움을 주었기 때문에 특히 좋았다고(I was particularly pleased with Kristie Fultz's talk, which helped me with the biggest challenge of my job) 했는데, 두 번째 지문인 워크숍 신청서에서 Tony Henning은 국제 고객들과의 의사소통 간극을 처리하는 것이 주된 어려움이라며, 취해야 하는 접근법이 문화에 따라 다르기 때문이라고(~ as the approach I should take varies depending on the culture) 한 것과 연계해 볼 때, Fultz 씨는 Henning 씨가 어려움을 느끼는 문화적 차이에 관해 발표한 것으로 유추할 수 있으므로 정답은 (C)이다.
| 어휘 | create 만들다, 창조하다　duty 임무, 직무　method 방법

195. 세부 사항을 묻는 문제

Terrell 씨와 Henning 씨 둘 다 언급하는 워크숍의 이점은 무엇인가?
(A) 자신감을 키우는 것
(B) 동료들을 알게 되는 것
(C) 매출 수치를 향상시키는 것
(D) 지식을 공유하는 것

| 해설 | 기사 첫 번째 단락에서 Kevin Terrell은 몇몇 직원들을 더 잘 알게 되었다고(I became better acquainted with some of the staff members) 했고, 두 번째 단락에서 Tony Henning은 다른 직원들과 인맥을 쌓고 그들과 더 친밀한 관계를 발전시킬 수 있었다고(I was able to network with other staff members and develop closer relationships with them) 했으므로 정답은 (B)이다.

| 어휘 | confidence 자신감 sales figures 매출 수치 knowledge 지식

| 패러프레이징 | became better acquainted with some of the staff members / was able to network with other staff members and develop closer relationships with them → Getting to know coworkers

196-200 다음 기사, 편지, 쿠폰을 참조하시오.

식목일을 기념하는 나무 심기 프로젝트
Carol Rollins 작성

4월 18일—Trevino 시는 나무가 공중 보건과 환경에 미치는 영향을 인식하는 휴일인 식목일을 기념하기 위해 사상 최초의 행사를 개최할 것이다. 도시 전역에 있는 4개의 공원들에서 나무들이 심어질 것인데, 이 나무들은 지방 자치 기금과 민간 기부금의 결합으로 구입되었다. 나무를 새로 심고 물을 주는 것뿐만 아니라 나무를 심을 지역을 개간하고 준비하기 위해 자원봉사자들이 필요하다. 자원봉사자로 참여하는 사람들은 자신의 소유지에 심을 무료 나무 쿠폰을 받을 것이다. ²⁰⁰지역 사회 단체들도 프로젝트에 참여하도록 권장되는데, 이 경우 구성원들과 나눠 가질 나무 10그루 쿠폰이 단체장들에게 주어질 것이다. 나무 심기는 다음 일정에 따라 진행될 것이다:

¹⁹⁶4월 25일 월요일: Maxwell 공원, 피크닉 구역
4월 27일 수요일: Spring 공원, 북쪽 주차장 인근
4월 29일 금요일: Avoca 공원, 조깅로를 따라
4월 30일 토요일: Cedar 공원, 동쪽 놀이터 인근

더 많은 정보는 www.trevinocity.gov/events를 방문하면 된다.

| 어휘 | commemorate 기념하다 Arbor Day 식목일 recognize 인식하다 impact 영향 public health 공중 보건 environment 환경 combination 결합 municipal 지방 자치의 private 개인적인, 민간의 donation 기부 volunteer 자원봉사자; 자원봉사를 하다 individual 개인 participate 참여하다 voucher 쿠폰, 상품권 property 소유지, 부동산 be encouraged to ~하도록 권장되다 take part in ~에 참여하다 share 나누다, 공유하다 playground 놀이터

Anastasia Whitcomb
207 Timbercrest Road

Omaha, NE 68102

Whitcomb 씨에게,

¹⁹⁶식목일 나무 심기 프로젝트의 첫날에 참여해 주셔서 감사드립니다. 귀하와 같은 자원봉사자들로 인해, 건강에 좋은 나무들의 이로움을 퍼트려 이곳 Trevino 시의 환경을 개선하는 저희 꿈을 ¹⁹⁷실현할 수 있었습니다. 신선한 산소와 그늘부터 새와 곤충들을 위한 자연 서식지까지, 나무는 진정으로 끊임없이 주는 선물입니다. Eastside 묘목장에서 쓸 수 있는 쿠폰이 동봉된 것을 확인하실 수 있으실 것입니다.

¹⁹⁸행사의 사진들을 가능한 한 많이 보여 드리고 싶으니, 뭔가 공유할 것이 있다면 www.trevinocity.gov/events를 방문해 그것들을 업로드해주세요. 이 행사를 연례 전통으로 만들 계획이니, 내년 행사에 참여하는 것을 고려해 주시기를 바랍니다.

안부를 전하며,

Lonzo Tocci

| 어휘 | participation 참여 realize one's dream 꿈을 실현하다 improve 개선하다 unleash 속박을 풀다, 촉발시키다 benefit 혜택, 이로움 health-giving 건강에 좋은 oxygen 산소 shade 그늘 insect 곤충 enclosed 동봉된 annual 연례의 tradition 전통 consider 고려하다

Eastside 묘목장 제품 쿠폰

이 쿠폰 소지자는 ___²⁰⁰무료 묘목 10그루___ 를 받을 수 있습니다.

쿠폰은 5월 1일부터 유효하며 재고가 있는 상기 제품 유형에 이용 가능합니다. ¹⁹⁹다른 할인 행사들과 함께 사용할 수 없습니다. Victoria Lane 지점은 나무들을 취급하지 않으니, Union Street 지점에서만 유효합니다.

___Lonzo Tocci [Trevino 시]___ 에 의해 ___²⁰⁰Anastasia Whitcomb___ 에게 발행됨

코드: 3959

| 어휘 | sapling 묘목 valid 유효한 in stock 재고가 있는 offer 할인 branch 지점 carry 취급하다

196. 연계 문제 – 세부 사항

Whitcomb 씨는 프로젝트를 위해 어디에서 자원봉사를 했나?
(A) Avoca 공원에서
(B) Cedar 공원에서
(C) Maxwell 공원에서
(D) Spring 공원에서

| 해설 | 두 번째 지문인 Whitcomb 씨에게 보낸 편지 도입부에서 식목일 나무 심기 프로젝트 첫날에 참여해 줘서 감사드린다고(Thank you for your participation on the first day of our Arbor Day tree-planting project) 한 것과, 첫 번째 지문인 기사의 일정에서 첫날의 장소로 Maxwell 공원이(Monday, April 25: Maxwell Park) 제시된 것을 연계하면 정답은 (C)이다.

🏠 고난도

197. 동의어 문제

편지에서 첫 번째 단락 두 번째 줄에 있는 단어 "realize"와 의미가 가장 유사한 것은

(A) 달성하다
(B) 이해하다
(C) 알아차리다
(D) 확인하다

| 해설 | 해당 단어가 들어간 문장은 '이곳 Trevino 시의 환경을 개선하는 저희 꿈을 실현할 수 있었다'라고 해석된다. 따라서 이와 가장 유사한 '달성하다, 성취하다'라는 뜻의 (A) achieve가 정답이다.

198. 세부 사항을 묻는 문제

Tocci 씨가 Whitcomb 씨에게 하도록 요청하는 것은?
(A) Eastside 묘목장에 있는 물품들을 예약하는 것
(B) 몇몇 사진들을 이메일로 보내는 것
(C) 의견을 공유하는 것
(D) 웹 사이트에 이미지를 게시하는 것

| 해설 | 편지의 두 번째 단락 도입부에 발신자인 Tocci 씨가 수신자인 Whitcomb 씨에게 행사의 사진들을 가능한 한 많이 보여 주고 싶으니, 공유할 것이 있다면 www.trevinocity.gov/events를 방문해 업로드해 달라고(~ show as many pictures as possible from the event, so if you have any to share, please visit www.trevinocity.gov/events to upload them) 했으므로 정답은 (D)이다.

| 어휘 | opinion 의견   post 게시하다
| 패러프레이징 | ·pictures → images
·upload → Post

199. True 문제

쿠폰에 관해 사실인 것은?
(A) 온라인으로 제출되어야 한다.
(B) 다른 할인 행사들과 같이 결합될 수 없다.
(C) 만료일은 5월 1일이다.
(D) 각각 다른 두 지점에서 이용될 수 있다.

| 해설 | 세 번째 지문인 쿠폰에 다른 할인 행사들과 함께 사용할 수 없다고(Not for use with other offers) 명시되어 있으므로 정답은 (B)이다.

| 어휘 | combine with ~와 결합하다   expiration date 만료일, 유통 기한
| 패러프레이징 | Not for use with → cannot be combined with

🏠 고난도

200. 연계 문제 – 추론

Whitcomb 씨에 관해 암시되는 것은 무엇인가?

(A) 그녀는 자신의 첫 쿠폰을 잃어버렸다.
(B) 그녀는 단체장이었다.
(C) 그녀는 내년에 참여할 계획이다.
(D) 그녀는 특별 주문을 했다.

| 해설 | Whitcomb 씨는 쿠폰을 받은 사람으로(Issued to Anastasia Whitcomb), 쿠폰 내용에서 무료 묘목 10그루를(10 complimentary tree saplings) 받은 것으로 확인되고, 기사에 지역 사회 단체들도 프로젝트에 참여하도록 권장되며, 이 경우 구성원들과 나눠 가질 나무 10그루 쿠폰이 단체장들에게 주어질 것이라고(in which case the group leader will be given a voucher for ten trees ~) 제시되어 있는 것을 연계해 볼 때, Whitcomb 씨는 프로젝트에 지역 사회 단체로 참여해 나무 10그루 무료 쿠폰을 받은 단체장이었음을 알 수 있으므로 정답은 (B)이다.

TEST 08

PART 5

101 (C)	102 (B)	103 (A)	104 (D)	105 (B)
106 (B)	107 (B)	108 (C)	109 (A)	110 (C)
111 (A)	112 (B)	113 (C)	114 (B)	115 (B)
116 (B)	117 (C)	118 (D)	119 (B)	120 (A)
121 (D)	122 (C)	123 (A)	124 (D)	125 (C)
126 (B)	127 (A)	128 (D)	129 (B)	130 (D)

PART 6

131 (B)	132 (D)	133 (B)	134 (C)	135 (B)
136 (C)	137 (D)	138 (A)	139 (D)	140 (B)
141 (C)	142 (D)	143 (B)	144 (C)	145 (C)
146 (D)				

PART 7

147 (C)	148 (D)	149 (C)	150 (B)	151 (A)
152 (C)	153 (B)	154 (B)	155 (D)	156 (A)
157 (A)	158 (B)	159 (D)	160 (C)	161 (A)
162 (C)	163 (D)	164 (B)	165 (A)	166 (C)
167 (C)	168 (A)	169 (C)	170 (D)	171 (B)
172 (C)	173 (D)	174 (A)	175 (B)	176 (B)
177 (B)	178 (C)	179 (C)	180 (C)	181 (C)
182 (D)	183 (B)	184 (B)	185 (C)	186 (C)
187 (B)	188 (D)	189 (C)	190 (D)	191 (A)
192 (D)	193 (C)	194 (B)	195 (D)	196 (C)
197 (A)	198 (C)	199 (D)	200 (A)	

PART 5

101. 인칭 대명사
귀하의 신용카드를 분실하거나 도난당한 경우, 즉시 이 24시간 고객 서비스 직통 전화로 저희에게 전화해 주세요.
| 해설 | 타동사 call 뒤 목적어 자리에 빈칸이 있으므로 빈칸에는 목적격 인칭 대명사와 재귀 대명사가 올 수 있다. 재귀 대명사는 주어와 목적어가 동일한 경우 목적어 자리에 올 수 있지만, 제시된 문장은 명령문으로, 명령문에서 생략된 주어는 you이므로 (D) ourselves는 오답이다. 따라서 목적격 인칭 대명사인 (C) us가 정답이다.
| 어휘 | immediately 즉시   hotline 직통 전화   lost 분실된   stolen 도난당한

102. 형용사 자리 - 주격 보어
팀원들은 프로젝트 관리자가 마감일을 4월 1일에서 4월 10일로 연장한 것을 고마워한다.
| 해설 | 빈칸은 be동사 are 뒤에 보어가 들어갈 자리이므로 동사 형태인 (A) thank와 (D) thanks, 부사인 (C) thankfully는 모두 답이 될 수 없고, 보어 자리에 올 수 있는 형용사인 (B) thankful이 정답이다.
| 어휘 | extend 연장하다   deadline 마감일, 마감 기한

103. 동사 자리
Henderson 씨는 방문객들은 방문 중에 항상 신분증 배지를 착용해야 한다고 주장한다.
| 해설 | 빈칸은 that절을 목적어로 가지는 문장의 동사가 들어갈 자리이므로 동사인 (A) insists가 정답이다.
| 어휘 | ID badge 신분증 배지   at all times 항상, 늘

104. 형용사 어휘
Marron 거리에 위치해 있는 주차장은 추가 공지가 있을 때까지 폐쇄될 것이다.
| 해설 | 빈칸은 명사 notice를 수식해줄 형용사가 들어갈 자리로, 문맥상 '추가 공지가 있을 때까지'라는 의미로 전개되는 것이 적절하므로 '추가의, 그 이상의'라는 뜻의 (D) further가 정답이다.
| 어휘 | parking lot 주차장   located on ~에 위치한   notice 공지   effective 효율적인, 효과적인   constant 지속적인, 끊임없는   periodic 주기적인, 정기적인   further 추가의, 그 이상의

105. 현재 분사 vs. 과거 분사
이 직책에 관심 있는 구직자들은 자기소개서 및 추천서와 함께 자신들의 이력서를 Ashley Waller에게 이메일로 보내야 한다.
| 해설 | be동사 뒤에 있는 빈칸에 명사가 오려면 주어와 동격이 되어야 하는데, 주어인 Job seekers와 (C) interests와 (D) interest는 동격이 될 수 없으므로 오답이고, '관심 있는 구직자들'이라는 의미가 되어야 하므로 'be interested in(~에 관심 있다)' 구문을 완성하는 (B) interested가 정답이다. (A) interesting은 '재미있는, 흥미로운'이라는 뜻으로 문맥상 적절치 않다.
| 어휘 | job seeker 구직자   résumé 이력서   cover letter 자기소개서   reference 추천서

106. 등위 접속사
소프트웨어가 최근에 업데이트되었고, 그래서 메뉴 항목에 몇 가지 변화가 있다.
| 해설 | 빈칸 앞뒤로 두 개의 완전한 절이 있으므로, 빈칸은 두 절을 연결해줄 접속사가 들어갈 자리이다. 따라서 부사인 (A) lastly와 (D) then은 오답이고, 문맥상 뒤의 절이 앞의 절의 결과로 전개되는 것이 적절하므로 (B) so가 정답이다.
| 어휘 | recently 최근에

107. 부사 자리 - 형용사 수식
그 약물에 대한 정보는 병원의 웹 사이트를 통해 환자들이 쉽게 이용할 수 있다.
| 해설 | be동사 is와 그 보어인 형용사 available 사이에 빈칸이 있으므로, 빈칸은 형용사를 수식할 부사가 들어갈 자리이다. 따라서 '손쉽게, 쉽게'라는 뜻의 부사인 (B) readily가 정답이다.
| 어휘 | drug 약물, 약   available 이용 가능한   patient 환자

108. 명사 어휘
여러 차례 주문품을 너무 익은 과일들로 받은 후에, Beechwood 출장 연회의 주인은 새로운 식품 공급업체를 찾으려고 노력했다.
| 해설 | 빈칸은 타동사 find의 목적어로 앞의 명사 food와 함께 복합 명사를 이루

는 명사가 들어갈 자리로, 문맥상 '새로운 식품 공급업체를 찾으려고'라는 의미로 전개되는 것이 적절하므로 '공급업체, 공급자'라는 뜻의 (C) supplier가 정답이다.
| 어휘 | overly ripe 너무 익은   presenter 발표자, 진행자   container 용기, 그릇   supplier 공급업체, 공급자   diner 식사 손님

109. 형용사 어휘
Spot-on 배송은 상승하는 연료비를 최소화하기 위해 하이브리드 차량들로 바꿀 것이다.
| 해설 | 빈칸은 minimize의 목적어인 복합 명사 fuel expenses를 수식해줄 형용사가 들어갈 자리로, 문맥상 '상승하는 연료비를 최소화하기 위해'라는 의미로 전개되는 것이 적절하므로 '상승하는'이라는 뜻의 (A) rising이 정답이다.
| 어휘 | spot-on 정확한, 정확히   switch 바꾸다, 전환하다   vehicle 차량   minimize 최소화하다   fuel expenses 연료비   limited 제한된   yielding 유연한

110. 동사 어휘
그 교육의 시작 시간은 Rudd 씨가 모두의 일정을 확인할 때까지 결정되지 않을 것이다.
| 해설 | 빈칸은 수동태 동사를 완성해줄 과거 분사가 들어갈 자리로, 문맥상 '모두의 일정을 확인할 때까지 결정되지 않을 것이다'라는 의미로 전개되는 것이 적절하므로 (C) decided가 정답이다.
| 어휘 | training 교육, 훈련   conclude 끝나다, 끝내다   persuade 설득하다   decide 결정하다   entitle 자격을 주다

111. 전치사 어휘
작가 Betty Glynn은 여러 텔레비전 인터뷰에 참여함으로써 자신의 새 소설에 대한 관심을 불러일으켰다.
| 해설 | 빈칸은 동명사 participating을 목적어로 받는 전치사가 들어갈 자리로, 문맥상 '인터뷰에 참여함으로써 관심을 불러일으켰다'라는 의미로 전개되는 것이 적절하므로 by+-ing(~함으로써) 구문을 완성하는 (A) by가 정답이다.
| 어휘 | author 작가, 저자   generate 발생시키다, 만들어 내다   interest 관심   novel 소설   participate 참여하다

112. 부사 자리 – 동사 수식
모든 자금은 잘 계획된 예산에 따라 현명하게 분배되고 사용되어야 한다.
| 해설 | 수동태 동사 뒤에 빈칸이 있고, 빈칸이 없어도 빠진 문장 성분이 없는 완전한 문장이므로, 빈칸에는 동사를 수식하는 부사가 와야 한다. 따라서 '빈틈없이, 현명하게'라는 뜻의 (B) wisely가 정답이다.
| 어휘 | fund 자금   allot 배분하다   budget 예산   wisdom 지혜, 현명함

113. 명사 자리 – 어휘
잠시 관찰한 후에, Wickham 씨는 연단에 있는 표지에 오타가 있다는 것을 알아차렸다.
| 해설 | 빈칸은 전치사 of의 목적어가 될 명사가 들어갈 자리이므로 형용사인 (B) observative와 동사인 (D) observe는 오답이고, 문맥상 '잠시 관찰한 후에'라는 의미로 전개되는 것이 적절하므로 '관찰'이라는 뜻의 (C) observation이 정답이다.
| 어휘 | realize 알아차리다, 깨닫다   sign 신호, 표지   podium 연단   misprint 오자, 오타   observer 관찰자   observative 관찰적인   observation 관찰   observe 관찰하다

114. 전치사 어휘
Crosby 제조사는 작년에 파산할 뻔했지만, 새로운 CEO가 회사를 호전시켰다.
| 해설 | be동사 was와 명사 bankruptcy 사이에 빈칸이 있는데, 주어인 Crosby Manufacturing과 bankruptcy가 동격이 될 수 없는 것으로 볼 때, 빈칸에는 이 명사와 함께 보어가 될 수 있는 전치사구를 완성해줄 전치사가 들어가야 함을 알 수 있다. 따라서 '파산할 뻔했지만'이라는 의미가 되도록 'be close to(~할 뻔하다, ~에 접근해 있다)'라는 표현을 완성해줄 (B) close to가 정답이다.
| 어휘 | bankruptcy 파산, 파탄   turn around (경기 등을) 호전시키다   nearby 인근의

115. 부사 자리 – 동사 수식
전문가들은 Belleview 호텔을 Austin의 비즈니스 여행자들에게 최고의 가치로 널리 간주한다.
| 해설 | 주어 Experts와 동사 regard 사이에 빈칸이 있으므로 빈칸은 동사를 수식하는 부사 자리이다. 따라서 '널리 간주한다'라는 의미를 완성해줄 '널리, 폭넓게'라는 뜻의 부사인 (B) widely가 정답이다.
| 어휘 | regard A as B A를 B로 간주하다, 여기다   value 가치   business traveler 비즈니스 여행자, 출장자   widen 넓히다, 넓어지다

116. 부사 어휘
대회의실은 영업 팀과 재무 팀 전체가 한번에 앉을 만큼 충분히 크다.
| 해설 | 빈칸은 형용사 large를 후치 수식해줄 부사가 들어갈 자리로, 문맥상 '충분히 크다'라는 의미로 전개되는 것이 적절하므로 '충분히'라는 뜻의 후치 수식 부사인 (B) enough가 정답이다.
| 어휘 | entire 전체의   finance team 재무 팀

117. 형용사 자리 – 명사 수식
Russell 씨는 그녀의 의사가 제한적인 식이 요법을 하라고 했기 때문에 연회에 참석하지 않았다.
| 해설 | 관사 a와 명사 diet 사이에 빈칸이 있으므로, 빈칸은 명사를 수식하는 형용사 자리이다. 따라서 '제한적인'이라는 뜻의 형용사인 (C) restrictive가 정답이다. 명사 앞에 명사가 올 수 있지만 restriction diet는 의미상 부적절하므로 (A)는 오답이다.
| 어휘 | banquet 연회   put A on a diet 식이 요법을 하도록 하다   restriction 제한, 규제   restrict 제한하다, 규정하다   restrictive 제한적인, 한정적인   restrictively 제한적으로

118. 명사 어휘
전시회의 대규모 개회식 후에, 주요 기부자들을 위한 비공개 리셉션이 있을 것이다.
| 해설 | 빈칸은 앞의 형용사 private의 수식을 받는 명사가 들어갈 자리로, 문맥상 '비공개 리셉션이 있을 것이다'라는 의미로 전개되는 것이 적절하므로 '리셉션, 환영 연회'라는 뜻의 (D) reception이 정답이다.
| 어휘 | following ~ 후에, 다음의   exhibit 전시회   private 비공개의, 사적인   donor 기부자   malfunction 오작동, 고장   direction 방향, 지시

occupation 직업, 점령   reception 리셉션, 환영 연회

🏠 고난도
119. 재귀 대명사
Sheila Slater는 청중들이 직접 작성한 질문을 기반으로 강연을 했다.
| 해설 | 완전한 문장 뒤에 있는 빈칸은 문장 구조에 영향을 주지 않는 강조 용법의 재귀 대명사가 들어갈 자리로, the audience members를 강조하는 재귀 대명사가 들어가야 하므로 (B) themselves가 정답이다.
| 어휘 | be based on ~을 기반으로 하다   audience member 청중, 관객

120. 부사 자리 - 문장 수식
항공권 가격이 예산을 훨씬 초과했기 때문에, 마케팅 팀은 대신에 학회에 기차를 타고 갔다.
| 해설 | 빈칸이 없어도 이유의 부사절 뒤에 주절이 연결된 완전한 문장이 되는 것으로 볼 때, 빈칸에는 문장 구조에 지장을 주지 않으며 수식 역할을 하는 부사가 들어가야 함을 알 수 있다. 따라서 전치사인 (B) against와 (C) despite는 답이 될 수 없고, '(비행기를 타는) 대신에 기차를 타고 갔다'라는 의미를 완성해줄 '대신에'라는 뜻의 (A) instead가 정답이다.
| 어휘 | exceed 초과하다, 넘다   budget 예산   conference 학회

121. 동사의 형태
Greenwood의 교통 상황이 더 나빠지게 되어 시 공무원들에 의해 다루어져야 한다.
| 해설 | Traffic conditions가 주어이고, 빈칸은 문장의 본동사가 들어갈 자리이므로 준동사인 (A) growing과 (B) to grow는 오답이고, 문맥상 '더 나빠지게 되어 공무원들에 의해 다루어져야 한다'라는 의미가 되는 것이 적절하므로 현재 완료 시제 동사인 (D) have grown이 정답이다.
| 어휘 | traffic conditions 교통 상황   address 다루다   city official 시 공무원

122. 관계 대명사
새로운 제안에 대한 문자 메시지 알림은 저희의 알림 서비스를 신청하신 분들이 이용할 수 있습니다.
| 해설 | 빈칸부터 service까지가 앞에 있는 those를 수식하는 구조이므로 빈칸은 관계 대명사 자리이다. 또한 빈칸 뒤에 주어가 빠져 있고, 수식을 받는 those는 사람이므로 사람 명사를 수식하는 주격 관계 대명사인 (C) who가 정답이다. those who(~인 사람들)를 하나의 덩어리 표현으로 알아 두자.
| 어휘 | text message alert 문자 메시지 알림   sign up for ~를 신청하다, ~에 등록하다   reminder 상기시키는 것

🏠 고난도
123. 부사 어휘
이전에 우체국이었던 Granger 빌딩이 최근에 댄스 스튜디오로 개조되었다.
| 해설 | 빈칸은 명사구 a post office를 수식할 부사가 들어갈 자리로, 문맥상 개조된 건물에 관해 '이전에 우체국이었던'이라는 의미로 전개되는 것이 적절하므로 '이전에'라는 뜻의 (A) Formerly가 정답이다.
| 어휘 | be converted to ~로 개조되다   formerly 이전에   solely 단독으로   needlessly 불필요하게   rarely 드물게

🏠 고난도
124. 동사 어휘
Pacheo의 시장은 Kemper 공원에 있는 분수를 시의 지역 소방관들에게 헌정하려고 한다.
| 해설 | 빈칸은 문장의 동사가 들어갈 자리로, 문맥상 '시장은 분수를 헌정하려고 한다'라는 의미로 전개되는 것이 적절하므로 '~하려고 하다'라는 뜻의 (B) intends가 정답이다.
| 어휘 | mayor 시장   dedicate A to B A를 B에게 바치다   fountain 분수   firefighter 소방관   declare 선언하다   intend ~하려고 하다, 의도하다   refer 참조하다   signify 의미하다

125. to부정사
대형 이삿짐 트럭을 합법적으로 운전하기 위해서는 주에서 발급하는 상업용 면허증이 필요하다.
| 해설 | 빈칸 앞에는 완전한 절이, 뒤에는 동사 원형이 제시되어 있으므로, 바로 뒤에 동사 원형이 올 수 없는 부사 (A) sometimes, 전치사 (B) regarding, 접속사 (D) as soon as는 모두 오답이다. 또한 문맥상으로도 빈칸 뒤의 내용은 앞의 절의 목적이 되므로 목적을 나타내는 to부정사 구문인 (C) in order to가 정답이다.
| 어휘 | commercial 상업적인   license 면허증, 허가   issue 발급하다, 발행하다   state 주   operate 가동하다, 조작하다   legally 합법적으로

126. 명사 자리 - 어휘
새로 고용된 인턴들은 자신들의 책무에 편안하게 될 때까지 지속적인 감독을 필요로 할 것이다.
| 해설 | 빈칸은 앞에 있는 타동사 require의 목적어이자 형용사 ongoing의 수식을 받는 명사가 들어갈 자리이므로 '감독'이라는 뜻의 명사인 (B) supervision이 정답이다.
| 어휘 | ongoing 지속적인, 계속되는   comfortable 편안한   responsibility 책무, 책임   supervisor 관리자   supervision 감독, 관리   supervise 감독하다, 관리하다

🏠 고난도
127. 부사절 접속사
Humphrey 은행은 불필요한 서류 작업을 없애면서 고객들에게 계속 소식을 알리기 위해 일하고 있다.
| 해설 | 빈칸 앞에는 완전한 절이, 뒤에는 분사 구문이 제시되어 있는 것으로 볼 때, 분사 구문을 이끌 수 없는 부사인 (D) therefore는 오답이고, 문맥상 '서류 작업을 없애면서 소식을 알리기 위해 일하고 있다'라는 의미로 동시 상황을 나타내는 구문을 완성해줄 부사절 접속사인 (B) while이 정답이다.
| 어휘 | keep A informed A에게 계속 소식을 알리다   eliminate 없애다, 제거하다   unnecessary 불필요한   paperwork 서류, 서류 작업

128. 형용사 어휘
신입 직원들은 60일의 수습 기간이 끝난 후에 계약 조건을 재협상할 자격이 있다.
| 해설 | 빈칸은 be동사 are의 보어가 될 형용사가 들어갈 자리로, 문맥상 '수습 기간이 끝난 후에 재협상할 자격이 있다'라는 의미로 전개되는 것이 적절하므로 '자격이 있는'이라는 뜻의 (D) eligible이 정답이다.
| 어휘 | renegotiate 재협상하다   contract term 계약 조건   trial period

수습 기간   completed 완료된, 마무리된   introductory 소개의, 서두의
familiar 익숙한, 친숙한   strict 엄격한   eligible 자격이 있는

129. 명사 자리 – 전치사의 목적어
상점 소유주의 상당한 낙관주의에도 불구하고, 대규모 개장식의 참가자 수가 많지 않았다.
| 해설 | 빈칸은 전치사 despite의 목적어 자리이며, 앞에 있는 형용사 considerable의 수식을 받는 명사가 들어갈 자리이므로 '낙관주의'라는 뜻의 명사인 (B) optimism이 정답이다.
| 어휘 | considerable 상당한   turnout 참가자 수   optimistic 낙관적인   optimism 낙관주의   optimize 낙관하다, 최적화하다   optimistically 낙관적으로

🔼 고난도
130. 동명사 자리 – 주어
퍼레이드로 도시의 설립일을 축하하는 것은 거의 100년 전으로 거슬러 올라가는 전통이다.
| 해설 | 빈칸 뒤에 명사구 the town's founding day와 문장의 동사인 is가 있는 것으로 볼 때, 빈칸에는 뒤에 있는 명사구를 목적어로 가지며 is의 주어 역할을 할 수 있는 동명사가 들어가야 함을 알 수 있으므로 (D) Celebrating이 정답이다.
| 어휘 | founding day 창립일   tradition 전통   go back 거슬러 올라가다   celebrate 축하하다, 기념하다   celebration 축하, 기념

PART 6

131-134 다음 광고를 참조하시오.

수신: Gladys Wheeler <g.wheeler@wheeler-studio.com>
발신: James Blackwell <blackwell_j@hammettdept.com>
날짜: 1월 23일
제목: Hammett 백화점

Wheeler 씨 귀하,

다가오는 겨울 시즌을 위한 재킷을 디자인해 주시겠다는 귀하의 의사를 확정해 주셔서 정말 기쁩니다. ¹³¹저는 귀하의 온라인 카탈로그에 있는 아이템들에 깊은 인상을 받았습니다. 그래서 이 프로젝트를 귀하와 함께 작업하는 것이 특히 흥분됩니다. 첫 번째 단계로, 모여서 색상과 기준 소매 가격에 관한 생각들을 브레인스토밍했으면 합니다. 저희 백화점은 ¹³²최신 유행 의류로 알려져 있기 때문에, 저희는 꼭 트렌드를 따르고 싶습니다. 저희 매장의 보조 구매자인 Diana Keasler가 회의에 저희와 ¹³³함께할 것입니다. 예비로 그린 그림들을 ¹³⁴봐주시면 감사하겠습니다. 귀하에게 어느 날짜가 좋을지 알려주세요.

진심으로,

James Blackwell

| 어휘 | confirm 확정하다, 확인하다   intention 의사, 의향   upcoming 다가오는, 곧 있을   especially 특히   exciting 흥분시키는, 신나는   price point 기준 소매 가격   be known for ~로 알려져 있다   follow 따르다   assistant buyer 보조 구매자   appreciate 감사하다, 고마워하다   preliminary 예비의   drawing 그림

🔼 고난도
131. 알맞은 문장 고르기
(A) 이 결정을 내리는 데는 여러 가지 방법이 있습니다.
(B) 저는 귀하의 온라인 카탈로그에 있는 아이템들에 깊은 인상을 받았습니다.
(C) 첨부된 것에서 필요한 변경 사항이 담긴 계약서를 보실 것입니다.
(D) 저는 이미 제 의류에 관해 많은 칭찬을 받았습니다.
| 해설 | 뒤이어 결과를 나타내는 접속 부사 Therefore로 시작하는 문장이 제시되어 있는 것으로 볼 때, 앞에는 그러한 이유가 될 수 있는 내용의 문장이 들어가야 함을 알 수 있다. 따라서 디자이너의 아이템들에 깊은 인상을 받은 사실을 전하는 문장이 그 이유로 적절하므로 (B)가 정답이다.
| 어휘 | decision 결정   be impressed with ~에 깊은 인상을 받다   attached 첨부된   contract 계약서   necessary 필요한   compliment 칭찬

132. 형용사 자리 – 명사 수식
| 해설 | 소유격 its와 명사 clothing 사이에 빈칸이 있으므로, 빈칸은 명사를 수식하는 형용사 자리이다. 따라서 '최신 유행의, 유행하는'이라는 뜻의 형용사인 (D) fashionable이 정답이다.

133. 동사 어휘
| 해설 | 빈칸은 문장의 동사가 들어갈 자리로, 뒤에 제시된 목적어 us와 연결되어 문맥상 '회의에 저희와 함께할 것이다'라는 의미로 전개되는 것이 적절하므로 '함께하다, 참여하다'라는 뜻의 (B) join이 정답이다.
| 어휘 | undergo 겪다   remind 상기시키다

🔼 고난도
134. 동명사 자리 – 동사의 목적어
| 해설 | 빈칸은 동사 appreciate의 목적어 자리로, appreciate는 동명사를 목적어로 취하는 동사이므로 동명사인 (C) viewing이 정답이다.

135-138 다음 편지를 참조하시오.

Webster 시 거주민 귀하,

Webster 시립 도서관 시스템은 오신 분들이 공부하고, 읽고, 연구를 하기에 편안한 환경을 ¹³⁵조성하기 위해 노력합니다. 이런 관점에서, 저희 Hollis 거리 지점에 개조를 할 예정입니다. 그 프로젝트는 총 6개월 ¹³⁶동안 두 단계 공사로 구성될 것입니다.

그 작업은 2월 16일에 시작될 것이고 지역 회사인 Benley 디자인에 의해 수행될 것입니다. 도서관의 일부 구역이 폐쇄될 것이고, 시끄러운 장비가 작동될 것입니다. ¹³⁷오시는 분들께 끼칠 모든 방해에 대해 유감스럽게 생각합니다. 조용한 환경이 필요하시면, 다른 장소들은 정규 개관 ¹³⁸시간 동안 이용이 가능할 것입니다.

진심으로,

Douglas Braun
Webster 시립 도서관 시스템 관리 책임자

| 어휘 | resident 거주민   strive 노력하다, 분투하다   comfortable 편안한, 편한   environment 환경   patron 고객   conduct 수행하다, 하다   in light of ~의 관점에서, ~에 비추어   renovation 개조   location 지점   consist of ~로 구성되다   phase 단계   construction 공사, 건설   carry out 수행하다, 시행하다   section 구역, 부분   noisy 시끄러운   equipment 장비   be in operation 작동/가동 중에 있다

135. to부정사 자리 – 동사의 목적어
| 해설 | 빈칸은 동사 strive의 목적어 자리로, strive는 to부정사를 목적어로 받는 동사이기 때문에 빈칸에는 to부정사가 와야 하고, 또한 빈칸 뒤에 목적어 a comfortable environment가 있기 때문에 능동태가 되어야 한다. 따라서 능동의 to부정사인 (B) to create가 정답이다.

136. 전치사 어휘
| 해설 | 빈칸은 뒤에 있는 명사구를 목적어로 가지는 전치사가 들어갈 자리로, 뒤에 목적어가 특정 기간에 해당하므로 '총 6개월 동안'이라는 의미를 완성해줄 기간 표현 전치사인 (C) for가 정답이다.

137. 알맞은 문장 고르기
(A) 저희의 새로운 도서 선집들은 매우 인기가 있습니다.
(B) 유감스럽게도, 귀하의 카드는 더 이상 유효하지 않습니다.
(C) 도서관 벌금은 즉시 납부되어야 합니다.
(D) 오시는 분들께 끼칠 모든 방해에 대해 유감스럽게 생각합니다.
| 해설 | 앞서 도서관 일부 구역 폐쇄 및 시끄러운 장비 작동에 대해서 알리는 내용이 제시되어 있는 것으로 볼 때, 그 연장선상에서 앞서 제시된 사항으로 인해 고객들에게 발생할 불편(방해)에 대해 유감의 뜻을 나타내는 문장이 이어지는 것이 가장 적절하므로 정답은 (D)이다.
| 어휘 | selection 선집, 선택   unfortunately 유감스럽게도   valid 유효한   fine 벌금   regret 유감스럽게 생각하다   disturbance 방해

138. 명사 어휘
| 해설 | 빈칸은 앞의 명사 opening과 함께 복합 명사를 이루어 전치사 during의 목적어가 될 명사가 들어갈 자리로, 문맥상 '정규 개관 시간 동안'이라는 의미로 전개되는 것이 적절하므로 'opening hours(개관 시간, 영업 시간)'라는 의미를 완성해줄 (A) hours가 정답이다.
| 어휘 | statement 성명, 진술   branch 지점, 지사

139-142 다음 이메일을 참조하시오.

수신: stephenshaw@bvmail.com
발신: corrine@odinsalesconference.com
날짜: 3월 28일
제목: Odin 영업 학회

Shaw 씨 귀하,

다가오는 Odin 영업 학회의 발표자가 되는 것에 동의해 주셔서 감사드리고 싶습니다.

저희의 특별 연사들 중 한 분으로서, 귀하는 대강당에서 5천 명이 넘는 청중들에게 ¹³⁹연설하게 될 것입니다. 수입과 수출을 둘러싼 규제에 관한 많은 관심이 있으니, 저희는 귀하께서 이러한 활동들에 영향을 미치는 ¹⁴⁰규제 기관들에 관해 이야기해 주셨으면 합니다.

귀하의 디지털 파일이 저희 시스템과 호환되는 것을 확실히 하기 위해, 5월 17일에 있을 학회 ¹⁴¹전에 귀하의 프레젠테이션 전자 사본을 저희에게 보내주세요. 귀하의 유인물은 인쇄하는 것이 아니라 저희 웹 사이트에 업로드해주셔야 합니다. ¹⁴²참가자들이 그 자료들을 미리 다운로드받을 것입니다.

진심으로,

Corrine Roland

| 어휘 | presenter 발표자   featured speaker 특별 연사   audience 청중, 관객   main auditorium 대강당   a great deal of 많은, 다량의   regulation 규제, 규정   surrounding 둘러싼, 관련된   import 수입   export 수출   agency 기관, 대행사   affect 영향을 미치다   ensure 확실히 하다, 보장하다   be compatible with ~와 호환되다   electronic 전자의   handout 유인물

139. 동사의 시제
| 해설 | 빈칸은 문장의 동사가 들어갈 자리로, 앞 단락에 발표자가 되는 것에 동의했다는 문장을 단서로, 연설하는 것은 미래에 진행될 일임을 알 수 있으므로 미래 시제 동사인 (D) will be addressing이 정답이다.

140. 형용사 자리 – 명사 수식
| 해설 | 관사 the와 명사 agencies 사이에 빈칸이 있으므로, 빈칸은 명사를 수식하는 형용사 자리이다. 따라서 '규제의'라는 뜻의 형용사인 (B) regulatory가 정답이다.
| 어휘 | regulating 조절하는   regulate 규제하다, 조절하다

141. 전치사 어휘
| 해설 | 빈칸은 뒤에 있는 명사구 the conference를 목적어로 가지는 전치사가 들어갈 자리로, 문맥상 '5월 17일에 있을 학회 전에 보내달라'는 의미로 전개되는 것이 적절하므로 '~ 전에, 이전에'라는 뜻의 (C) before가 정답이다.

142. 알맞은 문장 고르기
(A) 저희는 귀하의 창의적인 제안에 감사드립니다.
(B) 그 직책은 가능한 한 빨리 채워져야 합니다.
(C) 저희 수입 사업이 상당히 성장해 왔습니다.
(D) 참가자들이 그 자료들을 미리 다운로드받을 것입니다.

| 해설 | 앞서 인쇄물을 웹 사이트에 업로드해야 한다고 알리는 내용이 제시되어 있는 것으로 볼 때, 그 연장선상에서 웹 사이트에 올려진 자료들을 참가자들이 미리 다운로드할 것임을 알리는 문장이 이어지는 것이 가장 적절하므로 정답은 (D)이다.

| 어휘 | creative 창의적인   suggestion 제안   position 직책   fill 채우다, 충원하다   substantially 상당히   participant 참가자   material 자료   in advance 미리

143-146 다음 편지를 참조하시오.

Valdez 보험
4309 Holmes Street
Dallas, TX 75240

관계자에게:

저는 최근 귀사의 영업직에 지원한 Ana Robinson을 위해서 이 편지를 쓰고 있습니다. Robinson 씨는 지난 3년 동안 Hampton 산업에서 선임 영업 사원으로 143근무해 왔습니다. 저희 팀의 핵심 멤버로서, 신규 고객들을 144유치하는 것에서부터 홍보 자료를 개발하는 것에 이르기까지 많은 직무들을 처리했습니다. Robinson 씨는 사교적인 사람이고, 의사소통에 천부적인 재능을 가지고 있습니다. 비록 분야가 다르더라도 이러한 145능력들의 대부분은 귀사의 직책에 딱 맞을 것입니다.

저는 기꺼이 Robinson 씨의 업무 성과에 대해 더 자세히 이야기하고자 합니다. 146제 사무실로 저에게 편하게 연락해 주세요. 아래 기재된 주요 전화 교환대에서 제 내선 전화번호는 35입니다.

진심으로,

Maria Yokota
Hampton 산업, 영업 이사
469-555-6489

| 어휘 | whom it may concern 관계자   on behalf of ~을 대신하여, 위해서   apply for ~에 지원하다   sales position 영업직   senior 선임의   sales associate 영업 사원   handle 처리하다   duty 직무   develop 개발하다   promotional material 홍보 자료   people person 사교적인 사람   natural talent 천부적인 재능   field 분야   work performance 업무 성과   in detail 자세히, 상세히   extension 내선 번호   switchboard 교환대   listed 기재된, 열거된

고난도
143. 동사 어휘

| 해설 | 새로운 회사에 지원한 Ana Robinson을 위해 이전 회사(Hampton 산업)의 영업 이사가 쓴 추천서로, 문맥상 '지난 3년 동안 Hampton 산업에서 근무했다'라는 의미로 전개되는 것이 적절하므로 (B) served가 정답이다.

| 어휘 | accomplish 성취하다, 달성하다   serve 일하다, 근무하다   recognize 인정하다, 인식하다

144. 동명사 자리 – 전치사의 목적어 | 병치

| 해설 | 빈칸은 전치사 from의 목적어가 들어갈 자리로, 앞뒤에 제시된 from A to B 구문에서 A와 B는 서로 병렬 구조가 되어야 하므로, 뒤에 있는 developing과 같은 형태인 (C) attracting이 정답이다.

145. 명사 어휘

| 해설 | 빈칸은 형용사 these의 수식을 받는 명사가 들어갈 자리로, 앞에 제시된 Robinson 씨의 장점들이 제시되어 있는 것으로 볼 때, 문맥상 '이러한 능력들'이라는 의미로 전개되는 것이 적절하므로 (C) skills가 정답이다.

| 어휘 | agreement 동의   concern 염려, 관심사

146. 알맞은 문장 고르기
(A) 그녀가 그 일자리의 지원서를 검토할 것입니다.
(B) 제가 귀하를 다음 단계의 면접에 초대할 것입니다.
(C) 그녀가 더 정확한 데이터로 최신 정보를 제공해줄 것입니다.
(D) 제 사무실로 저에게 편하게 연락해 주세요.

| 해설 | 뒤이어 자신의 내선 번호를 알려주는 것으로 볼 때, 앞서 자신에게 연락할 것을 요청하는 내용의 문장이 삽입되는 것이 적절하므로 정답은 (D)이다.

| 어휘 | application 지원서   precise 정확한

PART 7

147-148 다음 쿠폰을 참조하시오.

RDC
움직이는 아이디어들
방문 15% 할인

입장료 15% 할인

이 쿠폰은 RDC에서 최대 4명까지 15% 입장료 할인을 위해 사용할 수 있습니다. 유효 기간은 없지만, 이 쿠폰은 다른 할인들과 결합될 수 없습니다. 147방문객들은 모든 전시들과 직접 해보는 실험 활동들 그리고 생물학 강연들의 이용이 허용됩니다(강연 일정은 저희 웹 사이트를 보세요).

여름 시간 (6월-8월): 월요일-토요일, 148오전 9시-오후 7시
148표준 시간 (9월-5월): 화요일-일요일, 오전 11시-오후 7시

| 어휘 | valid 유효한   admission 입장료   up to 최대 ~까지   expiration date 유효 기간, 만료 일자   be combined with ~와 결합

되다 permit 허용하다, 허락하다 access 이용, 입장, 접속 hands-on 직접 해보는, 실습의 lab 실험실 biology 생물학 lecture 강연, 강의

147. 추론 문제
RDC는 무엇일 것 같은가?
(A) 영화관
(B) 공익 기업
(C) 과학 센터
(D) 백화점

| 해설 | 방문객들은 모든 전시들과 직접 해보는 실험 활동들 그리고 생물학 강연들의 이용이 허용된다고(Visitors are permitted access to all displays, hands-on lab activities, and biology lectures) 한 것에서, 과학 센터일 것으로 유추할 수 있으므로 정답은 (C)이다.

148. True 문제
9월의 RDC에 대해 사실인 것은?
(A) 마감 시간이 더 이르다.
(B) 아침에 문을 닫는다.
(C) 며칠 더 문을 연다.
(D) 더 적은 시간 문을 연다.

| 해설 | 후반부에 9월이 속한 표준 시간(9월-5월)의 운영 시간은 오전 11시-오후 7시(11 A.M.-7 P.M.)로, 여름 운영 시간인 오전 9시-오후 7시(9 A.M.-7 P.M.)보다 문을 여는 시간이 짧은 것을 알 수 있으므로 정답은 (D)이다.

149-150 다음 이메일을 참조하시오.

수신: bruce_garmon@writersunite.com
발신: reneevarney@alabasterediting.com
날짜: 10월 3일
제목: 작가 연합 소식지

Garmon 씨 귀하,

저는 약 3년 동안 작가 연합 월간 소식지의 구독자였습니다. 저는 그것을 매달 받는 것을 기대하고 있는데, [149]늘 현재 프리랜서들을 고용하고 있는 회사들에 관한 폭넓은 색인을 제공하기 때문입니다. 실제로 그것은 제가 여러 프로젝트들을 찾는 데 도움을 주었기 때문에, 그런 유용한 정보원을 가지고 있는 것에 감사하고 있습니다.

저는 가끔 특집 기사들을 읽는데, [150]제가 그 간행물을 받기 시작한 이래로 다뤄지지 않았던 여러 가지 잠재적인 주제들이 있는 것 같습니다. 앞으로 나올 소식지들에 대한 제안을 받으시나요? 그렇다면, 여기 제가 생각하고 있었던 것들이 있습니다:

· 책 제안서 작성하기
· 작가의 글쓰기 막힘 현상을 극복하는 팁들

저와 다른 프리랜서들에게 주셨던 모든 도움에 감사드립니다!

진심으로,

Renée Varney

| 어휘 | subscriber 구독자 look forward to -ing ~하기를 기대하다, 고대하다 extensive 폭넓은, 광범위한 index 색인 currently 현재 resource 정보원, 자원 featured article 특집 기사 potential 잠재적인 cover 다루다 publication 간행물, 발행 accept 받다, 수락하다 overcome 극복하다 writer's block 작가의 글쓰기 막힘 현상

149. 세부 사항을 묻는 문제
Varney 씨는 월간 소식지의 어떤 면을 칭찬하는가?
(A) 프로젝트 관리 팁들
(B) 쉬운 검색 기능들
(C) 구직 기회 목록
(D) 할인 관련 정보

| 해설 | 첫 번째 단락에 매달 소식지를 받는 것을 기대하는 이유로, 프리랜서들을 고용하고 있는 회사들에 관한 폭넓은 색인을 제공하기 때문이라고(it always provides an extensive index of companies that are currently hiring freelancers) 했으므로 정답은 (C)이다.

| 어휘 | management 관리, 경영 feature 기능, 특징 job opportunity 구직 기회

| 패러프레이징 | an extensive index of companies that are currently hiring freelancers → Its list of job opportunities

고난도

150. 세부 사항을 묻는 문제
Varney 씨가 이메일에서 지적하는 것은 무엇인가?
(A) 그녀가 다른 이들에게 전달한 게시물들
(B) 그녀가 관심이 필요하다고 생각하는 주제들
(C) 부정확한 것들이 포함된 기사들
(D) 변경되어야 하는 정책들

| 해설 | 두 번째 단락에 그 간행물을 받기 시작한 이래로 다뤄지지 않았던 여러 가지 잠재적인 주제들이 있는 것 같다며(there are several potential topics that have not been covered since I started receiving the publication) 본인의 제안을 제시했으므로 정답은 (B)이다.

| 어휘 | post 게시물 forward 전달하다 subject 주제, 화제 attention 관심 contain 포함하다 inaccuracy 부정확한 것, 부정확 policy 정책, 방침

| 패러프레이징 | topics → Subjects

151-152 다음 문자 메시지 대화를 참조하시오.

Shirley Campbell (오전 10:33)
제가 막 South Bend 매장에 Summer Breeze 향수 박스들을 갖다 놓았어요. [151]Oakland에 있는 귀하의 지점을 위한 것도 세 박스 가지고

있는데요. 당신 교대 근무가 언제 끝나나요?

Chiara Feliciano (오전 10:35)
막 시작했으니까, 저희가 문 닫기 전에 언제든 편하게 들르세요.

Shirley Campbell (오전 10:36)
알겠어요. South Bend 지점이 향수 진열대를 아주 잘 설치했던데요. ¹⁵²진열 구역을 비치 타월, 비치 볼, 화려한 풍선들로 장식했어요.

Chiara Feliciano (오전 10:37)
그것 저희와 꼭 같은 것 같은데요. 물품들을 내리는 데 도움이 필요하실까요?

Shirley Campbell (오전 10:38)
네, 그러니 제가 도착하면 누군가를 보내 주세요. 그때 제가 문자를 보낼게요.

| 어휘 | drop off 갖다 놓다   perfume 향수   branch 지점, 지사   shift 교대 근무   stop by 잠시 들르다   decorate 장식하다   colorful 화려한, 알록달록한   balloon 풍선   exactly 꼭, 정확히   unload (짐을) 내리다

151. 주제/목적 문제
Campbell 씨는 왜 Feliciano 씨에게 메시지를 보냈나?
(A) 상품의 배달을 확인하기 위해
(B) 신상품에 관해 문의하기 위해
(C) 시연을 위한 시간을 정하기 위해
(D) South Bend 상점까지 가는 길을 안내받기 위해

| 해설 | 도입부에 South Bend 상점에 향수 박스들을 갖다 놓은 사실을 알린 후, Oakland에 있는 귀하의 지점을 위한 것도 세 박스 가지고 있는데(I have three boxes for your branch in Oakland) 교대 근무가 언제 끝나는지(When does your shift end) 물었으므로, 상품 배달과 관련하여 메시지를 보낸 것임을 알 수 있다. 따라서 정답은 (A)이다.

| 어휘 | inquire 문의하다   demonstration 시연   get directions 길 안내를 받다

| 패러프레이징 | three boxes → goods

🔺고난도
152. 의도 파악 문제
오전 10:37에 Feliciano 씨가 "그것 저희와 꼭 같은 것 같은데요"라고 쓸 때 암시하는 것은 무엇인가?
(A) Oakland는 South Bend와 비슷한 매출 수치를 가지고 있다.
(B) Feliciano 씨가 South Bend 관리자로부터 조언을 얻을 것이다.
(C) 일부 장식들이 Oakland에 설치되어 있다.
(D) Campbell 씨가 요청했던 타월들을 구입할 수 있다.

| 해설 | 이는 앞서 Shirley Campbell이 South Bend 지점이 향수 진열대를 아주 잘 설치했다며, 진열 구역을 비치 타월, 비치 볼, 화려한 풍선들로 장식했다고(They decorated the display area with beach towels, beach balls, and colorful balloons) 덧붙인 것에 대한 응답으로, 저희와 꼭 같은 것 같다는 말

로 Oakland 지점도 South Bend 지점처럼 그렇게 장식되어 있음을 나타낸 것임을 알 수 있으므로 정답은 (C)이다.

| 어휘 | sales figures 매출 수치, 매출액

153-155 다음 보고서를 참조하시오.

Houghton 건설

고객: Cecilia Irwin
주소: 429 Jaksa Lane, Baltimore, MD 21202
지붕널/타일 유형: 슬레이트   ¹⁵³**방문 날짜:** 9월 29일
지난 방문 이후 시간: 1년   ¹⁵³**Houghton 담당자:** Andrew Lahti

¹⁵³지붕 부분	등급	담당자의 의견:
지붕널들	3	사용 중인 특정 버전이 곧 생산이 중단될 것이기 때문에 보관용으로 슬레이트 타일들을 더 주문할 것을 권장했습니다. 고객 승인을 기다리고 있습니다.
타일들	0	
¹⁵⁴홈통들	4	
배수관	1	
지붕 데크	2	
¹⁵⁵태양 전지판들	0	
굴뚝 (밀폐 부분 포함)	3	

등급 상세: ¹⁵⁵0: 현재 없음 / 1: 훌륭함: 조치 불필요 / 2: 경미한 품질 저하: 1년 후에 재점검 / 3: 중간 수준 품질 저하: 6개월 후에 재점검 / ¹⁵⁴4: 중대한 품질 저하: 3개월에서 6개월 이내에 교체 / 5: 심각한 품질 저하: 즉시 교체

| 어휘 | representative 담당자, 대표자   feature 특성, 특징   shingle 지붕널   gutter 홈통   drainpipe 배수관   chimney 굴뚝   storage 보관, 저장   particular 특정한   discontinue (생산을) 중단하다   await 기다리다   approval 승인   present 있는, 현재의   minor 경미한, 사소한   deterioration 악화, (품질) 저하   severe 심각한

153. 추론 문제
Lahti 씨는 9월 29일에 무엇을 했을 것 같은가?
(A) 주문
(B) 지붕 상태 평가
(C) 일부 부품들 수리
(D) 수송품 배달

| 해설 | 9월 29일과 Lahti 씨의 이름은 보고서의 방문 날짜와(Date of Visit) 담당자(Houghton Representative) 항목에서 확인할 수 있고, 보고서의 내용이 지붕 상태에 대한 것이므로, 그날 Lahti 씨가 지붕 상태를 평가하여 보고서를 작성했을 것으로 유추할 수 있다. 따라서 정답은 (B)이다.

| 어휘 | assess 평가하다, 사정하다   component 부품

154. 세부 사항을 묻는 문제
어느 부분이 가장 빨리 교체되어야 하는가?
(A) 지붕널들
(B) 홈통들

(C) 배수관
(D) 지붕 데크

| 해설 | 등급 상세에서 등급 번호가 높을수록 빠른 교체가 필요함을 알 수 있는데, 도표에서 등급 번호가 가장 높은 것은 4로 표시된 홈통들(Gutters)로 확인되므로 정답은 (B)이다.

155. 추론 문제

Irwin 씨의 지붕에 대해 암시되는 것은 무엇인가?
(A) 원래 아마추어에 의해 설치되었다.
(B) 즉시 교체될 것이다.
(C) 9월에 굴뚝 가장자리가 다시 밀폐되었다.
(D) 태양으로부터 에너지를 발생시키는 장비는 갖춰져 있지 않다.

| 해설 | 표에 태양 전지판들(Solar panels)의 등급이 0으로 표시되어 있는데, 아래 등급 상세에서 0은 현재 없는(Not present) 상태로 확인되므로 정답은 (D)이다.

| 어휘 | originally 원래   edge 가장자리   reseal 다시 밀폐하다
equip 갖추다   generate 생성하다

| 패러프레이징 | Not present → not equipped

156-157 다음 정보를 참조하시오.

Logan 커뮤니티 센터
8월 10일 주에 시작하는 4주 수업들

DIY 마케팅
전문가들을 고용하기 위해 많은 돈을 쓰지 않고 여러분의 업체를 홍보하는 것의 기초를 배우세요.

등록 번호	강사	날짜/시간	장소
839586-01	156Patricia DeRosa	월요일/오후 6-8시	103호
839586-02	Stewart Crompton	목요일/오후 1-3시	206호

여러분의 청중을 알기
157청중에게 하는 여러분의 발언을 조정함으로써 다음 연설을 최대한 이용하는 것을 배우세요.

등록 번호	강사	날짜/시간	장소
842771-01	156Patricia DeRosa	목요일/오후 2-4시	205호
842771-02	157Abhinav Patel	토요일/오전 9-11시	102호

| 어휘 | promote 홍보하다   expert 전문가   enrollment 등록
instructor 강사   make the most of ~을 최대한 이용하다   tailor 재단하다, 맞추다, 조정하다   comment 발언, 언급

156. True 문제

DeRosa 씨에 관해 사실인 것은 무엇인가?
(A) 일주일에 이틀을 가르친다.
(B) 금융 전문가다.
(C) Crompton 씨에 의해 고용되었다.
(D) 자신의 업체를 운영한다.

| 해설 | DeRosa 씨는 DIY 마케팅(DIY Marketing Mondays)의 월요일(Mondays) 수업과 여러분의 청중을 알기(Knowing Your Audience)의 목요일(Thursdays) 수업을 담당하고 있음을 알 수 있으므로 정답은 (A)이다.

| 어휘 | financial expert 금융 전문가   operate 운영하다

157. 추론 문제

사람들은 왜 Patel 씨의 강좌에 등록할 것이겠는가?
(A) 대중에게 말하는 능력을 향상시키기 위해
(B) 기본적인 법에 관한 조언을 얻기 위해
(C) 의견들을 분석하는 방법을 배우기 위해
(D) 광고를 만드는 것을 실습하기 위해

| 해설 | Patel 씨는 두 번째 도표의 강사 목록에 있는 사람으로, 주제가 청중에게 하는 발언을 조정함으로써 다음 연설을 최대한 이용하는 것을 배우는(Learn to make the most of your next speech by tailoring your comments to the audience) 것으로 확인되므로 정답은 (A)이다.

| 어휘 | improve 향상시키다, 개선하다   public speaking 대중에게 말하기
analyze 분석하다

| 패러프레이징 | make the most of your next speech by tailoring your comments to the audience → improve public speaking skills

158-160 다음 이메일을 참조하시오.

수신: Muldoon Enterprises 직원들
발신: Navin Kamath
날짜: 2월 20일
제목: 유념해 주세요

Muldoon Enterprises 직원 여러분 귀하,

가장 최근의 직원 회의에서 논의된 대로, 인사 부서에서 휴가 정책을 변경했습니다. —[1]—. 158이제부터 한 부서에서 최대 3명까지 주어진 시간에 자리를 비울 수 있습니다. 저희는 이것이 우리가 높은 수준의 생산성과 고객 서비스를 유지하는 데 도움이 되기를 바랍니다. —[2]—. 계획된 부재에 관한 최신 일정이 우리 회사 웹 사이트에서 이용 가능할 것이니, 160그것이 먼저 확인되어야 합니다. 또한 휴가 계획에 관해 여러분의 동료들에게도 이야기해야 합니다. —[3]—.

최대 4개월 전에 휴가 시간을 요청할 수 있으므로, 159EZ-Cal 스마트폰 앱을 다운로드하는 것을 고려하고 싶을 수 있는데요. —[4]—. 159특정 날짜에 휴가 시간을 요청하는 것을 상기시키도록 설정할 수 있습니다.

귀하의 협조에 감사드립니다.

진심으로,

Navin Kamath
Muldoon Enterprises, 인사 부장

| 어휘 | human resources department 인사 부서　vacation policy 휴가 정책　maximum 최대, 최고　absent 자리를 비운, 부재한　maintain 유지하다　productivity 생산성　up-to-date 최신의　calendar 일정　absence 부재, 결근　available 이용 가능한　colleague 동료　certain 특정　cooperation 협조

158. 추론 문제
Muldoon Enterprises에 관해 암시되는 것은 무엇인가?
(A) 더 이상 직원들에게 유급 휴가를 제공하지 않을 것이다.
(B) 휴가를 내는 것에 대한 조건을 제한할 것이다.
(C) 업무 일을 빠뜨리지 않는 직원들에게 보너스를 줄 것이다.
(D) 직원들에게 휴가 일정에 관한 업데이트를 이메일로 보낼 것이다.
| 해설 | 첫 번째 단락에 인사 부서에서 휴가 정책을 변경했다며, 이제부터 한 부서에서 최대 3명까지 주어진 시간에 자리를 비울 수 있다고(From now on, a maximum of three people can be absent from a department at any given time) 한 것에서 휴가를 내는 것에 대한 조건에 제한을 둘 것임을 유추할 수 있으므로 정답은 (B)이다.
| 어휘 | paid vacation 유급 휴가　restrict 제한하다, 한정하다　take time off 휴가를 내다　miss 빠뜨리다, 놓치다
| 패러프레이징 | a maximum of three people can be absent from a department at any given time → restrict the conditions for taking time off

159. 세부 사항을 묻는 문제
Kamath 씨에 따르면, EZ-Cal 스마트폰 애플리케이션은 무엇을 할 수 있나?
(A) 직원들 사이에 메시지를 공유하는 것
(B) 일하는 데 보낸 시간의 양을 추적하는 것
(C) 촉박한 통지에 회의 일정을 잡는 것
(D) 업무에 관해 상기시키는 것을 보내는 것
| 해설 | 두 번째 단락에 EZ-Cal 스마트폰 앱을 언급한 후, 특정 날짜에 휴가 시간을 요청하는 것을 상기시키도록 설정할 수 있다고(You can set it to remind you to request vacation time on a certain date) 덧붙였으므로 정답은 (D)이다.
| 어휘 | share 공유하다　track 추적하다　on short notice 촉박한 통지에　reminder 상기시키는 것
| 패러프레이징 | remind you to request vacation time on a certain date → Send a reminder about a task

160. 문장 삽입 문제
[1], [2], [3], [4]로 표시된 곳 중에 다음 문장이 들어가기에 가장 적절한 곳은?
"여러분의 신청이 거부되지 않도록 확실히 하기 위해 이런 조치들을 취하기 바랍니다."
(A) [1]
(B) [2]
(C) [3]
(D) [4]
| 해설 | 제시된 문장은 '이러한 조치'가 언급된 문장 뒤에 들어가야 함을 알 수 있는데, 이는 첫 번째 단락 후반부에 있는 최신 일정을 먼저 확인하는 것과(that should be checked first), 동료들에게 휴가 계획을 이야기하는 것으로(You should also talk to your colleagues about their vacation plans) 파악할 수 있으므로 그 문장 바로 뒤의 (C)가 정답이다.
| 어휘 | take measures 조치를 취하다　ensure 확실히 하다, 보장하다　application 신청　reject 거부하다, 거절하다

161-163 다음 기사를 참조하시오.

Vaka가 사업 호황을 보다

[163]주로 인기 있는 Spirex-80 기기에 의해 이끌려 Vaka Tech의 매출이 작년 같은 기간에 비해 200% 이상 증가했다. 올해 초 [161]EU(유럽 연합)가 미네랄 함량을 이전 기준치보다 훨씬 낮게 제한하는 [161]병에 든 생수에 대한 엄격한 규정을 추가했다. 많은 음료 회사들이 그들의 제품들이 그것을 준수하도록 하기 위해 추가적인 자금을 쓸 수밖에 없었다.

그 변화는 3월 초에 발표되었다. 그 [162]시점부터 [163]물을 효과적으로 정화하는 시스템인 Spirex-80의 매출이 급증했다. 모든 음료 회사들이 필요로 하는 해결책을 제공하는 Spirex-80은 확실히 적절한 때에 적절한 장소에 있는 것으로 보인다.

| 어휘 | boom 호황, 붐　increase 증가하다　compared to ~와 비교하여　period 기간　driven by ~에 이끌린　device 기기　strict 엄격한　regulation 규정, 규제　limit 제한하다　mineral content 미네랄 함량　threshold 기준치, 한계점　be forced to ~할 수밖에 없다, ~하도록 강요받다　finance 자금　compliance 준수, 따름　effectively 효과적으로　purify 정화하다　skyrocket 급증하다　solution 해결책

161. 세부 사항을 묻는 문제
기사에 따르면, 무엇이 음료 회사들의 비용을 증가시켰나?
(A) 새로운 관리 규정
(B) 재료 부족
(C) 직원들 급여 지급
(D) 상승하는 연료비
| 해설 | 첫 번째 단락에 EU(유럽 연합)가 생수에 대한 엄격한 규정을 추가했다고(the EU added strict regulations on bottled water ~) 한 후, 음료 회사들이 그 규정을 준수하기 위해 추가적인 자금을 쓸 수밖에 없었다고(Many beverages companies were forced to use additional finances to bring their products into compliance) 제시되어 있으므로 정답은 (A)이다.
| 어휘 | government 정부, 관리, 행정　regulation 규정　shortage 부족　ingredient 재료　wage 급여, 임금　payment 지급, 지불　rising 상승하는　fuel price 연료비

🔺 고난도
162. 동의어 문제
두 번째 단락 첫 번째 줄에 있는 단어 "point"와 의미가 가장 유사한 것은
(A) 장소, 위치
(B) 세부 사항

(C) 순간
(D) 목적

| 해설 | 해당 단어가 들어간 문장은 '그 시점부터 물을 효과적으로 정화하는 시스템인 Spirex-80의 매출이 급증했다'라고 해석된다. 따라서 '시점'이라는 의미와 유사하여 대체해 쓸 수 있는 '순간'이라는 뜻의 (C) instant가 정답이다.

163. 세부 사항을 묻는 문제

기사에서 Vaka Tech가 했다고 제시한 것은 무엇인가?
(A) Spirex-80의 디자인을 바꾼 것
(B) 유럽의 한 나라로 이사한 것
(C) 경쟁사 중 한 곳을 인수한 것
(D) 정화 시스템을 만들어낸 것

| 해설 | 첫 번째 단락에 Vaka Tech의 매출이 자사의 Spirex-80 기기에 의해 이끌려 증가했다고(Sales at Vaka Tech ~ mainly driven by its popular Spirex-80 device) 한 것과 두 번째 단락에서 물을 효과적으로 정화하는 시스템인 Spirex-80이라고(the Spirex-80—a system that effectively purifies water—skyrocketed) 한 것을 연계해 볼 때, Vaka Tech가 물 정화 시스템인 Spirex-80를 만들어냈음을 알 수 있으므로 정답은 (D)이다.

| 어휘 | take over 인수하다, 인계받다 competitor 경쟁사, 경쟁자 create 만들어내다 purification 정화

| 패러프레이징 | a system that effectively purifies water → a purification system

164-167 다음 온라인 채팅 토론을 참조하시오.

Kirby Auyer (오전 9:08)
안녕하세요, Deandra와 Paola. 10시 대신 오후쯤에 세법 준수 책임자 직책의 이력서들을 검토할 수 있을까요? ¹⁶⁴제가 이사회에서 Hong 씨의 발표를 대신해야 해서요.

Deandra Calteaux (오전 9:09)
¹⁶⁷오후 3시 어때요? ¹⁶⁵우리가 회의실에 모여서 모두 검토할 수 있을 거예요.

Paola Gomez (오전 9:10)
¹⁶⁷저한테는 딱 좋아요. 제가 오후 1시까지 제출해야 하는 보고서를 아직 작업 중이었거든요.

Kirby Auyer (오전 9:10)
그것은 문제가 될 텐데요. 온라인 일정표에 따르면, ¹⁶⁵IT 팀이 그들의 분기별 교육을 위해 하루 종일 그곳에 있을 것이라서요.

Deandra Calteaux (오전 9:11)
¹⁶⁵우리는 직원 휴게실에서 만날 수 있어요. 그곳은 대개 비어 있어요.

Paola Gomez (오전 9:12)
좋아요. 파일들의 전자 버전을 볼 수 있도록 ¹⁶⁶제 노트북을 가져가야 할까요?

Deandra Calteaux (오전 9:13)
그럴 필요 없어요. 제가 모두를 위해 종이에 인쇄할게요.

Kirby Auyer (오전 9:14)
¹⁶⁷그때 봐요. 저한테 맞춰줘서 고마워요.

| 어휘 | résumé 이력서 tax 세금 compliance officer 준법 감시인 cover 대신하다 board meeting 이사회 go over 검토하다, 살펴보다 due 마감이 ~까지인 quarterly 분기별의 empty 비어 있는 electronic 전자의 necessary 필요한 accommodate 맞추다, 수용하다

🔺고난도

164. 세부 사항을 묻는 문제

Auyer 씨는 아침에 왜 바쁜가?
(A) 이사진들을 견학시켜 줄 것이다.
(B) 동료 대신에 이야기를 해야 한다.
(C) 다른 지점을 방문해야 한다.
(D) 끝내야 할 긴급한 보고서가 있다.

| 해설 | 오전 9:08에 Kirby Auyer가 이력서 검토를 오후에 할 수 있을지 물은 후, 이사회에서 Hong 씨의 발표를 대신해야 한다고(I need to cover Mr. Hong's presentation at the board meeting) 그 이유를 덧붙였으므로 정답은 (B)이다.

| 어휘 | colleague 동료 urgent 긴급한 complete 완료하다, 작성하다

| 패러프레이징 | need to cover Mr. Hong's presentation → has to give a talk in place of a colleague

165. 세부 사항을 묻는 문제

Calteaux 씨는 왜 그들이 직원 휴게실에서 만나야 한다고 생각하는가?
(A) 회의실이 사용 중일 것이기 때문에
(B) 그 구역에서 음식이 허용되기 때문에
(C) Auyer 씨의 사무실에서 가장 가깝기 때문에
(D) 방문객들을 위한 여유 공간이 있기 때문에

| 해설 | 오전 9:09에 Deandra Calteaux가 회의실에 모여서 검토할 수 있을 것이라고(We could get together in the meeting room to go over everything) 한 말에 대해, Kirby Auyer가 IT 팀이 하루 종일 그곳에 있을 것이라고(the IT team will be in there all day) 했고, 이에 Deandra Calteaux가 직원 휴게실에서 만날 수 있다고(We could meet in the employee lounge) 답했으므로 정답은 (A)이다.

| 어휘 | be in use 사용 중이다 allow 허용하다, 허락하다 extra space 여유 공간, 추가 공간

| 패러프레이징 | IT team will be in there all day → the meeting room will be in use

166. 의도 파악 문제

오전 9:13에 Calteaux 씨가 "그럴 필요 없어요"라고 쓸 때 암시하는 것은 무엇인가?
(A) Auyer 씨는 프로젝트를 도울 필요가 없다.

(B) 그는 이미 몇몇 입사 지원자들에게 연락했다.
(C) **Gomez 씨는 노트북을 사용할 필요가 없을 것이다.**
(D) Gomez 씨는 파일들을 미리 검토하지 말아야 한다.
| 해설 | 오전 9:12에 Paola Gomez가 노트북을 가져가야 할지(Should I bring my laptop) 물은 것에 대해 그럴 필요가 없다고 대답한 것이므로 정답은 (C)이다.
| 어휘 | contact 연락하다   job candidate 입사 지원자

167. 세부 사항을 묻는 문제
글쓴이들은 오늘 언제 만날 것인가?
(A) 오전 10시에
(B) 오후 1시에
(C) 오후 3시에
(D) 오후 4시에
| 해설 | 오전 9:09에 Deandra Calteaux가 오후 3시 어떤지(How about 3 P.M.) 묻는 말에 Paola Gomez가 딱 좋다고(That works perfectly for me) 했고, 마지막에 Kirby Auyer도 그때 보자고(See you then) 했으므로 정답은 (C)이다.

168-171 다음 편지를 참조하시오.

Brian Streich
502 Carissa Avenue
Aberdeen, SD 57401

4월 3일

Streich 씨 귀하,

[168]저는 최근에 삶의 질 향상을 도모하기 위한 지역 사회 봉사 활동 콘테스트를 담당하고 있는 제 동료를 만났습니다. 저희의 지난 Millennial Leaders Club 회의에서 귀하가 제시했던 아이디어들에 기반하여, [168]귀하가 이 행사에 아주 적격일 것이라고 생각하고 있습니다. [169]스트레스를 줄이고 질병을 예방하기 위한 이완 기법들에 관한 귀하의 프로그램이 분명 심사 위원단에게 깊은 인상을 줄 것입니다.

관심이 있으시면, 귀하의 프로그램과 그것이 어떻게 다른 이들을 도울 수 있는지에 관한 300자 설명을 제공하셔야 합니다. 귀하는 쉽게 참가 기준을 [170]충족시키니, 분명 심사 단계를 통과할 것이라고 생각합니다. 그 후에, 귀하의 프로그램에 관해 간단히 이야기하고 질문에 대답하도록 초청될 것인데요. 수상자는 5,000달러의 상금을 받게 될 테니, 분명 시도해 볼 만한 가치가 있을 것 같습니다.

제가 실례를 무릅쓰고 신청서를 다운로드하여 출력했으니, 동봉된 것을 발견하실 것입니다. [171]늦어도 4월 30일까지 귀하의 프로그램 설명과 신원 확인을 위한 여권이나 운전 면허증 사본과 함께 그것을 작성하여 보내셔야 합니다.

따뜻한 안부를 전하며,

Elaina Urmanski

| 어휘 | colleague 동료   be in charge of ~을 담당하다, 맡다   outreach 봉사 활동   quality-of-life improvements 삶의 질 향상   present 제시하다   fit 딱 맞음, 적합   relaxation techniques 이완 기법, 정신적 긴장 해소 방법   reduce 줄이다   prevent 예방하다, 막다   illness 질병, 병   impress 깊은 인상을 주다   judging panel 심사 위원단   description 설명서, 설명   entry criteria 참가 기준   definitely 분명히   screening phase 심사 단계   brief 간단한, 짧은   worth ~의 가치가 있는   give it a try 시도해보다, 한번 해보다   take the liberty of 실례를 무릅쓰고 ~하다   application form 신청서   enclosed 동봉된   identification 신원 확인

168. 주제/목적 문제
Urmanski 씨는 왜 편지를 보냈나?
(A) 대회에 참가하도록 제안하기 위해
(B) 심사 위원 한 명을 패널로 모집하기 위해
(C) 클럽에 가입하도록 초대장을 보내기 위해
(D) Streich 씨에게 일자리 공석에 관해 알리기 위해
| 해설 | 첫 번째 단락에 최근에 지역 사회 봉사 활동 콘테스트를 담당하고 있는 동료를 만났다고(I recently met with a colleague of mine who is in charge of the Community Outreach Contest ~) 한 후, 귀하가 이 행사에 아주 적격이라고 생각한다고(I believe that you would be an excellent fit for this event) 한 것에서, 콘테스트 참가를 제안할 목적으로 편지를 보낸 것임을 알 수 있으므로 정답은 (A)이다.
| 어휘 | competition 대회   recruit 모집하다   extend an invitation 초대장을 보내다, 초대하다

고난도
169. 추론 문제
Streich 씨의 전문 분야는 무엇일 것 같은가?
(A) 투자
(B) 기술
(C) 건강
(D) 제조
| 해설 | 첫 번째 단락 후반부에 스트레스를 줄이고 질병을 예방하기 위한 이완 기법들에 관한 귀하의 프로그램이라고(Your program of relaxation techniques for reducing stress and preventing illness) 한 것을 통해, 건강 관련 전문가인 것으로 유추할 수 있으므로 정답은 (C)이다.
| 어휘 | invest 투자하다   manufacture 제조하다, 생산하다

170. 동의어 문제
두 번째 단락 두 번째 줄에 있는 단어 "meet"과 의미가 가장 유사한 것은
(A) 수집하다, 모으다
(B) 인사하다
(C) 유지하다
(D) 충족시키다

| 해설 | 해당 단어가 들어간 문장은 '귀하는 쉽게 참가 기준을 충족시키니 ~'라고 해석된다. 따라서 이와 가장 유사한 '충족시키다, 채우다'라는 뜻의 (D) fulfill이 정답이다.

171. 세부 사항을 묻는 문제
streich 씨가 4월 30일까지 해야 하는 것은 무엇인가?
(A) 서식을 다운로드하는 것
(B) 필요한 서류들을 제출하는 것
(C) 질문들에 응답하는 것
(D) 여권을 갱신하는 것

| 해설 | 마지막 단락 후반부에, 늦어도 4월 30일까지 프로그램 설명과 여권이나 운전 면허증 사본과 함께 신청서를 작성하여 보내야 한다고(You must complete and send it, along with your program description and a copy of your passport or driver's license for identification purposes, no later than April 30) 했으므로 정답은 (B)이다.

| 어휘 | respond 응답하다, 답신하다   renew 갱신하다

| 패러프레이징 | the application form / your program description and a copy of your passport or driver's license → the required documents

172-175 다음 기사를 참조하시오.

<Surabaya Herald>
3월 24일

¹⁷²인도네시아의 새로운 인터넷 고객의 수는 같은 1년의 기간 동안 다른 나라들의 수에 거의 3배다. 인터넷 서비스 제공업체들 사이의 경쟁은 특히 시골 지역 사회에서 점점 더 많은 사람들이 온라인에 접속함에 따라 가열되어 왔다. —[1]—.

Lumbra 커뮤니케이션은 주로 주요 도시에 초점을 맞춘 오래된 인터넷 서비스 제공업체였다. ¹⁷⁵그곳은 한때 많은 곳에서 인터넷 사용자들의 유일한 옵션이었지만, 그것이 변화하고 있다. —[2]—. 결과적으로, 대부분의 신규 고객들은 인터넷 최초 사용자들이 아니라, 오히려 다른 회사에서 이동한 고객들이다.

선택할 회사들이 아주 많아서, 고객들은 더 이상 장기간의 작동 정지 시간을 참고 견디지 않는다. ¹⁷³고객들이 안정적인 연결을 믿을 수 없으면, 그들은 그저 다른 공급업체로 바꾼다. 그것이 Dhanas 웹의 몰락을 야기한 것인데, 그곳은 이전에 두 번째로 높은 시장 점유율을 차지하고 있었는데 두 달 전 폐업했다. —[3]—.

Lumbra 커뮤니케이션이 여전히 시장을 이끌고 있지만, Sandang 테크가 점점 강해지고 있다. —[4]—. Sandang 테크는 단지 18개월 동안 운영해오고 있지만, 전화와 인터넷 패키지를 통해 소비자들의 관심을 끌고 있다. ¹⁷⁴ ⁽ᶜ⁾그곳은 더 빠른 인터넷 속도를 제공하기 위해 끊임없이 노력하고 있는데, 그것은 비디오 스트리밍을 위해 인터넷을 이용하는 이들에게 특히 중요한 것이다. ¹⁷⁴ ⁽ᴮ⁾Sandang 테크의 초점은 젊은 전문직 종사자들에게 맞춰져 있고, 그들을 평생 고객으로 만들고 싶어한다.

¹⁷⁴ ⁽ᴰ⁾그곳은 또한 고장 난 회선과 라우터들을 당일 수리하는 것으로 명성을 가지고 있다. 현명하고 적응력 있는 사업 모델이 인터넷 사용의 급증을 극대화하는 비결이 될 수 있다.

| 어휘 | period 기간   competition 경쟁   provider 제공업체   heat up 가열되다   rural 시골의   focus on ~에 초점을 맞추다   transfer 옮기다, 이전하다   put up with ~을 참고 견디다   downtime 작동 정지 시간   rely on ~을 믿다, 의존하다   stable 안정적인   connection 연결   downfall 몰락   go out of business 폐업하다, 파산하다   previously 이전에   market share 시장 점유율   gain ground 더 강력해지다[성공하다]   be in operation 운영 중이다   grab the attention of ~의 관심을 끌다   continually 끊임없이, 계속해서   lifelong 평생의   have a reputation for ~에 명성을 가지고 있다   adaptable 적응력 있는, 적응할 수 있는   maximize 극대화하다   surge 급증

172. 주제/목적 문제
기사의 주된 화제는 무엇인가?
(A) 인터넷 기반 사업들의 인기
(B) 가장 흔한 마케팅 방법들
(C) 한 산업의 빠른 성장
(D) 인도네시아에서 가장 일하기 좋은 회사들

| 해설 | 첫 번째 단락 도입부에 인도네시아의 새로운 인터넷 고객의 수는 같은 1년의 기간 동안 다른 나라들의 수에 거의 3배라고(The number of new Internet customers in Indonesia is nearly three times that of other countries over the same one-year period) 한 후, 인터넷 서비스 산업의 성장 및 변화에 관해 구체적으로 제시하고 있으므로 정답은 (C)이다.

| 어휘 | popularity 인기   common 흔한, 일반적인   rapid 빠른   growth 성장

173. 추론 문제
Dhanas 웹에 관해 암시되는 것은 무엇인가?
(A) 가격이 너무 높았다.
(B) 주요 사업이 전화 패키지였다.
(C) 지역에서 가장 오래 운영된 업체였다.
(D) 신뢰할 수 없는 서비스를 가지고 있었다.

| 해설 | 세 번째 단락에 고객들이 안정적인 연결을 믿을 수 없으면, 그들은 그저 다른 공급업체로 바꾸는데(If customers cannot rely on a stable connection, they simply change to another provider), 그것이 Dhanas 웹의 몰락을 야기한 것이라고(This is what caused the downfall of Dhanas Web) 했으므로 정답은 (D)이다.

| 어휘 | unreliable 신뢰할 수 없는, 믿을 수 없는

| 패러프레이징 | cannot rely on a stable connection → had unreliable service

174. NOT True 문제
Sandang 테크의 전략으로 제시되지 않은 것은 무엇인가?

(A) 비디오 스트리밍 서비스를 제공하는 것
(B) 젊은 소비자들을 타깃으로 하는 것
(C) 인터넷 속도를 증가시키는 것
(D) 기술적인 문제들을 신속히 해결하는 것

| 해설 | 마지막 단락에 Sandang 테크에 대해 더 빠른 인터넷 속도를 제공하기 위해 끊임없이 노력하고 있다고(It works continually to provide faster Internet speeds) 한 것에서 (C), Sandang 테크의 초점은 젊은 전문직 종사자들에게 맞춰져 있다고(Sandang Tech's focus is on young professionals) 한 것에서 (B), 또한 고장 난 회선과 라우터들을 당일 수리하는 것으로 명성을 가지고 있다고(It also has a reputation for making same-day repairs to broken lines and routers) 한 것에서 (D)가 확인된다. 따라서 정답은 (A)이다.

| 어휘 | target 타깃으로 하다, 목표로 하다   resolve 해결하다

| 패러프레이징 | · provide faster Internet speeds → Increasing its Internet speed
· focus is on young professionals → Targeting young consumers
· making same-day repairs to broken lines and routers → Resolving technical issues quickly

🔺고난도

175. 문장 삽입 문제

[1], [2], [3], [4]로 표시된 곳 중에 다음 문장이 들어가기에 가장 적절한 곳은?

"그 고객 풀은 높은 시장 포화로 인해 줄어들기 시작할 것으로 예상된다."

(A) [1]
(B) [2]
(C) [3]
(D) [4]

| 해설 | 제시된 문장은 높은 고객 풀을 보유하고 있던 회사의 변화를 예측하는 내용이므로, 이러한 변화 사항이 언급된 것으로 두 번째 단락에 Lumbra 커뮤니케이션이 한때 많은 곳에서 인터넷 사용자들의 유일한 옵션이었지만, 그것이 변하고 있다고(It used to be the only option for Internet users in many places, but that is changing) 한 문장 뒤인 (B)가 정답이다.

| 어휘 | shrink 줄어들다   market saturation 시장 포화

176-180 다음 이메일들을 참조하시오.

수신: Gregorio Dellucci <dellucci@kokomohotel.com>
발신: Joyful 청소 <c_emmerson@joyfulcleaning.com>
날짜: 11월 19일, 오전 9:23
제목: 계정 #5872-R2003

Dellucci 씨 귀하,

Joyful 청소를 통해 최근 청소 용품을 주문해 주셔서 감사드립니다. 저희는 특히 귀하께서 Lemontime 바닥 세제로 우수한 결과를 얻으시기를 바라는데, 그것의 제조법이 최근에 더 효과적이 되도록 변경되었습니다. ¹⁷⁹수송품은 현재 11월 24일에 도착할 예정입니다.

이 주문으로 귀하는 "High-Volume 고객"의 범주에 들어가게 되시는데, 이는 ¹⁷⁶이제 귀하께서 저희 High-Volume 고객 보상 프로그램(HVCR)에 가입할 자격이 되신다는 것을 의미합니다. 이 프로그램 가입하면, 귀하와 같은 업체들은 95달러의 회원 카드 연회비를 지불하시게 됩니다. 이 카드로 12개월 동안 ¹⁷⁷ ⁽ᴬ⁾모든 주문에 대해 5% 할인을 받으실 수 있습니다. 심지어 사전 통지 없이, 저희의 보통 5일 배송 대신에 ¹⁷⁷ ⁽ᴰ⁾익일 배송을 신청하실 수도 있습니다. ¹⁷⁸이는 귀하의 세 호텔 지점들 어느 곳에나 적용될 것입니다. 또한 신제품들이 나오면 ¹⁷⁷ ⁽ᶜ⁾무료 샘플들을 받게 될 것입니다.

가입하시려면, 이 이메일에 답신해 주세요. ¹⁷⁹오늘 오후 5시까지 그렇게 하실 경우, 귀하의 현재 주문품을 하루 일찍 받으실 수 있을 것입니다.

따뜻한 안부를 전하며,

Connie Emmerson

| 어휘 | cleaning supplies 청소 용품   formula 제조법   effective 효과적인, 효율적인   shipment 수송품   put into ~에 들어가다   be eligible to ~할 자격이 있다   reward 보상   annual fee 연회비   period 기간   sign up for ~을 신청하다   advance notice 사전 통지   apply to ~에 적용되다

수신: Joyful 청소 <c_emmerson@joyfulcleaning.com>
발신: Gregorio Dellucci <dellucci@kokomohotel.com>
날짜: 11월 19일, 오후 1:48
제목: 회신: 계정 #5872-R2003

Emmerson 씨 귀하,

¹⁷⁹저는 HVCR 회원에 관심이 있으니, 제 계정에 95달러의 회비를 청구해 주세요. 또한 지난번 수송품에 대해, ¹⁸⁰배달원이 접수 담당자가 잠깐 자리를 비운 사이에 접수 데스크에 박스를 놓고 갔고, 그래서 그것을 지켜보는 사람 없이 몇 분 동안 그곳에 있었습니다. 새로운 배송 날짜에는 이런 일이 일어나지 않기를 바랍니다.

감사합니다!

Gregorio Dellucci

| 어휘 | be interested in ~에 관심 있다   bill 청구하다, 청구서를 보내다   account 계정   receptionist 접수 담당자   step out 잠시 자리를 비우다, 나가다   keep an eye on ~을 지켜보다, 눈을 떼지 않다   happen 일어나다

176. 주제/목적 문제

첫 번째 이메일의 한 가지 목적은 무엇인가?

(A) 서비스에 대한 피드백을 얻는 것

(B) 업체를 위한 한 가지 기회를 설명하는 것
(C) 청소 용품을 홍보하는 것
(D) 새로운 고객 보상 프로그램을 광고하는 것
| 해설 | 두 번째 단락에 이제 High-Volume 고객 보상 프로그램(HVCR)에 가입할 자격이 된다고(~ you are now eligible to join our High-Volume Customer Rewards program (HVCR)) 알려주고 있으므로 정답은 (B)이다.
| 어휘 | advertise 광고하다   loyalty program 고객 보상 프로그램

177. NOT True 문제
HVCR의 이점으로 제시되지 않은 것은 무엇인가?
(A) 더 낮은 제품 가격
(B) 사전 할인 알림
(C) 무료 샘플
(D) 익일 배송
| 해설 | 두 번째 단락에 모든 주문에 대해 5% 할인을 받을 수 있다고(The card allows you to get five percent off all orders) 한 것에서 (A), 익일 배송을 신청할 수 있다고(You'll also be able to sign up for next-day delivery) 한 것에서 (D), 무료 신제품 샘플들을 받게 될 것이라고(You'll also be sent free samples of new products) 한 것에서 (C)는 확인된다. 따라서 정답은 (B)이다.
| 어휘 | complimentary 무료의   overnight 밤사이에, 야간의
| 패러프레이징 | · five percent off all orders → Lower prices on products
· next-day delivery → Overnight shipments
· free samples → Complimentary samples

178. 추론 문제
Dellucci 씨에 관해 암시되는 것은 무엇인가?
(A) Lemontime 바닥 세제에 대한 후기를 작성했다.
(B) 자신의 주문에 물품들을 더 추가하기를 원했다.
(C) 한 곳 이상의 지점을 감독한다.
(D) 일부 품목들의 빠른 배송 비용을 지불했다.
| 해설 | Dellucci 씨는 첫 번째 이메일의 수신자로, 두 번째 단락 후반부에 회원 혜택에 대해 귀하의 세 호텔 지점들 어느 곳에나 적용될 것이라고(This would apply to any of your three hotel branches) 한 것을 통해, Dellucci 씨는 세 개의 호텔 지점을 감독하는 것으로 유추할 수 있으므로 정답은 (C)이다.
| 어휘 | oversee 감독하다   express 급행의, 속달의

고난도
179. 연계 문제 - 추론
Dellucci 씨는 언제 자신의 주문품을 받을 것 같은가?
(A) 11월 19일에
(B) 11월 20일에
(C) 11월 23일에
(D) 11월 24일에
| 해설 | 첫 번째 이메일 첫 번째 단락에 수송품은 현재 11월 24일에 도착할 예정이라고(The shipment is currently scheduled to arrive on November 24) 알린 후, 마지막 단락에 오늘 오후 5시까지 회원 가입을 위해 이메일에 답신하면 주문품을 하루 일찍 받을 수 있을 것이라고(~ you'll be able to receive your current order one day early) 했는데, 이를 두 번째 이메일에 Dellucci 씨가

HVCR 회원에 관심이 있으니, 제 계정에 95달러의 회비를 청구해 달라고(I am interested in HVCR membership, so please bill my account for the $95 membership fee) 한 것을 연계해 볼 때, 11월 23일에 주문품을 받을 것으로 유추할 수 있으므로 정답은 (C)이다.

180. 세부 사항을 묻는 문제
Dellucci 씨는 Emmerson 씨에게 어떤 문제에 관해 말하는가?
(A) 소포에 잘못된 물품들이 들어 있었다.
(B) 소포가 지켜보는 사람 없이 놓여 있었다.
(C) 그는 손상된 물품을 받았다.
(D) 그는 배송 비용을 과다하게 청구받았다.
| 해설 | 지난번 수송품에 대해 배달원이 접수 담당자가 잠깐 자리를 비운 사이에 접수 데스크에 박스를 놓고 갔고, 그래서 그것을 지켜보는 사람 없이 몇 분 동안 그곳에 있었다고(~ it sat there for several minutes with no one keeping an eye on it) 했으므로 정답은 (B)이다.
| 어휘 | unattended 지켜보는 사람 없는   overcharge 과다하게 청구하다
| 패러프레이징 | · the box → A package
· sat there ~ with no one keeping an eye on it → was left unattended

181-185 다음 편지와 주문서를 참조하시오.

Kimberly Shaw
1358 Wilmington Avenue
Winnipeg, MB R3G 3P4
캐나다

2월 6일

Shaw 씨 귀하,

[181]귀하의 업데이트된 사진 양도 계약서를 보내주셔서 감사드리며, 그것에는 귀하께서 저희에게 대금을 지불받으면 저희가 제한된 목적에 사진을 이용할 허가를 얻게 된다는 것이 나와 있습니다. 늘 그렇듯, [182]아직 지급되지 않은 귀하의 모든 수수료는 이번 달 20일에 지급될 것입니다.

[183]또한 Kirwan 출판이 다가오는 몇 달 내에 여러 새로운 출판물들을 출간할 것이어서, 저희가 어느 때보다 프리랜서 사진 촬영 서비스에 의존하게 될 것임을 알려드리게 되어 기쁩니다. [184]저희는 지난달에 저희의 어느 잡지에든 기고해 주셨던 프리랜서들에게 모든 잡지들에 50% 할인을 제공해 드리고 있습니다. 그 할인은 온라인 결제 페이지에서 코드 REF561를 이용함으로써 받으실 수 있습니다.

귀하와 계속해서 작업하기를 고대합니다!

따뜻한 안부를 전하며,

Calvin Leroy

| 어휘 | release form 양도 계약서   permission 허가, 승인   limited

제한된, 한정된   payment 대금, 지불금   outstanding 미지불된
commission 수수료   issue 지급하다, 발급하다   launch 출간하다,
출시하다   publication 출판물, 간행물   rely on ~에 의존하다, 기대다
contribute to ~에 기고하다, 기여하다   obtain 받다, 얻다   checkout
계산

---

www.kirwanpublishing.com/checkout

귀하의 주문이 처리되었습니다!

¹⁸⁵2월 특별 상품: 셋 이상의 잡지를 구독하시고 무료 달력을 받으세요.

¹⁸⁴이름: José Hudson
이메일 주소: jose@hudsonphotoshowcase.com
주문 날짜: 2월 19일
지불 방법: 신용 카드 XXXX-XXXX-XXXX-4574
청구지 주소: José Hudson, 925 Bolman Court, Vancouver,
BC V6J 4A1, 캐나다
배송 주소: 위와 동일

제품 상세
¹⁸⁵<Outdoor Monthly> 1년 구독	20.00달러
¹⁸⁵<Under the Stars> 1년 구독	15.00달러
¹⁸⁵<Wildlife Insider> 1년 구독	18.00달러
¹⁸⁴할인 코드 (REF561)	-26.50달러
총 내야 할 금액	26.50달러

귀하의 주문 다음 달 5일에 구독하신 것의 첫 번째 호를 받게 될 것입니다. 고객들은 구독이 만료되기 2개월 전에 구독을 갱신할 서류를 받게 됩니다.

| 어휘 | process 처리하다   subscribe 구독하다   complimentary 무료의   due 내야 할 돈   issue (잡지 등의) 호   subscription 구독   following 다음의   paperwork 서류, 서류 작업   renew 갱신하다   expire 만료되다

---

181. 주제/목적 문제

Leroy 씨는 왜 편지를 보냈나?
(A) 사진에 수정을 요청하기 위해
(B) Shaw 씨에게 일자리를 제안하기 위해
(C) 서식의 수령을 알리기 위해
(D) 지연에 대해 사과하기 위해

| 해설 | 도입부에 업데이트된 사진 양도 계약서를 보내줘서 감사하다고(Thank you for sending in your updated photo release form) 한 후, 그 계약서에 관한 내용이 이어지고 있으므로 정답은 (C)이다.

| 어휘 | adjustment 조정, 조절   acknowledge (편지·소포 등을) 받았음을 알리다, 인정하다   apologize for ~에 대해 사과하다   delay 지연

---

182. 세부 사항을 묻는 문제

이번 달에 Shaw 씨에게 무엇이 보내질 것인가?
(A) 업무 배당
(B) 새로운 잡지
(C) 계약서
(D) 지불금

| 해설 | Shaw 씨에게 보낸 편지 첫 번째 단락 후반부에 아직 지급되지 않은 모든 수수료는 이번 달 20일에 지급될 것이라고(your payment for any outstanding commissions will be issued on the 20th of this month) 했으므로 정답은 (D)이다.

| 어휘 | assignment 배당, 할당, 임무   contract 계약(서)

---

183. True 문제

Kirwan 출판에 대해 사실인 것은 무엇인가?
(A) 새로운 사진 촬영 부서를 개설할 것이다.
(B) 제품 범위를 확장할 계획이다.
(C) 독자 수의 감소를 겪어왔다.
(D) 상의 후보로 지명되었다.

| 해설 | 편지 두 번째 단락에 또한 Kirwan 출판이 다가오는 몇 달 내에 여러 새로운 출판물들을 출간할 것이라고(~ Kirwan Publishing will launch several new publications in the coming months) 한 것에서 제품 범위를 확대하려 한다는 것을 알 수 있으므로 정답은 (B)이다.

| 어휘 | expand 확장하다   experience 경험하다   decline 감소   readership 독자 수   be nominated for ~의 후보로 지명되다   award 상

| 패러프레이징 | will launch several new publications → plans to expand its product range

---

🔺고난도

184. 연계 추론 문제

Hudson 씨에 관해 암시되는 것은 무엇인가?
(A) Shaw 씨를 위해 추천서를 제공했다.
(B) 최근 Kirwan 출판을 통해 작품을 출간했다.
(C) Kirwan 출판의 단골 고객이다.
(D) <Outdoor Monthly>의 편집자이다.

| 해설 | Hudson 씨는 주문서에 제시된 고객으로, 제품 상세 마지막에 할인 코드 REF561를(Discount Code (REF561)) 이용하여 할인을 받은 것으로 확인되고, 이를 편지 두 번째 단락 후반부에 지난달에 저희의 어느 잡지에든 기고했던 프리랜서들에게 50% 할인을 제공한다며(~ freelancers who have contributed to any of our magazines in the past month) 온라인 결제 페이지에서 코드 REF561를 이용함으로써 받을 수 있다고(The discount can be obtained by using the code REF561 on the online checkout page) 한 것과 연계해 볼 때, Hudson 씨는 Kirwan 출판의 잡지에 기고해서 할인을 받게 된 것임을 알 수 있으므로 정답은 (B)이다.

| 어휘 | a letter of reference 추천서   regular customer 단골 고객   editor 편집자, 편집장

| 패러프레이징 | have contributed to any of our magazines in the past month → recently published work through Kirwan Publishing

고난도

185. 추론 문제

Hudson 씨의 주문에 대해 암시되는 것은 무엇인가?
(A) 자동으로 갱신될 것이다.
(B) 여러 주소들로 발송될 것이다.
(C) 무료 선물을 포함할 것이다.
(D) 약 2개월 후에 만료될 것이다.

| 해설 | 주문서 초반부에 2월 특별 상품으로 셋 이상의 잡지를 구독하고 무료 달력을 받으라고(February Special: Subscribe to three or more magazines and receive a complimentary calendar) 제시되어 있고, 제품 상세에 총 세 개의 잡지를 구독하는 것으로 나와 있으므로, 무료 달력을 받게 될 것임을 알 수 있다. 따라서 정답은 (C)이다.

| 어휘 | automatically 자동으로   multiple 많은, 여러 개의   include 포함하다

| 패러프레이징 | a complimentary calendar → a free gift

186-190 다음 이메일, 전단, 일정표를 참조하시오.

수신: Carolyn Dana <dana_c@ingrameden.com>
발신: Matthew Wallace <wallace_m@ingrameden.com>
날짜: 3월 8일
제목: 문화 활동들

안녕하세요, Caroly.

안녕하세요? **187**귀하가 Covington 지사와 우리 지사 사이의 차이에 익숙해지고 있기를 바랍니다. 저희는 귀하를 팀의 일원으로 보유하게 되어 기쁩니다. **186**귀하가 가장 최근 팀장 회의에 참석하실 수 없었기 때문에, 어떤 일이 있었는지 알려드리고 싶었는데요. 저희는 주로 다음 달 봄철 팀 단합 활동을 위해 무엇을 할 것인지를 논의했습니다. 저희가 이전에 직원들로부터 받았던 피드백에 기반하여, 전통 무용 공연이 가장 좋을 것이라고 생각했습니다.

저희가 아직 날짜는 발표하지 않았는데, 제가 아직 티켓 구입 옵션들을 알아보고 있기 때문입니다. 행사일에 모두가 오전에 반나절 근무를 하고, **190**오후에 공연을 보러 가고, 이른 저녁까지 사무실로 돌아올 것입니다. 모두 참여할 수 있도록 제가 비회원용 단체 티켓을 구입할 것입니다. **189**500달러의 우리 예산으로 주차 비용을 조금 남겨두면서 전 직원들을 위한 티켓 비용을 충당하게 될 것 같습니다.

일단 그것들이 확정되면 더 많은 세부 사항들을 제공해 드리겠습니다.

진심으로,

Matthew Wallace
Ingram Eden, 인사 팀장

| 어휘 | get used to ~에 익숙해지다   team-building 팀 구축, 팀 단합   based on ~에 기반하여   previously 이전에   traditional 전통적인

look into ~을 알아보다   participate 참여하다   budget 예산   cover 충당하다   fee 요금   details 세부 사항

Horizon 극장에서 전통 무용 공연과 함께 과거로 여행을 떠나보세요!

Moon Bay 무용단이 전 세계 관객들에게 전통 무용의 즐거움을 공유해오고 있습니다. 세대를 거쳐 전해 내려온 무용들의 모습과 음향을 즐겨보세요. 저희 매표소를 방문하여 여러분의 티켓을 예약하세요. 또는 **188**티켓 취급 수수료를 피하기 위해 온라인으로 예약하세요.

여러분의 티켓을 어떻게 구매하시든 단체 요금은 이용 가능합니다.
티켓 10장: 140달러
티켓 20장: 250달러
189티켓 40장: 480달러
티켓 50장: 550달러

매표소: 806 Kent Street, (649) 555-3198
웹 사이트: www.htheaterboxoffice.com

| 어휘 | dance troupe 무용단   share 공유하다   sight 모습, 광경   pass down through generations 세대를 거쳐 전해 내려오다   box office 매표소   reserve 예약하다   avoid 피하다   handling fee 취급 수수료

**Horizon 극장
Moon Bay 무용단의 곧 있을 공연들**

날짜	시작 시간	출연 공연가	**190**티켓 제한
4월 2일	오후 8:00	Salini Chetti	없음
4월 5일	오후 2:00	Salini Chetti	회원 전용
4월 9일	오후 8:00	Ayush Kamal	회원 전용
1904월 12일	오후 2:00	Ayush Kamal	**190**없음

Horizon 극장의 전체 행사 목록을 위해서는 www.htheaterboxoffice.com을 방문하세요.

| 어휘 | upcoming 곧 있을, 다가오는   featured 출연하는   performer 공연가, 연기자   restriction 제한   complete 전체의, 완전한

---

186. 주제/목적 문제

Wallace 씨의 이메일의 목적은 무엇인가?
(A) 피드백 서식을 요청하는 것
(B) 회의 일정을 다시 잡는 것
(C) 결정을 알리는 것
(D) 취업 면접 일정을 잡는 것

| 해설 | 첫 번째 단락에 회의에 불참한 Dana 씨에게 어떤 일이 있었는지 알려준다며(As you were unable to attend the most recent team leader meeting, I wanted to let you know what happened) 결정 사항에 관해 구

체적으로 설명하고 있으므로 정답은 (C)이다.

| 어휘 | reschedule 일정을 다시 잡다   decision 결정

187. 추론 문제

이메일에서 Dana 씨에 관해 암시되는 것은 무엇인가?
(A) Horizon 극장에서 일했었다.
(B) 최근에 새로운 지점으로 옮겼다.
(C) 더 많은 문화 행사에 참석할 것을 제안했다.
(D) 공연 티켓 몇 장을 잃어버렸다.

| 해설 | 첫 번째 단락 도입부에 Dana 씨에게 Covington 지사와 우리 지사 사이의 차이에 익숙해지고 있기를 바란다고(I hope you are getting used to the differences between the Covington branch and our branch) 한 후, 팀의 일원으로 보유하게 되어 기쁘다고(We're glad to have you as part of the team) 덧붙인 것을 통해, Covington 지사에서 Wallace 씨가 있는 지사로 전근해 온 것으로 유추할 수 있으므로 정답은 (B)이다.

| 어휘 | used to ~했었다, ~하고는 했다   transfer 전근하다, 이전하다   cultural 문화적인   lose 잃어버리다, 분실하다

188. 세부 사항을 묻는 문제

전단에 언급된 온라인 예약의 이점은 무엇인가?
(A) 주차장을 미리 고르는 것
(B) 더 많은 좌석 선택권을 가지는 것
(C) 다과에 할인을 받는 것
(D) 취급 수수료를 피하는 것

| 해설 | 전단 첫 번째 단락 후반부에 티켓 취급 수수료를 피하기 위해 온라인으로 예약하라고(book online to avoid the ticket handling fee) 제시되어 있으므로 정답은 (D)이다.

| 어휘 | select 고르다   refreshment 다과

| 패러프레이징 | the ticket handling fee → a handling charge

고난도
189. 연계 문제 - 추론

Ingram Eden에는 몇 명의 사람들이 일하는 것 같은가?
(A) 10
(B) 20
(C) 40
(D) 50

| 해설 | 이메일 두 번째 단락 후반부에 500달러의 예산으로 주차 비용을 조금 남겨두면서 전 직원들을 위한 티켓 비용을 충당하게 될 것 같다고(~ our budget of five hundred dollars will cover the tickets for all staff members with a little left over for the parking fees) 했고, 전단에서 500달러에서 약간 금액을 남길 수 있는 것은 티켓 40장: 480달러(40 tickets: $480)일 것이므로 정답은 (C)이다.

고난도
190. 연계 문제 - 추론

Ingram Eden 직원들은 언제 공연을 보러 갈 것 같은가?
(A) 4월 2일
(B) 4월 5일
(C) 4월 9일
(D) 4월 12일

| 해설 | 이메일 두 번째 단락에 오후에 공연을 보러 가고(attend the show in the afternoon), 이른 저녁에 사무실로 돌아올 것이라며(return to the office by early evening), 모두 참여할 수 있도록 비회원용 단체 티켓을 구입할 것이라고(I'll buy group tickets for non-members so that everyone can participate) 했는데, 일정표에서 티켓 제한이(Ticket Restrictions) 없고(None), 이른 저녁에 사무실로 돌아올 수 있는 오후 공연은 4월 12일(April 12) 공연으로 확인되므로 정답은 (D)이다.

191-195 다음 회람, 일정표, 공지를 참조하시오.

수신: 전 직원
발신: Natalie Lantz, 사무실 관리자
주제: 보수

4월 17일

5월 2일에 시작되는 Perine Enterprises 건물 전체 보수 공사로 인해, 2층에 있는 회의실 두 개가 직원들을 위한 업무 공간으로 이용될 것입니다. 이것이 불편한 일임은 이해하지만, 필요에 따라 임시 배치로 [191]그럭저럭 해 나갈 수 있을 것임을 확신합니다. 부서들은 다음 일정에 따라 회의실을 이용할 것입니다:

첫째 주(5월 2-8일): 영업 마케팅
[192]둘째 주(5월 9-15일): 회계
셋째 주(5월 16-22일): 연구 개발
넷째 주(5월 23-29일): 인사

[194]다섯 째 주에는(5월 30일-6월 5일) 보수 공사가 로비에서 이루어질 것입니다. 이 기간 동안에는 정문 출입구가 폐쇄될 것이니, 직원들과 방문객들은 건물의 동쪽 문을 이용해야 합니다.

여러분의 협조에 감사드립니다.

| 어휘 | renovation 보수 공사   conference room 회의실   workspace 업무 공간, 작업 공간   inconvenience 불편, 불편한 일   get by with ~로 그럭저럭 해 나가다   temporary 임시의, 일시적인   setup 배치, 설치   as necessary 필요에 따라   following 다음의   take place 일어나다   entrance 출입구   cooperation 협조

O'Malley 건설

작업 일정: Perine Enterprises, 5월 2일-6월 5일
작업 공정: #58305 / 연락 담당자: Natalie Lantz

주	장소	작업
첫째 주	4층	벽면 재 페인트칠, 카펫 뜯어내기, 바닥 타일 설치

192둘째 주	5층	벽면 재 페인트칠, 193 (D)복도 끝에 찬장들 만들기
셋째 주	2층	벽면 재 페인트칠, 193 (B)창문 설치 x 12
넷째 주	3층	벽면 재 페인트칠, 193 (A)깨진 바닥 타일들 수리
다섯째 주	1층 (로비)	입구 확장, 대리석 바닥 설치, 천장 조명들 재 배선

| 어휘 | remove 없애다, 빼다　cupboard 찬장　hallway 복도　broken 깨진　expand 확장하다　marble 대리석　rewire 배선을 다시 하다　ceiling light 천장 조명

PERINE ENTERPRISES 직원들에 공지

194우리 건물의 Saginaw Avenue 출입구는 보수 공사 작업의 일환으로 5월 30일부터 6월 5일까지 폐쇄될 것입니다. Turner Street 출입구의 보안 카드가 필요한 분들은 보안 책임자 Li Wan을 만나시기 바랍니다. 이 기간 동안 접수 구역은 폐쇄될 것이지만, 엘리베이터 근처에 테이블이 설치되어 그곳에서 접수 담당자들이 정규 업무를 수행할 것입니다. 방문객들에게 변경 사항을 알려 주시기 바랍니다. 외부 장소에서 방문객들을 만나는 것이 더 편하다면, 195회사 자금으로 비용을 충당받을 자격이 있을 수 있습니다. Eleanor Butler를 만나 미리 허가를 받으세요. 보수 공사의 진행에 관한 문의들은 Gina Lombardi에게 보낼 수 있습니다.

| 어휘 | security card 보안 카드　reception area 접수 구역　set up 설치하다　receptionist 접수 담당자　carry out 시행하다　regular 정규적인　duty 의무, 업무　off-site 외부　be eligible to ~할 자격이 있다　expense 비용　fund 자금　permission 허가, 승인　in advance 미리　progress 진행　direct to ~에게 보내다

🏠 고난도

191. 동의어 문제
회람에서 첫 번째 단락 세 번째 줄에 있는 관용구 "get by"와 뜻이 가장 유사한 것은
(A) 그럭저럭 해내다
(B) 받다
(C) 승인하다
(D) 능가하다
| 해설 | 해당 관용구가 들어간 문장은 '필요에 따라 임시 배치로 그럭저럭 해 나갈 수 있을 것임을 확신한다'라고 해석된다. 따라서 이와 가장 유사한 '그럭저럭 해내다'라는 뜻의 동사인 (A) manage가 정답이다.

192. 연계 문제 – 세부 사항
회계 부서는 Perine Enterprises 건물의 어디에 위치해 있나?
(A) 2층에
(B) 3층에
(C) 4층에
(D) 5층에
| 해설 | 첫 번째 지문인 회람에서 회계 부서는(Accounting) 둘째 주에(5월 9–15) 보수 작업 일정이 잡혀 있고, 두 번째 지문인 일정표에서 둘째 주 작업 위치는 5층으로(5th Floor) 확인되므로 정답은 (D)이다.

193. NOT True 문제
보수 공사 프로젝트의 일환으로 언급되지 않은 것은?
(A) 바닥을 보수하는 것
(B) 새로운 창문을 설치하는 것
(C) 카펫을 까는 것
(D) 보관 구역을 추가하는 것
| 해설 | 일정표 둘째 주에 있는 복도 끝에 찬장들 만들기(build cupboards at end of hallway)에서 (D), 셋째 주에 있는 창문 설치(window installation)에서 (B), 넷째 주에 있는 깨진 바닥 타일 수리(fix broken floor tiles)에서 (A)는 확인된다. 따라서 정답은 (C)이다.
| 어휘 | lay 깔다　storage 보관, 저장
| 패러프레이징 | · fix broken floor tiles → Repairing some flooring
· window installation → Installing new windows
· cupboards → a storage area

🏠 고난도

194. 연계 문제 – True
Perine Enterprises에 관해 사실인 것은 무엇인가?
(A) 건물 벽면들이 모두 다시 페인트칠 될 것이다.
(B) 정문 출입구는 Saginaw Avenue에 있다.
(C) 직원들이 장소 개선을 요청했다.
(D) 접수 서비스를 일주일 동안 이용할 수 없을 것이다.
| 해설 | 회람 후반부에 다섯째 주에는(5월 30일–6월 5일) 보수 공사가 로비에서 이루어질 것이고, 이 기간 동안 정문 출입구가 폐쇄될 것이라고(In Week 5 (May 30–June 5), ~ The main entrance will be closed during this time) 한 것과 공지 도입부에 건물의 Saginaw Avenue 출입구가 5월 30일부터 6월 5일까지 폐쇄될 것이라고(The Saginaw Avenue entrance to our building will be closed from May 30 to June 5 ~) 한 것을 연계시키면, Saginaw Avenue 출입구가 정문 출입구임을 알 수 있으므로 (B)가 정답이다.
| 어휘 | improvement 개선　unavailable 이용할 수 없는

195. 세부 사항을 묻는 문제
직원들은 왜 Butler 씨에게 연락하도록 권고되는가?
(A) 방문객들의 이름을 제공하기 위해
(B) 자금 지원 승인을 받기 위해
(C) 보안 출입증을 요청하기 위해
(D) 프로젝트에 관한 최신 정보를 받기 위해
| 해설 | 공지 후반부에 외부 장소에서 방문객들을 만나는 것이 더 편하다면, 회사 자금으로 비용을 충당받을 자격이 있을 수 있다고(you may be eligible to have the expenses covered by company funds) 한 후 Eleanor Butler을 만나 미리 허가를 받으라고(See Eleanor Butler to get permission in advance) 했으므로 정답은 (B)이다.
| 어휘 | funding 자금 제공, 자금 지원　approval 승인　security 보안

| 패러프레이징 | permission → approval

196-200 다음 일정표, 이메일, 기사에 관한 문제입니다.

Gaskell Creations
샘플 주문 제작 진행
상세: Skylark 전신 드레스

날짜	제작 계획
5월 12일, 일요일	- Anja Rembert에 의해 디자인 확정
¹⁹⁶5월 13일, 월요일	- ¹⁹⁶Stroop Supplies의 원단 선택 프레젠테이션 - ¹⁹⁶선택한 물품에 대한 긴급 주문 요청
¹⁹⁸5월 16일, 목요일	- 열 벌의 드레스 제작 - ¹⁹⁸품질 관리 점검 (치수 확인, 지퍼 테스트, 시각적 분석)
5월 17일, 금요일	- 전체 샘플 생산
5월 18일, 토요일	- 완료된 샘플들을 Orchard 패션에 발송

| 어휘 | production 제작, 생산   description 상세, 설명   full-length dress 전신 드레스   fabric 원단, 천   rush 급한, 긴급한   selected 선택된, 선정된   quality control 품질 관리   inspection 점검   dimension 치수   visual 시각의, 시각적인   analysis 분석

수신: Beth Ehmann <ehmannb@orchardfashions.com>
발신: Tammy Culver <culvert@orchardfashions.com>
날짜: ¹⁹⁹5월 21일
제목: Skylark 드레스

Ehmann 씨 귀하,

Gaskell Creations로부터 Skylark 전신 드레스의 샘플을 받았습니다. ¹⁹⁷제작 비용과 완성된 샘플의 높은 품질을 검토해 보니, Gaskell Creations가 이 프로젝트를 위한 올바른 선택이라고 생각합니다.

¹⁹⁸지난 목요일에 저는 첫 열 벌의 드레스에 대한 품질 관리 점검에 참여했습니다. 다음 날 아침에 공장 감독관을 만나서 고르지 않은 단 끝에 관해 우려를 표명했습니다. 그가 제작을 재개하기 전에 절단기를 적절히 조정했습니다. 전체 샘플의 어떤 드레스에도 문제가 발생하지 않았습니다.

¹⁹⁹제가 오늘 아침에 Lily Zemanski와 화상 회의를 했는데, 그때 제가 우리의 잠재적인 제휴에 있어 유일한 문제는 Gaskell Creations가 우리의 사훈(사명 선언)과 맞지 않는 것이라고 설명했습니다. ¹⁹⁹Zemanski 씨가 저희가 만족하도록 회사가 다음 달에 그 문제를 해결하기 위한 조치를 취할 것이라고 약속했습니다. 그래서 우리가 계속 진전할 수 있다는 것이라고 말하게 되어 기쁩니다.

Tammy Culver

| 어휘 | foreman 감독   express one's concerns about ~에 대한 우려를 표명하다   uneven 고르지 않은   hemline (드레스 등의) 단 끝   appropriate 적절한   adjustment 조정   resume 재개하다   occur 발생하다   teleconference 화상 회의   potential 잠재적인   fit with ~에 맞다, 적합하다   mission statement 사명 선언, 사훈   take measures 조치를 취하다, 대책을 강구하다   to one's satisfaction ~가 만족하도록   move forward 진전하다, 앞으로 나아가다

소도시 공장이 거대 기업과 연계하다

8월 8일 — Clairsville의 남쪽 지역에 위치한 제조업체인 Gaskell Creations가 그 회사 역사상 가장 큰 고객과 제휴를 시작했다. Gaskell은 현재 Orchard 패션을 위한 의류들을 제작하고 있다. ¹⁹⁹그 계약을 확보하기 위해, Gaskell은 6월에 여러 번의 교육과 장비 업그레이드를 실시하여 안전 등급을 높였다.

"저희는 이 협의를 진행시키도록 확실히 하고자 기꺼이 변화를 주었습니다." Gaskell의 전무 이사인 Lily Zemanski가 말했다. "큰 계약은 저희의 투자액을 빠르게 회수할 수 있다는 것을 의미하고, 그 변화는 저희 직원들에게 크게 도움이 됩니다. ²⁰⁰처음으로 우리는 구직자들을 위한 자리가 없기 때문에 그들을 거절하고 있습니다."

| 어휘 | manufacturer 제조업체, 제조사   located 위치한   garment 의복   secure 확보하다, 획득하다   equipment 장비   safety rating 안전 등급   agreement 합의, 협정   go forward 진행시키다, 진전하다   executive director 전무 이사   investment 투자, 투자액   benefit 도움이 되다, 유용하다   turn away 외면하다, 거절하다   job applicant 구직자

196. 세부 사항을 묻는 문제

5월 13일에 어떤 활동이 완료되었나?
(A) 디자인들이 광고되었다.
(B) 프레젠테이션이 배정되었다.
(C) 원단이 주문되었다.
(D) 샘플이 운송되었다.

| 해설 | 일정표에서 5월 13일 제작 계획에 Stroop Supplies의 원단 선택 프레젠테이션(Presentation of fabric options by Stroop Supplies)과 선택한 물품에 대한 긴급 주문 요청(Request rush order on selected items)이 제시되어 있으므로 원단을 선택하여 주문했음을 알 수 있다. 따라서 정답은 (C)이다.

| 패러프레이징 | fabric options / Request rush order → Fabrics were ordered

197. 추론 문제

Culver 씨가 완성된 샘플 제품에 관해 암시하는 것은 무엇인가?
(A) 회사의 요구에 적합하다.
(B) 그것의 품질이 판매 가격에 영향을 미칠 수 있다.
(C) 경험 없는 작업자들에 의해 만들어졌다.

(D) 원래 예정된 것보다 더 늦게 도착했다.

| 해설 | Culver 씨가 보낸 이메일의 첫 번째 단락에 제작 비용과 완성된 샘플의 높은 품질을 검토해 보니, Gaskell Creations가 이 프로젝트를 위한 올바른 선택이라고 생각한다고(~ I believe Gaskell Creations is the right choice for this project) 한 것에서 샘플 제품이 회사의 요구에 적합하다고 생각함을 알 수 있으므로 정답은 (A)이다.

| 어휘 | suitable 적합한, 알맞은   inexperienced 경험 없는

198. 연계 문제 – 추론
Culver 씨는 언제 공장 관리자를 만났던 것 같은가?
(A) 5월 12일
(B) 5월 16일
(C) 5월 17일
(D) 5월 18일

| 해설 | Culver 씨가 보낸 이메일의 두 번째 단락에 지난 목요일에 품질 관리 점검에 참여했고, 다음 날 아침에 공장 감독관을 만났다고(The following morning, I met with the factory foreman ~) 했는데, 일정표에서 품질 관리 점검을 (Quality control inspection) 한 것은 5월 16일로 확인되므로, 그 다음 날인 (C)가 정답이다.

고난도
199. 연계 문제 – 세부 사항
Zemanski 씨가 5월 21일에 약속한 것은 무엇인가?
(A) 즉시 더 많은 작업자들이 고용될 것이다.
(B) 제품이 촉박한 통지에 제작될 수 있을 것이다.
(C) 환경친화적인 원단이 이용될 것이다.
(D) Gaskell Creations가 안전 등급을 향상시킬 것이다.

| 해설 | Culver 씨가 5월 21일에 보낸 이메일의 세 번째 단락에 오늘 아침에 Zemanski 씨와 화상 회의를 했는데 Gaskell Creations와의 제휴에 있어 문제가 되는 것을 설명하니 그가 다음 달에 회사가 그 문제를 해결하기 위한 조치를 취할 것이라고 약속했다고(Ms. Zemanski promised that the company would take measures next month to resolve that issue to our satisfaction) 했다. 또한 기사 첫 번째 단락에 그 계약을 확보하기 위해, Gaskell은 6월에 여러 번의 교육과 장비 업그레이드를 실시하여 안전 등급을 높였다고(~ Gaskell made several training and equipment upgrades in June to bring its safety rating up) 했는데, 이 둘을 연계하면 Zemanski 씨가 5월 21일에 안전 등급 향상을 약속한 것임을 유추할 수 있으므로 정답은 (D)이다.

| 어휘 | guarantee 보장하다, 약속하다   short notice 촉박한 통지 environmentally friendly 환경친화적인

| 패러프레이징 | made several training and equipment upgrades in June to bring its safety rating up → improve its safety rating

200. 추론 문제
Zemanski 씨가 자신의 회사에 관해 암시하는 것은 무엇인가?
(A) 일자리에 대한 수요가 많다.
(B) 새로운 지점을 열 계획이 있다.
(C) Clairsville에 가장 큰 고용업체이다.
(D) 현재 새로운 투자자들을 찾고 있다.

| 해설 | 기사 후반부에 Zemanski 씨가 처음으로 구직자들을 위한 자리가 없기 때문에 그들을 거절하고 있다고(For the first time ever, we're turning away job applicants because we don't have room for them) 한 것에서, 일자리에 대한 수요가 많음을 유추할 수 있으므로 정답은 (A)이다.

| 어휘 | be in high demand 수요가 많다   seek 찾다   investor 투자자

TEST 09

PART 5				
101 (C)	102 (B)	103 (C)	104 (D)	105 (B)
106 (C)	107 (C)	108 (D)	109 (C)	110 (C)
111 (D)	112 (A)	113 (C)	114 (B)	115 (B)
116 (B)	117 (B)	118 (B)	119 (C)	120 (C)
121 (A)	122 (D)	123 (B)	124 (C)	125 (C)
126 (C)	127 (C)	128 (A)	129 (A)	130 (B)

PART 6				
131 (A)	132 (B)	133 (C)	134 (C)	135 (B)
136 (D)	137 (D)	138 (A)	139 (D)	140 (C)
141 (A)	142 (D)	143 (C)	144 (D)	145 (A)
146 (B)				

PART 7				
147 (B)	148 (A)	149 (B)	150 (A)	151 (D)
152 (B)	153 (C)	154 (D)	155 (D)	156 (A)
157 (D)	158 (C)	159 (C)	160 (D)	161 (C)
162 (D)	163 (C)	164 (C)	165 (D)	166 (B)
167 (C)	168 (A)	169 (C)	170 (B)	171 (C)
172 (B)	173 (A)	174 (C)	175 (D)	176 (B)
177 (C)	178 (D)	179 (B)	180 (B)	181 (B)
182 (D)	183 (C)	184 (B)	185 (A)	186 (C)
187 (A)	188 (C)	189 (D)	190 (B)	191 (B)
192 (B)	193 (D)	194 (C)	195 (C)	196 (A)
197 (D)	198 (B)	199 (A)	200 (C)	

PART 5

101. 전치사 어휘
작업반이 시내 도로들에 새로운 차선 경계선을 페인트칠하는 동안 교통이 우회되었다.
해설 빈칸은 뒤에 있는 명사구를 목적어로 가지는 전치사가 들어갈 자리로, the downtown streets는 장소를 나타내는 명사구이므로 '시내 도로들에'라는 의미를 완성해줄 장소 전치사인 (C) on이 정답이다.
어휘 traffic 교통 | reroute 우회하다 | work crew 작업반 | downtown 시내

102. 인칭 대명사
최고 품질의 주방 가전에 관심 있는 고객들께서는 저희 안내서를 읽어보셔야 합니다.
해설 빈칸은 타동사 read의 목적어인 명사 brochure를 한정 수식하는 자리이므로 소유격 대명사가 들어가야 한다. 따라서 (B) our가 정답이다.
어휘 top-quality 최고 품질의 | kitchen appliance 주방 가전

🔺고난도
103. 형용사 어휘
이번 달의 저널에 포함된 기사들 중에, 대부분의 독자들은 Cavalcanti 박사의 글이 가장 유익했다는 것에 동의한다.
해설 빈칸은 be동사 was의 보어로 앞의 최상급 부사의 수식을 받는 형용사가 들어갈 자리로, 'Cavalcanti 박사의 글이 가장 유익했다는 것에 동의한다'라는 의미로 전개되는 것이 적절하므로 '유익한'이라는 뜻의 (C) informative가 정답이다.
어휘 included 포함된 | piece 기사, 글 | prompt 즉각적인 | dissatisfied 불만스러워하는 | informative 유익한 | constant 지속적인

104. 명사 자리 - 주어
은행 직원은 그 서류의 기밀이 보호될 것이라고 Reeves 씨에게 장담했다.
해설 빈칸은 that절의 주어 자리로 관사 the와 전치사 of 사이에 있으므로 명사 자리이다. 따라서 '기밀, 비밀'이라는 뜻의 명사인 (D) confidentiality가 정답이다.
어휘 bank teller 은행 직원 | assure 장담했다, 보장하다 | confident 자신감 있는, 확신하는 | confidentially 비밀리에, 은밀히 | confidential 비밀의, 기밀의

105. 명사 어휘
Winchell 무용단의 인상적인 공연이 비평가들로부터 극찬을 낳았다.
해설 빈칸은 형용사 impressive와 뒤의 of 전치사구의 수식을 받는 명사가 들어갈 자리로, '무용단의 인상적인 공연이 극찬을 낳았다'라는 의미로 전개되는 것이 적절하므로 '공연'이라는 뜻의 (B) performance가 정답이다.
어휘 impressive 인상적인 | result in ~을 낳다, 야기하다 | rave review 극찬, 호평 | critic 비평가 | disposal 처리, 폐기 | performance 공연, 연기 | renovation 개조, 수리 | compensation 보상, 보수

106. 동사의 형태
최근에 전문 세미나에 참석했던 직원들은 피드백을 제공하도록 요청받는다.
해설 빈칸은 주어인 Employees를 수식하는 형용사절의 본동사가 들어갈 자리로, 앞에 have가 있으므로 have와 함께 현재 완료 시제 동사를 완성해줄 (C) attended가 정답이다.
어휘 recently 최근에 | professional 전문의; 전문직 종사자

107. 형용사 자리 - 명사 수식
그 물 필터의 혁신적인 디자인이 표면 위 곰팡이와 박테리아의 성장을 감소시킨다.
해설 소유격 표현 's와 명사 design 사이에 빈칸이 있으므로, 명사를 수식해줄 형용사나 복합 명사를 만들어줄 명사가 들어갈 자리임을 알 수 있다. (D) innovations는 복합 명사를 만들기에 의미상 부적절하므로 '필터의 혁신적인 디자인'이라는 의미를 완성해줄 '혁신적인'이라는 뜻의 형용사인 (C) innovative가 정답이다.
어휘 reduce 감소시키다, 줄이다 | growth 성장, 증가 | mold 곰팡이 | surface 표면 | innovatively 혁신적으로 | innovating 혁신하는 | innovation 혁신

108. 비교급
새로운 Yao 자동차 광고는 작년의 캠페인보다 더 명확하게 젊은 전문직 종사자들을 겨냥한다.

| 해설 | 빈칸 앞의 절은 빈칸이 없어도 하나의 완전한 절이 되는 것으로 볼 때, 빈칸에는 문장 구조에 지장을 주지 않는 부사가 들어가야 함을 알 수 있는데, 뒤에 비교급 전치사 than이 제시되어 있으므로 비교급 부사인 (D) more specifically가 정답이다.
| 어휘 | commercial 광고   target 겨냥하다, 목표로 삼다   specifically 명확하게, 구체적으로   specific 구체적인, 특정한

109. 동사 어휘
늦어도 금요일까지는 행사 기획자들에게 신청서를 꼭 제출해 주세요.
| 해설 | 빈칸은 to부정사를 완성해줄 동사 원형이 들어갈 자리로, 뒤에 제시된 목적어 the registration form과 연결 지어 '~에게 신청서를 제출해 주세요'라는 의미로 전개되는 것이 적절하므로 (C) submit이 정답이다.
| 어휘 | registration form 신청서   event planner 행사 기획자   no later than 늦어도 ~까지는   obtain 얻다   accept 수락하다   praise 칭찬하다

고난도
110. 부정 대명사
위원회가 발표된 각각의 신제품에 관해 논의하고 시장 성공 가능성이 가장 큰 하나를 선택할 것이다.
| 해설 | 빈칸은 타동사 select의 목적어가 될 대명사가 들어갈 자리이므로 대명사가 아닌 (A) other는 오답이고, 또한 빈칸을 수식하는 형용사절의 동사가 has로 단수이므로 복수 대명사인 (B) some과 (D) both도 오답이다. 따라서 단수의 부정 대명사인 (C) one이 정답이다.
| 어휘 | committee 위원회   present 발표하다   select 선택하다   chance 가능성   success 성공

고난도
111. 명사 어휘
영업 부장이 프레젠테이션의 슬라이드 몇 장의 수정을 요청했다.
| 해설 | 빈칸은 타동사 requested의 목적어이자 to 이하 전치사구의 수식을 받는 명사가 들어갈 자리로, '슬라이드의 수정을 요청했다'라는 의미로 전개되는 것이 적절하므로 '수정'이라는 뜻의 (D) revisions가 정답이다.
| 어휘 | transfer 이전, 전근   standard 기준, 표준

112. 전치사 자리
몇 주간의 치열한 협상 후에, GW 스포츠와 Poncia 주식회사의 합병이 마침내 합의되었다.
| 해설 | 빈칸은 뒤에 있는 명사구를 목적어로 가지는 전치사가 들어갈 자리이므로, 부사 혹은 형용사인 (D) Even은 답이 될 수 없고, '협상 후에, ~ 마침내 합의되었다'라는 의미로 전개되는 것이 적절하므로 '~ 후에'라는 뜻의 (A) After가 정답이다.
| 어휘 | intense 치열한, 집중적인   negotiation 협상   merger 합병   agree 합의하다

113. 부사절 접속사
직원들의 의견을 고려하는 것은 중요하지만, 리더들은 자신만의 본능을 따를 수 있어야 한다.
| 해설 | 빈칸 뒤로 두 개의 완전한 절이 있으므로, 빈칸은 두 절을 연결해 줄 접속사가 들어갈 자리이다. 따라서 부사절 접속사인 (C) Although가 정답이다. (A) Meanwhile, (B) Rather, (D) Regardless는 모두 부사이므로 오답이다.
| 어휘 | consider 고려하다   opinion 의견   be capable of ~할 수 있다   follow 따르다   instinct 본능

114. 명사절 접속사
공원 방문객들은 비 오는 날씨에는 길이 아주 미끄러워질 수 있다는 것을 알고 있어야 한다.
| 해설 | 빈칸 앞에 있는 형용사 aware는 'be aware of+명사' 혹은 'be aware that+절'의 구조로 쓰이는데 빈칸 뒤에 완전한 절이 있으므로 (B) that이 정답이다.
| 어휘 | aware 알고 있는   trail 오솔길, 코스   slippery 미끄러운   rainy 비 오는

고난도
115. 명사 자리 - 복합 명사
Nashville의 시 공무원들은 자금이 풀리자마자 사회 기반 시설 투자를 할 계획이다.
| 해설 | 타동사 make와 명사 an infrastructure 뒤에 빈칸이 있고, 빈칸 뒤에는 부사절이 있는데, 주절과 부사절에 각각 동사가 있으므로 동사인 (C) invest는 오답이고, 문맥상 앞의 명사와 함께 복합 명사를 이루는 명사가 들어가서 '사회 기반 시설 투자를 할 계획이다'라는 의미로 전개되는 것이 적절하므로 명사인 (B) investment가 정답이다. (D) investors는 의미상으로도 부적절하며 또한 복수이므로 관사 an과 함께 쓰일 수 없다.
| 어휘 | city official 시 공무원   infrastructure 사회 기반 시설   funds 자금   release 풀다   invest 투자하다   investor 투자자

고난도
116. 동사 어휘
Maxwell 청소용품은 자사의 식기 세척제가 다른 어떤 브랜드보다 기름을 잘 녹인다고 주장한다.
| 해설 | 문장의 본동사가 들어갈 자리로, that절을 목적어로 가지는 타동사가 들어가야 하고, 문맥상 '~라고 주장한다'라는 의미로 전개되는 것이 적절하므로 (B) claims가 정답이다.
| 어휘 | dishwashing liquid 식기 세척제   dissolve 녹이다, 용해시키다   grease 기름   modify 수정하다   claim 주장하다   attempt 시도하다   involve 관련시키다

117. 명사 어휘
Lansberry 비즈니스 협회는 많은 분야의 전문직 종사자들에게 폭넓은 범위의 강좌들을 제공한다.
| 해설 | 문맥상 '폭넓은 범위의 강좌들을 제공한다'라는 의미로 전개되는 것이 적절하므로 (B) range가 정답이다. a broad range of(다양하고 폭넓은, 광범위한)를 하나의 덩어리 표현으로 알아두자.
| 어휘 | broad 폭넓은   field 분야   method 방법   range 범위   parcel 꾸러미, 소포   surplus 잉여, 흑자

118. 동사의 형태
미술품 수집가들은 화가 Ella Padovesi의 새로운 전시회에서 보여진 그 재능을 매우 가치 있게 생각해야 한다.

| 해설 | 조동사 should 뒤에 부사 highly만 있고 동사 원형이 없으므로 빈칸은 동사 원형이 들어갈 자리이다. 따라서 (B) value가 정답이다.
| 어휘 | art collector 미술품 수집가   talent 재능   demonstrate 보여주다, 입증하다   exhibition 전시회   value 가치 있게 생각하다   valuable 귀중한

고난도
119. 부사 어휘
그 브랜드에 익숙한 사람들은 시골 지역들을 포함하여 어디에서나 디자이너 Paula Mazzi의 의류를 알아차릴 것이다.
| 해설 | 빈칸은 앞의 동사 notice의 의미를 보충 수식해줄 부사가 들어갈 자리로, 문맥상 '어디에서나 알아차릴 것이다'라는 의미로 전개되는 것이 적절하므로 (C) everywhere가 정답이다.
| 어휘 | be familiar with ~에 익숙하다, 잘 알고 있다   notice 알아차리다   clothing 의류   including ~을 포함하여   rural area 시골 지역   mutually 상호간에

120. 형용사 자리 - 주격 보어
연중 가장 추운 달에 지역 사회 퍼레이드를 여는 것은 계획자들에게는 합리적이지 않을 것이다.
| 해설 | 빈칸은 be동사의 보어가 들어갈 자리로, 동사와 명사로 쓰이는 (A) senses와 (D) sense는 명사인 경우 주어인 Holding과 동격이 되어 부적절하므로 답이 될 수 없고, '합리적이지 않을 것이다'라는 의미를 완성해줄 형용사인 (C) sensible이 정답이다.
| 어휘 | hold 열다, 개최하다   sense 감각, 지각; 감지하다, 느끼다

121. 형용사 어휘
귀하의 소포가 귀하의 청구서에 열거된 물품들을 모두 포함하고 있지 않으면, 고객 서비스로 연락하세요.
| 해설 | 빈칸은 명사 items를 수식해줄 과거 분사형 형용사가 들어갈 자리로, '열거된 물품들을 모두 포함하고 있지 않으면'이라는 의미로 전개되는 것이 적절하므로 (A) listed가 정답이다.
| 어휘 | include 포함하다   invoice 청구서, 송장   list 목록을 작성하다, 열거하다   reassure 안심시키다   dominate 지배하다   address 다루다

122. 접속사 자리
일단 투표 용지들이 모두 집계되면 그 선거의 승자가 공식적으로 발표될 것이다.
| 해설 | 빈칸 앞뒤에 두 개의 완전한 절이 있으므로, 빈칸에는 두 절을 연결해줄 접속사가 들어가야 한다. 따라서 부사절 접속사인 (D) once가 정답이다. (A) ever는 부사, (B) from은 전치사, (C) these는 대명사이자 형용사이므로 두 개의 절을 연결할 수 없다.
| 어휘 | winner 승자, 당선자   election 선거   officially 공식적으로, 정식으로   announce 발표하다   ballot 투표 용지   count 집계하다, 세다

고난도
123. 부사 어휘
채용 위원회의 선정 회의가 짧았는데, 위원들이 Steele 씨에게 일자리를 제안하는 것에 만장일치로 투표했기 때문이다.
| 해설 | 빈칸은 뒤의 동사를 수식해줄 부사가 들어갈 자리로, 이유를 나타내는 접속사 as로 연결되어 있는 것으로 볼 때, '만장일치로 투표했기 때문이다'라는 의미로 전개되는 것이 적절하므로 '만장일치로'라는 뜻의 (B) unanimously가 정답이다.
| 어휘 | hiring committee 채용 위원회   selection meeting 선정 회의   vote 투표하다   unanimously 만장일치로   intensively 집중적으로   frequently 자주, 종종

124. 명사 자리 - 복합 명사
업체들이 상업적인 용도로 상품을 수입하기 위해서는 보통 정부 허가를 받아야 한다.
| 해설 | 타동사 get과 명사 government 뒤에 빈칸이 있는데, government를 get의 목적어로 보기에는 문맥상 부적절하므로 government와 함께 복합 명사를 이룰 명사가 빈칸에 들어가야 한다. 따라서 '정부 허가'라는 의미의 복합 명사를 완성해줄 (B) permission이 정답이다.
| 어휘 | government 정부   import 수입하다   goods 상품, 제품   commercial use 상업적인 용도   permit 허용하다, 허락하다   permission 허가

125. 부사절 접속사
모두가 서로 더 쉽게 알 수 있도록 워크숍 참가자들에게 이름표가 배포되었다.
| 해설 | 빈칸 앞뒤에 두 개의 완전한 절이 있으므로, 빈칸에는 두 절을 연결해줄 접속사가 들어가야 한다. 또한 뒤의 절이 앞의 절의 이유/목적으로 볼 수 있으므로 이유/목적을 나타내는 부사절 접속사인 (C) so that이 정답이다.
| 어휘 | nametag 이름표, 명찰   distribute 배포하다, 나누어 주다   participant 참가자   except ~을 제외하고는

고난도
126. 분사 구문
완전히 편집되었을 때, 그 부서별 보고서들은 높은 직원 만족도에 대한 추세를 보여줬다.
| 해설 | 빈칸 앞에는 접속사 When과 부사 fully가 있고, 빈칸 뒤로는 완전한 절이 있으므로, 빈칸이 포함된 절은 분사 구문이 되어야 함을 알 수 있다. 따라서 'When (they were) fully complied ~'에서 주절의 주어와 같은 주어와 be동사가 생략된 분사 구문을 완성해줄 과거 분사인 (C) compiled가 정답이다.
| 어휘 | departmental 부서(별)의   trend 추세, 동향   satisfaction 만족   compile 엮다, 편집하다   compiler 편집자, 편찬자

고난도
127. 전치사 어휘
한쪽 당사자가 이번 회의에서 합의된 것들 이상의 계약 수정을 하길 원하면, 또 다른 회의가 필요하다.
| 해설 | 빈칸은 뒤에 명사를 목적어로 가지는 전치사가 들어갈 자리로, 뒤의 목적어와 연결 지어 '합의된 것 이상의'라는 의미로 전개되는 것이 적절하므로 '~ 이상, 넘어서는'이라는 뜻의 (C) beyond가 정답이다.
| 어휘 | party 당사자   contract 계약, 계약서   adjustment 조정, 수정   agree upon ~에 합의하다

고난도
128. 부사 자리
Shine 치과가 3층 특실로 이사한 날에 임대주가 아래층 건물 안내판에 그 이름을 추가했다.

| 해설 | 완전한 절 뒤에 빈칸이 있으므로, 빈칸은 부사가 들어갈 자리이며, 문맥상 건물 안내판이 있는 위치를 나타내 '아래층에 건물 안내판에 이름을 추가했다'라는 의미로 전개되는 것이 적절하므로 (A) downstairs가 정답이다.

| 어휘 | dental clinic 치과   suite 특실   landlord 임대주, 건물주   directory 건물 안내판   all in all 대체로

고난도
129. 동사 어휘 – 문법
기자 회견 시작 부분에 회사 대변인이 기자들에게 합병에 관한 세부 사항에 대해 간단히 말했다.

| 해설 | 빈칸 뒤에 사람 목적어 reporters가 있으므로, 빈칸의 동사는 사람 목적어를 갖는 동사여야 한다. 또한 문맥상 '기자들에게 간단히 말했다'라는 의미로 전개되는 것이 적절하므로 (A) briefed가 정답이다. (B) recounted, (C) discussed, (D) expressed 뒤에는 주로 이야기할 주제를 나타내는 사물 목적어가 온다.

| 어휘 | press conference 기자 회견   spokesperson 대변인   reporter 기자   details 세부 사항   merger 합병   brief 간단히 말하다   recount 이야기하다   express 표현하다

130. 형용사 자리 – 명사 수식
BT Kitchens는 완전 맞춤형 수납장들을 제작함으로써 여러분의 공간을 가장 효율적으로 사용하도록 만듭니다.

| 해설 | 부사 completely와 명사 cabinets 사이에 빈칸이 있으므로, 부사의 수식을 받으며 명사를 수식해줄 수 있는 형용사가 들어갈 자리이다. 따라서 형용사 역할을 할 수 있는 (B) customized가 정답이다.

| 어휘 | make the most efficient use of ~을 가장 효율적으로 이용하다   create 만들어내다, 창출하다   completely 완전히   customize 주문 제작하다   customization 주문 제작

PART 6

131-134 다음 이메일을 참조하시오.

수신: Ravi Harish <harishravi@dolainteriors.com>
발신: Angelina Kohl <angelina@homedecmag.com>
날짜: 10월 3일
제목: <홈 데코레이팅 매거진> 기사

Harish 씨 귀하,

축하합니다! Dola 인테리어가 이번 분기의 '스타일 스타'로 선정되었습니다. 저희 잡지가 11월호에 귀사를 ¹³¹특집으로 다룰 것인데요. 저희 잡지의 '스타일 스타' 코너는 인테리어 디자인의 유행을 창출하는 ¹³²업체들의 작업을 집중 조명합니다.

저희 직원들 중 한 명과의 전화 인터뷰를 할 시간이 있으신가요? ¹³³귀하의 말씀을 인용하는 것이 도움이 될 것입니다. 그것들이 귀사의 디자인 전략뿐만 아니라 사명을 개괄적으로 설명할 것입니다. 이것이 기사에 신뢰성을 가져올 것이고요. 저희 출간 마감일을 맞추기 위해 저희가 10월 ¹³⁴25일까지 귀하와 연락을 해야 할 것입니다.

진심을 담아,

Angelina Kohl
<홈 데코레이팅 매거진> 부편집장

| 어휘 | be chosen as ~로 선정되다   quarter 분기   firm 회사   issue (잡지 등의) 호   highlight 강조하다, 집중 조명하다   set trends 유행을 창출하다   outline 개요를 서술하다, 개괄하다   mission 사명   strategy 전략   authenticity 신뢰성, 확실성   be in touch with ~와 연락하다   deadline 마감일

131. 동사의 형태
| 해설 | be동사와 명사구 your firm 사이에 빈칸이 있으므로, 동사와 명사로 쓰이는 (C) features와 (D) feature는 오답이다. 또한 뒤에 명사구 your firm을 목적어로 받으려면 능동태가 되어야 하므로 앞에 있는 will be와 함께 미래 진행 시제를 만드는 현재 분사인 (A) featuring이 정답이다.

132. 명사 어휘
| 해설 | 빈칸은 전치사 of의 목적어가 될 명사이자 that절의 수식을 받는 명사가 들어갈 자리로, '유행을 창출하는 업체들의 작업을 집중 조명한다'는 의미로 전개되는 것이 적절하므로 (B) enterprises가 정답이다.

| 어휘 | procedure 절차   enterprise 기업, 회사   material 재료

고난도
133. 알맞은 문장 고르기
(A) 위원회가 질문들을 선택할 것입니다.
(B) 저희 잡지의 독자 수가 증가해오고 있습니다.
(C) 귀하의 말씀을 인용하는 것이 도움이 될 것입니다.
(D) 저희는 장식된 방의 사진들이 마음에 들었습니다.

| 해설 | 빈칸 앞에 전화 인터뷰를 할 시간이 있는지 물었고, 뒤이어 대명사 They가 제시되어 있는 것으로 볼 때, 빈칸에는 They가 가리키는 대상이 구체적으로 나타나 있는 문장이 삽입되어야 함을 알 수 있다. 따라서 인터뷰를 진행할 경우에 나올 수 있는 A few quotes가 언급되어 있는 문장인 (C)가 정답이다.

| 어휘 | readership 독자 수   quote 인용구   decorated 장식된

134. 전치사 어휘
| 해설 | 빈칸은 시간 명사를 목적어로 가지는 전치사가 들어갈 자리로, '마감을 맞추기 위해 10월 25일까지 연락을 해야 할 것이다'라는 의미로 전개되는 것이 적절하므로 특정 시점까지 완료되어야 하는 상태를 나타낼 때 쓰는 전치사인 (C) by가 정답이다.

135-138 다음 이메일을 참조하시오.

수신: Livia Castro
발신: Souza 전자
날짜: 8월 3일
제목: 주문 #52490

Castro 씨 귀하,

귀하의 주문이 저희 온라인 시스템을 통해 성공적으로 이루어졌습니다. 포장 과정 ¹³⁵완료 시, 물품들이 발송되었음을 알리기 위해 다시 이메일을 보내 드릴 것입니다. ¹³⁶그러면 추적 코드를 받으시게 될 것입니다. 그것을 이용해 귀하의 배송 상태를 확인하실 수 있습니다.

귀하의 주문품을 받으시자마자, 그 소포의 내용물을 확인하실 것을 ¹³⁷권장드립니다. 문제가 있으면, 저희가 배송 일에 그것을 더 쉽게 ¹³⁸해결할 수 있습니다.

진심을 담아,

Souza 전자

| 어휘 | successfully 성공적으로   packaging 포장   process 과정   inform 알리다   dispatch 발송하다, 보내다   status 상태   verify 확인하다   contents 내용물   issue 문제   solve 해결하다

고난도

135. 명사 어휘

| 해설 | 빈칸은 전치사 Upon의 목적어가 될 명사가 들어갈 자리로, 뒤에 제시된 물품들이 발송되는 것과 관련 지어 '포장 과정 완료 시'라는 의미로 전개되는 것이 적절하므로 (B) completion이 정답이다.

| 어휘 | elimination 제거   completion 완료   intersection 교차로   generation 세대

136. 알맞은 문장 고르기

(A) 그 부품은 현재 재고가 없습니다.
(B) 귀하의 계정에 차액이 입금될 것입니다.
(C) 저희가 조립을 도와드릴 수 있습니다.
(D) 그러면 추적 코드를 받으시게 될 것입니다.

| 해설 | 뒤이어 그것을 이용해 배송 상태를 확인할 수 있다고 알린 것을 단서로, 그 앞에는 it이 가리키는 대상이 구체적으로 제시된 문장이 삽입되어야 함을 알 수 있다. 배송 상태를 확인할 수 있게 하는 it이 될 수 있는 a tracking code가 언급되어 있는 문장인 (D)가 정답이다.

| 어휘 | component 부품   be out of stock 재고가 없다, 품절되다   currently 현재   credit 입금하다   difference 차액   assist 돕다   assembly 조립   tracking code 추적 코드

137. 동사의 시제

| 해설 | 빈칸은 본동사가 들어갈 자리로, 부사절의 동사가 receive로 현재 시제이고, '주문품을 받자마자, 소포의 내용물을 확인할 것을 권장한다'는 내용이므로 현재 시제인 (D) encourage가 정답이다.

138. 형용사 어휘

| 해설 | 빈칸은 be동사 are의 보어가 들어갈 자리로, 뒤에 제시된 to부정사와 연결 지어 '그것을 더 쉽게 해결할 수 있습니다'라는 의미로 전개되는 것이 적절하므로 (A) able이 정답이다.

| 어휘 | be able to ~할 수 있다   comprehensive 종합적인, 포괄적인   talented 재능 있는   acceptable 허용할 수 있는, 받아들일 만한

139-142 다음 정보를 참조하시오.

사무실 모든 전화기에서 국제 전화번호로 전화를 걸 수 있습니다. 먼저, 9번을 누르고 발신음이 들리면 전체 번호를 입력하세요. 전화가 ¹³⁹연결되자마자, 분당 요금이 발생하기 시작할 것입니다. 이 요금들은 비쌀 수 있기 때문에, 재무 팀이 여러분에게 연락하여 통화의 이유를 ¹⁴⁰확인할 수도 있습니다. 국제 전화의 통화 시간에 대한 공식적인 제한은 없습니다. ¹⁴¹하지만 저희는 그것이 최소로 유지되도록 요청드립니다. 특정한 달의 총 통화 시간이 걱정되면, 상사에게 확인하는 것이 ¹⁴²바람직합니다. 그러면 합리적인 금액 이내로 유지하는 것을 확실히 하는 데 도움이 될 것입니다.

| 어휘 | international 국제적인   input 입력하다   entire 전체의   dial tone 발신음   per-minute charge 분당 요금   accrue 발생하다   expensive 비싼   finance team 재무 팀   formal 공식적인, 정식의   limit 제한   duration 시간, 기간   amount 총액, 양   supervisor 관리자   ensure 확실히 하다   reasonable 합리적인, 합당한

139. 동사의 형태

| 해설 | 빈칸은 부사절의 단수 주어 your call 뒤에 본동사가 들어갈 자리이므로 준동사인 (A) connecting과 (C) to connect는 오답이다. 또한 전화가 연결되는 수동의 의미가 되어야 하므로 수동태가 되어야 하고, 시간/조건 부사절에서는 현재 시제가 미래 시제를 대신하므로 수동태의 현재 시제 동사인 (D) is connected가 정답이다.

140. 동사 어휘

| 해설 | 빈칸은 to부정사를 완성해줄 동사 원형이 들어갈 자리로, '재무 팀이 연락하여 통화의 이유를 확인할 수도 있다'라는 의미로 전개되는 것이 적절하므로 (C) confirm이 정답이다.

| 어휘 | adjust 조정하다   relocate 이전하다   confirm 확인하다   terminate 종료하다

141. 알맞은 문장 고르기

(A) 하지만 저희는 그것이 최소로 유지되도록 부탁드립니다.
(B) 예산을 주의 깊게 검토해 주셔서 감사합니다.
(C) 귀하의 전화가 IT 부서를 통해 업그레이드될 수 있습니다.
(D) 다른 직원들이 그 소리에 방해를 받을 수 있습니다.

| 해설 | 앞서 국제 전화의 통화 시간에 대한 공식적인 제한이 없다는 문장이 제시

되어 있는 것으로 볼 때, 그 연장선상에서 국제 전화(international calls)를 대명사 they로 받아 그것을 최소로 유지해 줄 것을 요청하는 내용의 문장이 삽입되는 것이 적절하므로 (A)가 정답이다.

| 어휘 | keep ~ to a minimum ~을 최소로 유지하다   budget 예산   be disturbed by ~에 의해 방해받다

고난도
142. 형용사 어휘
| 해설 | 뒤에 제시된 진주어인 that절과 연결 지어 '확인하는 것이 바람직합니다'라는 의미로 전개되는 것이 적절하므로 '바람직한'이라는 뜻의 (D) advisable이 정답이다.
| 어휘 | portable 휴대용의   significant 상당한   visible 가시적인, 눈에 띄는   advisable 바람직한, 권할 만한

143-146 다음 회람을 참조하시오.

수신: 전 직원
발신: Stella Reynell, 현장 관리자
주제: 엔터테인먼트 코디네이터
날짜: 4월 3일

직원들 귀하,

다음 주부터 Laguna 식물원이 정규직 엔터테인먼트 코디네이터를 위한 구인 광고를 할 것입니다. 저희가 최근 열었던 'Daisy 댄스 쇼'의 [143]인기가 현장에서 더 많은 활동들의 필요성을 증명해 주었는데요, 그것들이 평소보다 더 많은 방문객들을 끌어모으기 때문입니다. 경영 팀은 5월 첫째 주에 이 직책에 대한 1차 면접을 [144]시작할 것입니다. [145]저희가 선호하는 것은 현 직원을 승진시키는 것입니다. 일반 대중의 지원서도 고려될 것인데, 그래서 저희가 취업 웹 사이트들에 채용 공고를 낼 계획입니다. [146]자격을 갖춘 사람들은 행정 사무실에서 지원서를 가져가셔야 합니다.

진심을 담아,

Stella

| 어휘 | botanical garden 식물원   job opening 일자리 공석   full-time 정규직의   demonstrate 증명하다, 보여주다   on site 현장에   attract 끌어모으다   management team 경영 팀   application 지원(서)   general public 일반 대중   post 게시하다, 올리다   pick up 가져가다, 수령하다   administrative office 행정 사무실

143. 명사 어휘
| 해설 | 빈칸은 뒤에 있는 of 이하의 전치사구의 수식을 받는 문장의 주어가 될 명사가 들어갈 자리로, 뒤에 제시된 타동사 및 그 목적어인 demonstrated the need와 연결 지어 '~ 인기가 ~ 필요성을 증명해 주었다'라는 의미로 전개되는 것이 적절하므로 (C) popularity가 정답이다.
| 어휘 | popularity 인기   courtesy 호의, 공손함

144. 동사의 시제
| 해설 | 빈칸은 문장의 본동사가 들어갈 자리로, 회람을 보낸 날짜가 4월 3일이고 문장에 제시된 5월 첫째 주(the first week of May)는 미래이므로, 미래 시제 동사인 (D) will begin이 정답이다.

145. 알맞은 문장 고르기
(A) 저희가 선호하는 것은 현 직원을 승진시키는 것입니다.
(B) 관리자들은 보통 한 달에 한 번 만납니다.
(C) 저희는 여러분 모두 그 공연을 즐기기를 바랍니다.
(D) 성수기는 작년에 그랬던 것보다 훨씬 더 바쁠 수 있습니다.
| 해설 | 뒤이어 또한 일반 대중의 지원서도 고려될 것임을 알리는 문장이 제시되어 있는 것으로 볼 때, 현재 내부 직원을 승진시키는 것을 선호함을 알리는 내용의 문장이 삽입되는 것이 적절하므로 정답은 (A)이다.
| 어휘 | preference 선호 사항, 선호도   promote 승진시키다   current 현재의   peak season 성수기

146. 형용사 어휘
| 해설 | 빈칸은 be동사 are의 보어가 들어갈 자리로, 뒤에 제시된 pick up an application과 관련 지어 지원서를 가져가야 할 대상자는 '자격을 갖춘 사람들'일 것이므로 (B) qualified가 정답이다.
| 어휘 | renegotiated 재협상된   qualified 자격 있는   enrolled 등록된   affected 영향을 받은

PART 7

147-148 다음 초대장을 참조하시오.

Business Builders 오찬

3월 8일 목요일
오전 11:30 – 오후 1:00

Thai Garden, 전용 미팅 룸
1926 Lang Avenue
Bloomington, IL 61701

연사: Georgia Rufin
'[147]예산 내에서 여러분의 고객 기반 확장하기'

티켓은 1인당 12달러이고, 세 가지 코스 식사가 포함되어 있습니다. 저희가 출장 연회 주문을 준비할 수 있도록 [148]3월 1일까지 참석 여부를 회신해 주세요.
행사 기획자 Tyson Lee: 555-7833

| 어휘 | luncheon 오찬   expand 확장하다, 확대하다   customer

base 고객 기반, 고객층   per -당   RSVP 참석 여부를 회신해 주다
catering 출장 연회

147. 세부 사항을 묻는 문제
손님들은 행사에서 무엇에 관해 배울 것인가?
(A) 로고를 만드는 것
(B) 더 많은 고객들을 얻는 것
(C) 예산 편성 소프트웨어를 이용하는 것
(D) 직원을 확대하는 것

| 해설 | 연사 밑에 제목이 '예산 내에서 여러분의 고객 기반 확장하기(Expanding Your Customer Base on a Budget)'로 제시되어 있으므로 정답은 (B)이다.
| 어휘 | create 만들다   gain 얻다   budgeting 예산 편성
| 패러프레이징 | Expanding Your Customer Base → Gaining more customers

148. 추론 문제
행사에 관해 암시되는 것은 무엇인가?
(A) 손님들은 참석할 계획인지 여부를 알려야 한다.
(B) 단체는 입장권 할인을 받을 수 있다.
(C) 식사 요금은 주문되는 것에 달려 있다.
(D) 3월 매주 목요일에 열린다.

| 해설 | 후반부에 출장 연회 주문을 준비할 수 있도록 3월 1일까지 참석 여부를 회신해 달라고(Please RSVP by March 1) 제시되어 있으므로 정답은 (A)이다.
| 어휘 | indicate 말하다, 표현하다   admission ticket 입장권   charge 요금   depend on ~에 달려 있다
| 패러프레이징 | RSVP → indicate whether they plan to attend

149. 주제/목적 문제
이메일은 왜 작성되었나?
(A) 고객들에게 그들의 충성에 감사하기 위해
(B) 고급 패키지의 매출을 증가시키기 위해
(C) 성수기를 위한 투어 가이드들을 모집하기 위해
(D) 일정 변경을 알리기 위해

| 해설 | 초반부에 최신 투어 패키지 R360으로 멋지게 로마를 여행하라며(Tour Rome in style with Roma Day Tours' newest tour package: R360) 호화로운 투어 패키지(extravagant tour package)를 소개하고 있으므로 정답은 (B)이다.
| 어휘 | loyalty 충성(심)   boost 신장시키다, 증가하다   recruit 모집하다   peak season 성수기   publicize 알리다, 홍보하다
| 패러프레이징 | extravagant tour package → a luxury package

🔼 고난도

150. True 문제
R360 티켓에 관해 제시된 것은 무엇인가?
(A) 함께 예약하는 사람들의 단체들을 위한 것이다.
(B) 성인들로만 한정된다.
(C) 그날 내내 모든 식사가 포함되어 있다.
(D) 전화로 주문되어야 한다.

| 해설 | 단체 규모가 작게 유지된다고(group sizes are kept small) 하였고, 한 차례 예약에 최대 10명까지 이용될 수 있다고(The R360 ticket can be used by up to ten people on one reservation) 제시되어 있으므로 정답은 (A)이다.
| 패러프레이징 | up to ten people → groups of people

149-150 다음 이메일을 참조하시오.

수신: 미공개 수신자들
발신: <service@romadaytours.it>
날짜: 5월 19일
제목: 로마가 부르고 있어요!

¹⁴⁹로마 일일 투어의 최신 투어 패키지 R360으로 아주 멋지게 로마를 여행하세요. 저희가 제한된 시간 동안 단 875유로에 그것을 제공하고 있으며, 입장료를 포함한 가격입니다. 이 ¹⁴⁹호화로운 투어 패키지는 고급 리무진으로 여러분을 로마 최고의 장소들로 데리고 가고, 투어 가이드로부터 각별한 관심을 받을 수 있도록 ¹⁵⁰단체 규모들이 작게 유지됩니다. R360 티켓은 한 차례 예약에 최대 10명까지 이용될 수 있습니다. 여기를 클릭하셔서 여러분의 여행을 시작하세요!

| 어휘 | undisclosed 미공개의, 비밀에 부쳐진   in style 아주 멋지게   limited 제한된, 한정된   include 포함하다   entrance fee 입장료   extravagant 호화로운, 사치스러운   luxurious 고급의, 호화로운   extra attention 각별한 관심   reservation 예약   journey 여행

151-152 다음 문자 메시지 대화를 참조하시오.

Isabelle Chauncy (오전 9:03)
안녕하세요, Beau. 제가 신입 사원을 위한 몇 가지 물품들을 가지러 지하실의 창고 구역에 있는데요. ¹⁵¹여기 여러분의 컴퓨터 모니터가 하나 있는 것을 봤어요. 당신의 책상에 하나 더 필요하다고 하지 않으셨어요?

Beau Esson (오전 9:05)
네, 그랬는데, 새로운 구매에 대해 승인을 받지 못했거든요. 우리에게 여분이 있었다는 것은 몰랐네요. 작동을 하는지 테스트를 해봐야겠네요.

Isabelle Chauncy (오전 9:06)
¹⁵²제가 다른 물품들과 함께 그것을 당신에게 가져다 주기를 원하나요?

Beau Esson (오전 9:07)
그것은 당신이 결정해요. ¹⁵²짐이 이미 너무 많으면, 제가 나중에 가서 가져올 수 있어요. 고마워요.

| 어휘 | storage area 보관 구역   basement 지하실, 지하층   spare 여분의; 여분   approve 승인하다   purchase 구입(품)   call 결정, 판단

151. 주제/목적 문제

Chauncy 씨는 왜 Esson 씨에게 연락했는가?
(A) 책상을 옮기는 것에 도움을 요청하기 위해
(B) 창고에 더 많은 물품들을 넣도록 제안하기 위해
(C) 직원의 도착 시간을 확인하기 위해
(D) 그가 어떤 장비를 원하는지 알아보기 위해

| 해설 | 오전 9:03에 Isabelle Chauncy가 자신의 위치를 알린 후, 여분의 컴퓨터 모니터가 하나 있는데, 하나 더 필요하다고 하지 않았냐고(I saw that there's a spare computer monitor in here. Didn't you say you needed a second one for your desk) 물은 것을 통해, 여분의 컴퓨터 모니터를 원하는지 알아보고자 연락한 것임을 알 수 있으므로 정답은 (D)이다.

| 어휘 | assistance 도움   find out 알아보다   equipment 장비

| 패러프레이징 | a spare computer monitor → some equipment

152. 의도 파악 문제

오전 9:07에 Esson 씨가 "그것은 당신이 결정해요"라고 쓸 때 의미하는 것은 무엇인가?
(A) Chauncy 씨가 어떤 구역을 정리하는 것에 관해 결정을 해야 한다.
(B) Chauncy 씨가 물건을 가져올 것인지 아닌지 판단해야 한다.
(C) 그는 주문이 경영진에 의해 승인될 때까지 기다릴 것이다.
(D) 그는 Chauncy 씨의 컴퓨터를 고칠 시간이 없다.

| 해설 | 이는 앞서 오전 9:06에 Isabelle Chauncy가 다른 물품들과 함께 그것을 당신에게 가져다 주기를 원하는지(Do you want me to bring it up to you with the other items) 물은 것에 대한 응답으로, 뒤이어 짐이 이미 너무 많으면 자신이 나중에 가서 가져올 수 있다고(If you have too much already, I can go and get it later) 덧붙인 것을 통해, 여분의 컴퓨터 모니터를 가져오는 것에 관해서 Chauncy 씨에게 결정권을 넘기는 것임을 알 수 있으므로 정답은 (B)이다.

| 어휘 | make a decision 결정을 하다   organize 준비하다, 조직하다   management 경영진   fix 고치다

153-154 다음 공지를 참조하시오.

Aldridge 직물
¹⁵⁴관리 책임자: Michelle Struble
생산 관리자: Allen Buchanan

Aldridge 직물에서 즐거운 시간을 보내시기 바랍니다. 여러분의 안전과 저희 직원들의 안전 그리고 저희 제품의 품질을 위해, ¹⁵³여러분의 투어 내내 아래 규칙들을 따라 주시기 바랍니다. 추가 장비는 생산 관리자로부터 받아 이용할 수 있습니다. ¹⁵⁴여러분의 매장에서 Aldridge 직물을 취급하는 것에 관해 질문이 있으면, 관리 책임자에게 이야기해 주시기 바랍니다.

해야 할 것
· 항상 가이드의 지시 사항을 따르는 것.
· 여러분의 임시 신분증이 잘 보이도록 두는 것.
· 기계를 작동하고 있지 않은 작업자들에게 질문을 하는 것.
· 사진을 찍는 것 (플래시가 꺼진 상태로).

하지 말아야 할 것
· 기계를 작동시키는 작업자들을 산만하게 하는 것.
· 생산 구역에 음식이나 음료를 가져오는 것.
· 여러분의 그룹에서 분리되는 것.

| 어휘 | production 생산   safety 안전   quality 품질   follow 따르다   rule 규칙   gear 장비   available 이용 가능한   carry 취급하다   instruction 지시 사항, 지침   temporary 임시의   visible 보이는   operate 작동시키다   machinery 기계   turn off 끄다   distract 산만하게 하다   beverage 음료   get separated from ~에서 분리되다

153. 추론 문제

공지는 누구를 위해 작성되었을 것 같은가?
(A) 직물 디자이너들
(B) 채용 담당자들
(C) 공장 방문객들
(D) 보안 전문가들

| 해설 | 첫 단락에 투어 내내 아래 규칙들을 따라 주기 바란다고(please follow the rules below throughout your tour) 한 것에서 방문객들을 위한 공지임을 알 수 있고, 기계 작동(operating machinery), 생산 구역(production area) 등의 어휘를 통해 공장임을 유추할 수 있다. 따라서 정답은 (C)이다.

고난도

154. 세부 사항을 묻는 문제

공지에 따르면, Struble 씨는 무엇을 할 것인가?
(A) 일부 필요한 장비를 나누어 주는 것
(B) 제품 카탈로그들을 제공하는 것
(C) 현장의 규정을 정기적으로 업데이트하는 것
(D) 판매와 관련된 문의들을 처리하는 것

| 해설 | Struble 씨는 도입부에 관리 책임자(Managing Director)로 제시되어 있는데, 첫 번째 단락 후반부에 매장에서 Aldridge 직물을 취급하는 것에 관해 질문이 있으면, 관리 책임자에게 이야기하라고(Should you have any questions about carrying Aldridge Fabrics in your store, please speak to the managing director) 제시되어 있으므로 정답은 (D)이다.

| 어휘 | distribute 나누어 주다, 배포하다   necessary 필요한   regularly 정기적으로   handle 처리하다

| 패러프레이징 | questions about carrying Aldridge Fabrics in your store → inquiries regarding sales

155-157 다음 서식을 참조하시오.

Emerson 아파트 요청서
건물 관리자: Diego Landeros
d.landeros@emersonapt.com / 555-4848

¹⁵⁵세입자: Elizabeth Swanson   요청 유형:
타워: C   세입자의 가구 [✓]

가구: 518	공동 구역 – 실내 [ ]
연락 번호: 555-4510	공동 구역 – 실외 [ ]

문제 설명: ¹⁵⁵가스 벽난로의 밸브가 꽉 닫혀 있어서, 켜지지 않습니다. 부동산 관리자인 Denise Platt는 (가스 냄새가 없기 때문에) 안전 문제는 아니라고 말했습니다.

메모: ¹⁵⁵방문하려고 계획하실 때 미리 저에게 알려주세요. ¹⁵⁶그 벽난로 위 벽면에 그림 두 점이 걸려 있는데요. 기술자에게 여유 공간을 제공하기 위해 ¹⁵⁶작업을 시작하기 바로 전에 이것들을 치울 것입니다.

사무실 전용
¹⁵⁷요청 일자: 1월 9일   접수한 이: Jerry Tobin
등급: 긴급한 [ ] 잠재적으로 긴급한 [✓] 최우선 사항 [ ] 일반 [ ]
¹⁵⁷배정된 이: Ryan Marrero

지침: ¹⁵⁷세입자에게 전화해서 오늘 방문할 것이라고 알려주세요. 당신의 점검 결과 필요하다고 판단되면 사무실은 전문가를 예약할 수 있습니다.

| 어휘 | request form 요청서, 신청서 supervisor 관리자 tenant 세입자 unit 가구 common area 공동 구역 description 설명, 기술 fireplace 벽난로 stuck closed 꽉 닫힌 turn on 켜다 property manager 부동산 관리자 safety issue 안전 문제 gas odor 가스 냄새 in advance 미리 painting 그림 hang 걸리다, 매달리다 shortly 곧 장 extra 추가의, 여분의 ranking 등급 urgent 긴급한 potentially 잠재적으로 high priority 최우선 사항 assigned 배정된, 할당된 specialist 전문가 determine 결정하다 inspection 점검

155. 주제/목적 문제
Swanson 씨는 왜 서식을 제출했나?
(A) 건물을 둘러보기 위해
(B) 청구 방법을 업데이트하기 위해
(C) 임대 계약을 갱신하기 위해
(D) 수리 일정을 잡기 위해

| 해설 | Swanson 씨는 서식을 제출한 세입자로, 문제 설명에 가스 벽난로의 밸브가 꽉 닫혀 있어 켜지지 않는다고(The valve for the gas fireplace is stuck closed, so it does not turn on) 문제 사실을 알린 후, 메모에 방문하려고 계획할 때 미리 알려달라고(Please let me know in advance when you plan to visit) 한 것을 통해, 문제가 있는 가스 벽난로 밸브의 수리 일정을 잡고자 서식을 제출한 것임을 알 수 있으므로 정답은 (D)이다.

| 어휘 | billing method 청구 방법 renew 갱신하다 lease 임대차 계약

156. 세부 사항을 묻는 문제
Swanson 씨는 그림들에 관해 뭐라고 언급하는가?
(A) 벽에서 제거될 것이다.
(B) 선물로 받았다.
(C) 특이한 냄새가 난다.
(D) 잘못하여 훼손되었다.

| 해설 | 메모 부분에 그 벽난로 위에 그림 두 점이 있는데, 작업을 시작하기 전에 치울 것이라고(I have two paintings hanging on the wall above the fireplace. I'll take these down shortly before the work begins) 제시되어 있으므로 정답은 (A)이다.

| 어휘 | remove 제거하다, 치우다 unusual 특이한 accidentally 잘못하여, 우연히

| 패러프레이징 | take these down → be removed

157. 세부 사항을 묻는 문제
1월 9일에 누가 Swanson 씨에게 전화할 것인가?
(A) Landeros 씨
(B) Platt 씨
(C) Tobin 씨
(D) Marrero 씨

| 해설 | 아래 사무실 전용 부분에 1월 9일은 요청 일자(Date of Request: January 9), 작업에 배정된 이는 Ryan Marrero(Assigned to: Ryan Marrero)로 확인되고, 지침에 세입자에게 전화해서 오늘 방문할 것이라고 알려달라고(Please call the tenant to inform her that you will visit today) 제시되어 있는 것에서, 1월 9일에 방문할 Ryan Marrero가 Swanson 씨에게 전화할 것임을 알 수 있으므로 정답은 (D)이다.

158-160 다음 기사를 참조하시오.

타이베이(10월 7일)—필리핀에 본사를 둔 가정용 가구 매장인 Sampaga가 약 3개월 전 대만에서 첫 지점을 열었다. 그 브랜드는 밝은 색상과 즐거운 패턴들로 이루어진 저렴한 가격의 가정용 제품 컬렉션으로 알려져 있다. Sampaga는 필리핀 전역에서 누구나 아는 이름이다. —[1]—.

신규 매장은 타이베이에서 인기 있는 Ximending 동네에 위치해 있다. 그 매장은 필리핀에 있는 대부분의 지점들만큼 크지 않다. —[2]—. 하지만 ¹⁵⁸그 매니저인 Mei-hua Liu는 자신만의 아이디어를 추가했는데, 여러 작은 방들을 집의 방들처럼 구성한 것이다. 그곳들은 천장에서 바닥까지 Sampaga 제품들로 장식되어 있다. Liu 씨는 이것이 고객들이 각자의 집 안에 제품들을 시각화하는 데 도움이 된다고 생각한다.

—[3]—. ¹⁵⁹가장 잘 팔리는 제품은 그 매장의 양탄자 라인이다. 그것들은 다양한 사이즈로 나오고 어떤 방에도 톡톡 튀는 색을 연출한다. ¹⁵⁹손으로 짠 이 제품들이 대만 가정에서 최신 유행하는 액세서리가 되고 있다.

¹⁶⁰타이베이 지점은 Sampaga 체인에서 가장 최근에 문을 연 매장일지도 모르지만, 이미 가장 인기 있는 곳이다. —[4]—.

| 어휘 | based 본사를 둔, 기반한 furnishing 가구, 비품 branch 지점 be known for ~로 알려져 있다 affordable 가격이 저렴한, 알맞은 joyful 기쁨을 주는, 즐거운 household name 누구나 아는 이름 neighborhood 인근, 이웃 set up 구성하다, 마련하다 decorate 장식

하다 visualize 시각화하다 top-selling 가장 잘 팔리는 rug 양탄자, 깔개 a variety of 다양한 pop of color 톡톡 튀는 색 hand-woven 손으로 짠 trendy 최신 유행의

158. 세부 사항을 묻는 문제
타이베이 매장의 독특한 특징은 무엇인가?
(A) 경험 많은 직원들
(B) 상당한 크기
(C) 전시장들
(D) 편리한 위치
| 해설 | 두 번째 단락에 매니저인 Mei-hua Liu가 아이디어를 추가해 여러 작은 방들을 집의 방들처럼 구성했는데(several small rooms set up like rooms in a house) 그곳들은 천장에서 바닥까지 Sampaga 제품들로 장식되어 있다고(They are decorated from top to bottom with Sampaga products) 제시되어 있으므로 정답은 (C)이다.
| 어휘 | experienced 경험 많은   considerable 상당한   convenient 편리한

159. True 문제
Sampaga의 양탄자들에 관해 언급된 것은 무엇인가?
(A) 지속 가능한 재료를 쓴다.
(B) 지점에 따라 다르다.
(C) 손으로 만들어진다.
(D) 맞춤 사이즈로 구입 가능하다.
| 해설 | 세 번째 단락에 가장 잘 팔리는 제품은 그 매장의 양탄자 라인이라고(One top-selling product is the store's line of rugs) 했고, 그것이 손으로 짠 제품(These hand-woven items)이라고 제시되어 있으므로 정답은 (C)이다.
| 어휘 | sustainable (환경 파괴 없이) 지속 가능한   vary 달라지다, 다르다   depending on ~에 따라   available 구입 가능한   custom 맞춤의
| 패러프레이징 | hand-woven → made by hand

160. 문장 삽입 문제
[1], [2], [3], [4]로 표시된 곳 중에 다음 문장이 들어가기에 가장 적절한 곳은?
"실제로, 그 지점은 첫 달에 오래된 회사 매출 기록을 깼다."
(A) [1]
(B) [2]
(C) [3]
(D) [4]
| 해설 | 제시된 문장의 주어인 the branch는 3개월 전 문을 연 타이베이 지점임을 알 수 있는데, 회사 매출 기록을 깼다는 것은 인기 있는 매장이라는 의미이므로, 이에 관해 언급된 문장 뒤인 (D)가 정답이다.
| 어휘 | long-standing 오래된   sales record 매출 기록

161-163 다음 보도 자료를 참조하시오.

즉각적인 보도용
Ulyerra, 홍보 책임자 Sharon Lindquist 315-555-7190

Ulyerra가 Ryker 제약이 에너지 사용을 줄이도록 돕다

브리스틀(5월 22일)—Ryker 제약이 에너지 소비를 줄이고 공과금 비용을 절감하기 위해 Ulyerra의 조명 시스템을 도입했다. 타이머와 광 센서의 조합을 이용하여, 그 시스템은 그 목적에 완벽하게 부합하도록 그 단지 내에 있는 모든 건물의 조명을 프로그래밍할 수 있다. 조명은 자연광 레벨이 높을 때 밝기가 낮아질 수 있고, 자주 사용되지 않는 구역들에서는 조명이 자동으로 꺼지도록 설정될 수 있다.

현장 관리자인 Glenn Bradley는 결과에 만족했다. [161]"제가 직접 그 전체 시스템을 설치할 수 있었고, 그것은 예상했던 것보다 훨씬 더 쉬웠어요."라고 그가 말했다.

"제가 유사한 시스템들을 조사해 봤습니다." Ryker의 총괄 매니저인 Marc Coronado가 전했다. "그런데 저희가 그런 투자를 할 준비가 되어 있는지 확신이 없었습니다. [162]Ulyerra가 우리가 만족하지 않으면 전액 환불을 제안했기 때문에, 그것이 옳은 선택이라는 것을 알았죠."

[163]바로 지난달, Ryker 제약은 영국에서 네 번째로 큰 제약 공급업체에서 세 번째로 큰 곳으로 발돋움했다. 혁신적인 기술을 수용하려는 그 의지가 분명히 그곳을 훨씬 더 멀리 도약하게 할 것이다.

| 어휘 | immediate 즉각적인   PR Director 홍보 책임자   pharmaceuticals 제약 (회사)   implement 도입하다, 시행하다   lighting 조명   reduce 줄이다   consumption 소비   utilities 공과금   combination 조합, 결합   complex (건물) 단지   match 부합하다, 맞다   dim (밝기를) 낮추다, 어둑하게 하다   turn off 꺼지다   automatically 자동으로   frequently 자주   install 설치하다   look into ~을 조사하다, 살펴보다   investment 투자   a full refund 전액 환불   satisfied 만족해하는, 만족스러운   supplier 공급업체   willingness 의지, 의사   embrace 수용하다, 받아들이다   innovative 혁신적인

161. 추론 문제
Bradley 씨에 관해 암시되는 것은 무엇인가?
(A) 광 센서 시스템을 발명했다.
(B) 자연광에서 일하는 것을 선호한다.
(C) 여러 건물들에서 설치를 진행했다.
(D) 에너지 사용의 감소를 기록했다.
| 해설 | 두 번째 단락에 현장 관리자인 Glenn Bradley가 전체 시스템을 직접 설치할 수 있었다고(I was able to install the entire system myself) 말했다고 했으므로 정답은 (C)이다.
| 어휘 | invent 발명하다   perform 진행하다, 실시하다   installation 설치   drop 감소, 하락

162. 세부 사항을 묻는 문제

Coronado 씨는 왜 경쟁사들이 아닌 Ulyerra를 선택했나?
(A) 그 종류에 해당하는 유일한 시스템을 판매했다.
(B) 시중에서 가장 저렴한 제품을 보유하고 있다.
(C) 동료에 의해 추천되었다.
(D) 환불 보장이 딸려 있었다.

| 해설 | 세 번째 단락에 있는 Marc Coronado의 인터뷰 내용에 Ulyerra가 불만족 시 전액 환불을 제안했기 때문에, 옳은 선택이라는 것을 알았다고(Since Ulyerra offered a full refund if we weren't satisfied, I knew it was the right choice) 제시되어 있으므로 정답은 (D)이다.
| 어휘 | colleague 동료   come with ~이 딸려 있다   money-back guarantee 환불 보장
| 패러프레이징 | offered a full refund → came with a money-back guarantee

🔺 고난도

163. True 문제

Ryker 제약에 관해 제시된 것은 무엇인가?
(A) Ulyerra에 의해 인수되었다.
(B) 해외 지점을 개설할 계획이다.
(C) 최근 시장 점유율을 늘렸다.
(D) 정부와의 계약을 따냈다.

| 해설 | 마지막 단락에 바로 지난달, Ryker 제약은 영국에서 네 번째로 큰 제약 공급업체에서 세 번째로 큰 곳으로 발돋움했다고(Just last month, Ryker Pharmaceuticals moved from the fourth-largest to the third-largest supplier of pharmaceuticals in the UK) 제시되어 있는 것에서, 시장 점유율을 높였다는 것을 알 수 있으므로 정답은 (C)이다.
| 어휘 | acquire 인수하다, 취득하다   overseas 해외의   gain 늘리다, 증가하다   secure 확보하다   government 정부
| 패러프레이징 | ·just last month → recently
· moved from the fourth-largest to the third-largest supplier → has recently gained market share

164-167 다음 정보를 참조하시오.

Feeney Accounting 구내 다과

¹⁶⁴Feeney Accounting이 직원들과 방문객들에게 약간의 다과를 제공합니다. 이것들은 공유되기 위한 것이지만, 우리 비용이 합리적인 범위 내에서 유지되도록 하면서 우리가 가장 좋은 인상을 주도록 돕기 위해 일부 구역은 다른 곳들과 다르게 구비되어 있습니다.

- 포장된 사탕 한 그릇은 접수 구역에 놓여 있고 단기 방문객을 위한 것입니다.
- 직원 회의실인 222호에는 인스턴트 커피와 티백, 그리고 엄선된 크래커와 쿠키가 있습니다. 알레르기가 있는 분들은 드시기 전에 포장지를 확인해야 합니다.

– ¹⁶⁵301호에는 내린 커피와 신선한 페이스트리가 있습니다. 이것들은 고객들과의 회의 중에만 제공되어야 합니다.

무엇이든 상하지 않는 음식들을 다시 채워야 할 경우, 335호에서 그것들을 찾으실 수 있습니다. 냅킨과 컵들도 그곳에 보관되어 있습니다. 어떤 물품이든 다 떨어지면, Vernita Neilsen에게 알려 주세요. 하지만 ¹⁶⁶그 달의 예산이 이미 모두 지출된 경우, 다음 달까지 다시 채워지지 않을 수 있습니다. ¹⁶⁷어떤 구역이 정돈되지 않은 것을 알게 되고 그곳을 직접 정리할 시간이 없을 경우, David Haas에게 연락해 주세요.

| 어휘 | accounting 회계   on-site 구내의   refreshments 다과   be intended to ~하기 위해 의도되다   stock (식품 따위로) 채우다   impression 인상   reasonable 합리적인   range 범위   bowl 그릇   wrapped 포장된   position (특정한 장소에) 놓다   reception area 접수 구역   short-term 단기의   contain 들어 있다   consumption 섭취, 소비   restock 다시 채우다, 보충하다   non-perishable 상하지 않는   be out of ~이 다 떨어지다   supplies 물품, 용품   refill 다시 채우다   disorganized 정돈되지 않은   tidy up 정리하다, 치우다

164. 주제/목적 문제

정보는 왜 작성되었나?
(A) 주문 전에 음식 요청을 수집하기 위해
(B) 건물에 새로 온 방문객들을 환영하기 위해
(C) 어떤 팀의 구조 조정을 설명하기 위해
(D) 회사의 정책을 개괄하기 위해

| 해설 | 도입부에 Feeney Accounting이 직원들과 방문객들에게 약간의 다과를 제공한다고(Feeney Accounting provides some refreshments to employees and visitors) 한 후, 그와 관련된 내용이 이어지고 있으므로 정답은 (D)이다.
| 어휘 | gather 수집하다, 모으다   describe 서술하다, 기술하다   restructuring 구조 조정   outline 개괄하다   policy 정책, 방침

165. 추론 문제

Feeney Accounting 고객들은 어디에서 미팅을 가질 것 같은가?
(A) 222호에서
(B) 301호에서
(C) 335호에서
(D) 접수 구역에서

| 해설 | 중반부의 세 번째 항목에 301호에는 내린 커피와 신선한 페이스트리가 있고(Room 301 has brewed coffee and fresh pastries) 이것들은 고객들과의 회의 중에만 제공되어야 한다고(These are to be served during meetings with clients only) 제시되어 있으므로, 고객 회의는 301호실에서 진행되는 것으로 유추할 수 있다. 따라서 정답은 (B)이다.

166. 세부 사항을 묻는 문제

정보에 따르면, 왜 일부 구역들에 음식이 없을 수 있는가?
(A) 일부 민감한 장비가 가동 중이다.

(B) 월 예산에 도달되었다.
(C) 담당하는 사람이 부재중이다.
(D) 보건 규정이 위반되어서는 안 된다.

| 해설 | 마지막 단락에 어떤 물품이든 다 떨어지면, Vernita Neilsen에게 알려 달라고 한 후, 그 달의 예산이 이미 모두 지출된 경우, 그것들이 다음 달까지 다시 채워지지 않을 수 있다고(if the budget for the month has already been spent, they may not be refilled until the following month) 제시되어 있으므로 정답은 (B)이다.

| 어휘 | delicate 정교한, 민감한   be in operation 가동 중이다   reach 도달하다   in charge 담당인, 맡은   absent 부재의

| 패러프레이징 | the budget for the month has already been spent → A monthly budget has been reached

167. 세부 사항을 묻는 문제
직원들은 왜 Haas 씨에게 연락해야 하는가?
(A) 예산을 확인하기 위해
(B) 더 많은 물품을 요구하기 위해
(C) 지저분한 구역을 알리기 위해
(D) 음식 알레르기를 설명하기 위해

| 해설 | 마지막 부분에 정돈되지 않은 구역을 알게 됐는데 정리할 시간이 없으면, David Haas에게 연락해 달라고(If you notice that an area is disorganized and you do not have time to tidy it up yourself, please contact David Haas) 제시되어 있으므로 정답은 (C)이다.

| 어휘 | messy 지저분한

| 패러프레이징 | an area is disorganized → a messy area

168-171 다음 온라인 채팅 토론을 참조하시오.

Liberty 호텔 온라인 채팅 서비스

Wen Shao (오후 2:14)
제가 귀사의 웹 사이트에 광고하신 최근 할인 행사를 이용했는데요. ¹⁷¹ ⁽ᴬ⁾2월 1일과 3월 31일 사이에 Liberty 호텔이나 체인 호텔 어디에서든 3박 이상 숙박하는 Liberty 리워즈 회원들은 무료 하루 숙박 쿠폰을 받을 수 있다고 되어 있었거든요. 제가 Gateway 호텔에서 체크아웃을 했을 때, ¹⁶⁸프런트 데스크 직원이 제가 우편으로 그 쿠폰을 받을 것이라고 말했는데, 그것에 대한 아무런 소식이 없어서요.

Claudia McLeish (오후 2:15)
¹⁷¹ ⁽ᴮ⁾그 쿠폰은 Liberty 호텔과 저희 제휴 호텔들 모두에서 유효하고, ¹⁷¹ ⁽ᴰ⁾유효 기간이 없는데요. 제가 Jasper Rautio를 이 대화에 추가할 것인데요, 그가 Gateway의 행정을 처리하기 때문입니다. ¹⁶⁹귀하의 리워즈 회원 번호를 알려주시겠어요? 그것이 이 문제를 확인하는 데 도움이 될 것입니다.

Jasper Rautio (오후 2:17)
그것이 여기 저한테 있어요. 우리 시스템에서 Shao 씨를 찾았는데, 2월 8일부터 2월 15일까지 숙박하여 확실히 그 쿠폰을 받을 자격이 됩니다.

Wen Shao (오후 2:18)
R389-07164이에요.

Jasper Rautio (오후 2:19)
¹⁷¹ ⁽ᴬ⁾그 쿠폰은 프로모션이 끝난 다음 날 발송될 것입니다. 저희가 파일에 귀하의 우편 주소를 가지고 있습니다. ¹⁷⁰귀하의 Liberty 리워즈 계정을 프리미엄 레벨로 업그레이드하는 것을 도와드릴까요? 그것은 더 많은 혜택을 제공합니다.

Wen Shao (오후 2:20)
고맙지만, 그것에는 관심이 없어요. 쿠폰을 기다리도록 할게요.

| 어휘 | take advantage of ~을 이용하다   voucher 쿠폰, 상품권   clerk 직원   valid 유효한   expiration date 유효 기간, 만료 일자   handle 처리하다   administration 행정, 관리   definitely 확실히, 분명히   eligible for ~에 자격이 되는   account 계정   benefit 혜택

168. 주제/목적 문제
Shao 씨는 왜 온라인 채팅 서비스를 이용했는가?
(A) 물품을 받지 못했음을 알리기 위해
(B) 로열티 프로그램 회원을 갱신하기 위해
(C) 쿠폰을 이용하는 방법에 관해 문의하기 위해
(D) 호텔 객실 예약을 취소하기 위해

| 해설 | 도입부에 호텔의 프로모션 및 자신의 숙박 상황에 관해 설명한 뒤, 프런트 데스크 직원이 우편으로 쿠폰을 받을 것이라고 말했는데, 아무런 소식이 없다고(the front desk clerk said I'd get the voucher in the mail, but there's no sign of it) 한 것을 통해, 자신이 받아야 할 쿠폰을 받지 못했음을 알리고자 온라인 채팅 서비스를 이용해 문의한 것임을 알 수 있으므로 정답은 (A)이다.

| 어휘 | renew 갱신하다   inquire 문의하다

🔺고난도

169. 의도 파악 문제
오후 2:17에 Rautio 씨가 "그것이 여기 저한테 있어요"라고 썼을 때 암시하는 것은 무엇인가?
(A) 그는 청구서 번호를 알려줄 수 있다.
(B) 그는 분실된 개인 물품을 찾았다.
(C) 그는 이미 일부 정보를 찾아보았다.
(D) 그는 잔고를 확인할 수 있었다.

| 해설 | 이는 앞서 오후 2:15에 Claudia McLeish가 Shao 씨에게 리워즈 회원 번호를 알려달라고(Could you give me your rewards membership number) 한 것에 대해 Rautio 씨가 먼저 응답한 것으로, 리워즈 회원 번호를 이미 찾아봐서 갖고 있다는 의미임을 알 수 있으므로 정답은 (C)이다.

| 어휘 | invoice 청구서, 송장   lost 분실된   personal item 개인 물품   look up 찾아보다   balance 잔고, 잔액

170. 세부 사항을 묻는 문제
Rautio 씨가 제안하는 것은 무엇인가?
(A) Shao 씨의 객실 예약을 업그레이드하는 것

(B) Shao 씨의 멤버십 유형을 변경하는 것
(C) Shao 씨에게 계정 개요를 보내는 것
(D) Shao 씨에게 환불을 해주는 것

| 해설 | 오후 2:19에 Jasper Rautio가 Liberty 리워즈 계정을 프리미엄 레벨로 업그레이드하는 것을 도와주는(Could I help you to upgrade your Liberty Rewards account to the Premium level, which gives you more benefits) 것을 제안했으므로 정답은 (B)이다.

| 어휘 | summary 개요, 요약   issue a refund 환불을 해주다

| 패러프레이징 | upgrade your Liberty Rewards account to the Premium level → Change Ms. shao's membership type

고난도

171. NOT True 문제
Liberty 호텔 쿠폰에 관해 제시되지 않은 것은 무엇인가?
(A) 4월 1일에 우편으로 보내질 것이다.
(B) Liberty 호텔 이외의 장소들에서 이용될 수 있다.
(C) 이용자에게 무료 3박을 제공한다.
(D) 유효 기간이 없다.

| 해설 | 오후 2:14에 Wen Shao가 프로모션 기간으로 2월 1일과 3월 31일 사이(between February 1 and March 31)라고 한 것과 2:19에 Jasper Rautio가 쿠폰은 프로모션이 끝난 다음 날에 발송될 것이라고(The voucher will be sent the day after the promotion finishes) 한 것을 연계해볼 때 (A), 2:15에 Claudia McLeish가 쿠폰은 Liberty 호텔과 저희 파트너 호텔들 모두에서 유효하다고(The voucher is valid at both Liberty Hotel and our partners' hotels) 한 것에서 (B), 유효 기간이 없다고(it does not have an expiration date) 한 것에서 (D)는 모두 확인되므로 정답은 (C)이다.

| 패러프레이징 | is valid → can be used

172-175 다음 편지를 참조하시오.

Sandra Duarte
1881 McCabe Drive
Oak Hill, VA 20171

Manuel Bruckner
590 Caynor Avenue
Herndon, VA 22090

Bruckner 씨 귀하,

¹⁷²제가 Fairfax County 웹 사이트에 이제 디지털 버전으로 올라가 있는 오래된 기록들을 찾아보고 있었는데, 귀하가 Herndon의 Varner 가 559번지에 있는 부동산의 현 소유주인 것으로 그 기록에 나타나 있었습니다. —[1]—. ¹⁷⁴이 건물이 Herndon에서 가장 오래된 것들 중 하나이고, 이 지역에서 좀처럼 찾아보기 힘든 몇몇 건축 요소를 특별히 포함하고 있다는 것을 아마도 알고 계실 것입니다. —[2]—.

이 건물과 관련하여 파트너십을 형성하고 싶으신지 궁금합니다. ¹⁷³제가

알기로 그것이 건축 규정을 충족시키지 않고, 그래서 현재 주거용이나 상업용으로 허용되지 않고 있는데요. ¹⁷⁴그렇게 오래된 건물이 버려지거나 훼손된다면 유감스러운 일이 될 것입니다. —[3]—. ¹⁷⁴이를 막을 방법이 있다면, 그것이 최상의 시나리오가 될 것입니다.

이 건물이 예전의 영광을 되찾기 위해 협력할 것을 제안합니다. ¹⁷⁵제가 일종의 파트너십 협정의 일환으로 그 건물을 복원할 자금을 제공할 수 있습니다. —[4]—. 그것이 가치 있는 프로젝트가 될 것임을 아시게 될 것이라고 생각합니다.

제 제안에 관심이 있으시면, 그 문제를 더 논의할 수 있도록 저에게 전화해 주세요. 제 번호는 703-555-7193입니다. 귀하로부터 곧 소식 듣기를 바랍니다.

따뜻한 안부를 전하며,

Sandra Duarte

Sandra Duarte

| 어휘 | indicate 보여 주다, 나타내다   current 현재의   owner 소유주   property 부동산, 건물   feature 특별히 포함하다   architectural element 건축 요소   rarely 좀처럼 ~않는   form 형성하다, 구축하다   building codes 건축 규정   permit 허용하다   residential 주거의, 거주의   commercial use 상업용   shame 유감스러운 일   abandon 버리다   destroy 훼손하다, 파괴하다   prevent 막다, 예방하다   best-case scenario 최상의 시나리오   former 이전의   glory 영광   capital 자금   restore 복원하다   arrangement 협약   worthwhile 가치 있는

172. True 문제
Fairfax County에 관해 사실인 것은 무엇인가?
(A) 더 엄격한 건축 규정들을 통과시켰다.
(B) 일부 기록들을 디지털 형태로 전환시켰다.
(C) 본사가 Herndon 시에 있다.
(D) 부동산을 등록하는 일에 요금을 부과한다.

| 해설 | 도입부에 발신자가 Fairfax County 웹 사이트에 디지털 버전으로 올라가 있는 오래된 기록들을 찾아보고 있었다고(I was searching through some old records that have now been uploaded as digital copies to the Fairfax County Web site) 제시되어 있으므로 정답은 (B)이다.

| 어휘 | pass 통과시키다   strict 엄격한   convert 전환시키다   charge 청구하다   register 등록하다

| 패러프레이징 | some old records that have now been uploaded as digital copies → converted some records to digital form

173. 추론 문제
Bruckner 씨 소유의 Varner 가 부동산에 관해 암시되는 것은 무엇인가?
(A) 현재 상태로는 사용될 수 없다.
(B) 주거지 주소로 등록되어 있다.

TEST 09   **181**

(C) 한때 공공 도서관이었다.
(D) 최근에 매물로 나와 있는 상태이다.
| 해설 | 두 번째 단락에 그것이 건축 규정을 충족시키지 않아서 현재 주거용이나 상업용으로 허용되지 않고 있다고(it does not meet the building codes, and, therefore, is not permitted for residential or commercial use at this time) 제시되어 있으므로 정답은 (A)이다.
| 어휘 | put up for sale 팔려고 내놓다
| 패러프레이징 | is not permitted for residential or commercial use
→ cannot be used

174. 추론 문제
Duarte 씨는 왜 파트너십을 형성하기를 원하는 것 같은가?
(A) 건축술에 대해 배우는 것에 관심이 있다.
(B) 자신의 상점을 운영할 장소를 찾고 있다.
(C) 역사적인 건물을 보호하기를 원한다.
(D) 최근 부동산 사업에 발을 들여놓았다.
| 해설 | 첫 번째 단락에 이 건물이 Herndon에서 가장 오래된 것들 중 하나라고(this building is one of the oldest in Herndon) 한 것과 두 번째 단락에 그렇게 오래된 건물이 버려지거나 파괴된다면 유감스러운 일이 될 것이라며(It would be a shame if such an old building were to be abandoned or destroyed) 이를 막을 방법이 있다면, 그것이 최상의 시나리오가 될 것이라고(If there is a way to prevent this, that would be the best-case scenario) 한 것을 연계해볼 때, 역사적인 건물을 보호하기 위해 파트너십 형성을 제안하는 것임을 알 수 있으므로 정답은 (C)이다.
| 어휘 | architecture 건축술, 건축 양식   run 운영하다   historical 역사적인   enter 들어가다, 시작하다   real estate 부동산

🏠 고난도
175. 문장 삽입 문제
[1], [2], [3], [4]로 표시된 곳 중에 다음 문장이 들어가기에 가장 적절한 곳은?
"예를 들어, 그 소유권의 지분을 저에게 주실 수 있습니다."
(A) [1]
(B) [2]
(C) [3]
(D) [4]
| 해설 | 제시된 문장은 파트너십 협정의 한 가지 예시 사항으로, 세 번째 단락에서 발신자가 일종의 파트너십 협정의 일환으로 그 건물을 복원할 자금을 제공할 수 있다고(I could provide capital to restore the building as part of some kind of partnership arrangement) 한 이후에, 그에 따라 소유주인 Bruckner 씨는 소유권의 지분을 줄 수 있다는 제시된 문장이 이어지는 것이 적절하므로 (D)가 정답이다.
| 어휘 | share 지분, 몫   ownership 소유권

176-180 다음 이메일과 안건을 참조하시오.

수신: 부서 목록 <departmentstaff@myraco.net>
발신: Ranjan Naidu <r_naidu@myraco.net>

[177]날짜: 7월 18일
제목: 월간 회의

팀 귀하,

Myra 사의 다음 월간 부서 회의는 7월 20일 목요일 오후 3시에 대 회의실에서 열릴 것입니다. [176]제가 Robert Sabo와 그의 부서를 저희와 함께하도록 초청했는데, 그 연사들이 두 팀 모두에 이득을 줄 수 있기 때문입니다. 제가 보내드렸던 안건에서 한 가지 변경이 있습니다. Sabo 씨가 Crawford 씨의 시간대를 맡을 것이고, [177]Crawford 씨의 강연은 다음 달 안건으로 옮겨질 것입니다.

[178]고객 피드백 설문지를 돕기로 자원했던 분들께서는, 회의 전에 여러분의 질문 아이디어를 작성해 주세요. 본 회의 후에 만나서 어느 것을 포함시킬지에 관해 논의할 것입니다.

회의에서 봅시다!

Ranjan

| 어휘 | departmental 부서별의   take place 열리다, 개최되다   benefit 득이 되다, 도움이 되다   take over 맡다, 인계받다   time slot 시간대   volunteer 자원하다   questionnaire 설문지

Myra 사 월간 부서 회의 안건
7월 20일, 오후 3:00 - 오후 6:30

연사	주제	세부 사항
Pamela Toth	고객 관리	고객들과 상호 작용을 하기 위한 팁 [180]화장품 구매에 동반할 물품들을 제안하는 방법
[177]Darrell Crawford	소셜 미디어 전략	소셜 미디어 마케팅 계획의 검토
[179]Maria Elliot, 환경 커넥트의 창립자	지역 봉사 활동	Myra 사 직원들을 위한 [179]이 환경 자선 단체에서 주말 자원봉사 기회들
Augusta Ramos	제품 시연	[180]회사의 새로운 핸드 크림 샘플 체험 그 제품의 포장에 관한 간단한 피드백 시간
Lori Vogel	소식지 발간	고객들을 위한 월간 소식지에 대한 정보와 기사를 기고하는 방법

| 어휘 | interact with ~와 상호 작용하다   accompany 동반하다, 수반하다   strategy 전략   founder 창립자, 설립자   outreach 봉사 활동   environmental charity 환경 자선 단체   demonstration 시연   brief 간단한, 짧은   contribute 기고하다

고난도
176. 추론 문제
Naidu 씨가 이메일에서 회의에 관해 암시하는 것은 무엇인가?
(A) 참석자들이 회의 후에 함께 식사를 나눌 것이다.
(B) 애초에 예상된 것보다 더 많은 사람들이 참석할 것이다.
(C) 회의 장소가 다른 곳이 될 것이다.
(D) 많은 연사들이 그들의 강연을 취소해야 했다.

| 해설 | 이메일 첫 번째 단락에 발신자가 Robert Sabo와 그의 부서를 초청했다고(I've invited Robert Sabo and his department to join us) 한 것을 통해, 월간 회의에 기존 참석자 외에 더 많은 사람들이 참석할 것임을 유추할 수 있으므로 정답은 (B)이다.

| 어휘 | participant 참석자 share a meal 식사를 나누다
be in attendance 참석하다 initially 애초에, 처음에

| 패러프레이징 | invited Robert Sabo and his department → More people will be in attendance

고난도
177. 연계 문제 - 추론
회의 참석자들은 8월에 어떤 주제에 관해 들을 것인가?
(A) 소식지 발간
(B) 고객 관리
(C) 소셜 미디어 전략
(D) 제품 시연

| 해설 | 이메일을 보낸 날짜가 7월 18일이고, 첫 번째 단락 후반부에 Crawford 씨의 강연이 다음 달 안건으로 옮겨질 것이라고(Mr. Crawford's talk will be moved to next month's agenda) 했는데, 두 번째 지문인 회의 안건에서 Darrell Crawford가 진행할 주제는 소셜 미디어 전략(Social Media Strategy)으로 확인되므로 정답은 (C)이다.

178. 세부 사항을 묻는 문제
회의 전에 하도록 일부 직원들에게 요청되는 것은 무엇인가?
(A) 시장 동향을 조사하는 것
(B) 일부 제품 샘플을 주문하는 것
(C) 매출 수치를 검토하는 것
(D) 몇몇 설문 조사 질문들을 준비하는 것

| 해설 | 이메일 두 번째 단락에 고객 피드백 설문지를 돕기로 자원했던 사람들은 회의 전에 질문 아이디어를 작성해 달라고(For those of you who have volunteered to assist with the customer feedback questionnaire, please write down your question ideas before the meeting) 요청하는 내용이 제시되어 있으므로 정답은 (D)이다.

| 어휘 | trend 동향, 추세

| 패러프레이징 | customer feedback questionnaire / write down your question ideas → Prepare some survey questions

179. True 문제
안건에 따르면, Elliot 씨에 관해 사실인 것은 무엇인가?
(A) Myra 사의 가장 새로운 팀원이다.
(B) 지역 자선 단체를 시작했다.
(C) 회의에 늦게 도착할 것이다.
(D) Naidu 씨의 부서에서 일한다.

| 해설 | Elliot 씨는 세 번째 연사로 확인되는데, 환경 커넥트의 창립자(founder of Environment Connect)라고 덧붙인 것과 세부 사항에 이 환경 자선 단체(this environmental charity)라고 제시된 것을 통해, 환경 자선 단체를 시작했음을 알 수 있으므로 정답은 (B)이다.

| 패러프레이징 | environmental charity → local charity

고난도
180. 추론 문제
Myra 사는 어떤 종류의 상품을 파는 것 같은가?
(A) 신발
(B) 화장품
(C) 사무 용품
(D) 전동 공구

| 해설 | 안건에서 첫 번째 연사의 세부 사항에 제시된 화장품(makeup)과 네 번째 연사의 세부 사항에 제시된 회사의 새로운 핸드 크림(the company's new hand cream)을 통해, Myra 사는 화장품을 판매하는 회사인 것으로 유추할 수 있으므로 정답은 (B)이다.

| 패러프레이징 | makeup / hand cream → Cosmetics

181-185 다음 이메일과 정책 정보를 참조하시오.

수신: Margaret Wenski <m_wenski@edr1.com>
발신: Tae-min Lim <limtaemin@anaheimco.com>
날짜: 3월 2일
제목: Anaheim 사로부터
첨부: anaheimstaff.dox

Wenski 씨 귀하,

Anaheim 사에 입사하신 것을 환영합니다. [183]귀하의 근무 시작일은 3월 6일 월요일이 될 것입니다. 제 동료인 Janet Baxter가 귀하가 교육 자료를 미리 받으면 아주 좋을 것이라고 [182]생각했다는 것을 알고 있습니다. 그런데 [181]그녀가 귀하에게 보냈던 정책 정보 파일은 작년 것입니다. 그 파일을 삭제하고 대신에 첨부된 파일을 참조하세요.

월요일과 화요일은 교육 활동들로 구성되어 있을 것이고, 그런 다음 [183]금요일에 고객의 사무실에 처음 방문하게 될 것입니다. Vincent Trevisan이 동행할 것이니, 귀하는 주로 참관인 역할을 맡게 될 것입니다.

첫날에 [184]특별한 소프트웨어가 탑재되어 있는 회사 노트북을 지급받게 될 것임을 유념해 주세요. 첫 출근일 전에 어떤 질문이 있으면, 편하게 저에게 이메일을 보내주세요.

따뜻한 안부를 전하며,

Tae-min Lim

| 어휘 | colleague 동료 figure 판단하다, 생각하다 policy information 정책 정보 refer to ~를 참고하다 attached 첨부된 instead 대신에 be made up of ~로 구성되다 accompany 동행하다 take on 맡다, 떠맡다 observer 관찰자, 참관인 role 역할 load (프로그램을) 로딩하다 feel free to ~ 편하게 ~하다

Anaheim 사 정책 정보	
주차	전자 장비
¹⁸⁵북쪽 주차장은 직원들만을 위해 지정된 곳입니다. ¹⁸⁵이 주차장에 필요한 주차권은 인사과에서 수령할 수 있습니다. ¹⁸⁵남쪽 주차장은 방문객들을 위한 곳으로, 그들은 출입구에서 시간당 주차권을 구입할 수 있습니다. 출구에서 확인 도장을 받은 주차권을 보여주면 비용이 환불될 수 있습니다. ¹⁸⁵동쪽과 서쪽의 주차장은 방문객과 직원 주차장이 합쳐져 있습니다. ¹⁸⁵그곳 둘 다 유효한 주차권이 필요합니다. 야간 주차는 허용되지 않습니다.	직원들은 자신들에게 할당되는 전자 장비를 관리할 책임이 있습니다. 데스크에서 하나의 컴퓨터를 공유하는 관리 부서에 있는 접수 담당자들을 제외하고 각 직원은 한 대의 데스크톱 컴퓨터를 받게 됩니다. ¹⁸⁴그래픽 디자이너들은 1인당 하나씩 노트북이 추가로 지급됩니다. 이것은 노트북에 설치된 소프트웨어 때문에 재택 근무를 할 때 이용되어야 합니다. 영업 팀원들은 외부 영업 프레젠테이션을 위해 필요한 경우 IT 부서에서 노트북을 대여할 수 있습니다. 일반적인 대여 기간은 최대 3일이지만, 이것은 관리자의 승인으로 연장될 수 있습니다.

| 어휘 | reserved 지정된 pick up 수령하다 refund 환불하다 validated ticket 주차 확인 도장을 받은 티켓 combination 조합, 결합 valid 유효한 overnight 야간의 permit 허용하다 electronic equipment 전자 장비 be responsible for ~에 책임이 있다 take care of ~을 관리하다 assigned 할당되는, 배정되는 receptionist 접수 담당자 administration department 관리 부서 share 공유하다 check out 대출하다 off-site 외부의 maximum 최대치 extend 연장하다 approval 승인

181. 주제/목적
Lim 씨는 왜 이메일을 보냈나?
(A) 오리엔테이션의 주제들을 설명하기 위해
(B) 업데이트된 문서를 제공하기 위해
(C) 신입 사원에게 일정 변경에 관해 알리기 위해
(D) 고용 계약 변경을 확인하기 위해
| 해설 | 첫 번째 단락 후반부에 자신의 동료가 보냈던 정책 정보 파일은 작년 것이라고(the policy information file that she sent you is from last year) 한 후, 그 파일을 삭제하고 첨부된 파일을 참조하라고(Please delete that file and refer to the attached one instead) 한 것을 통해, 업데이트된 문서를 제공할 목적으로 보낸 이메일임을 알 수 있으므로 정답은 (B)이다.
| 어휘 | confirm 확인하다, 확정하다 employment contract 고용 계약서

182. 동의어 문제
이메일에서 첫 번째 단락 두 번째 줄의 단어 "figured"와 의미가 가장 유사한 것은
(A) 나타났다
(B) 뒤따랐다
(C) 계산했다
(D) 생각했다
| 해설 | 해당 단어가 들어간 문장은 '제 동료인 Janet Baxter가 귀하가 교육 자료를 미리 받으면 아주 좋을 것이라고 생각했다'라고 해석된다. 따라서 figured는 '생각했다'라는 의미로 쓰인 것이므로 이와 가장 의미가 유사한 (D) thought가 정답이다.

183. 추론 문제
Wenski 씨에 대해 암시되는 것은 무엇인가?
(A) Baxter 씨에게 교육을 받을 것이다.
(B) 자신의 컴퓨터 장비를 제공해야 한다.
(C) 3월에 고객을 만날 것이다.
(D) 첫날에 교육 시험에 통과해야만 한다.
| 해설 | Wenski 씨에게 보낸 이메일의 첫 단락에 근무 시작일이 3월 6일 월요일이라고(Your start date will be Monday, March 6) 하였고, 두 번째 단락에 첫 주 일정을 설명하며 금요일에 고객의 사무실에 처음 방문하게 될 것이라고(you'll have your first visit to a client's office on Friday) 하였으므로, 3월에 고객을 만날 것임을 알 수 있다. 따라서 정답은 (C)이다.
| 패러프레이징 | have your first visit to a client's office → meet with a client

184. 연계 문제 – 추론
Wenski 씨는 어떤 부서에서 일할 것 같은가?
(A) 행정
(B) 그래픽 디자인
(C) IT
(D) 영업
| 해설 | 이메일 마지막 단락에 특별한 소프트웨어가 탑재되어 있는 회사 노트북을 지급받게 될 것이라고(you will be issued your own company laptop with special software loaded onto it) 했고, 이를 정책 정보 오른쪽 내용에 그래픽 디자이너들은 1인당 하나씩 노트북이 추가로 지급된다고(Graphic designers have an additional assigned laptop, one per person) 제시된 것과 연계해 볼 때, Wenski 씨는 그래픽 디자이너인 것으로 유추할 수 있으므로 정답은 (B)이다.

185. True 문제
정책 정보에 따르면, 모든 Anaheim 사 주차장에 관해 사실인 것은 무엇인가?
(A) 주차권이 필요하다.
(B) 방문객은 무료로 주차하는 것이 허용된다.
(C) 그곳들 각각은 같은 수의 공간을 제공한다.
(D) 직원들은 필요 시 밤새 주차할 수 있다.
| 해설 | 북쪽 주차장(The northern parking lot)에 대해 이 주차장에 필요한 주차권은 인사과에서 수령할 수 있다고(The pass needed for this lot can be

picked up in the HR office) 한 것과 남쪽 주차장은 방문객들을 위한 곳으로, 그들은 출입구에서 시간당 주차권을 구입할 수 있다고(The southern lot is for visitors, who can purchase an hourly pass at the gate) 한 것, 동쪽과 서쪽의 주차장(The east and west parking lots)에 대해 둘 다 유효한 주차권이 필요하다고(They both require a valid pass) 한 것을 통해, 모든 주차장에서 주차권이 필요한 것으로 확인되므로 정답은 (A)이다.

| 어휘 | at no cost 무료로

186-190 다음 이메일들과 회람을 참조하시오.

수신: Eugenia Arcuri <e.arcuri@cunhasoftware.com>
발신: Sunder Pandya <s.pandya@cunhasoftware.com>
날짜: 11월 3일
제목: 몇 가지 제안들

Arcuri 씨 귀하,

저는 우리 건물의 회의 공간 부족에 관해 계속해서 많은 불평을 받고 있습니다. 다른 팀장들에게도 이야기했는데, 그들도 같은 문제를 보고했습니다. 팀 의사소통은 우리의 운영에 필수적입니다. 이것 때문에 186팀은 직원들이 추가 수당도 받지 못하고 정기적으로 사무실 마감 시간 이후에 회의를 열어야 하는 상황인데, 그것이 빈 회의실을 잡을 유일한 방법이기 때문입니다.

저는 팀들이 인근 커피숍에서 만날 수 있도록 회사가 음료와 음식의 비용을 환급해 주어야 한다고 생각합니다. 187또한 부담을 완화하도록 돕기 위해 외부에 추가 회의실을 대여하는 것도 검토해야 하고요. 또 다른 옵션은 모두가 회의실을 이용할 기회를 갖도록 매주 팀 회의의 수를 제한하는 것입니다. 제 아이디어들을 고려해 주셔서 감사합니다.

진심을 담아,

Sunder Pandya

| 어휘 | complaint 불평, 항의   lack 부족   essential 필수적인   operation 운영   regularly 정기적으로   additional pay 추가 급여   reimburse 환급하다   nearby 인근의   rent 대여하다   off-site 외부에; 외부의   relieve 완화하다   pressure 압력, 부담   limit 제한하다, 한정하다   consider 고려하다

수신: Cunha 소프트웨어 직원들
발신: Eugenia Arcuri
날짜: 11월 24일
제목: 회의실

우리 회사의 회의실 상황을 개선하기 위한 노력으로, 187우리 옆 건물인 Bowman 타워에 전용실을 하나 임대했습니다. 그 방은 화요일과 목요일에는 하루 종일 이용이 가능합니다. 189또한 우리 자체 대회의실을

위해 Zuniga 평면 스크린 TV를 주문했는데, 그것은 11월 27일에 배달될 것입니다.

188여러분 중 몇몇은 휴게실에서 소규모 모임을 열어오고 있는데요. 그렇게 하는 것을 삼가 주세요. 이곳은 휴식 공간으로 마련된 것이라서 188가능한 한 조용히 유지되어야 하기 때문입니다. 3층의 보관실을 리모델링하여 최대 6명이 이용할 수 있는 작은 회의실을 만들 것입니다. 위의 해결책들이 문제를 해결하는 데 도움이 되기를 바랍니다.

| 어휘 | in an effort to ~하기 위한 노력으로   improve 개선하다   flat-screen 평면 스크린   conference room 대회의실   break room 휴게실   refrain from -ing ~하는 것을 삼가다   storage room 보관실   create 만들다   solution 해결책   resolve 해결하다

수신: Eugenia Arcuri <e.arcuri@cunhasoftware.com>
발신: Zuniga <orders@zuniga.com>
날짜: 11월 25일
제목: Zuniga 주문

Arcuri 씨 귀하,

Zuniga 고객이 되어주셔서 감사합니다! 저희는 저희 제품들의 품질을 보증합니다. 그래서 189고객들께서 배송일로부터 6주 이내에 물품들을 매장으로 다시 보내실 수 있습니다. 이는 어떤 이유에서든 가능하고, 저희가 전액 환불을 해 드릴 것입니다. 원래 포장재들이 모두 포함되어야 한다는 것을 유념해 주시기 바랍니다.

일반 쓰레기로 버릴 수 없어서 결함이 있거나 구식인 전자 기기를 계속 보관하고 계신가요? 저희가 환경을 돕기 위한 새로운 프로그램을 막 시작했습니다. 190유해한 화학 물질이 우리 생태계로 새어 들어가는 것을 막기 위해 저희가 낡은 가전제품을 수거하고 그것들을 적절히 재활용할 것입니다. 더 알아보시려면, 저희 웹 사이트를 방문하세요.

안부를 전하며,

Albert Mills
Zuniga 고객 서비스

| 어휘 | stand by 보증하다, 지지하다   quality 품질   original 원래의   packaging material 포장재   hang onto (팔거나 버리지 않고) 보관하다   faulty 결함 있는   outdated 구식의   electronic device 전자 기기   regular trash 일반 쓰레기   environment 환경   pick up 수거하다   recycle 재활용하다   properly 적절히, 제대로   prevent 막다, 예방하다   harmful 유해한   chemicals 화학 물질   leak into ~에 새어 들어가다   ecosystem 생태계

186. 세부 사항을 묻는 문제
Pandya 씨에 따르면, 회의 공간의 부족이 직원들에게 어떻게 영향을 미쳤나?

(A) 이메일로 더 많은 정보를 보냈다.
(B) 팀의 규모를 변경했다.
(C) 사무실에 늦게까지 머물러야 했다.
(D) 자신들의 장비를 가져와야 했다.
| 해설 | Pandya 씨가 보낸 이메일 첫 번째 단락에 팀들은 정기적으로 사무실 마감 시간 이후에 회의를 열어야 하는 상황이라고(teams are regularly having to hold meetings after the office closing time) 했으므로 정답은 (C)이다.
| 패러프레이징 | hold meetings after the office closing time → stay late at the office

187. 연계 문제 - 추론
Arcuri 씨는 Pandya 씨가 한 어떤 추천을 채택했나?
(A) 외부 장소를 임대하는 것
(B) 화상 회의로 회의를 여는 것
(C) 카페 지출을 환급하는 것
(D) 회의 시간을 제한하는 것
| 해설 | Pandya 씨가 보낸 이메일 두 번째 단락에 문제 해결 방법을 추천하면서 외부에 추가 회의실을 대여하는 것도 검토해야 한다고(We should also look into renting an additional meeting room off-site to help relieve the pressure) 제안했고, Arcuri 씨가 보낸 회람 첫 번째 단락에 우리 옆 건물인 Bowman 타워에 전용실을 하나 임대했다고(we have rented a private room at Bowman Tower, which is the building next to ours) 했으므로 정답은 (A)이다.
| 어휘 | teleconference 화상 회의
| 패러프레이징 | an additional meeting room off-site → an off-site location

188. True 문제
회람에서 Arcuri 씨가 휴게실에 관해 언급한 것은 무엇인가?
(A) 3층에 위치해 있다.
(B) 리모델링 프로젝트를 진행할 것이다.
(C) 소음 수준이 낮게 유지되어야 한다.
(D) 공간이 소규모 회의들에 적합하다.
| 해설 | 회람 두 번째 단락에 몇몇 사람들이 휴게실에서 소규모 모임을 열고 있다는(Some of you have been holding small meetings in the break room) 사실을 알린 후, 그곳이 가능한 한 조용히 유지되어야 한다고(it should be kept as quiet as possible) 했으므로 정답은 (C)이다.
| 어휘 | located 위치해 있는   undergo 진행하다   noise level 소음 수준   suitable 적합한, 적당한
| 패러프레이징 | should be kept as quiet as possible → Its noise levels should be kept low

고난도

189. 연계 문제 - True
Cunha 소프트웨어에 의해 구입된 새로운 모니터에 관해 제시된 것은 무엇인가?
(A) Bowman 타워에 설치될 것이다.
(B) 팀장들에 의해 요청되었다.
(C) 11월 27일에 주문되었다.
(D) 12월에 언제든 반품될 수 있다.
| 해설 | Arcuri 씨가 보낸 회람 첫 번째 단락에 대회의실을 위해 Zuniga 평면 스크린 TV를 주문했고, 11월 27일에 배달될 것이라고(We've also ordered a Zuniga flat-screen TV for our own conference room, which will be delivered on November 27) 한 것과 Zuniga 고객 서비스에서 보낸 이메일 첫 번째 단락에 고객들은 배송일로부터 6주 이내에 물품들을 매장으로 다시 보낼 수 있다고(That's why customers may send items back to the store within 6 weeks of the delivery date) 한 것을 연계해볼 때, 12월 중에 언제든 반품될 수 있다는 것을 알 수 있으므로 정답은 (D)이다.
| 패러프레이징 | send items back to the store → be returned

190. 세부 사항을 묻는 문제
Zuniga가 최근에 추가한 서비스는 무엇인가?
(A) 품질 보증 기간 연장
(B) 중고 전자제품 재활용
(C) 주말 배송
(D) 온라인 추적
| 해설 | Zuniga 고객 서비스에서 보낸 이메일 두 번째 단락에 새로운 프로그램을 시작했다며, 유해한 화학 물질이 생태계로 새어 들어가는 것을 막기 위해 낡은 가전 제품을 수거하고 그것들을 적절히 재활용할 것이라고(We will pick up your old electronics and recycle them properly to prevent harmful chemicals from leaking into our ecosystem) 제시되어 있으므로 정답은 (B)이다.
| 어휘 | extended 연장된   tracking 추적
| 패러프레이징 | old → Used

191-195 다음 기사, 이메일, 프로그램을 참조하시오.

Galway 전통 음악 축제

GALWAY (8월 7일) – 대중들의 요구에 힘입어, Galway 전통 음악 축제가 올해 10월 10일부터 16일까지 예정되어 있다. 그 축제는 더 다양한 관객들과 자신들의 음악을 공유하기를 원했던 바이올린 연주자 그룹에 의해 시작되었다. 시작된 이래로, ¹⁹¹그 축제는 규모가 커졌고 사람들이 아일랜드 전통 음악에 다시 관심을 갖게 만들었다.

그 축제는 주로 Straffan 공원에서 열릴 것이다. 입장료는 대중에게 무료이고, 총 50명의 음악가들이 야외 무대에서 공연을 펼칠 것이다. 폐막식은 축제 마지막 날에 그 공원에 인접한 Bluebell 센터에서 열릴 것이다. 이는 축제에서 유일하게 초대받은 사람들만 입장할 수 있다.

공연 전체 목록은 www.galwaymusic.ie에서 확인할 수 있다. Straffan 공원은 주차 공간이 한정되어 있기 때문에, 방문객들은 행사장까지 대중 교통을 이용하도록 권장된다.

| 어휘 | back by popular demand 대중의 요구에 따라   found 설립하다   fiddler 바이올린 연주자   audience 관객   admission 입장료   put on performances 공연을 펼치다   outdoor stage 야외 무대   closing ceremony 폐막식   adjacent to ~에 인접한   by invitation

only 초대받은 사람들만 입장할 수 있는 complete 전체의, 완전한
public transportation 대중 교통

수신: Calvin Vaughn
발신: Adrienne Kenner
날짜: 8월 10일
제목: 회신: 뮤직 페스티벌 시상식

192Vaughn 씨 귀하,

192귀하가 축제 시상식에 참석하기 위해 일정을 조정하실 수 있었다는 것을 듣게 되어 기쁩니다. 저희가 화상 회의를 통해 귀하의 상을 수여할 준비가 되어 있었지만, 192그곳에 오셔서 직접 수상하시는 것이 훨씬 더 좋습니다. Bluebell 센터의 문은 초대 손님들을 위해 오후 6시 30분에 열릴 것입니다. 195축제의 행사 기획자인 Bonnie Forbes가 귀하를 소개하고 상을 수여할 것입니다.

193귀하에게 우편으로 티켓 한 장이 발송될 것이니, 가급적 빨리 귀하의 우편 주소를 저에게 주시기 바랍니다. 193그것은 귀하와 선택하신 손님 한 분에게 유효합니다. 티켓들은 행사 위원회를 통해서만 구할 수 있으며 일반에게 판매되지 않는다는 것을 유념해 주시기 바랍니다.

따뜻한 안부를 전하며,

Adrienne Kenner
Galway 전통 음악 축제, 관리자

| 어휘 | delighted 기쁜 adjust 조정하다 accommodate 수용하다
awards ceremony 시상식 present 수여하다 award 상 via ~을 통해 teleconferencing 화상 회의 진행 introduce 소개하다
mailing address 우편 주소 at one's earliest convenience 가급적 빨리 valid 유효한

Galway 전통 음악 축제 폐막식
행사 순서

오후 6:30	문 개방
오후 7:00	Amy McDaniel 시장의 환영사
오후 7:10	음악 공연: 아일랜드 바이올린, Darcy Byrne과 Lark 무용단
오후 8:00	Robert Wright의 음악 상 수여
오후 8:20	195Bonnie Forbes의 기부자 감사 상 수여
오후 8:30	Aidan Quinn의 공로상 수여
오후 8:40	194음악 공연: 켈트 하프, Dylan Flynn
오후 9:30	Amy McDaniel의 폐회사

| 어휘 | welcome speech 환영사 mayor 시장 presentation 공연 fiddle 바이올린 dance troupe 무용단 donor 기부자

appreciation 감사 lifetime achievement award 공로상 closing speech 폐회사

고난도
191. True 문제
축제에 관해 제시된 것은 무엇인가?
(A) 올해 무대 공연의 수를 늘릴 것이다.
(B) 어떤 예술 형태에 대한 관심을 새롭게 했다.
(C) 50년 동안 계속돼 오고 있다.
(D) 전통 악기들을 팔려고 내놓는다.
| 해설 | 기사 첫 번째 단락 후반부에 축제는 규모가 커졌고 사람들이 아일랜드 전통 음악에 다시 관심을 갖게 만들었다고(the festival has grown in size and has made people interested in traditional Irish music again) 제시되어 있으므로 정답은 (B)이다.
| 어휘 | increase 늘리다, 증가시키다 renew 재개하다, 새롭게 하다
offer for sale 팔려고 내놓다
| 패러프레이징 | has made people interested in traditional Irish music again → has renewed an interest in an art form

고난도
192. 세부 사항을 묻는 문제
Kenner 씨는 무엇에 대해 기뻐하는가?
(A) Vaughn 씨가 어떤 상의 후보로 그녀를 지명했다.
(B) Vaughn 씨가 직접 참석할 것이다.
(C) 그녀는 마지막 티켓을 구할 수 있을 것이다.
(D) 그녀는 연설을 하도록 선발되었다.
| 해설 | Kenner 씨가 Vaughn 씨에게 보낸 이메일 초반부에 귀하가 축제 시상식에 참석하기 위해 일정을 조정할 수 있었다는 것을 듣게 되어 기쁘다고(I'm delighted to hear that you were able to adjust your schedule to accommodate the festival awards ceremony) 한 후, 그곳에 와서 직접 수상하는 것이 훨씬 더 좋다고(it's even better that you'll be there to accept it yourself) 덧붙였으므로 정답은 (B)이다.
| 어휘 | nominate 지명하다 make an appearance 참석하다, 등장하다
in-person 직접의, 본인이 직접 출연하는 last-minute 막판의

193. 추론 문제
폐막 행사 티켓들에 관해 암시되는 것은 무엇인가?
(A) Bluebell 센터에서 수령되어야 한다.
(B) 축제를 후원할 돈을 창출할 것이다.
(C) 고객들에 의해 온라인으로 구매될 수 있다.
(D) 같은 티켓으로 두 사람이 입장하는 것을 허용한다.
| 해설 | 이메일 두 번째 단락에 우편으로 티켓 한 장이 발송될 것이라고(You will be sent one ticket in the mail) 한 것과 그것은 본인과 선택한 손님 한 명에게 유효하다고(It is valid for yourself and a guest of your choice) 한 것을 통해, 티켓 한 장으로 두 사람이 입장할 수 있는 것으로 유추할 수 있으므로 정답은 (D)이다.
| 어휘 | pick up 수령하다 generate 발생시키다, 창출하다 permit 허용하다

| 패러프레이징 | valid for yourself and a guest of your choice → permit two people to enter with the same ticket

194. 추론 문제
Dylan Flynn은 누구일 것 같은가?
(A) 행사 기획자
(B) 시 공무원
(C) 연주자
(D) 기자

| 해설 | Dylan Flynn은 프로그램에서 오후 8:40에 진행되는 음악 공연에서 켈트 하프(Musical Presentation: Celtic harp)를 연주할 사람으로 확인되므로 정답은 (C)이다.

| 어휘 | city official 시 공무원

고난도
195. 연계 문제 - 추론
Vaughn 씨는 왜 상을 받을 것 같은가?
(A) 자신의 음악 그룹을 결성했다.
(B) 음악에 자신의 일생을 바쳤다.
(C) 행사에 기부를 했다.
(D) 음악 수업을 가르친다.

| 해설 | Vaughn 씨에게 보낸 이메일 첫 번째 단락에 Bonnie Forbes가 귀하를 소개하고 상을 수여할 것이라고(Bonnie Forbes, the festival's event planner, will introduce you and present the award) 했는데, 이를 프로그램에서 오후 8:20에 예정된 Bonnie Forbes의 기부자 감사 상 수여(Donor Appreciation Award presented by Bonnie Forbes)와 연계해볼 때, 기부에 대한 감사로 상을 받을 것임을 알 수 있으므로 정답은 (C)이다.

| 어휘 | dedicate 바치다, 헌신하다   make a donation 기부를 하다

| 패러프레이징 | Donor → made a donation

196-200 다음 이메일들과 편지를 참조하시오.

수신: Sasha Juarez <sashaj@arroya.com.au>
발신: Connor Walkom <c_walkom@montagu.com.au>
날짜: 7월 19일
제목: 추천서

Juarez 씨 귀하,

Carnegie 출판에 제가 지원하는 것을 위해 추천서를 써 주셔서 감사합니다. 이 기회에 떠올려 있었지만, 결국 그 직책에 제가 선정되진 않았습니다. ¹⁹⁶온라인 선발 시험을 치르도록 요구되었는데, 그 시험에서 아주 낮은 점수를 받았습니다. ¹⁹⁷/¹⁹⁸저는 Montagu에서 근무할 때 기술 장비들의 취급 설명서를 편집했던 저의 경험을 잘 이어갈 수 있을 거라 생각했습니다. 그런데 그 일자리가 문학 잡지를 위한 것이었기 때문에 시험에 문학 문제들이 많이 포함되어 있었고, 제 학위와 경험은 그 분야가 아닙니다. 제 구직 활동에 대해 계속 알려 드리겠습니다.

따뜻한 안부를 전하며,

Connor

| 어휘 | reference 추천(서)   application 지원   opportunity 기회   ultimately 결국, 궁극적으로   be required to ~하도록 요구되다   screening test 선발 시험   score 점수를 받다   instruction manual 취급 설명서   technical device 기술 장비   carry over (다른 상황에서 계속) 이어지다   literary 문학적인, 문학의   degree 학위   field 분야   keep ~ posted ~에게 계속 알려주다   job hunt 구직

Connor Walkom
708 Moruya Road
BRISBANE QLD 4001

8월 5일

Walkom 씨 귀하,

Bayview 제조사를 대표하여, 귀하를 저희 팀에 환영하고 싶습니다. 저희 본사 면접에서 귀하는 저희의 요구에 대한 철저한 이해를 보여주었습니다. ¹⁹⁷귀하가 제공하신 Montagu에서의 작업 샘플이 저희가 원하는 것에 딱 들어맞았는데, 이곳에서 아주 유사한 직책을 가지게 될 것이기 때문입니다.

동봉된 것에서 ¹⁹⁹8월 12일 귀하의 업무 첫날을 위한 오리엔테이션 자료를 보실 텐데요. 오전 9시에 출근해 주세요. 먼저 211호인 제 사무실로 오셔야 합니다. ¹⁹⁸그곳에서 귀하의 직속 상사가 될 Marvin Carillo를 만날 것입니다. 그가 귀하를 교육하고 나머지 팀원에게 소개해줄 것입니다. ¹⁹⁹오전 11시 30분에는 보안 부서에서 귀하의 사원증을 수령할 것이고요. 점심 식사 계획은 아직 확정되지 않았지만, 아마도 귀하의 팀과 함께 구내 식당에서 하게 될 것 같습니다.

8월 12일에 뵙겠습니다!

Rafael Prescott

| 어휘 | on behalf of ~을 대표하여, 대신하여   head office 본사   thorough 철저한   understanding 이해   enclosed 동봉된   report to work 출근하다   immediate supervisor 직속 상관   conduct 하다, 실시하다   ID badge 사원증, 신분증   security department 보안 부서   cafeteria 구내 식당

수신: Sasha Juarez <sashaj@arroya.com.au>
발신: Connor Walkom <c_walkom@montagu.com.au>
날짜: 8월 7일
제목: 성공!

Juarez 씨 귀하,

제가 Bayview 제조사에서 일자리를 제안받았습니다. 사실, ²⁰⁰면접이 끝날 때 고용 계약서를 받았습니다! 이 일자리는 저에게 딱 맞고, 제 구직 활동 내내 추천서들을 써주신 일에 감사드립니다.

따뜻한 안부를 전하며,

Connor

| 어휘 | employment contract 고용 계약서 appreciate 감사하다, 고마워하다 throughout 내내 job search 구직

(A) 금융 전문가
(B) 선임 편집자
(C) 회사 투자자
(D) 인사 관리자

| 해설 | Walkom 씨에게 보낸 편지 첫 번째 단락 후반부에 Montagu에서와 유사한 직책을 가지게 될 것이라고 했고 중반부에 직속 상사가 될 Marvin Carillo를 만날 것이라고(There you will meet Marvin Carillo, who will be your immediate supervisor) 했는데, 이를 Walkom 씨가 보낸 첫 번째 이메일 중반부에 Montagu에서 근무할 때 기술 장비들의 취급 설명서를 편집했던 경험을(my experience editing instruction manuals for technical devices when I worked at Montagu) 언급한 것과 연계해볼 때, Walkom 씨의 직속 상사가 될 Carillo 씨도 편집 작업을 하는 사람으로 유추할 수 있으므로 정답은 (B)이다.

| 어휘 | financial 금융의, 재무의 senior 선임의 investor 투자자

196. 세부 사항을 묻는 문제
Walkom 씨는 왜 Carnegie 출판의 일자리를 제안받지 못했나?
(A) 시험 성적이 좋지 않았다.
(B) 자신의 학위 사본을 제공할 수 없었다.
(C) 면접에 늦게 도착했다.
(D) 너무 높은 급여를 요구했다.

| 해설 | 첫 번째 이메일에 그 직책에 선정되지 않았음을 알린 후, 그 이유로 온라인 선발 시험에서 아주 낮은 점수를 받았다고(I was required to take an online screening test, which I scored very low on) 했으므로 정답은 (A)이다.

| 어휘 | poorly 형편없이, 저조하게

| 패러프레이징 | scored very low on → performed poorly on

199. 세부 사항을 묻는 문제
편지에 따르면, 8월 12일 오전 11시 30분에 Walkom 씨는 어디로 가야 하는가?
(A) 보안 사무실로
(B) 휴게실로
(C) 구내 식당으로
(D) Prescott 씨 사무실로

| 해설 | 편지 두 번째 단락에 Walkom 씨의 업무 첫날이 8월 12일(your first day of work, August 12)로 제시되어 있고, 이후 그날 오전 11시 30분에는 보안 부서에서 사원증을 수령할 것이라고(At 11:30 A.M., you'll pick up your ID badge from the security department) 했으므로 정답은 (A)이다.

| 패러프레이징 | the security department → a security office

197. 연계 문제 - 추론
Walkom 씨에 대해 암시되는 것은 무엇인가?
(A) 최근에 대학 교육을 마쳤다.
(B) Prescott 씨의 팀에서 일했었다.
(C) 새로운 도시로 이사했기 때문에 Montagu에서 일하는 것을 그만두었다.
(D) Bayview 제조사의 기술 매뉴얼을 검토할 것이다.

| 해설 | 첫 번째 이메일 중반부에 Montagu에서 근무할 때 기술 장비들의 취급 설명서를 편집했던 경험을 잘 이어갈 수 있을 거라 생각했다고(I thought my experience editing instruction manuals for technical devices when I worked at Montagu would carry over well) 한 것과 편지 첫 번째 단락 후반부에 귀하가 제공한 Montagu에서의 작업 샘플이 회사에서 원하는 것에 딱 들어맞았는데, 이곳에서 아주 유사한 직책을 가지게 될 것이기 때문이라고(The sample work you provided from Montagu was a perfect fit, as you will have a very similar position here) 한 것을 연계해볼 때, Walkom 씨는 Bayview 제조사에서 기술 장비의 취급 설명서 편집하는 것과 유사한 일을 할 것으로 유추할 수 있으므로 정답은 (D)이다.

| 패러프레이징 | editing instruction manuals for technical devices → review technical manuals

200. 세부 사항을 묻는 문제
Walkom 씨는 자신의 계약서를 어떻게 받았나?
(A) 이메일로
(B) 팩스로
(C) 직접
(D) 우편으로

| 해설 | Walkom 씨가 보낸 두 번째 이메일에 면접이 끝날 때 고용 계약서를 받았다고(I was given the employment contract at the close of my interview) 했으므로 정답은 (C)이다.

| 패러프레이징 | at the close of my interview → In person

198. 연계 문제 - 추론
Carillo 씨는 누구일 것 같은가?

TEST 10

PART 5

101 (B)	102 (D)	103 (A)	104 (C)	105 (C)
106 (A)	107 (D)	108 (B)	109 (A)	110 (D)
111 (C)	112 (B)	113 (A)	114 (B)	115 (C)
116 (B)	117 (C)	118 (A)	119 (D)	120 (B)
121 (A)	122 (A)	123 (D)	124 (C)	125 (B)
126 (D)	127 (D)	128 (D)	129 (C)	130 (C)

PART 6

131 (A)	132 (D)	133 (D)	134 (B)	135 (A)
136 (A)	137 (C)	138 (D)	139 (B)	140 (C)
141 (B)	142 (D)	143 (C)	144 (B)	145 (A)
146 (C)				

PART 7

147 (B)	148 (A)	149 (D)	150 (B)	151 (B)
152 (B)	153 (B)	154 (C)	155 (D)	156 (A)
157 (B)	158 (B)	159 (C)	160 (C)	161 (C)
162 (B)	163 (A)	164 (C)	165 (C)	166 (B)
167 (B)	168 (C)	169 (D)	170 (A)	171 (C)
172 (D)	173 (A)	174 (C)	175 (C)	176 (B)
177 (B)	178 (A)	179 (B)	180 (C)	181 (D)
182 (A)	183 (D)	184 (C)	185 (C)	186 (D)
187 (B)	188 (C)	189 (D)	190 (B)	191 (C)
192 (C)	193 (D)	194 (C)	195 (A)	196 (C)
197 (B)	198 (B)	199 (B)	200 (B)	

PART 5

101. 동사의 형태
Floyd 씨가 그 정보를 자신의 직원들 모두에게 전달할 것이다.
| 해설 | 조동사 will 뒤에 빈칸이 있으므로 동사 원형이 들어갈 자리이다. 따라서 (B) forward가 정답이다.
| 어휘 | forward 전달하다

102. 전치사 어휘
최근 경제 위기에도 불구하고, Richland 제조사는 노동력을 15% 늘렸다.
| 해설 | 빈칸은 뒤에 있는 명사구를 목적어로 가지는 전치사가 들어갈 자리이며, 경제 위기와 노동력을 늘리는 것은 대조적인 내용이므로 '~에도 불구하고'라는 뜻의 (D) Despite가 정답이다. (B) Instead와 (C) Very는 부사이므로 오답이다.
| 어휘 | economic crisis 경제 위기 increase 늘리다 workforce 노동력

103. 동사 어휘
HR 부서가 새로운 최고 재무 책임자인 Ariel Pacheco를 환영하기 위한 파티를 열 것이다.
| 해설 | 빈칸은 to부정사를 완성해줄 동사가 들어갈 자리로, '새로운 최고 재무 책임자를 환영하기 위해 파티를 열 것'이라는 의미로 전개되는 것이 적절하므로 '환영하다'라는 뜻의 (A) welcome이 정답이다.
| 어휘 | throw a party 파티를 열다 chief financial officer 최고 재무 책임자 replace 교체하다 transfer 옮기다 retire 퇴직하다

104. 형용사 자리 - 명사 수식
스위스의 가장 인기 있는 초콜릿 제조 판매회사가 곧 독일로 진출할 것이다.
| 해설 | 최상급 표현 부사인 most와 명사 chocolatier 사이에 빈칸이 있으므로, 부사의 수식을 받으며 명사를 수식해줄 수 있는 형용사가 들어가야 한다. 따라서 '인기 있는'이라는 뜻의 형용사인 (C) popular가 정답이다.
| 어휘 | chocolatier 초콜릿 제조 판매업(자) expand into ~로 확장하다, 진출하다 popularity 인기 popularly 일반적으로, 통속적으로 popularize 대중화하다

105. 동사의 형태와 시제
신제품을 내놓았음에도 Norman Technologies의 매출이 지난 분기에 감소했다.
| 해설 | 빈칸은 복수 주어 뒤에 문장의 본동사가 들어갈 자리이므로 수 일치가 되지 않는 단수 동사인 (B) falls와 단독으로 본동사 자리에 올 수 없는 과거 분사인 (D) fallen은 오답이고, 빈칸 뒤에 과거 시점 표현인 in the last quarter가 있으므로 과거 시제 동사인 (C) fell이 정답이다.
| 어휘 | quarter 분기 introduce 소개하다, 내놓다

106. 명사 어휘
Akron 쇼핑몰에 할인 체인점들을 추가하면 저예산 쇼핑객들을 더 불러올 수 있다.
| 해설 | 문장의 주어가 될 명사가 들어갈 자리로, 문맥상 저예산 쇼핑객들을 더 불러올 수 있는 것은 할인 체인점의 '추가'일 것이므로 '추가'라는 뜻의 (A) addition이 정답이다.
| 어휘 | discount chain store 할인 체인점 bring 불러오다, 데려오다 low-budget 저 예산 addition 추가, 부가 vendor 판매회사

107. 동사의 형태
더 많은 서빙 직원이 고용되어야 할지 알아보기 위해 Cohen 씨가 조사를 하고 있다.
| 해설 | 빈칸은 조동사 should 뒤 if절의 동사가 들어갈 자리로, 동사 hire는 타동사인데 빈칸 뒤에 목적어가 없으므로 수동태가 되어야 한다. 따라서 수동태인 (D) be hired가 정답이다.
| 어휘 | conduct 하다, 수행하다

▲ 고난도
108. 전치사 어휘
도서관 열람 시간 외에 책을 반납할 때는 입구 근처에 있는 책 수거함을 이용해 주세요.
| 해설 | 빈칸은 뒤에 있는 전치사 of와 함께 전치사구를 완성해줄 단어가 들어갈 자리로, 문맥상 '도서관 열람 시간 외에'라는 의미가 되어야 함을 알 수 있으므로

outside of(~을 넘어서)라는 전치사구를 완성해줄 (B) outside가 정답이다.
| 어휘 | drop box 드롭 박스, 수거함   entrance 입구

🔺고난도
109. 형용사 어휘
단골 고객들은 추가 보상 포인트를 위해 Ramsey Sporting의 회원으로 가입하는 것이 장려된다.
| 해설 | 빈칸은 명사 customers를 수식해줄 형용사가 들어갈 자리로, 문맥상 '단골 고객들'이라는 의미로 전개되는 것이 적절하므로 (A) Frequent가 정답이다.
| 어휘 | be encouraged to ~하도록 장려되다   extra 추가의   reward 보상   frequent 빈번한, 잦은

110. 명사 자리 – 전치사의 목적어
이 일자리 공석의 이상적인 지원자는 마케팅에 폭넓은 경험을 가지고 있을 것이다.
| 해설 | 빈칸은 전치사 for의 목적어로 보이는 this job과 조동사 would 사이에 위치해 있으므로, 형용사이자 동사 원형인 (A) open, 3인칭 단수 동사인 (C) opens, 후치 수식하는 과거 분사로 볼 경우 의미상 부적절한 (B) opened는 모두 답이 될 수 없고, 앞에 있는 job과 함께 '일자리 공석'이라는 의미의 복합 명사를 완성해줄 명사인 (D) opening이 정답이다.
| 어휘 | ideal 이상적인   candidate 지원자, 후보자   extensive 폭넓은   experience 경험

111. 부사절 접속사
새로운 계약서를 철할 때 발송 주소를 확인하는 것을 잊지 마세요.
| 해설 | 빈칸 앞에 완전한 절이 있고, 뒤에 분사 구문이 제시되어 있는 것으로 볼 때, 분사 구문을 이끌 수 없는 전치사인 (A) from과 (B) to는 답이 될 수 없고, '제출할 때 ~ 잊지 마세요'라는 의미를 완성해줄 부사절 접속사인 (C) when이 정답이다.
| 어휘 | confirm 확인하다, 확정하다   file 철하다, 정리하다   contract 계약서

🔺고난도
112. 부사 자리 – 부사 수식
Ripley Power 주식회사가 동종의 다른 어떤 것보다 상당히 더 혁신적인 새로운 태양 전지판을 생산했다.
| 해설 | be동사 is와 비교급을 만드는 부사 more 사이에 빈칸이 있으므로, 빈칸은 부사를 수식해줄 부사가 들어가야 함을 알 수 있다. 따라서 '상당히, 현저히'라는 뜻의 부사인 (B) considerably가 정답이다.
| 어휘 | solar panel 태양 전지판   innovative 혁신적인   considerable 상당한   considerably 상당히

🔺고난도
113. 동사 어휘 – 문법
Neo Producers의 CEO가 자사의 Eastland 사 인수가 거의 마무리되었다고 언론에 말했다.
| 해설 | 빈칸은 문장의 본동사가 들어갈 자리로, 뒤에 목적어가 두 개(the press, that절) 있으므로, 이와 같은 '동사+목적어1+목적어2(that절)' 구조로 쓰일 수 있는 4형식 동사인 (A) told가 정답이다. (C) spoke는 주로 자동사로 쓰이고, (B) stated와 (D) mentioned는 목적어(that절)를 하나만 갖는 3형식 동사이므로 오

답이다.
| 어휘 | press 언론   acquisition 인수

🔺고난도
114. 부사 어휘
새로운 회계 소프트웨어에 관한 모든 문의들은 기술 지원 팀의 관리자에 의해 직접 답변될 것이다.
| 해설 | 빈칸은 동사 answered를 수식해줄 부사가 들어갈 자리로, '관리자에 의해 직접 답변될 것이다'라는 의미로 전개되는 것이 적절하므로 '직접'이라는 뜻의 (B) personally가 정답이다.
| 어휘 | inquiry 문의   regarding ~에 관한   accounting 회계   currently 현재   personally 직접   smoothly 부드럽게   equally 동일하게

115. 동명사 자리 – 전치사의 목적어
어제 정기 점검을 완료하자마자, Maki 씨가 자신의 관리자에게 낼 결과 보고서를 작성했다.
| 해설 | 빈칸 앞에는 전치사 Upon이, 뒤에는 명사구가 제시되어 있으므로 빈칸에는 전치사의 목적어 자리에 올 수 있으면서 명사구를 목적어로 가질 수 있는 동명사가 들어가야 함을 알 수 있다. 따라서 (C) completing이 정답이다.
| 어휘 | regular inspection 정기 점검   supervisor 관리자   complete 완료하다, 작성하다   completion 완료

116. 명사 어휘
9월에 퇴직하려는 Reyes 씨의 계획 때문에, Dorsey 산업은 그녀의 후임자를 회사 내부에서 모집하기로 결정했다.
| 해설 | 빈칸은 타동사 recruit의 목적어로 소유격 대명사 her의 수식을 받는 명사가 들어갈 자리로, 앞에 언급된 퇴직과 연결시켜 볼 때 '후임자를 모집하기로 결정했다'는 의미로 전개되는 것이 적절하므로 '후임자'라는 뜻의 (B) replacement가 정답이다.
| 어휘 | retire 퇴직하다   recruit 모집하다   achievement 성취   replacement 후임자, 대체   ceremony 의식   organization 기관, 조직

🔺고난도
117. 현재 분사 vs. 과거 분사
Coyote Cable에 의해 제공되는 고속 인터넷 서비스가 고객들로부터 호평을 받았다.
| 해설 | 빈칸 앞에는 문장의 주어가, 뒤에는 전치사구가 제시되어 있고, 문장의 본동사인 has been received가 있는 것으로 볼 때, 본동사 자리에 들어갈 수 있는 일반 동사 형태인 (A) provide와 (B) provides는 답이 될 수 없고, 후치 수식하는 분사가 들어갈 자리임을 알 수 있는데, 뒤에 전치사 by로 시작하는 전치사구가 있고, '~ 의해 제공되는'이라는 수동의 의미가 되는 것이 적절하므로 과거 분사인 (C) provided가 정답이다.
| 어휘 | be received favorably 호평을 받다

118. 부사절 접속사
도쿄에 있는 자리에 받아들여지자마자, Kim 씨는 해외로 이사할 준비를 하기 시작했다.
| 해설 | 빈칸 뒤로 완전한 두 개의 절이 있으므로 빈칸은 두 절을 연결해줄 접속사

가 들어갈 자리이며, 문맥상 '받아들여지자마자, 준비를 하기 시작했다'라는 의미로 전개되는 것이 적절하므로 '~하자마자'라는 뜻의 부사절 접속사인 (A) As soon as가 정답이다.

| 어휘 | accept 수락하다, 받아들이다 overseas 해외로

고난도
119. 소유격 관계 대명사
매출 수치가 연간 목표를 초과한 영업 사원들에게 특별 휴가 보너스가 지급될 것이다.

| 해설 | 빈칸 뒤에 있는 절(sales figures ~ goals)을 이끌어 앞의 명사 salespeople을 적절히 수식하는 관계사를 찾는 문제로, 빈칸 뒤에 있는 관계사 절이 주어나 목적어가 빠짐없이 모두 있는 완전한 절의 형태이므로, 완전한 절과 결합하는 소유격 관계 대명사인 (D) whose가 정답이다.

| 어휘 | sales figures 매출 수치, 매출액 exceed 초과하다, 넘다 annual goal 연간 목표

120. 형용사 어휘
이 안내서는 전문적인 엔지니어링 면허를 위한 필수적인 기술들 각각을 설명한다.

| 해설 | 빈칸은 뒤에 있는 명사 skills를 수식해줄 형용사가 들어갈 자리로, 문맥상 '면허를 위한 필수적인 기술들'이라는 의미로 전개되는 것이 적절하므로 '필수적인'이라는 뜻의 (B) essential이 정답이다.

| 어휘 | handbook 안내서 describe 설명하다, 기술하다 license 면허, 자격증 competing 경쟁하는 essential 필수적인 dedicated 헌신적인 dependent 의존적인

고난도
121. 동사 어휘 - 문법
BoBo Tech의 새로운 태블릿이 매우 수익성 있는 것으로 판명되어, 회사는 그것을 계속 생산하기로 결정했다.

| 해설 | 빈칸은 문장의 본동사가 들어갈 자리로, 뒤에 '부사+형용사'가 제시되어 있으므로 목적어가 필요한 타동사인 (B) created와 (C) earned는 답이 될 수 없고, 문맥상 '수익성 있는 것으로 판명되다'라는 의미로 전개되는 것이 적절하므로 '판명되다'라는 뜻의 (A) proved가 정답이다.

| 어휘 | profitable 수익성 있는 prove 드러나다, 판명되다 create 만들다 earn 벌다 apply 적용되다

고난도
122. 부사 어휘
Gates 씨가 새로운 금전 등록기를 설치하기 바로 전에 매장 동료들 모두를 위한 교육 세션을 열었다.

| 해설 | 빈칸은 뒤에 있는 before를 수식해줄 부사가 들어갈 자리로, before와 함께 쓰여 '바로 전에, 직전에'라는 의미를 만드는 (A) right가 정답이다.

| 어휘 | sales floor associate 매장 동료 install 설치하다 cash registers 금전 등록기

123. 현재 분사 vs. 과거 분사
Longwood 노인 마을은 편안하고 안전한 동네가 있는 것으로 잘 알려져 있다.

| 해설 | 형용사 safe와 등위 접속사 and로 연결된 빈칸은 safe와 함께 명사 neighborhood를 수식할 형용사가 들어갈 자리로, '편안하고 안전한 이웃'이라는 의미로 전개되는 것이 적절하므로 '편안한, 느긋한'이라는 뜻의 (D) relaxing이 정답이다. (C) relaxed는 주로 사람이나 분위기(atmosphere) 등을 수식할 때 사용된다.

| 어휘 | be well-known for ~로 잘 알려져 있다 neighborhood 이웃, 동네 relaxation 휴식 relax 휴식을 취하다 relaxed 느긋한, 여유 있는 relaxing 편안한, 느긋한

124. to부정사
엔지니어가 더 고르게 차량의 균형을 잡기 위해 자동차의 뒤쪽 끝에 엔진을 놓았다.

| 해설 | 빈칸 앞에 완전한 문장이 있고, 뒤에는 동사 원형이 있으므로, 동사 원형 앞에 올 수 없는 전치사구인 (A) in addition to와 (B) as a result of, (D) on behalf of는 모두 오답이다. 따라서 뒤에 동사 원형이 올 수 있는 to부정사 관용 표현인 (C) in order to가 정답이다.

| 어휘 | rear 뒤쪽의 evenly 고르게 balance 균형을 잡다 on behalf of ~을 대신하여

125. 부사 어휘
Chester 홀은 매우 다양한 음악 공연을 위한 충분한 공간을 제공하도록 의도적으로 설계되었다.

| 해설 | 빈칸은 동사 designed를 수식해줄 부사가 들어갈 자리로, 문맥상 '의도적으로 설계되었다'라는 의미로 전개되는 것이 적절하므로 '의도적으로'라는 뜻의 (B) intentionally가 정답이다.

| 어휘 | accommodate 충분한 공간을 제공하다, 수용하다 a wide variety of 매우 다양한 punctually 정각에, 엄수하여 intentionally 의도적으로 aggressively 공격적으로 enormously 엄청나게

126. 명사 자리 - 주어
성공한 회사들에 취업을 하기 위한 경쟁이 치열하기 때문에, 구직자들은 인상적인 이력서를 써야 한다.

| 해설 | 빈칸은 뒤에 있는 전치사구의 수식을 받는 문장의 주어가 될 명사가 들어갈 자리이므로 동사인 (B) Compete와 형용사인 (C) Competitive는 답이 될 수 없고, 뒤에 제시된 형용사 보어인 strong과 연결 지어 '경쟁이 치열하다'라는 의미로 전개되는 것이 적절하므로 '경쟁'이라는 뜻의 명사인 (D) Competition이 정답이다. '경쟁자, 경쟁업체'라는 뜻의 (A) Competitor는 가산 명사이기 때문에 관사나 소유격 없이 단독으로 단수로 쓰일 수 없다.

| 어휘 | employment 고용, 취업 job applicant 취업 지원자, 구직자 impressive 인상적인 résumé 이력서 competitor 경쟁자, 경쟁업체 compete 경쟁하다 competitive 경쟁력 있는, 경쟁적인 competition 경쟁

고난도
127. 명사절 접속사
회사를 매각해야 할지 여부를 결정하고자 이사진이 Middleton 지점에 모였다.

| 해설 | 빈칸은 뒤의 절(they ~ company)을 이끌어 타동사 decide의 목적어가 될 명사절 접속사가 들어갈 자리로, 뒤에 완전한 문장이 제시되어 있고 '매입할지 여부를 결정하고자'라는 의미로 전개되는 것이 적절하므로 (D) whether가 정답이다.

| 어휘 | board members 이사진 gather 모이다 branch 지점

고난도
128. 명사 어휘
Rainbow 카페는 국립 역사 박물관과 인접한 덕분에 항상 관광객들로 붐빈다.

| 해설 | 빈칸은 thanks to의 목적어인 명사가 들어갈 자리로, 카페가 붐비는 이유가 될 수 있는 것은 국립 역사 박물관과의 '인접성'이므로 (D) proximity가 정답이다.

| 어휘 | be crowded with ~로 붐비다 National History Museum 국립 역사 박물관 navigation 항해, 운항 attraction 매력, 끌림 necessity 필요성, 필수품 proximity 인접성, 근접성

고난도
129. 동사 어휘
Hirohito Robostars가 새로운 조립 로봇이 올여름 도쿄 엑스포에서 공개될 것이라고 발표했다.

| 해설 | 빈칸은 수동태 동사를 만들어줄 과거 분사가 들어갈 자리로, that절의 주어 its new assembly robot과 연결 지어 '새로운 조립 로봇이 공개될 것'이라는 의미로 전개되는 것이 적절하므로 (C) unveiled가 정답이다.

| 어휘 | assembly 조립 decrease 줄다, 줄이다 refer 조회하다, 참조시키다 unveil 공개하다, 발표하다

고난도
130. 동사의 형태
영업 팀장인 Travis Barber가 모든 신입 영업 사원들과 일대일 면담을 하겠다고 요청했다.

| 해설 | '요청/주장/명령/제안'의 의미를 나타내는 동사가 나오면 그 목적어로 쓰인 that절의 동사는 '(should)+동사 원형'의 형태가 되어야 하는데, 빈칸은 요청을 나타내는 동사 requested의 목적어로 쓰인 that절의 동사 자리이므로 동사의 형태는 '(should)+동사 원형'이 되어야 한다. 따라서 동사 원형인 (C) conduct가 정답이다.

| 어휘 | one-on-one interview 일대일 면접

PART 6

131-134 다음 편지를 참조하시오.

Huiling Lee
Pasir Pajang Road
싱가포르 619998

Lee 씨에게,

저희 분기별 카탈로그에 **131**잘못 인쇄된 것에 관해 알려 드리고자 합니다. 저희가 CTR-60 외장 하드 드라이브의 생산을 중단하여, 그것은 포함되지 않아야 했습니다. 제가 업데이트된 카탈로그를 한 부 동봉했습니다. **132**그것이 현재 저희에게서 이용 가능한 것을 정확히 보여줄 것입니다. CTR-60에 대한 귀하의 주문은 취소되었습니다. 향후 2주 **133**이내에 새로 주문을 하신다면, 저희의 가을 세일로 인해 무료 배송의 자격이

되실 것이며, 그것은 10월 10일까지 진행됩니다. 귀하의 주문을 제때 받도록 **134**확실히 하기 위해, 저희 웹 사이트 www.ophirelectronics.com을 통해 주문하실 것을 권장합니다.

진심으로,

Ophir 전자제품

| 어휘 | quarterly 분기별의 discontinue (생산을) 중단하다 external hard drive 외장 하드 드라이브 include 포함시키다 enclose 동봉하다 be eligible for ~에 자격이 되다 in time 제때, 제시간에 via ~을 통해

131. 명사 어휘
| 해설 | 빈칸은 전치사 about의 목적어가 될 명사가 들어갈 자리로, 뒤에 제시된 내용 전개상 '카탈로그에 잘못 인쇄된 것에 관해 알리고 싶다'라는 의미가 되어야 함을 알 수 있으므로 '잘못 인쇄된 것, 오타'라는 뜻의 (A) misprint가 정답이다.

| 어휘 | collection 수집품

132. 알맞은 문장 고르기
(A) 저희는 초기 버전들에서 발견됐던 안전 문제들을 해결했습니다.
(B) 이것들은 고객에게 무료로 다운로드될 수 있습니다.
(C) 그 하드 드라이브는 이전보다 더 많은 데이터를 저장할 수 있습니다.
(D) 그것이 현재 저희에게서 이용 가능한 것을 정확히 보여줄 것입니다.

| 해설 | 앞서 업데이트된 카탈로그를 동봉했다는 문장이 제시되어 있으므로 뒤이어 그 업데이트된 카탈로그에서 확인 가능한 것에 관한 내용이 제시되는 것이 적절하다. 따라서 the updated copy of catalog를 대명사 it으로 받아 현재 이용 가능한 것을 정확히 보여준다고 하는 문장인 (D)가 정답이다.

| 어휘 | resolve 해결하다 safety issue 안전 문제 at no cost 무료로 exactly 정확히 available 이용 가능한

133. 전치사 어휘
| 해설 | 빈칸은 뒤에 있는 시간 명사구 the next two weeks를 목적어로 가지는 전치사가 들어갈 자리로, '향후 2주 이내에 새로 주문을 하면 ~ 자격이 될 것이다'라는 의미로 전개되는 것이 적절하므로 '~ 이내에'라는 뜻의 (D) within이 정답이다.

고난도
134. to부정사
| 해설 | 빈칸 뒤로 that절과 주절이 어어져 있으므로, 3인칭 현재 시제 동사인 (C) Ensures는 답이 될 수 없고, 내용 전개상 '귀하의 주문이 제때 도착하도록 확실히 하기 위해'라는 목적을 나타내 줄 준동사가 들어가는 것이 적절하므로 목적을 나타내줄 to부정사 형태인 (B) To ensure가 정답이다.

135-138 다음 회람을 참조하시오.

수신: Romani 컨설팅 전 직원
발신: Philip Shealey

날짜: 5월 4일
주제: Yamal Gupte

안녕하세요, 여러분.

아주 많은 사람들이 처음 두 차례 전문성 개발 기술 행사에 참가했기 때문에, 여러분에게 Yamal Gupte가 이끄는 이 ¹³⁵전용 워크숍을 제공하게 되어 기쁩니다. 저희는 그가 5월 22일에 우리 회사에 방문하도록 했습니다. Gupte 씨는 제품 홍보를 위해 소셜 미디어를 극대화하는 많은 전략들을 ¹³⁶소개할 것입니다. 이것은 모든 직원들이 이용할 수 있는 유일한 워크숍입니다. ¹³⁷다른 것들은 관리자급 직원들만을 위한 것입니다. Gupte 씨는 선두적인 동기 부여 연설가이니, 이것은 그에게서 배울 훌륭한 기회입니다. 행정 사무실의 Yates 씨가 참가자 명단 ¹³⁸작성을 맡고 있으니, 신청하려면 그녀에게 이야기해 주세요.

감사합니다.

| 어휘 | participate in ~에 참가하다   professional development 전문성 개발   bring 가져다주다, 제공해 주다   arrange for 준비하다, 계획을 짜다   strategy 전략   maximize 극대화하다   promotion 홍보   leading 선두적인   motivation speaker 동기 부여 연설가   fantastic 훌륭한, 환상적인   administration office 행정 사무실   be responsible for ~을 책임지다, 맡다   sign up 등록하다

135. 형용사 어휘
| 해설 | 빈칸은 명사 workshop을 수식할 형용사가 들어갈 자리로, 'Yamal Gupte가 이끄는 (직원들만을 위한) 이 전용 워크숍을 제공하게 되어 기쁘다'라는 의미로 전개되는 것이 적절하므로 '전용의'라는 뜻의 (A) private가 정답이다.
| 어휘 | private 전용의, 개인의   initial 초기의

136. 동사의 시제
| 해설 | 빈칸은 문장의 본동사가 들어갈 자리로, 그가 5월 22일에 우리 회사에 방문하도록 했다고 한 앞 문장을 단서로, 많은 전략들을 소개하는 것은 미래 상황일 것임을 알 수 있으므로 미래 시제 동사인 (A) will introduce가 정답이다.

137. 알맞은 문장 고르기
(A) 여러 해 동안 Gupte 씨는 작은 웹 사이트를 운영했습니다.
(B) 각 활동들에 자체 안내서가 딸려 있습니다.
(C) 다른 것들은 관리 레벨의 직원들만을 위한 것입니다.
(D) 여러분은 아마 최소한 하나의 소셜 미디어 계정은 가지고 있을 겁니다.
| 해설 | 앞서 이번이 모든 직원들이 이용 가능한 유일한 워크숍이라고 했으므로, 뒤이어 또 다른 워크숍에 관해 언급한 내용의 문장이 삽입되는 것이 적절하다. 따라서 다른 워크숍은 관리 레벨 직원들만을 위한 것이라는 내용의 (C)가 정답이다.
| 어휘 | operate 운영하다   activity 활동   come with ~이 딸려 있다   handbook 안내서   management 관리, 경영   account 계정

🔺고난도
138. 전치사의 목적어
| 해설 | 빈칸은 전치사 for의 목적어가 들어갈 자리이므로, '관계 대명사+동사'인 (A) who created와 동사인 (B) creates는 오답이다. 뒤에 제시된 명사 a participant list와 연결 지어 '참가자 명단 작성을 맡고 있다'라는 의미로 전개되는 것이 적절하므로 '~의 작성'이라고 해석되는 (D) the creation of가 정답이다.

139-142 다음 이메일을 참조하시오.

수신: Fang Jin <fangjin@grand-mail.net>
발신: Noah Cole <n.cole@hartway101.net>
날짜: 9월 16일
제목: 프리랜서 프로젝트

Jin 씨 귀하,

저는 화장품 업계의 뉴스를 게시하는 웹 사이트의 편집자입니다. 저희는 내년 말까지 저희 콘텐츠를 다섯 개의 다른 언어들로 ¹³⁹제공할 목표를 세웠습니다. 영어를 중국어로 번역하는 것은 귀하의 ¹⁴⁰전문 분야이기 때문에, 귀하가 이 프로젝트에 적격일 것 같습니다. 화장품 업계에서 일하고 있지 않다면, 저희 기사들 중 일부는 ¹⁴¹다소 지루해 보일 수도 있지만, 그것들은 전 세계 많은 회사들에 유용합니다. 번역되어야 하는 수백 개의 기사가 있습니다. 함께 잘 일할 수 있을지 알아보기 위해, 먼저 5개의 기사를 번역해 주셨으면 합니다. ¹⁴²이것이 성공적이라면, 정규직 계약서를 드릴 것입니다. 귀하께서 가능 여부를 알려주시기 바랍니다.

감사합니다!

Noah Cole

| 어휘 | editor 편집자   post 게시하다   cosmetics 화장품   industry 업계, 산업   set a goal 목표를 세우다   perform 하다, 수행하다   translation 번역   boring 지루한   at first 우선, 먼저   availability 이용 가능성

139. 동명사 자리 - 전치사의 목적어
| 해설 | 빈칸은 전치사 of의 목적어가 들어갈 자리인데, 뒤에 있는 명사 our contents를 목적어로 가질 수 있어야 하므로 동명사가 들어가야 한다. 따라서 (B) offering이 정답이다.

140. 명사 어휘
| 해설 | 빈칸은 be동사 is의 주격 보어가 될 명사가 들어갈 자리로, 뒤이어 귀하가 이 프로젝트에 적격일 것 같다고 했으므로 그렇게 생각하는 이유가 되도록 '영어를 중국어로 번역하는 것이 귀하의 전문 분야이기 때문이다'라고 전개되는 것이 적절하다. 따라서 '전문 분야'라는 뜻의 (C) specialty가 정답이다.
| 어휘 | capacity 능력, 수용력   requirement 요건   specialty 전문 분야   response 응답, 회신

141. 부사 어휘

| 해설 | 빈칸은 동사 seem의 보어인 형용사 boring을 수식해 줄 부사가 들어갈 자리로, 문맥상 '다소 지루해 보일 있지만, 많은 회사들에 유용하다'라는 의미로 전개되는 것이 적절하므로 '다소, 꽤'라는 뜻의 (B) rather가 정답이다.

142. 알맞은 문장 고르기

(A) 가능하다면 그 화장품은 빠르게 운송되어야 합니다.
(B) 애석하게도 저희는 서비스 수준에 실망했습니다.
(C) 이 방문객들은 제공된 정보로부터 많이 배울 수 있습니다.
(D) 이것이 성공적이라면, 정규직 계약서를 드릴 것입니다.

| 해설 | 앞서 함께 잘 일할 수 있을지 알아보기 위해, 먼저 5개의 기사를 번역해 주셨으면 한다고 언급했으므로 그 작업 의뢰와 관련하여 그 일이 성공적이라면, 정규직 계약서를 드릴 것이라는 내용의 문장이 이어지는 것이 적절하다. 따라서 (D)가 정답이다.

| 어휘 | sadly 애석하게도   be disappointed with ~에 실망하다   full-time contract 정규직 계약서

143-146 다음 기사를 참조하시오.

곧 있을 듯한 통근자들이 안도할 소식

1월 5일—어제 시청에서 열렸던 회의에서 디트로이트 고속도로 협회(DHA)가 도시의 서부 지역의 교통 혼잡을 완화하기 위해 유료 도로를 만들 계획을 발표했다. ¹⁴³그 도로는 I-94 경로의 대안을 제공할 것이다. 현재 도로를 이용하는 통근자들은 특히 러시아워 동안 교통 체증에 대해 종종 불평한다. ¹⁴⁴그 결과 시는 납세자들에게 불필요한 부담을 가하지 않으면서 이러한 압박을 완화할 방안들을 모색하고 있다. 새로운 도로에서의 작업은 빠르면 이번 여름에 시작할 수 있을 것이다. 도급업체들로부터 입찰을 ¹⁴⁵받기 위한 위원회가 설치되었다. 위원회 위원들에 의한 ¹⁴⁶결정은 4월 1일에 이루어질 것이다.

| 어휘 | relief 안도   on the horizon 곧 일어날 듯한   toll road 유료 도로   ease 완화하다   traffic congestion 교통 혼잡   commuter 통근자   complain 불평하다   explore 모색하다, 찾아보다   relieve 완화하다   pressure 부담, 압박   burden 부담   taxpayer 납세자   committee 위원회   bid 입찰   contractor 도급업체, 계약자

143. 알맞은 문장 고르기

(A) 그 지역은 인구 감소를 보여왔다.
(B) 그 도시는 주 전역에서 오는 작업자들을 환영한다.
(C) 그 도로는 I-94 경로의 대안을 제공할 것이다.
(D) DHA는 최종 결과에 만족스러워한다.

| 해설 | 앞서 교통 혼잡을 완화하기 위해 유료 도로를 만들 계획을 발표했다고 제시되어 있으므로 그 유료 도로의 역할이 될 만한 것으로 기존 도로의 대안을 제공할 것이라는 내용의 문장이 삽입되는 것이 적절하다. 따라서 (C)가 정답이다.

| 어휘 | population 인구   alternative to ~에 대한 대안   be pleased with ~에 만족하다, 기뻐하다

---

144. 접속 부사

| 해설 | 빈칸은 앞뒤 두 문장의 내용을 자연스럽게 연결해줄 접속 부사가 들어갈 자리로, 앞 문장의 내용은 통근자들이 교통 체증에 대해 종종 불평한다는 것이고, 뒤 문장의 내용은 시가 이를 완화할 방안을 모색하고 있다는 것이다. 뒤 문장은 앞 문장의 결과로 볼 수 있으므로 '그 결과로, 결과적으로'라는 뜻의 (B) As a result가 정답이다.

| 어휘 | in conclusion 마지막으로   in contrast 대조적으로

145. 동사 어휘

| 해설 | 빈칸은 to부정사를 완성해줄 동사 원형이 들어갈 자리로, '도급업체들로부터의 입찰을 받기 위한 위원회가 설치되었다'는 의미로 전개되는 것이 적절하므로 '받다, 수락하다'라는 뜻의 (A) accept가 정답이다.

| 어휘 | insist 주장하다   convince 확신시키다   launch 출시하다

146. 명사 자리 – 주어

| 해설 | 빈칸은 주어 자리이며, 관사 A와 전치사 by 사이에 있으므로 명사 자리이다. 따라서 명사인 (C) decision이 정답이다.

PART 7

147-148 다음 공지를 참조하시오.

Tony's 스테이크 하우스

무료로 제공되는 애피타이저를 즐기세요!

¹⁴⁷Tony's 스테이크 하우스의 어느 지점에서든 식사를 하신 후에, 온라인 www.tonyssteak.com/survey로 가셔서 모든 식사 구매 시 무료 애피타이저를 선택할 수 있는 쿠폰을 받으세요!

¹⁴⁸전화로 포장 주문을 하시고 여러분의 청구서에 애피타이저 쿠폰을 적용하고 싶으신 경우, 여러분의 총액이 정확하도록 확실히 하기 위해 주문을 찾으러 오시기 전에 ¹⁴⁸그것을 꼭 언급해 주세요.

| 어휘 | on the house 무료로 제공되는   win 얻다   place a takeout order 포장 주문을 하다   apply 적용하다   bill 청구서   pick up 찾아가다   ensure 확실히 하다   total 총계, 총액   accurate 정확한

147. True 문제

Tony's 스테이크 하우스에 관해 제시된 것은 무엇인가?
(A) 식사 손님들에게 보상 포인트를 제공한다.
(B) 여러 지점들이 있다.
(C) 별도의 포장 메뉴가 있다.
(D) 온라인 예약을 받는다.

| 해설 | 도입부에 Tony's 스테이크 하우스의 어느 지점에서든(at any of Tony's Steakhouse locations)이라고 제시되어 있는 것에서 여러 지점이 있다는 것을 알 수 있다. 따라서 정답은 (B)이다.

| 어휘 | reward points 보상 포인트   diner 식사 손님   multiple 여럿의, 많은   separate 별도의   reservation 예약
| 패러프레이징 | any ~ locations → multiple locations

148. 세부 사항을 묻는 문제
포장 고객들이 무료 애피타이저를 받기 위해 하도록 요청되는 것은 무엇인가?
(A) 쿠폰을 언급하는 것
(B) 미리 전화하는 것
(C) 회원이 되는 것
(D) 픽업 카운터를 이용하는 것
| 해설 | 두 번째 단락에 포장 주문을 하고 청구서에 애피타이저 쿠폰을 적용하고 싶으면 그것을 꼭 언급해 달라고(If you are placing a takeout order on the phone and want to apply an appetizer coupon to your bill, please be sure to mention it) 제시되어 있으므로 정답은 (A)이다.
| 어휘 | complimentary 무료의   in advance 미리

149-150 다음 제품 후기를 참조하시오.

> **Armor Shell**
>
> 비록 제가 전문 사진사는 아니지만, 제 고급 디지털 카메라인 DP-150으로 일상 순간들의 사진을 찍는 것을 즐겨왔습니다. 그것을 조심하여 다루고자 최선을 다하지만, 닳고 긁히는 것은 일상적 사용에 있어 불가피한 일이죠. 때로 제 손에서 미끄러져 바닥에 떨어지기도 합니다. ¹⁴⁹그래서 제 카메라를 금이 가고 깨지는 것으로부터 보호하기 위해 Armor Shell 케이스를 써본 것인데요. 벽과 물체들에 부딪치기도 했지만, Armor Shell을 사용한 이후로 손상의 흔적이 없었습니다. 이 제품은 디지털 카메라를 가진 모든 사람들에게 추천합니다. 회의적이라면, 그것은 100% 만족 정책을 제공한답니다. ¹⁵⁰그것에 만족하지 않으면 언제든 전액 환불을 위해 반품하실 수 있죠.
>
> | 어휘 | high-end 고급의   handle 다루다   with care 조심하여   worn out 닳은   scratched 긁히는   unavoidable 불가피한, 피할 수 없는   slip out of ~에서 미끄러져 나가다   crack 금이 가다   bump into ~에 부딪치다   object 물체, 물건   damage 손상, 파손   skeptical 회의적인   satisfaction policy 만족 정책   return 반품하다   a full refund 전액 환불

149. 세부 사항을 묻는 문제
어떤 제품의 후기가 작성된 것인가?
(A) 이어폰 세트
(B) 디지털 카메라
(C) 배터리 충전기
(D) 카메라 케이스
| 해설 | 중반부에 카메라를 보호하기 위해 Armor Shell 케이스를 써본 것이라고(That is why I tried the Armor Shell casing to protect my camera from cracking or breaking) 한 것에서 카메라 케이스에 관한 제품 후기임을 알 수 있으므로 정답은 (D)이다.

| 어휘 | charger 충전기
| 패러프레이징 | the Armor Shell casing to protect my camera → A camera case

150. True 문제
제품에 관해 언급되는 것은 무엇인가?
(A) 업계 전문가들로부터 호의적인 평가를 받았다.
(B) 환불 보증이 있다.
(C) 다른 유사 제품들보다 더 가볍다.
(D) 내열성과 내수성을 가지고 있다.
| 해설 | 후반부에 100% 만족 정책을 제공한다며, 만족하지 않으면 언제든 전액 환불을 위해 반품할 수 있다고(You can always return it for a full refund if you are not happy with it) 제시되어 있으므로 정답은 (B)이다.
| 어휘 | favorable 호의적인   money-back guarantee 환불 보증   water resistant 내수성
| 패러프레이징 | can always return it for a full refund → has a money-back guarantee

151-152 다음 문자 메시지 대화를 참조하시오.

> **Troy Whitlock**   오전 10:11
> ¹⁵²Getz 기업 직원들이 우리 봄 광고 캠페인을 위한 아이디어를 제시하기 위해 오늘 오후에 여기 올 거예요.
>
> **Lian Zou**   오전 10:12
> 그건 우리의 Angus Athletic 라인을 위한 것이죠, 그렇죠?
>
> **Troy Whitlock**   오전 10:14
> 네. 제품 개발자들 중 일부도 거기 갈 거예요. 당신도 갈 건가요?
>
> **Lian Zou**   오전 10:15
> 아마도 아니요. ¹⁵¹그 회의가 회의실 C에서 열리기로 되어 있어 실망스러웠어요. 너무 작아서 많은 사람들이 들어갈 수 없잖아요.
>
> **Troy Whitlock**   오전 10:16
> 그건 변경되었어요.
>
> **Lian Zou**   오전 10:19
> 오, 정말이요? 이제 어디인데요?
>
> **Troy Whitlock**   오전 10:21
> 주 회의실에서요. ¹⁵²첫 발표자는 오후 1시에 Carol Dodson이 될 거예요.
>
> **Lian Zou**   오전 10:22
> 알겠어요. 그런 경우라면, 관리자가 괜찮다고 하면 그곳에 갈게요.
>
> | 어휘 | representative 대표, 직원   present 제시하다   ad 광고   disappointed 실망한   take place 열리다   include 포함시키다   as long as ~하는 한

🔺고난도

151. 의도 파악 문제

오전 10:16에 Whitlock 씨가 "그건 변경되었어요"라고 쓸 때 의미하는 것은 무엇인가?

(A) 새로운 정책이 승인되었다.
(B) 미팅이 늦게 시작할 것이다.
(C) 참석이 현재 의무적이다.
(D) 문제가 해결되었다.

| 해설 | 이는 앞서 오전 10:15에 Lian Zou가 회의가 회의실 C에서 열리기로 되어 있어 실망스러웠다며(I was disappointed that the meeting is scheduled to take place in Conference Room C) 그 이유로, 너무 작아서 많은 사람들이 들어갈 수 없다고(That's too small to include many people) 덧붙인 것에 대한 응답으로, 회의실이 변경되어 문제가 해결되었음을 알리는 것으로 볼 수 있으므로 정답은 (D)이다.

| 어휘 | approve 승인하다 attendance 참석 mandatory 의무적인 resolve 해결하다

152. 추론 문제

Dodson 씨는 누구일 것 같은가?

(A) 제품 개발자
(B) Getz 기업 직원
(C) Zou 씨의 관리자
(D) Angus Athletic 투자자

| 해설 | Troy Whitlock이 오전 10:21에 첫 발표자는 Dodson 씨일 것이라고(The first presenter will be Carol Dodson at 1 P.M.) 했는데, 도입부에 Getz 기업 직원들이 광고 캠페인을 위한 아이디어를 제시하기 위해 오늘 오후에 여기 올 것이라고(The Getz Corporation representatives will be here this afternoon to present ideas for our spring ad campaign) 한 것과 연계해 볼 때, Getz 기업 직원일 것으로 유추할 수 있으므로 정답은 (B)이다.

| 어휘 | investor 투자자

153-155 다음 공지를 참조하시오.

> **다가오는 행사들**
>
> **Aurora** 극장이 이번 여름 7월 6일부터 8월 30일까지 일련의 공연들을 특별히 포함할 것입니다. ¹⁵³지난달 극장의 수석 관리자로 막 일을 맡게 된 Jackie Astor가 올여름에 뭔가 새로운 것을 하고 싶다고 발표했습니다. 이전 해들과 달리 올여름은 특별히 오직 솔로 아티스트들만 공연할 것입니다. ¹⁵⁴그 변화는 <Monthly Entertainment in Aurora>의 5월 호에 실린 Nancy Short의 기사에서 찬사를 받았습니다. 다가오는 몇몇 솔로 공연들에는 스탠드업 코미디를 하는 Mario Torres와 ¹⁵⁵피아노로 모차르트 곡을 연주하는 Jillian Villa, 셰익스피어의 원작들을 바탕으로 독백극을 하는 Hector Fray가 포함되어 있습니다. Short 씨의 5월 기사에서 그녀는 "¹⁵⁵Golden 피아노 상 수상자의 야외 단독 콘서트를 즐기는 것은 매일 있는 일이 아닙니다."라고 언급했습니다. 관심 있는 사람은 누구나 Aurora 극장의 웹 사이트 www.auroratheater.com에서 혹은 매표소에서 팸플릿을 가져감으

로써 행사에 관한 더 많은 세부 사항을 찾아볼 수 있습니다.

| 어휘 | feature 특징으로 하다, 특별히 포함하다 a series of 일련의 performance 공연 take over 맡다, 떠맡다 previous 이전의 solely 오로지, 단지 move 움직임, 변화 praise 칭찬하다 monologue 독백극 original work 원작 recipient 수상자, 수령인 details 세부 사항 box office 매표소

🔺고난도

153. True 문제

극장에 관해 언급되는 것은 무엇인가?

(A) 무대가 대형 그룹들에게는 너무 작다.
(B) 새로운 경영진에 의해 운영되고 있다.
(C) 계절적으로만 운영한다.
(D) 최근에 개조가 진행되었다.

| 해설 | 초반부에 지난달 극장의 수석 관리자로 막 일을 맡게 된 Jackie Astor라고(Jackie Astor, who just took over as the theater's head manager last month) 한 것에서 지난달부터 새로운 경영진에 의해 운영되고 있음을 알 수 있으므로 정답은 (B)이다.

| 어휘 | operate 운영하다 management 경영진 seasonally 계절적으로 undergo 진행하다, 겪다 renovation 개조

| 패러프레이징 | just took over as the theater's head manager
→ is being operated by new management

154. 추론 문제

Short 씨는 누구일 것 같은가?

(A) 연주자
(B) 영화 평론가
(C) 기자
(D) 감독

| 해설 | 중반부에 그 변화는 <Monthly Entertainment in Aurora>의 5월 호에 실린 Nancy Short의 기사에서 찬사를 받았다고(The move was praised by Nancy Short in her article in the May edition of *Monthly Entertainment in Aurora*) 제시되어 있는 것을 통해, Short 씨가 기자일 것으로 유추할 수 있으므로 정답은 (C)이다.

🔺고난도

155. 세부 사항을 묻는 문제

누가 상을 받았나?

(A) Hector Fray
(B) Nancy Short
(C) Mario Torres
(D) Jillian Villa

| 해설 | 후반부에 Short 씨가 기사에서 Golden 피아노 상 수상자의 단독 콘서트를 즐기는 것은 매일 있는 일이 아니라고(It's not every day you get to enjoy an outdoor concert solo by a recipient of a Golden Piano prize) 언급한 것이 나와 있는데, 솔로 공연 명단을 소개하며 피아노 연주자로 제시된 사람은

Jillian Villa(Jillian Villa playing Mozart on the piano)이므로, Jillian Villa가 수상자임을 알 수 있다. 따라서 정답은 (D)이다.

156-157 다음 계약 서식을 참조하시오.

프로젝트 조정 세부 사항

계약자: Connie McCarthy – McCarthy Roofing & Siding – 444 Bronson Road, Hardenville, MO 65666

의뢰인: Gregory Houston – 4425 Court Street, Olivette, MO 63132

시작일: 8월 7일

[157]마감일: 8월 16일

이 문서는 7월 28일에 서명된 원래 계약서에 이루어진 조정을 명시한다.

추가/취소 작업: [156]Houston 씨의 요청에 따라 외벽에 일반 페인트 대신에 비바람에 잘 견디는 페인트가 쓰일 것이다.

원래 비용(인건비 & 자재비 포함): 4,700달러
순수 요금 변경: 400달러
최종 합의된 비용: 5,100달러
기타 메모: 10%(510달러)는 기한이 시작일까지입니다. [157]나머지 (4,590달러)의 기한은 명시된 작업의 완료 시까지입니다.

계약자: *Connie McCarthy*   의뢰인: *Gregory Houston*
Connie McCarthy   Gregory Houston

| 어휘 | adjustment 조정   contractor 계약자, 도급업자   client 의뢰인, 고객   specify 명시하다   original 원래의, 본래의   additional 추가의   weatherproof 비바람에 잘 견디는   siding 사이딩(가로 널로 붙이는 외부 마감재)   regular 일반의, 정기적인   as per ~에 따라   net 순   be due ~까지이다   remainder 나머지   completion 완료

[고난도]

156. 세부 사항을 묻는 문제

왜 원래 계약이 변경되었나?
(A) 다른 재료가 선택되었다.
(B) 작업 날짜가 연기되어야 했다.
(C) 추가 작업이 요청되었다.
(D) 작업이 더 일찍 마무리되어야 했다.

| 해설 | 추가/취소 작업에 Houston 씨의 요청에 따라 외벽에 일반 페인트 대신에 비바람에 잘 견디는 페인트가 쓰일 것이라고(Weatherproof paint will be used on the siding instead of regular paint as per request of Mr. Houston) 제시되어 있는 것에서, 재료 변경으로 인해 계약서 조정이 이루어졌음을 알 수 있으므로 정답은 (A)이다.

| 어휘 | material 재료   postpone 연기하다

| 패러프레이징 | Weatherproof paint will be used on the siding instead of regular paint → A different material was selected.

157. 추론 문제

Houston 씨는 8월 16일에 McCarthy Roofing & Siding에 얼마를 빚지고 있을 것 같은가?
(A) 510달러
(B) 4,590달러
(C) 4,700달러
(D) 5,100달러

| 해설 | 초반부에 마감일이 8월 16일(Finish By: 16 August)로 되어 있고, 이를 후반부의 기타 메모 내용에 나머지(4,590달러)는 명시된 작업의 완료 시까지라고(The remainder ($4,590) is due upon completion of the specified work) 제시되어 있는 것과 연계해볼 때, Houston 씨는 8월 16일에 4,590달러를 지급해야 할 것임을 알 수 있으므로 정답은 (B)이다.

158-160 다음 이메일을 참조하시오.

수신: Lorna Parnell <lornaparnell@exactagencyteam.com>
발신: Asif Mustafi <asif.mustafi@miventerprises.net>
날짜: 8월 15일
제목: 사진들

Parnell 씨 귀하,

귀하의 [158]광고 캠페인을 위해 저희 컬렉션에서 다운로드한 사진들에 있는 워터마크에 대해 알려 주셔서 감사합니다. 정확하게 지적하셨듯이, 귀하는 유료 구독자이기 때문에 사진에 저희 워터마크가 없어야 합니다. —[1]—. 그 문제는 귀하의 비서가 비즈니스 계정이 아닌 개인 이메일 계정으로 구매 요청을 보냈던 사실에서 기인한 듯합니다. —[2]—. [159 (A)]저희는 매일 수천 건의 이미지 요청을 처리하고 있어 자동화된 시스템을 이용합니다. [159 (B)]요청이 기업 사용을 위한 풀 버전인 "유료 구독자 요청"이 됐어야 했는데, 이미지가 복사될 수 없도록 워터마크가 포함된 "일회성 요청"으로 표시되었습니다. [160]제가 저희 시스템에서 그 요청을 수동으로 업데이트했습니다. —[3]—.

앞으로 [159 (D)]시스템에 등록된 이메일 주소를 사용하여 요청을 처리하는 한 더 이상 문제가 없을 것입니다. —[4]—. 다시 한 번, 야기된 불편에 대해 제 사과를 받아 주시길 부탁드립니다.

안부를 전하며,

Asif Mustafi
고객 서비스 매니저
MIV Enterprises

| 어휘 | advertising 광고   watermark 워터마크, 복사 방지 마크   correctly 정확하게   point out 지적하다   paid subscriber 선급금 이용자   stem from ~에서 기인하다   assistant 비서, 보조   process 처리하다   automated 자동화된   be flagged as ~로 표시되다   contain 포함되다   corporate 회사의, 기업의   manually 수동으로   process 처리하다   registered 등록된   inconvenience 불편

🔼 고난도
158. 추론 문제
MIV Enterprises는 어떤 유형의 회사일 것 같은가?
(A) 인터넷 제공업체
(B) 사진 라이브러리
(C) 광고 대행사
(D) 그래픽 디자인 연구소

| 해설 | MIV Enterprises는 이메일을 보낸 회사인데, 도입부에 귀하의 광고를 위해 저희 컬렉션에서 다운로드한 사진들(the photos you downloaded from our collection for your advertising campaign)이 언급된 것과 유료 회원은 사진에 워터마크가 없다는 것 등을 단서로 고객들에게 사진 다운로드 서비스를 제공하는 업체일 것으로 유추할 수 있으므로 정답은 (B)이다.

159. NOT True 문제
Mustafi 씨에 의해 언급된 것이 아닌 것은?
(A) 매일 처리되는 요청의 양
(B) 계정 타입들 사이의 차이점
(C) 시스템 업그레이드 요건들
(D) 선호되는 로그인 방법

| 해설 | 첫 번째 단락 중반부에 매일 수천 건의 이미지 요청을 처리하고 있다고(As we process thousands of requests for images each day) 한 것에서 (A), "일회성 요청"과 "유료 구독자 요청"을 비교한(The request was flagged as a "One-Time Request," which contains a watermark ~ "Paid Subscriber Request," which is the full version for corporate use) 것에서 (B), 두 번째 단락에 시스템에 등록된 이메일 주소를 사용하여 요청을 처리하는 한(as long as you process requests using the e-mail address registered on the system) 문제가 없을 것이라고 한 것에서 (D)는 모두 언급된 내용으로 확인되므로, 정답은 (C)이다.

| 어휘 | requirement 필요, 요건   preferred 선호되는

160. 문장 삽입 문제
[1], [2], [3], [4]로 표시된 곳 중에 다음 문장이 들어가기에 가장 적절한 곳은?

"이제 정상적으로 로그인하고 필요하신 파일의 올바른 버전을 다운로드하실 수 있습니다."

(A) [1]
(B) [2]
(C) [3]
(D) [4]

| 해설 | 제시된 문장은 문제 해결 후 가능해진 일에 관해 설명하는 것으로, 이는 문제 해결 조치가 언급된 문장 뒤에 삽입되어야 함을 알 수 있으므로 첫 번째 단락 후반부에 시스템에서 그 요청을 수동으로 업데이트했다고(I have updated the request on our system manually) 알리는 문장 뒤인 (C)가 정답이다.

| 어휘 | normally 정상적으로   correct 올바른, 제대로 된

161-164 다음 공지를 참조하시오.

Rational 러닝

[161]Rational 러닝이 4월 7일 일요일에 Lewiston으로 옵니다! 이 기금 모금 행사에서 달릴 여러분을 기꺼이 후원할 지역 업체를 찾아보세요. 더 많은 사람들이 달릴수록, 더 많이 모아질 것입니다!

[162]Rational 러닝 행사들에서 모아진 모든 돈은 지역의 음식 나눔 운동을 지원하기 위해 사용됩니다. 이번 행사의 수익금은 Lewiston Soup Kitchen에 전달될 것입니다. [163]달리기 주자나 보조 코디네이터로 이 행사에 참가를 자원하는 것도 또한 지역 사회 봉사 시간으로 인정됩니다. 확인 서명을 받으려면 Soup Kitchen 담당자를 만나세요.

경주는 Lewiston 고등학교의 야외 트랙에서 열릴 것입니다. 인근에 살며 행사에 참가하지 않는 이들은 누구나 오셔서 달리기 주자들을 응원해주실 것이 장려됩니다.

수속 부스는 옥외 관람석의 북쪽에 설치될 것입니다. 그 부스에서 기념 티셔츠도 판매할 것입니다. 또한 [164]자원봉사자들이 각 달리기 주자의 이름과 그 후원자들 모두의 이름이 특별히 포함된 전단을 나누어드릴 것입니다.

자원봉사를 하거나 Lewiston Soup Kitchen에 기부하는 것에 관한 더 많은 정보를 위해서는 www.lewistonrationalrunning.org를 방문해 주세요.

| 어휘 | rational 이성적인, 합리적인   be willing to 기꺼이 ~하다   sponsor 후원하다   fundraising 기금 모금   raise 모으다   drive (조직적인) 운동   proceeds 수익금   volunteer 자원하다; 자원봉사자   count 인정되다   representative 담당자   validation signature 확인 서명   outdoor 야외의   be encouraged to ~하도록 장려되다   cheer 응원하다   check-in booth 수속 부스   bleacher 야외 관람석   memorabilia 기념품   hand out 나누어 주다   flyer 전단   make a donation 기부하다

161. 주제/목적 문제
공지의 주된 목적은 무엇인가?
(A) 규칙적으로 운동하도록 사람들을 장려하는 것
(B) 정책 변경을 발표하는 것
(C) 자선 행사를 홍보하는 것
(D) 지역 업체의 프로필을 알려주는 것

| 해설 | 도입부에 Rational 러닝이 4월 7일 일요일에 Lewiston으로 온다고(Rational Running is coming to Lewiston on Sunday, April 7) 한 후, 이 기금 모금 행사에 대해서 설명하고 있으므로 정답은 (C)이다.

| 어휘 | exercise 운동하다   regularly 규칙적으로, 정기적으로   promote 홍보하다   charity 자선, 자선 단체   profile 프로필을 알려주다

고난도
162. 추론 문제
Lewiston Soup Kitchen은 무엇일 것 같은가?
(A) 레스토랑
(B) 푸드 뱅크
(C) 동물 보호소
(D) 농장

| 해설 | 두 번째 단락에 Rational 러닝 행사들에서 모아진 모든 돈은 지역의 음식 나눔 운동을 지원하기 위해 사용되고(All of the money raised by Rational Running events is used to support local food drives), 이번 행사의 수익금은 Lewiston Soup Kitchen으로 가게 될 것이라고(The proceeds from this event will go to the Lewiston Soup Kitchen) 한 것에서 Lewiston Soup Kitchen은 음식 나눔 운동에 동참하는 푸드 뱅크의 하나인 것으로 유추할 수 있으므로 정답은 (B)이다.

| 어휘 | food bank 푸드 뱅크(가난한 사람들이 무료로 음식을 얻는 곳) shelter 보호소

고난도
163. True 문제
참가하는 주자들에 관해 언급된 것은 무엇인가?
(A) 참가에 대해 공식적인 인정을 받는다.
(B) 등록비를 지불하도록 요구된다.
(C) 오리엔테이션에 참석할 것으로 예상된다.
(D) 무료 티셔츠를 받을 것이다.

| 해설 | 두 번째 단락 후반부에 달리기 주자나 보조 코디네이터로 행사 참가를 자원하는 것도 지역 사회 봉사 시간으로 인정된다고(Volunteering to participate in this event as either a runner or an assistant coordinator also counts as community service time) 제시되어 있으므로 정답은 (A)이다.

| 어휘 | official 공식적인, 정식의   recognition 인정   registration fee 등록비
| 패러프레이징 | counts as community service time → receive official recognition

164. 세부 사항을 묻는 문제
참석자들은 어디에서 행사 후원자들에 관해 더 알아볼 수 있나?
(A) 웹 사이트에서
(B) 등록 부스에서
(C) 행사 팜플렛에서
(D) 지역 신문에서

| 해설 | 네 번째 단락에 자원봉사자들이 각 달리기 주자의 이름과 그 후원자들 모두의 이름이 특별히 포함된 전단을 나누어드릴 것이라고(volunteers will hand out flyers that feature the names of each runner and all of his or her sponsors) 제시되어 있으므로 정답은 (C)이다.

| 패러프레이징 | flyers → event pamphlet

165-167 다음 편지를 참조하시오.

피트니스 매거진
PO Box 51854
Denver, CO 80907

9월 3일

Jacquie Berman
1872 Berry Street
Colorado Springs, CO 80903

Berman 씨 귀하,

<피트니스 매거진> 구독을 1년 더 갱신하신 것을 축하드립니다! 귀하의 갱신으로 귀하는 또한 저희 출판사가 운영하는 다른 잡지를 무료로 체험 구독할 수 있는 자격이 됩니다. ¹⁶⁵그것은 일반적인 4개월 체험 기간보다 2개월 더 긴 것입니다. ¹⁶⁶동봉된 것에서 저희 출판사의 전체 잡지 목록을 보실 수 있습니다.

귀하께서 저희 잡지를 1년 동안 읽어오고 계시니, 귀하로부터 의견을 듣고 싶습니다. ¹⁶⁷이 페이지의 뒷면에 있는 설문을 작성하여 그것을 저희에게 다시 보내주세요. 귀하의 편의를 위해 우체국에 가지 않으셔도 되도록 ¹⁶⁷미리 수신 주소를 써둔 우편 요금이 지불된 봉투를 포함해 두었습니다.

진심으로,

Michael Boles
고객 서비스 담당자

| 어휘 | renew 갱신하다   subscription 구독   renewal 갱신   qualify 자격을 주다   free trial 무료 체험   run 운영하다, 관리하다   publisher 출판사   enclosed 동봉된   fill out 작성하다   convenience 편의   pre-addressed 미리 수신 주소를 써둔   postage-paid envelope 우편 요금이 지불된 봉투

165. 세부 사항을 묻는 문제
Berman 씨는 얼마 동안 무료 잡지를 받을 수 있나?
(A) 3개월 동안
(B) 4개월 동안
(C) 6개월 동안
(D) 12개월 동안

| 해설 | 첫 번째 단락에 무료 체험에 대해 일반적인 4개월 체험 기간보다 2개월 더 긴 것이라고(That's two months longer than normal four-month trial periods) 제시되어 있으므로 정답은 (C)이다.

| 패러프레이징 | two months longer than normal four-month → 6 months

166. 세부 사항을 묻는 문제
편지에 무엇이 동봉되어 있나?
(A) 회원 카드
(B) 정기 간행물의 목록
(C) 주문서
(D) 식권

| 해설 | 첫 번째 단락 후반부에 동봉된 것에서 출판사의 전체 잡지 목록을 볼 수 있다고(Enclosed you can find a full list of our publisher's magazines) 제시되어 있으므로 정답은 (B)이다.
| 어휘 | periodical 정기 간행물
| 패러프레이징 | a full list of our publisher's magazines → A list of periodicals

167. 세부 사항을 묻는 문제
Berman 씨가 하도록 요청받은 것은 무엇인가?
(A) 제때 결제를 하는 것
(B) 피드백 서식을 우편으로 다시 보내는 것
(C) 온라인으로 의견을 작성하는 것
(D) 연락처를 업데이트하는 것

| 해설 | 두 번째 단락에 이 페이지의 뒷면에 있는 설문을 작성하여 다시 보내달라고(Please fill out the survey on the back side of this page and return it to us) 요청한 후, 미리 수신 주소를 써둔 우편 요금이 지불된 봉투를 포함해 두었다고(we included a pre-addressed postage-paid envelope) 덧붙였으므로 정답은 (B)이다.
| 어휘 | make a payment 결제하다   comment 의견   contact information 연락처
| 패러프레이징 | the survey → a feedback form

168-171 다음 온라인 채팅 토론을 참조하시오.

John Bautista [오전 9:54]
오늘 오후 기획 회의 전에 질문이 있나요? ¹⁶⁸Eunha Baek이 우리 박물관에서 강연하는 것에 동의해 줘서 정말 기뻐요.

Satya Kamei [오전 9:55]
저도요. ¹⁶⁸저는 저널에 실린 그녀의 여러 연구들을 읽었고, 그녀의 연구에 관해 더 듣는 것을 고대하고 있어요. ¹⁶⁹Marshall 센터가 보통 요금의 절반에 우리에게 홀을 빌려주기로 동의했어요.

Kun Quan [오전 9:56]
그것 정말 좋은 소식이네요!

Maura Genovesi [오전 9:57]
네, 그래요! 그들이 그것을 찬성할 거라고 생각하지 않았거든요.

Satya Kamei [오전 9:59]
음, 평일이라서 표준 요금으로 예약을 받을 수 있을 거라고 생각하지 않았나 봐요. 모든 게 완벽하게 잘 진행되고 있네요, 그렇지 않나요?

John Bautista [오전 10:01]
그렇기도 하고 아니기도 해요. ¹⁷⁰지역 음악 협회가 같은 날 밤에 Flynn 강당에서 록 페스티벌을 개최할 것이라는 걸 방금 알았어요. 사람들이 그것에 매우 관심이 있을 거예요.

Kun Quan [오전 10:02]
그것은 그저 우리 행사를 더 강하게 홍보해야 한다는 걸 의미하죠. 제가 <Stoneybrook Times>의 편집자에게 연락해 우리가 무료 신문 보도를 좀 할 수 있을지 알아볼게요.

John Bautista [오전 10:03]
고마워요! ¹⁷¹Renee Abraham에게 다과 준비를 다시 부탁하도록 하죠. 지난번에 아주 잘해줬잖아요.

Maura Genovesi [오전 10:06]
훌륭한 생각이에요. ¹⁷¹제가 우리 회의 전에 전화해서 가능한지 알아볼게요.

| 어휘 | give a talk 강연하다   look forward to ~를 고대하다   go for ~에 찬성하다, 지지하다   standard rate 표준 요금   come together 잘 풀리다, 좋게 진행되다   editor 편집자   news coverage 신문 보도   cater 음식을 준비하다, 공급하다   refreshment 다과

168. 세부 사항을 묻는 문제
토론에 참여하는 이들은 어떤 행사를 준비하고 있나?
(A) 음악 축제
(B) 시상식
(C) 학술 강연
(D) 박물관 개관식

| 해설 | 오전 9:54에 John Bautista가 Eunha Baek이 강연하는 것에 동의해 줘서 정말 기쁘다고(I'm so pleased that Eunha Baek agreed to give a talk at our museum) 한 것과 오전 9:55에 Satya Kamei도 동의하며 저널에 실린 그녀의 여러 연구들을 읽었고, 더 듣는 것을 고대하고 있다고(I've read several of her studies in journals, and I'm looking forward to hearing more about her research) 한 것에서, 학술 강연을 준비하고 있음을 알 수 있으므로 정답은 (C)이다.
| 패러프레이징 | talk → lecture

고난도
169. 의도 파악 문제
오전 9:57에 Genovesi 씨가 "그들이 그것을 찬성할 거라고 생각하지 않았거든요"라고 쓸 때 의미하는 것은 무엇일 것 같은가?
(A) 그녀는 시에서 행사가 열리도록 허락할 것이라고 생각하지 않았다.
(B) 그녀는 장소가 예약되지 않은 것에 놀랐다.
(C) 그녀는 위원회가 다른 누군가를 선출할 것이라고 생각했다.
(D) 그녀는 할인율이 제공될지에 대해 의문스러웠다.

| 해설 | 이는 앞서 Satya Kamei가 Marshall 센터가 보통 요금의 절반에 홀을 빌려주기로 동의했다고(The Marshall Center agreed to let us rent the hall

for half off the usual rate) 쓴 것에 대한 응답으로, 그들이 찬성하리라고 생각하지 않았다는 것은 반값으로 할인을 해 주지 않을 거라고 생각했었다는 뜻이므로 정답은 (D)이다.

| 어휘 | allow 허락하다, 허용하다   venue 장소   committee 위원회   elect 선출하다   doubt 의심스럽다, 의문을 가지다   discount rate 할인율

170. 세부 사항을 묻는 문제
Bautista 씨는 무슨 일이 있을 것이라고 생각하는가?
(A) 경쟁 행사가 많은 사람들을 끌어들일 것이다.
(B) 신문이 일찍 배달될 것이다.
(C) 군중을 다루기가 힘들 것이다.
(D) 동료가 승진될 것이다.
| 해설 | 오전 10:01에 John Bautista가 같은 날에 Flynn 강당에서 록 페스티벌이 열린다는 걸 방금 알았다며, 사람들이 그것에 매우 관심이 있을 것이라고(I just found out that the Regional Music Association will hold a rock festival at Flynn Auditorium on the same night. People will be highly interested in that) 쓴 것을 통해, 경쟁 행사에 사람들이 많이 갈 것이라고 생각함을 알 수 있으므로 정답은 (A)이다.
| 어휘 | competing 경쟁하는   draw 끌어들이다   crowd 군중, 사람들   handle 다루다, 다스리다   promotion 승진   coworker 동료
| 패러프레이징 | a rock festival ~ on the same night → A competing event

171. 추론 문제
Genovesi 씨는 오늘 누구에게 연락할 것 같은가?
(A) 시 공무원
(B) 기자
(C) 출장 연회업자
(D) 음악가
| 해설 | 오전 10:03에 John Bautista가 Renee Abraham에게 다과 준비를 다시 부탁하자며(Let's have Renee Abraham cater the refreshments again) 지난번에 아주 잘해줬다고 한 것에 대해 Maura Genovesi가 훌륭한 생각이라며, 회의 전에 전화해서 가능한지 알아보겠다고(I'll call her before our meeting to see if she is available) 했으므로, Genovesi 씨는 Renee Abraham에게 연락할 것임을 알 수 있고, Renee Abraham은 음식을 준비하고 공급하는 것을 전문으로 하는 사람임을 유추할 수 있다. 따라서 정답은 (C)이다.

172-175 다음 공지를 참조하시오.

HIGHTOWN LITHO 고객들 모두에게 알림:

¹⁷⁴10월 11일부터 14일까지 제조업체에 의해 이루어지는 정기 관리와 업그레이드로 인해 ¹⁷²Rockford 지점에서 가장 큰 기계(DC 10506)의 서비스가 중단될 것입니다. ¹⁷³이러한 조정은 대량 주문의 처리 시간을 최대 15%까지 개선하도록 도움을 줄 것입니다. ─[1]─. 그러나 이것은 그 기간 동안 Rockford에서 다음 서비스들을 일시적으로 이용할 수 없음을 의미할 것입니다: A0 & A1 복사, 배너(천과 비닐 모두), ¹⁷⁴광고 포스터들 그리고 A2보다 큰 플라스틱 간판. Cedar Falls와 Westerville

의 운영에는 변화가 없을 것입니다. ─[2]─.

¹⁷³/¹⁷⁴저희는 여전히 위에 있는 유형의 인쇄 작업을 받고 있지만, 그것들은 모두 Cedar Falls 지점에서 처리될 것입니다. ¹⁷⁵보통 작업을 다른 지점에 위탁하면 운송 요금이 부과되지만, 유지 관리 작업 기간에는 이것들이 면제될 것입니다. ─[3]─.

저희는 10월 15일부터 Rockford에서 정상적인 서비스가 재개될 것으로 예상합니다. ─[4]─. 이것이 요청된 프로젝트들에 어떤 영향을 미치는지 알아보려면 고객들은 저희 직원들 중 한 명과 이야기하거나 customerservices@hightownlitho.com으로 저희 본사에 이메일을 보내 주셔야 합니다. 고객들은 더 많은 정보를 위해 www.hightownlitho.com을 방문하실 수도 있습니다.

| 어휘 | be out of service 서비스가 중단되다   maintenance 유지 보수   manufacturer 제조업체   adjustment 조정   improve 개선하다   turnaround time 처리 시간   signage 광고판   operation 운영   process 처리하다   charge 요금   apply 적용하다   outsource 외부에 위탁하다   waive 면제하다   resume 재개하다   headquarters 본사

172. 주제/목적 문제
공지의 목적은 무엇인가?
(A) 일시적인 매장 휴업을 알리는 것
(B) 새롭게 이용할 수 있는 서비스를 소개하는 것
(C) 추가 지점의 개점을 알리는 것
(D) 고객들에게 줄어든 서비스들에 관해 알리는 것
| 해설 | 첫 번째 단락에 Rockford 지점에서 가장 큰 기계의 서비스가 중단될 것이라며(the largest machine (DC 10506) at the Rockford branch will be out of service), 그 기간 동안 이용할 수 없는 서비스들을 구체적으로 알리고 있으므로 정답은 (D)이다.
| 어휘 | temporary 일시적인, 임시의   closure 폐쇄, 휴업   reduced 줄어든

🔺고난도
173. 세부 사항을 묻는 문제
회사가 얻기를 바라는 이점은 무엇인가?
(A) 인쇄 속도 증가
(B) 확장된 고객 기반
(C) 새로운 아웃렛의 위치
(D) 가격 하락
| 해설 | 첫 번째 단락 초반부에 이러한 조정은 대량 주문의 처리 시간을 최대 15%까지 개선하도록 도움을 줄 것이라고(These adjustments will help us to improve our turnaround time on large orders by up to 15%) 한 것을 통해 속도 증가를 기대하고 있음을 알 수 있고, 여전히 인쇄 작업을 받고 있다(We are still accepting print jobs)고 한 것을 통해 인쇄를 하는 곳임을 알 수 있으므로 정답은 (A)이다.
| 어휘 | increase 증가, 상승   expanded 확장된, 확대된   customer base 고객층   decrease 하락, 감소
| 패러프레이징 | improve our turnaround time → An increase in

printing speed

174. 세부 사항을 묻는 문제
10월 11일부터 14일까지 광고 포스터 주문들은 어디에서 처리될 것인가?
(A) 본사에서
(B) Rockford 지점에서
(C) Cedar Falls 지점에서
(D) Westerville 지점에서

| 해설 | 첫 번째 단락을 보면, 10월 11일부터 14일은 Rockford 지점에서 일부 서비스가 중단되는 기간이고, 중단된 서비스에 광고 포스터가 포함되어 있는 걸 알 수 있는데, 두 번째 단락 도입부에 이런 작업들은 모두 Cedar Falls 지점에서 처리될 것이라고(We are still accepting print jobs for the above types, but they will all be processed at our Cedar Falls branch) 제시되어 있으므로 광고 포스터는 Cedar Falls 지점에서 인쇄될 것임을 알 수 있다. 따라서 정답은 (C)이다.

175. 문장 삽입 문제
[1], [2], [3], [4]로 표시된 곳 중에 다음 문장이 들어가기에 가장 적절한 곳은?
"이 경우 배송에 추가 하루를 허용해 주시기 바랍니다."

(A) [1]
(B) [2]
(C) [3]
(D) [4]

| 해설 | 제시된 문장에서 이 경우(this case)가 말하는 것이 무엇인지 파악해야 되는데, 인쇄가 다른 지점에서 처리되는 것이 배송에 하루가 더 필요한 경우로 볼 수 있다. 따라서 다른 지점에 위탁하여 처리되는 것을 설명한 문장(Shipping charges usually apply when work is outsourced to another branch, but these will be waived during the maintenance work) 다음에 들어가는 것이 적절하므로 정답은 (C)이다.

176-180 다음 광고와 이메일을 참조하시오.

Pearl 해변 숙소 임대

며칠 동안 일상의 스트레스에서 벗어나 Pearl 해변에 위치해 있는 임대 하우스에서 느긋함을 즐겨보세요! 아래 옵션들 중에서 하나를 선택하세요. 가족들과 오시든 아니면 친구들과 오시든 여러분의 필요에 맞는 장소를 가지고 있으며, ¹⁷⁶모두 해변 전망입니다.

임대 건물	특징	일일 요금(달러)
커플 스위트	침실 1개(투숙객 2명) 뷔페 이용권	140
¹⁷⁷허니문 스위트	침실 1개(투숙객 2명) 요청 시 룸 서비스	170
가족 휴양지	침실 2개(투숙객 최대 4명) 바비큐 화덕	260
파티 하우스	침실 3개(투숙객 6명) 바비큐 화덕	310

객실들은 제시된 수 이상의 투숙객을 수용할 수 있지만, 1인당 1박에 20달러의 요금이 있습니다. 추가 비용으로 추가 침대를 이용할 수 있습니다. 음식 메뉴는 계절에 따라 다릅니다.

*¹⁷⁹4세 미만의 모든 어린이는 모든 추가 요금이 면제될 것입니다.

| 어휘 | escape from ~에서 벗어나다, 탈출하다   match one's needs 필요에 맞다, 필요에 부합하다   beachfront view 해변 경관   barbecue pit 바비큐 화덕   accommodate 수용하다   suggested 제시된, 제안된   extra 추가의   differ 다르다   based on ~에 기반하여   under the age of ~세 미만의   be exempt from ~에서 면제되다

수신: Pearl 해변 숙소 임대 <custserv@pbvr.com>
발신: John Woodall <j.woodall@jmail.net>
날짜: 3월 8일
제목: 임대 질문

¹⁷⁷제가 이번 여름에 제 아내와 아들과 함께 여행을 할 계획인데, 귀사의 건물들 중 하나에서 며칠 보내는 것에 관심이 있습니다. ¹⁷⁸저희가 귀사의 모회사인 Global 리조트에 의해 운영되는 다른 리조트에 머물렀는데, 그곳에서 아주 즐거웠거든요. 그런데 예약을 하기 전에 귀하의 건물들에 관해 몇 가지 질문이 있습니다. 우선, ¹⁷⁹객실에 추가 인원이 있는 것이 허용되나요? ¹⁷⁷저희 아들이 겨우 2살이라 아직 같은 방에서 저희와 함께 자거든요. 또한 ¹⁷⁷저희는 객실에서 개인적으로 식사를 하는 것이 더 좋고요. 마지막으로, 귀사의 리조트가 위치해 있는 지역에 걸어서 다닐 수 있는 상점들과 레스토랑들이 있는지 또는 리조트에서 셔틀 버스 서비스를 제공하는지 알고 싶습니다. ¹⁸⁰예산이 빠듯해서 차를 빌리거나 택시를 타는 것 같은 교통에 드는 돈을 좀 절약하고 싶어서요.

미리 감사드립니다.

John Woodall

| 어휘 | spend (시간을) 보내다, (돈을) 쓰다   property 건물, 부동산   parent company 모회사   in private 개인적으로, 사적으로   wander around 돌아다니다   on foot 걸어서   tight budget 빠듯한 예산   transportation 교통, 수송

176. 세부 사항을 묻는 문제
Pearl 해변 숙소 임대의 건물들이 공통으로 가지고 있는 특징은 무엇인가?
(A) 침실의 수
(B) 가지고 있는 경관
(C) 식사 옵션
(D) 제시된 투숙객들의 수

| 해설 | 도표 위 단락에 누구와 오든 필요에 맞는 장소를 가지고 있다며 모두 해변 전망이라고(all with beachfront views) 제시되어 있으므로 정답은 (B)이다.

177. 연계 문제 – 추론
Woodall 씨는 어떤 종류의 건물을 대여할 것 같은가?
(A) 커플 스위트
(B) 허니문 스위트
(C) 가족 휴양지
(D) 파티 하우스

| 해설 | Woodall 씨가 보낸 이메일 도입부에 아내와 아들과 함께 여행을 할 계획인데(I plan on taking a trip with my wife and son this summer), 아이가 2살이라 같은 방을 쓴다(Our son is only 2 years old and still sleeps in the same room with us)고 했고, 객실에서 개인적으로 식사를 하는 것이 더 좋다고(we would prefer to have our meals in private in the guest room) 했으므로, 침실 1개(투숙객 2명)인 곳 중에 요청 시 룸 서비스가 되는 (B)가 정답이다.

178. 세부 사항을 묻는 문제
Pearl 해변 숙소 임대에 관해 명시된 것은 무엇인가?
(A) 자회사이다.
(B) 보통 대기자 명단이 있다.
(C) 유명한 주방 직원이 있다.
(D) 여름에만 운영한다.

| 해설 | Woodall 씨가 보낸 이메일 초반부에 귀사의 모회사인 Global 리조트에 의해 운영되는 다른 리조트에 머물렀다고(We have stayed at other resorts run by your parent company, Global Resorts) 한 것에서, Pearl 해변 숙소 임대는 Global 리조트의 자회사임을 알 수 있으므로 정답은 (A)이다.
| 어휘 | subsidiary company 자회사   wait list 대기자 명단   operate 운영하다
| 패러프레이징 | your parent company → a subsidiary company

179. 연계 문제 – 추론
Woodall 씨에 대해 암시되는 것은?
(A) 출장을 자주 간다.
(B) 추가 침대에 대한 비용을 지불하지 않을 것이다.
(C) 직접 식사를 요리하는 것을 선호한다.
(D) 전에 Pearl 해변에 가본 적이 있다.

| 해설 | Woodall 씨가 보낸 이메일 중반부에 객실에 추가 인원이 있는 것이 허용되는지(are we allowed to have an extra person in the room) 물은 후, 아들이 겨우 2살이라 아직 같은 방에서 함께 잔다고(Our son is only 2 years old and still sleeps in the same room with us) 이를 광고 마지막 별표에 4세 미만의 모든 어린이는 모든 추가 요금이 면제될 것이라고(Any child under the age of 4 will be exempt from all extra fees) 제시된 것과 연계해볼 때, 추가 침대에 대해 요금을 면제받을 것임을 알 수 있으므로 정답은 (B)이다.
| 패러프레이징 | will be exempt from all extra fees → won't pay for an extra bed

180. 추론 문제
이메일에서 Woodall 씨가 자신의 휴가 계획에 관해 암시하는 것은 무엇인가?
(A) 해변에서 시간을 보내고 싶어한다.
(B) 사교 행사들에 참석할 것이다.
(C) 오전 비행기를 예약할 것이다.
(D) 차를 빌리지 않으려고 한다.

| 해설 | 이메일 후반부에 예산이 빠듯해서 차를 빌리거나 택시를 타는 것 같은 교통에 드는 돈을 절약하고 싶다고(I have a tight budget and want to save some money on transportation such as renting a car or taking a taxi) 한 것에서, 차를 빌리지 않으려고 함을 알 수 있으므로 정답은 (D)이다.
| 어휘 | social event 사교 행사   reserve 예약하다

181-185 다음 전단과 온라인 서식을 참조하시오.

Bristow 문화 박물관

¹⁸¹Bristow 문화 박물관 회원으로 가입하시고 다양한 혜택을 누리세요.
¹⁸⁴월 25달러의 적은 요금으로 하실 수 있는 것:

– 박물관의 월간 소식지를 받는 것
– 매일 "역사 속의 오늘" 문자 메시지를 받는 것
– ¹⁸³ ⁽ᶜ⁾/¹⁸⁴모든 행사 티켓에 5달러 할인을 받는 것(보통 20달러)과 문화 행사 티켓들을 일찍 입수하는 것
– 박물관 전시 구역에 무료로 입장하는 것(보통 10달러)

¹⁸³ ⁽ᴬ⁾연극이나 뮤지컬 공연 같은 문화 행사들이 매 주말마다 열립니다.
¹⁸³ ⁽ᴮ⁾다가오는 행사들의 일정을 위해 박물관의 웹 사이트를 방문하세요.
¹⁸²/¹⁸⁵날씨가 허락하면, 4월부터 9월까지 행사가 야외에서 열립니다. 모든 야외 문화 행사들은 모든 박물관 방문객들에게 무료로 제공됩니다.

| 어휘 | sign up for ~을 신청하다   a variety of 다양한   benefit 혜택   fee 요금   access 이용, 접근   enter 입장하다   exhibit 전시, 전시회   theatrical 연극의   upcoming 다가오는, 곧 있을   weather permitting 날씨가 허락하면, 날씨가 좋으면   outdoors 야외에

---

www.bristowculturalmuseum.org/tickets
Bristow 문화 박물관

행사 티켓

¹⁸⁵행사 일자: 2월 7일
¹⁸⁵행사: 전통 러시아 댄스
¹⁸⁴티켓 가격: 15.00달러
티켓 수량: 2
총비용: 30.00달러

개인 정보
¹⁸⁴이름: Elias Dorsey
주소: 944 Ridge Drive, Bristow
전화번호: 555-8492
카드 종류: 비자
카드에 있는 이름: ELIAS DORSEY
카드 번호: xxxx-xxxx-xxxx-7021

저는 회원 약관에 동의합니다: 네

| 어휘 | traditional 전통적인   personal information 개인 정보
agree to ~에 동의하다   terms 조건

181. 주제/목적 문제
전단의 주된 목적은 무엇인가?
(A) 공연을 광고하는 것
(B) 새로운 전시회를 소개하는 것
(C) 자격 있는 직원들을 모집하는 것
(D) 회원 프로그램을 홍보하는 것

| 해설 | 도입부에 Bristow 문화 박물관 회원으로 가입하고 다양한 혜택을 누리라고(Sign up for a membership at Bristow Cultural Museum to enjoy a variety of benefits) 한 후, 회원 혜택을 구체적으로 제시하였으므로 정답은 (D)이다.

| 어휘 | recruit 모집하다   qualified 자격 있는   publicize 홍보하다

182. 추론 문제
Bristow 문화 박물관에 관해 암시되는 것은 무엇인가?
(A) 야외무대를 가지고 있다.
(B) 무료 회원권을 제공한다.
(C) 매월 전시회를 변경한다.
(D) 여러 언어를 하는 직원들을 고용한다.

| 해설 | 전단의 마지막 단락에 날씨가 허락하면 4월에서 9월까지 행사가 야외에서 열린다고(Weather permitting, events are held outdoors) 제시되어 있는 것을 통해, 야외에 공연 행사들이 진행될 무대가 있는 것으로 유추할 수 있으므로 정답은 (A)이다.

| 어휘 | multilingual 여러 언어를 하는, 다중 언어의

| 패러프레이징 | events are held outdoors → has an outdoor stage

183. NOT True 문제
문화 행사들에 관해 명시되지 않은 것은 무엇인가?
(A) 1년 내내 열린다.
(B) 일정표가 온라인에 게시된다.
(C) 회원들은 할인된 티켓을 받는다.
(D) 모두 뮤지컬 콘서트다.

| 해설 | 전단 마지막 단락에 문화 행사들이 매 주말마다 열린다고(Cultural events ~ are held every weekend) 한 것에서 (A), 행사 일정을 위해 박물관의 웹 사이트를 방문하라고(Visit the museum's Web site for a schedule of upcoming events) 한 것에서 (B), 회원 혜택 세 번째에 모든 행사 티켓에 5달러 할인을 받는다고($5 off any event ticket) 한 것에서 (C)는 모두 명시된 내용으로 확인되므로 정답은 (D)이다.

| 어휘 | throughout the year 1년 내내   post 게시하다, 올리다

| 패러프레이징 | · every weekend → throughout the year
· Web site → online
· $5 off any event ticket → discounted tickets

184. 연계 문제 - 추론
Dorsey 씨에 관해 사실일 것 같은 것은 무엇인가?
(A) Bristow 문화 박물관의 직원이다.
(B) 전시회를 볼 때 할인을 받는다.
(C) 매달 25달러를 지불한다.
(D) 최근에 러시아에 갔었다.

| 해설 | Dorsey 씨는 온라인 서식의 개인 정보에 제시된 이름으로, 티켓 가격(Ticket Price)으로 15달러를 청구받았는데, 이를 전단에 있는 회원 혜택 중 행사 티켓이 보통 20달러인데 5달러 할인을 받는다는($5 off any event ticket (Normally $20)) 것과 연계해볼 때, Dorsey 씨는 회원 할인을 받았다는 것을 알 수 있고, 전단 도입부에 회원 요금이 월 25달러(a small monthly fee of $25)라고 제시되어 있으므로 정답은 (C)이다.

| 어휘 | recently 최근에

185. 연계 문제 - 추론
전통 러시아 댄스 행사에 관해 암시되는 것은 무엇인가?
(A) 티켓이 매진되었다.
(B) 원래 야외에서 열릴 예정이었다.
(C) 실내에서 열릴 것이다.
(D) 모든 댄서들이 러시아에서 온다.

| 해설 | 온라인 서식에서 전통적인 러시아 댄스의 행사 일자는 2월 7일(Event Date: 7 February)로 확인되는데, 이를 전단 마지막 단락에 날씨가 허락하면, 4월부터 9월까지 행사가 야외에서 열린다고(Weather permitting, events are held outdoors from April to September) 한 것과 연계해볼 때, 2월 행사는 실내에서 열릴 것으로 유추할 수 있으므로 정답은 (C)이다.

| 어휘 | be sold out 매진되다, 다 팔리다   originally 원래   be scheduled to ~할 예정이다

186-190 다음 편지들과 청구서를 참조하시오.

Eastland 스포츠 기념품
623 Stafford Road
Eastland, TX 76448

7월 18일

관계자에게:

저는 약 7년 동안 야구 카드들과 수집품들의 열렬한 수집가였습니다. 최근 Eastland에 있는 친척들을 방문하는 동안 귀하의 상점을 우연히 발견하게 되어 기뻤습니다. 저는 당시 여러 제품들을 구입했습니다. 그런데 집에 돌아와서 그 제품들을 더 자세히 봤더니, 186그것들 중 하나가 가짜라는 것에 걱정을 하게 되었습니다. 187Alfonzo Deluca가 서명한 야구공에 있는 사인은 제가 가지고 있는 그의 다른 사인 포스터들과 야구 카드에 있는 사인과 상당히 다릅니다. 물론 공에 있는 것이 그의 진짜 사인이 아니라면, 저 같은 수집가에게는 전혀 쓸모가 없습니다. 이 문제를 가능한 한 빨리 검토해 주셨으면 좋겠습니다. 귀하의 편의를 위해 송장 사본을 동봉했습니다. 답변을 기다리고 있겠습니다.

진심을 담아,

Luis Sullivan

| 어휘 | avid 열렬한, 열심인   collector 수집가   collectible 수집물   approximately 대략   come across ~을 우연히 발견하다   relative 친척   fake 가짜인   signature 사인, 서명   autographed by ~에 의해 서명된   completely 완전히   worthless 가치 없는   matter 문제   enclose 동봉하다   for one's convenience 편의를 위해

고객 청구서 · EASTLAND 스포츠 기념품
623 Stafford Road, Eastland, TX 76448 · 254-555-6211

날짜: 6월 29일   고객: Luis Sullivan

물품 번호	상세	가격
1094	¹⁹⁰야구공 진열 케이스 (비어 있는, 나무 바닥, 측면 유리)	49.99달러
1722	가죽 장정 야구 카드 바인더 (카드 9장 진열/페이지)	39.99달러
2948	¹⁸⁷Alfonzo Deluca가 사인한 Wildcats 챔피언십 야구공	495.99달러
2659	Wildcats 경기장 홈 플레이트 (1994 시즌)	565.99달러
3029	Alex McManus가 입은 Eagles 배팅 연습용 셔츠 (1999 시즌)	295.99달러
	총액	1,447.95달러

¹⁸⁸판매할 스포츠 기념품이나 수집품들이 있으신가요? 오늘 저희에게 전화해 견적을 받아보세요.

| 어휘 | memorabilia 기념품   display case 진열 케이스   leather-bound 가죽 장정   practice 연습   jersey 운동용 셔츠   wear 입다   quote 견적

Luis Sullivan
3271 Troy Avenue
Whitestone, NY 11357

7월 23일

Sullivan 씨에게,

Eastland 스포츠 기념품에서 귀하께서 가장 최근에 구입하신 것과 관련하여, 저는 저희의 모든 제품들이 독립된 기관에 의해 인증된다는 것을 확실히 말씀드릴 수 있고, 귀하가 언급하신 제품의 인증서가 동봉되어 있습니다. 야구공의 경우, 둥근 표면에 쓰는 것의 어려움 때문에 때로 서명이 약간 다릅니다. 그래도 구매가 만족스럽지 않다고 느끼신다면, ¹⁸⁷기꺼이 전액 환불을 해 드리겠습니다. ¹⁸⁹그러나 이 경우 저희가 구매일로부터 45일 이내에만 반품을 처리할 수 있기 때문에 신속히 조치를 취하실 것을 권장합니다.

어떻게 하기로 결정하시든, 저희의 선물로 간직하시도록 ¹⁹⁰야구공 진열 케이스를 추가로 보내드리겠습니다.

진심으로,

William Mason

| 어휘 | assure 보증하다, 확신하다   be certified by ~에 의해 인증되다   independent agency 독립 기관   certificate 인증서   slightly 다소, 약간   rounded surface 둥근 표면   unsatisfactory 만족스럽지 않은   refund 환불을 해주다   take action 조치를 취하다   process 처리하다

186. 주제/목적 문제
Sullivan 씨 편지의 목적은 무엇인가?
(A) 배송 문제에 관해 항의하는 것
(B) 일부 파손된 상품을 알리는 것
(C) 청구서에 초과 청구된 것의 환불을 요청하는 것
(D) 제품의 진위에 의문을 제기하는 것

| 해설 | 편지 중반부에 구매한 제품 중 하나가 가짜라는 것에 걱정을 하게 되었다고 (I became concerned that one of them was fake) 한 것을 통해, 제품의 진위에 대해 우려하는 상황을 알리고자 쓴 편지임을 알 수 있으므로 정답은 (D)이다.

| 어휘 | broken 파손된   merchandise 상품, 제품   overcharge 초과 청구   authenticity 진위, 진짜

187. 연계 문제 – 세부 사항
Mason 씨는 어떤 제품에 환불을 제공하는가?
(A) 1094
(B) 2948
(C) 2659
(D) 3029

| 해설 | 첫 번째 편지 중반부에 Alfonzo Deluca가 야구공에 한 사인(The signature on the baseball autographed by Alfonzo Deluca)이 다른 것들과 상당히 다르다고 한 것에 대해, 두 번째 편지 중반부에 서명이 다른 이유를 설명한 후, 그래도 구매가 만족스럽지 않다고 느끼면, 전액 환불을 해 주겠다고(we would be happy to refund the full price) 했고, 청구서상에 그 제품은 Alfonzo Deluca가 사인한 Wildcats 챔피언십 야구공(Wildcats Championship Baseball signed by Alfonzo Deluca)으로 제품 번호가 2948로 확인되므로 정답은 (B)이다.

188. 추론 문제
Eastland 스포츠 기념품에 관해 암시되는 것은 무엇인가?
(A) Sullivan 씨의 집 근처에 지점이 있다.

(B) 빠른 배송 옵션을 제공한다.
(C) 고객들로부터 중고품들을 매입한다.
(D) 약 7년 동안 영업을 해 오고 있다.
| 해설 | Eastland 스포츠 기념품의 청구서 마지막에 판매할 스포츠 기념품이나 수집품들이 있는지 물으며 견적을 받아보라고(Do you have sports memorabilia or collectible items to sell? Call us today to get a quote) 한 것을 통해, 중고품을 매입하는 것을 유추할 수 있으므로 정답은 (C)이다.
| 어휘 | expedited shipping 빠른 배송
| 패러프레이징 | memorabilia or collectible items → used items

189. True 문제

Mason 씨에 의해 언급된 것은 무엇인가?
(A) 영수증이 요청서에 함께 포함되어야 한다.
(B) 반품은 매장에서 직접 이루어져야만 한다.
(C) 제품의 가격이 최근에 변경되었다.
(D) 해결책이 제한된 시간 동안만 가능하다.
| 해설 | Mason 씨는 두 번째 편지를 보낸 업체의 직원으로, 전액 환불을 해 주겠다고 해결책을 제시하면서, 하지만 구매일로부터 45일 이내에만 반품을 처리할 수 있기 때문에 신속히 조치를 취할 것을 권장한다고(However, in this case I would recommend taking action quickly because we can only process returns within 45 days of the purchase date) 했으므로 정답은 (D)이다.
| 어휘 | receipt 영수증   in person 직접   solution 해결   limited 제한된, 한정된
| 패러프레이징 | within 45 days of the purchase date → for a limited time

190. 연계 문제 – 세부 사항

Sullivan 씨에게 무료로 보내질 제품의 가격은 얼마인가?
(A) 39.99달러
(B) 49.99달러
(C) 295.99달러
(D) 495.99달러
| 해설 | 두 번째 편지 마지막에 야구공 진열 케이스를 추가로 보내겠다고(I will send you an additional baseball display case) 했고, 청구서에서 야구공 진열 케이스(baseball display case)에 해당하는 금액은 49.99달러로 확인되므로 정답은 (B)이다.

191-195 다음 회람, 이메일, 기사를 참조하시오.

수신: Balentine Labs 전 직원
발신: Saeko Nagao
주제: 읽어주시기 바랍니다

3월 3일

Lavelle 교육 기관의 화학과 학생 그룹이 3월 17일 목요일에 우리 본사를 방문할 예정입니다. [191]반드시 여러분이 방문객들에 대한 우리 회사의 방침들을 잊지 않기를 바라는데, 지난달 언론 행사에 앞서 논의된 동일한 것들입니다. 직원들은 업무와 시중에 나와 있는 우리의 기존 제품들에 관한 일반적인 질문에는 답할 수 있습니다. 회사 프라이버시를 위해, 현재 프로젝트에 관해서 이야기해서는 안 됩니다. 우리의 기업 비밀들을 [192]안전하게 유지하는 것이 중요합니다. 방문 중에 현장 관리자가 학생들에게 투어를 제공할 것이고, 그런 다음 그들은 [194]연구 부서의 책임자가 이끄는 질의응답 세션에 참석할 것입니다. 여러분의 협조에 감사드립니다.

| 어휘 | chemistry 화학, 화학과   headquarters 본사   regulation 규정   prior to ~에 앞서   press event 언론 행사   general 일반적인   work duty 업무   existing 기존의   for the sake of ~을 위하여   current 현재의   trade secrets 기업 비밀   secure 안전한   site manager 현장 관리자   cooperation 협조   appreciated 감사하는

수신: Saeko Nagao <saeko.negao@balentinelabs.com>
발신: Karen Dupree <dupreek@lavelleinstitute.edu>
날짜: 3월 10일
제목: 다가오는 방문

Nagao 씨에게,

제 학급이 계획했던 날에 귀하의 시설을 방문할 수 없을 것임을 알려 드리게 되어 유감입니다. 유감스럽게도, 일정상의 문제들이 좀 있었습니다. 가능하다면, 저희는 여전히 귀하의 업체를 꼭 보고 싶습니다. 저희가 가능한 시간은 다음과 같습니다: 3월 15일 화요일(9–정오), 3월 18일 금요일(2–5), 또는 [193]3월 19일 토요일(1–4). 이 시간대 중 귀하의 일정과 맞는 것이 있는지 알려주시기 바라며, 저희를 받아주시는 것에 감사를 드립니다.

안부를 전하며,

Karen Dupree
Lavelle 교육 기관 화학과 강사

| 어휘 | regret 후회하다, 유감스럽다   scheduling problem 일정상의 문제   operation 기업, 사업체, 운영   time slot 시간대   accommodate 수용하다

Lavelle 교육 기관 4월 소식지-Vol. 254

학생들이 작업이 진행 중인 실험실을 둘러보다
Corey Ramey 작성

Lavelle 교육 기관의 화학과 대학생 그룹이 강사 Karen Dupree와 함께 지난달 Balentine Labs를 방문했습니다. 그들은 그곳에서 시설을 둘러봤고, 장비 시연을 보았고, 운영에 관해 배웠습니다. [193]주말이었음에도 불구하고, 그 시설은 언제나처럼 여전히 분주했는데, 시간에 민감한 연구를 수용하기 위해 일주일에 7일 문을 열기 때문이다. "저는 그 투어에서 많은 것을 배웠습니다." 2학년 학생인 Cynthia Lester가 말했다.

"저희는 195최근 문을 연 건물 증축 부분을 선보이게 되어 특히 자랑스럽습니다." 194투어에 뒤이은 특별 세션에서 그룹의 질문들에 응답하면서 Mira Prakash가 말했다. "그 새로운 공간 덕택에, 195이제 우리는 바로 여기 본사에서 환자들에게 시험을 진행하고 있죠. 이는 이러한 목적으로 진료 공간을 찾을 필요가 없으니 많은 시간과 번거로움을 덜어주고 있습니다."

| 어휘 | undergraduate 대학생   along with ~와 함께   instructor 강사   equipment 장비   demonstration 시연   time-sensitive 시간에 민감한   be proud to ~해서 자랑스럽다   particularly 특히   show off 선보이다, 자랑하다   extension 확장   following ~에 뒤이어   trial 실험, 시험   hassle 귀찮은 일, 번거로움

191. 주제/목적 문제
Nagao 씨는 왜 회람을 보냈나?
(A) 규정 변경을 알리기 위해
(B) 투어를 위한 자원봉사자들을 요청하기 위해
(C) 직원들에게 정책을 상기시키기 위해
(D) 취업 기회를 소개하기 위해

| 해설 | 도입부에서 한 그룹의 방문 예정을 알리고, 뒤이어 반드시 방문객들에 대한 회사 방침들을 잊지 않기를 바란다고(I want to make sure that you don't forget our company regulations on visitors) 당부한 후, 구체적으로 해야 할 일에 관해 제시했으므로 정답은 (C)이다.
| 어휘 | volunteer 자원봉사자   remind 상기시키다
| 패러프레이징 | company regulations → policy

192. 동의어 문제
회람에서 첫 번째 단락 여섯 번째 줄에 있는 단어 "secure"와 그 의미가 가장 유사한 것은
(A) 자신 있는
(B) 닫힌, 폐쇄된
(C) 보호된
(D) 매어진, 고정된

| 해설 | 해당 단어가 들어간 문장은 '우리 기업 비밀들을 안전하게 유지하는 것이 중요하다'라고 해석된다. 따라서 secure는 '안전한'라는 의미이므로 이와 가장 유사한 '보호된'이라는 뜻의 (C) protected가 정답이다.

고난도
193. 연계 문제 – 추론
Dupree 씨의 그룹은 언제 Balentine Labs을 방문했던 것 같은가?
(A) 3월 15일
(B) 3월 17일
(C) 3월 18일
(D) 3월 19일

| 해설 | 먼저 두 번째 지문에서 Dupree 씨가 제시한 시간대는 3월 15일 화요일, 3월 18일 금요일, 3월 19일 토요일인데, 세 번째 지문에서 업체 방문 상황에 대해 주말이었음에도 불구하고(Even though it was a weekend) 분주했다고 한 것에서, 3월 19일 토요일에 방문했던 것으로 유추할 수 있으므로 정답은 (D)이다.

194. 연계 문제 – 추론
Prakash 씨에 관해 암시된 것은 무엇인가?
(A) Balentine Labs의 현장 관리자이다.
(B) 2년 동안 학교에 있었다.
(C) 부서장이다.
(D) 곧 다른 투어를 계획하고 있다.

| 해설 | 회람 후반부에 학생들이 연구 부서의 책임자가 이끄는 질의응답 세션에 참석할 것이라고(they will attend a question-and-answer session led by the director of the research department) 했고, 기사 두 번째 단락에 특별 세션에서 그룹의 질문들에 응답하면서 Mira Prakash가 말했다고(said Mira Prakash as she responded to inquiries from the group at a special session) 한 것을 통해, 질의응답 세션을 이끈 Prakash는 연구 부서의 책임자일 것으로 유추할 수 있으므로 정답은 (C)이다.
| 어휘 | head of a department 부서장
| 패러프레이징 | director of the research department → head of a department

고난도
195. 추론 문제
Balentine Labs에 관해 암시된 것은 무엇인가?
(A) 처음으로 환자들과 현장 시험을 실시하고 있다.
(B) 오직 Lavelle 교육 기관 졸업생들만 채용한다.
(C) 연구를 위해 환자들을 모집하는 것에 어려움이 있다.
(D) 의료를 제공하는 무료 진료소를 운영한다.

| 해설 | Balentine Labs는 Lavelle 교육 기관 학생들이 방문했던 곳으로, 마지막 지문에서 Prakash 씨가 최근 문을 연 건물 증축 부분(our recently opened building extension)을 선보이게 되어 자랑스럽다며, 그 새로운 공간 덕택에, 이제 본사에서 환자들에게 시험을 진행하고 있다고(Thanks to the new space, we are now running trials with patients right here at our headquarters) 한 것을 통해, 최근에 건물을 증축하여 처음으로 현장에서 시험을 실시하고 있음을 알 수 있으므로 정답은 (A)이다.
| 어휘 | conduct 하다, 시행하다   exclusively 오직, 독점적으로   graduate 졸업생   medical care 의료
| 패러프레이징 | running → conducting

196-200 다음 광고, 서식, 이메일을 참조하시오.

Morris Fabrics

낡은 가구를 교체하지 마세요. 대신에 새것을 구입하는 비용의 극히 일부로 저희 숙련된 기술자들이 닳아 해진 천을 교체하도록 하시는 것은 어떤가요? 여기 Morris Fabrics에서 저희는 거의 20년 동안 오직 최고 품질의 재료들로 가구의 천 장식을 해 왔습니다. 저희 직원들은 최고 수

준으로 교육을 받고 관리되며, ¹⁹⁶저희는 100년이 넘은 의자와 소파들의 작업에만 집중하는 경험 많은 작업 팀도 보유하고 있습니다. ¹⁹⁷5개 이상의 유사한 품목들의 주문에 대해 9월 말까지 20% 할인을 제공할 것입니다. 이는 호텔과 사무실들에 최적이죠. 더 많은 정보를 위해 (302) 555-9898로 전화하시거나 www.morrisfabrics.com을 방문하세요.

| 어휘 | worn 닳아 해진   fabric 직물   skilled 숙련된   technician 기술자   fraction 일부, 아주 조금   upholster 천을 대다   finest-quality 최고 품질의   material 재료   standard 수준   experienced 경험 많은   concentrate on ~에 집중하다   solely 오로지

작업 주문 #3299

직원: Holly Weston #145   날짜: 9월 23일
완료 예정일: 9월 25일   ²⁰⁰배송 예정일: 9월 26일
고객 이름: ¹⁹⁷David Greaves

상세: ¹⁹⁷마호가니로 된 조지 왕조 시대 스타일 의자 6개. 각각 모든 좌석 천을 벗겨냄. 표준 고정 핀을 이용하여 교체 직물 진홍색 펠트(#13437B) 적용. 반드시 밑면에 이중 솔기. 앞쪽 바와 팔걸이에 닳아 해진 부분들 다시 광내기. 다리에 있는 헐거워진 크로스바 확인. 필요 시 투명한 접착제 바르기.

| 어휘 | completion 완료, 완성   due 예정된   replacement 교체   apply 사용하다, 적용하다, 바르다   pinning 핀 고정   ensure 보장하다, 확보하다   double seam 이중 솔기   underside 밑면   re-polish 다시 광을 내다   arm 팔걸이   loose 헐거워진, 느슨한   transparent 투명한   adhesive 접착제

수신: Morris Fabrics <customerservices@morrisfabrics.com>
발신: David Greaves <david.greaves@localmail.net>
날짜: 9월 28일
제목: 추가적인 요청

관계자에게:

저의 가장 최근 주문에 대한 작업 품질에 매우 만족스러웠고, ²⁰⁰제 의자들을 예정보다 하루 일찍 받아서 기분 좋게 놀랐습니다. 특히 가격을 고려하면 그것들에 이루어진 작업은 훌륭합니다. 저희의 현관 홀에 자리한 의자들을 볼 기회가 있었는데, 이제 보니 새 커버가 현재 가지고 있는 커튼들과 ¹⁹⁹어울리지 않네요. 그 천을 파시는지 궁금했습니다. 동일한 천을 추가로 36야드 더 살 수 있다면, 의자들과 정확히 동일한 커튼을 만들 수 있을 겁니다.

그것이 구매 가능하다면 제가 가서 다른 보완적인 옵션들과 더불어 ¹⁹⁸그 천을 다시 볼 수 있도록 시간을 정하기 위해 저에게 이메일로 답장을 해 주시기 바랍니다.

진심을 담아,

David Greaves

| 어휘 | additional 추가의, 추가적인   extremely 매우, 극도로   fantastic 훌륭한, 환상적인   consider 고려하다, 감안하다   covering 덮개   go with ~와 어울리다   currently 현재, 지금   exactly 정확히, 똑같이   arrange a time 시간을 정하다   complementary 상호 보완적인

196. 추론 문제

Morris Fabrics에 관해 암시된 것은 무엇인가?
(A) 온라인에 완료된 프로젝트들의 사진 갤러리가 있다.
(B) 재활용을 위해 중고 가구들을 받는다.
(C) 골동품을 전문으로 하는 팀이 있다.
(D) 최근에 소유권이 변경되었다.

| 해설 | 광고의 첫 번째 단락 후반부에 100년이 넘은 의자와 소파들의 작업에만 집중하는 경험 많은 작업 팀도 보유하고 있다고(we have an experienced crew that concentrates solely on working with chairs and sofas that are over one hundred years old) 한 것을 통해, 골동품을 전문으로 작업하는 팀이 있음을 알 수 있으므로 정답은 (C)이다.

| 어휘 | recycling 재활용   specialize in ~을 전문으로 하다   antique 고풍의, 골동품의   ownership 소유권

| 패러프레이징 | chairs and sofas that are over one hundred years old → antique pieces

🔺고난도

197. 연계 문제 - True

Greaves 씨에 관해 사실인 것은?
(A) 인테리어 디자이너로 일한다.
(B) 대량 주문 할인을 받았다.
(C) 호텔의 직원이다.
(D) 프로젝트를 위해 두 개의 천을 골랐다.

| 해설 | Greaves 씨는 서식에서 작업을 의뢰한 고객으로, 상세 내역에서 마호가니로 된 조지 왕조 시대 스타일 의자 6개(6 Mahogany Georgian-style chairs)를 주문한 것을 알 수 있는데, 이를 첫 번째 지문의 두 번째 단락에 5개 이상의 유사한 품목들의 주문에 대해 9월 말까지 20% 할인을 할 것이라고(For orders of five or more similar items, we will be offering a discount of 20%) 제시된 것과 연계하면 할인을 받았을 것임을 알 수 있으므로 정답은 (B)이다.

| 어휘 | bulk discount 대량 주문 할인

198. 세부 사항을 묻는 문제

Greaves 씨가 Morris Fabrics에 요청하는 것은 무엇인가?
(A) 직물 샘플을 보내는 것
(B) 약속을 정하는 것
(C) 제품 스타일들을 추천하는 것
(D) 커튼들을 맡아두는 것

| 해설 | Greaves 씨가 보낸 이메일의 두 번째 단락에 가서 천을 다시 볼 수 있도록 시간을 정하기 위해 이메일로 답장을 해 주기 바란다고(Please e-mail me back

to arrange a time for me to come in and look at the fabric again) 했으므로 정답은 (B)이다.
| 어휘 | set up 정하다   put on reserve 맡아 두다, 확보해 두다
| 패러프레이징 | arrange a time → Set up an appointment

199. 동의어 문제
이메일에서 첫 번째 단락 네 번째 줄에 있는 문구 "go with"와 의미가 가장 유사한 것은
(A) 제공하다
(B) 어울리다, 일치하다
(C) 수용하다, 받아들이다
(D) 동반하다, 동행하다
| 해설 | 해당 단어가 들어간 문장은 '이제 보니 새 커버가 현재 가지고 있는 커튼들과 어울리지 않는다'라고 해석된다. 따라서 go with는 '어울리다'라는 의미로 쓰인 것이므로, 이와 가장 유사한 '어울리다, 일치하다'라는 뜻인 (B) match가 정답이다.

200. 연계 문제 – 세부 사항
Greaves 씨는 자신의 제품들을 언제 받았나?
(A) 9월 23일에
(B) 9월 25일에
(C) 9월 26일에
(D) 9월 27일에
| 해설 | 서식에서 배송 예정일이 9월 26일(Scheduled delivery date: September 26)로 확인되는데, 이메일 초반부에 의자들을 예정보다 하루 일찍 받아서 기분 좋게 놀랐다고(I was pleasantly surprised to receive my chairs a day earlier than scheduled) 했으므로 9월 25일에 제품을 받았음을 알 수 있다. 따라서 정답은 (B)이다.

Memo

Memo

Memo

Memo

Memo

1

영단기 토익
실전 1000제 RC 해설집
vol.1

영단기
eng.conects.com

영단기
eng.conects.com